# Maestro Owners Workshop Manual

## John S Mead

**Models covered**
All Austin Maestro 1.3 & 1.6 models, including
Automatic, Vanden Plas and special/limited editions;
1275 cc & 1598 cc
MG Maestro 1600; 1598 cc
Austin Maestro 500 & 700 Vans; 1275 cc & 1598 cc

*Does not cover MG Maestro 2.0 EFi, Turbo or Diesel engine models*

(922-2X13)    ABCD

2

**Haynes Publishing**
Sparkford Nr Yeovil
Somerset BA22 7JJ England

**Haynes North America, Inc**
861 Lawrence Drive
Newbury Park
California 91320 USA

**Acknowledgements**
Thanks are due to Champion Spark Plug who supplied the illustrations showing spark plug conditions, to Holt Lloyd Limited who supplied the illustrations showing bodywork repair, and to Duckhams Oils who provided lubrication data. Certain other illustrations are the copyright of BL Cars Limited (now Rover Group plc) and are used with their permission. Thanks are also due to Sykes-Pickavant, who provided some of the workshop tools, and all the staff at Sparkford who helped in the production of this manual.

© **Haynes Publishing 1995**

A book in the **Haynes Owners Workshop Manual Series**

Printed by J. H. Haynes & Co. Ltd., Sparkford, Nr Yeovil, Somerset BA22 7JJ, England

ISBN 1 85960 057 3

**British Library Cataloguing in Publication Data**
A catalogue record for this book is available from the British Library

We take great pride in the accuracy of information given in this manual, but vehicle manufacturers make alterations and design changes during the production run of a particular vehicle of which they do not inform us. No liability can be accepted by the authors or publishers for loss, damage or injury caused by any errors in, or omissions from, the information given.

# Restoring and Preserving our Motoring Heritage

**Few people can have had the luck to realise their dreams to quite the same extent and in such a remarkable fashion as John Haynes, Founder and Chairman of the Haynes Publishing Group.**

Since 1965 his unique approach to workshop manual publishing has proved so successful that millions of Haynes Manuals are now sold every year throughout the world, covering literally thousands of different makes and models of cars, vans and motorcycles.

A continuing passion for cars and motoring led to the founding in 1985 of a Charitable Trust dedicated to the restoration and preservation of our motoring heritage. To inaugurate the new Museum, John Haynes donated virtually his entire private collection of 52 cars.

Now with an unrivalled international collection of over 210 veteran, vintage and classic cars and motorcycles, the Haynes Motor Museum in Somerset is well on the way to becoming one of the most interesting Motor Museums in the world.

A 70 seat video cinema, a cafe and an extensive motoring bookshop, together with a specially constructed one kilometre motor circuit, make a visit to the Haynes Motor Museum a truly unforgettable experience.

Every vehicle in the museum is preserved in as near as possible mint condition and each car is run every six months on the motor circuit.

Enjoy the picnic area set amongst the rolling Somerset hills. Peer through the William Morris workshop windows at cars being restored, and browse through the extensive displays of fascinating motoring memorabilia.

From the 1903 Oldsmobile through such classics as an MG Midget to the mighty 'E' Type Jaguar, Lamborghini, Ferrari Berlinetta Boxer, and Graham Hill's Lola Cosworth, there is something for everyone, young and old alike, at this Somerset Museum.

## Haynes Motor Museum
*Situated mid-way between London and Penzance, the Haynes Motor Museum is located just off the A303 at Sparkford, Somerset (home of the Haynes Manual) and is open to the public 7 days a week all year round, except Christmas Day and Boxing Day.*

# Contents

*Spark plug condition and bodywork repair colour section between pages 32 and 33*

Austin Maestro 1.6L

Austin Maestro 1.6HLS

# Fault diagnosis

## Introduction

The vehicle owner who does his or her own maintenance according to the recommended schedules should not have to use this section of the manual very often. Modern component reliability is such that, provided those items subject to wear or deterioration are inspected or renewed at the specified intervals, sudden failure is comparatively rare. Faults do not usually just happen as a result of sudden failure, but develop over a period of time. Major mechanical failures in particular are usually preceded by characteristic symptoms over hundreds or even thousands of miles. Those components which do occasionally fail without warning are often small and easily carried in the vehicle.

With any fault finding, the first step is to decide where to begin investigations. Sometimes this is obvious, but on other occasions a little detective work will be necessary. The owner who makes half a dozen haphazard adjustments or replacements may be successful in curing a fault (or its symptoms), but he will be none the wiser if the fault recurs and he may well have spent more time and money than was necessary. A calm and logical approach will be found to be more satisfactory in the long run. Always take into account any warning signs or abnormalities that may have been noticed in the period preceding the fault – power loss, high or low gauge readings, unusual noises or smells, etc – and remember that failure of components such as fuses or spark plugs may only be pointers to some underlying fault.

The pages which follow here are intended to help in cases of failure to start or breakdown on the road. There is also a Fault Diagnosis Section at the end of each Chapter which should be consulted if the preliminary checks prove unfruitful. Whatever the fault, certain basic principles apply. These are as follows:

**Verify the fault.** This is simply a matter of being sure that you know what the symptoms are before starting work. This is particularly important if you are investigating a fault for someone else who may not have described it very accurately.

**Don't overlook the obvious.** For example, if the vehicle won't start, is there petrol in the tank? (Don't take anyone else's word on this particular point, and don't trust the fuel gauge either!) If an electrical fault is indicated, look for loose or broken wires before digging out the test gear.

**Cure the disease, not the symptom.** Substituting a flat battery with a fully charged one will get you off the hard shoulder, but if the underlying cause is not attended to, the new battery will go the same way. Similarly, changing oil-fouled spark plugs for a new set will get you moving again, but remember that the reason for the fouling (if it wasn't simply an incorrect grade of plug) will have to be established and corrected.

**Don't take anything for granted.** Particularly, don't forget that a 'new' component may itself be defective (especially if it's been rattling round in the boot for months), and don't leave components out of a fault diagnosis sequence just because they are new or recently fitted. When you do finally diagnose a difficult fault, you'll probably realise that all the evidence was there from the start.

## Electrical faults

Electrical faults can be more puzzling than straightforward mechanical failures, but they are no less susceptible to logical analysis if the basic principles of operation are understood. Vehicle electrical wiring exists in extremely unfavourable conditions – heat, vibration and chemical attack – and the first things to look for are loose or corroded connections and broken or chafed wires, especially where the wires pass through holes in the bodywork or are subject to vibration.

All metal-bodied vehicles in current production have one pole of the battery 'earthed', ie connected to the vehicle bodywork, and in nearly all modern vehicles it is the negative (–) terminal. The various electrical components – motors, bulb holders etc – are also connected to earth, either by means of a lead or directly by their mountings. Electric current flows through the component and then back to the battery via the bodywork. If the component mounting is loose or corroded, or if a good path back to the battery is not available, the circuit will be incomplete and malfunction will result. The engine and/or gearbox are also earthed by means of flexible metal straps to the body or subframe; if these straps are loose or missing, starter motor, generator and ignition trouble may result.

Assuming the earth return to be satisfactory, electrical faults will be due either to component malfunction or to defects in the current supply. Individual components are dealt with in Chapter 9. If supply wires are broken or cracked internally this results in an open-circuit, and the easiest way to check for this is to bypass the suspect wire temporarily with a length of wire having a crocodile clip or suitable connector at each end. Alternatively, a 12V test lamp can be used to verify the presence of supply voltage at various points along the wire and the break can be thus isolated.

If a bare portion of a live wire touches the bodywork or other earthed metal part, the electricity will take the low-resistance path thus formed back to the battery: this is known as a short-circuit. Hopefully a short-circuit will blow a fuse, but otherwise it may cause burning of the insulation (and possibly further short-circuits) or even a fire. This is why it is inadvisable to bypass persistently blowing fuses with silver foil or wire.

## Spares and tool kit

Most vehicles are supplied only with sufficient tools for wheel changing; the *Maintenance and minor repair* tool kit detailed in *Tools and working facilities*, with the addition of a hammer, is probably sufficient for those repairs that most motorists would consider attempting at the roadside. In addition a few items which can be fitted without too much trouble in the event of a breakdown should be carried. Experience and available space will modify the list below, but the following may save having to call on professional assistance:

*Spark plugs, clean and correctly gapped*
*HT lead and plug cap – long enough to reach the plug furthest from the distributor*
*Distributor rotor*
*Drivebelt(s) – emergency type may suffice*
*Spare fuses*
*Set of principal light bulbs*
*Tin of radiator sealer and hose bandage*
*Exhaust bandage*
*Roll of insulating tape*
*Length of soft iron wire*
*Length of electrical flex*
*Torch or inspection lamp (can double as test lamp)*
*Battery jump leads*
*Tow-rope*
*Ignition water dispersant aerosol*
*Litre of engine oil*
*Sealed can of hydraulic fluid*
*Emergency windscreen*
*Worm drive clips*

If spare fuel is carried, a can designed for the purpose should be used to minimise risks of leakage and collision damage. A first aid kit and a warning triangle, whilst not at present compulsory in the UK, are obviously sensible items to carry in addition to the above.

When touring abroad it may be advisable to carry additional spares which, even if you cannot fit them yourself, could save having to wait while parts are obtained. The items below may be worth considering:

Clutch and throttle cables
Cylinder head gasket
Alternator brushes
Tyre valve core

One of the motoring organisations will be able to advise on availability of fuel etc in foreign countries.

## Engine will not start

### Engine fails to turn when starter operated
Flat battery (recharge, use jump leads, or push start)
Battery terminals loose or corroded
Battery earth to body defective
Engine earth strap loose or broken
Starter motor (or solenoid) wiring loose or broken
Automatic transmission selector in wrong position, or inhibitor switch faulty
Ignition/starter switch faulty
Major mechanical failure (seizure)
Starter or solenoid internal fault (see Chapter 9)

### Starter motor turns engine slowly
Partially discharged battery (recharge, use jump leads, or push start)
Battery terminals loose or corroded
Battery earth to body defective
Engine earth strap loose
Starter motor (or solenoid) wiring loose
Starter motor internal fault (see Chapter 9)

### Starter motor spins without turning engine
Flat battery
Flywheel gear teeth damaged or worn
Starter motor mounting bolts loose

### Engine turns normally but fails to start
Damp or dirty HT leads and distributor cap (crank engine and check for spark) – try moisture dispersant such as Holts Wet Start
No fuel in tank (check for delivery at carburettor)
Excessive choke (hot engine) or insufficient choke (cold engine)
Fouled or incorrectly gapped spark plugs (remove and regap, or renew)
Other ignition system fault (see Chapter 4)
Other fuel system fault (see Chapter 3)
Poor compression (see Chapter 1)
Major mechanical failure (eg camshaft drive)

### Engine fires but will not run
Insufficient choke (cold engine)
Air leaks at carburettor or inlet manifold
Fuel starvation (see Chapter 3)
Other ignition fault (see Chapter 4)

## Engine cuts out and will not restart

### Engine cuts out suddenly – ignition fault
Loose or disconnected LT wires
Wet HT leads or distributor cap (after traversing water splash)
Coil failure (check for spark)
Other ignition fault (see Chapter 4)

### Engine misfires before cutting out – fuel fault
Fuel tank empty
Fuel pump defective or filter blocked (check for delivery)
Fuel tank filler vent blocked (suction will be evident on releasing cap)
Carburettor needle valve sticking
Carburettor jets blocked (fuel contaminated)
Other fuel system fault (see Chapter 3)

### Engine cuts out – other causes
Serious overheating
Major mechanical failure (eg camshaft drive)

## Engine overheats

### Ignition (no-charge) warning light illuminated
Slack or broken drivebelt – retension or renew (Chapter 9)

### Ignition warning light not illuminated
Coolant loss due to internal or external leakage (see Chapter 2)
Thermostat defective
Low oil level
Brakes binding
Radiator clogged externally or internally
Electric cooling fan not operating correctly
Engine waterways clogged
Ignition timing incorrect or automatic advance malfunctioning
Mixture too weak

**Note**: *Do not add cold water to an overheated engine or damage may result*

## Low engine oil pressure

### Gauge reads low or warning light illuminated with engine running
Oil level low or incorrect grade
Defective gauge or sender unit
Wire to sender unit earthed
Engine overheating
Oil filter clogged or bypass valve defective
Oil pressure relief valve defective
Oil pick-up strainer clogged
Oil pump worn or mountings loose
Worn main or big-end bearings

**Note**: *Low oil pressure in a high-mileage engine at tickover is not necessarily a cause for concern. Sudden pressure loss at speed is far more significant. In any event, check the gauge or warning light sender before condemning the engine.*

## Engine noises

### Pre-ignition (pinking) on acceleration
Incorrect grade of fuel
Ignition timing incorrect
Distributor faulty or worn
Worn or maladjusted carburettor
Excessive carbon build-up in engine

### Whistling or wheezing noises
Leaking vacuum hose
Leaking carburettor or manifold gasket
Blowing head gasket

### Tapping or rattling
Incorrect valve clearances
Worn valve gear
Worn timing chain or belt
Broken piston ring (ticking noise)

### Knocking or thumping
Unintentional mechanical contact (eg fan blades)
Worn drivebelt
Peripheral component fault (alternator, water pump etc)
Worn big-end bearings (regular heavy knocking, perhaps less under load)
Worn main bearings (rumbling and knocking, perhaps worsening under load)
Piston slap (most noticeable when cold)

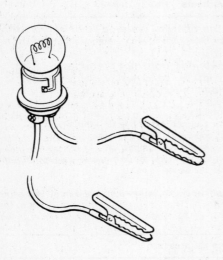

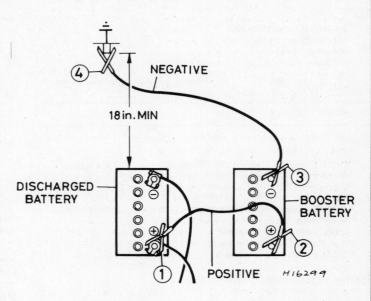

NEGATIVE

18 in. MIN

DISCHARGED BATTERY

BOOSTER BATTERY

POSITIVE

H16299

A simple test lamp is useful for tracing electrical faults

Jump start lead connections for negative earth vehicles – connect leads in order shown

Carrying a few spares may save you a long walk

# Safety first!

Professional motor mechanics are trained in safe working procedures. However enthusiastic you may be about getting on with the job in hand, do take the time to ensure that your safety is not put at risk. A moment's lack of attention can result in an accident, as can failure to observe certain elementary precautions.

There will always be new ways of having accidents, and the following points do not pretend to be a comprehensive list of all dangers; they are intended rather to make you aware of the risks and to encourage a safety-conscious approach to all work you carry out on your vehicle.

### Essential DOs and DON'Ts

**DON'T** rely on a single jack when working underneath the vehicle. Always use reliable additional means of support, such as axle stands, securely placed under a part of the vehicle that you know will not give way.

**DON'T** attempt to loosen or tighten high-torque nuts (e.g. wheel hub nuts) while the vehicle is on a jack; it may be pulled off.

**DON'T** start the engine without first ascertaining that the transmission is in neutral (or 'Park' where applicable) and the parking brake applied.

**DON'T** suddenly remove the filler cap from a hot cooling system – cover it with a cloth and release the pressure gradually first, or you may get scalded by escaping coolant.

**DON'T** attempt to drain oil until you are sure it has cooled sufficiently to avoid scalding you.

**DON'T** grasp any part of the engine, exhaust or catalytic converter without first ascertaining that it is sufficiently cool to avoid burning you.

**DON'T** allow brake fluid or antifreeze to contact vehicle paintwork.

**DON'T** syphon toxic liquids such as fuel, brake fluid or antifreeze by mouth, or allow them to remain on your skin.

**DON'T** inhale dust – it may be injurious to health (see *Asbestos* below).

**DON'T** allow any spilt oil or grease to remain on the floor – wipe it up straight away, before someone slips on it.

**DON'T** use ill-fitting spanners or other tools which may slip and cause injury.

**DON'T** attempt to lift a heavy component which may be beyond your capability – get assistance.

**DON'T** rush to finish a job, or take unverified short cuts.

**DON'T** allow children or animals in or around an unattended vehicle.

**DO** wear eye protection when using power tools such as drill, sander, bench grinder etc, and when working under the vehicle.

**DO** use a barrier cream on your hands prior to undertaking dirty jobs – it will protect your skin from infection as well as making the dirt easier to remove afterwards; but make sure your hands aren't left slippery. Note that long-term contact with used engine oil can be a health hazard.

**DO** keep loose clothing (cuffs, tie etc) and long hair well out of the way of moving mechanical parts.

**DO** remove rings, wristwatch etc, before working on the vehicle – especially the electrical system.

**DO** ensure that any lifting tackle used has a safe working load rating adequate for the job.

**DO** keep your work area tidy – it is only too easy to fall over articles left lying around.

**DO** get someone to check periodically that all is well, when working alone on the vehicle.

**DO** carry out work in a logical sequence and check that everything is correctly assembled and tightened afterwards.

**DO** remember that your vehicle's safety affects that of yourself and others. If in doubt on any point, get specialist advice.

**IF,** in spite of following these precautions, you are unfortunate enough to injure yourself, seek medical attention as soon as possible.

### Asbestos

Certain friction, insulating, sealing, and other products – such as brake linings, brake bands, clutch linings, torque converters, gaskets, etc – contain asbestos. *Extreme care must be taken to avoid inhalation of dust from such products since it is hazardous to health.* If in doubt, assume that they *do* contain asbestos.

### Fire

Remember at all times that petrol (gasoline) is highly flammable. Never smoke, or have any kind of naked flame around, when working on the vehicle. But the risk does not end there – a spark caused by an electrical short-circuit, by two metal surfaces contacting each other, by careless use of tools, or even by static electricity built up in your body under certain conditions, can ignite petrol vapour, which in a confined space is highly explosive.

Always disconnect the battery earth (ground) terminal before working on any part of the fuel or electrical system, and never risk spilling fuel on to a hot engine or exhaust.

It is recommended that a fire extinguisher of a type suitable for fuel and electrical fires is kept handy in the garage or workplace at all times. Never try to extinguish a fuel or electrical fire with water.

**Note:** *Any reference to a 'torch' appearing in this manual should always be taken to mean a hand-held battery-operated electric lamp or flashlight. It does NOT mean a welding/gas torch or blowlamp.*

### Fumes

Certain fumes are highly toxic and can quickly cause unconsciousness and even death if inhaled to any extent. Petrol (gasoline) vapour comes into this category, as do the vapours from certain solvents such as trichloroethylene. Any draining or pouring of such volatile fluids should be done in a well ventilated area.

When using cleaning fluids and solvents, read the instructions carefully. Never use materials from unmarked containers – they may give off poisonous vapours.

Never run the engine of a motor vehicle in an enclosed space such as a garage. Exhaust fumes contain carbon monoxide which is extremely poisonous; if you need to run the engine, always do so in the open air or at least have the rear of the vehicle outside the workplace.

If you are fortunate enough to have the use of an inspection pit, never drain or pour petrol, and never run the engine, while the vehicle is standing over it; the fumes, being heavier than air, will concentrate in the pit with possibly lethal results.

### The battery

Never cause a spark, or allow a naked light, near the vehicle's battery. It will normally be giving off a certain amount of hydrogen gas, which is highly explosive.

Always disconnect the battery earth (ground) terminal before working on the fuel or electrical systems.

If possible, loosen the filler plugs or cover when charging the battery from an external source. Do not charge at an excessive rate or the battery may burst.

Take care when topping up and when carrying the battery. The acid electrolyte, even when diluted, is very corrosive and should not be allowed to contact the eyes or skin.

If you ever need to prepare electrolyte yourself, always add the acid slowly to the water, and never the other way round. Protect against splashes by wearing rubber gloves and goggles.

When jump starting a car using a booster battery, for negative earth (ground) vehicles, connect the jump leads in the following sequence: First connect one jump lead between the positive (+) terminals of the two batteries. Then connect the other jump lead first to the negative (–) terminal of the booster battery, and then to a good earthing (ground) point on the vehicle to be started, at least 18 in (45 cm) from the battery if possible. Ensure that hands and jump leads are clear of any moving parts, and that the two vehicles do not touch. Disconnect the leads in the reverse order.

### Mains electricity and electrical equipment

When using an electric power tool, inspection light etc, always ensure that the appliance is correctly connected to its plug and that, where necessary, it is properly earthed (grounded). Do not use such appliances in damp conditions and, again, beware of creating a spark or applying excessive heat in the vicinity of fuel or fuel vapour. Also ensure that the appliances meet the relevant national safety standards.

### Ignition HT voltage

A severe electric shock can result from touching certain parts of the ignition system, such as the HT leads, when the engine is running or being cranked, particularly if components are damp or the insulation is defective. Where an electronic ignition system is fitted, the HT voltage is much higher and could prove fatal.

# General dimensions, weights and capacities

*For modifications, and information applicable to later models, see Supplement at end of manual*

## Dimensions

| | |
|---|---|
| Turning circle (between kerbs) | 406 in (10312 mm) |
| Wheelbase | 98.5 in (2502 mm) |
| Overall length: | |
|     1.3 litre base model | 157.5 in (4001 mm) |
|     All other models | 159.5 in (4051 mm) |
| Overall width (excluding mirrors) | 66.2 in (1681 mm) |
| Overall height: | |
|     1.3 base model | 55.7 in (1414 mm) |
|     1.3L and HLE | 56 in (1422 mm) |
|     1.6L, HLS, Vanden Plas and MG | 56.5 in (1435 mm) |
| Ground clearance: | |
|     1.3 base model | 5.2 in (127 mm) |
|     1.3L and HLE | 5.5 in (140 mm) |
|     1.6L, HLS, Vanden Plas and MG | 6 in (152 mm) |
| Track: | |
|     All models except MG: | |
|         Front | 57.7 in (1465.5 mm) |
|         Rear | 56.7 in (1440 mm) |
|     MG models: | |
|         Front | 58.2 in (1478 mm) |
|         Rear | 57.2 in (1452 mm) |

## Weights

| | |
|---|---|
| Kerb weight: | |
|     1.3 base model | 1929 lb (875 kg) |
|     1.3L | 1995 lb (905 kg) |
|     1.3 HLE | 2017 lb (915 kg) |
|     1.6L | 2083 lb (945 kg) |
|     1.6 HLS | 2116 lb (960 kg) |
|     Vanden Plas | 2171 lb (985 kg) |
|     MG | 2127 lb (965 kg) |
| Maximum roof rack weight (distributed) | 165 lb (75 kg) |
| Towing hitch downward load | 75 to 100 lb (35 to 45 kg) |

## Capacities

| | |
|---|---|
| Engine oil (refill with filter change): | |
|     1.3 litre models | 4.75 pt (2.7 litres) |
|     1.6 litre models | 5.5 pt (3.2 litres) |
| Transmission: | |
|     Four-speed gearbox | 2.75 pt (1.5 litres) |
|     Five-speed gearbox | 3.5 pt (2.0 litres) |
| Cooling system: | |
|     1.3 litre models | 11.75 pt (6.6 litres) |
|     1.6 litre models | 14.5 pt (8.2 litres) |
| Fuel tank | 11.75 gal (53 litres) |

# About this manual

## Its aim

The aim of this manual is to help you get the best value from your vehicle. It can do so in several ways. It can help you decide what work must be done (even should you choose to get it done by a garage), provide information on routine maintenance and servicing, and give a logical course of action and diagnosis when random faults occur. However, it is hoped that you will use the manual by tackling the work yourself. On simpler jobs it may even be quicker than booking the car into a garage and going there twice, to leave and collect it. Perhaps most important, a lot of money can be saved by avoiding the costs a garage must charge to cover its labour and overheads.

The manual has drawings and descriptions to show the function of the various components so that their layout can be understood. Then the tasks are described and photographed in a step-by-step sequence so that even a novice can do the work.

## Its arrangement

The manual is divided into Chapters, each covering a logical sub-division of the vehicle. The Chapters are each divided into numbered Sections, which are headed in bold type between horizontal lines. Where required for ease of reference, some Sections are divided into sub-Sections, and in some cases into sub-sub-Sections; all such sub-divisions are indicated by appropriately-sized sub-headings. Each Section contains individual paragraphs which (except in the case of purely-descriptive "General description" Sections) are consecutively numbered; this numbering sequence is applied throughout the Section, regardless of any sub-division.

It is freely illustrated, especially in those parts where there is a detailed sequence of operations to be carried out. There are two forms of illustration: figures and photographs. The figures are numbered in sequence with decimal numbers, according to their position in the Chapter – eg Fig. 6.4 is the fourth drawing/illustration in Chapter 6. Photographs carry the same number (either individually or in related groups) as the Section and paragraph to which they relate.

There is an alphabetical index at the back of the manual as well as a contents list at the front. Each Chapter is also preceded by its own individual contents list.

References to the 'left' or 'right' of the vehicle are in the sense of a person in the driver's seat facing forwards.

Unless otherwise stated, nuts and bolts are removed by turning anti-clockwise, and tightened by turning clockwise.

Vehicle manufacturers continually make changes to specifications and recommendations, and these, when notified, are incorporated into our manuals at the earliest opportunity.

**We take great pride in the accuracy of information given in this manual, but vehicle manufacturers make alterations and design changes during the production run of a particular vehicle of which they do not inform us. No liability can be accepted by the authors or publishers for loss, damage or injury caused by any errors in, or omissions from, the information given.**

# Introduction to the Maestro

Introduced early in 1983, the Maestro marks a departure from traditional BL front wheel drive technology with the introduction of this all-new medium range hatchback saloon. Coil spring suspension and a Volkswagen gearbox mounted on the end of (rather than below) the engine are just two of the features signalling the change from a design approach dating back nearly 25 years to the introduction of the first Minis.

Another breakthrough for a British manufacturer is the use of high technology solid-state instrumentation and a voice synthesis unit, as well as computer-controlled engine management systems. These features place the Maestro at the forefront of modern vehicle technology which is rapidly becoming dominated by the micro-chip.

The Maestro range is powered by the 1.3 litre 'A +' engine, similar to the unit used in Metro models, or the 1.6 litre 'R' series engine which is derived from the unit previously used in the highly successful Maxi range.

Various models are offered in the line up, ranging from the 1.3 litre base model to the sporty sophistication of the MG 1600 version. Standard and optional equipment on the mid-range models provides a range of vehicles which should prove highly successful in a very competitive market.

Later 1.6 litre models are powered by the 'S' series engine which is derived from the 'R' series unit, and is covered in the Supplement at the back of this manual.

An MG 2.0 litre EFi model is also now available, which supersedes the MG 1600 model, but is not covered by this manual.

Details of later models, and modifications which may affect procedures covered in the main chapters are given in the Supplement at the back of this manual.

BL Cars Limited is now known as The Rover Group plc, with dealers operating under the flag of Austin Rover. All references in the text to BL should be regarded with this in mind.

# Buying spare parts and vehicle identification numbers

## Buying spare parts

Spare parts are available from many sources, for example: BL garages, other garages and accessory shops, and motor factors. Our advice regarding spare parts sources is as follows:

*Officially appointed BL garages* – This is the best source for parts which are peculiar to your car and are not generally available (eg complete cylinder heads, internal gearbox components, badges, interior trim etc). It is also the only place at which you should buy parts if your vehicle is still under warranty – non-BL components may invalidate the warranty. To be sure of obtaining the correct parts it will always be necessary to give the storeman your car's vehicle identification number, and if possible, to take the 'old' part along for positive identification. Many parts are available under a factory exchange scheme – any parts returned should always be clean. It obviously makes good sense to go straight to the specialists on your car for this type of part as they are best equipped to supply you

*Other garages and accessory shops* – These are often very good places to buy materials and components needed for the maintenance of your car (eg oil filters, spark plugs, bulbs, drivebelts, oils and greases, touch-up paint, filler paste, etc). They also sell general accessories, usually have convenient opening hours, charge lower prices and can often be found not far from home.

*Motor factors* – Good factors will stock all of the more important components which wear out relatively quickly (eg clutch components, pistons, valves, exhaust systems, brake pipes/seals and pads etc). Motor factors will often provide new or reconditioned components on a part exchange basis – this can save a considerable amount of money.

## Vehicle identification numbers

Modifications are a continuing and unpublicised process in vehicle manufacture quite apart from major model changes. Spare parts manuals and lists are compiled upon a numerical basis, the individual vehicle numbers being essential to correct identification of the component required.

When ordering spare parts, always give as much information as possible. Quote the car model, year of manufacture, body and engine numbers as appropriate.

The vehicle identification number is stamped on a plate attached to the front body panel.

The vehicle identification number (VIN) is stamped on a plate which is located at the base of the left-hand centre door pillar (B-Post). The number is also stamped into the centre of the front scuttle drain channel.

The body number plate is fixed to the bonnet lock panel just above the right-hand headlamp.

The engine number is stamped on a plate attached to the cylinder block below No. 1 spark plug.

The gearbox number is stamped on the bottom face of the gearbox casing.

# General repair procedures

Whenever servicing, repair or overhaul work is carried out on the car or its components, it is necessary to observe the following procedures and instructions which will assist in carrying out the operation efficiently and to a professional standard of workmanship.

## Joint mating faces and gaskets

Where a gasket is used between the mating faces of two components ensure that it is renewed on reassembly and fit it dry unless otherwise stated in the repair procedure. Make sure that the mating faces are clean and dry with all traces of old gasket removed. When cleaning a joint face, use a tool which is not likely to score or damage the face, and remove any burrs or nicks with an oilstone or fine file.

Make sure that tapped holes are cleaned with a pipe cleaner, and keep them free of jointing compound if this is being used.

Ensure that all orifices, channels or pipes are clear and blow through them, preferably using compressed air.

## Oil seals

Whenever an oil seal is removed from its working location, either individually or as part of an assembly, it should be renewed.

The very fine sealing lip of the seal is easily damaged and will not seal if the surface it contacts is not completely clean and free from scratches, nicks or grooves. If the original sealing surface of the component cannot be restored, the component should be renewed.

Protect the lips of the seal from any surface which may damage them in the course of fitting. Use tape or a conical sleeve where possible. Lubricate the seal lips with oil before fitting and, on dual lipped seals, fill the space between the lips with grease.

Unless otherwise stated, oil seals must be fitted with their sealing lips toward the lubricant to be sealed.

Use a tubular drift or block of wood of the appropriate size to install the seal and, if the seal housing is shouldered, drive the seal down to the shoulder. If the seal housing is unshouldered, the seal should be fitted with its face flush with the housing top face.

## Screw threads and fastenings

Always ensure that a blind tapped hole is completely free from oil, grease, water or other fluid before installing the bolt ot stud. Failure to do this could cause the casting to crack due to the hydraulic action of the bolt or stud as it is screwed in.

Always renew a fastening if the threads are in any way corroded or damaged. The strength of the thread fit will be weakened if it is renovated with a tap, die or thread chaser. If the thread in a housing is damaged, the hole should be drilled oversize and retapped. An oversize bolt or stud should then be used for retention. Damaged threads in aluminium components can often be renovated using 'helicoil' inserts.

When tightening a castellated nut to accept a split pin, tighten the nut to the specified torque, where applicable, and then tighten further to the next split pin hole. Never slacken the nut to align a split pin hole unless stated in the repair procedure.

When checking or retightening a nut or bolt to a specified torque setting, slacken the nut or bolt by a quarter of a turn, and then retighten to the specified setting.

## Locknuts, locktabs and washers

Any fastening which will rotate against a component or housing in the course of tightening should always have a washer between it and the relevant component or housing.

Spring or split washers should always be renewed when they are used to lock a critical component such as a big-end bearing retaining nut or bolt.

Locktabs which are folded over to retain a nut or bolt should always be renewed.

Self-locking nuts can be reused in non-critical areas, providing resistance can be felt when the locking portion passes over the bolt or stud thread.

Split pins must always be renewed with new ones of the correct size for the hole.

## Special tools

Some repair procedures in this manual entail the use of special tools such as a press, two or three-legged pullers, spring compressors etc. Whenever possible, suitable readily available alternatives to the manufacturer's special tools are described, and are shown in use. In some instances, where no alternative is possible, it has been necessary to resort to the use of a manufacturer's tool and this has been done for reasons of safety as well as the efficient completion of the repair operation. Unless you are highly skilled and have a thorough understanding of the procedure described, never attempt to short cut the use of any special tool when the procedure described specifies its use. Not only is there a very great risk of personal injury, but expensive damage could be caused to the components involved.

# Tools and working facilities

## Introduction

A selection of good tools is a fundamental requirement for anyone contemplating the maintenance and repair of a motor vehicle. For the owner who does not possess any, their purchase will prove a considerable expense, offsetting some of the savings made by doing-it-yourself. However, provided that the tools purchased meet the relevant national safety standards and are of good quality, they will last for many years and prove an extremely worthwhile investment.

To help the average owner to decide which tools are needed to carry out the various tasks detailed in this manual, we have compiled three lists of tools under the following headings: *Maintenance and minor repair, Repair and overhaul,* and *Special.* The newcomer to practical mechanics should start off with the *Maintenance and minor repair* tool kit and confine himself to the simpler jobs around the vehicle. Then, as his confidence and experience grow, he can undertake more difficult tasks, buying extra tools as, and when, they are needed. In this way, a *Maintenance and minor repair* tool kit can be built-up into a *Repair and overhaul* tool kit over a considerable period of time without any major cash outlays. The experienced do-it-yourselfer will have a tool kit good enough for most repair and overhaul procedures and will add tools from the *Special* category when he feels the expense is justified by the amount of use to which these tools will be put.

It is obviously not possible to cover the subject of tools fully here. For those who wish to learn more about tools and their use there is a book entitled *How to Choose and Use Car Tools* available from the publishers of this manual.

Fixings on the Maestro may be UNF or metric to ISO standards.

## Maintenance and minor repair tool kit

The tools given in this list should be considered as a minimum requirement if routine maintenance, servicing and minor repair operations are to be undertaken. We recommend the purchase of combination spanners (ring one end, open-ended the other); although more expensive than open-ended ones, they do give the advantages of both types of spanner.

*Combination spanners - 10, 11, 12, 13, 14 & 17 mm*
*Combination spanners — $\frac{7}{16}$, $\frac{1}{2}$, $\frac{9}{16}$, $\frac{5}{8}$, $\frac{3}{4}$, $\frac{13}{16}$, $\frac{7}{8}$ and $\frac{15}{16}$ in AF*
*Adjustable spanner - 9 inch*
*Gearbox drain plug key*
*Spark plug spanner (with rubber insert)*
*Spark plug gap adjustment tool*
*Set of feeler gauges*
*Brake bleed nipple spanner*
*Screwdriver - 4 in long x $\frac{1}{4}$ in dia (flat blade)*
*Screwdriver - 4 in long x $\frac{1}{4}$ in dia (cross blade)*
*Combination pliers - 6 inch*
*Hacksaw (junior)*
*Tyre pump*
*Tyre pressure gauge*
*Oil can*
*Fine emery cloth (1 sheet)*
*Wire brush (small)*
*Funnel (medium size)*
*Oil filter removal tool (1.6 litre models)*

## Repair and overhaul tool kit

These tools are virtually essential for anyone undertaking any major repairs to a motor vehicle, and are additional to those given in the *Maintenance and minor repair* list. Included in this list is a comprehensive set of sockets. Although these are expensive they will be found invaluable as they are so versatile - particularly if various drives are included in the set. We recommend the $\frac{1}{2}$ in square-drive type, as this can be used with most proprietary torque wrenches. If you cannot afford a socket set, even bought piecemeal, then inexpensive tubular box spanners are a useful alternative.

The tools in this list will occasionally need to be supplemented by tools from the *Special* list.

*Sockets (or box spanners) to cover range in previous list*
*Reversible ratchet drive (for use with sockets)*
*Extension piece, 10 inch (for use with sockets)*
*Universal joint (for use with sockets)*
*Torque wrench (for use with sockets)*
*'Mole' wrench - 8 inch*
*Ball pein hammer*
*Soft-faced hammer, plastic or rubber*
*Screwdriver - 6 in long x $\frac{5}{16}$ in dia (flat blade)*
*Screwdriver - 2 in long x $\frac{5}{16}$ in square (flat blade)*
*Screwdriver - 1$\frac{1}{2}$ in long x $\frac{1}{4}$ in dia (cross blade)*
*Screwdriver - 3 in long x $\frac{1}{8}$ in dia (electricians)*
*Pliers - electricians side cutters*
*Pliers - needle nosed*
*Pliers - circlip (internal and external)*
*Cold chisel - $\frac{1}{2}$ inch*
*Scriber*
*Scraper*
*Centre punch*
*Pin punch*
*Hacksaw*
*Valve grinding tool*
*Steel rule/straight-edge*
*Allen keys*
*Selection of files*
*Wire brush (large)*
*Axle-stands*
*Jack (strong scissor or hydraulic type)*

## Special tools

The tools in this list are those which are not used regularly, are expensive to buy, or which need to be used in accordance with their manufacturers' instructions. Unless relatively difficult mechanical jobs are undertaken frequently, it will not be economic to buy many of these tools. Where this is the case, you could consider clubbing together with friends (or joining a motorists' club) to make a joint purchase, or borrowing the tools against a deposit from a local garage or tool hire specialist.

The following list contains only those tools and instruments freely available to the public, and not those special tools produced by the vehicle manufacturer specifically for its dealer network. You will find occasional references to these manufacturers' special tools in the text of this manual. Generally, an alternative method of doing the job without the vehicle manufacturers' special tool is given. However, sometimes, there is no alternative to using them. Where this is the case and the relevant tool cannot be bought or borrowed, you will have to entrust the work to a franchised garage.

*Valve spring compressor*
*Piston ring compressor*
*Balljoint separator*
*Universal hub/bearing puller*
*Impact screwdriver*
*Micrometer and/or vernier gauge*
*Dial gauge*
*Stroboscopic timing light*
*Dwell angle meter/tachometer*
*Universal electrical multi-meter*
*Cylinder compression gauge*
*Lifting tackle*
*Trolley jack*
*Light with extension lead*

## Buying tools

For practically all tools, a tool factor is the best source since he will have a very comprehensive range compared with the average garage or accessory shop. Having said that, accessory shops often offer excellent quality tools at discount prices, so it pays to shop around.

There are plenty of good tools around at reasonable prices, but always aim to purchase items which meet the relevant national safety standards. If in doubt, ask the proprietor or manager of the shop for advice before making a purchase.

## Care and maintenance of tools

Having purchased a reasonable tool kit, it is necessary to keep the tools in a clean serviceable condition. After use, always wipe off any dirt, grease and metal particles using a clean, dry cloth, before putting the tools away. Never leave them lying around after they have been used. A simple tool rack on the garage or workshop wall, for items such as screwdrivers and pliers is a good idea. Store all normal wrenches and sockets in a metal box. Any measuring instruments, gauges, meters, etc, must be carefully stored where they cannot be damaged or become rusty.

Take a little care when tools are used. Hammer heads inevitably become marked and screwdrivers lose the keen edge on their blades from time to time. A little timely attention with emery cloth or a file will soon restore items like this to a good serviceable finish.

## Working facilities

Not to be forgotten when discussing tools, is the workshop itself. If anything more than routine maintenance is to be carried out, some form of suitable working area becomes essential.

It is appreciated that many an owner mechanic is forced by circumstances to remove an engine or similar item, without the benefit of a garage or workshop. Having done this, any repairs should always be done under the cover of a roof.

Wherever possible, any dismantling should be done on a clean, flat workbench or table at a suitable working height.

Any workbench needs a vice: one with a jaw opening of 4 in (100 mm) is suitable for most jobs. As mentioned previously, some clean dry storage space is also required for tools, as well as for lubricants, cleaning fluids, touch-up paints and so on, which become necessary.

Another item which may be required, and which has a much more general usage, is an electric drill with a chuck capacity of at least $\frac{5}{16}$ in (8 mm). This, together with a good range of twist drills, is virtually essential for fitting accessories such as mirrors and reversing lights.

Last, but not least, always keep a supply of old newspapers and clean, lint-free rags available, and try to keep any working area as clean as possible.

## Spanner jaw gap comparison table

| Jaw gap (in) | Spanner size |
|---|---|
| 0.250 | $\frac{1}{4}$ in AF |
| 0.276 | 7 mm |
| 0.313 | $\frac{5}{16}$ in AF |
| 0.315 | 8 mm |
| 0.344 | $\frac{11}{32}$ in AF; $\frac{1}{8}$ in Whitworth |
| 0.354 | 9 mm |
| 0.375 | $\frac{3}{8}$ in AF |
| 0.394 | 10 mm |
| 0.433 | 11 mm |
| 0.438 | $\frac{7}{16}$ in AF |
| 0.445 | $\frac{3}{16}$ in Whitworth; $\frac{1}{4}$ in BSF |
| 0.472 | 12 mm |
| 0.500 | $\frac{1}{2}$ in AF |
| 0.512 | 13 mm |
| 0.525 | $\frac{1}{4}$ in Whitworth; $\frac{5}{16}$ in BSF |
| 0.551 | 14 mm |
| 0.563 | $\frac{9}{16}$ in AF |
| 0.591 | 15 mm |
| 0.600 | $\frac{5}{16}$ in Whitworth; $\frac{3}{8}$ in BSF |
| 0.625 | $\frac{5}{8}$ in AF |
| 0.630 | 16 mm |
| 0.669 | 17 mm |
| 0.686 | $\frac{11}{16}$ in AF |
| 0.709 | 18 mm |
| 0.710 | $\frac{3}{8}$ in Whitworth; $\frac{7}{16}$ in BSF |
| 0.748 | 19 mm |
| 0.750 | $\frac{3}{4}$ in AF |
| 0.813 | $\frac{13}{16}$ in AF |
| 0.820 | $\frac{7}{16}$ in Whitworth; $\frac{1}{2}$ in BSF |
| 0.866 | 22 mm |
| 0.875 | $\frac{7}{8}$ in AF |
| 0.920 | $\frac{1}{2}$ in Whitworth; $\frac{9}{16}$ in BSF |
| 0.938 | $\frac{15}{16}$ in AF |
| 0.945 | 24 mm |
| 1.000 | 1 in AF |
| 1.010 | $\frac{9}{16}$ in Whitworth; $\frac{5}{8}$ in BSF |
| 1.024 | 26 mm |
| 1.063 | $1\frac{1}{16}$ in AF; 27 mm |
| 1.100 | $\frac{5}{8}$ in Whitworth; $\frac{11}{16}$ in BSF |
| 1.125 | $1\frac{1}{8}$ in AF |
| 1.181 | 30 mm |
| 1.200 | $\frac{11}{16}$ in Whitworth; $\frac{3}{4}$ in BSF |
| 1.250 | $1\frac{1}{4}$ in AF |
| 1.260 | 32 mm |
| 1.300 | $\frac{3}{4}$ in Whitworth; $\frac{7}{8}$ in BSF |
| 1.313 | $1\frac{5}{16}$ in AF |
| 1.390 | $\frac{13}{16}$ in Whitworth; $\frac{15}{16}$ in BSF |
| 1.417 | 36 mm |
| 1.438 | $1\frac{7}{16}$ in AF |
| 1.480 | $\frac{7}{8}$ in Whitworth; 1 in BSF |
| 1.500 | $1\frac{1}{2}$ in AF |
| 1.575 | 40 mm; $\frac{15}{16}$ in Whitworth |
| 1.614 | 41 mm |
| 1.625 | $1\frac{5}{8}$ in AF |
| 1.670 | 1 in Whitworth; $1\frac{1}{8}$ in BSF |
| 1.688 | $1\frac{11}{16}$ in AF |
| 1.811 | 46 mm |
| 1.813 | $1\frac{13}{16}$ in AF |
| 1.860 | $1\frac{1}{8}$ in Whitworth; $1\frac{1}{4}$ in BSF |
| 1.875 | $1\frac{7}{8}$ in AF |
| 1.969 | 50 mm |
| 2.000 | 2 in AF |
| 2.050 | $1\frac{1}{4}$ in Whitworth; $1\frac{3}{8}$ in BSF |
| 2.165 | 55 mm |
| 2.362 | 60 mm |

# Jacking and towing

*For modifications, and information applicable to later models, see Supplement at end of manual*

To change a roadwheel, remove the spare wheel and tool kit from the well in the rear compartment (photos). Apply the handbrake and chock the wheel diagonally opposite the one to be changed. Make sure that the car is located on firm level ground. Lever off the hub cover (photo) and slightly loosen the wheel nuts with the spanner provided. Position the jack at the nearest jacking point to the wheel being removed. Using the handle provided, raise the jack until the wheel is free of the ground. Unscrew the wheel nuts and remove the wheel, then remove the wheel finisher, if fitted.

Fit the finisher to the spare wheel and fit the wheel on the studs.

Fit and tighten the wheel nuts with their tapered ends towards the wheel. Lower the jack, then finally tighten the wheel nuts and refit the hub cover. Remove the chock, and refit the wheel and tool kit in the rear compartment.

When jacking up the car with a trolley jack, position the head of the jack under the jacking bracket/towing hook in the centre of the front crossmember (position 1 in the illustration) to raise both front wheels. To raise both rear wheels use a suitable length of square steel tubing securely located between the rear suspension strut lower

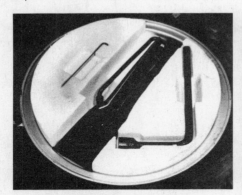

The toolkit is located in a tray ...

... which fits in the rim of the spare wheel

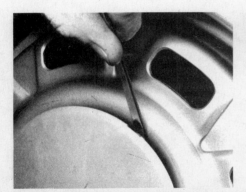

Use the tool provided or a screwdriver to lever off the wheel trim

Ensure that the jack is properly located under the appropriate jacking point

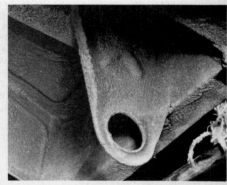

The rear lashing eyes are not to be used for towing

mountings on the trailing arms. To raise one side of the car at the front or rear, place the jack head beneath the front or rear jacking points. In all cases make sure the handbrake is firmly applied and the wheels chocked before raising the car. Always position axle stands or suitable supports under a structural member, such as a chassis member or crossmember, to support the car securely when it is raised.

The car may be towed using the towing hook provided on the front crossmember. The lashing eyes at the rear (photo) are only intended for use when the vehicle is on a transporter, and *should not be used for towing another vehicle.*

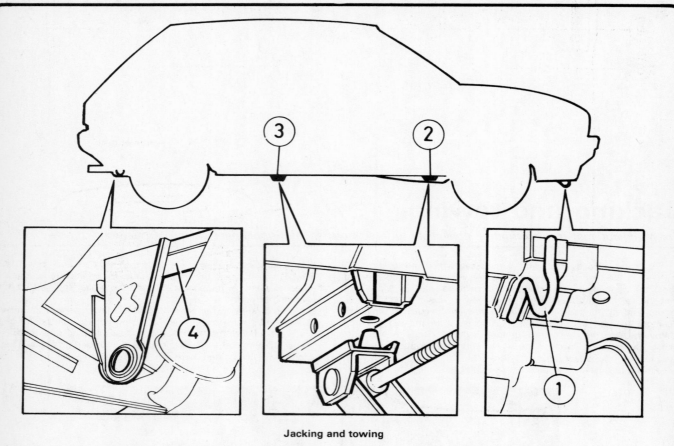

**Jacking and towing**

1   *Front jacking bracket/ towing hook*

2   *Front jacking points*
3   *Rear jacking points*

4   *Position axle stands under structural members when the car is raised*

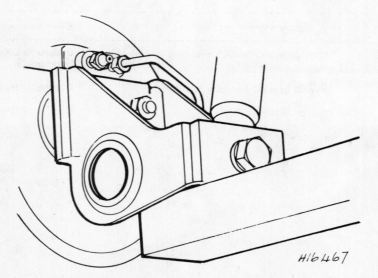

**Use a suitable length of square steel tubing between the rear trailing arms if both rear wheels are to be raised**

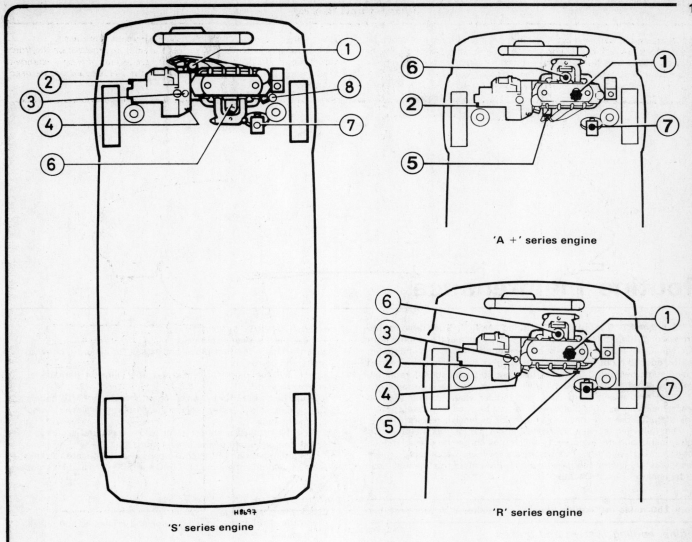

'A +' series engine

'S' series engine

'R' series engine

# Recommended lubricants and fluids

| Component or system | Lubricant type/specification | Duckhams recommendation |
|---|---|---|
| 1 Engine* | Multigrade engine oil, viscosity SAE 10W/40 | Duckhams QXR, QS, Hypergrade Plus, or Hypergrade |
| 2 Manual gearbox | Hypoid gear oil, viscosity SAE 80EP | Duckhams Hypoid 80 |
| 3 Automatic transmission | Dexron II D type ATF | Duckhams Uni-Matic |
| 4 Final drive (automatic transmission) | Hypoid gear oil, viscosity SAE 90EP | Duckhams Hypoid 90S |
| 5 Distributor ('A+' and 'R' series only) | Multigrade engine oil, viscosity SAE 10W/40 | Duckhams QXR, QS, Hypergrade Plus, or Hypergrade |
| 6 Carburettor piston damper | Multigrade engine oil, viscosity SAE 10W/40 | Duckhams QXR, QS, Hypergrade Plus, or Hypergrade |
| 7 Brake fluid reservoir | Hydraulic fluid to FMVSS 116 DOT 4 or SAE J1703 C | Duckhams Universal Brake and Clutch Fluid |
| 8 Power steering | Dexron II D type ATF | Duckhams Uni-Matic |

**\* Note:** *Austin Rover specify a 10W/40 oil to meet warranty requirements for models produced after August 1983. Duckhams QXR is available to meet these requirements*

# Routine maintenance

Maintenance is essential for ensuring safety and desirable for the purpose of getting the best in terms of performance and economy from your car. Over the years the need for periodic lubrication has been greatly reduced if not totally eliminated. This has unfortunately tended to lead some owners to think that because no such action is required, the items either no longer exist, or will last forever. This is certainly not the case; it is essential to carry out regular visual examination as comprehensively as possible in order to spot any possible defects at an early stage before they develop into major expensive repairs.

The following service schedules are a list of the maintenance requirements and the intervals at which they should be carried out, as recommended by the manufacturers. Where applicable these procedures are covered in greater detail throughout this manual, near the beginning of each Chapter.

## Every 250 miles (400km) or weekly – whichever occurs first

### Engine, cooling system and brakes
Check the oil level and top up, if necessary (photo)
Check the coolant level and top up, if necessary (photo)
Check the brake fluid level in the master cylinder and top up, if necessary (photo)

### Lights and wipers
Check the operation of all interior and exterior lights, wipers and washers
Check and, if necessary, top up the washer reservoir, adding a screen wash such as Turtle Wax High Tech Screen Wash

### Tyres
Check the tyre pressures
Visually examine the tyres for wear or damage

## Every 12 000 miles (20 000 km) or 12 months – whichever occurs first

### Engine
Renew the engine oil and filter (photos)
Check and, if necessary, adjust the valve clearances on 1.3 litre models
Visually check the engine for oil leaks and for the security and condition of all related components and attachments

### Cooling system
Check the hoses, hose clips and visible joint gaskets for leaks and any signs of corrosion or deterioration
Check and, if necessary, top up the cooling system
Check the condition of the alternator and power steering drivebelts and renew if worn. Adjust the tension of the drivebelts

### Fuel and exhaust system
Renew the air cleaner element
Visually check the fuel pipes and hoses for security, chafing, leaks and corrosion
Check the fuel tank for leaks and any signs of damage or corrosion
Top up the carburettor piston damper (photo) – not MG models
Check and, if necessary, adjust the carburettor slow running characteristics
Check the exhaust system for corrosion, leaks and security
Check the operation of the accelerator
Check the operation of the choke control and lubricate the linkage with a few drops of engine oil – 500 and 700 vans and MG models

### Ignition system
Check the spark plugs
Clean the distributor cap, coil tower and HT leads, and check for tracking

### Clutch
Check the operation of the clutch and clutch pedal
Check and, if necessary, adjust the clutch cable

### Gearbox
Visually check for oil leaks around the gearbox joint faces and oil seals
Check and, if necessary, top up the gearbox oil (photo)
Lubricate gearchange linkage

### Automatic transmission
Visually check for oil leaks around the transmission joint faces and oil seals
Check and, if necessary, top up the automatic transmission fluid
Check and, if necessary, top up the oil in the final drive unit

### Driveshafts
Check the driveshaft constant velocity joints for wear or damage and check the rubber gaiters for condition

### Braking system
Check visually all brake pipes, hoses and unions for corrosion, chafing, leakage and security
Check and, if necessary, top up the brake fluid
Check the operation of the brake warning indicators
Check the brake servo vacuum hose for condition and security
Check load-sensitive (pressure regulating) valve (Van only)

Check, and if necessary, top up the engine oil level ...

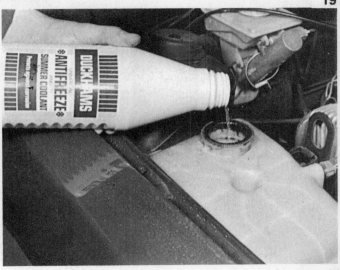

... the coolant level ...

... and the brake fluid level

Sump drain plug location on 1.3 litre models (arrowed) ...

... and 1.6 litre models (arrowed)

Oil filter location on 1.3 litre engines

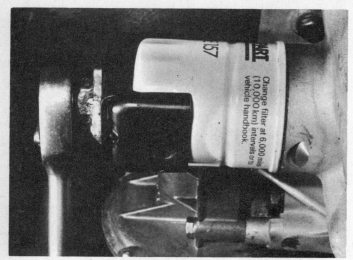

Using an oil filter removal tool on a 1.6 litre engine

Top up the carburettor piston damper with engine oil to the top of the hollow piston rod

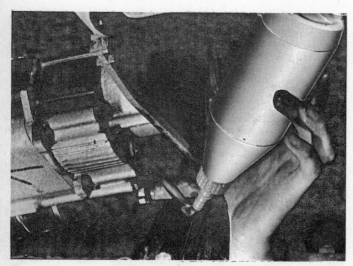

Topping up the gearbox oil

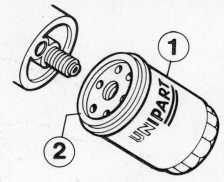

H16464

**Oil filter renewal**

1   Oil filter
2   Sealing ring – lubricate
    with engine oil before
    fitting

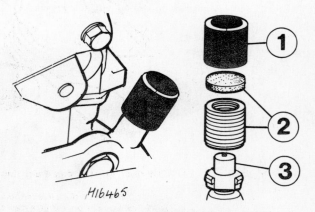

H16465

**Engine breather assembly (1.6 litre models)**

1   Cover                        3   Adaptor
2   Filter and felt pad

Check the operation of the hand and footbrake
Check the front brake pads for wear, and the discs for condition
Check the rear brake shoes for wear, and the drums for condition

## Electrical system

Check the condition and security of all accessible wiring connectors, harnesses and retaining clips
Check the operation of all electrical equipment and accessories (lights, indicators, horn, wipers etc)
Check and adjust the operation of the screen washer and, if necessary, top up the reservoir
Clean the battery terminals and smear with petroleum jelly
Have the headlamp alignment checked and, if necessary, adjusted
Check the tension and condition of the alternator drivebelt

## Suspension, steering, wheels and tyres

Check the front and rear suspension struts for fluid leaks
Check the condition and security of the steering gear, steering and suspension joints, and rubber gaiters
Check the front wheel toe setting
Check and adjust the tyre pressures
Check the tyres for damage, tread depth and uneven wear
Inspect the roadwheels for damage
Check the tightness of the wheel nuts
Check the power steering fluid level
Check the tension and condition of the power steering drivebelt

## Bodywork

Carefully inspect the paintwork for damage and the bodywork for corrosion

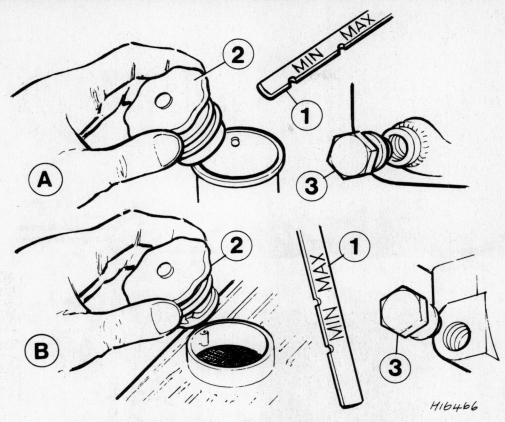

**Oil filler, dipstick and drain plug details (A 1.3 litre models, B 1.6 litre models)**

1 Maintain the oil level between the MAX and MIN marks on the dipstick
2 Oil filler cap – on 1.3 litre models, renew the cap every 24 000 miles or 24 months
3 Oil drain plug – renew the sealing washer if it is at all distorted

Check the condition of the underseal
Oil all hinges, door locks and the bonnet release mechanism with a few drops of light oil

## Road test
Check the operation of all instruments and electrical equipment
Check the operation of the seat belts
Check for any abnormalities in the steering, suspension, handling or road feel
Check the performance of the engine, clutch and transmission
Check the operation and performance of the braking system

---

**Every 24 000 miles (40 000 km) or 24 months – whichever occurs first**

---

In addition to all the items in the annual service, carry out the following:

## Engine
Renew the engine oil filler cap on 1.3 litre models
Clean (1.6 litre 'S' series) or renew (1.6 litre 'R' series) the engine breather filter
Check and, if necessary, adjust the valve clearances on 1.6 litre engines

## Cooling system
Flush the cooling system and renew the antifreeze solution
Renew the water pump and alternator drivebelt

## Fuel system
Check and adjust the carburettor idle speed and mixture settings

On MG models balance the airflow through the carburettors
Renew the in-line fuel filter – MG 1600 models with 'S' series engine (and all models with solid-state instruments)

## Ignition system
Renew the spark plugs
Check and, if necessary, adjust the ignition timing

## Clutch
Check and adjust operating cable free play

## Automatic transmission
Drain the transmission fluid, clean the oil strainer and refill with fresh fluid
Check the operation of the parking pawl

## Braking system
Renew the brake fluid

---

**Every 36 000 miles (60 000 km) or 36 months – whichever occurs first**

---

In addition to the items in the annual service, carry out the following:

## Braking system
Renew the flexible rubber hoses and the rubber seals in the calipers, wheel cylinders and master cylinder
Renew the air filter and non-return valve in the servo unit

---

**Every 48 000 miles (80 000 km) or 4 years – whichever occurs first**

---

## Engine
Renew the timing belt – 1.6 litre models with 'S' series engine

1 Brake master cylinder
2 Ignition coil
3 Ignition amplifier
4 Braking system twin GP valve
5 Battery positive terminal
6 Clutch cable adjuster
7 Starter motor and solenoid
8 Radiator bottom hose
9 Oil filter
10 Distributor cap
11 Engine oil dipstick
12 Oil filler cap
13 Thermostat housing
14 Cooling system expansion tank
15 Radiator top hose
16 Brake servo vacuum hose
17 Ambient air temperature sensor
18 Carburettor
19 Carburettor piston damper
20 Vacuum pipe banjo union
21 Main vacuum line connector
22 Front body panel

Engine and under bonnet component location on 1.3 litre models (air cleaner removed for photographic access)

1 Suspension lower arm rear mounting
2 Anti-roll bar clamp
3 Anti-roll bar
4 Suspension lower arm
5 Engine oil drain plug
6 Oil filter
7 Towing hook
8 Gearbox oil drain plug
9 Gearbox oil filler plug
10 Brake caliper
11 Steering tie-rod outer balljoint

**Front underbody view of a 1.6 litre model**

**Rear underbody view of a 1.6 litre model**

1 Rear suspension strut lower mounting
2 Handbrake cable connectors
3 Fuel tank
4 Fuel tank rear mounting bolts
5 Fuel tank front mounting bolts
  and stiffener plates
6 Rear axle transverse member
7 Rear axle trailing arm
8 Rear flexible brake hose
9 Rear axle mounting pivot bolt
10 Exhaust mounting
11 Handbrake cable adjuster
12 Exhaust tailpipe silencer

# Chapter 1 Engine

*For modifications, and information applicable to later models, see Supplement at end of manual*

**Contents**

**Specifications**

*Part A – 1.3 litre engine*
## General
| | |
|---|---|
| Type ................................................................................ | Four-cylinder in-line, overhead valve |
| Bore ................................................................................ | 2.780 in (70.61 mm) |
| Stroke .............................................................................. | 3.200 in (81.28 mm) |
| Capacity ........................................................................... | 1275 cc (77.8 cu in) |
| Firing order ...................................................................... | 1-3-4-2 (No 1 cylinder at crankshaft pulley end) |

## Crankshaft
| | |
|---|---|
| Main journal diameter ........................................................ | 1.7505 to 1.7512 in (44.46 to 44.48 mm) |
| Main bearing running clearance ............................................ | 0.0007 to 0.0029 in (0.018 to 0.074 mm) |
| Main journal minimum regrind diameter ................................. | 1.7305 in (43.96 mm) |
| Crankpin journal diameter .................................................... | 1.6252 to 1.6259 in (41.28 to 41.298 mm) |
| Crankpin running clearance .................................................. | 0.001 to 0.0027 in (0.025 to 0.069 mm) |
| Crankpin minimum regrind diameter ...................................... | 1.6052 in (40.77 mm) |
| Endfloat ........................................................................... | 0.002 to 0.003 in (0.051 to 0.076 mm) |

## Connecting rods
| | |
|---|---|
| Length between centres ....................................................... | 5.75 in (146.05 mm) |

## Pistons
| | |
|---|---|
| Skirt clearance in cylinder: | |
|     Top ......................................................................... | 0.0021 to 0.0033 in (0.053 to 0.084 mm) |
|     Bottom .................................................................... | 0.0004 to 0.0014 in (0.010 to 0.036 mm) |
| Oversizes available ............................................................. | 0.020 in (0.51 mm) |

## Piston rings
| | |
|---|---|
| Clearance in groove: | |
|     Top compression ...................................................... | 0.002 to 0.0035 in (0.051 to 0.089 mm) |
| 2nd and 3rd compression .................................................... | 0.002 to 0.004 in (0.051 to 0.102 mm) |
| End gap: | |
|     Compression ............................................................ | 0.007 to 0.012 in (0.178 to 0.305 mm) |
|     Oil control rails ........................................................ | 0.014 to 0.041 in (0.38 to 1.04 mm) |

## Gudgeon pins
| | |
|---|---|
| Diameter ........................................................................... | 0.8123 to 0.8125 in (20.63 to 20.64 mm) |
| Clearance in piston ............................................................. | Hand push fit at 20°C (68°F) |
| Interference fit in connecting rod ......................................... | 0.0008 to 0.0015 in (0.02 to 0.04 mm) |

## Camshaft
| | |
|---|---|
| Journal diameter: | |
|     Front ....................................................................... | 1.6655 to 1.6660 in (42.304 to 42.316 mm) |
|     Centre ..................................................................... | 1.62275 to 1.62325 in (41.218 to 41.231 mm) |
|     Rear ........................................................................ | 1.37275 to 1.3735 in (34.868 to 34.887 mm) |
| Running clearance in bearings .............................................. | 0.001 to 0.00225 in (0.025 to 0.057 mm) |
| Endfloat ........................................................................... | 0.003 to 0.007 in (0.076 to 0.178 mm) |
| Valve lift .......................................................................... | 0.318 in (8.08 mm) |
| Cam followers outside diameter ............................................ | 0.812 in (20.62 mm) |

## Valves
| | |
|---|---|
| Seat angle ........................................................................ | 45° |
| Head diameter: | |
|     Inlet ........................................................................ | 1.307 to 1.312 in (33.20 to 33.32 mm) |
|     Exhaust .................................................................... | 1.1515 to 1.1565 in (29.25 to 29.38 mm) |
| Stem diameter: | |
|     Inlet ........................................................................ | 0.2793 to 0.2798 in (7.094 to 7.107 mm) |
|     Exhaust .................................................................... | 0.2788 to 0.2793 in (7.082 to 7.094 mm) |
| Clearance in guide: | |
|     Inlet ........................................................................ | 0.0015 to 0.0025 in (0.038 to 0.064 mm) |
|     Exhaust .................................................................... | 0.002 to 0.003 in (0.051 to 0.076 mm) |
| Valve guides: | |
|     Length ..................................................................... | 1.687 in (42.85 mm) |
|     Outside diameter ...................................................... | 0.470 to 0.471 in (11.94 to 11.96 mm) |
|     Inside diameter ........................................................ | 0.2813 to 0.2818 in (7.145 to 7.158 mm) |
|     Fitted height above head ........................................... | 0.540 in (13.72 mm) |
| Valve springs: | |
|     Free length .............................................................. | 1.95 in (49.53 mm) |
| Valve timing (at valve clearance of 0.021 in/0.53 mm): | |
|     1.3 and 1.3L models: | |
|         Inlet opens ......................................................... | 20° BTDC |
|         Inlet closes ......................................................... | 52° ABDC |
|         Exhaust opens .................................................... | 55° BBDC |
|         Exhaust closes .................................................... | 17° ATDC |

1.3 HLE models
    Inlet opens ............................................................... 9° BTDC
    Inlet closes .............................................................. 41° ABDC
    Exhaust opens .......................................................... 49° BBDC
    Exhaust closes ......................................................... 11° ATDC
Valve clearances (cold):
    1.3 and 1.3L models ............................................... 0.014 in (0.38 mm)
    1.3 HLE models ........................................................ 0.013 in (0.35 mm)

## Lubrication system
Oil type/specification* ................................................ Multigrade engine oil, viscosity SAE 10W/40 (Duckhams QXR, QS, Hypergrade Plus, or Hypergrade)
Oil filter (without oil cooler) ...................................... Champion D102
Oil filter (with oil cooler) .......................................... Champion B101
Oil pump:
    Type ......................................................................... Bi-rotor
    Outer rotor endfloat ................................................ 0.005 in (0.127 mm)
    Inner rotor endfloat ................................................ 0.005 in (0.127 mm)
    Outer rotor-to-body clearance ................................. 0.010 in (0.254 mm)
    Rotor lobe clearance ............................................... 0.006 in (0.15 mm)
System pressure:
    Idling ....................................................................... 15 lbf/in$^2$ (1.0 bar)
    Running ................................................................... 60 lbf/in$^2$ (4.1 bar)
Warning light switch operating pressure ..................... 6 to 10 lbf/in$^2$ (0.4 to 0.7 bar)
Pressure relief valve operating pressure ..................... 60 lbf/in$^2$ (4.1 bar)
Pressure relief valve spring free length ...................... 2.86 in (72.63 mm)

* **Note:** *Austin Rover specify a 10W/40 oil to meet warranty requirements for models produced after August 1983. Duckhams QXR is available to meet these requirements*

## Torque wrench settings

| | lbf ft | Nm |
| --- | --- | --- |
| Camshaft locating plate bolts ...................................... | 8 | 11 |
| Camshaft retaining nut ................................................ | 65 | 88 |
| Connecting rod big-end cap nuts ................................. | 30 | 40 |
| Crankshaft pulley bolt ................................................. | 105 | 142 |
| Cylinder head nuts ...................................................... | 55 | 75 |
| Front plate to main bearing cap .................................. | 5 | 7 |
| Front plate to cylinder block ....................................... | 16 | 22 |
| Gearbox adaptor plate bolts ....................................... | 18 | 25 |
| Main bearing cap bolts ................................................ | 65 | 85 |
| Oil pressure switch ..................................................... | 18 | 25 |
| Oil pump retaining bolts .............................................. | 8 | 11 |
| Oil pressure relief valve cap nut ................................. | 45 | 61 |
| Oil separator bolts ...................................................... | 16 | 22 |
| Rocker cover bolts ...................................................... | 3 | 4 |
| Rocker shaft pedestal nuts ......................................... | 24 | 32 |
| Sump drain plug .......................................................... | 28 | 38 |
| Sump retaining bolts ................................................... | 8 | 11 |
| Timing cover to front plate: | | |
|     $\frac{1}{4}$ in bolts | 5 | 7 |
|     $\frac{5}{16}$ in bolts | 12 | 16 |
| Vacuum hose banjo union bolt ..................................... | 37 | 50 |
| Left-hand engine mounting bracket to body ................. | 16 | 22 |
| Left-hand engine mounting-to-bracket retaining bolts ......... | 16 | 22 |
| Left-hand engine mounting through-bolt ...................... | 70 | 95 |
| Left-hand engine mounting to gearbox ........................ | 30 | 40 |
| Right-hand engine mounting support strap bolts .......... | 16 | 22 |
| Right-hand engine mounting bracket-to-engine side bolts ....... | 16 | 22 |
| Right-hand engine mounting bracket top and bottom bolts ...... | 30 | 40 |
| Right-hand engine mounting through-bolt ..................... | 70 | 95 |
| Tie-rod bracket bolts .................................................. | 33 | 45 |
| Tie-rod to engine bracket ........................................... | 67 | 90 |
| Tie-rod to crossmember .............................................. | 33 | 45 |

## *Part B – 1.6 litre engine ('R' Series)*
## General
Type ............................................................................ Four-cylinder in-line overhead camshaft
Bore ............................................................................ 3.000 in (76.20 mm)
Stroke ......................................................................... 3.448 in (87.38 mm)
Capacity ...................................................................... 1598 cc (97.5 cu in)
Firing order ................................................................. 1-3-4-2 (No 1 cylinder at crankshaft pulley end)

## Crankshaft
Main journal diameter .................................................. 2.2515 to 2.2520 in (57.19 to 57.20 mm)
Main bearing running clearance .................................... 0.002 to 0.0035 in (0.05 to 0.08 mm)
Main journal minimum regrind diameter ........................ 2.2115 in (56.19 mm)
Crankpin journal diameter ............................................ 1.8759 to 1.8765 in (47.62 to 47.64 mm)
Crankpin running clearance .......................................... 0.0015 to 0.003 in (0.04 to 0.08 mm)
Crankpin minimum regrind diameter .............................. 1.8359 in (46.63 mm)

Endfloat ................................................................................ 0.004 to 0.007 in (0.10 to 0.18 mm)

## Connecting rods
Length between centres ...................................................... 5.830 in (148.07 mm)

## Pistons
Skirt clearance in cylinder:

    Top .............................................................................. 0.0028 to 0.0044 in (0.071 to 0.112 mm)

    Bottom ........................................................................ 0.001 to 0.002 in (0.03 to 0.05 mm)

Oversizes available .............................................................. 0.020 in (0.51 mm)

## Piston rings
Clearance in grooves ......................................................... 0.0015 to 0.0035 in (0.03 to 0.08 mm)

Fitted gap:

    Compression ............................................................... 0.012 to 0.022 in (0.30 to 0.56 mm)

    Oil control rails .......................................................... 0.015 to 0.045 in (0.38 to 1.14 mm)

## Gudgeon pins
Diameter ................................................................................ 0.8123 to 0.8125 in (20.63 to 20.64 mm)

Clearance in piston ............................................................ Hand push fit at 20°C (68°F)

Interference fit in connecting rod ..................................... 0.0008 to 0.0015 in (0.02 to 0.04 mm)

## Camshaft
Journal diameter:

    Front ........................................................................... 1.9355 to 1.9365 in (49.19 to 49.20 mm)

    Centre ......................................................................... 1.9668 to 1.9678 in (49 .98 to 49.99 mm)

Rear ...................................................................................... 1.998 to 1.999 in (50.76 to 50.78 mm)

Running clearance in bearings .......................................... 0.001 to 0.0023 in (0.025 to 0.057 mm)

Endfloat ................................................................................ 0.002 to 0.007 in (0.05 to 0.18 mm)

Valve lift:

    Inlet ............................................................................ 0.342 to 0.344 in (8.68 to 8.74 mm)

    Exhaust ...................................................................... 0.338 to 0.340 in (8.58 to 8.62 mm)

## Tappets
Adjustment ........................................................................... Selected shims

Outside diameter ................................................................ 1.1865 in (30.14 mm)

## Valves
Seat angle ............................................................................ $45\frac{1}{4}°$

Head diameter:

    Inlet ............................................................................ 1.500 in (38 mm)

    Exhaust ...................................................................... 1.218 in (31 mm)

Stem diameter (standard) .................................................. 0.3115 to 0.3120 in (7.91 to 7.93 mm)

Stem diameter (oversize) ................................................... 0.3331 to 0.3336 in (8.46 to 8.47 mm)

Stem-to-guide clearance .................................................... 0.0015 in (0.038 mm)

Valve springs free length .................................................. 1.797 in (45.70 mm)

Valve timing (at tappet clearance of 0.21 in/0.53 mm):

    Inlet opens ................................................................. 17° BTDC

    Inlet closes ................................................................. 59° ABDC

    Exhaust opens ........................................................... 57° BBDC

    Exhaust closes .......................................................... 19° ATDC

Tappet clearances (cold):

    Inlet ............................................................................ 0.014 to 0.016 in (0.35 to 0.41 mm)

    Exhaust ...................................................................... 0.017 to 0.019 in (0.43 to 0.49 mm)

Adjust only if less than ..................................................... 0.012 in (0.30 mm))

Valve sequence (from front of head):

    Inlet ............................................................................ 2, 3, 6, 7

    Exhaust ...................................................................... 1, 4, 5, 8

## Cylinder head
Height:

    New ............................................................................. 3.322 in (84.17 mm)

    Minimum ..................................................................... 3.312 in (83.92 mm)

Maximum clearance under straight-edge across surface ...................... 0.002 in (0.05 mm)

## Lubrication system
Oil type/specification* ........................................................ Multigrade engine oil, viscosity SAE 10W/40 (Duckhams QXR, QS, Hypergrade Plus, or Hypergrade)

Oil filter ................................................................................ Champion B101

Oil pump:

    Type ............................................................................ Bi-rotor

    Outer rotor endfloat ................................................. 0.005 in (0.13 mm)

    Inner rotor endfloat ................................................. 0.005 in (0.13 mm)

    Outer rotor-to-body clearance ............................... 0.010 in (0.25 mm)

    Rotor lobe clearance ................................................ 0.006 in (0.15 mm)

System pressure:

    Idling .......................................................................... 15 lbf/in² (1.0 bar)

    Running ...................................................................... 60 lbf/in² (4.1 bar)

| | |
|---|---|
| Warning light switch operating pressure ........................................ | 6 to 10 lbf/in² (0.4 to 0.7 bar) |
| Pressure relief valve operating pressure ....................................... | 60 lbf/in² (4.1 bar) |
| Pressure relief valve spring free length ....................................... | 2.86 in (72.63 mm) |

**\* Note:** *Austin Rover specify a 10W/40 oil to meet warranty requirements for models produced after August 1983. Duckhams QXR is available to meet these requirements*

## Torque wrench settings

| | lbf ft | Nm |
|---|---|---|
| Camshaft carrier bolts ............................................................... | 23 | 31 |
| Camshaft cover bolts ................................................................ | 12 | 16 |
| Camshaft sprocket bolt ............................................................. | 35 | 47 |
| Connecting rod big-end nuts ...................................................... | 33 | 45 |
| Crankshaft pulley bolt ............................................................... | 93 | 126 |
| Cylinder head bolts (see text) ................................................... | 60 | 80 |
| Gearbox adaptor plate: | | |
| $\frac{5}{16}$ in bolts ...................................... | 24 | 32 |
| M12 bolts ............................................. | 38 | 51 |
| Lifting bracket bolts .................................................................. | 20 | 27 |
| Main bearing cap bolts .............................................................. | 69 | 94 |
| Oil pump bolts ......................................................................... | 19 | 26 |
| Oil pressure switch ................................................................... | 18 | 25 |
| Sump drain plug ....................................................................... | 28 | 38 |
| Sump bolts .............................................................................. | 16 | 22 |
| Timing chain guide bolts ............................................................ | 20 | 27 |
| Timing chain fixed guide dowel bolt ............................................. | 20 | 27 |
| Vacuum hose banjo union bolt .................................................... | 37 | 50 |
| Left-hand engine mounting bracket to body ................................... | 16 | 22 |
| Left-hand engine mounting to bracket retaining bolts ...................... | 16 | 22 |
| Left-hand engine mounting through-bolt ........................................ | 70 | 95 |
| Left-hand engine mounting to gearbox .......................................... | 30 | 40 |
| Right-hand engine mounting support strap bolts .............................. | 16 | 22 |
| Right-hand engine mounting bracket-to-engine side bolts ................. | 16 | 22 |
| Right-hand engine mounting bracket top and bottom bolts ................ | 30 | 40 |
| Right-hand engine mounting through-bolt ....................................... | 70 | 95 |
| Tie-rod bracket to sump ............................................................ | 18 | 25 |
| Tie-rod to sump ....................................................................... | 55 | 75 |
| Tie-rod to crossmember ............................................................ | 33 | 45 |

# PART A: 1.3 LITRE ENGINE

## 1 General description

The engine is of four-cylinder, in-line overhead valve type, mounted transversely at the front of the car.

The crankshaft is supported in three shell type main bearings. Thrust washers are fitted at the centre main bearing to control crankshaft endfloat.

The connecting rods are attached to the crankshaft by horizontally split shell type big-end bearings, and to the pistons by interference fit gudgeon pins. The aluminium alloy pistons are of the slipper type and are fitted with three piston rings; two compression rings and a three piece oil control ring.

The camshaft is chain driven from the crankshaft and operates the rocker arms via pushrods. The inlet and exhaust valves are each closed by a single valve spring and operate in guides pressed into the cylinder head. The valves are actuated directly by the rocker arms.

Engine lubrication is by an eccentric rotor type oil pump. The pump is mounted on the gearbox end of the cylinder block and is driven by the camshaft, as are the distributor and fuel pump.

## 2 Maintenance and inspection

1   At regular intervals (see Routine Maintenance), carry out the following maintenance operations on the engine.
2   Visually inspect the engine joint faces, gaskets and seals for any sign of oil or water leaks. Pay particular attention to the areas around the rocker cover, cylinder head, timing cover and sump joint faces. Rectify any leaks by referring to the appropriate Sections of this Chapter.
3   Place a suitable container beneath the oil drain plug on the right-hand side of the sump. Unscrew the plug using spanner or socket and allow the oil to drain. Inspect the condition of the drain plug sealing washer and renew it, if necessary. Refit and tighten the plug after draining.
4   Refill the engine using the correct grade of oil, through the filler neck on the rocker cover. Fill until the level reaches the 'MAX' mark on the dipstick. The quantity of oil required to raise the level from 'MIN' to 'MAX' is 0.9 pint (0.5 litre).
5   Move the bowl to the rear of the engine, under the oil filter.
6   Using a strap wrench, or filter removal tool, slacken the filter and then unscrew it from the engine and discard.
7   Wipe the mating face on the cylinder block with a rag and then lubricate the seal of a new filter using clean engine oil.
8   Screw the filter into position and tighten it by hand only, do not use any tools.
9   With the engine running, check for leaks around the filter seal.
10  Adjust the valve clearances using the procedure described in Section 44.
11  At less frequent intervals (see Routine Maintenance) renew the oil filler cap on the rocker cover.

## 3 Major operations possible with the engine in the car

The following operations can be carried out without having to remove the engine from the car:

(a)  *Removal and refitting of the cylinder head*
(b)  *Removal and refitting of the timing cover, chain and gears*
(c)  *Removal and refitting of the sump*
(d)  *Removal and refitting of the piston and connecting rod assemblies (after removal of the cylinder head)*
(e)  *Renewal of the engine mountings*

## 4 Major operations requiring engine removal

The following operations can only be carried out after removal of the engine from the car:

(a)  *Removal and refitting of the camshaft*
(b)  *Removal and refitting of the oil pump*
(c)  *Removal and refitting of the crankshaft and main bearings*
(d)  *Removal and refitting of the tappets (cam followers)*

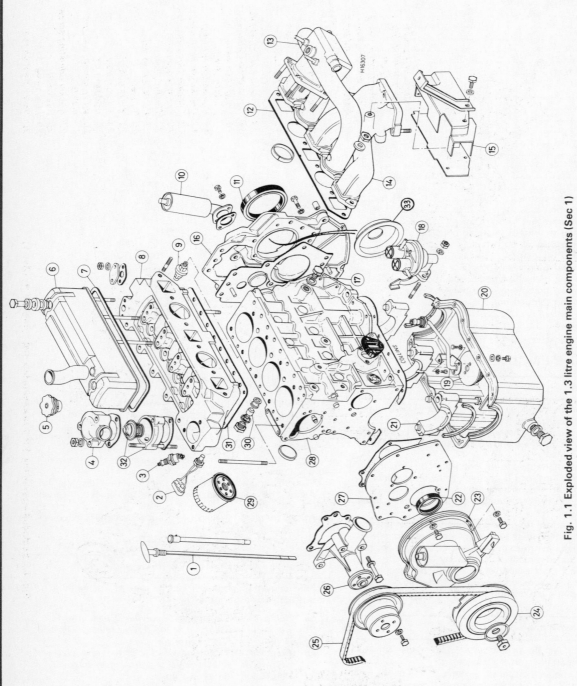

**Fig. 1.1 Exploded view of the 1.3 litre engine main components (Sec 1)**

| | | | |
|---|---|---|---|
| 1 | Dipstick | 15 | Hot air box |
| 2 | Temperature gauge sensor | 16 | Gearbox adaptor plate |
| 3 | Spark plug | 17 | Drain plug |
| 4 | Thermostat housing cover | 18 | Fuel pump |
| 5 | Oil filler cap | 19 | Oil pick-up pipe and |
| 6 | Rocker cover | | strainer |
| 7 | Gasket | 20 | Sump |
| 8 | Cylinder head | 21 | Main bearing cap |
| 9 | Oil pressure switch | 22 | Timing cover oil seal |
| 10 | Oil separator | 23 | Timing cover |
| 11 | Crankshaft oil seal | 24 | Crankshaft pulley |
| 12 | Manifold gasket | 25 | Drivebelt |
| 13 | Inlet manifold | 26 | Water pump |
| 14 | Exhaust manifold | 27 | Engine front plate |
| | | 28 | Cylinder block |
| | | 29 | Oil filter |
| | | 30 | Oil pressure relief valve |
| | | 31 | Cylinder head gasket |
| | | 32 | Thermostat and housing |
| | | 33 | Oil pump cover |

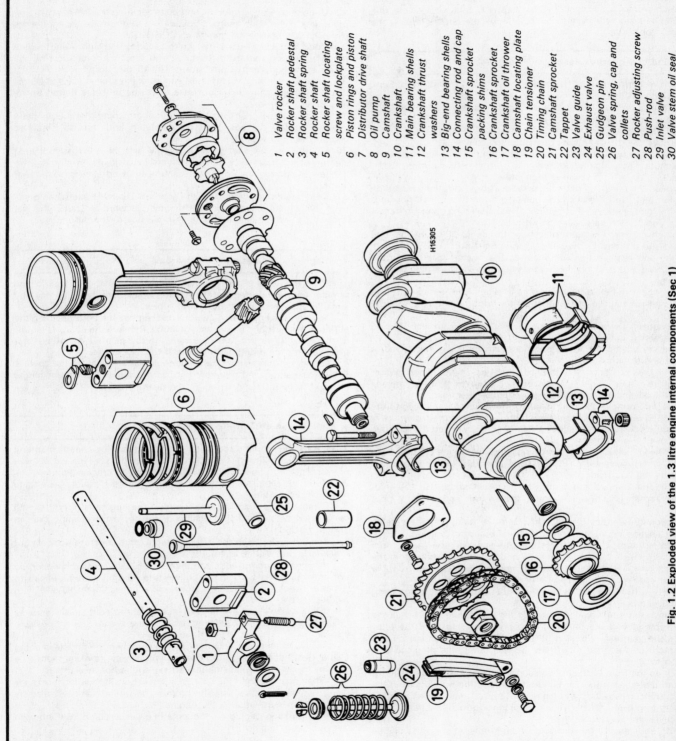

1 Valve rocker
2 Rocker shaft pedestal
3 Rocker shaft spring
4 Rocker shaft
5 Rocker shaft locating screw and lockplate
6 Piston rings and piston
7 Distributor drive shaft
8 Oil pump
9 Camshaft
10 Crankshaft
11 Main bearing shells
12 Crankshaft thrust washers
13 Big-end bearing shells
14 Connecting rod and cap
15 Crankshaft sprocket packing shims
16 Crankshaft sprocket
17 Crankshaft oil thrower
18 Camshaft locating plate
19 Chain tensioner
20 Timing chain
21 Camshaft sprocket
22 Tappet
23 Valve guide
24 Exhaust valve
25 Gudgeon pin
26 Valve spring, cap and collets
27 Rocker adjusting screw
28 Push-rod
29 Inlet valve
30 Valve stem oil seal

Fig. 1.2 Exploded view of the 1.3 litre engine internal components (Sec 1)

## 5  Methods of engine removal

The engine and gearbox assembly can be lifted from the car as a complete unit, as described in the following Section, or the gearbox may first be removed, as described in Chapter 6. It is not possible, due to the limited working clearances, to remove the engine leaving the gearbox in position.

## 6  Engine and gearbox assembly – removal

1  Remove the bonnet, as described in Chapter 11, and the battery, as described in Chapter 9.
2  Undo and remove the bolts securing the battery tray to the body and remove the tray.
3  Drain the cooling system, as described in Chapter 2.
4  Remove the air cleaner as described in Chapter 3.
5  Slacken the retaining clips and detach the radiator top hose from the thermostat housing, the bottom hose from the water pump and the two heater hoses from the inlet manifold.
6  Slacken the clips and detach the supply hose from the base of the expansion tank, and the overflow hose from the thermostat housing.
7  Undo and remove the retaining bolts, noting their different lengths, and lift off the expansion tank.
8  Detach the main vacuum pipe from the banjo union on the inlet manifold and disconnect the pipes at the connector.
9  Undo and remove the bolt securing the heater hose clip to the cylinder head and position the heater hose and vacuum pipe clear of the engine.
10  Disconnect the electrical wiring multi-plugs from the carburettor.
11  Spring back the clip and disconnect the wiring multi-plug from the alternator.
12  Disconnect the distributor wiring multi-plug from the ignition amplifier wiring connector.
13  Note the position of the wiring connections at the starter motor solenoid and disconnect the wires.
14  Note the positions of the oil pressure switch and water temperature gauge wires and disconnect them from their sensors. Detach the reversing lamp switch wires at the gearbox.
15  Undo and remove the bolt securing the wiring harness clip to the gearbox, and release the clips securing the harness to the rocker cover brackets. Check that all the wiring has been disconnected and move the harness clear of the engine.
16  Pull the HT leads off the spark plugs and detach the HT lead from the coil and rubber boot. Spring back the clips and remove the distributor cap and leads.
17  Undo and remove the banjo union retaining bolt at the inlet manifold and lift off the union, noting the arrangement of the copper washers.
18  Slacken the retaining screw and remove the accelerator cable from the linkage connector and from the carburettor bracket.
19  Undo and remove the bolt securing the speedometer cable to the gearbox. Withdraw the cable, squarely and without twisting, from the gearbox. *If care is not taken the pinion may become detached from the cable and drop into the gearbox.*
20  Refer to Chapter 5 and detach the clutch cable from the operating lever and gearbox bracket.
21  Remove the retaining clip and slide the gearchange rod out of the selector shaft lever. Disconnect the rear selector rod from the relay lever on the gearbox by prising off the balljoint with a screwdriver.
22  Detach the fuel inlet pipe from the fuel pump and plug the pipe after removal.
23  Jack up the front of the car and support it securely on axle stands.
24  From underneath the car undo and remove the nuts securing the exhaust front pipes to the manifold. Remove the hot air box as necessary to provide access. Release the pipe-to-manifold flange joint and recover the gasket.
25  Undo and remove the nut and through-bolt securing the engine tie-rod and stay to the engine bracket.
26  Undo and remove the two nuts and bolts securing the tie-rod bracket to the engine and withdraw the bracket from the engine and tie-rod.
27  Mark the relationship of the driveshaft inner constant velocity joints to the differential drive flanges.
28  Lift off the protective caps and unscrew the joint-to-drive flange retaining bolts using an Allen key.

29  Undo and remove the screws securing the left-hand access panel under the wheel arch and lift out the panel.
30  Remove the axle stands and lower the car to the ground.
31  Position a jack under the gearbox and just take the weight of the engine and gearbox assembly on the jack.
32  Undo and remove the nuts and bolts securing the left-hand engine mounting to the body and gearbox bracket and remove the mounting. Note the location of the engine earth strap.
33  Undo and remove the two bolts securing the right-hand engine mounting support strap to the body and the two bolts securing the strap to the body mounting bracket. Lift off the strap.
34  Attach a suitable hoist to the engine using chains or rope slings, or by attaching the chains or ropes to sturdy brackets bolted to the engine and gearbox.
35  Make a final check that everything attaching the engine and gearbox to the car has been disconnected and that all detached components are well clear.
36  Lift the engine and gearbox slightly and, as soon as sufficient clearance exists, release the driveshaft inner joints from the drive flanges. Support or tie up the driveshafts to avoid straining the outer joints.
37  Continue lifting the engine and gearbox assembly and when it has been raised sufficiently, draw the hoist forward or push the car backwards and lower the engine and gearbox to the ground.

## 7  Engine – separation from gearbox

1  With the engine and gearbox removed from the car, undo and remove the two starter motor retaining bolts using an Allen key and suitable spanner. Lift off the starter motor.
2  Support the engine and gearbox and remove the bolts securing the stiffener plates to the engine and gearbox. Remove the stiffener plates.
3  Undo and remove the bolts securing the gearbox to the adaptor plate, noting the different lengths and their locations.
4  Withdraw the gearbox from the engine after releasing the dowels. Draw the gearbox off squarely and do not allow the weight of the gearbox to hang unsupported on the gearbox shaft.

## 8  Engine dismantling – general

1  If possible mount the engine on a stand for the dismantling procedure, but failing this, support it in an upright position with blocks of wood placed under each side of the sump or crankcase.
2  Drain the oil into a suitable container before cleaning the engine or major dismantling.
3  Cleanliness is most important, and if the engine is dirty it should be cleaned with paraffin or a suitable solvent while keeping it in an upright position.
4  Avoid working with the engine directly on a concrete floor, as grit presents a real source of trouble.
5  As parts are removed, clean them in a paraffin bath. However, do not immerse parts with internal oilways in paraffin as it is difficult to remove, usually requiring a high pressure hose. Clean oilways with nylon pipe cleaners.
6  It is advisable to have suitable containers to hold small items, as this will help when reassembling the engine and also prevent possible losses.
7  Always obtain complete sets of gaskets when the engine is being dismantled, but retain the old gaskets with a view to using them as a pattern should a replacement if a new one is not available.
8  When possible, refit nuts, bolts, and washers in their location after being removed, as this helps to protect the threads and will also be helpful when reassembling the engine.
9  Retain unserviceable components in order to compare them with the new parts supplied.

## 9  Ancillary components – removal

With the engine separated from the gearbox the externally mounted ancillary components, as given in the following list, can be removed. The removal sequence need not necessarily follow the order given:

# Are your plugs trying to tell you something?

**Normal.**
Grey-brown deposits, lightly coated core nose. Plugs ideally suited to engine, and engine in good condition.

**Heavy Deposits.**
A build up of crusty deposits, light-grey sandy colour in appearance.
Fault: Often caused by worn valve guides, excessive use of upper cylinder lubricant, or idling for long periods.

**Lead Glazing.**
Plug insulator firing tip appears yellow or green/yellow and shiny in appearance.
Fault: Often caused by incorrect carburation, excessive idling followed by sharp acceleration. Also check ignition timing.

**Carbon fouling.**
Dry, black, sooty deposits.
Fault: over-rich fuel mixture.
Check: carburettor mixture settings, float level, choke operation, air filter.

**Oil fouling.**
Wet, oily deposits. Fault: worn bores/piston rings or valve guides; sometimes occurs (temporarily) during running-in period.

**Overheating.**
Electrodes have glazed appearance, core nose very white – few deposits. Fault: plug overheating. Check: plug value, ignition timing, fuel octane rating (too low) and fuel mixture (too weak).

**Electrode damage.**
Electrodes burned away; core nose has burned, glazed appearance. Fault: pre-ignition. Check: for correct heat range and as for 'overheating'.

**Split core nose.**
(May appear initially as a crack). Fault: detonation or wrong gap-setting technique.
Check: ignition timing, cooling system, fuel mixture (too weak).

# WHY DOUBLE COPPER IS BETTER FOR YOUR ENGINE.

**Unique Trapezoidal Copper Cored Earth Electrode** — **50% Larger Spark Area** — **Copper Cored Centre Electrode**

Champion Double Copper plugs are the first in the world to have copper core in both centre <u>and</u> earth electrode. This innovative design means that they run cooler by up to 100°C – giving greater efficiency and longer life. These double copper cores transfer heat away from the tip of the plug faster and more efficiently. Therefore, Double Copper runs at cooler temperatures than conventional plugs giving improved acceleration response and high speed performance with no fear of pre-ignition.

TRAPEZOIDAL COPPER CORED EARTH ELECTRODE

NEW TRAPEZOIDAL COPPER CORED EARTH ELECTRODE / CONVENTIONAL SOLID NICKEL ALLOY EARTH ELECTRODES

50% INCREASE IN SPARK AREA

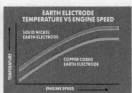

EARTH ELECTRODE TEMPERATURE VS ENGINE SPEED

SOLID NICKEL EARTH ELECTRODE

COPPER CORED EARTH ELECTRODE

TEMPERATURE / ENGINE SPEED

Champion Double Copper plugs also feature a unique trapezoidal earth electrode giving a 50% increase in spark area. This, together with the double copper cores, offers greatly reduced electrode wear, so the spark stays stronger for longer.

 **FASTER COLD STARTING**

 **FOR UNLEADED OR LEADED FUEL**

 **ELECTRODES UP TO 100°C COOLER**

 **BETTER ACCELERATION RESPONSE**

 **LOWER EMISSIONS**

 **50% BIGGER SPARK AREA**

**THE LONGER LIFE PLUG**

**Plug Tips/Hot and Cold.**
Spark plugs must operate within well-defined temperature limits to avoid cold fouling at one extreme and overheating at the other.
Champion and the car manufacturers work out the best plugs for an engine to give optimum performance under all conditions, from freezing cold starts to sustained high speed motorway cruising.
Plugs are often referred to as hot or cold. With Champion, the higher the number on its body, the hotter the plug, and the lower the number the cooler the plug.

**Plug Cleaning**
Modern plug design and materials mean that Champion no longer recommends periodic plug cleaning. Certainly don't clean your plugs with a wire brush as this can cause metal conductive paths across the nose of the insulator so impairing its performance and resulting in loss of acceleration and reduced m.p.g.
However, if plugs are removed, always carefully clean the area where the plug seats in the cylinder head as grit and dirt can sometimes cause gas leakage.
Also wipe any traces of oil or grease from plug leads as this may lead to arcing.

**CHAMPION**

**DOUBLE COPPER**

This photographic sequence shows the steps taken to repair the dent and paintwork damage shown above. In general, the procedure for repairing a hole will be similar; where there are substantial differences, the procedure is clearly described and shown in a separate photograph.

First remove any trim around the dent, then hammer out the dent where access is possible. This will minimise filling. Here, after the large dent has been hammered out, the damaged area is being made slightly concave.

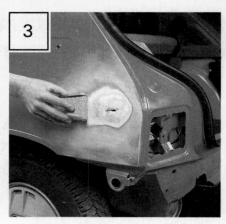

Next, remove all paint from the damaged area by rubbing with coarse abrasive paper or using a power drill fitted with a wire brush or abrasive pad. 'Feather' the edge of the boundary with good paintwork using a finer grade of abrasive paper.

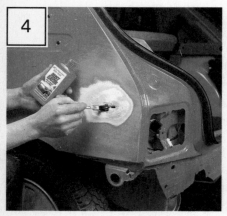

Where there are holes or other damage, the sheet metal should be cut away before proceeding further. The damaged area and any signs of rust should be treated with Turtle Wax Hi-Tech Rust Eater, which will also inhibit further rust formation.

*For a large dent or hole* mix Holts Body Plus Resin and Hardener according to the manufacturer's instructions and apply around the edge of the repair. Press Glass Fibre Matting over the repair area and leave for 20-30 minutes to harden. Then ...

... brush more Holts Body Plus Resin and Hardener onto the matting and leave to harden. Repeat the sequence with two or three layers of matting, checking that the final layer is lower than the surrounding area. Apply Holts Body Plus Filler Paste as shown in Step 5B.

*For a medium dent*, mix Holts Body Plus Filler Paste and Hardener according to the manufacturer's instructions and apply it with a flexible applicator. Apply thin layers of filler at 20-minute intervals, until the filler surface is slightly proud of the surrounding bodywork.

*For small dents and scratches* use Holts No Mix Filler Paste straight from the tube. Apply it according to the instructions in thin layers, using the spatula provided. It will harden in minutes if applied outdoors and may then be used as its own knifing putty.

Use a plane or file for initial shaping. Then, using progressively finer grades of wet-and-dry paper, wrapped round a sanding block, and copious amounts of clean water, rub down the filler until glass smooth. 'Feather' the edges of adjoining paintwork.

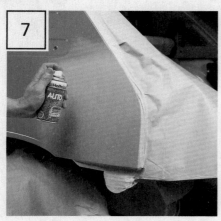

**7** Protect adjoining areas before spraying the whole repair area and at least one inch of the surrounding sound paintwork with Holts Dupli-Color primer.

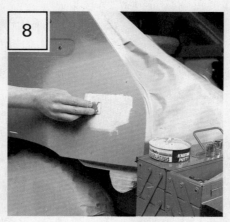

**8** Fill any imperfections in the filler surface with a small amount of Holts Body Plus Knifing Putty. Using plenty of clean water, rub down the surface with a fine grade wet-and-dry paper – 400 grade is recommended – until it is really smooth.

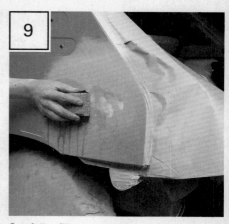

**9** Carefully fill any remaining imperfections with knifing putty before applying the last coat of primer. Then rub down the surface with Holts Body Plus Rubbing Compound to ensure a really smooth surface.

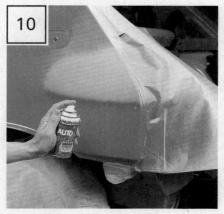

**10** Protect surrounding areas from overspray before applying the topcoat in several thin layers. Agitate Holts Dupli-Color aerosol thoroughly. Start at the repair centre, spraying outwards with a side-to-side motion.

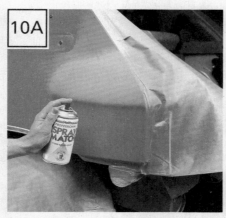

**10A** If the exact colour is not available off the shelf, local Holts Professional Spraymatch Centres will custom fill an aerosol to match perfectly.

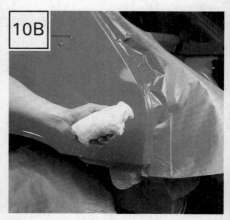

**10B** To identify whether a lacquer finish is required, rub a painted unrepaired part of the body with wax and a clean cloth.

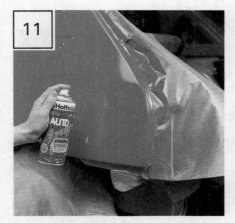

**11** If *no* traces of paint appear on the cloth, spray Holts Dupli-Color clear lacquer over the repaired area to achieve the correct gloss level.

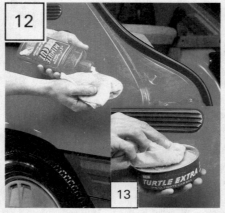

**12** **13** The paint will take about two weeks to harden fully. After this time it can be 'cut' with a mild cutting compound such as Turtle Wax Minute Cut prior to polishing with a final coating of Turtle Wax Extra.

**14** When carrying out bodywork repairs, remember that the quality of the finished job is proportional to the time and effort expended.

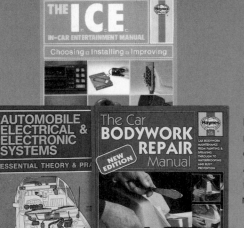

# HAYNES No1 for DIY

Haynes publish a wide variety of books besides the world famous range of *Haynes Owners Workshop Manuals*. They cover all sorts of DIY jobs. Specialist books such as the *Improve and Modify* series and the *Purchase and DIY Restoration Guides* give you all the information you require to carry out everything from minor modifications to complete restoration on a number of popular cars. In addition there are the publications dealing with specific tasks, such as the *Car Bodywork Repair Manual* and the *In-Car Entertainment Manual*. The *Household DIY* series gives clear step-by-step instructions on how to repair everyday household objects ranging from toasters to washing machines.

Whether it is under the bonnet or around the home there is a Haynes Manual that can help you save money. Available from motor accessory stores and bookshops or direct from the publisher.

*Inlet and exhaust manifolds and carburettor (Chapter 3)*
*Fuel pump (Chapter 3)*
*Alternator (Chapter 9)*
*Spark plugs (Chapter 4)*
*Distributor (Chapter 4)*
*Water pump (Chapter 2)*
*Thermostat housing and thermostat (Chapter 2)*
*Oil filter (Section 2 of this Chapter)*
*Dipstick*
*Engine right-hand mounting (Section 29 of this Chapter)*
*Clutch and flywheel (Chapter 5)*

## 10 Cylinder head – removal

**Note**: *If the engine is still in the car, first carry out the following operations with reference to the relevant Sections and Chapters of this manual:*

(a) *Disconnect the battery negative lead*
(b) *Drain the cooling system*
(c) *Remove the inlet and exhaust manifold complete with carburettor*
(d) *Disconnect the cooling system top hose, heater hose, and expansion tank hose from the thermostat housing*
(e) *Remove the HT leads and spark plugs*
(f) *Disconnect the lead from the water temperature sensor*
(g) *Release the engine mounting bracket on the thermostat housing*
(h) *Remove the bolt securing the heater hose clip to the cylinder head*

1   Unscrew the two rocker cover retaining bolts and lift off the wiring harness support brackets. Collect the washers and lift off the rocker cover and gasket (photos).
2   Unscrew the rocker shaft pedestal small nuts and remove the washers. Note the lockwasher fitted to the second pedestal from the front.

3   Unscrew the cylinder head nuts half a turn at a time in the reverse order to that shown in Fig. 1.11, and then remove the nuts.
4   Lift the rocker shaft and pedestals from the studs.
5   Shake the pushrods free from the tappets (cam followers), then withdraw them from the cylinder head keeping them in strict order to ensure correct refitting (photo).
6   Lift the cylinder head from the block. If it is stuck, tap it free with a wooden mallet. *Do not insert a lever into the gasket joint – you may damage the mating surfaces.*
7   Remove the cylinder head gasket from the cylinder block.

## 11 Cylinder head – dismantling

1   Using a valve spring compressor, compress each valve spring in turn until the split collets can be removed (photo). Release the compressor and remove the cup and spring. If the cups are difficult to release, do not continue to tighten the compressor, but gently tap the top of the tool with a hammer. Always make sure that the compressor is held firmly over the cup.
2   Remove the oil seals from the inlet valve guides (photo). A small seal may also be fitted at the bottom of the collet groove on the valve stems.
3   Remove each valve from the combustion chambers keeping them in their order of removal, together with the respective valve springs and cups (photos). Identify each valve according to the cylinder, remembering that No 1 cylinder is at the thermostat end of the cylinder head.

## 12 Timing cover, chain, and gears – removal

**Note**: *If the engine is still in the car, carry out the following operations with reference to the relevant Sections and Chapters of this manual:*

(a) *Disconnect the battery negative lead*
(b) *Remove the drivebelt and the water pump pulley*
(c) *Remove the access panel from the right-hand wheel arch*

10.1a Remove the rocker cover washer and seal

10.1b Lift off the rocker cover and gasket

10.5 Removing a pushrod

11.1 With the valve spring compressed lift out the split collets

11.2 Withdraw the valve oil seals from the inlet valve guides

11.3a Remove the valves ...

11.3b ... and keep all the components together

1   Disconnect the crankcase ventilation hose from the oil separator on the timing cover and release the fuel pipe clips from the timing cover studs.

2   Using a spanner or socket on the crankshaft pulley bolt, rotate the engine until No 4 piston is at top-dead-centre on the compression stroke. This will align the timing gear marks.

3   Undo and remove the crankshaft pulley bolt after releasing the lockwasher. If the engine is removed, lock the crankshaft using a bar or stout screwdriver across two bolts fitted to the crankshaft rear boss. If the engine is in the car, engage top gear and apply the handbrake.

4   Lever the pulley and damper off the front of the crankshaft (photo).

5   Unbolt and remove the timing cover, and remove the gasket (photo).

6   Remove the oil thrower, noting which way round it is fitted (photo).

7   Flatten the lockwasher, the unscrew the camshaft gear retaining nut (photo). Use a screwdriver through one of the gear holes to restrain the gear. Remove the lockwasher.

8   Check that the alignment marks on the timing gears are facing each other, then unbolt and remove the chain tensioner.

9   Using two levers, ease the two gears and chain from the camshaft and crankshaft.

10   Remove the gears from the chain but identify the outer face of the chain so that it can be refitted in its original position.

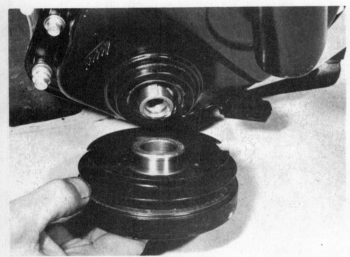

12.4 Remove the crankshaft pulley and damper

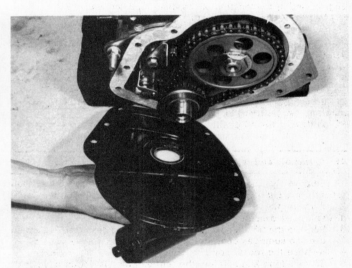

12.5 Removing the timing cover

12.6 Note the fitted position of the oil thrower

12.7 Remove the camshaft gear retaining nut

## 13 Sump – removal

**Note:** *If the engine is still in the car carry out the following operations with reference to the relevant Sections and Chapters of this manual:*

    (a) *Disconnect the battery negative lead*
    (b) *Drain the engine oil*
    (c) *Unbolt and remove the engine tie-rod*

1   Undo and remove the bolts securing the sump to the crankcase and withdraw the sump. If it is initially stuck, give it a tap with a hide or plastic mallet to break the seal. Remove the gaskets and the end seals.
2   To remove the oil pick-up pipe and strainer, unscrew the bolt securing the support bracket to the main bearing cap. Undo the pipe union nut and withdraw the pipe and strainer.

## 14 Gearbox adaptor plate – removal

1   Remove the engine and gearbox, as described in Section 6, separate the gearbox and remove the clutch assembly, as described in Chapter 5.
2   Remove the sump, as described in the previous Section.
3   Undo and remove the bolts securing the adaptor plate to the engine, noting the location of the three long screws.
4   Withdraw the adaptor plate and recover the gasket.

## 15 Oil pump – removal

1   Remove the gearbox adaptor plate, as described in the previous Section.
2   Bend back the locktabs and unscrew the bolts securing the oil pump to the cylinder block.
3   Withdraw the oil pump and recover the gasket.

## 16 Camshaft and tappets – removal

1   Remove the engine and gearbox, as described in Section 6, then separate the gearbox from the engine, as described in Section 7.
2   Remove the fuel pump, as described in Chapter 3, and the distributor, as described in Chapter 4.
3   Remove the timing cover chain and gears, as described in Section 12, and the sump, as described in Section 13.
4   Remove the rocker cover, rocker shaft and the pushrods.
5   Screw a long $\frac{5}{16}$ in bolt into the centre of the distributor drive shaft and withdraw the shaft from its location in the cylinder block (photo).
6   Undo and remove the three bolts securing the camshaft locating plate to the front of the cylider block and lift off the plate (photo).
7   Turn the engine on its side to prevent the tappets fouling the camshaft as it is withdrawn.
8   Turn the camshaft through one complete turn to move all the tappets away from the cam lobes and then withdraw the camshaft from the cylinder block (photo). Take care not to damage the three camshaft bearings as the cam lobes pass through them.
9   Withdraw each of the eight tappets through the crankcase (photo) and keep them in strict order as they must be refitted in their original locations unless they are to be renewed.

## 17 Pistons and connecting rods – removal

**Note** *If the engine is still in the car, carry out the following operations with reference to the relevant Sections and Chapters of this manual:*

    (a) *Remove the sump and oil pick-up pipe*
    (b) *Remove the cylinder head (this is not necessary if only the big-end bearings are to be removed)*

1   Check the big-end caps for identification marks. If necessary, use a centre-punch on the caps and connecting rods to identify them; mark them on the camshaft side to ensure correct refitting.
2   Turn the crankshaft so that No 1 crankpin is at its lowest point. Using a suitable socket, undo and remove the nuts securing the connecting rod cap to the rod.

16.5 Use a bolt to withdraw the distributor driveshaft

16.6 Remove the camshaft locating plate

16.8 Withdraw the camshaft from the engine

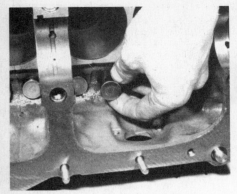

16.9 Remove the tappets from their bores

17.3 Removing a big-end bearing cap

18.5 Engine front plate removal

18.7 Checking the crankshaft endfloat

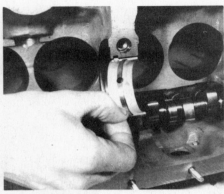

18.10 Main bearing shell removal

21.1 Remove the screw and lift off the oil pump cover

21.5a Checking the oil pump inner rotor endfloat ...

21.5b ... outer rotor endfloat ...

21.5c ... outer rotor clearance ...

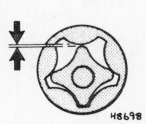

Fig. 1.3 Oil pump rotor lobe clearance checking point (Sec 21)

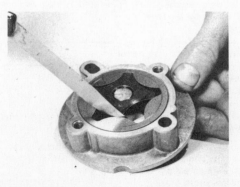

21.5d ... rotor lobe clearance

3   Withdraw the cap complete with the bearing shell (photo).
4   Using the handle of a hammer, tap the piston and connecting rod from the bore and withdraw it from the top of the cylinder block.
5   Loosely refit the cap to the connecting rod.
6   Repeat the procedure given in paragraphs 1 to 5 on No 4 piston and connecting rod, then turn the crankshaft through half a turn and repeat the procedure on No 2 and No 3 pistons.

## 18 Crankshaft and main bearings – removal

1   Remove the engine and gearbox from the car, as described in Section 6, and separate the gearbox, as described in Section 7.
2   Remove the timing cover gears and chain, as described in Section 12.
3   Remove the gearbox adaptor plate, as described in Section 14.
4   Follow the procedure for removing the pistons and connecting rods described in Section 17, but it is not necessary to completely withdraw them from the cylinder block.
5   Unbolt the front plate from the engine, and remove the gasket (photo). Invert the engine.
6   Check the main bearing caps for identification marks, and if necessary use a centre-punch to identify them.
7   Before removing the crankshaft, check that the endfloat is within the specified limits by inserting a feeler blade between the centre crankshaft web and the thrust washers (photo). This will indicate whether new thrust washers are required or not.
8   Unscrew the bolts and remove the main bearing caps complete with bearing shells. Recover the thrust washers from the centre main bearing cap.
9   Lift the crankshaft from the crankcase and remove the remaining centre bearing thrust washers.
10  Extract the bearing shells from the crankcase recesses and the caps, and identify them for location (photo).

## 19 Crankcase ventilation system – description

The crankcase ventilation system consists of hoses from the crankcase area linked and connected to a port on the carburettor.

One hose is attached to an oil separator bolted to the gearbox adaptor plate and the other is attached to an oil separator on the timing cover.

Periodically the hoses should be examined for security and condition. Cleaning them will not normally be necessary except when the engine is well worn and sludge has accumulated.

## 20 Examination and renovation – general

With the engine completely stripped, clean all the components and examine them for wear. Each part should be checked, and where necessary renewed or renovated as described in the following Sections. Renew main and big-end shell bearings as a matter of course, unless you know that they have had little wear and are in perfect condition.

## 21 Oil pump – examination

1   Remove the retaining screw and withdraw the cover from the locating dowels (photo).
2   Lift the two rotors from the pump body.
3   Clean the components with paraffin and wipe dry.
4   Refit the rotors to the pump body, making sure that the chamfer on the outer rotor enters the body first.
5   Using a feeler blade, and where necessary a straight-edge, check that the rotor clearances are as given in the Specifications (photos). If any clearance is outside that specified, or if damage is evident on any component, renew the complete oil pump.
6   If the oil pump is serviceable, refit the cover and tighten the retaining screw. Operate the pump in clean engine oil to prime it.

## 22 Crankshaft and main bearings – examination and renovation

1   Examine the bearing surfaces of the crankshaft for scratches or scoring and, using a micrometer, check each journal and crankpin for ovality. Where this is found to be in excess of 0.001 in (0.0254 mm) the crankshaft will have to be reground and undersize bearings fitted.
2   Crankshaft regrinding should be carried out by a suitable engineering works, who will normally supply the matching undersize main and big-end shell bearings.
3   If the crankshaft endfloat is more than the maximum specified amount, new thrust washers should be fitted to the centre main bearing; these are usually supplied together with the main and big-end bearings on a reground crankshaft.

## 23 Cylinder block and crankcase – examination and renovation

1   The cylinder bores must be examined for taper, ovality, scoring, and scratches. Start by examining the top of the bores; if these are worn, a slight ridge will be found which marks the top of the piston ring travel. If the wear is excessive, the engine will have had a high oil consumption rate accompanied by blue smoke from the exhaust.
2   If available, use an inside dial gauge to measure the bore diameter just below the ridge and compare it with the diameter at the bottom of the bore, which is not subject to wear. If the difference is more than 0.006 in (0.152 mm), the cylinders will normally require boring with new oversize pistons fitted.
3   Provided the cylinder bore wear does not exceed 0.008 in (0.203 mm), however, special oil control rings and pistons can be fitted to restore compression and stop the engine burning oil.
4   If new pistons are being fitted to old bores, it is essential to roughen the bore walls slightly with fine glasspaper to enable the new piston rings to bed in properly.
5   Thoroughly examine the crankcase and cylinder block for cracks and damage and use a piece of wire to probe all oilways and waterways to ensure they are unobstructed.
6   Check the tappet bores for wear and scoring; if excessive, they can be reamed and oversize tappets fitted.
7   Unscrew the oil pressure relief valve cap and remove the valve and spring. Check the valve seating for excessive wear and check that the spring free length is as specified. Renew the valve and spring as necessary, and refit them to the cylinder block.

## 24 Pistons and connecting rods – examination and renovation

1   Examine the pistons for ovality, scoring, and scratches. Check the connecting rods for wear and damage (photo).

24.1 Piston and connecting rod components

2   If the pistons or connecting rods are to be renewed it is recommended that this work is carried out by a BL garage, who will have the necessary tooling to extract the gudgeon pins from the connecting rods.

3   If new rings are to be fitted to the original pistons, expand the old rings over the top of the pistons. The use of two or three old feeler blades will be helpful in preventing the rings dropping into empty grooves. Note that the oil control ring is in three sections.

4   Before fitting the new rings to the piston, insert them into the cylinder bore and use a feeler gauge to check that the end gaps are within the specified limits.

5   After fitting the rings, check the compression rings for groove clearances using a feeler blade (photo). Make sure that the word 'Top', where marked on the compression rings, is toward the top of the piston. Arrange the compression ring gaps at 90 degrees to each other on the camshaft side of the piston.

## 25  Camshaft and tappets – examination

1   Examine the camshaft bearing surfaces, cam lobes, and skew gear for wear. If excessive, renew the shaft.

2   Check the locating plate for wear, and renew it if necessary.

3   Check the camshaft bearings for wear and if necessary remove them with a suitable diameter length of tubing. Fit the new prefinished bearings with their oil holes aligned with the oilways in the cylinder block.

4   Examine the tappets for wear, and renew them if necessary.

## 26  Timing cover, chain, and gears – examination

1   Examine all the teeth on the camshaft and crankshaft sprockets. If these are 'hooked' in appearance, renew the sprockets.

2   Examine the chain tensioner for wear, and renew it if necessary.

3   Examine the timing chain for wear. If it has been in operation for a considerable time, or if when held horizontally (rollers vertical) it takes on a deeply bowed appearance, renew it.

4   Check the timing cover for damage, and renew it if necessary. It is good practice to renew the timing cover oil seal whenever the timing cover is removed. To do this, drive out the old seal with a suitable drift, and install the new seal using a block of wood to make sure that it enters squarely (photo).

## 27  Gearbox adaptor plate – examination and renovation

1   The oil seal in the gearbox adaptor plate should be renewed as a matter of course if the engine is being overhauled.

2   Remove the old seal by prising or drifting it out of its location.

3   Lubricate a new seal in engine oil and place it in position on the adaptor plate, with its sealing lip towards the engine.

4   Using a block of wood and a hammer, drive the seal into its location until it is flush with the adaptor plate face.

## 28  Cylinder head – decarbonising, valve grinding, and renovation

1   The operation will normally only be required at comparatively high mileages. However, if persistent pinking occurs and performance has deteriorated even though the engine adjustments are correct, de-carbonising and valve grinding may be required.

2   With the cylinder head removed, use a scraper to remove the carbon from the combustion chambers and ports. Remove all traces of gasket from the cylinder head surface, then wash it thoroughly with paraffin.

3   Use a straight-edge and feeler blade to check that the cylinder head surface is not distorted. If it is, it must be resurfaced by a suitably equipped engineering works.

4   If the engine is still in the car, clean the piston crowns and cylinder bore upper edges, but make sure that no carbon drops between the pistons and bores. To do this, locate two of the pistons at the top of their bores and seal off the remaining bores with paper and masking tape. Press a little grease between the two pistons and their bores to collect any carbon dust; this can be wiped away when the piston is lowered. To prevent carbon build-up, polish the piston crown with

24.5 Checking the piston ring-to-groove clearance

26.4 Fitting the timing cover oil seal

metal polish, but remove all traces of polish afterwards.

5   Examine the heads of the valves for pitting and burning, especially the exhaust valve heads. Renew any valve which is badly burnt. Examine the valve seats at the same time. If the pitting is very slight, it can be removed by grinding the valve heads and seats together with coarse, then fine, grinding paste.

6   Where excessive pitting has occurred, the valve seats must be recut or renewed by a suitably equipped engineering works.

7   Valve grinding is carried out as follows. Place the cylinder head upside down on a bench with a block of wood at each end to give clearance for the valve stems.

8   Smear a trace of coarse carborundum paste on the seat face and press a suction grinding tool onto the valve head. With a semi-rotary action, grind the valve head to its seat, lifting the valve occasionally to redistribute the grinding paste. When a dull matt even surface is produced on both the valve seat and the valve, wipe off the paste and repeat the process with fine carborundum paste. A light spring placed under the valve head will greatly ease this operation. When a smooth unbroken ring of light grey matt finish is produced on both the valve and seat, the grinding operation is complete.

9   Scrape away all carbon from the valve head and stem, and clean away all traces of grinding compound. Clean the valves and seats with a paraffin-soaked rag, then wipe with a clean rag.

10  If the valve guides are worn, indicated by a side-to-side motion of the valve, new guides must be fitted. To do this, use a suitable mandrel

to press the worn guides downwards and out through the combustion chamber. Press the new guides into the cylinder head in the same direction until they are at the specified fitted height.

11 If the original valve springs have been in use for 20 000 miles (32 000 km) or more renew them. Where fitted, the inlet valve oil seals should also be renewed whenever the cylinder head is dismantled.

12 Examine the pushrods and rocker shaft assembly for wear, and renew them as necessry. Dismantling and reassembly of the rocker components is straightforward if reference is made to Figs. 1.2 and 1.5.

## 29 Engine mountings – removal and refitting

### Left-hand mounting

1 Place a jack beneath the gearbox, with a block of wood between the jack head and the gearbox. Raise the jack and just take the weight of the gearbox.

2 Undo and remove the through-bolt securing the engine mounting to the gearbox bracket. Lift off the upper rebound washer, lower the jack slightly and slide out the lower rebound washer.

3 Undo and remove the two bolts and withdraw the mounting from the body bracket.

4 Refitting is the reverse sequence to removal.

### Right-hand mounting

5 Jack up the front of the car so that the front wheels are just clear of the ground and support it securely on axle stands.

6 Undo and remove the securing screws and withdraw the access panel from under the right-hand wheel arch.

7 Undo and remove the bolts securing the cooling system expansion tank to the body and move the tank to one side.

8 Position a jack beneath the right-hand side of the sump with a block of wood placed between the jack head and sump. Raise the jack and just take the weight of the engine.

9 Slacken the mounting centre through-bolt, undo and remove the bolts securing the support strap to the body and body mounting bracket. Lift off the support strap.

10 Undo and remove the bolts securing the mounting and brackets to the engine and withdraw the mounting assembly.

11 To refit the mounting assembly, first position it with the spacer offset towards the top, and place the reinforced buffer plate on one side, engaging the top location hole on the mounting.

12 Place the support straps on the mounting, refit the through-bolt and refit the assembly to the mounting bracket and buffer plates.

13 Place this assembly on the body mounting bracket and refit the retaining bolts, but do not tighten at this stage.

14 Refit the bolts securing the mounting assembly to the engine and tighten fully. Tighten the through-bolt.

15 Refer to Fig. 1.7 and move the support straps as necessary to give the specified clearances, then tighten the support strap retaining bolts.

16 Refit the access panel, remove the axle stands and lower the car to the ground.

## 30 Engine tie-rod – removal and refitting

1 Jack up the front of the car and support it securely on axle stands.

2 Undo and remove the through-bolts securing the tie-rod to the engine support bracket (photo) and the crossmember bracket. Withdraw the tie-rod from its location.

3 If necessary the tie-rod engine support bracket can be removed after unscrewing the two nuts and bolts securing the bracket to the engine (photo).

4 Refitting is the reverse sequence to removal.

## 31 Engine reassembly – general

1 To ensure maximum life with minimum trouble from a rebuilt engine, not only must everything be correctly assembled, but it must also be spotlessly clean. All oilways must be clear, and locking washers and spring washers must be fitted where indicated. Oil all bearings and other working surfaces thoroughly with engine oil during assembly.

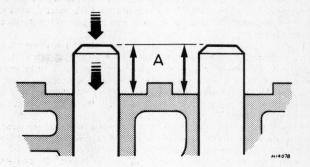

**Fig. 1.4 Valve guide fitted height dimension 'A' (Sec 28)**

*Arrow indicates direction of removal and refitting*

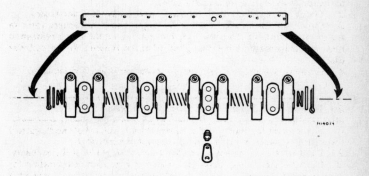

**Fig. 1.5 Rocker shaft components (Sec 28)**

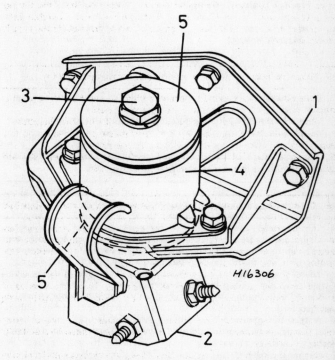

**Fig. 1.6 Left-hand engine mounting details (Sec 29)**

| | | | |
|---|---|---|---|
| 1 | Engine mounting to body bracket | 4 | Mounting |
| 2 | Gearbox mounting bracket | 5 | Rebound washers |
| 3 | Through-bolt | | |

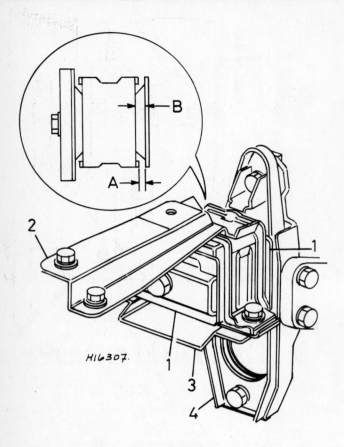

**Fig. 1.7 Right-hand engine mounting details (Sec 29)**

| | |
|---|---|
| *1   Buffer plates* | *A  = 0.16 to 0.20 in* |
| *2   Support strap* | *(4 to 5 mm) both sides* |
| *3   Body mounting bracket* | *B  = Gap to be parallel* |
| *4   Engine mounting bracket* | *over full length* |

2    Before assembly begins, renew any bolts or studs with damaged threads.
3    Gather together a torque wrench, oil can, clean rags and a set of engine gaskets and oil seals, together with a new oil filter.

## 32  Crankshaft and main bearings – refitting

1    Clean the backs of the bearing shells and the bearing recesses in both the cylinder block and main bearing caps.
2    Press the main bearing shells into the cylinder block and caps and oil them liberally.
3    Using a little grease, stick the thrust washers to each side of the centre main bearings with their oilways facing away from the bearing (photo). Similarly fit the thrust washers to the centre main bearing cap.
4    Lower the crankshaft into position, then fit the main bearing caps in their previously noted locations (photo).
5    Insert and tighten evenly the main bearing cap bolts to the specified torque (photo). Check that the crankshaft rotates freely, then check that the endfloat is within the specified limits by inserting a feeler blade between the centre crankshaft web and the thrust washers. Oversize thrust washers are available to enable endfloat adjustment if required.
6    Smear the front plate gasket with sealing compound and locate it on the front of the cylinder block. Fit the engine front plate and tighten the two lower retaining bolts.
7    With the engine upright, refit the timing cover, chain, and gears, as described in Section 38.
8    Refit the pistons and connecting rods as described in Section 33.

30.2 Tie-rod to engine and crossmember bracket through-bolts (arrowed)

30.3 Tie-rod engine support bracket retaining bolts (arrowed)

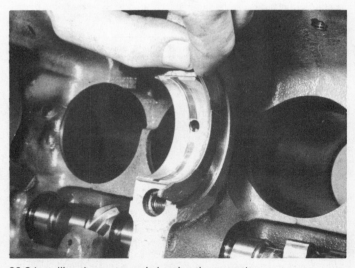

32.3 Installing the centre main bearing thrust washers

32.4 Installing the centre main bearing cap and thrust washers

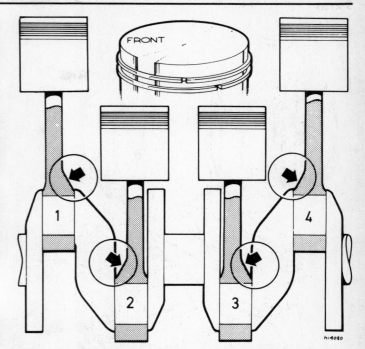

Fig. 1.8 Connecting rod offset positioning – arrowed (Sec 33)

### 34 Oil pump – refitting

**Note:** *Prime the pump with clean engine oil before fitting*

1    Make sure that the mating faces of the oil pump and cylinder block are clean, then fit the oil pump together with a new gasket, and tighten the retaining bolts evenly to the specified torque. Make sure that the cut-outs in the gasket are correctly aligned with the pump, and, if the camshaft is already in position, make sure that the pump spindle engages the slot in the camshaft.
2    Bend the lockwashers to lock the bolts.
3    If the engine and gearbox were removed purposely to remove the oil pump refit the gearbox adaptor plate, with reference to Section 36, and attach the gearbox. Refit the engine and gearbox, as described in Section 42.

### 35 Camshaft and tappets – refitting

1    Lubricate the tappets with engine oil and insert them into their bores. If the original tappets are being refitted, insert them in their original locations.
2    Oil the camshaft bearings and carefully insert the camshaft from the timing chain end of the cylinder block. Make sure that the oil pump spindle engages the slot in the camshaft.
3    Fit the locating plate to the front plate and tighten the bolts evenly.
4    Temporarily refit the camshaft sprocket, then, using a dial gauge, vernier calipers, or feeler blade and bridging piece, check that the camshaft endlfoat is within the specified limits. If not, renew the locating plate.
5    With the engine upright, refit the timing cover, chain, and gears as described in Section 38.
6    Turn the engine until No 1 piston is at top-dead-centre (TDC) on the compression stroke. If the cylinder head is not yet fitted, use two pushrods to determine the point when No 4 cylinder valves are rocking – in this position No 1 piston is at TDC compression.
7    Using the $\frac{5}{16}$ in bolt, insert the distributor driveshaft into the cylinder block with the slot in the vertical position and the larger offset section towards the crankshaft pulley (Fig. 1.9). As the driveshaft engages it will turn anti-clockwise so that the slot is parallel with the engine block, and the larger offset is towards the engine centreline. Remove the bolt after fitting.
8    Refit the distributor (Chapter 4) and the fuel pump (Chapter 3).
9    Refit the pushrods and rocker shaft and adjust the valve clearances, as described in Section 44. Refit the rocker cover.
10   Attach the gearbox to the engine (Section 41) and refit the engine and gearbox, as described in Section 42.

32.5 Tightening the main bearing bolts with a torque wrench

### 33 Pistons and connecting rods – refitting

1    Clean the backs of the bearing shells and the recesses in the connecting rods and big-end caps.
2    Press the big-end bearing shells into the connecting rods and caps in their correct position and oil them liberally.
3    Fit a ring compressor to No 1 piston, then insert the piston and connecting rod into No 1 cylinder. With No 1 crankpin at its lowest point, drive the piston carefully into the cylinder with the wooden handle of a hammer, and at the same time guide the connecting rod onto the crankpin. Make sure that the 'Front' mark on the piston crown is facing the timing chain end of the engine, and that the connecting rod offset is as shown in Fig. 1.8.
4    Fit the big-end bearing cap in its previously noted position, then tighten the nuts evenly to the specified torque.
5    Check that the crankshaft turns freely.
6    Repeat the procedure given in paragraphs 3 to 5 for No 4 piston and connecting rod, then turn the crankshaft through half a turn and repeat the procedure on No 2 and No 3 pistons.
7    Refit the gearbox adaptor plate, as described in Section 36.
8    Refit the sump, as described in Section 37.
9    Refit the cylinder head, as described in Section 39.
10   Attach the gearbox to the engine (Section 41) and then refit the engine and gearbox assembly, as described in Section 42.

2    Lubricate the crankshaft oil seal with engine oil and refit the adaptor plate to the cylinder block.
3    Refit the retaining bolts and tighten them evenly to the specified torque.
4    Refit the sump, as described in Section 37.
5    Refit the clutch assembly, as described in Chapter 5, attach the gearbox to the engine (Section 41) and refit the engine and gearbox as described in Section 42.

### 37  Sump – refitting

1    If the oil pick-up pipe and strainer were removed, refit the pipe to the crankcase and engage the union nut.
2    Refit and tighten the bolt securing the support bracket to the main bearing cap and then tighten the union nut.
3    Ensure that the sump and crankcase mating faces are clean and free from all traces of old gasket.
4    Apply jointing compound to both sides of the new side gaskets and position them on the sump.
5    Locate the new end seals in the sump recesses so that when they are pushed fully into place, an equal amount of gasket at each side protrudes above the sump face.
6    Refit the sump to the crankcase and secure with the retaining bolts. Tighten the bolts in a diagonal sequence to the specified torque in two or three stages.
7    If the engine is in the car, refit the tie-rod as described in Section 30, fill the engine with oil and reconnect the battery.

### 38  Timing cover, chain and gears – refitting

1    Locate the timing gears on the crankshaft and camshaft without the chain, and check their alignment using a straight-edge.
2    Remove the gears, and if necessary extract the Woodruff key and fit shims to the crankshaft to obtain the alignment (photo). Refit the key.
3    Turn the crankshaft so that the Woodruff key is at top-dead-centre, and turn the camshaft so that the key is at 2 o'clock. In this position No 4 cylinder is at TDC compression.
4    Loop the timing chain over the two gears so that the timing marks are facing each other on the centre line (see Fig. 1.10).
5    Locate the two gears on the crankshaft and camshaft and press them firmly home. Using a straight-edge check that the timing marks are still on the centre line.
6    Fit the camshaft gear retaining nut and lockwasher, and tighten the nut while using a screwdriver through one of the gear holes to restrain the gear (photo). Bend the lockwasher to lock the nut (photo).

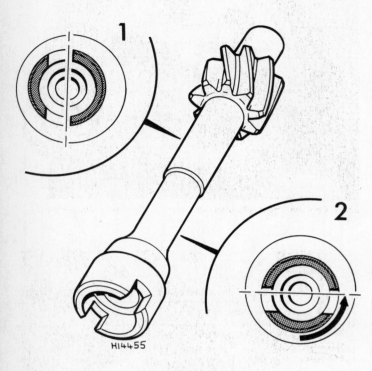

Fig. 1.9 Distributor driveshaft and fitting procedure (Sec 35)

*1   Initial fitting position        2   Fitted position*

### 36  Gearbox adaptor plate – refitting

1    Ensure that the mating faces are perfectly clean and place a new gasket in position on the cylinder block.

38.2 Crankshaft gear shim location (arrowed)

38.6a Tightening the camshaft gear retaining nut

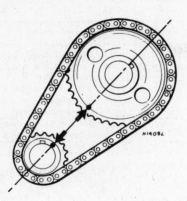

Fig. 1.10 Timing gear alignment marks (arrowed) and centre line (Sec 38)

38.6b Camshaft gear retaining nut locked, and timing marks aligned

7 Fit the chain tensioner and tighten the bolts, while keeping firm thumb pressure against the top of the bracket to provide the preload (photo).

8 Locate the oil thrower on the crankshaft with the side marked 'F' facing outwards.

9 Stick the timing cover gasket to the front plate, then fit the timing cover and retain it with two upper bolts inserted loosely.

10 Oil the timing cover oil seal, then temporarily fit the crankshaft pulley to centralize the timing cover. Insert and tighten evenly the upper retaining bolts, then remove the pulley and fit the lower bolts.

11 Fit the crankshaft pulley on the crankshaft followed by the lockwasher and bolt. Tighten the bolt to the specified torque (photo) and bend over the lockwasher tab. Adopt the same procedure as used during removal to lock the crankshaft as the bolt is tightened (Section 12).

12 Connect the crankcase ventilation hose to the oil separator and attach the fuel pipe clips to the timing cover studs.

13 If the engine is in the car, refit the access panel to the wheel arch, refit the water pump pulley and drivebelt, with reference to Chapter 2, and reconnect the battery.

38.7 Fitting the timing chain tensioner

## 39 Cylinder head – reassembly and refitting

1 Fit the valves in their original sequence or, if new valves have been obtained, in the seat to which they have been ground.

2 Oil the valve stems liberally and fit the oil seals to the inlet valve guides and collet grooves, where applicable.

3 Working on one valve, fit the spring and cup, then compress the spring with the compressor and insert the split collets. Release the compressor and remove it.

4 Repeat the procedure given in paragraph 3 on the remaining valves. Tap the end of each valve stem with a non-metallic mallet to settle the collets.

5 Make sure that the faces of the cylinder head and block are perfectly clean, then fit the new gasket over the studs with the words 'TOP' and 'FRONT' correctly positioned, 'FRONT' being the crankshaft pulley end of the engine. Do not use jointing compound.

6 Lower the cylinder head over the studs and onto the gasket.

7 Insert the pushrods in their original locations, then lower the rocker shaft and pedestals over the studs, at the same time guiding the adjusting screws into the pushrods.

8 Locate the coil and bracket on the stud furthest from the crankshaft pulley, and fit the rocker shaft lockwasher to the second pedestal from the front (crankshaft pulley end).

9 Fit the cylinder head nuts and tighten them to half the specified torque in the order shown in Fig. 1.11 (photo). After several minutes, tighten the nuts to the final torque, again in the order recommended.

10 Fit the rocker shaft pedestal washers and nuts and tighen them evenly to the specified torque (photo).

11 Adjust the valve clearances, as described in Section 44.

12 Fit the rocker cover with a new gasket, place the wiring harness

38.11 Tightening the crankshaft pulley bolt

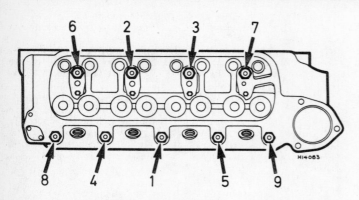

Fig. 1.11 Cylinder head nut tightening sequence – 1.3 litre engine (Sec 39)

support brackets in position and refit the rocker cover retaining bolts and washers. Tighten the bolts to the specified torque.

13  If the engine is in the car, reverse the introductory procedure given in Section 10, and refill the cooling system, with reference to Chapter 2.

14  Drive the car for five to ten miles then allow the engine to cool, and remove the rocker cover. Working in the order shown in Fig. 1.11, slacken half a turn, then immediately tighten each cylinder head nut to the specified torque. Readjust the valve clearances then refit the rocker cover.

## 40  Ancillary components – refitting

Refer to Section 9 and refit the listed components with reference to the Chapters indicated.

## 41  Engine – attachment to gearbox

Refer to Section 7 and attach the gearbox to the engine using the reverse of the removal procedure. Tighten the retaining bolts to the specified torque.

## 42  Engine and gearbox assembly – refitting

Refer to Section 6 and refit the engine and gearbox using the reverse of the removal procedure, noting the following additional points:

(a)  Align the marks on the driveshaft joints and drive flanges made during removal. Fit and tighten the bolts to the specified torque and fit new protective caps

(b)  Adjust the accelerator cable, as described in Chapter 3, and the clutch cable, as described in Chapter 5.

(c)  Refill the engine with oil
(d)  Refill the cooling system, as described in Chapter 2.

## 43  Engine – adjustments after major overhaul

1  With the engine and gearbox refitted to the car, make a final check to ensure that everything has been reconnected and that no rags or tools have been left in the engine compartment.

2  Make sure that the oil and water levels are topped up and then start the engine; this may take a little longer than usual as the fuel pump and carburettor float chamber may be empty.

3  As soon as the engine starts, watch for the oil pressure light to go out and check for any oil, fuel or water leaks. Don't be alarmed if there are some odd smells and smoke from parts getting hot and burning off oil deposits.

4  Drive the car until normal operating temperature is reached and then allow it to cool. Re-torque the cylinder head nuts, as described in Section 39, and adjust the valve clearances, as described in Section 44.

5  If new pistons, rings or crankshaft bearings have been fitted the engine must be run-in for the first 500 miles (800 km). Do not exceed 45 mph (72 kph), operate the engine at full throttle or allow it to labour in any gear.

6  After the initial 6 000 miles (10 000 km) has been covered, the engine oil and oil filter should be changed. Thereafter, oil and filter changes should be carried out at the usual intervals specified in Routine Maintenance.

## 44  Valve clearances – adjustment

1  The valve clearances must be adjusted with the engine cold.

2  Remove the rocker cover and gasket.

3  Turn the engine with a spanner on the crankshaft pulley bolt until No 8 valve (no 4 cylinder exhaust) is fully open.

4  Insert a feeler blade of the correct thickness between the rocker arm and valve stem of No 1 valve (No 1 cylinder exhaust). If the blade is not a firm sliding fit, loosen the locknut on the rocker arm with a ring spanner and turn the adjusting screw with a screwdriver (photo). Tighten the locknut whilst holding the adjusting screw stationary, then recheck the adjustment.

5  Repeat the procedure given in paragraphs 3 and 4 on the remaining valves using the 'rule of nine' method as given below:

| Valve open | Adjust valve |
| --- | --- |
| 8 exhaust | 1 exhaust |
| 6 inlet | 3 inlet |
| 4 exhaust | 5 exhaust |
| 7 inlet | 2 inlet |
| 1 exhaust | 8 exhaust |
| 3 inlet | 6 inlet |
| 5 exhaust | 4 exhaust |
| 2 inlet | 7 inlet |

6  Check the rocker cover gasket for damage, and renew it if necessary. Refit the rocker cover and gasket with the filler cap towards the crankshaft pulley end of the engine. Tighten the nuts to the specified torque.

39.9 Tightening the cylinder head ...

39.10 ... and rocker pedestal nuts using a torque wrench

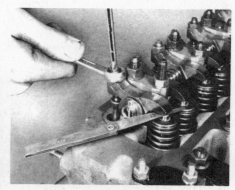

44.4 Checking the valve clearances

## PART B: 1.6 LITRE ENGINE ('R' SERIES)

### 45 General description

The engine is of four-cylinder, in-line overhead camshaft type, mounted transversely at the front of the car.

The crankshaft is supported in five shell type main bearings. Thrust washers are fitted to No 4 main bearing to control crankshaft endfloat.

The connecting rods are attached to the crankshaft by horizontally split shell type big-end bearings, and to the pistons by interference fit gudgeon pins. The aluminium alloy pistons are of the slipper type and have their gudgeon pins offset to the thrust side to reduce piston slap. Two compression rings and a three piece oil control ring are fitted to each piston.

The overhead camshaft is mounted in a carrier attached to the cylinder head, and is chain driven by the crankshaft. The camshaft operates the valves via inverted bucket type tappets which are also housed in the camshaft carrier. Tappet adjustment is by shims fitted between the valve stems and the tappet buckets. The inlet and exhaust valves are mounted at an angle in the cylinder head and are each closed by a single valve spring.

A gear mounted on the front of the crankshaft drives the distributor and a shaft connected to this gear drives the oil pump, which is mounted externally on the front of the engine.

The oil filter is located on the front face of the aluminium alloy sump. The sump is removable with the engine in the car to allow access to the crankshaft bearings.

The fuel pump is attached to the camshaft cover and is operated by an eccentric on the camshaft.

### 46 Maintenance and inspection

1   At regular intervals (see Routine Maintenance) carry out the following maintenance operations on the engine.
2   Visually inspect the engine joint faces, gaskets and seals for any sign of oil or water leaks. Pay particular attention to the areas around the camshaft cover, cylinder head, crankshaft front oil seal and sump joint faces. Rectify any leaks by referring to the appropriate Sections of this Chapter.
3   Place a suitable container beneath the oil drain plug located on the rear right-hand side of the sump. Unscrew the plug using a spanner or socket and allow the oil to drain. Inspect the condition of the drain plug sealing washer, and renew it if necessary. Refit and tighten the plug after draining.
4   Move the bowl to the front of the engine under the oil filter.
5   Using a strap wrench or filter removal tool, slacken the filter and unscrew it from the engine and discard (photo).
6   Wipe the filter mating face on the sump with a rag and then

lubricate the seal of a new filter using clean engine oil.
7   Screw the filter into position and tighten it by hand only, do not use any tools.
8   Refill the engine using the correct grade of oil through the filler on the camshaft cover. Fill until the level reaches the 'MAX' mark on the dipstick. The quantity of oil required to raise the level from 'MIN' to 'MAX' is 0.9 pint (0.5 litre).
9   With the engine running, check for leaks around the filter seal.
10   At less frequent intervals (see Routine Maintenance), check and, if necessary, adjust the tappet clearances, as described in Section 95.
11   At the same service interval, unscrew the crankcase breather filter located at the rear left-hand side of the engine on the gearbox adaptor plate (photo). Refit a new filter and plastic container assembly to its location on the adaptor plate.

### 47 Major operations possible with the engine in the car

The following operations can be carried out without having to remove the engine from the car:

(a)   Removal and refitting of the camshaft and tappets
(b)   Removal and refitting of the timing chain, tensioner and guides (providing a suitable chain link removal tool is available)
(c)   Removal and refitting of the cylinder head
(d)   Removal and refitting of the sump
(e)   Removal and refitting of the big-end bearings
(f)   Removal and refitting of the piston and connecting rod assemblies (after removal of the cylinder head)
(g)   Removal and refitting of the oil pump
(h)   Removal and refitting of the engine mountings

### 48 Major operations requiring engine removal

Strictly speaking it is only necessary to remove the engine if the crankshaft or main bearings require attention. However, due to the possibility of dirt entry, and to allow greater working access, it is preferable to remove the engine if working on the piston and connecting rod assemblies, or when carrying out any major engine overhaul or repair.

### 49 Methods of engine removal

The engine and gearbox assembly can be lifted from the car as a complete unit, as described in the following Section, or the gearbox may first be removed, as described in Chapter 6. It is not possible, due

46.5 Using a filter removal tool to unscrew the oil filter

46.11 The crankcase breather filter is located on the gearbox adaptor plate

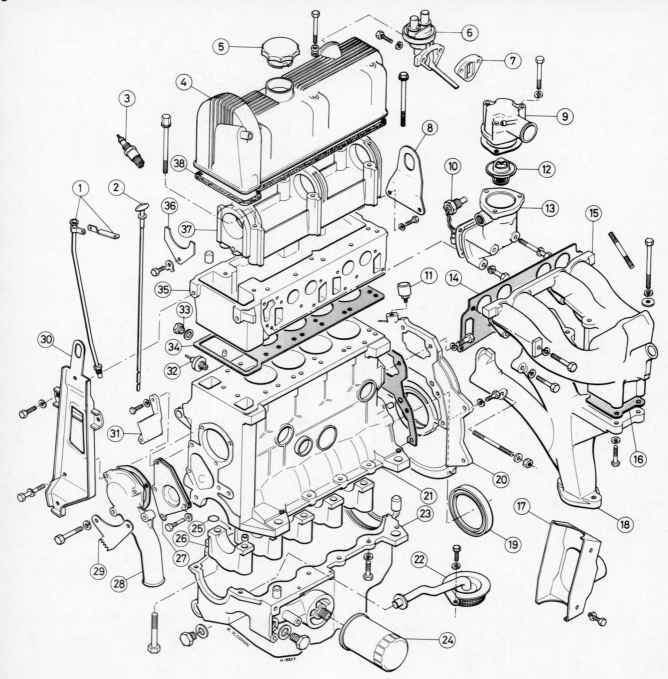

**Fig. 1.12 Exploded view of the 1.6 litre engine main components (Sec 45)**

| | | |
|---|---|---|
| 1 Dipstick tube and support bracket | 14 Manifold gasket | 27 Front cover |
| 2 Dipstick | 15 Inlet manifold | 28 Water inlet elbow |
| 3 Spark plug | 16 Gasket | 29 Timing plate |
| 4 Camshaft cover | 17 Hot air box | 30 Engine mounting bracket |
| 5 Oil filler cap | 18 Exhaust manifold | 31 LED timing sensor bracket |
| 6 Fuel pump | 19 Crankshaft oil seal | 32 Oil pressure switch |
| 7 Insulation block | 20 Gearbox adaptor plate | 33 Cylinder block drain plug |
| 8 Engine lifting bracket | 21 Cylinder block | 34 Cylinder head gasket |
| 9 Thermostat housing cover | 22 Oil pick-up tube and strainer | 35 Cylinder head |
| 10 Temperature gauge sensor | 23 Sump | 36 Camshaft locating plate |
| 11 Crankcase breather filter | 24 Oil filter | 37 Camshaft carrier |
| 12 Thermostat | 25 O-ring seal | 38 Gasket |
| 13 Thermostat housing | 26 Main bearing cap | |

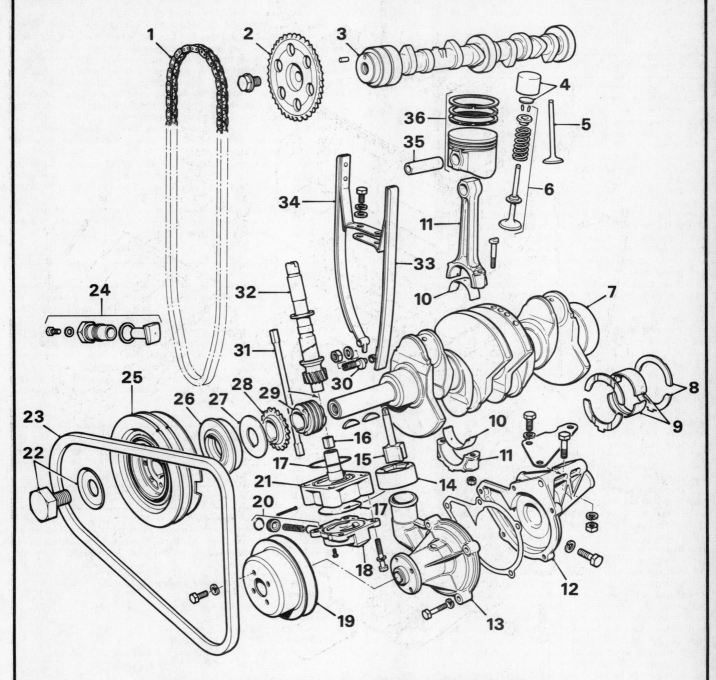

Fig. 1.13 Exploded view of the 1.6 litre engine internal components (Sec 45)

| | | | |
|---|---|---|---|
| 1 Timing chain | 10 Big-end bearing shells | 17 O-ring seals | 26 Crankshaft oil seal |
| 2 Camshaft sprocket | 11 Connecting rod and cap | 18 Oil pump cover | 27 Oil thrower |
| 3 Camshaft | 12 Water pump body – rear | 19 Water pump pulley | 28 Crankshaft sprocket |
| 4 Tappet and shim | 13 Water pump body – front | 20 Oil pressure relief valve | 29 Distributor and oil pump drivegear |
| 5 Exhaust valve | 14 Oil pump outer rotor | 21 Oil pump body | 30 Chain guide adjuster |
| 6 Inlet valve, oil seal, spring, cap and collets | 15 Oil pump shaft and inner rotor | 22 Pulley bolt and lockwasher | 31 Oil pump driveshaft |
| 7 Crankshaft | 16 Driveshaft adaptor | 23 Drivebelt | 32 Distributor driveshaft |
| 8 Crankshaft thrust washers | | 24 Timing chain tensioner | 33 Adjustable chain guide |
| 9 Main bearing shells | | 25 Crankshaft pulley | 34 Fixed chain guide |
| | | | 35 Gudgeon pin |
| | | | 36 Piston rings and piston |

to the limited working clearances, to remove the engine leaving the gearbox in position.

## 50 Engine and gearbox assembly – removal

1   Remove the bonnet, as described in Chapter 11, and the battery, as described in Chapter 9.
2   Undo and remove the bolts securing the battery tray to the body and remove the tray.
3   Drain the cooling system, as described in Chapter 2.
4   Remove the air cleaner, as described in Chapter 3.
5   Slacken the retaining clips and detach the radiator top hose, heater hose and expansion tank overflow hose from the thermostat housing.
6   Slacken the retaining clips and detach the radiator bottom hose from the water pump (photo), and the lower heater hose from its connection at the engine compartment bulkhead.
7   Undo and remove the bolt securing the heater hose clip to the cylinder head lifting bracket (photo) and move all the disconnected hoses clear of the engine.
8   Slacken the clip and detach the supply hose from the base of the expansion tank (photo).
9   Undo and remove the screws and bolt securing the expansion tank to the body panel and lift off the tank. Note the spacer and position of the bolt securing the brake servo vacuum pipe clip.
10  Detach the main vacuum pipe from the banjo union on the inlet manifold and disconnect the pipes at the connector.
11  Undo and remove the banjo union retaining bolt at the inlet manifold and lift off the union (photo) noting the arrangement of the copper washers.
12  Disconnect the electrical wiring multi-plugs from the carburettor.
13  Spring back the clip and disconnect the wiring multi-plug from the alternator.
14  Disconnect the distributor wiring multi plug from the ignition amplifier wiring connector.
15  Note the position of the wiring connections at the starter motor solenoid and disconnect the wires.
16  Note the positions of the oil pressure switch and water temperature gauge wires and disconnect them from their sensors. Detach the reversing lamp switch wires at the gearbox.
17  Undo and remove the bolt securing the wiring harness clip to the gearbox, and release the clips securing the harness to the camshaft cover brackets. Check that all wiring has been disconnected and move the harness clear of the engine.
18  Pull the HT leads off the spark plugs and detach the HT lead from the coil and rubber boot. Spring back the clips and remove the distributor cap and leads.
19  Release the accelerator cable from the carburettor linkage and bracket (photo). On MG models release the choke cable from the carburettor levers and flange. Position the cable(s) clear of the engine.
20  Undo and remove the bolt securing the speedometer cable or speed transducer cable to the gearbox. Withdraw the cable squarely and without twisting from the gearbox. *If care is not taken the pinion may become detached from the cable and drop into the gearbox.*
21  Refer to Chapter 5 and detach the clutch cable from the operating lever and gearbox bracket.
22  Remove the retaining clip and slide the gearchange rod out of the selector shaft lever. Disconnect the rear selector rod from the relay lever on the gearbox by prising off the balljoint with a screwdriver.
23  Detach the fuel inlet pipe from the fuel pump (photo) and plug the pipe after removal.
24  Jack up the front of the car and support it securely on axle stands.
25  From underneath the car, undo and remove the nuts securing the exhaust front pipes to the manifold. Remove the hot air box and manifold support bracket as necessary to provide access. Release the pipe-to-manifold flange joint (photo) and recover the gasket.
26  Refer to Section 80 and remove the engine tie-rod.
27  Mark the relationship of the driveshaft inner constant velocity joints to the differential drive flanges.
28  Lift off the protective caps and unscrew the joint-to-drive flange retaining bolts using an Allen key.
29  Undo and remove the screws securing the left-hand access panel under the wheel arch and lift out the panel.
30  Remove the axle stands and lower the car to the ground.
31  Position a jack under the gearbox and just take the weight of the

engine and gearbox assembly on the jack.
32  Undo and remove the nuts and bolts securing the left-hand engine mounting to the body and gearbox bracket, and remove the complete mounting assembly. Remove the engine earth strap.
33  Undo and remove the two bolts securing the right-hand engine mounting support strap to the body and the two bolts securing the strap to the body mounting bracket (photo). Lift off the strap.
34  Attach a suitable hoist to the engine using chains or ropes through the engine lifting brackets on the side of the cylinder head. Refit the previously removed bolt to the left-hand bracket.
35  Make a final check that everything attaching the engine and gearbox to the car has been disconnected and that all detached components are well clear.
36  Lift the engine and gearbox slightly and as soon as sufficient clearance exists, release the driveshaft inner joints from the drive flanges. Support or tie up the driveshafts to avoid straining the outer joints.
37  Continue lifting the engine and gearbox assembly and when it has been raised sufficiently (photo) draw the hoist forward or push the car backwards and lower the engine and gearbox to the ground.

## 51 Engine – separation from gearbox

1   With the engine and gearbox removed from the car, undo and remove the two starter motor retaining bolts using an Allen key and suitable spanner. Lift off the starter motor (photo).
2   Support the engine and gearbox and remove the bolts securing the stiffener plates to the engine and gearbox. Lift away the plates.
3   Undo and remove the bolts securing the gearbox to the adaptor plate, noting the different lengths and their locations.
4   Withdraw the gearbox off the engine after releasing the dowels (photo). Draw the gearbox off squarely and do not allow the weight of the gearbox to hang unsupported on the gearbox shaft.

## 52 Engine dismantling – general

Refer to Section 8.

## 53 Ancillary components – removal

With the engine separated from the gearbox the externally mounted ancillary components, as given in the following list, can be removed, with reference to the relevant Chapters of this manual where necessary. The removal sequence need not necessarily follow the order given:

*Inlet and exhaust manifolds and carburettor (Chapter 3)*
*Fuel pump (Chapter 3)*
*Alternator (Chapter 9) – photo*
*Spark plugs (Chapter 4)*
*Distributor (Chapter 4)*
*Water pump (Chapter 2) – photo*
*Thermostat housing and thermostat (Chapter 2) – photos*
*Oil filter (Section 46 of this Chapter) – photo*
*Dipstick – photo*
*Engine right-hand mounting (Section 29 of this Chapter)*
*Clutch and flywheel (Chapter 5)*
*Water inlet elbow and timing plate – photo*

## 54 Cylinder head removal – engine in car

1   Disconnect the battery negative terminal.
2   Refer to Chapter 2 and drain the cooling system.
3   Refer to Chapter 3 and remove the air cleaner.
4   Disconnect the fuel inlet and outlet hoses at the fuel pump and plug the disconnected hoses.
5   Detach the vacuum pipe from the inlet manifold banjo union. Undo and remove the retaining bolt and lift off the banjo union and the two copper washers (photo).
6   Detach the carburettor vacuum pipe at the connector and move the pipe to one side.
7   Detach the distributor vacuum advance pipe from the carburettor.

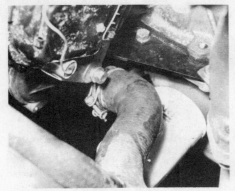

50.6 Detach the bottom hose from the water pump

50.7 Remove the heater hose retaining clip

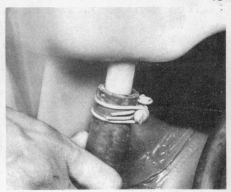

50.8 Detach the expansion tank hose

50.11 Disconnect the banjo union

50.19 Release the accelerator cable from the linkage connector (A) and support bracket (B)

50.23 Detach the fuel inlet pipe from the pump

50.25 Separate the exhaust pipe-to-manifold flange joint

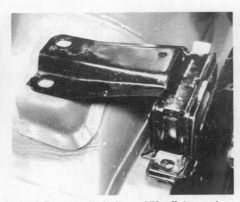

50.33 Remove the bolts and lift off the engine mounting support strap

50.37 Removing the engine and gearbox assembly from the car

51.1 Removing the starter motor

51.4 Separating the gearbox from the engine

53.1a Remove the alternator ...

53.1b ... water pump ...

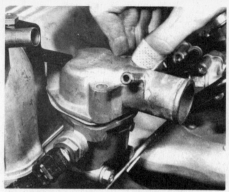

53.1c ... thermostat housing cover ...

53.1d ... thermostat and housing ...

53.1e ... oil filter ...

53.1f ... dipstick tube at the attachments arrowed ...

53.1g ... the water inlet elbow and timing plate

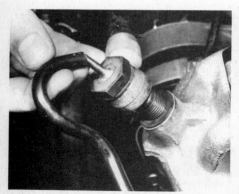

54.5 Detach the vacuum pipe and unscrew the banjo union

54.9 Removing the camshaft cover

54.18 Camshaft sprocket and carrier timing marks (arrowed) aligned

54.19 Using an 1/8 in Allen key (arrowed) to retract the tensioner slipper

54.20 Withdraw the sprocket and lay the chain over the guides

54.22 Cylinder head retaining bolt slackening sequence

8   Disconnect the accelerator cable from the carburettor linkage and support bracket. On MG models disconnect the choke cable from the levers on the carburettors and from its support bracket.

9   Undo and remove the bolts and washers securing the camshaft cover to the cylinder head. Lift off the wiring harness support brackets, detach the breather hose and lift off the cover and gasket (photo).

10   Slacken the retaining clips and disconnect the top hose, heater hose and expansion tank hose from the thermostat housing. On MG models slacken the retaining clips and disconnect the heater hoses from the inlet manifold.

11   Undo and remove the bolt securing the heater hose clip to the side of the cylinder head. Position all the disconnected hoses clear of the cylinder head.

12   Undo and remove the bolt securing the fuel drain pipe to the thermostat housing. Detach the hose from the carburettor and remove the pipe and hose from the engine.

13   Make a note of their locations and disconnect the electrical wiring connectors and multi plug from the carburettor.

14   Pull the spark plug HT leads off the plugs and disconnect the HT lead from the coil and rubber boot.

15   Disconnect the electrical connector at the water temperature gauge sensor.

16   Undo and remove the nuts securing the exhaust pipe flange to the manifold. Detach the support bracket, separate the flanges and recover the gasket.

17   Jack up the front of the car and support it securely on axle stands. Undo and remove the retaining screws and withdraw the access panel from under the right-hand wheel arch.

18   Using a suitable socket on the crankshaft pulley bolt, rotate the crankshaft in the normal direction of rotation until the camshaft carrier and sprocket timing marks are aligned (photo), and the crankshaft pulley timing notch is at TDC.

19   Undo and remove the small bolt in the centre of the timing chain tensioner and then, using a $\frac{1}{8}$ in Allen key inserted in the bolt hole, engage and turn the tensioner 90° clockwise to retract the tensioner slipper from the chain (photo).

20   Undo and remove the bolt securing the sprocket to the camshaft. Withdraw the sprocket from the camshaft, disengage the chain from the sprocket teeth, and allow the chain to lie over the guides (photo).

21   Undo and remove the bolts securing the right-hand engine mounting to the cylinder head.

22   Gradually slacken the cylinder head retaining bolts half a turn at a time in the order shown (photo) until they are loose, and then remove them.

23   Lift the cylinder head and manifold assembly from the engine (photo). If it is stuck, tap it free with a soft-faced mallet, *do not attempt to prise it free using a lever between the head and cylinder block,* or the mating faces may be damaged.

24   Remove the cylinder head gasket from the cylinder block.

### 55 Cylinder head removal – engine on bench

The procedure for removing the cylinder head with the engine on the bench is similar to that for removal when the engine is in the car, with the exception of disconnecting the controls and services. Refer to Section 54 and follow the procedure given in paragraph 9, and

paragraphs 18 to 24 inclusive.

### 56 Camshaft and tappets – removal

**Note:** *If the engine is still in the car, carry out the following operations with reference to the relevant Sections and Chapters of this manual:*

   *(a)   Disconnect the battery negative terminal*
   *(b)   Remove the air cleaner*
   *(c)   Remove the camshaft cover*
   *(d)   Jack up the front of the car, support it securely on axle stands and remove the right-hand access panel from under the wheel arch*

1   Using a suitable socket on the crankshaft pulley bolt, rotate the crankshaft in the normal direction of rotation until the camshaft carrier and sprocket timing marks are aligned and the crankshaft pulley timing notch is at TDC.

2   Undo and remove the small bolt in the centre of the timing chain tensioner and then, using a $\frac{1}{8}$ in Allen key inserted in the bolt hole, engage and turn the tensioner 90° clockwise to retract the tensioner slipper from the chain.

3   Undo and remove the bolt securing the sprocket to the camshaft. Withdraw the sprocket from the camshaft, disengage the chain from the sprocket teeth and allow the chain to lie over the guides.

4   Progressively undo and remove the six bolts securing the camshaft carrier to the cylinder head.

5   Lift off the camshaft carrier and, as soon as it is clear of the valves, turn it on its side to prevent the tappet buckets dropping out. Some of the buckets may stay in place on the valves as the carrier is removed. If so lift them off and place them in their correct bore in the carrier. Make sure that there is a tappet adjusting shim in each bucket and that none of these are left sitting on top of the valves.

6   Push the tappet buckets halfway out of their bores so that the cam lobes will clear, remove the camshaft locating plate and withdraw the camshaft from the carrier.

7   If the tappet buckets are to be removed, keep them in order, as each bucket and shim must be refitted in its original carrier bore unless they are being renewed.

### 57 Cylinder head – dismantling

1   Using a valve spring compressor, compress each valve spring in turn until the split collets can be removed (photo). Release the compressor and lift off the cap and spring (photos).

2   If, when the valve spring compressor is screwed down, the valve spring cap refuses to free and expose the split collets, gently tap the top of the tool, directly over the cap with a light hammer. This will free the cap.

3   Withdraw the oil seal off the top of the valve guide (photo) and then remove the valve through the combustion chamber (photo).

4   It is essential that the valves are kept in their correct sequence unless they are so badly worn that they are to be renewed. If they are going to be kept and used again, place them in a sheet of card having

54.23 Removing the cylinder head with the engine in the car

57.1a Compress the valve springs and extract the split collets

57.1b Lift off the valve spring cap ...

57.1c ... followed by the spring

57.3a Remove the valve oil seal ...

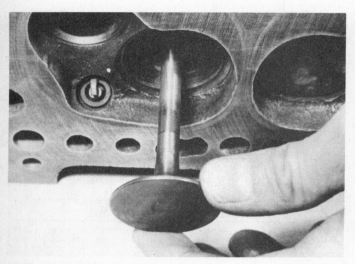

57.3b ... and the valve

58.5 Removing the crankshaft pulley

eight holes numbered 1 to 8 – corresponding to the relative fitted positions of the valves. Note that No 1 valve is nearest to the timing chain end of the engine.

## 58  Timing chain and sprockets – removal

**Note:** *It is not possible to remove the chain in continuous form with the crankshaft in place. If a chain link removal/refitting tool can be obtained, the chain can be split at the special link provided for this purpose and removed. If the engine is on the bench and this operation forms part of the dismantling sequence, leave the chain in place until the crankshaft is removed.*

If the engine is still in the car, carry out the following operations with reference to the relevant Sections and Chapters of this manual:

    (a)  *Disconnect the battery negative terminal*
    (b)  *Remove the air cleaner*
    (c)  *Remove the camshaft cover*
    (d)  *Jack up the front of the car and support it securely on axle stands*
    (e)  *Remove the right-hand access cover from under the wheel arch*

1    Using a suitable socket on the crankshaft pulley bolt, rotate the crankshaft in the normal direction of rotation until the camshaft carrier and sprocket timing marks are aligned and the crankshaft pulley timing notch is at TDC.

2    Undo and remove the small bolt in the centre of the timing chain tensioner and then, using a $\frac{1}{8}$ in Allen key inserted in the bolt hole, engage and turn the tensioner 90° clockwise to retract the tensioner slipper from the chain (photo 54.19).

3    Undo and remove the bolt securing the sprocket to the camshaft, disengage the chain from the sprocket teeth and allow the chain to lie over the guides.

4    Release the lockwasher and then undo and remove the bolt securing the crankshaft pulley to the crankshaft. If the engine is removed, lock the crankshaft using a bar or stout screwdriver across two bolts fitted to the crankshaft rear boss. If the engine is in the car, engage top gear and apply the handbrake.

5    Using two screwdrivers, if necessary, lever the pulley off the front of the crankshaft (photo).

6    Slacken the locknut and, using a screwdriver, turn the chain guide adjuster anti-clockwise to the back of the cam – approximately half a turn (see Fig. 1.14).

7    Using a screwdriver, prise the front oil seal from its location. It is recommended that a new seal is obtained for reassembly.

8    Slide the oil thrower off and then withdraw the sprocket from the crankshaft.

**Fig. 1.14 Timing chain tensioner removal (Secs 58 and 59)**

| | |
|---|---|
| 1 Tensioner centre screw | 5 Fixed chain guide |
| 2 Tensioner | dowel bolt |
| 3 Tensioner slipper | 6 Chain guide adjuster |
| 4 Front cover | 7 Cam and spring |

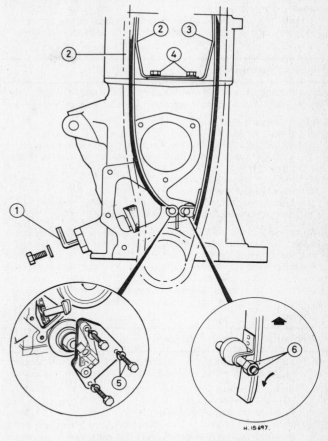

**Fig. 1.15 Timing chain guide removal (Sec 60)**

| | |
|---|---|
| 1 Allen key to retract | 5 Dowel bolt and sealing |
| tensioner slipper | washer |
| 2 Fixed guide | 6 Chain guide adjuster |
| 3 Adjustable guide | and locknut |
| 4 Guide retaining bolts | |

9 Move the chain around until the bright link is located. Using a chain removal/refitting tool extract the bright link rivets, withdraw the link, and separate the chain.
10 If a new chain is to be fitted temporarily connect one end of the new chain to one end of the old one and then use the old chain to pull the new one through the crankcase and into position. Detach the old chain and join the new one, as described in Section 86.

## 59 Timing chain tensioner – removal

**Note:** *If the engine is still in the car, carry out the following operations with reference to the relevant Sections and Chapters of this manual:*

*(a) Disconnect the battery negative terminal*
*(b) Remove the air cleaner*
*(c) Remove the camshaft cover*
*(d) Jack up the front of the car and support it securely on axle stands. Remove the right-hand access cover from under the wheel arch*
*(e) Refer to Section 58 and carry out the operations described in paragraphs 1 to 6 inclusive*

1 Undo and remove the four bolts securing the front cover to the engine. Note that two of the bolts also retain the LED timing light sensor bracket and that the bolt nearest to the chain guide adjuster is a dowel bolt used to locate the lower end of the fixed chain guide. Note also that this dowel bolt has a sealing washer.
2 With the bolts removed, lift off the sensor bracket and the engine front plate with gasket.
3 Unscrew the chain tensioner and withdraw it from the engine while at the same time removing the tensioner slipper through the front cover aperture.

## 60 Timing chain guides – removal

**Note:** *If the engine is still in the car, refer to Section 59 and carry out all the operations described in the introductory note to that Section.*
1 Undo and remove the four bolts securing the front cover to the engine. Note that two of the bolts also retain the LED timing light sensor bracket and that the bolt nearest to the chain guide adjuster is a dowel bolt used to locate the lower end of the fixed chain guide. Note also that this bolt has a sealing washer.
2 With the bolts removed, lift off the sensor bracket and the engine front plate with gasket.
3 Lift the timing chain away from the chain guide upper retaining bolts and tie it to the engine lifting bracket.
4 Undo and remove the two upper retaining bolts securing the guides to the cylinder block.
5 Lift out the fixed guide, disengage the lower end of the adjustable guide from the adjuster, and lift out the adjustable guide. It may be necessary to turn the adjuster further anti-clockwise to enable the hooked end of the guide to clear the adjuster cam.

## 61 Oil pump – removal

**Note:** *If the engine is still in the car, carry out the following operations with reference to the relevant Sections and Chapters of this manual:*

*(a) Disconnect the battery negative terminal*
*(b) Drain the engine oil*

1 Undo and remove the bolts securing the oil pump to the sump and

withdraw the pump (photo).
2    Remove the O-ring seal from the mating face of the pump body
and withdraw the pump driveshaft from the distributor driveshaft.

## 62  Sump – removal

**Note**: *If the engine is still in the car, carry out the following operations
with reference to the relevant Sections and Chapters of this manual:*

(a)   *Remove the oil pump*
(b)   *Drain the cooling system*
(c)   *Raise the front of the car, support it securely on axle stands
      and remove the access cover from under the right-hand
      wheel arch*
(d)   *Remove the engine tie-rod*
(e)   *Remove the water pump*
(f)   *Disconnect the exhaust pipe at the manifold flange*
(g)   *Remove the dipstick tube from the sump*

1    Undo and remove the bolts securing the engine stiffener plates to
the sump and gearbox adaptor plate. Remove the stiffener plates.
2    Undo and remove the bolts securing the sump to the crankcase.
Tap the sump from side-to-side using a hide or plastic mallet to release
it from the locating dowels.
3    Withdraw the sump and remove the rear main bearing cap sealing
strip and the O-ring seal from the sump mating face.

## 63  Distributor driveshaft – removal

**Note**: *If the engine is still in the car, carry out the following operations
with reference to the relevant Sections and Chapters of this manual:*

(a)   *Remove the sump*
(b)   *Remove the air cleaner*
(c)   *Remove the camshaft cover*
(d)   *Refer to Section 58 and carry out the operations described in
      paragraphs 1 to 8 inclusive, with the exception of paragraph
      6*
(e)   *Remove the distributor cap*

1    If the engine is still in the car, note the position of the distributor
rotor arm which should be at the 2 o-clock position when viewed
toward the cylinder head.
2    Withdraw the distributor drivegear from the end of the crankshaft,
using a screwdriver as a lever if it is tight.
3    If the distributor is still in place note that the rotor arm will now
have moved to the 5 o-clock position.
4    Withdraw the distributor driveshaft and thrust washer from the
crankcase.

## 64  Gearbox adaptor plate – removal

1    Remove the engine and gearbox, as described in Section 50,
separate the gearbox (Section 51) and remove the clutch assembly, as
described in Chapter 5.
2    Remove the sump, as described in Section 62.
3    Undo and remove the bolts securing the adaptor plate to the
engine (photo), noting the two long bolts at the bottom.
4    Withdraw the adaptor plate and recover the gasket.

## 65  Pistons and connecting rods – removal

**Note**: *If the engine is still in the car, carry out the following operations
with reference to the relevant Sections and Chapters of this manual:*

(a)   *Remove the sump*
(b)   *Remove the cylinder head (this is not necessary if only the
      big-end bearings are to be removed)*

1    Check the big-end caps for identification marks. If necessary, use
a centre-punch on the caps and connecting rods to identify them; mark
them on the distributor side to ensure correct refitting.
2    Turn the crankshaft so that No 1 crankpin is at its lowest point.
Using a suitable socket undo and remove the nuts securing the
connecting rod cap to the rod.
3    Withdraw the cap complete with bearing shell.
4    Using the handle of a hammer, push the piston and connecting rod
up through the bore and withdraw it from the top of the cylinder block.
5    Loosely refit the cap to the connecting rod.
6    Repeat the procedure given in paragraphs 1 to 5 on No 4 piston
and connecting rod, then turn the crankshaft through half a turn and
repeat the procedure on No 2 and No 3 pistons.

## 66  Crankshaft and main bearings – removal

1    Remove the engine and gearbox from the car, as described in
Section 50, and separate the gearbox, as described in Section 51.
2    Remove the timing chain and sprockets, as described in Section
58, and the sump, as described in Section 62.
3    Remove the distributor driveshaft, as described in Section 63, and
the gearbox adaptor plate, as described in Section 64.
4    Follow the procedure for removing the pistons and connecting
rods described in Section 65, but it is not necessary to completely
withdraw them from the cylinder block.
5    Check the main bearing caps for identification marks and if
necessary use a centre-punch to identify them (photo).
6    Before removing the crankshaft, check that the endfloat is within

61.1 Removing the oil pump

64.3 Gearbox adaptor plate retaining bolt locations (arrowed)

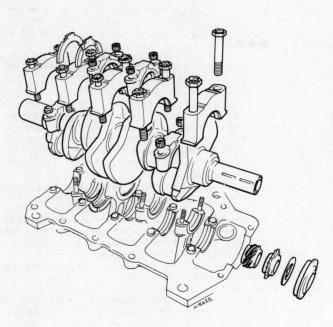

**Fig. 1.16 Crankshaft and main bearing components (Sec 66)**

66.5 Main bearing cap and crankcase identification marks (arrowed)

the specified limits by inserting feeler gauges between No 4 crankshaft web and the thrust washers. This will indicate whether new thrust washers are required or not.

7   Undo and remove the bolts securing the main bearing caps to the crankcase and remove the bearing caps complete with bearing shells. Recover the thrust washers from No 4 bearing cap.

8   Lift the crankshaft from the crankcase (photo) and release it from the timing chain. Remove the remaining thrust washers from No 4 bearing.

9   Extract the bearing shells from the crankcase recesses and the caps, and identify them for location.

## 67  Crankcase ventilation system – description

The crankcase ventilation system consists of an oil separator in the camshaft cover, a hose connecting the camshaft cover to the carburettor, and a breather filter located on the gearbox adaptor plate.

Air is drawn into the crankcase through the breacher filter. Inlet manifold depression draws the crankcase fumes through the oil separator and into the carburettor airstream where they mix with the incoming mixture passing to the cylinders for combustion.

The breather filter should be renewed at the intervals specified in Section 46 and the hose should also be checked for condition and security.

## 68  Examination and renovation – general

Refer to Section 20.

## 69  Crankshaft and main bearings – examination and renovation

Refer to Section 22.

## 70  Cylinder block and crankcase – examination and renovation

Refer to Section 23, paragraphs 1 to 5.

66.8 Removing the crankshaft

## 71  Pistons and connecting rods – examination and renovation

Refer to Section 24. Note that when arranging the piston rings, the compression ring gaps should be positioned at 90 degrees to each other, away from the distributor side of the engine.

## 72  Camshaft and camshaft bearings – examination and renovation

1   The camshaft itself should show no sign of wear, but if very slight score marks on the cams are noticed, they can be removed by very gently rubbing down with very fine emery cloth or an oilstone. The greatest care should be taken to keep the cam profiles smooth.

2   Carefully examine the camshaft bearing surfaces for wear and, if evident, the camshaft must be renewed.

3   Check the camshaft fit in the cast aluminium carrier and, if side movement is evident, a new housing must be obtained. The camshaft runs directly in the aluminium carrier and does not have white metal bushes.

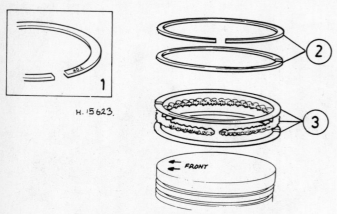

H. 15623.

**Fig. 1.17 Piston ring details (Sec 71)**

1   *Compression ring face
    marked 'TOP'*
2   *Compression ring gaps
    positioned at 90° to each
    other, away from
    distributor side of
    engine*
3   *Oil control ring rails
    and spreader spring*

## 73 Tappets – examination

1   The little shims found inside the tappet bucket must be kept with the relative tappet and not interchanged.
2   The faces of the tappets which bear on the camshaft lobes should show no signs of pitting, scoring, fracturing or other forms of wear. They should not be a loose fit in the aluminium carrier. Wear is normally encountered at very high mileages or in cases of neglected engine lubrication. Renew the tappets or carrier as necessary.

## 74 Gearbox adaptor plate – examination and renovation

Refer to Section 27.

## 75 Timing sprockets and chain – examination

1   Carefully examine the teeth on both the crankshaft and camshaft sprockets for wear. Each tooth forms an inverted V with the gear wheel periphery and if worn, the side of each tooth under tension will be slightly concave in shape when compared with the other side of the tooth. If any sign of wear is present, the sprockets must be renewed.
2   Examine the links of the chain for side slackness and renew the chain if any slackness is noticeable when compared with a new chain. It is a sensible precaution to renew the chain at about 30 000 miles (50 000 km) and at a lesser mileage if the engine is stripped down for major overhaul. The actual rollers on a very badly worn chain may be slightly grooved.

## 76 Timing chain tensioner and guides – examination

1   Examine the contact pad of the tensioner slipper and renew the tensioner assembly if the pad is deeply grooved.
2   Refit the slipper to the tensioner and check the release action of the assembly as follows. Insert the Allen key into the tensioner and turn it anti-clockwise, then clockwise. Check that the slipper retracts and that the action is smooth.
3   Examine the guides and renew them if the contact faces are grooved.

## 77 Cylinder head – decarbonising, valve grinding and renovation

1   Decarbonising can be carried out with the engine either in or out of the car. With the cylinder head off, carefully remove, with a wire brush and blunt scraper, all traces of carbon deposits from the combustion spaces and the ports. The valve stems and valve guides should also be free from any carbon deposits. Wash the combustion spaces and ports down with paraffin and scrape the cylinder head surface free of any foreign matter with the side of a steel rule or similar article. Take care not to scratch the surfaces.
2   Clean the pistons and top of the cylinder bores. If the pistons are still in the cylinder bores, it is essential that great care is taken to ensure that no carbon gets into the bores as this could scratch the cylinder walls or cause damage to the piston and rings. To ensure that this does not happen first turn the crankshaft so that two of the pistons are at the top of the bores. Place clean lint-free rags into the two bores, or seal them off with paper and masking tape. The water and oil ways should also be covered with a small piece of masking tape to prevent particles of carbon entering the cooling system and damaging the water pump, or entering the lubrication system and causing damage to a bearing surface.
3   Before starting, press a little grease into the gap between the cylinder walls and the two pistons which are to be worked on. With a blunt scraper carefully scrape away the carbon from the piston crowns, taking care not to scratch the aluminium. Also scrape away the carbon from the surrounding lip of the cylinder wall. When all carbon has been removed, scrape away the grease which will now be contaminated with carbon particles, taking care not to press any into the bores. To assist prevention of carbon build-up, the piston crown can be polished with metal polish. Remove the rags or masking tape from the other two cylinders and turn the crankshaft so that the two pistons which were at the bottom are now at the top. Place rag into the other two bores, or seal them with paper and masking tape. Do not forget the waterways and oilways as well. Proceed as previously described.
4   With the valves removed from the cylinder head, examine the heads for signs of cracking, burning away and pitting of the edges where they seat in the ports. The seats of the valves in the cylinder head should also be examined for the same signs. Usually it is the valve that deteriorates first, but if a bad valve is not rectified the seat will suffer and this is more difficult to repair.
5   Provided there are no obvious signs of serious pitting, the valve should be ground into its seat. This may be done by placing a smear of carborundum paste on the edge of the valve head and using a suction type valve holder, grinding the valve *in situ*. Use a semi-rotary action, rotating the handle of the valve holder between the hands and lifting it occasionally to re-distribute the traces of paste. Start with a coarse paste and finish with a fine paste.
6   As soon as a matt grey unbroken line appears on both the valve and seat, the valve is 'ground in'. All traces of carbon should also be cleaned from the head and neck of the valve stem. A wire brush mounted in a power drill is a quick and effective way of doing this.
7   If the valve requires renewal, the new one should be ground into the seat in the same way as the old valve.
8   Another form of valve wear can occur on the stem where it runs in the guide in the cylinder head. This can be detected by trying to rock the valve from side-to-side. If there is any movement at all, it is an indication that the valve stem or guide is worn. Check the stem first with a micrometer at points along and around its length, and if they are not within the specified tolerance new valves will probably solve the problem. If the guides are worn, however, they will need reboring for oversize valves to be fitted. The valve seats will also need recutting to ensure they are concentric with the stems. This work should be given to your local BL garage or engineering works.
9   When the valve seats are badly burnt or pitted, requiring renovation, inserts may be fitted – or renewed if previously fitted – and once again this is a specialist task to be carried out by a suitable engineering firm.
10  When all valve grinding is completed, it is essential that every trace of grinding paste is removed from the valves and ports in the cylinder head. This should be done by thorough washing in paraffin and blowing out with a jet of air. If particles of carborundum paste should work their way into the engine this would cause havoc with bearings or cylinder walls.

## 78 Oil pump – examination

1   Undo and remove the retaining screws and separate the pump body from the relief valve body (photo). Recover the O-ring seal.
2   Remove the two rotors from the pump body and clean the

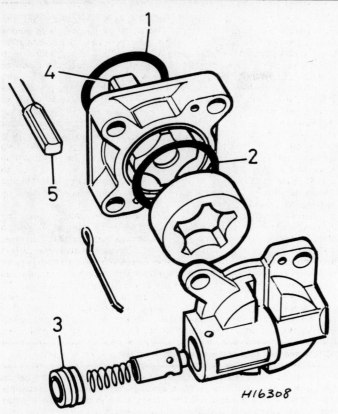

Fig. 1.18 Exploded view of the oil pump (Sec 78)

1  Pump to sump O-ring seal        4  Driveshaft adaptor
2  Cover to body O-ring seal       5  Pump driveshaft
3  Relief valve plug O-ring
   seal

78.1 Separate the oil pump bodies and recover the O-ring

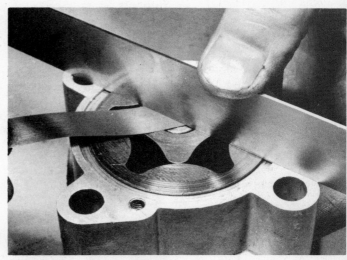

78.4a Checking the rotor endfloat ...

78.4b ... outer rotor-to-body clearance ...

components with paraffin. Dry with a lint-free rag.
3   Refit the rotors to the pump body, making sure that the chamfer on the outer rotor enters the body first.
4   Using a feeler gauge and, where necessary, a straight-edge, check that the rotor clearances are as given in the Specifications (photos).
5   To check the pressure relief valve, extract the split pin and force the plug from the valve. Withdraw the spring and valve.
6   Check the condition of the valve and compare the spring length with the dimension given in the Specifications.
7   If any clearance is outside that specified, or if any of the components show signs of scoring, wear or damage, renew the complete oil pump.
8   If the pump is serviceable, refit the pressure relief valve using a new O-ring to seal the plug. Secure the plug using a new split pin.
9   Place a new O-ring on the pump body and refit the relief valve body and retaining screws. Operate the pump in clean engine oil to prime it.

## 79 Engine mountings – removal and refitting

Refer to Section 29.

## 80 Engine tie-rod – removal and refitting

1   Jack up the front of the car and support it securely on axle stands.
2   Undo and remove the two bolts securing the tie-rod support bracket to the sump.
3   Undo and remove the bolt securing the tie-rod to the support bracket and sump, and to the crossmember bracket (photo).
4   Lift the tie-rod up at the front, withdraw it from the crossmember and remove it from the car.
5   Refitting is the reverse sequence to removal.

78.4c ... and the rotor lobe clearance

80.3 Tie-rod to sump and crossmember attachments

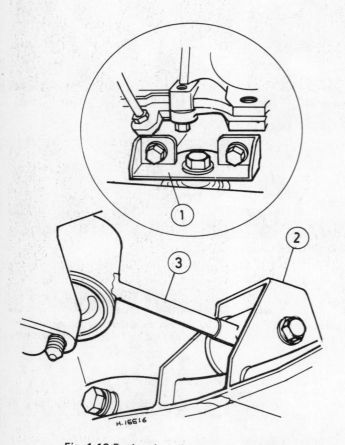

H. 16616

**Fig. 1.19 Engine tie-rod attachments (Sec 80)**

1   Tie-rod support bracket
2   Tie-rod crossmember
    bracket
3   Tie-rod

## 81  Engine reassembly – general

Refer to Section 31.

## 82  Crankshaft and main bearings – refitting

1   Refit the main bearing shells by placing the five upper halves of the shells in their location in the crankcase, after wiping the location clean. If the old bearings are being used ensure that they are fitted in their original location.

2   Note that on the back of each is a tab which engages in locating grooves in either the crank or the main bearing cap housing (photo).

3   New shells are coated with protective grease; carefully clean away all traces of this with paraffin and then fit the bearing shells, noting that the shell having a coloured edge is fitted to No 4 position.

4   With the five upper bearing shells securely in place, wipe the lower bearing cap housings and fit the five lower shell bearings to their caps ensuring that the right shell goes into the right cap if the old bearings are being refitted.

5   Wipe the recesses either side of the number 4 main bearing which locate the upper halves of the thrust washers.

6   Smear a little grease onto the recesses for the upper thrust washers within the crankcase. Fit the thrust washers with their grooves facing outwards (photo).

7   Fit the innermost Woodruff key to the nose of the crankshaft.

8   Generously lubricate the crankshaft journals and the upper and lower main bearing shells and carefully lower the crankshaft into position (photos). Slip the timing chain over the front of the crankshaft as it is fitted.

9   Fit the main bearing caps into position, ensuring that they locate properly on the dowels and that the mating numbers correspond.

10  Apply a little grease to the location for the thrust washers on number 4 main bearing cap. Fit the thrust washers with the grooves facing outwards. Refit the cap to the main bearing web (photo).

11  Refit the long bolts that secure the main bearing caps and screw them up finger tight.

12  Test the crankshaft for freedom of rotation. Should it be very stiff to turn, or possesses high spots, a most careful inspection must be made, preferably by a skilled mechanic with a micrometer, to trace the cause of the trouble. It is very seldom that any trouble of this nature will be experienced when fitting the crankshaft.

13  Tighten the main bearing bolts to the specified torque (photo) and recheck the crankshaft for freedom of rotation.

14  The endfloat of the crankshaft should be checked next. Using a screwdriver as a lever at one of the crankshaft webs and main bearing caps, move the crankshaft longitudinally as far as possible in one direction. Measure the gap between the side of number 4 journal and the thrust washer (photo). Ensure that the endfloat is within the specified limits. Oversize thrust washers are available to enable endfloat adjustment if required.

15  Refit the pistons and connecting rods, as described in Section 83.

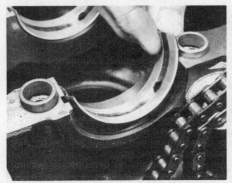

82.2 Engaging the main bearing shell tab with the crankcase groove

82.6 Upper crankshaft thrust washer halves in position

82.8a Lubricate the main bearing shells ...

82.8b ... and place the crankshaft in position

82.10 Refitting No 4 main bearing cap with thrust washers in position

82.13 Tighten the main bearing bolts to the specfied torque

82.14 Checking the crankshaft endfloat

83.3a With the piston ring compressor in position ...

83.3b ... insert the piston and connecting rod and tap it into the bore using a hammer handle

## 83 Pistons and connecting rods – refitting

1   Clean the backs of the bearing shells and the recesses in the connecting rods and big-end caps, If new shells are being fitted ensure that all traces of the protective grease are cleaned off using paraffin.
2   Press the big-end bearing shells into the connecting rods and caps in their correct positions and oil them liberally.
3   Fit a ring compressor to No 1 piston then insert the piston and connecting rod into No 1 cylinder (photo). With No 1 crankpin at its lowest point, drive the piston carefully into the cylinder with the wooden handle of a hammer (photo), and at the same time guide the connecting rod onto the crankpin. Make sure that the 'FRONT' mark on the piston crown or the arrow is facing the timing chain end of the engine (photo).
4   Fit the big-end bearing cap in its previously noted position (photo), then tighten the nuts to the specified torque (photo).

5   Check that the crankshaft turns freely.
6   Repeat the procedure given in paragraphs 3 to 5 for No 4 piston and connecting rod, then turn the crankshaft through half a turn and repeat the procedure on No 2 and No 3 pistons.
7   Refit the gearbox adaptor plate, distributor driveshaft, sump, timing gear components and cylinder head, as applicable, using the procedures described in the following Sections.

## 84 Gearbox adaptor plate – refitting

1   Ensure that the mating faces are perfectly clean and place a new gasket in position on the cylinder block.
2   Lubricate the crankshaft oil seal with engine oil and refit the adaptor plate to the cylinder block (photo).
3   Refit the retaining bolts and tighten them evenly to the specified torque. Note that the two long bolts are fitted at the bottom.

83.3c The word 'FRONT' on the piston must be toward the timing chain end of the engine

83.4a Fit the big-end bearing caps ...

83.4b ... and tighten the nuts to the specified torque

84.2 Refitting the gearbox adaptor plate

85.3 Refitting the distributor driveshaft and thrust washer

85.4a With the Woodruff key in place on the crankshaft ...

85.4b ... slide on the distributor drivegear

86.1 Engage the end of the adjustable guide with the adjuster cam (arrowed)

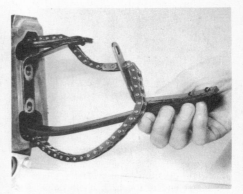

86.2a Refit the fixed guide ...

86.2b ... and secure the guides with the retaining bolts

86.3 Refit the crankshaft sprocket

86.4 Refit the oil thrower

4   Refit the sump, as described in Section 87.
5   Refit the clutch assembly, as described in Chapter 5, attach the gearbox to the engine (Section 92) and refit the engine and gearbox as described in Section 93.

## 85 Distributor driveshaft – refitting

1   Turn the crankshaft to bring No 1 piston to TDC.
2   If the engine is in the car, with the distributor in position, turn the rotor arm to the 5 o'clock position when viewed toward the cylinder head.
3   Place the thrust washer over the driveshaft and insert the driveshaft into its bore (photo). If the engine is in the car engage the driveshaft with the distributor, making sure that the rotor arm remains at the 5 o'clock position. If the engine is on the bench, position the driveshaft slot at 5 o'clock with the large offset towards the engine centre line.
4   Make sure that the Woodruff key is in place on the crankshaft (photo), and slide on the distributor drivegear (photo). As the gear meshes with the driveshaft the distributor rotor arm, or the driveshaft slot, will move to the 2 o'clock position. If the engine is on the bench, temporarily refit the distributor and check that the rotor arm is correctly positioned.
5   Refit the timing gear components, sump, camshaft cover and air cleaner with reference to the appropriate Sections and Chapters of this manual.
6   Adjust the ignition timing, as described in Chapter 4.

## 86 Timing chain guides, chain, sprockets and tensioner – refitting

1   Place the adjustable guide in the crankcase and manipulate its lower end to engage the hooked part over the adjuster (photo).
2   Fit the fixed guide next and secure the upper ends of both guides with the two retaining bolts (photos).
3   Make sure that the inner Woodruff key is in position on the crankshaft and slide the crankshaft sprocket into place (photo). Engage the timing chain with the sprocket teeth.
4   Refit the oil thrower to the crankshaft (photo).
5   Assemble the chain tensioner by inserting one end of the spring into the slipper cylinder. Compress the spring with the cam until the cam enters the plunger cylinder, ensuring that the peg engages in the cam helical slot. Insert and turn the Allen key clockwise until the end of the cam is below the peg and the spring is held in compression.
6   Oil the slipper cylinder and insert it through the front cover aperture with the slipper contacting the chain (photo).
7   Refit the tensioner and washer to the cylinder block and tighten it fully (photo).
8   Place a new gasket in position on the front cover and refit the cover and lower retaining bolt. Refit the dowel bolt with a sealing washer to the front cover bolt hole (photo) and engage the dowel with the lower end of the fixed chain guide. Refit the LED timing sensor bracket and the remaining two bolts (photo), and tighten all the bolts to the specified torque.
9   At this stage the remaining paragraphs are only applicable if the engine is in the car.
10  Using the chain link removal/refitting tool used during removal, fit a new bright link to the chain ends and secure the link by riveting the link pins with the tool.
11  Lubricate a new crankshaft front oil seal with engine oil and place it in position over the crankshaft. Drive the seal into its location using a hammer and block of wood, or the old seal and a suitable tube.
12  Refit the crankshaft pulley and screw in the retaining bolt, using a new lockwasher. Tighten the bolt to the specified torque and bend over the lockwasher.
13  Ensure that the engine is at TDC with No 1 cylinder on compression.
14  Temporarily place the camshaft sprocket on the end of the camshaft and, if necessary, move the camshaft to align the timing marks on the carrier and sprocket. Remove the sprocket.
15  Slip the timing chain over the sprocket teeth and refit the sprocket to the camshaft, ensuring that the timing marks are still aligned. Refit the sprocket retaining bolt and tighten it to the specified torque.
16  Insert a screwdriver into the slot of the chain guide adjuster and

turn the adjuster clockwise until the chain is tight, but not taut. Hold the adjuster in this position and tighten the locknut.

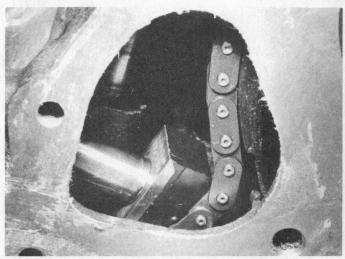

86.6 With the timing chain slipper in place against the chain ...

86.7 ... refit the tensioner to the cylinder block

86.8a Refit the front cover dowel bolt and engage the fixed guide

86.8b Refit the remaining front cover bolts and the LED sensor bracket

87.1 Refit the oil strainer and pick-up pipe to the sump

87.2 Fitting a new cork seal to the rear of the sump

87.3 Place the crankshaft front oil seal in position

87.4 Locate a new O-ring in the sump face groove

87.5 Position the sump on the crankcase ...

87.6 ... and refit the stiffener plates and sump retaining bolts

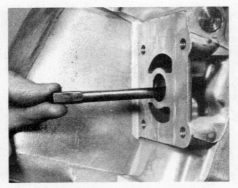

88.2a Locate the oil pump driveshaft in the distributor driveshaft ...

88.2b ... and refit the oil pump

17  Insert the Allen key into the timing chain tensioner and turn it 90° anti-clockwise to release the slipper. Refit the small bolt and washer to the centre of the tensioner.

18  Refit the camshaft cover, air cleaner and battery negative terminal. Refit the access cover and lower the car to the ground.

## 87 Sump – refitting

1  If removed, refit the oil pick-up tube and strainer to the base of the sump and secure with the retaining bolt (photo).

2  Locate a new cork seal in the rear sealing groove of the sump and push the seal squarely into place. Do not trim off any protruding edges of the seal above the joint face (photo).

3  Lubricate a new oil seal and place it over the crankshaft and into position in the crankcase (photo).

4  Locate a new O-ring seal in the groove of the sump mating face (photo).

5  Apply a fairly thin bead of RTV silicone sealant along the centre of the sump-to-crankcase joint faces and immediately fit the sump to the crankcase (photo).

6  With the two stiffener plates in position refit the sump retaining bolts (photo) and progressively tighten the retaining bolts to the specified torque.

7  If the engine is in the car, refit the dipstick tube, oil pump, exhaust pipe flange, water pump and engine tie-rod. Lower the car to the ground and refill the cooling system.

## 88 Oil pump – refitting

1  Having primed the pump in engine oil, position a new O-ring in the groove in the pump body and make sure that the adaptor is pressed fully onto the pump spindle.

2  Locate the pump driveshaft in the distributor driveshaft and place the pump in position on the sump (photos).

3 Refit the retaining bolts and progressively tighten them to the specified torque.

4 If the engine is in the car, refill the engine with oil and refit the battery negative terminal.

## 89 Cylinder head – reassembly and refitting

1 Fit the valves to their original guides or, if new valves have been obtained, to the seat in which they have been ground.

2 Oil the valve stems liberally and fit the oil seals to the inlet valve guides. Note that, if valves with oversize stems are being fitted, oil seals with two rings on their flange must be used (Fig. 1.20).

3 Working on one valve at a time, fit the spring and cap then compress the spring with the compressor and insert the split collets. Release the compressor and remove it.

4 Repeat the procedure given in paragraph 3 on the remaining valves. Tap the end of each valve stem with a mallet to settle the collets.

5 Make sure that the faces of the cylinder block and head are perfectly clean and locate a new head gasket over the cylinder block dowels (photo). Do not use jointing compound.

6 Lower the cylinder head onto the gasket (photo).

7 Lightly oil the threads of the cylinder head retaining bolts and screw them into their locations. Refer to Fig. 1.21 and tighten the cylinder head bolts to half the specified torque, in the order shown, then to the full torque, and finally a further $1/4$ turn (90°).

8 If the engine is in the car reverse the procedure given in paragraphs 1 to 21 of Section 54.

## 90 Camshaft and tappets – refitting

1 Smear the tappet shims with petroleum jelly and then locate the shims in the recesses of their respective tappet buckets (photo).

2 Lubricate the camshaft bearings and carefully slide the camshaft into the carrier (photo). Engage the camshaft locating plate with the groove in the camshaft and secure with the retaining bolt and lockwasher. Tighten the bolt fully and bend over the lockwasher tabs.

3 Insert each tappet bucket into its correct bore in the carrier (photo).

4 Position the carrier, on its side, next to the valves (photo), and then very quickly turn it the right way up and position it on the cylinder head before the tappet buckets have a chance to fall out.

5 Refit the six camshaft carrier retaining bolts and tighten them evenly and in a diagonal sequence to the specified torque.

6 Temporarily refit the sprocket to the camshaft and turn the camshaft to align the timing marks on the sprocket and carrier. Remove the sprocket.

89.5 Lay a new cylinder head gasket on the block face

89.6 ... and lower the cylinder head into place

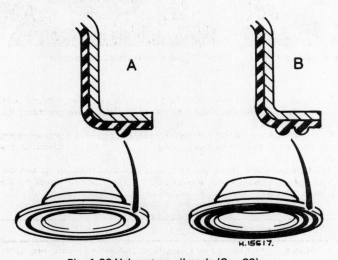

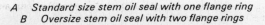

**Fig. 1.20 Valve stem oil seals (Sec 89)**

A  Standard size stem oil seal with one flange ring
B  Oversize stem oil seal with two flange rings

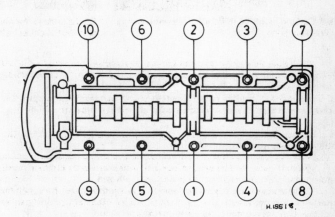

**Fig. 1.21 Cylinder head bolt tightening sequence – 1.6 litre engine (Sec 89)**

90.1 Refit the shims in their respective tappet buckets

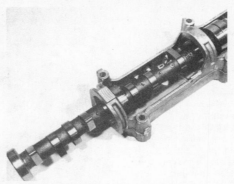

90.2 Slide the camshaft into the carrier ...

90.3 ... and insert each tappet bucket into its correct bore

90.4 Refit the camshaft carrier to the cylinder head

90.8 Sprocket and carrier timing marks aligned

90.9 Refit the sprocket retaining bolt

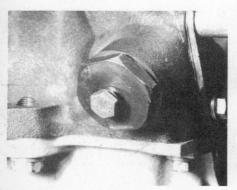

90.11 Refit the small bolt to the tensioner

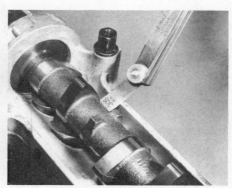

95.4 Checking the tappet clearances

95.15 The shim thickness is stamped on the shim

7  Check that the crankshaft is at TDC with No 1 cylinder on compression.

8  Engage the timing chain over the sprocket teeth and refit the sprocket to the camshaft. Ensure that the timing marks are still aligned (photo).

9  Refit the camshaft sprocket retaining bolt (photo) and tighten the bolt to the specified torque.

10  Engage a screwdriver in the slot of the movable chain guide adjuster and turn the adjuster clockwise until the timing chain is tight, but not taut. Hold the adjuster in this position and tighten the locknut.

11  Engage the Allen key in the hole in the centre of the timing chain tensioner (photo 54.19) and turn the Allen key 90° anti-clockwise to release the tensioner slipper. Remove the Allen key and refit the tensioner centre bolt and washer (photo).

12  If the crankshaft pulley has not yet been refitted, slide it on the end of the crankshaft pulley and refit the retaining bolt and lockwasher. Tighten the bolt to the specified torque and bend over the lockwasher.

13  The tappet clearances should now be checked, as described in Section 95.

14  If the engine is in the car, refit the access cover under the wheel arch and lower the car to the ground.

## 91  Ancillary components – refitting

Refer to Section 53 and refit the listed components with reference to the Sections and Chapters specified.

## 92  Engine – attachment to gearbox

Refer to Section 51 and attach the gearbox to the engine using the reverse of the removal procedure. Tighten the retaining bolts to the specified torque.

## 93 Engine and gearbox assembly – refitting

Refer to Section 50 and refit the engine and gearbox using the reverse of the removal procedure, noting the following additional points:

(a) *Align the marks on the driveshaft joints and drive flanges made during removal. Fit and tighten the bolts to the specified torque and fit new protective caps*

(b) *Adjust the accelerator cable, as described in Chapter 3, and the clutch cable, as described in Chapter 5*

(c) *Refill the engine with oil*

(d) *Refill the cooling system, as described in Chapter 2*

## 94 Engine – adjustments after major overhaul

Refer to Section 43, but note that it is not necessary to retorque the cylinder head retaining bolts.

## 95 Tappet clearances – adjustment

1   Disconnect the battery negative terminal and remove the air cleaner, as described in Chapter 3.

2   Disconnect the fuel inlet and outlet pipes at the fuel pump and plug them after removal.

3   Undo and remove the bolts securing the camshaft cover to the cylinder head and recover the sealing washers. Detach the breather hose and lift off the camshaft cover. Place the wiring harness support brackets to one side.

4   Using a feeler gauge, check the clearance between the cam lobe and the tappet bucket of each valve (photo) in the order given in the following table and record each clearance. The engine may be turned using a spanner or socket on the crankshaft pulley bolt. If necessary remove the access cover from under the right-hand wheel arch to provide greater access to the pulley bolt.

*Check No 1 tappet with No 8 valve fully open*
*Check No 3 tappet with No 6 valve fully open*
*Check No 5 tappet with No 4 valve fully open*
*Check No 2 tappet with No 7 valve fully open*
*Check No 8 tappet with No 1 valve fully open*
*Check No 6 tappet with No 3 valve fully open*
*Check No 4 tappet with No 5 valve fully open*
*Check No 7 tappet with No 2 valve fully open*

5   Once the readings have been tabulated for all valves it should be noted that, unless new parts have been fitted or the valve seats reground, adjustment of the valve tappet clearance to the standard setting is only necessary if the clearance of either inlet or exhaust is less than the specified minimum.

6   If adjustment is necessary, align the timing marks on the camshaft sprocket and camshaft carrier and check that the crankshaft pulley timing notch is at the TDC position.

7   Jack up the front of the car and support it securely on axle stands. Undo and remove the securing screws and lift off the access cover from under the right-hand wheel arch.

8   Undo and remove the small bolt from the centre of the timing chain tensioner and insert a 1/8 in Allen key in the bolt hole. Turn the Allen key 90° clockwise to retract the tensioner slipper.

9   Undo and remove the two retaining bolts and lift off the left-hand side engine lifting bracket from the cylinder head.

10   Undo and remove the bolt securing the camshaft sprocket to the camshaft. Place a cloth pad beneath the sprocket, ease the sprocket and chain off the camshaft and rest it on the pad.

11   Bend back the locktab, undo and remove the retaining bolt and lift off the camshaft locating plate.

12   Progressively slacken the camshaft carrier retaining bolts until all the valve spring tension is released and remove the bolts.

13   Lift the carrier slightly, push down all the tappet buckets and withdraw the camshaft from the left-hand side of the carrier.

14   Remove each maladjusted tappet bucket in turn and recover the adjusting shim from inside the bucket.

15   Note the thickness of the shim originally fitted (photo) and by using the following calculation, determine the thickness of the new shim required to give the correct tappet clearance.

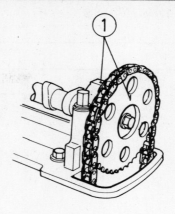

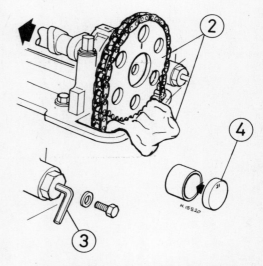

**Fig. 1.22 Tappet clearance adjustment (Sec 95)**

1   *Camshaft sprocket and carrier alignment marks*
2   *Camshaft sprocket resting on pad*
3   *Allen key to retract tensioner slipper*
4   *Tappet shim*

$A$ = *clearance measured in paragraph 4*
$B$ = *thickness of existing shim*
$C$ = *correct clearance*
*New shim thickness required* = $A + B - C$

16   Although the shim thickness is stamped on the face of the shim it is advisable to double check this with a micrometer.

17   Refit the shims into their respective buckets using petroleum jelly to retain them. Refit the buckets to the camshaft carrier.

18   Slide the camshaft into the carrier and refit the locating plate, retaining bolt and lockwasher. Tighten the bolt and bend over the lockwasher tabs.

19   Refit the camshaft carrier retaining bolts and tighten them finger tight only at this stage.

20   Note the position of the dowel hole in the camshaft sprocket and turn the camshaft until its dowel is in approximately the same position.

21   Progressively tighten the camshaft carrier retaining bolts to the specified torque.

22   Refit the camshaft sprocket and secure with the retaining bolt tightened to the specified torque.

23   Engage the Allen key with the timing chain tensioner, turn the key 90° anti-clockwise to release the tensioner slipper and then refit the small centre bolt and sealing washer.

24   Refit the engine lifting bracket to the cylinder head

25   Refit the camshaft cover using a new gasket, if necessary. Refit the cover retaining bolts and reconnect the fuel pipes.

26   Refit the air cleaner, battery negative terminal and access cover. Lower the car to the ground.

## PART C: FAULT DIAGNOSIS

### 96 Fault diagnosis – engine

| Symptom | Reason(s) |
| --- | --- |
| Engine fails to start | Discharged battery<br>Loose battery connection<br>Loose or broken ignition leads<br>Moisture on spark plugs, distributor cap, or HT leads<br>Incorrect spark plug gaps<br>Cracked distributor cap or rotor<br>Other ignition system fault<br>Dirt or water in carburettor<br>Empty fuel tank<br>Faulty fuel pump<br>Other fuel system fault<br>Faulty starter motor<br>Low cylinder compressions |
| Engine idles erratically | Intake manifold air leak<br>Leaking cylinder head gasket<br>Worn rocker arms, timing chain, and gears<br>Worn camshaft lobes<br>Faulty fuel pump<br>Incorrect valve clearances<br>Loose crankcase ventilation hoses<br>Carburettor adjustment incorrect<br>Uneven cylinder compressions |
| Engine misfires | Spark plugs worn or incorrectly gapped<br>Dirt or water in carburettor<br>Carburettor adjustment incorrect<br>Burnt out valve<br>Leaking cylinder head gasket<br>Distributor cap cracked<br>Incorrect valve clearances<br>Uneven cylinder compressions<br>Worn carburettor |
| Engine stalls | Carburettor adjustment incorrect<br>Intake manifold air leak<br>Ignition timing incorrect |
| Excessive oil consumption | Overfilling<br>Worn pistons, cylinder bores or piston rings<br>Valve guides and valve stem seals worn<br>Oil leaking from rocker cover, differential drive flange oil seals, or timing cover oil seal |
| Engine backfires | Carburettor adjustment incorrect<br>Ignition timing incorrect<br>Incorrect valve clearances<br>Intake manifold air leak<br>Sticking valve |

# Chapter 2 Cooling system

*For modifications, and information applicable to later models, see Supplement at end of manual*

## Contents

## Specifications

**System type** ................................................. Pressurized, water pump assisted thermo-syphon with front mounted radiator and electric cooling fan

**Expansion tank cap pressure** ..................... 15 lbf/in² (1.0 kgf/cm²)

**Thermostat**
Opening temperature ........................................ 88°C (190°F)
Lift height .......................................................... 0.32 in (8.1 mm)

**Drivebelt tension** ...................................... 0.3 to 0.5 in (7.0 to 12.0 mm) deflection between pulleys under load of 10 lbf (4.5 kgf)

**System capacity (including heater)**
1.3 litre models ................................................ 11.75 Imp pints (6.6 litres)
1.6 litre models ................................................ 14.5 Imp pints (8.2 litres)

**Antifreeze type/specification** .................. Ethylene glycol-based antifreeze to BS6580 (Duckhams Universal Antifreeze and Summer Coolant)

**Antifreeze properties and quantities**
33% Antifreeze (by volume):
Commences freezing ......................................... -19°C (-2°F)
Frozen solid ...................................................... -36°C (-33°F)

| | Antifreeze | Water |
|---|---|---|
| Quantities (system refill): | | |
| 1.3 litre models | 3.92 Imp pints (2.20 litres) | 7.83 Imp pints (4.40 litres) |
| 1.6 litre models | 4.83 Imp pints (2.73 litres) | 9.67 Imp pints (5.47 litres) |

50% Antifreeze (by volume):
Commences freezing ......................................... -36°C (-33°F)
Frozen solid ...................................................... -48°C (-53°F)

| | Antifreeze | Water |
|---|---|---|
| Quantities (system refill): | | |
| 1.3 litre models | 5.88 Imp pints (3.30 litres) | 5.88 Imp pints (3.30 litres) |
| 1.6 litre models | 7.25 Imp pints (4.10 litres) | 7.25 Imp pints (4.10 litres) |

**Torque wrench settings**

*1.3 litre models*

| | lbf ft | Nm |
|---|---|---|
| Temperature gauge sensor | 40 | 54 |
| Coolant outlet elbow | 16 | 22 |
| Water pump bolts | 16 | 22 |
| Water pump pulley | 8 | 11 |
| Cylinder block drain plug | 27 | 37 |

*1.6 litre models*

| | lbf ft | Nm |
|---|---|---|
| Temperature gauge sensor | 14 | 19 |
| Thermostat housing | 9 | 12 |
| Water pump to sump | 18 | 25 |
| Water pump front body to rear body | 9 | 12 |
| Water pump pulley | 8 | 11 |
| Cylinder block drain plug | 27 | 37 |
| Coolant outlet elbow to cylinder block | 18 | 25 |

## 1  General description

The cooling system is of the pressurised, pump-assisted thermo-syphon type. The system consists of the radiator, water pump, thermostat, electric cooling fan, expansion tank and associated hoses.

The system functions as follows. Cold coolant in the bottom of the radiator left-hand tank passes through the bottom hose to the water pump where it is pumped around the cylinder block and head passages. After cooling the cylinder bores, combustion surfaces and valve seats, the coolant reaches the underside of the thermostat, which is initially closed, and is diverted through the heater inlet hose to the heater. After passing through the heater the coolant is returned to the water pump inlet hose. On 1.3 litre models the coolant first passes through the water jacket of the inlet manifold before returning to the pump inlet hose. When the engine is cold the thermostat remains closed and the coolant circulates only through the engine and heater. When the coolant reaches a predetermined temperature (see Specifications) the thermostat opens and the coolant passes through the top hose to the radiator right-hand tank. As the coolant circulates around the radiator it is cooled by the inrush of air when the car is in forward motion. Airflow is supplemented by the action of the electric cooling fan when necessary. Upon reaching the left-hand side of the

radiator, the coolant is now cooled and the cycle is repeated.

When the engine is at normal operating temperature the coolant expands and some of it is displaced into the expansion tank. This coolant collects in the tank and is returned to the radiator when the system cools.

The electric cooling fan mounted in front of the radiator is controlled by a thermostatic switch located in the radiator side tank. At a predetermined coolant temperature the switch contacts close, thus actuating the fan.

## 2  Maintenance and inspection

1  Check the coolant level in the system weekly and, if necessary, top up with a water and antifreeze mixture until the level is up to the indicator in the expansion tank. With a sealed type cooling system, topping-up should only be necessary at very infrequent intervals. If this is not the case and frequent topping-up is required, it is likely there is a leak in the system. Check all hoses and joint faces for any staining, or actual wetness, and rectify if necessary. If no leaks can be found it is advisable to have the system pressure tested, as the leak could possibly be internal. It is a good idea to keep a check on the engine oil level as a serious internal leak can often cause the level in the sump

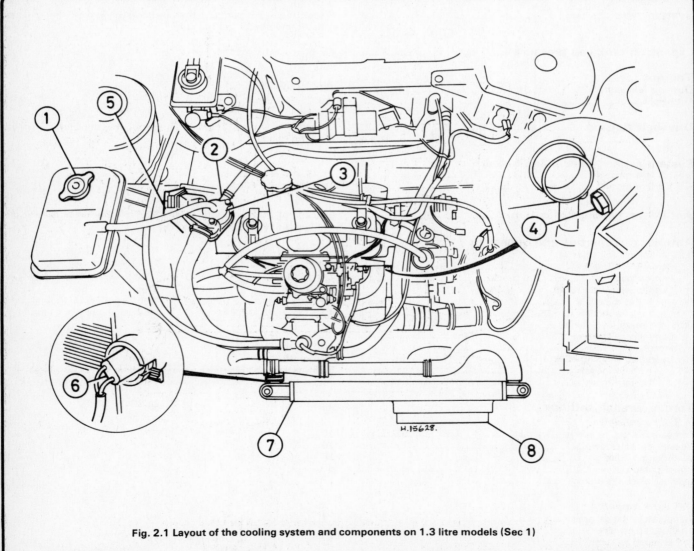

H.15628.

**Fig. 2.1 Layout of the cooling system and components on 1.3 litre models (Sec 1)**

| 1 Expansion tank filler cap | 4 Cylinder block drain plug | 6 Cooling fan thermostatic | 8 Electric cooling fan |
|---|---|---|---|
| 2 Coolant outlet elbow | (if fitted) | switch | and cowl |
| 3 Thermostat housing | 5 Water pump | 7 Radiator | |

to rise, thus confirming suspicions.

2    At regular intervals (see Routine Maintenance) carefully inspect all the hoses, hose clips and visible joint gaskets of the system for cracks, corrosion, deterioration or leakage. Renew any hoses and clips that are suspect, and also renew any gaskets, if necessary.

3    At the same service interval check the condition of the drivebelt and renew it if there is any sign of cracking or fraying. Check and adjust the tension of the belt, as described in Section 13.

4    At less frequent service intervals (see Routine Maintenance) drain, flush and refill the cooling system using fresh antifreeze, as described in Sections 3, 4, and 5 respectively.

5    Renew the drivebelt also at this service interval, using the procedure described in Section 13.

## 3    Cooling system – draining

1    It is preferable to drain the cooling system when the engine is cold. *If the engine is hot the pressure in the cooling system must be released before attempting to drain the system.* Place a cloth over the pressure cap of the expansion tank and turn the cap anti-clockwise until it reaches its stop.

2    Wait until the pressure has escaped, then press the cap downwards and turn it further in an anti-clockwise direction. Release the downward pressure on the cap very slowly and, after making sure that all the pressure in the system has been relieved, remove the cap.

3    Place a suitable container beneath the left-hand side of the radiator. Slacken the hose clip and carefully ease the bottom hose off the radiator outlet. Allow the coolant to drain into the container.

4    Check and adjust the cylinder block drain plug. If fitted, the plug is located on the front left-hand side of the engine on 1.3 litre models and on the rear left-hand side on 1.6 litre models. Unscrew the plug and drain the coolant into the container.

5    If the system needs to be flushed after draining see the next Section, otherwise refit the drain plug and secure the bottom hose to the radiator.

## 4    Cooling system – flushing

1    With time the cooling system may gradually lose its efficiency as the radiator core becomes choked with rust, scale deposits from the water, and other sediment.

2    To flush the system, first drain the coolant, as described in the previous Section.

3    Disconnect the top hose at the thermostat housing and leave the

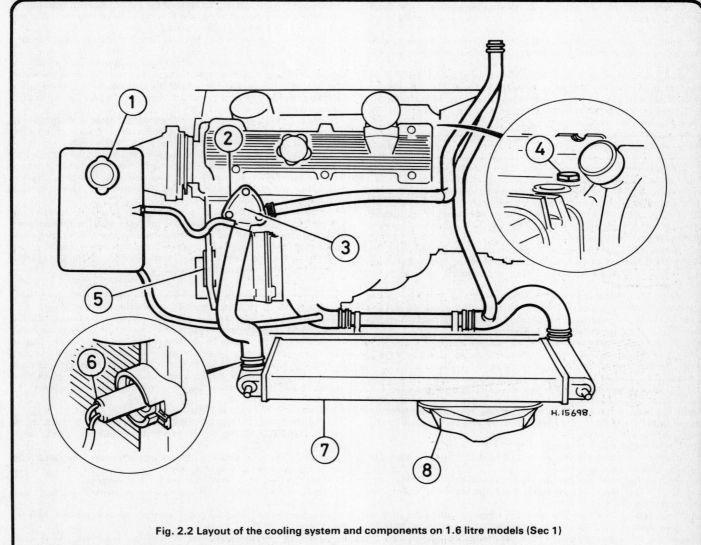

**Fig. 2.2 Layout of the cooling system and components on 1.6 litre models (Sec 1)**

| | | | |
|---|---|---|---|
| 1    Expansion tank filler cap | 4    Cylinder block drain plug | 6    Cooling fan thermostatic switch | 7    Radiator |
| 2    Coolant outlet elbow | 5    Water pump | | 8    Electric cooling fan and cowl |
| 3    Thermostat housing | | | |

bottom hose disconnected at the radiator outlet.

4   Insert a hose into the top hose and allow water to circulate through the radiator until it runs clear from the outlet.

5   If, after a reasonable period the water still does not run clear, the radiator can be flushed with a good proprietary cleaning agent such as Holts Radflush or Holts Speedflush.

6   Disconnect the heater inlet hose from the thermostat housing. Insert the hose and allow water to circulate through the heater and out through the bottom hose until clear.

7   In severe cases of contamination the system should be reverse flushed. To do this remove the radiator, as described in Section 7, invert it and insert a hose in the bottom outlet. Continue flushing until clean water runs from the top hose outlet.

8   The engine should also be flushed. To do this remove the thermostat, as described in Section 8, and insert the hose into the cylinder head. Remove the cylinder block drain plug (if fitted) and flush the system until clear water runs from the drain plug orifice and bottom hose.

9   The use of chemical cleaners should only be necessary as a last resort. The regular renewal of antifreeze should prevent the contamination of the system.

## 5   Cooling system – filling

1   If removed, refit the thermostat housing, reconnect the radiator top and bottom hoses and heater hose, refit the cylinder block drain plug.

2   Pour the appropriate mixture of water and antifreeze (see Section 6) into the expansion tank until the tank is half-full, and then refit the cap.

3   Run the engine at a fast idling speed for approximately three minutes then stop the engine and check the level in the expansion tank. If necessary, top up the level to just above the indicator in the tank, *being careful to release pressure from the system before removing the filler cap completely.*

## 6   Antifreeze mixture

1   The antifreeze should be renewed at regular intervals (see Routine Maintenance). This is necessary not only to maintain the antifreeze properties, but also to prevent corrosion which would otherwise occur as the corrosion inhibitors become progressively less effective.

2   Always use an ethylene glycol based antifreeze which is suitable for use in mixed metal cooling systems (Duckhams Universal Antifreeze and Summer Coolant).

3   Before adding antifreeze the cooling system should be completely drained and flushed, and all hoses checked for condition and security.

4   The quantity of antifreeze and levels of protection are indicated in the Specifications.

5   After filling with antifreeze, a label should be attached to the radiator stating the type and concentration of antifreeze used and the date installed. Any subsequent topping-up should be made with the same type and concentration of antifreeze.

6   Do not use engine antifreeze in the screen washer system, as it will cause damage to the vehicle paintwork. Screen wash antifreeze is available from most motor accessory shops.

## 7   Radiator – removal, inspection, cleaning and refitting

**Note:** *If a leaking radiator is suspected, minor leaks may be cured by adding Holts Radweld to the cooling system in accordance with the manufacturers instructions.*

1   Disconnect the battery negative terminal.

2   Drain the cooling system, as described in Section 3. Leave the bottom radiator hose disconnected.

3   Slacken the retaining clip and detach the radiator top hose.

4   Detach the electrical connector from the radiator cooling fan thermostatic switch (photo).

5   Undo and remove the upper retaining screws securing the grille to the front body panel. Tip the grille forward at the top and lift it to release the lower mounting lugs from their locations (photo).

6   Detach the wiring connector from the terminal at the rear of the horn.

7   Undo and remove the three screws each side securing the front body panel in position (photo). Release the air cleaner cold air intake hose from the panel (photo) and then withdraw the panel (photo) and

place it to one side, leaving the bonnet release catch still attached.

8   The radiator may now be carefully lifted out and inspected for damage. If major repairs are necessary this is best left to a specialist.

9   Reverse flush the radiator, as described in Section 4. Renew the top and bottom hoses and clips if they are damaged or have deteriorated.

10  Refitting is a reversal of removal. Fill the cooling system, as described in Section 5.

## 8   Thermostat – removal, testing and refitting

1   Remove the expansion tank filler cap. *If the engine is hot, place a cloth over the cap and turn it slowly anti-clockwise until the first stop is reached.* Wait until all the pressure had been released and then remove the cap completely.

2   Place a suitable container beneath the radiator bottom hose outlet. Disconnect the bottom hose and drain approximately 4 pints (2.3 litres) of the coolant. Reconnect the bottom hose and tighten the clip.

3   Slacken the clips and detach the radiator top hose, heater hose and expansion tank overflow hose from the coolant outlet elbow (photo).

4   Undo and remove the three bolts (or nuts) securing the water outlet elbow to the cylinder head and lift off the elbow. On 1.3 litre models it will be necessary to remove the upper retaining bolt and lift away the engine mounting support bracket to facilitate removal of the elbow. After removal, recover the gasket.

5   Withdraw the thermostat from its seat in the thermostat housing (photo).

6   To test whether the unit is serviceable, suspend it on a string in a saucepan of cold water together with a thermometer. Heat the water and note the temperature at which the thermostat begins to open. Continue heating the water until the thermostat is fully open and then remove it from the water.

7   The temperature at which the thermostat should start to open is given in the Specifications. If the thermostat does not start to open at the specified temperature, does not fully open in boiling water, or does not fully close when removed from the water, then it must be discarded and a new one fitted. *Under no circumstances should the car be used without a thermostat,* as uneven cooling of the cylinder walls and head passages will occur, causing distortion and possible seizure of the engine internal components.

8   Refitting the thermostat is the reverse sequence to removal. Ensure that all traces of old gasket are removed from the mating faces of the coolant outlet elbow and thermostat housing. Use a new gasket lightly smeared with jointing compound and tighten the retaining nuts or bolts to the specified torque. On completion top up the cooling system, with reference to Section 5.

## 9   Water pump (1.3 litre models) – removal and refitting

**Note:** *Water pump failure is indicated by water leaking from the gland at the front of the pump, or by rough and noisy operation. This is usually accompanied by excessive play of the pump spindle which can be checked by moving the pulley from side to side. Repair or overhaul of a faulty pump is not possible, as internal parts are not available separately. In the event of failure a replacement pump must be obtained.*

1   Disconnect the battery negative terminal.

2   Slacken the alternator adjusting arm and mounting bolts, move the alternator toward the engine and slip the drivebelt off the three pulleys.

3   Remove the adjusting arm bolt and the mounting nuts and bolts and place the alternator to one side.

4   Refer to Section 3, and drain the cooling system.

5   Undo and remove the four water pump pulley retaining bolts and lift off the pulley.

6   Slacken the retaining clip and disconnect the inlet water hose from the pump.

7   Undo and remove the water pump retaining bolts, noting their lengths and location.

8   Using a soft-faced mallet, tap the pump body to release it from the locating dowels. Lift away the pump and remove the gasket.

9   Refitting is the reverse sequence to removal, bearing in mind the following points:

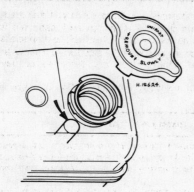

**Fig. 2.3 Expansion tank level indicator (Sec 5)**

7.4 Cooling fan thermostatic switch electrical connector (arrowed)

7.5 Grille lower mounting lug and location in lower front panel

7.7a Remove the three screws each side (arrowed) ...

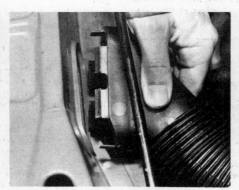

7.7b ... withdraw the cold air intake hose ...

7.7c ... and lift off the upper front panel

8.3 Radiator top hose (A), heater hose (B) and expansion tank overflow hose (C), to coolant outlet elbow and thermostat housing (1.6 litre model shown)

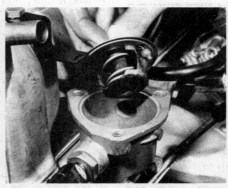

8.5 Removing the thermostat (1.6 litre model shown)

10.4 Access panel retaining screw locations under front wheel arch (arrowed). Additional screw situated out of picture on left

> (a) Remove all traces of old gasket from the cylinder block and pump faces, and ensure that both mating surfaces are clean and dry
> (b) Use a new gasket, lightly smeared with jointing compound
> (c) Adjust the drivebelt tension, as described in Section 13, and refill the cooling system as described in Section 5

**10 Water pump (1.6 litre models) – removal and refitting**

1   Refer to the introductory note at the beginning of Section 9 before proceeding.
2   Disconnect the battery negative terminal.
3   Apply the handbrake, prise off the right-hand front wheel trim and slacken the wheel nuts. Jack up the front of the car, support it securely on axle stands and remove the right-hand roadwheel.
4   Undo and remove the retaining screws and lift off the access panel from the right-hand inner wing (photo).

5   Refer to Section 3, and drain the cooling system.
6   Slacken the retaining clip and detach the coolant inlet hose from the rear of the pump body (photo).
7   Slacken the alternator adjusting arm bolt and the two lower mounting nuts and bolts. Move the alternator towards the engine and slip the drivebelt off the three pulleys.
8   Remove the alternator adjusting arm and lower mounting bolts and place the alternator to one side. Note the arrangement of spacers and distance washers on the mounting bolts.
9   Undo and remove the four bolts securing the water pump to the side of the sump (photos). Slacken the small hose retaining clips and withdraw the pump from under the wheel arch (photo).
10  If the pump is to be renewed, undo and remove the four bolts securing the pulley to the pump spindle (photo).
11  The bolts securing the pump inner and outer bodies together can now be undone and the halves separated (photos).
12  Refitting is the reverse sequence to removal, bearing in mind the following points:

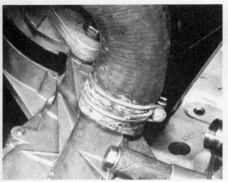

10.6 Water pump inlet hose location at rear of pump body

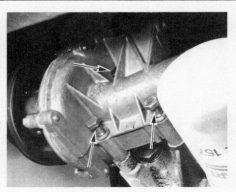

10.9a Remove the three lower ...

10.9b ... and one upper water pump retaining bolts (arrowed)

10.9c Slacken the small connecting hose clips and withdraw the pump

10.10 Remove the four bolts (arrowed) and lift off the pulley

10.11a Remove the five bolts (arrowed) ...

10.11b ... and separate the pump halves

11.5 Lift the fan assembly to release the lower mounting lugs (arrowed) from their locations

12.3 Detach the wiring plug and release the thermostatic switch by turning the retaining plate (arrowed) anti-clockwise

(a) Remove all traces of old gasket from the faces of the pump bodies, and ensure that both surfaces are clean and dry
(b) Apply RTV sealant to the pump mating faces
(c) Tighten the pump body, pulley and retaining bolts to the specified torque
(d) Adjust the drivebelt tension, as described in Section 13, and refill the cooling system as described in Section 5

## 11 Cooling fan assembly – removal and refitting

1   Disconnect the battery negative terminal.
2   Undo and remove the upper retaining screws securing the grille to the front body panel. Tip the grille forward at the top and lift it to release the lower mounting lugs from their locations.
3   Detach the wiring connector from the terminal at the rear of the horn.
4   Undo and remove the three screws each side securing the front

body panel in position. Release the air cleaner cold air intake hose from the panel and then withdraw the panel, leaving the bonnet release cable still attached. Place the panel to one side (photos 7.7a, b and c).
5   Detach the wiring connector and lift up the fan assembly to release the lower mounting lugs from their locations (photo). Remove the unit from the car.
6   If required the fan blades can be withdrawn from the motor spindle after extracting the retaining circlip.
7   Refitting is the reverse sequence to removal.

## 12 Cooling fan thermostatic switch – testing, removal and refitting

1   If the thermostatic switch located on the right-hand side of the radiator develops a fault, it is most likely to fail open circuited. This will cause the fan motor to remain stationary even though the coolant may

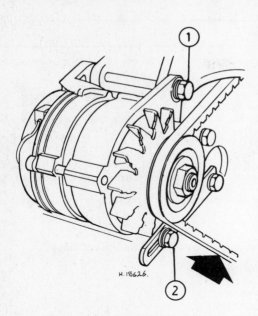

Fig. 2.4 Drivebelt adjustment points – 1.3 litre models (Sec 13)

    1   Alternator mounting bolt
    2   Adjusting arm bolt
    Arrow indicates tension checking point

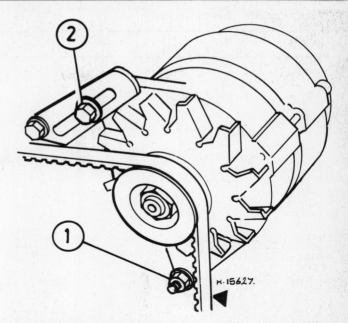

Fig. 2.5 Drivebelt adjustment points – 1.6 litre models (Sec 13)

    1   Alternator mounting bolt
    2   Adjusting arm bolt
    Arrow indicates tension checking point

reach boiling point.

2   To test for a faulty thermostatic switch, disconnect the plug and connect a length of wire or suitable metal object between the two plug terminals. If the fan operates with the ignition switch on, the thermostatic switch is proved faulty and must be renewed.

3   Disconnect the battery negative terminal and remove the plug from the switch (photo). Remove the expansion tank filler cap.

4   Place a suitable clean container beneath the radiator outlet, then disconnect the bottom hose and drain approximately 4 pints (2.3 litres) of coolant. Reconnect the bottom hose and tighten the clip.

5   Release the retaining plate and withdraw the thermostatic switch and seal from the radiator.

6   Refitting is a reversal of removal, but use a new seal and top up the cooling system with reference to Section 5.

## 13  Drivebelt – renewal and adjustment

1   The drivebelt should be checked and re-tensioned at regular intervals (see Routine Maintenance). It should be renewed at these service intervals if it shows any sign of fraying or deterioration.

2   To remove the drivebelt, slacken the alternator mounting bolts and adjusting arm nut or bolt. Move the alternator toward the engine and slip the drivebelt off the three pulleys. On 1.6 models equipped with power steering, the power steering pump drivebelt will have to be removed first as described in Chapter 12, Section 15.

3   Fit the new drivebelt over the pulleys then lever the alternator away from the engine until the correct tension is obtained (see Specifications). The alternator must only be levered at the drive end bracket.

4   Hold the alternator in this position and tighten the adjusting arm nut or bolt followed by the mounting bolts.

5   Run the engine at a fast idle for approximately five minutes and then recheck the tension.

## 14  Temperature gauge sensor – removal and refitting

1   Remove the expansion tank filler cap. *If the engine is hot place a cloth over the cap and release it slowly to the first stop to allow the*

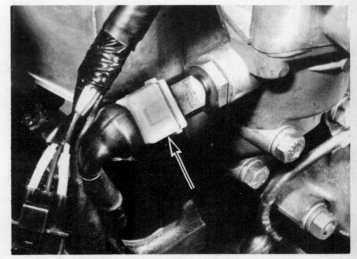

14.3 Temperature gauge sensor wiring plug (arrowed)

*pressure to escape.* When all pressure in the system has been relieved, remove the cap.

2   Place a suitable container beneath the radiator bottom hose outlet. Slacken the retaining clip and disconnect the bottom hose. Drain approximately 4 pints (2.3 litres) of coolant then refit the hose and tighten the clip.

3   Disconnect the electrical wiring plug and unscrew the sensor (photo). On 1.3 litre models the sensor is located on the rear face of the cylinder head below the thermostat housing. On 1.6 litre models the unit is situated on the side of the thermostat housing.

4   Refitting is the reverse sequence to removal. Tighten the sensor to the specified torque, and top up the cooling system, with reference to Section 5.

## 15 Fault diagnosis – cooling system

| Symptom | Reason(s) |
| --- | --- |
| Overheating | Low coolant level (this may be the result of overheating for other reasons) |
| | Drivebelt slipping or broken |
| | Radiator blockage (internal or external), or grille restricted |
| | Thermostat defective |
| | Ignition timing incorrect or distributor defective (automatic advance inoperative) |
| | Carburettor maladjustment |
| | Faulty cooling fan thermostatic switch |
| | Faulty cooling fan |
| | Blown cylinder head gasket (combustion gases in coolant) |
| | Water pump defective |
| | Expansion tank pressure cap faulty, or 5.0 mm hose stub on tank blocked |
| | Brakes binding |
| Overcooling | Thermostat missing, defective or wrong heat range |
| Water loss – external | Loose hose clips |
| | Perished or cracked hoses |
| | Radiator core leaking |
| | Heater matrix leaking |
| | Expansion tank pressure cap leaking |
| | Boiling due to overheating |
| | Water pump or thermostat housing leaking |
| | Core plug leaking |
| Water loss – internal | Cylinder head gasket blown |
| | Cylinder head cracked or warped |
| | Cylinder block cracked |
| Corrosion | Infrequent draining and flushing |
| | Incorrect antifreeze mixture or inappropriate type |
| | Combustion gases contaminating coolant |

# Chapter 3 Fuel and exhaust systems

*For modifications, and information applicable to later models, see Supplement at end of manual*

## Contents

## Specifications

**Air cleaner** ........................... Automatic air temperature control type, with renewable paper element (all models except MG 1600 – Champion W135)

### Fuel pump
Type ................................ Mechanical, operated by eccentric on camshaft
Make ................................ SU AUF800
Delivery pressure ................... 4lbf/in$^2$ (0.3 bar)

### Carburettor
Type:
All models except MG ........... SU HIF44 variable choke with electronic mixture control
MG models ...................... Twin Weber 40 DCNF dual throat downdraught

### SU carburettor specification
Type identification:
1.3 and 1.3L ................... FZX 1422
1.3 HLE ........................ FZX 1428
1.6L, HLS and Vanden Plas ...... FZX 1419
Piston spring colour ............... Red
Jet size ........................... 0.100 in
Needle identification:
1.3 and 1.3L ................... BCZ
1.3 HLE ........................ BCZ
1.6L, HLS and Vanden Plas ...... BES
Adjustment data:
Fast idle rod minimum clearance ... 0.005 in (0.13 mm)
Throttle lever lost motion gap .... 0.060 to 0.080 in (1.55 to 2.05 mm)
Float height (see text) ........... 0.040 to 0.020 in (1.00 to 1.50 mm)
Idling speed:
1.3 and 1.3L ................... 700 to 800 rpm
1.3 HLE ........................ 600 to 675 rpm
1.6L, HLS and Vanden Plas ...... 600 to 700 rpm
Fast idle speed:
1.3, 1.3L and HLE .............. 1050 to 1150 rpm
1.6L, HLS and Vanden Plas ...... 950 to 1050 rpm
CO mixture ......................... 1.5 to 3.5%
Piston damper oil type/specification .... Multigrade engine oil, viscosity SAE 10W/40 (Duckhams QXR, QS, Hypergrade Plus, or Hypergrade)

### Weber carburettor specification
Venturi diameter ................... 1.17 in (30 mm)
Jet sizes:
Main .......................... 145
Air correction ................ 210
Idle .......................... 57
Accelerator pump .............. 35
Emulsion tube ................. F22
Adjustment data:
Float setting dimension (see text) ... 1.95 in (50 mm)
Float stop dimension (see text) ...... 2.26 in (58 mm)
Idling speed ....................... 800 to 900 rpm
CO mixture ......................... 1.5 to 3.5%

**Fuel tank capacity** .................................................. 11.75 Imp gals (53 litres)

**Torque wrench settings**

|  | lbf ft | Nm |
|---|---|---|
| Carburettor retaining nuts ......................................... | 16 | 22 |
| Fuel pump retaining nuts ........................................... | 16 | 22 |
| Manifold retaining nuts and bolts ............................... | 16 | 22 |

## 1    General description

The fuel system consists of a centrally mounted fuel tank, camshaft operated mechanical fuel pump and, on all models except MG, an SU variable choke carburettor with electronic mixture control system. On MG models twin Weber downdraught dual throat carburettors are utilized.

The air cleaner is of the automatic air temperature control type and contains a disposable paper element.

The exhaust system is in three sections; the front section incorporates the twin downpipes and is fitted with a ball and socket type universal joint, the intermediate section incorporates the front silencer, and the rear section incorporates the rear silencer and tailpipe. The exhaust system is suspended on rubber mountings at the rear and is bolted to the cast iron manifold at the front.

**Warning:** *Many of the procedures in this Chapter entail the removal of fuel pipes and connections which may result in some fuel spillage. Before carrying out any operation on the fuel system refer to the precautions given in Safety First! at the beginning of this manual and follow them implicitly. Petrol is a highly dangerous and volatile liquid and the precautions necessary when handling it cannot be overstressed.*

## 2    Maintenance and inspection

1    At regular intervals (see Routine Maintenance) the following

checks and adjustments should be carried out on the fuel and exhaust system components.

2    With the car over a pit, raised on a vehicle lift, or securely supported on axle stands, carefully inspect the fuel pipes, hoses and unions for chafing, leaks and corrosion. Renew any pipes that are severely pitted with corrosion or in any way damaged. Renew any hoses that show signs of cracking or other deterioration.

3    Examine the fuel tank for leaks, particularly around the fuel gauge sender unit, and for signs of corrosion or damage.

4    Check the condition of the exhaust system, as described in Section 21.

5    From within the engine compartment, check the security of all fuel hose attachments and inspect the fuel hoses and vacuum hoses for kinks, chafing or deterioration.

6    Renew the air cleaner element and check the operation of the air cleaner automatic temperature control, as described in Section 3.

7    Check the operation of the accelerator linkage and lubricate the linkage, cable and pedal pivot with a few drops of engine oil. On MG models, check the operation of the choke control and linkage, as described in Section 16.

8    Top up the carburettor piston damper (not MG models) to the top of the hollow piston rod with engine oil. Note that although this operation is only considered necessary by the manufacturers at the annual major service interval, practical experience has shown that the damper oil may require topping-up more frequently.

9    At less frequent service intervals (see Routine Maintenance) check and, if necessary, adjust the carburettor idle, fast idle and mixture settings, as described in Sections 12 and 16. Additionally on MG

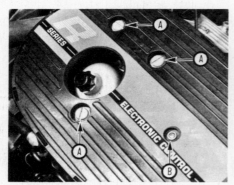

3.1a Air cleaner body retaining screws (A) and top cover retaining screw (B)

3.1b Release the top cover from the locating tags to gain access to the paper element

3.2 Removing the air cleaner element

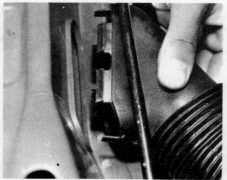

3.3 Air cleaner cold air intake hose attachment to front body panel

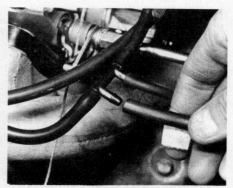

3.4 Air cleaner vacuum pipe connector in main vacuum line

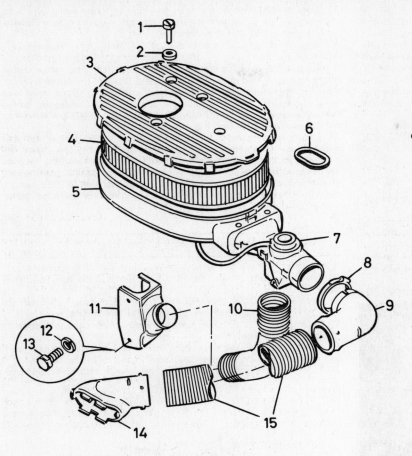

**Fig. 3.1 Air cleaner assembly and related components – all models except MG (Sec 3)**

1  *Retaining screw*
2  *Washer*
3  *Top cover*
4  *Paper element*
5  *Air cleaner body*
6  *Sealing washer*
7  *Control flap vacuum motor*
8  *Retaining clip*
9  *Intake elbow*
10  *Hot air hose*
11  *Hot air box (1.6 litre model shown)*
12  *Washer*
13  *Bolt*
14  *Cold air intake hose adaptor*
15  *Cold air intake hose*

models the air flow through the carburettors should be balanced, as described in Section 16.

### 3  Air cleaner and element (all models except MG) – removal and refitting

1  To remove the air cleaner element unscrew the three large screws and one small screw securing the air cleaner top cover and body (photo). Withdraw the screws, release the cover from the locating tags and withdraw it from the air cleaner body (photo).
2  The paper element can now be removed (photo).
3  If the air cleaner body is to be removed, detach the cold air intake hose from its location in the front body panel (photo).
4  Lift up the air cleaner and detach the vacuum pipe from the connector in the main vacuum line adjacent to the carburettor (photo). Detach the air cleaner hose from the hot air box on the exhaust manifold and remove the air cleaner from the engine.
5  Thoroughly clean the inside of the air cleaner and check the vacuum pipes and vacuum/temperature switch for condition and security.
6  To test the operation of the air temperature control system, first slacken the retaining clip and remove the cold air intake hose at the elbow.
7  Observe the position of the air temperature control flap which should be set to receive air from the cold air intake. Apply suction to the air cleaner vacuum pipe that was previously disconnected, and ensure that the flap moves to the hot air delivery position. The flap should move to the cold air delivery position when the ambient temperature reaches 30°C (86°F). This can be tested by heating the vacuum/temperature switch in the air cleaner body with a hair dryer while applying suction to the hose. If the operation of the unit is in doubt it should be renewed.
8  Refitting the air cleaner body and element is the reverse sequence to removal. Ensure that the rubber sealing washer is in position around the lip of the carburettor intake flange on the air cleaner body. Also

make sure that the element seats correctly in the body before fitting the cover.

### 4  Air cleaner and element (MG models) – removal and refitting

1  Detach the crankcase breather hose from the air cleaner cover and unscrew the three retaining nuts and washers.
2  Spring back the retaining clips and lift off the cover.
3  The air cleaner paper element can now be withdrawn.
4  To remove the air cleaner body, detach the cold air intake hose

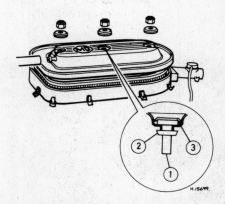

**Fig. 3.2 Air cleaner assembly – MG models (Sec 4)**

1  *Spacer*               3  *Washer*
2  *Seal*

from its location in the front body panel.

5    Undo and remove the nuts securing the air intake throats to the carburettor studs. Lift off the washers and the intake throats.

6    Lift up the air cleaner and detach the vacuum pipe from the connector in the main vacuum line. Detach the air cleaner hose from the hot air box on the element manifold and remove the air cleaner from the engine.

7    Thoroughly clean the inside of the air cleaner and check the vacuum pipes and vacuum/temperature switch for condition and security.

8    The operation of the air temperature control system can be checked, as described in paragraphs 6 and 7 of the previous Section.

9    Refitting the air cleaner and element is the reverse sequence to removal. Ensure that the spacers are in position over the air cleaner cover retaining studs before fitting the cover.

---

## 5    Fuel pump – removal, testing and refitting

1    The mechanical fuel pump is located in the front lower right-hand side of the cylinder block on 1.3 litre engines, and at the rear of the camshaft cover on 1.6 litre units. The pump is of sealed construction and in the event of faulty operation must be renewed as a complete unit.

2    To remove the pump first disconnect the battery negative terminal.

5.3 Removing the fuel inlet pipe from the pump nozzle

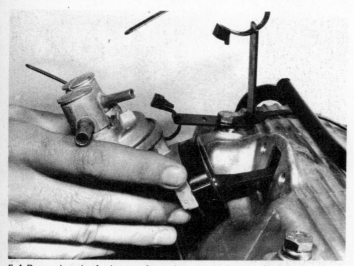

5.4 Removing the fuel pump from the camshaft cover (1.6 litre models)

3    Note the location of the fuel inlet pipe and fuel outlet pipe and then remove the pipes from the pump (photo). Plug the pipe ends with a metal rod or old bolt after removal.

4    Undo and remove the two nuts, or bolts, and washers and withdraw the pump and insulating block from the engine (photo).

5    To test the pump operation, refit the fuel inlet pipe to the pump inlet and hold a wad of rag near the outlet. Operate the pump lever by hand and if the pump is in a satisfactory condition a strong jet of fuel should be ejected from the pump outlet as the lever is released. If this is not the case, check that fuel will flow from the inlet pipe when it is held below the tank level, if so the pump is faulty.

6    Before refitting the pump, clean all traces of old gasket from the pump flange, insulating block and engine face. Use a new gasket on each side of the insulator block and refit the pump using the reverse sequence to removal. Ensure that the pump lever locates over the top of the camshaft eccentric as the pump is installed. If this proves difficult, turn the engine over until the large offset of the eccentric is facing downward.

---

## 6    Fuel tank – removal, servicing and refitting

**Note**: *Refer to the warning note in Section 1 before proceeding.*

1    Disconnect the battery negative lead. Remove the fuel tank filler cap.

2    A drain plug is not provided and it will therefore be necessary to syphon, or hand pump, all the fuel from the tank before removal.

3    Having emptied the tank jack up the rear of the car and support it securely on axle stands.

4    Disconnect the electrical leads from the fuel gauge sender unit and release the clips securing the leads to the tank (photo).

5    Using pliers, release the fuel feed hose retaining clip and

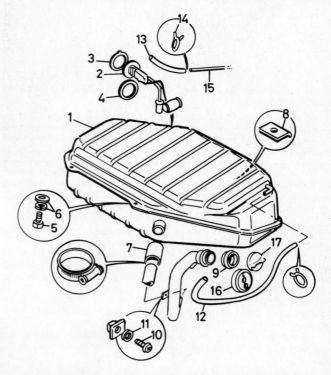

Fig. 3.3 Fuel tank, fittings and related components (Sec 6)

| | |
|---|---|
| 1    Fuel tank | 10    Screw |
| 2    Sender unit | 11    Washer |
| 3    Locking ring | 12    Breather hose |
| 4    Seal | 13    Fuel feed hose |
| 5    Bolt | 14    Clip |
| 6    Washers | 15    Fuel pipe |
| 7    Filler hose | 16    Filler cap (lockable) |
| 8    Stiffener plate | 17    Filler cap (non-lockable) |
| 9    Filler neck grommet | |

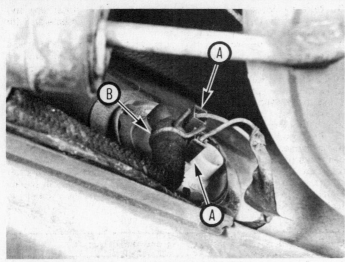

6.4 Electrical leads (A) and fuel feed hose (B) locations at the fuel gauge sender unit

6.8a One of the two fuel tank rear retaining bolts (arrowed) ...

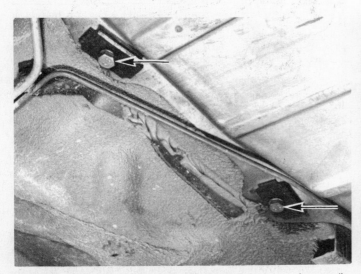

6.8b ... and the two front retaining bolts and stiffener plates (arrowed)

disconnect the hose from the outlet on the sender unit.

6   Unscrew the retaining clip securing the fuel filler hose to the tank and disconnect the hose.

7   Release the right-hand rear brake pipe retaining clip from the front of the tank.

8   Support the tank on blocks, or with a jack, and undo the two rear and two front retaining bolts and stiffener plates (photos).

9   Move the tank to the left to clear the brake pipe and lower it sufficiently to allow the breather hose to be detached. Now lower the tank to the ground and withdraw it from under the car.

10  If the tank is contaminated with sediment or water, remove the sender unit, as described in Secion 7, and swill the tank out with clean fuel. If the tank is damaged, or leaks, it should be repaired by a specialist or, alternatively, renewed. **Do not** *under any circumstances solder or weld the tank.*

11  Refitting the tank is the reverse sequence to removal.

## 7   Fuel gauge sender unit – removal and refitting

**Note:** *Refer to the warning note in Section 1 before proceeding.*

1   Follow the procedure given in Section 6, paragraphs 1 to 5 inclusive.

2   Engage a screwdriver, flat bar or other suitable tool with the lugs of the locking ring, and turn the ring anti-clockwise to release it.

3   Withdraw the locking ring, seal and sender unit.

4   Refitting is the reverse sequence to removal, but always use a new seal.

## 8   Accelerator cable and pedal – removal and refitting

1   Disconnect the battery negative terminal.

2   Remove the air cleaner, as described in Section 3 or 4, and then slacken the screw to release the inner cable from the connector on the throttle linkage (photo). Slide the cable from the carburettor bracket. On MG models, open the throttle and detach the cable end from the lever.

3   Working inside the car, prise the retaining clip from the top of the accelerator pedal, and disconnect the inner cable.

4   Release the accelerator cable from the engine compartment bulkhead and withdraw the complete cable from the car.

5   Refitting is a reversal of removal, but before tightening the throttle linkage connector, adjust the position of the inner cable to provide a small amount of free movement. Check that, with the accelerator pedal fully depressed, the throttle linkage is fully open, and with the pedal released the linkage is in the closed position.

6   To remove the accelerator pedal, detach the cable end, as previously described, and where fitted unhook the return spring.

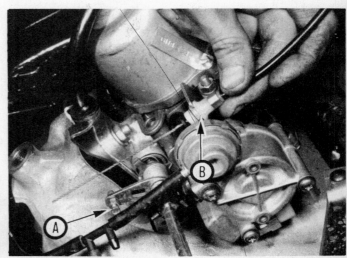

8.2 Accelerator inner cable linkage connector (A) and carburettor bracket fitting (B)

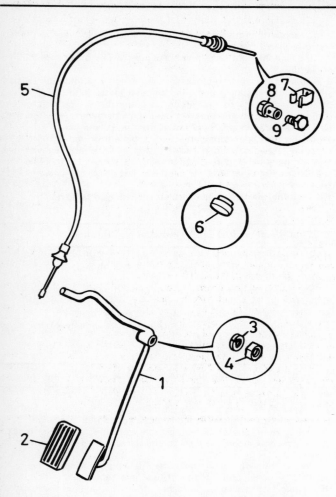

**Fig. 3.4 Accelerator cable and pedal components (Sec 8)**

| | | | |
|---|---|---|---|
| 1 | Accelerator pedal | 6 | Pedal stop |
| 2 | Pedal pad | 7 | Cable retaining clip |
| 3 | Washer | 8 | Cable connector |
| 4 | Retaining nut | 9 | Connector screw |
| 5 | Accelerator cable | | |

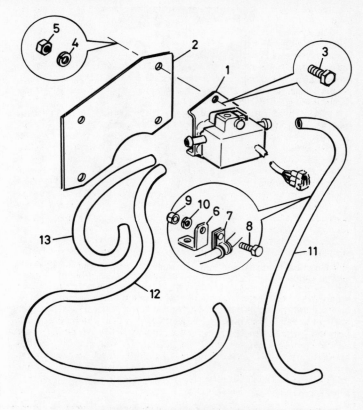

**Fig. 3.5 Fuel flow transducer and fittings (Sec 10)**

| | | | |
|---|---|---|---|
| 1 | Transducer and bracket | 9 | Nut |
| 2 | Adaptor plate | 10 | Washer |
| 3 | Bolt | 11 | Fuel outlet pipe |
| 4 | Washer | 12 | Fuel inlet pipe |
| 5 | Nut | | (1.3 litre models) |
| 6 | Pipe support bracket | 13 | Fuel inlet pipe |
| 7 | Pipe clip | | (1.6 litre models) |
| 8 | Bolt | | |

7  Undo the retaining nut and washer and slide the pedal off the shaft.

8  Refitting is the reverse sequence to removal.

### 9  Choke control cable (MG models) – removal and refitting

1  Disconnect the battery negative terminal and remove the air cleaner, as described in Section 4.

2  Slacken the two screws to release the inner cable from the carburettor choke lever connectors.

3  From inside the car remove the choke control knob by depressing the small retaining pin and pulling off the knob.

4  Unscrew the retaining ring and withdraw the cable from its panel location. Refer to Chapter 11 for details of the facia panel attachments, if necessary. Detach the warning light switch from the cable.

5  Pull the cable through the engine compartment bulkhead grommet and into the passenger compartment. Remove the cable from inside the car.

6  Refitting is the reverse sequence to removal. Ensure that the choke levers on the carburettors are fully returned when the choke knob is pushed in and fully opened when the knob is in the cold start position.

### 10  Fuel flow transducer – removal and refitting

1  On models equipped with a trip computer, a fuel flow transducer module is incorporated in the fuel line between the pump and carburettor. The unit is mounted on the engine compartment bulkhead adjacent to the ignition coil and provides information on fuel delivery and rate of flow to the trip computer.

2  To remove the unit first disconnect the battery negative terminal.

3  Disconnect the wiring multi-plug at the harness connector.

4  Release the fuel inlet and outlet pipes from the transducer nozzles and plug the pipes after removal.

5  Undo and remove the two nuts and bolts securing the transducer bracket to the adaptor plate and withdraw the unit. Note that the unit is only available as a complete assembly and cannot, therefore, be dismantled.

6  Refitting is the reverse sequence to removal.

### 11  SU carburettor – general description

The SU HIF (Horizontal Integral Float chamber) carburettor is of the variable choke, constant depression type incorporating a sliding piston which automatically controls the mixture of air and fuel supplied to the engine with respect to the throttle valve position and engine speed. In addition the carburettor is equipped wth an electronically operated mixture control device. This alters the mixture strength and engine speed when starting and during slow running, and also controls the operation of a fuel shut-off valve when decelerating or descending a hill.

The carburettor functions as follows. When the engine is started and is allowed to idle, the throttle valve passes a small amount of air. Because the piston is in a low position, it offers a large restriction, and the resultant pressure reduction draws fuel from the jet, and atomisation occurs to provide a combustible mixture. Since the inside section of the tapered needle is across the mouth of the jet, a relatively small amount of fuel is passed.

When the throttle valve is opened, the amount of air passing through the carburettor is increased, which causes a greater depression beneath the sliding piston. An internal passageway connects this depression with the suction chamber above the piston, which now rises. The piston offers less of a restriction and the depression is reduced, with the result that a point is reached where the forces of depression, gravity, and spring tension balance out. The tapered needle has now been raised, and more fuel passes from the jet.

Incorporated in the jet adjusting (mixture) screw mechanism is a bi-metal strip which alters the position of the jet to compensate for varying fuel densities resulting from varying fuel temperatures

Fuel enrichment for cold starting is by an internal valve which admits more fuel into the airstream passing through the carburettor. This valve is operated by a stepping motor which also controls the engine idling speed. An electronic control unit (ECU) which is a small microprocessor receives inputs from the coolant temperature sensor, ambient air temperature sensor, throttle switch and ignition amplifier, and adjusts the engine idle speed and mixture accordingly. The ECU also controls the operation of a fuel shut-off valve which comes into operation when decelerating or descending a hill. If, during these conditions, the engine speed is in excess of 1300 rpm the valve is opened and closed at half second intervals, thus weakening the mixture. When accelerating, a vacuum operated switch acts upon the mixture control, allowing more fuel to be drawn through, resulting in the necessary richer mixture.

The overall effect of this type of carburettor is that it will remain in tune during the lengthy service intervals and also under varying operating conditions and temperature changes. The design of the unit and its related systems ensures a fine degree of mixture control over the complete throttle range, coupled with enhanced engine fuel economy.

## 12 SU carburettor – adjustments

**Note**: *Before carrying out any carburettor adjustment, ensure that the ignition timing, spark plug gaps and valve clearances are correct and that the distributor is operating correctly. To carry out the adjustments an accurate tachometer will be required. The use of an exhaust gas analyser (CO meter) is also preferable, although not essential.*

1   Begin by removing the air cleaner assembly, as described in Section 3.

2   Unscrew and remove the piston damper from the suction chamber.

3   Undo and remove the three securing screws and lift off the suction chamber, complete with piston and piston spring. After removal avoid rotating the piston in the suction chamber.

4   Invert the suction chamber assembly and drain the oil from the hollow piston rod. Check that the needle guide is flush with the piston face and is secure. Do not be concerned that the needle appears loose in the guide, this is perfectly normal.

5   Observe the position of the jet in relation to the jet guide located in the centre of the carburettor venturi. The jet will probably be slightly below the top face of the jet guide. Turn the mixture adjusting screw until the top of the jet is flush with the top of the jet guide. Now turn the adjusting screw two complete turns clockwise. If the mixture adjusting screw is covered by a small blue or red tamperproof plug, hook this out with a small screwdriver and discard it.

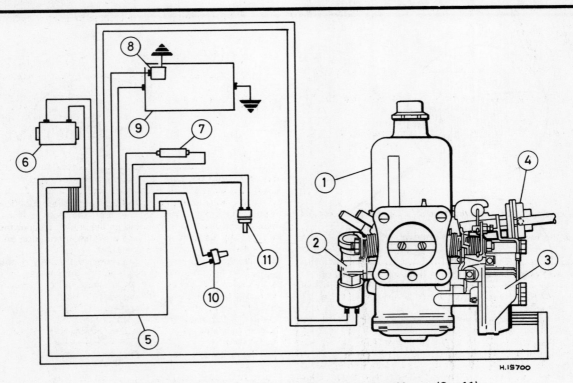

H.15700

**Fig. 3.6 SU carburettor and electronic mixture control layout (Sec 11)**

| | | | |
|---|---|---|---|
| 1 | Carburettor | 4 | Vacuum switch |
| 2 | Fuel shut-off valve and solenoid | 5 | Electronic control unit – ECU* |
| 3 | Mixture control stepping motor | | |

| | | | |
|---|---|---|---|
| 6 | Ignition amplifier | 9 | Engine temperature gauge |
| 7 | Ambient temperature sensor | 10 | Accelerator pedal switch |
| 8 | High engine temperature warning light | 11 | Engine temperature gauge sensor |

*Located at rear of driver's facia shelf (held by two screws)*

6   Refit the piston and suction chamber assembly, taking care not to turn the piston in the suction chamber any more than is necessary to align the piston groove with its guide. If the piston is turned excessively the spring will be wound up and the assembly will have to be dismantled, as described in Section 14.

7   Check that the piston is free to move in the suction chamber by lifting it and allowing it to drop under its own weight. A definite metallic click should be heard as the piston falls and contacts the bridge in the carburettor body. If this is not the case, dismantle and clean the suction chamber, as described in Section 14. If satisfactory, top up the damper oil with engine oil to the top of the hollow piston rod, and refit the damper.

8   Check that the throttle linkage operates smoothly and that there is a small amount of free play in the accelerator cable.

9   Connect a tachometer to the engine in accordance with the manufacturer's instructions, and also a CO meter if this is to be used.

10  Reconnect the air cleaner vacuum pipe to the connector in the vacuum line and lay the air cleaner alongside the carburettor.

11  Start the engine and run it at a fast idle speed until it reaches its normal operating temperature. Continue to run the engine for a further five minutes before commencing adjustment.

12  Increase the engine speed to 2500 rpm for 30 seconds and repeat this at three minute intervals during the adjustment procedure. This will ensure that any excess fuel is cleared from the inlet manifold.

13  Allow the engine to idle and check the idling speed against that given in the Specifications. If necessary, turn the idle speed adjustment screw clockwise to increase the speed and anti-clockwise to decrease it (see Fig. 3.7).

14  To adjust the mixture, slowly turn the mixture adjustment screw clockwise (to enrich) or anti-clockwise (to weaken), until the fastest idling speed which is consistent with smooth even running is reached. If a CO meter is being used, adjust the mixture screw to obtain the specified idling exhaust gas content.

15  Reset the engine idling speed using the idle speed adjustment screw.

16  Check the clearance between the fast idle rod and fast idle adjustment screw using feeler gauges (position B in Fig. 3.7). Turn the fast idle adjustment screw as necessary to obtain the specified clearance.

17  Check the throttle lever lost motion gap using feeler gauges (position A in Fig. 3.7) and, if necessary, turn the throttle lever adjustment screw to obtain the specified clearance.

18  To adjust the fast idle speed, disconnect the two wires at the engine ambient air temperature sensor located behind the right-hand headlight unit in the engine compartment. Join the two disconnected wires together using a suitable length of wire.

19  Detach the wiring connector at the engine temperature gauge sensor (refer to Chapter 2, if necessary). Bridge the terminals of the connector using a resistor, the value of which is determined by the colour coding of the electronic control unit (ECU). Observe the ECU, which is located under the facia shelf on the driver's side, and determine the resistor required as follows:

| | |
|---|---|
| 1.3 litre engines with yellow spot or no spot on ECU | 1000 ohms |
| 1.3 litre engines with blue spot on ECU | 600 ohms |
| 1.6 litre engines | 600 ohms |

### See also Chapter 12, Section 7

Resistor of 0.5 watt rating with a 1% tolerance should be used; these are available from electrical component suppliers. Two 1200 ohm resistors may be used in parallel in place of a 600 ohm resistor, if necessary.

20  With the connections made, start the engine and note the fast idling speed. If necessary adjust the fast idle adjustment screw to obtain the specified setting.

21  Switch off the engine, remove the resistor and link wire and refit

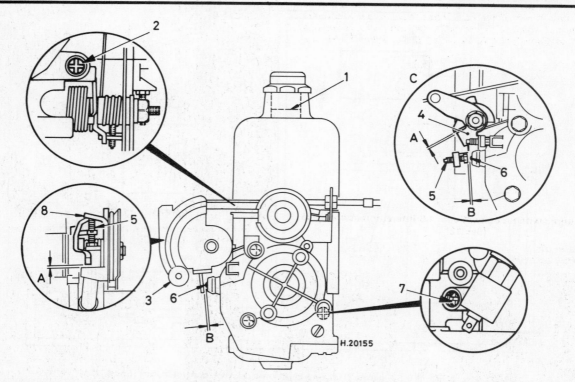

**Fig. 3.7 SU carburettor adjustment points. On some models gap 'B' is adjusted by bending tag '8' (inset, bottom left)**
**(Sec 12)**

| | | |
|---|---|---|
| 1  Piston damper oil level | 5  Fast idle adjustment screw | A  Lost motion gap |
| 2  Idle speed adjustment screw | 6  Fast idle pushrod | B  Fast idle clearance |
| 3  Accelerator cable cam | 7  Mixture adjustment screw | C  Alternative throttle linkage |
| 4  Throttle lever adjustment screw | 8  Lost motion adjustment tag | |

the wiring connectors. **Note**: *after carrying out this adjustment, ensure that the specified minimum clearance still exists between rod and screw, as described in paragraph 16. Adjust the screw if the clearance is less than specified.*

22 Make a final check that the mixture and idling speed are correct after refitting the air cleaner, then switch off the engine and disconnect the instruments.

23 On 1.6 litre models with automatic transmission, there have been problems with warm starting due to excessively rich mixture, normally after the car has been driven a short distance and then stopped for a minute or two. Where problems of this nature are noted, check the idle speed and CO settings as described above. If this fails to resolve the fault, you should remove the vacuum switch and replace it with a restricted air bleed as follows. You will need the following parts, obtainable through Austin Rover dealers:

| | |
|---|---|
| 6 mm diameter tube | Part No. JZX 2000 |
| Restrictor assembly | Part No. LZX 1098 |
| Fuel hose | Part No. JZV 1228 |
| Hose clip | Part No. UKC 3796 |

24 Refer to Fig. 3.8. Disconnect and remove the vacuum switch as described in Section 13. Push the straight end of the 6 mm tube into the end of either one of the two short rubber pipes from the carburettor body, and fit the restrictor assembly into the end of the other rubber pipe.

25 Using a sharp knife, cut off 5 mm from each end of the fuel hose (3) and use the shortened hose to connect the bulbous end of the 6 mm tube to the projecting end of the restrictor, fitting a clip to secure the fuel hose to the restrictor.

26 Disconnect the vacuum switch signal pipe and T-piece, and discard them. Using the existing elbow, connect the signal pipe to the carburettor.

## 13 SU carburettor – removal and refitting

**Note**: *Due to the position of the stepping motor and vacuum switch, access to the bottom right-hand carburettor retaining nut is severely limited. A special spanner is available for this purpose and is manufactured by Snap-On tools, part No S5911. Without this tool*

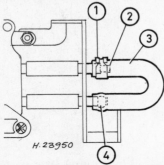

**Fig. 3.8 Vacuum switch modification – 1.6 litre automatic models (Sec 12)**

| | | | |
|---|---|---|---|
| 1 | Retaining clip | 3 | Fuel hose |
| 2 | Restrictor assembly | 4 | 6 mm tube |

*access is only possible after removal of the vacuum switch and stepping motor and in practice this is often the method adopted. It must be pointed out, however, that this procedure is not recommended by the manufacturers. New stepping motor O-rings (paragraph 11) may not be available from dealers.*

1 Disconnect the battery negative terminal and then remove the air cleaner assembly, as described in Section 3.

2 Slacken the retaining screw and release the accelerator inner cable from the throttle lever connectors. Release the outer cable from the support bracket and place the cable to one side.

3 Detach the distributor vacuum advance pipe, crankcase, breather hose, fuel unit hose and float chamber vent hose from the carburettor (photo). Plug the fuel hose after removal.

4 Detach the wiring connectors at the fuel shut-off valve solenoid and stepping motor (photos).

5 If the special tool described in the introduction to this Section is available, the carburettor retaining nuts and washers can now be unscrewed, the hose at the vacuum switch outlet removed, and the carburettor lifted off the manifold studs. If the tool is not available, proceed as follows.

6 Pull the vacuum hose off the vacuum switch outlet and then remove the lower screw and upper nut and bolt securing the switch to the stepping motor and carburettor. Carefully ease the vacuum switch hoses off the carburettor outlets and withdraw the switch (photo).

7 Make a very careful note of the positioning of the throttle linkage return spring ends on the stepping motor and on the linkage levers.

8 Remove the two remaining securing screws and carefully withdraw the stepping motor from the side of the carburettor (photo).

9 Having removed the vacuum switch and stepping motor, it is now possible to gain access to the carburettor lower retaining nut (photo). Undo and remove this, and the other three nuts and washers securing the carburettor to the inlet manifold.

10 Withdraw the carburettor from the inlet manifold studs and, if

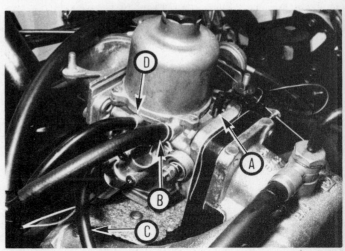

13.3 Distributor vacuum advance pipe (A), crankcase breather hose (B), fuel inlet hose (C), and float chamber vent hose (D) locations on carburettor body

13.4a Detach the fuel shut-off valve wiring connector ...

13.4b ... and the stepping motor wiring connector

13.6 Vacuum hose (A), vacuum switch lower retaining screw (B) and upper retaining nut and bolt (C) – *Caution, see text*

13.8 Removing the stepping motor – *Caution, see text*

13.9 Carburettor lower retaining nut

13.11 Ensure that the stepping motor O-ring seals (arrowed) are undamaged before refitting

14.3 Removing the carburettor suction chamber and piston assembly

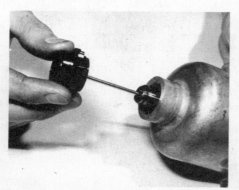

14.4 Unscrew the damper and drain the oil

14.5a Extract the retaining circlip ...

14.5b ... to allow removal of the piston and spring

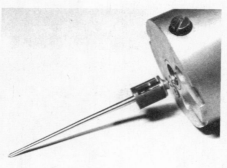

14.6 Slacken the needle guide locking screw and withdraw the needle, guide and spring

14.7 Lift off the float chamber cover after removing the four retaining screws

necessary, remove the air cleaner mounting bracket, gaskets and insulating block.

11  Refitting is the reverse sequence to removal. Ensure that all mating faces are perfectly clean and always use new gaskets, one each side of the insulating block and one between bracket and carburettor — three in all. Ensure that the O-rings on the stepping motor are undamaged (photo) and renew them, if necessary. Make sure that the linkage return springs are refitted as noted during removal and sufficiently wound up to provide return tension on the linkage. After refitting connect the accelerator cable, with reference to Section 8, and adjust the carburettor, as described in Section 12.

## 14  SU carburettor – dismantling, overhaul and reassembly

**Note:** *Check the availability of spare parts before deciding to overhaul the carburettor.*

1  Remove the carburettor, as described in the previous Section.
2  Clean off the exterior of the carburettor using paraffin, or a suitable solvent and wipe dry.

3  Unscrew the three retaining screws and lift off the suction chamber and piston assembly (photo).
4  Unscrew the damper from the suction chamber (photo), and drain the oil from the piston rod.
5  Push the piston up to expose the retaining circlip (photo). Extract the circlip and withdraw the piston and spring assembly (photo).
6  Unscrew the needle guide locking screw and withdraw the needle, guide and spring (photo).
7  Mark the relationship of the float chamber cover to the carburettor body. Unscrew the four retaining screws and lift off the cover and O-ring seal (photo).
8  Unscrew the jet adjusting lever retaining screw and withdraw the jet and adjusting lever assembly (photo). Disengage the jet from the lever.
9  Unscrew the float pivot screw (photo) and lift out the float and fuel needle valve (photo). Unscrew the needle valve seat from the base of the float chamber (photo).

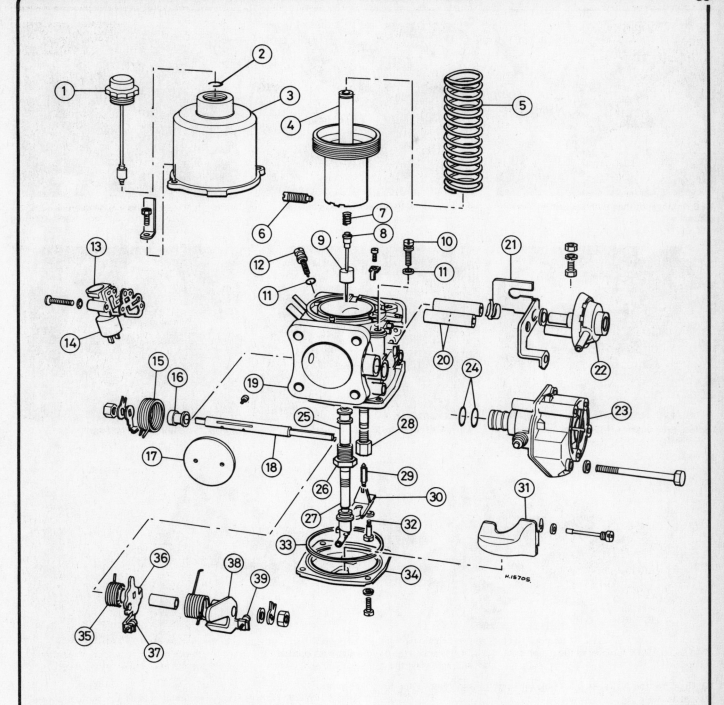

**Fig. 3.9 Exploded view of the SU carburettor (Sec 14)**

1 Piston damper
2 Retaining circlip
3 Suction chamber
4 Piston
5 Piston spring
6 Needle guide locking screw
7 Needle bias spring
8 Jet needle
9 Needle guide
10 Idle speed adjustment screw

11 Adjustment screw seal
12 Mixture adjustment screw
13 Fuel shut-off valve and housing
14 Fuel shut-off valve solenoid
15 Throttle return spring
16 Throttle spindle seal
17 Throttle plate
18 Throttle spindle
19 Carburettor body
20 Vacuum hoses

21 Mounting bracket
22 Vacuum switch
23 Mixture control stepping motor
24 Stepping motor O-rings
25 Jet bearing
26 Jet bearing nut
27 Jet assembly
28 Float needle seat
29 Float needle
30 Bi-metal jet lever
31 Float

32 Jet adjusting lever retaining screw
33 Float chamber cover seal
34 Float chamber cover
35 Throttle return spring
36 Lost motion link
37 Throttle lever adjustment screw
38 Throttle lever
39 Fast idle adjustment screw

14.8 Removal of the jet and adjusting lever assembly

14.9a Unscrew the float pivot screw and remove the float ...

14.9b ... followed by the fuel needle valve ...

14.9c ... then unscrew the needle valve seat

14.10a Unscrew the jet bearing locknut ...

14.10b ... and lift out the jet bearing

14.11 Remove the fuel shut-off valve and solenoid

14.13 Ensure that the filter in the fuel needle valve seat is clean

10  Unscrew the jet bearing locking nut (photo) and remove the jet bearing (photo).

11  Undo the three retaining screws and remove the fuel shut-off and solenoid assembly (photo). Recover the gasket.

12  Dismantling the remaining components is not recommended, as these parts are not available separately. If the throttle levers, linkage or spindle appear worn, or in any way damaged, it will be necessary to renew the complete carburettors.

13  Check the condition of the float needle valve and seat and renew these components if there is any sign of pitting or wear ridges, particularly on the needle. Ensure that the filter in the seat assembly is clean (photo).

14  Examine the carburettor body for cracks and damage, and ensure that the brass fittings and piston guide are secure.

15  Clean the inside of the suction chamber and the outer circumference of the piston with a petrol-moistened rag and allow to air dry. Insert the piston into the suction chamber without the spring. Hold the assembly in a horizontal position and spin the piston. If there is any tendency for the piston to bind, renew the piston and dashpot assembly.

16  Connect a 12 volt supply to the terminals of the fuel shut-off solenoid and ensure that the valve closes. If not, renew the solenoid.

17  If there is any doubt about the operation of the stepping motor, check the resistances at the motor wiring connector between the orange/white lead and each of the other four leads in turn, using an **ohmmeter**. If the resistance readings are outside the permitted range of 12 to 18 ohms, a new motor must be fitted. Do not apply voltage to the motor wiring during testing, or damage may result. Do not attempt to dismantle the motor; it is preset during manufacture, and is neither adjustable or repairable.

18  Check the piston needle and jet bearing for any signs of ovality, or wear ridges.

19  Shake the float and listen for any trapped fuel which may have entered through a tiny crack or fracture.

20  Check the condition of all gaskets, seals and connecting hoses and renew any that show signs of deterioration.

21  Begin reassembly by refitting the jet bearing and retaining nut to the carburettor body.

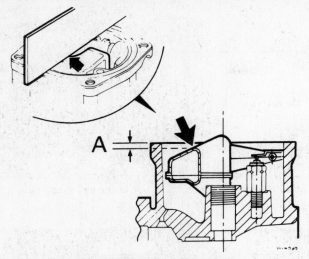

**Fig. 3.10 SU carburettor float height adjustment (Sec 14)**

*Arrows indicate checking and adjustment points*

14.27a Refit the needle, spring and guide to the piston ...

22 Refit the fuel needle valve and seat, followed by the float and float pivot screw.
23 Allow the float to close the needle valve under its own weight and measure the distance from the centre of the float to the face of the carburettor body, as shown in Fig 3.10. If the measured dimension is outside the float level height setting given in the Specifications, carefully bend the brass contact pad on the float to achieve the required setting.
24 Engage the jet with the cut-out in the adjusting lever, ensuring that the jet head moves freely. Position the jet in the jet bearing and, at the same time, engage the slot in the adjusting lever with the protruding tip of the mixture adjustment screw. Secure the assembly with the retaining screw.
25 Turn the mixture adjustment screw as necessary to bring the top of the jet flush with the jet bearing upper face when viewed from above. Now turn the adjustment screw two complete turns clockwise to obtain an initial mixture setting.
26 Refit the O-ring seal to the float chamber cover. Fit the cover with the previously made marks aligned and secure with the four retaining screws.
27 Refit the piston needle, spring and needle guide to the piston (photo), ensuring that the needle guide is flush with the underside of the piston and the triangular etch mark on the guide is between the two transfer holes in the piston (photo). Refit and tighten the locking screw.
28 Temporarily refit the piston and dashpot to the carburettor body without the spring. Engage the piston in its guide, and, with the suction chamber in its correct position relative to the retaining screws, mark the piston-to-suction chamber relationship. Remove the suction-chamber and piston.
29 Fit the spring to the piston, align the previously made marks and slide the suction chamber over the piston and spring. Avoid turning the piston in the suction chamber, otherwise the spring will be wound up.
30 Push the piston up and refit the circlip to the piston rod.
31 Refit the piston and suction chamber, and secure with the three retaining screws tightened evenly. Fill the piston damper with engine oil up to the top of the piston rod and refit the damper.
32 Refit the fuel shut-off valve using a new gasket, if necessary, and secure the unit with the three screws.
33 The vacuum switch and stepping motor should not be fitted until the carburettor has been refitted to the car, which can now be done, as described in Section 13.

## 15 Weber carburettor – general description

The Weber 40 DCNF carburettor is a downdraught dual throat unit operating in twin carburettor configuration on MG versions of the Maestro range. The carburettor features simultaneous operation of both throats via a common throttle shaft with all components except

14.27b ... with the guide flush with the piston base and the etch mark (arrowed) positioned as shown

the accelerator pump assembly duplicated in each throat. In the MG twin carburettor configuration, this effectively provides one complete carburettor for each engine cylinder.

The carburettor functions as follows. When the engine is idling, the depression in the inlet manifold causes fuel to be drawn from the float chamber to the idle jets, where it mixes with air drawn in through calibrated air bushes. This emulsified mixture passes down through drillings in the carburettor body and is discharged through the idle feed orifices below the throttle plates. The amount of emulsified mixture discharged through these orifices is controlled by the idle mixture screws.

As the throttle is partially opened, this same mixture is also discharged through the progression orifices located above the throttle plates. Additional opening of the throttle causes the depression in the carburettor throat to increase. Fuel is now drawn through the main jets and air is drawn through the air correction jets. The fuel and air mix in the emulsion tubes, and this mixture is then discharged through the spray nozzles in the auxiliary venturi. As this occurs the depression across the idle feed and progression orifices weakens, and the flow of mixture ceases.

As throttle movement increases further, the cam on the throttle shaft actuates the accelerator pump lever which in turn depresses the pump diaphragm. This causes neat fuel to be pumped via the pump jets. Sudden throttle movement is absorbed by the accelerator pump

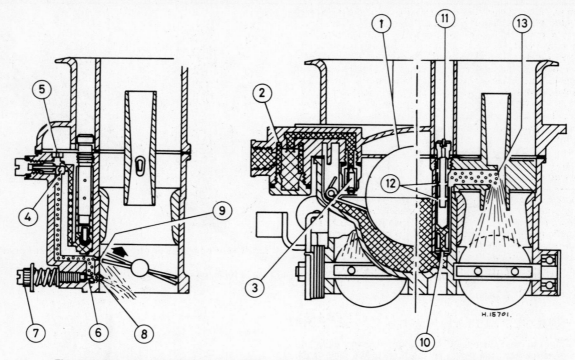

**Fig. 3.11 Operating principles of the Weber carburettor – idle and normal running (Sec 15)**

| 1 | Float | 5 | Air bush | 8 | Idle feed orifice | 11 | Air correction jet |
|---|---|---|---|---|---|---|---|
| 2 | Filter | 6 | Mixture passage | 9 | Progression orifice | 12 | Emulsion tube |
| 3 | Needle valve | 7 | Idle mixture adjustment | 10 | Main jet | 13 | Spray nozzle |
| 4 | Idle jet | | screw | | | | |

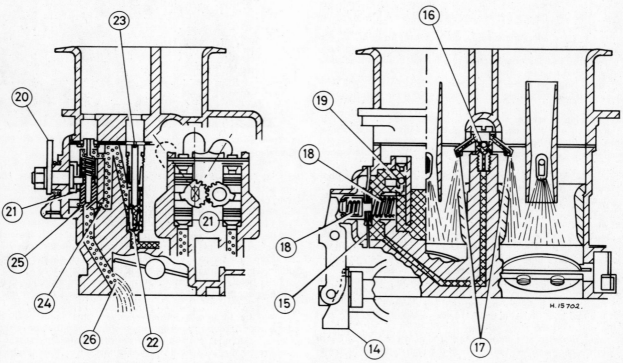

**Fig. 3.12 Operating principles of the Weber carburettor – cold starting and acceleration (Sec 15)**

| 14 | Throttle shaft cam | 17 | Pump jets | 20 | Choke control lever | 24 | Outlet |
|---|---|---|---|---|---|---|---|
| 15 | Accelerator pump | 18 | Pump operating | 21 | Mixture valves | 25 | Air orifice |
| | diaphragm | | springs | 22 | Starting jet | 26 | Discharge orifice |
| 16 | Delivery valve | 19 | One-way ball valve | 23 | Air jet | | |

operating spring, thus causing fuel delivery to be prolonged. Excess fuel is returned to the float chamber via a calibrated bush. A one-way ballvalve is used to admit fuel to the accelerator pump under the returning action of the diaphragm.

A cable operated cold start (choke) mechanism is employed, whereby operation of the choke control moves a lever on the carburettor body which raises two internal mixture valves. As the engine is cranked, fuel is drawn from the float chamber through the starting jets where it is mixed with air from the air jets. The mixture passes to the outlets above the mixture valve where it is further mixed with air before being drawn into the carburettor throats via the orifices below the throttle plates.

### 16 Weber carburettor – adjustments

**Note**: *Before carrying out any carburettor adjustment, ensure that the ignition timing, spark plug gaps and valve clearances are correct, and that the distributor is operating correctly. To carry out the adjustments an accurate tachometer and a vacuum gauge will be required. Part of the adjustment procedure entails the balancing of the airflow through each throat of each carburettor and, due to the design of the carburettor, a conventional balancing tool cannot be used effectively. The traditional method of listening to the hiss in each throat with a small bore pipe is considered to be far too inaccurate for satisfactory use on these units. A vacuum gauge is therefore necessary, and the following procedure entails the use of such an instrument. To accurately adjust the mixture strength an exhaust gas analyser (CO meter) is preferable, although not essential.*

1   Begin by removing the air cleaner assembly, as described in Section 4, but leave the vacuum pipe attached to the connector in the main vacuum line. Lay the air cleaner on top of the engine alongside the carburettors.

2   Check that the throttles open fully when the accelerator pedal is depressed, and close fully when the pedal is released. Ensure that there is a small amount of free play in the cable when the throttles are closed. Adjust the cable, if necessary.

3   With the choke knob pushed fully in, make sure that both mixture control levers on the carburettors are fully returned, and fully open when the choke knob is in the cold start position. Reset the levers on the cable, if necessary.

4   Lubricate the throttle linkage and choke linkage with a few drops of engine oil.

5   Commence the adjustment procedure by checking the throttle lever interconnection as follows.

6   Unscrew the idle speed adjustment screw (see Fig. 3.13) until a clearance exists between the end of the screw and its contact lever. Similarly, slacken the throttle interconnection screw until it is clear of its contact lever.

7   Hold the throttle of the right-hand carburettor (nearest the crankshaft pulley) closed, and turn the interconnection screw until it just touches its contact lever. Turn the idle speed adjustment screw until it just touches its contact lever, and then give it one complete turn clockwise. This will give an initial idle speed setting and enable the engine to be started.

8   If the carburettor has been dismantled or if the idle mixture adjustment screws have been disturbed, or their settings in any other way altered, screw them in fully, *but do not tighten*. Now unscrew each mixture screw four complete turns.

9   Connect a tachometer to the engine in accordance with the manufacturer's instructions.

10  Start the engine and run it at a fast idle until it reaches normal operating temperature, indicated by the electric cooling fan operating.

11  Connect the hose of a vacuum gauge to the vacuum adaptor on the inner throat of the right-hand carburettor (see Fig. 3.14). Open the adaptor by unscrewing it approximately half a turn. With the engine idling, record the reading on the vacuum gauge.

12  Close the adaptor, remove the vacuum hose and repeat the procedure on the outer throat of the right-hand carburettor.

13  If the readings are not identical, slacken the locknuts and screw both air bypass screws fully in. *Do not tighten the screws or the seats will be damaged.*

14  Unscrew the bypass screw of the throat having the highest vacuum reading by half a turn. Connect the vacuum gauge to the adaptor of that throat and open the adaptor. Adjust the air bypass screw until the vacuum reading is the same as recorded on the other

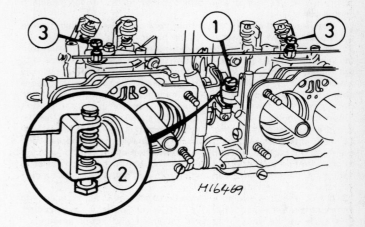

**Fig. 3.13 Weber carburettor linkage adjustment points (Sec 16)**

1   Idle speed adjustment screw
2   Throttle interconnection screw
3   Choke cable retaining screws

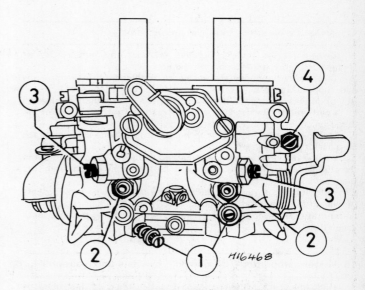

**Fig. 3.14 Weber carburettor adjustment points (Sec 16)**

1   Mixture adjustment screws
2   Vacuum adaptors
3   Air bypass screws
4   Idle speed adjustment screw

throat (ie the lowest vacuum reading). Having done that, tighten the adaptor and remove the vacuum hose. Hold the air bypass screws with a screwdriver to prevent them turning, and tighten the locknuts. **Note that:** *one air bypass screw must always remain screwed fully in and adjustment carried out on the screw with the highest vacuum reading only.*

15  Repeat the procedure described in paragraphs 11 to 14 on the left-hand carburettor.

16  In the same manner as described previously, check the vacuum readings between the inner throats of each carburettor. Obtain the same setting between the two carburettors by adjusting the interconnection screw.

17  Having equalised the flow of air through the four carburettor throats, the idle mixture setting can now be adjusted as follows.

18  Increase the engine speed to 2500 rpm for 30 seconds, and repeat this at three minute intervals during the adjustment procedure. This will ensure that any excess fuel is cleared from the inlet manifold.

19 Turn the idle speed adjustment screw to obtain the specified engine idle speed.

20 Withdraw and discard the tamperproof caps over the idle mixture adjustment screws if these are still in place.

21 Starting with the outer throat on the right-hand carburettor, turn the mixture adjustment screw clockwise to weaken the mixture until the engine speed just starts to drop. Now turn the screw slowly anticlockwise to richen the mixture until the maximum engine speed is obtained. Repeat this procedure for the inner screw on the right-hand carburettor, and then for two screws on the left-hand carburettor. Return the engine to the specified idling speed by means of the idle speed adjustment screw after each adjustment.

22 The engine should now be idling noticeably more smoothly and evenly, and it is advisable to repeat the mixture adjustment once more to obtain a fine degree of accuracy. It should now be much easier to detect any minute changes in engine rpm and smoothness of running as the mixture screws are turned.

23 If a CO meter is available, it can be connected in accordance with the manufacturer's instructions. If the CO reading is not as specified, turn each of the mixture screws by small and equal amounts — clockwise to weaken, anti-clockwise to richen — until the CO content is as specified.

24 Switch off the engine and refit the air cleaner, as described in Section 4.

25 Start the engine again and make a final check later that the settings are correct. If so, switch off and disconnect the measuring instruments.

## 17 Weber carburettor – removal and refitting

1 Disconnect the battery negative terminal and remove the air cleaner assembly, as described in Section 14.

2 Disconnect the choke and accelerator cables from their trunnions and support brackets.

3 Undo and remove the banjo union nuts securing the fuel pipes to each carburettor. Recover the copper washers from each side of the banjo union.

4 Undo and remove the four nuts and washers securing each carburettor to the inlet manifold.

5 Lift the carburettors off the mounting studs and then separate the throttle linkage. Withdraw the gaskets and heat shield from the manifold.

6 Refitting is the reverse sequence to removal. Use new gaskets between the carburettors and inlet manifold and adjust the carburettors, as described in Section 16, before refitting the air cleaner assembly.

## 18 Weber carburettor – dismantling, overhaul and reassembly

1 With the carburettor removed, as described in the previous Section, clean the exterior of the carburettor body using paraffin, or a suitable solvent, and dry with a lint-free cloth.

2 Place the carburettor on a clean uncluttered working surface and have a number of clean receptacles handy to store the small components after removal.

3 Undo and remove the screws securing the top cover to the carburettor body. Carefully lift off the cover and remove the gasket.

4 Tap out the float pivot pin and lift off the float. Take out the fuel needle valve and then undo and remove the needle valve seat and sealing washer. Undo and remove the filter plug and washer, and withdraw the filter.

5 From the side of the carburettor body, undo and remove the four retaining screws and lift off the accelerator pump cover, followed by the diaphragm and return spring.

6 Unscrew the accelerator pump jet and lift out the jet, delivery valve and sealing washers.

7 Carefully withdraw the main and auxiliary venturi assemblies from each throat.

8 Unscrew the two vacuum adaptors and seals from the outside of the carburettor body.

9 Undo and remove the two retaining screws and washers and lift off the mixture (choke) control cover and gasket.

10 Carefully extract the retaining clip, then withdraw the retainer and spring from each mixture valve. Remove the two mixture valves.

11 Undo and remove the two mixture (choke) jets and air jet assemblies.

12 Undo and remove the two main jets, and then withdraw the emulsion tube and air correction jet located beneath each main jet.

13 From the side of the carburettor body, unscrew the idle jet holder and remove the idle jet and O-ring.

14 Slacken the air bypass screw locknuts and then screw each screw fully in, counting the number of turns taken. Note which screw was already screwed in fully, and which one was open, and by how many turns. Now remove both air bypass screws.

15 Turn each idle mixture adjustment screw clockwise until it lightly contacts its seat and count the number of turns taken. Record the number of turns and then remove the screws.

16 It is not recommended that the levers and return springs on the throttle linkage be disturbed unless they are obviously worn or damaged. If removal is necessary, bend back the locking tabs and unscrew the linkage retaining nuts. Note the position of the return springs and withdraw the levers.

17 The throttle shaft and plates are not available as separate components and if worn, damaged, or showing signs of excessive play, the complete carburettor must be renewed.

18 Clean all components in petrol and allow to air dry.

19 Blow out all the jets and orifices in the carburettor body with an air line. Do not probe the jets or orifices with any metal object that is likely to cause burrs or increase their size.

20 Examine all the components for wear, or damage, and all the seals and gaskets for deterioration. It is strongly recommended that a repair kit consisting of new gaskets and seals be obtained for reassembly.

21 Check the condition of the top cover and carburettor body for cracks, damaged screw threads and the security of the pressed-in fittings.

22 Check the fuel needle valve and seat for any signs of scoring or wear ridges. Shake the float and listen for any trapped fuel which may indicate a small crack or fracture.

23 Renew all the components, as necessary, and ensure that everything is thoroughly clean. Apply one very small drop of light oil to each screw thread before fitting, and commence reassembly as follows.

24 Refit the idle mixture adjustment screws with their springs and seals. Set the mixture adjustment screws in their original positions as recorded during dismantling.

25 Refit the two air bypass screws and set them as previously recorded, one screwed fully in, and one opened slightly. Tighten the locknuts.

26 Refit the idle jet and O-ring, and the idle jet holder.

27 Refit the air correction jets, emulsion tubes and main jets to the carburettor body.

28 Refit the two mixture jets and air jet assemblies.

29 Place the mixture valves in position, followed by the spring and retainer over each valve. Secure the spring retainers with the C-shaped clips.

30 Position the gasket on the carburettor body and refit the mixture control cover and retaining screws.

31 Refit the two vacuum adaptors and O-ring seals.

32 Carefully insert the main and auxiliary venturis into each throat.

33 Refit the accelerator pump delivery valve, sealing washers and the pump jet.

34 Place the accelerator pump return spring in its location, place the pump diaphragm over the spring, and refit the cover and retaining screws.

35 Position the fuel filter in the top cover and refit the filter plug. Refit the fuel needle valve and seat assembly.

36 Hold the float in position in the top cover and tap in the pivot pin. Ensure that the float pivots freely on its pin.

37 Measure the float setting, with reference to Fig. 3.16, as follows. Hold the top cover vertically with the float resting against, but not depressing, the ball in the end of the needle valve. Measure the distance from the lower surface of the float to the face of the top cover. If the dimension is not as specified, carefully bend the float tongue as necessary. Now hold the cover horizontally and allow the float to hang under its own weight. Take a further measurement as before, and if necessary carefully bend the float stop to achieve the specified dimension.

38 Place a new gasket on the carburettor body and refit the top cover. Secure the cover with the retaining screws evenly tightened.

39 The carburettor can now be refitted to the car, as described in the previous Section.

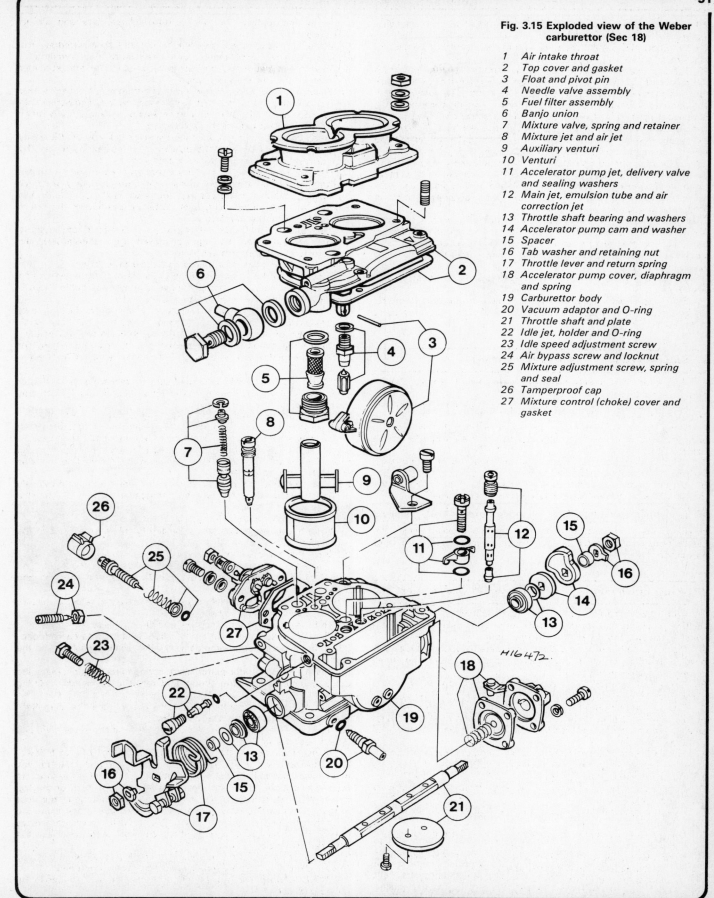

**Fig. 3.15 Exploded view of the Weber carburettor (Sec 18)**

1   Air intake throat
2   Top cover and gasket
3   Float and pivot pin
4   Needle valve assembly
5   Fuel filter assembly
6   Banjo union
7   Mixture valve, spring and retainer
8   Mixture jet and air jet
9   Auxiliary venturi
10  Venturi
11  Accelerator pump jet, delivery valve and sealing washers
12  Main jet, emulsion tube and air correction jet
13  Throttle shaft bearing and washers
14  Accelerator pump cam and washer
15  Spacer
16  Tab washer and retaining nut
17  Throttle lever and return spring
18  Accelerator pump cover, diaphragm and spring
19  Carburettor body
20  Vacuum adaptor and O-ring
21  Throttle shaft and plate
22  Idle jet, holder and O-ring
23  Idle speed adjustment screw
24  Air bypass screw and locknut
25  Mixture adjustment screw, spring and seal
26  Tamperproof cap
27  Mixture control (choke) cover and gasket

H16472.

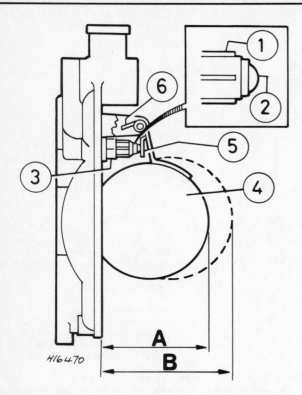

**Fig. 3.16 Weber carburettor float level settings (Sec 18)**

1   Needle valve              5   Float setting tongue
2   Needle valve ball         6   Float stop
3   Needle valve seat         A = Float setting dimension
4   Float                     B = Float stop dimension

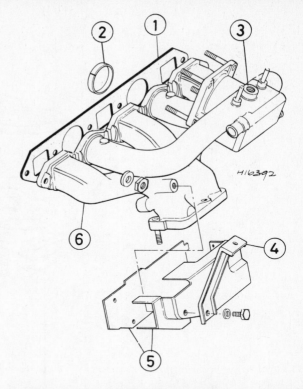

**Fig. 3.17 Inlet and exhaust manifold assemblies – 1.3 litre models
(Sec 19)**

1   Manifold gasket                4   Support bracket
2   Inlet manifold locating        5   Hot air box
    ring                           6   Exhaust manifold
3   Inlet manifold

## 19  Inlet and exhaust manifolds (all models except MG) – removal and refitting

### 1.3 litre models

1   Disconnect the battery negative terminal, and then remove the carburettor, as described in Section 13.
2   Pull the vacuum pipe off the banjo union connector in the centre of the inlet manifold (photo). Undo and remove the banjo union nut and recover the two washers. Place the servo vacuum hose to one side.
3   Remove the cooling system filler cap from the expansion tank. *If the engine is hot, unscrew the cap slowly to release the pressure and use a rag as protection against scalding.*
4   Place a suitable receptacle beneath the inlet manifold and slacken the two clips securing the water hoses to the manifold. Ease off the hoses and allow the water to drain into the receptacle.
5   Undo and remove the bolt securing the steady bracket to the exhaust manifold and the nuts and large washers securing the inlet manifold to the cylinder head. Withdraw the inlet manifold from the cylinder head.
6   To remove the exhaust manifold remove the front portion of the hot air box to provide access to the exhaust downpipe.
7   Undo and remove the nuts securing the downpipe to the manifold, and the remaining nuts and washers securing the manifold to the cylinder head. Withdraw the exhaust manifold from the cylinder head.
8   With the manifolds removed, recover the gaskets from the cylinder head and exhaust downpipe flange, and remove the inlet manifold locating rings.
9   Refitting the manifolds is the reverse sequence to removal. Use new gaskets and make sure all mating faces are clean. Tighten the manifold-to-cylinder head nuts evenly to the specified torque before fully tightening the downpipe and steady bracket nuts and bolts. Refit the carburettor, as described in Section 13, and top up the cooling system, as described in Chapter 2.

**19.2 Banjo union component sequence**

A   Vacuum pipe              D   Banjo union
B   Union nut                E   Sealing washer
C   Sealing washer

### 1.6 litre models

10  Disconnect the battery negative terminal, and then remove the carburettor, as described in Section 13.
11  Pull the vacuum pipe off the banjo union connector in the centre of the inlet manifold. Undo and remove the banjo union nut and recover the two washers. Place the servo vacuum hose to one side.
12  Undo and remove the bolts and clamp plates securing the inlet manifold to the cylinder head.

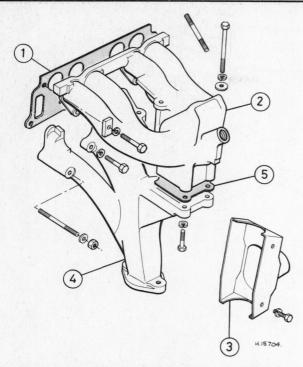

Fig. 3.18 Inlet and exhaust manifold assemblies – 1.6 litre models except MG (Sec 19)

| | | | |
|---|---|---|---|
| 1 | Manifold gasket | 4 | Exhaust manifold |
| 2 | Inlet manifold | 5 | Joint gasket |
| 3 | Hot air box | | |

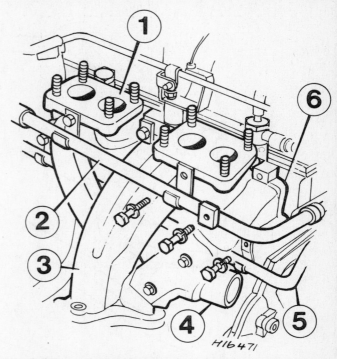

Fig. 3.19 Inlet and exhaust manifold assemblies – MG models (Sec 20)

| | | | |
|---|---|---|---|
| 1 | Inlet manifold | 4 | Hot air box |
| 2 | Heater inlet pipe | 5 | Heater outlet pipe |
| 3 | Exhaust manifold | 6 | Manifold gasket |

19.16 Removing the inlet and exhaust manifolds as an assembly (1.6 litre model with engine removed for clarity)

13  If the inlet manifold is to be removed separately, undo the two screws and remove the carburettor heat shield from the centre of the inlet manifold.

14  Undo and remove the bolts and washers securing the inlet manifold to the exhaust manifold and withdraw the inlet manifold from the car. Recover the gasket between the two manifolds.

15  If both manifolds are to be removed as an assembly, unscrew the nuts securing the exhaust downpipe to the manifold.

16  Undo and remove the nuts, bolts and washers securing the exhaust manifold to the cylinder head and withdraw the two manifolds (photo). Remove the manifold-to-cylinder head gasket.

17  Refitting is the reverse sequence to removal. Use new gaskets and make sure all mating faces are clean. Tighten the manifold-to-cylinder

head nuts and bolts evenly to the specified torque. Refit the carburettor, as described in Section 13.

## 20  Inlet and exhaust manifolds (MG models) – removal and refitting

1  Disconnect the battery negative terminal, and then remove the carburettors, as described in Section 17.

2  Pull the vacuum pipe off the banjo union connector, undo and remove the banjo union nut, and recover the two washers.

3  Undo and remove the bolts and washers securing the heater inlet and outlet pipe brackets to the manifolds.

4  Undo and remove the nuts and washers securing the exhaust downpipe to the manifold.

5  Undo and remove the nuts, bolts and clamp plates securing the manifolds to the cylinder head. Lift the heater pipes as necessary, and withdraw the inlet manifold and the exhaust manifold from their locations. Recover the manifold-to-cylinder-head gasket and the manifold-to-exhaust-downpipe gasket.

6  Refitting is the reverse sequence to removal. Use new gaskets and ensure that all mating surfaces are clean. Tighten the manifold retaining nuts and bolts evenly to the specified torque. Refit the carburettor, as described in Section 17.

## 21  Exhaust system – checking, removal and refitting

1  The exhaust system should be examined for leaks, damage and security at regular intervals (see Routine Maintenance). To do this, apply the handbrake and allow the engine to idle. Lie down on each side of the car in turn, and check the full length of the exhaust system for leaks while an assistant temporarily places a wad of cloth over the end of the tailpipe. If a leak is evident, stop the engine and use a proprietary repair kit to seal it. Holts Flexiwrap and Holts Gun Gum exhaust repair systems can be used for effective repairs to exhaust pipes and silencer boxes, including ends and bends. Holts Flexiwrap is an MOT approved permanent exhaust repair. If the leak is excessive, or damage is evident, renew the section. Note that Holts Firegum is suitable for the assembly of all exhaust system joints. Check the rubber mountings for deterioration, and renew them if necessary.

94

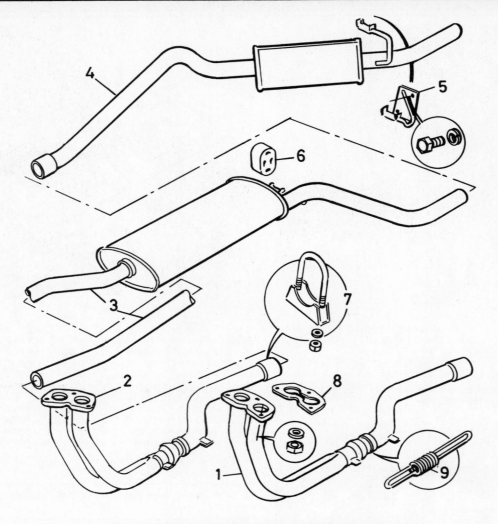

**Fig. 3.20 Component parts of the exhaust system (Sec 21)**

| | | |
|---|---|---|
| 1 Front section (1.3 litre models) | 4 Rear section | 7 Exhaust clamp |
| 2 Front section (1.6 litre models) | 5 Mounting bracket | 8 Downpipe-to-manifold gasket |
| 3 Intermediate section | 6 Mounting block | 9 Compression spring |

21.3a Exhaust rear section retaining clamp ...

21.3b ... and rubber mounting block

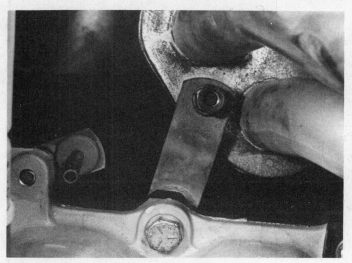

21.4a Exhaust downpipe support bracket ,...

21.4b ... and universal joint compression spring

2    To remove the exhaust system, jack up the front and/or rear of the car and support it securely on axle stands. Alternatively drive the front or rear wheels up on ramps.

3    The system consists of three sections which can be individually removed. If the intermediate section is to be removed, it will, however, be necessary to remove the front or rear section first. To remove the front or rear sections of the system, unscrew the retaining nuts and remove the U-shaped retaining clamps (photo). Release the mounting bracket from the rubber mounting block (photo) and twist the section free. If the joint is stubborn, liberally apply penetrating oil and leave it to soak. Tap the joint with a hammer and it should now be possible to twist it free. If necessary, carefully heat the joint with a blowlamp to assist removal, *but shield the fuel tank, fuel lines and underbody adequately from heat.*

4    To remove the front section, undo and remove the nuts securing the downpipes to the exhaust manifold and, where fitted, remove any additional support brackets (photo). Unhook the compression spring from the front pipe universal joint (not necessary if the intermediate pipe has been removed) and release the front section (photo).

5    Refitting is the reverse sequence to removal. Position the joints so that there is adequate clearance between all parts of the system and the underbody, and ensure that there is equal load on all mounting blocks. Always use a new gasket on the downpipe-to-manifold joint face and, if the compression spring was removed, refit the spring with the longer draw bar facing the front of the car.

'Fault diagnosis – fuel and exhaust systems' overleaf

## 22 Fault diagnosis – fuel and exhaust systems

Unsatisfactory engine performance, bad starting and excessive fuel consumption are not necessarily the fault of the fuel system or carburettor. In fact they more commonly occur as a result of ignition and timing faults. Before acting on the following, it is necessary to check the ignition system first. Even though a fault may lie in the fuel system, it will be difficult to trace unless the ignition system is correct. The faults below, therefore, assume that, where applicable, this has been attended to first. If during the fault diagnosis procedure it is suspected that the carburettor electronic mixture control or any of its related systems may be at fault, it is recommended that the help of a reputable BL dealer is sought. Accurate testing of the system and its components entails the use of a 31 step systematic checking procedure using specialist equipment and this is considered beyond the scope of the average home mechanic.

| Symptom | Reason(s) |
| --- | --- |
| Difficult starting when cold | Faulty electronic mixture control system or related component (not MG)<br>Carburettor piston sticking<br>Fuel tank empty or pump defective<br>Choke control inoperative or maladjusted (MG only)<br>Incorrect float chamber fuel level |
| Difficult starting when hot | Faulty electronic mixture control system or related component (not MG)<br>Choke control sticking on (MG only)<br>Air cleaner choked<br>Carburettor piston sticking (not MG)<br>Float chamber flooding or incorrect fuel level<br>Fuel tank empty or pump defective<br>Carburettor idle mixture adjustment incorrect |
| Excessive fuel consumption | Leakage from tank, pipes, pump or carburettor<br>Air cleaner choked<br>Carburettor idle mixture adjustment incorrect<br>Carburettor float chamber flooding<br>Faulty fuel shut-off solenoid or control system (not MG)<br>Carburettor worn<br>Excessive engine wear or other internal fault<br>Tyres underinflated<br>Brakes binding |
| Fuel starvation | Fuel level low<br>Leak on suction side of pump<br>Fuel pump faulty<br>Float chamber fuel level incorrect<br>Fuel tank breather restricted<br>Fuel tank inlet or carburettor inlet filter blocked |
| Poor performance, hesitation or erratic running | Carburettor idle mixture adjustment incorrect<br>Blocked carburettor jets or orifices (MG only)<br>Carburettor air by-pass and synchronisation maladjusted (MG only)<br>Carburettor piston damper oil level low (not MG)<br>Leaking manifold gasket<br>Fuel starvation<br>Carburettor worn<br>Excessive engine wear or other internal fault |

# Chapter 4 Ignition system

*For modifications, and information applicable to later models, see Supplement at end of manual*

## Contents

## Specifications

**System type** ..................................................... Electronic breakerless, inductive type

### Ignition coil
Type .................................................................... Ducellier 54041372 or 520029A
Current consumption – engine idling ................ 2.3 to 2.7 amps
Primary resistance at 20°C (68°F) ................... 0.77 to 0.87 ohms

### Distributor
Type:
    1.3 litre engines ........................................... Lucas 59 DM4
    1.6 litre engines ........................................... Lucas 62 DM4
Direction of rotation .......................................... Anti-clockwise
Reluctor air gap ................................................ 0.008 to 0.014 in (0.20 to 0.35 mm)
Lubricant type/specification ('A+' and 'R' series only) ...................... Multigrade engine oil, viscosity SAE 10W/40 (Duckhams QXR, QS, Hypergrade Plus, or Hypergrade)

### Ignition amplifier ............................................. Lucas AB14 or Ducellier

### Firing order ...................................................... 1–3–4–2
Location of No 1 cylinder .................................. Crankshaft pulley end

### Spark plugs
Type:
    All models except MG 1600 ........................... Champion RN9YCC or RN9YC
    MG 1600 ......................................................... Champion RN7YCC or RN7YC
Spark plug gap .................................................. 0.8 mm (0.031 in)

### HT leads ........................................................... Champion LS–O2 boxed set (1.3 and 1.6 R series)

### Ignition timing
*Stroboscopic with vacuum disconnected and plugged*
1.3 and 1.3L ..................................................... 12° BTDC at 1500 rpm
1.3 HLE .............................................................. 8° BTDC at 1500 rpm
1.6L, 1.6 HLS and Vanden Plas ...................... 16° BTDC at 1500 rpm
MG 1600 ............................................................ 21° BTDC at 2000 rpm

### Torque wrench settings

|  | lbf ft | Nm |
|---|---|---|
| Spark plugs | 18 | 25 |
| Distributor clamp bolt (1.3 litre models) | 16 | 22 |
| Distributor clamp and pinch bolts (1.6 litre models) | 3 | 4 |

## 1 General description

A breakerless inductive type electronic ignition system is fitted, the system consists of a battery, coil, distributor, ignition amplifier and spark plugs. The distributor is driven by a driveshaft in mesh with the camshaft on 1.3 litre models, and the crankshaft on 1.6 litre models.

In order that the engine can run correctly, it is necessary for an electrical spark to ignite the fuel/air mixture in the combustion chamber at exactly the right moment in relation to engine speed and load. The ignition system is based on feeding low tension voltage from the battery to the coil, where it is converted to high tension voltage. The high tension voltage is powerful enough to jump the spark plug gap in the cylinders many times a second under high compression, providing that the system is in good condition and that all adjustments are correct.

The ignition system is divided into two circuits, the low tension circuit and the high tension circuit. The low tension circuit consists of the battery, lead to the ignition switch, lead from the ignition switch to the low tension coil windings, leads from the coil windings to the ignition amplifier and leads from the ignition amplifier to the pick-up coil assembly in the distributor. The high tension circuit consists of the high tension coil windings, the heavy lead from the coil to the distributor cap, the rotor arm, spark plug leads and spark plugs.

The system functions in the following manner. Low tension voltage is changed in the coil into high tension voltage by the action of the ignition amplifier in conjunction with the pick-up coil assembly. As each of the reluctor teeth pass through the magnetic field of the pick-up coil in the distributor, an electrical signal is sent to the ignition amplifier which triggers the coil in the same way as the opening of the contact breaker points in a conventional system. High tension voltage is then fed via the carbon brush in the centre of the distributor cap to the distributor rotor arm. The voltage passes across to the appropriate metal segment in the cap and via the spark plug lead to the spark plug where it finally jumps the spark plug gap to earth. The ignition is advanced and retarded automatically, to ensure that the spark occurs at just the right instant for the particular load at the prevailing engine speed.

The ignition advance is controlled both mechanically and by a vacuum operated system. The mechanical governor mechanism consists of two weights, which move out from the distributor shaft as the engine speed rises due to centrifugal force. As they move outwards they rotate the cam relative to the distributor shaft, and so advance the spark. The weights are held in position by two light springs and it is the tension of the springs which is largely responsible for correct spark advancement.

The vacuum control consists of a diaphragm, one side of which is connected via a small bore tube to the carburettor, and the other side to the distributor baseplate. Depression in the inlet manifold and carburettor, which varies with engine speed and throttle opening, causes the diaphragm to move, so moving the baseplate, and advancing or retarding the spark. A fine degree of control is achieved by a spring in the vacuum assembly.

Due to the nature of the electronic ignition system, no current is consumed by the ignition coil with the ignition switched on and the

engine stationary. A ballast resistor is not required in the starting circuit.

Note that all photographs in this Chapter are of a 1.6 litre model. However, unless otherwise stated, the component shown, and the procedure highlighted, will be similar or identical on 1.3 litre versions.

## 2    Maintenance and inspection

1    At regular intervals (see Routine Maintenance) remove the distributor cap and thoroughly clean it inside and out with a dry lint-free rag. Examine the four HT lead segments inside the cap. If the segments appear badly burned or pitted, renew the cap. Make sure that the carbon brush in the centre of the cap is free to move and that it protrudes by approximately 0.1 in (3 mm) from its holder.
2    With the distributor cap removed, lift off the rotor arm and the plastic anti-flash shield. Carefully apply two drops of engine oil to the felt pad in the centre of the cam spindle. Also lubricate the centrifugal advance mechanism by applying two drops of oil through the square hole in the baseplate. Wipe away any excess oil and refit the anti-flash shield, rotor arm and distributor cap.
3    At the same service intervals, remove and check the spark plugs, using the procedure described in Section 8. Using a stroboscopic timing light check and, if necessary, reset the ignition timing, as described in Section 5.
4    It is recommended by the manufacturers that the spark plugs should be renewed every 24 000 miles (40 000 km), or two years, whichever occurs sooner. Practical experience has shown this, in some circumstances, to be considerably in excess of the practical working life of a spark plug. In terms of performance and reliability, it may be considered beneficial to renew the plugs at the 12 000 mile (20 000 km), or 12 month, service interval.

## 3    Distributor – removal and refitting

1    Disconnect the battery negative terminal.
2    Pull off the HT lead and remove No 1 spark plug (nearest the crankshaft pulley).
3    Place a finger over the plug hole and turn the engine in the normal direction of rotation (clockwise from the crankshaft pulley end) until pressure is felt in No 1 cylinder. This indicates that the piston is commencing its compression stroke. The engine can be turned with a socket and bar on the crankshaft pulley bolt (photo) after removing the access cover from the inner wheel arch.
4    Continue turning the engine until the notch in the crankshaft pulley is aligned with the TDC pointer on the timing scale (photo). This is the last pointer on the scale, nearest the front of the car.
5    Make a reference mark on the side of the distributor body adjacent to the No 1 cylinder spark plug lead position in the cap. Spring back the clips, or remove the two screws, and lift off the cap. Check that the rotor arm is pointing toward the reference mark.
6    Make a further mark on the cylinder block in line with the mark on the distributor body.
7    Detach the vacuum advance pipe and disconnect the ignition amplifier wiring harness at the connector (photo).
8    On 1.3 litre models, unscrew the distributor clamp retaining bolt,

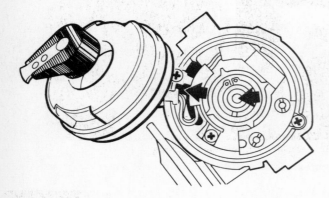

**Fig. 4.1 Distributor lubrication points (Sec 2)**

3.3 The engine can be turned using a socket and bar on the pulley bolt after removing the access cover

3.4 Crankshaft pulley timing notch aligned with TDC pointer on timing scale (arrowed)

3.7 Ignition amplifier to distributor wiring harness connector

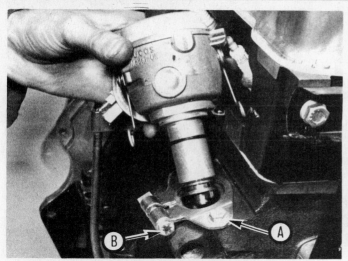

3.8 Distributor removal (engine removed for clarity)

*A Distributor clamp retaining bolt*     *B Clamp pinch-bolt*

4.3a Extract the circlip ...

lift away the clamp and withdraw the distributor from the engine. On 1.6 litre models, slacken the distributor clamp pinch-bolt and one of the bolts securing the clamp to the cylinder block (photo). Withdraw the distributor from the engine.

9   To refit the distributor, first check that the engine is still at the TDC position with No 1 cylinder on compression. If the engine has been turned while the distributor was removed, return it to the correct position, as previously described.

10  With the vacuum unit pointing toward No 1 spark plug (1.3 litre engines) or No 2 spark plug (1.6 litre engines), slide the distributor into the cylinder block and turn the rotor arm slightly until the offset slot on the distributor drive dog positively engages with the driveshaft.

11  Turn the distributor body until the rotor arm is pointing toward the No 1 spark plug lead segment in the distributor cap, or if the original distributor is being refitted, align the previously made reference marks. Hold the distributor in this position and refit the clamp and retaining bolt (1.3 litre engines) or tighten the pinch-bolt and clamp retaining bolt (1.6 litre engines).

12  Reconnect the vacuum advance pipe and the wiring harness connector. Refit the distributor cap, No 1 spark plug and the HT lead.

13  Reconnect the battery and, if removed, refit the access panel to the inner wheel arch.

14  The ignition timing should now be adjusted, as described in Section 5.

4.3b ... and lift off the washer and O-ring

## 4   Distributor – dismantling and reassembly

1    Remove the distributor, as described in the previous Section.

2    Lift off the rotor arm, followed by the anti-flash shield.

3    Using circlip pliers, extract the retaining circlip (photo) and lift off the washer and O-ring (photo).

4    Withdraw the reluctor and coupling ring (photos) using a screwdriver very carefully to ease them off the shaft if they are initially tight.

5    Undo and remove the screws securing the vacuum unit to the distributor body. Disengage the vacuum unit operating link from the peg on the underside of the baseplate using a twisting movement and withdraw the unit (photo).

6    Release the wiring harness rubber grommet and remove the two baseplate securing screws. Lift the baseplate out of its location in the distributor body (photo).

7    This is the limit of dismantling, as the parts located below the baseplate, the distributor shaft and distributor body can only be renewed as an assembly.

8    With the distributor dismantled, renew any parts that show signs of wear, or damage, and any that are known to be faulty. Pay close attention to the centrifugal advance mechanism (photo), checking for loose or broken springs, wear in the bob weight pivots and play in the distributor shaft.

4.4a Withdraw the reluctor ...

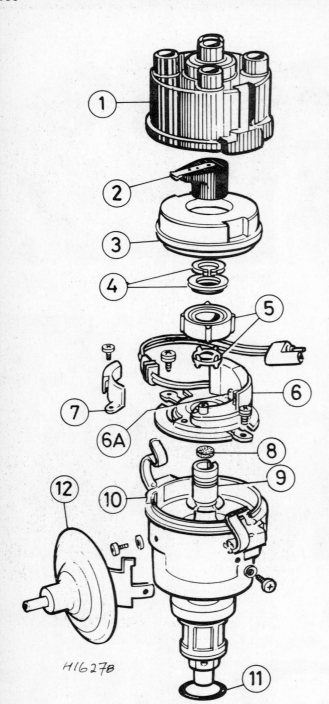

4.4b ... followed by the coupling ring

4.5 Disengage the vacuum unit operating link from the baseplate peg and withdraw the unit

4.6 Remove the screws and lift out the baseplate

H16278

**Fig. 4.2 Exploded view of the distributor – 1.3 litre engines (Sec 4)**

| | | | |
|---|---|---|---|
| 1 | Distributor cap | 6A | Pick-up limb |
| 2 | Rotor arm | 7 | Wiring guide |
| 3 | Anti-flash shield | 8 | Felt pad |
| 4 | O-ring, washer and circlip | 9 | Distributor shaft |
| 5 | Reluctor and coupling ring | 10 | Distributor body |
| | | 11 | O-ring |
| 6 | Pick-up coil and baseplate assembly | 12 | Vacuum unit |

4.8 Check the centrifugal advance mechanism bob weights, pivots and springs for wear

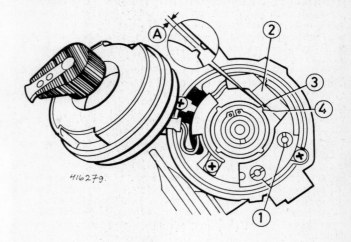

**Fig. 4.3 Reluctor air gap adjustment (Sec 4)**

*Dimension A = specified air gap*
1   *Adjusting nuts*
2   *Pick-up coil assembly*
3   *Pick-up limb*
4   *Reluctor tooth*

9   Begin reassembly by lubricating the distributor shaft, bob weight pivots, vacuum link and baseplate sliding surfaces with engine oil.
10   Place the baseplate assembly in position, with the peg on the underside adjacent to the vacuum unit aperture. Refit and tighten the two securing screws.
11   Refit the coupling ring to the underside of the reluctor and slide this assembly over the distributor shaft. Align the broad lug of the coupling ring with the broad slot in the shaft, and push the ring and reluctor fully into place.
12   Position the O-ring and washer over the shaft and secure them with the circlip.
13   Insert the vacuum unit operating link into its aperture and manipulate the unit and baseplate until the link can be engaged with the peg. Refit and tighten the retaining screws, noting that one also secures one of the distributor cap clips (1.6 litre models only).
14   Refit the harness leads and grommet to the slot in the distributor body.
15   Position the reluctor so that one of the teeth is adjacent to the limb on the pick-up assembly. Using feeler gauges, preferably of plastic or brass, measure the air gap between the reluctor tooth and pick-up assembly (photo). If the measured dimension is outside the tolerance given in the Specifications, slacken the adjusting nuts on the pick-up assembly and reposition the unit as necessary.
16   Refit the anti-flash shield and rotor arm, then refit the distributor, as described in Section 3.

## 5   Ignition timing – adjustment

**Note**: *With electronic ignition systems the only suitable method which may be used to accurately time the ignition is with a stroboscopic timing light. However, for initial setting up purposes (ie after major overhaul, or if the timing has been otherwise completely lost) a basic initial static setting may be used to get the engine started. Once the engine is running, the timing should be accurately set using the timing light. A further method, employing the light emitting diode (LED) sensor bracket, and timing disc on the crankshaft pulley may be used, but the equipment for use with this system is not normally available to the home mechanic.*

1   In order that the engine can run efficiently, it is necessary for a spark to occur at the spark plug and ignite the fuel/air mixture at the instant just before the piston on the compression stroke reaches the top of its travel. The precise instant at which the spark occurs is determined by the ignition timing, and this is quoted in degrees before top-dead-centre (BTDC).
2   If the timing is being checked as a maintenance or servicing procedure, refer to paragraph 11. If the distributor has been dismantled or renewed, or if its position on the engine has been altered, obtain an initial static setting as follows.

4.15 Using feeler gauges to measure the reluctor air gap

### Static setting

3   Pull off the HT lead and remove No 1 spark plug (nearest the crankshaft pulley).
4   Place a finger over the plug hole and turn the engine in the normal direction of rotation (clockwise from the crankshaft pulley end) until pressure is felt in No 1 cylinder. This indicates that the piston is commencing its compression stroke. The engine can be turned with a socket and bar on the crankshaft pulley bolt after removing the access cover from the inner wheel arch.
5   Continue turning the engine until the notch in the crankshaft pulley is aligned with the TDC pointer on the timing scale (photos 3.3 and 3.4). This is the last pointer on the scale, nearest the front of the car.
6   Remove the distributor cap and check that the rotor arm is pointing toward the No 1 spark plug HT lead segment in the cap.
7   Lift off the rotor arm and anti-flash shield and observe the position of the reluctor in relation to the pick-up coil. One of the teeth on the reluctor should be aligned with, or very near to, the small pip, or limb, of the pick-up coil.

8    Slacken the distributor clamp retaining bolt (1.3 litre engines), or the clamp pinch-bolt (1.6 litre engines) and turn the distributor body until the reluctor tooth and pick-up limb are directly in line (photo).
9    Tighten the distributor clamp, or pinch-bolt, refit the anti-flash shield, rotor arm and distributor cap. Refit No 1 spark plug and HT lead.
10   It should now be possible to start and run the engine enabling the timing to be accurately checked with a timing light as follows.

*Stroboscopic setting*
11   Disconnect the vacuum advance pipe at the distributor and plug its end.
12   The timing marks are located on a scale just above the crankshaft pulley, with a corresponding V-notch in the rim of the pulley (photo). The pointer peak at the far right of the scale (ie nearest the front of the car) is the TDC position and is marked with a '0'. The pointer peaks to the left of TDC are in increments of 4° BTDC. If a timing light with a strong light source is being used the marks will be clearly visible from above; however, for greater clarity, the access panel under the inner wheel arch may be removed – enabling the timing light to be held very close to the marks.
13   Refer to the Specifications for the timing setting applicable to the engine being worked on, and then highlight the appropriate mark and pulley V-notch with white chalk or paint.
14   Connect a timing light to the engine in accordance with the manufacturer's instructions (usually between No 1 spark plug and its HT lead). If the car is not equipped with a tachometer, connect a suitable unit to the engine in accordance with the manufacturer's instruction.
15   Start the engine and run it at the speed specified for ignition timing.
16   Point the timing light at the timing marks (photo) and they should appear to be stationary with the crank pulley notch in alignment with the appropriate pointer.
17   If adjustment is necessary (ie the pulley notch does not line up with the appropriate point), loosen the distributor clamp retaining bolt, or pinch-bolt, and turn the distributor body clockwise to advance the timing and anti-clockwise to retard it. Tighten the securing bolt when the setting is correct.
18   Gradually increase the engine speed while still pointing the timing light at the marks. The pulley notch should appear to advance further, indicating that the centrifugal advance mechanism is operating correctly. If the timing marks remain stationary when the engine speed is increased, or if the movement is erratic or jerky, then the distributor should be dismantled for inspection, as described in Section 4.
19   Reconnect the vacuum pipe to the distributor and check that the advance alters when the pipe is connected. If not, the vacuum unit on the distributor may be faulty.
20   Switch off the engine and disconnect the timing light and tachometer. Where applicable, refit the access panel to the inner wheel arch.

5.8 Reluctor tooth (A) aligned with pick-up limb (B)

5.12 Crankshaft pulley timing notch and timing scale. Pulley notch shown aligned with TDC pointer

## 6   Ignition coil – description and testing

1    The coil is bolted to the centre of the engine compartment bulkhead (photo), and it should be periodically wiped over to prevent high tension (HT) voltage loss through arcing.
2    To ensure correct HT polarity at the spark plugs, the LT coil leads must always be connected correctly. The LT leads from the ignition amplifier should be connected as follows. White/black leads to the coil **negative** terminal. White leads to the coil **positive** terminal. Incorrect connections can cause bad starting, misfiring and short spark plug life.
3    Apart from the tests of the low tension circuit contained in the ignition system test procedure (Section 9), accurate checking of the coil output requires special equipment and for the home mechanic the easiest test is by substitution of a new unit.
4    If a new coil is to be fitted, ensure that it is of the correct type and suitable for use on electronic ignition systems. Failure to do so could cause irreparable damage to the ignition amplifier or distributor pick-up assembly.
5    To remove the coil, slide back the protective rubber boot and disconnect the HT and LT wires from the terminals. Undo and remove the two retaining bolts and lift away the coil complete with bracket. Refitting is the reverse sequence to removal.

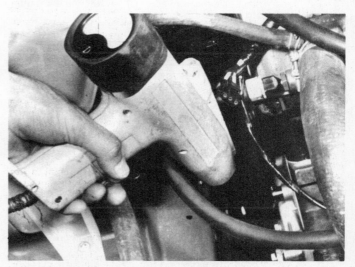

5.16 Using a stroboscope to check the ignition timing

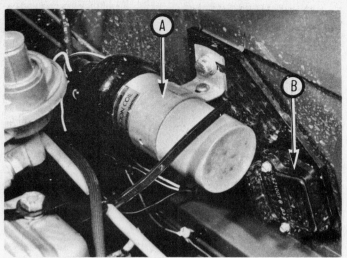

6.1 Location of the ignition coil (A) and ignition amplifier (B) on the engine compartment bulkhead

## 7  Ignition amplifier – general

1   The ignition amplifier is mounted on the engine compartment bulkhead, just below the coil (photo 6.1). The amplifier controls the function of the ignition coil in response to signals received from the pick-up coil in the distributor.
2   The unit may be tested using the procedure described in Section 9. If the amplifier is found to be faulty it must be renewed as a complete unit, repairs to the components or circuitry are not possible due to its sealed construction.
3   To remove the unit, disconnect the battery negative terminal and then disconnect the wiring plug from the end of the amplifier. Remove the two small retaining screws and withdraw the unit from the car. Refitting is the reverse sequence to removal.

## 8  Spark plugs and HT leads – general

1   The correct functioning of the spark plugs is vital for the correct running and efficiency of the engine. It is essential that the plugs fitted are appropriate for the engine, and the suitable type is specified at the beginning of this chapter. If this type is used and the engine is in good condition, the spark plugs should not need attention between scheduled replacement intervals. Spark plug cleaning is rarely necessary and should not be attempted unless specialised equipment is available as damage can easily be caused to the firing ends.
2   To remove the plugs, first mark the HT leads to ensure correct refitment, and then pull them off the plugs. Using a spark plug spanner, or suitable deep socket and extension bar, unscrew the plugs and remove them from the engine.
3   The condition of the spark plugs will also tell much about the overall condition of the engine.
4   If the insulator nose of the spark plug is clean and white, with no deposits, this is indicative of a weak mixture, or too hot a plug. (A hot plug transfers heat away from the electrode slowly – a cold plug transfers it away quickly).
5   If the tip and insulator nose are covered with hard black-looking deposits, then this is indicative that the mixture is too rich. Should the plug be black and oily, then it is likely that the engine is fairly worn, as well as the mixture being too rich.
6   If the insulator nose is covered with light tan to greyish brown deposits, then the mixture is correct and it is likely that the engine is in good condition.
7   The spark plug gap is of considerable importance, as, if it is too large or too small, the size of the spark and its efficiency will be seriously impaired. The spark plug gap should be set to the figure given in the Specifications at the beginning of this Chapter.
8   To set it, measure the gap with a feeler gauge, and then bend open, or close, the *outer* plug electrode until the correct gap is achieved. The centre electrode should *never* be bent as this may crack the insulation and cause plug failure, if nothing worse.

9   To fit the plugs, screw them in by hand initially and then fully tighten to the specified torque. If a torque wrench is not available, tighten the plugs until initial resistance is felt as the sealing washer contacts its seat and then tighten by a further eighth of a turn. Refit the HT leads in the correct order, ensuring that they are a tight fit over the plug ends. Periodically wipe the leads clean to reduce the risk of HT leakage by arcing.

## 9  Fault diagnosis – ignition system

There are two main symptoms indicating ignition faults. Either the engine will not start or fire, or the engine is difficult to start and misfires. If it is a regular misfire, ie the engine is only running on two or three cylinders, the fault is almost sure to be in the high tension circuit. If the misfiring is intermittent, the fault could be in either the high or low tension circuits. If the car stops suddenly, or will not start at all, it is likely that the fault is in the low tension circuit. Loss of power and overheating, apart from faulty carburation settings, are normally due to faults in the distributor or incorrect ignition timing.

The first part of this Section deals with the diagnosis of faults in the high tension circuit. If these tests prove negative or indicate a possible fault in the electronic ignition or low tension circuit, a separate test procedure should be followed. This is contained in the second part of this Section and entails the use of a 0 to 12 volt voltmeter and an ohmmeter.

## PART 1

### *Engine fails to start*

1   If the engine fails to start and the car was running normally when it was last used, first check there is fuel in the petrol tank. If the engine turns over normally on the starter motor and the battery is evidently well charged, then the fault may be in either the high or low tension circuits. First check the HT circuit. If the battery is known to be fully charged, the ignition light comes on, and the starter motor fails to turn the engine, check the tightness of the leads on the battery terminals and the security of the earth lead to its connection to the body. It is quite common for the leads to have worked loose, even if they look and feel secure. If one of the battery terminal posts gets very hot when trying to work the starter motor, this is a sure indication of a faulty connection to that terminal.
2   One of the most common reasons for bad starting is wet or damp spark plug leads and distributor. Remove the distributor cap to see if condensation is visible inside. If condensation is present wipe the cap internally with a clean lint-free rag and then refit. At the same time wipe clean and dry all the HT leads. Once some Holts Wet Start moisture dispersant is sprayed onto the distributor the engine should be easy to start. To prevent poor starting occurring in future Holts Damp Start may be used to provide a sealing coat, so excluding any further moisture from the ignition system. In extreme starting difficulty due to a weak spark Holts Cold Start should prove useful.
3   If the engine still fails to start, check that current is reaching the plugs, by disconnecting each plug lead in turn at the spark plug end, and holding the end of the cable about $\frac{3}{16}$ inch (5 mm) away from the cylinder block. Spin the engine on the starter motor.
4   Sparking between the end of the cable and the block should be fairly strong with a regular blue spark. (Hold the lead with rubber to avoid electric shocks). If current is reaching the plugs, then remove them and regap them. The engine should now start.
5   If there is no spark at the plug leads, take off the HT lead from the centre of the distributor cap and hold it to the block as before. Spin the engine on the starter once more. A rapid succession of blue sparks between the end of the lead and the block indicate that the coil is in order and that the distributor cap is cracked, the rotor arm faulty or the carbon brush in the top of the distributor cap is not making good contact with the rocker arm.
6   If there are no sparks from the end of the lead from the coil, check the connections at the coil end of the lead. If it is in order carry out the checks contained in the electronic ignition test procedure (Part 2).

### *Engine misfires*

7   If the engine misfires regularly, run it at a fast idling speed. Pull off

each of the plug caps in turn and listen to the note of the engine. Hold the plug cap in a dry cloth or with a rubber glove as additional protection against a shock from the HT supply.

8    No difference in engine running will be noticed when the lead from the defective circuit is removed. Removing the lead from one of the good cylinders will accentuate the misfire.

9    Remove the plug lead from the end of the defective plug and hold it about $\frac{3}{16}$ inch (5 mm) away from the block. Restart the engine. If the sparking is fairly strong and regular, the fault must lie in the spark plug.

10   The plug may be loose, the insulation may be cracked, or the points may have burnt away, giving too wide a gap for the spark to jump. Worse still, one of the points may have broken off. Either renew the plug, or reset the gap, and then test it.

11   If there is no spark at the end of the plug lead, or if it is weak and intermittent, check the ignition lead from the distributor to the plug. If the insulation is cracked or perished, renew the lead. Check the connections at the distributor cap.

12   If there is still no spark, examine the distributor cap carefully for tracking. This can be recognised by a very thin black line running between two or more electrodes, or between an electrode and some other part of the distributor. These lines are paths which now conduct electricity across the cap, thus letting it run to earth. The only answer in this case is a new distributor cap.

13   Apart from the ignition timing being incorrect, other causes of misfiring have already been dealt with under the section dealing with the failure of the engine to start. To recap, these are that:

> (a)   The coil may be faulty giving an intermittent misfire
> (b)   There may be a damaged wire or loose connection in the low tension circuit
> (c    There may be a fault in the electronic ignition system
> (d)   There may be a mechanical fault in the distributor

14   If the ignition timing is too far retarded it should be noted that the engine will tend to overheat, and there will be a quite noticeable drop in power. If the engine is overheating and the power is down, and the ignition timing is correct, then the carburettor should be checked, as it is likely that this is where the fault lies.

## PART 2

*Electronic ignition system test procedure*

| Test | Remedy |
| --- | --- |
| 1  Is the reluctor air gap set to the specified dimension? | Yes  Proceed to Test 2<br>No:  Adjust the gap, as described in Section 4 |
| 2  Is the battery voltage greater than 11.5 volts? | Yes:  Proceed to Test 3<br>No:  Recharge the battery |
| 3  Is the voltage at the coil '+' terminal more than 1 volt below battery voltage? | Yes:  Faulty wiring or connector between ignition switch and coil. Faulty ignition switch<br>No:  Proceed to Test 4 |
| 4  Is the voltage at the coil '–' terminal more than 2 volts? | Yes:  Disconnect the wiring connector between distributor and ignition amplifier and proceed to Test 7<br>No:  Disconnect the ignition amplifier lead at the coil '–' terminal and proceed to Test 5 |
| 5  Is the voltage at the coil '–' terminal now more than 2 volts? | Yes:  Proceed to Test 6<br>No:  Renew the ignition coil |
| 6  Is the voltage at the ignition amplifier earth more than 0.1 volts? | Yes:  Clean and/or repair the earth connection<br>No:  Renew the ignition amplifier |
| 7  Is the pick-up coil resistance measured at the wiring connector terminals between 2.2 ohms and 4.8 ohms? | Yes:  Reconnect the wiring connector between distributor and ignition amplifier and proceed to Test 8<br>No:  Renew the pick-up coil assembly in the distributor |
| 8  Does the voltage at the coil '–' terminal drop when the starter motor is operated? | Yes:  Check and adjust the ignition timing. If the fault still exists the problem may lie with the engine internal components<br>No:  Renew the ignition amplifier |

# Chapter 5 Clutch

*For modifications, and information applicable to later models, see Supplement at end of manual*

## Contents

## Specifications

**Type** ........................................................................ Single dry plate, non-fulcrum diaphragm spring pressure plate, cable actuation

### Clutch disc diameter
1.3 litre models, except HLE ...................................... 7.48 in (190 mm)
1.3 litre HLE models .................................................... 7.0 in (178 mm)
1.6 litre models ............................................................ 7.87 in (200 mm)

### Clutch cable adjustment
Clearance ....................................................................... 0.5 in (12 mm)
Clutch pedal free play .................................................. 0.56 to 1.00 in (15 to 25 mm)

### Torque wrench settings

| | lbf ft | Nm |
| --- | --- | --- |
| Pressure plate to crankshaft | 55 | 75 |
| Flywheel to pressure plate | 11 | 15 |
| Gearbox end cover (four-speed gearbox) | 11 | 15 |

## 1 General description

Unlike the clutch on most engines, the clutch pressure plate is bolted to the crankshaft flange. The flywheel, which is dish shaped, is bolted to the pressure plate with the friction disc being held between them. This is, in effect, the reverse of the more conventional arrangement where the flywheel is bolted to the crankshaft flange and the clutch pressure plate bolted to the flywheel.

The release mechanism consists of a metal disc, called the release plate, which is clamped in the centre of the pressure plate by a retaining ring. In the centre of the release plate is a boss into which the clutch pushrod is fitted. The pushrod passes through the centre of the gearbox input shaft and is actuated by a release bearing located in the gearbox end housing. A single finger lever presses on this bearing when the shaft to which it is splined is turned by operation of the cable from the clutch pedal. In effect the clutch lever pushes the clutch pushrod, which in turn pushes the centre of the release plate inwards towards the crankshaft. The outer edge of the release plate presses on the pressure plate fingers forcing them back towards the engine and removing the pressure plate friction face from the friction disc, thus disconnecting the drive. When the clutch pedal is released the pressure plate reasserts itself, clamping the friction disc firmly against the flywheel and restoring the drive.

As the friction linings on the disc wear, the pressure plate will gradually move closer to the flywheel and the cable free play will decrease. Periodic adjustment must therefore be carried out, as described in Section 2.

## 2 Clutch – adjustment

1   The clutch adjustment should be checked regularly (see Routine Maintenance). To do this grasp the clutch outer cable at the gearbox mounting bracket and pull the cable upwards until resistance is felt. Using feeler gauges measure the clearance between the adjusting nut and the rubber guide sleeve. If the clearance is not as given in the Specifications, adjust as follows.
2   Slacken the locknut and turn the adjusting nut clockwise to decrease the clearance or anti-clockwise to increase it. Recheck using the feeler gauges, and when the clearance is correct tighten the locknut.
3   After adjustment check that the clutch pedal free play is within the limits given in the Specifications.

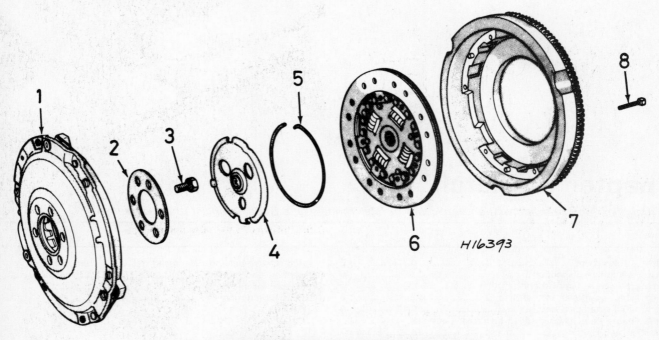

**Fig. 5.1 Exploded view of the clutch assembly (Sec 1)**

| | | | |
|---|---|---|---|
| 1 | Pressure plate | 3 | Pressure plate bolts | 5 | Retaining ring | 7 | Flywheel |
| 2 | Locking plate | 4 | Release plate | 6 | Friction disc | 8 | Flywheel bolt |

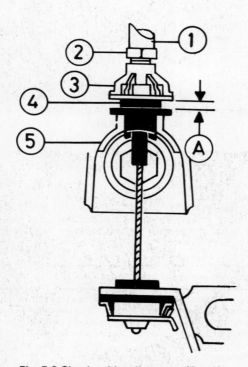

**Fig. 5.2 Clutch cable adjustment (Sec 2)**

1   Outer cable      4   Rubber guide sleeve
2   Locknut         5   Gearbox bracket
3   Adjusting nut     A = specified clearance

### 3   Clutch cable – removal and refitting

1   Working in the engine compartment, slacken the outer cable locknut at the gearbox bracket. Back off the cable adjusting nut by turning it anti-clockwise until there is considerable slack in the cable.
2   Release the inner cable from the operating lever by sliding out the retaining clip and cable seating plate located on the underside of the lever (photos).
3   Withdraw the inner cable end from the operating lever rubber pad (photo), release the rubber retainer and withdraw the cable assembly from the gearbox bracket (photo).
4   From inside the car unhook the cable end from the clutch pedal and withdraw the cable complete with rubber guide and retainer into the engine compartment. Release the retaining clip and remove the cable from the car.
5   To refit the cable, feed the hooked end through the engine compartment bulkhead and connect it to the pedal. Ensure that the outer cable is located correctly in the bulkhead tube.
6   Route the cable through the engine compartment and refit the cable retaining clip.
7   With the guide sleeve and rubber retainer in place, feed the cable through the gearbox bracket and hook the lower half of the rubber retainer over the guide sleeve to secure the cable. Position the rubber retainer, as shown in Fig. 5.4, so that the flap of the rubber retainer covers the gearbox breather.
8   Feed the inner cable end through the rubber pad of the operating lever and slide on the cable seating plate and retaining clip.
9   Adjust the clutch cable, as described in Section 2.

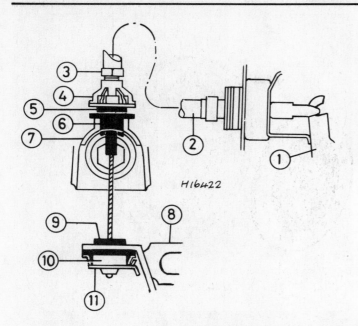

**3.2b ... followed by the cable seating plate**

**Fig. 5.3 Clutch cable attachments (Sec 3)**

| | | | |
|---|---|---|---|
| 1 | Clutch pedal | 7 | Gearbox bracket |
| 2 | Outer cable | 8 | Operating lever |
| 3 | Locknut | 9 | Rubber pad |
| 4 | Adjusting nut | 10 | Cable seating plate |
| 5 | Rubber guide sleeve | 11 | Cable retaining clip |
| 6 | Rubber retainer | | |

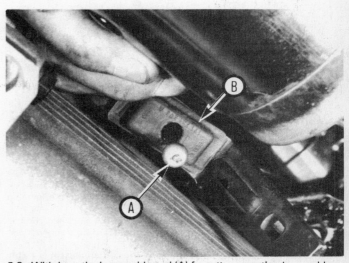

**3.3a Withdraw the inner cable end (A) from the operating lever rubber pad (B) ...**

**3.2a Slide out the clutch cable retaining clip (arrowed) ...**

### 4  Clutch pedal – removal and refitting

The clutch pedal and brake pedal are hinged on a common pivot and reference should be made to Chapter 8, Section 20, for the removal and refitting procedures.

### 5  Clutch assembly – removal and refitting

1  Refer to Chapter 6, and remove the gearbox.
2  In a diagonal sequence, half a turn at a time, slacken the six bolts securing the flywheel to the pressure plate. Hold the crankshaft pulley

**3.3b ... release the rubber retainer, and remove the cable from the gearbox bracket**

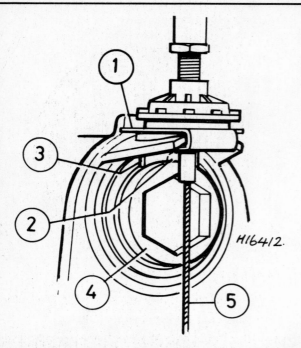

**Fig. 5.4 Correct positioning of clutch cable in gearbox bracket (Sec 3)**

1   *Rubber retainer upper*        4   *Selector shaft*
    *half*                            *end cap*
2   *Gearbox breather*             5   *Clutch cable*
3   *Rubber retainer flap*

5.7a Place the pressure plate in position on the crankshaft ...

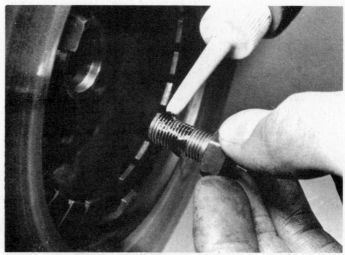

5.7b ... and refit the retaining bolts after applying a thread locking compound

5.8 Ensure that the release plate retaining ring is correctly located under the diaphragm spring lugs (arrowed) – 1.6 litre unit shown

bolt with a large spanner or socket during this operation to prevent the crankshaft turning.

3   When all the bolts are slack, take them out and lift off the flywheel and the clutch friction disc. It may be necessary to carefully ease the flywheel off using a screwdriver, due to the tight fit of the locating dowels.

4   Note the fitted position of the clutch release plate retaining ring as a guide to reassembly, and then prise the ring out using a screwdriver. Lift off the release plate.

5   It is not necessary to remove the pressure plate unless it is visibly worn or is to be renewed for other reasons. If the unit is to be removed, lock the crankshaft pulley bolt using a spanner or socket and slacken the pressure plate bolts in a diagonal sequence. Remove the bolts and locking plate, then withdraw the pressure plate.

6   After removal, refer to the following Section and carry out a careful inspection of the clutch components.

7   To refit the clutch, place the pressure plate in position on the end of the crankshaft (photo) and refit the retaining bolts, using a thread locking compound (photo). Tighten the bolts evenly in a diagonal sequence to the specified torque.

8   Position the release plate over the pressure plate diaphragm fingers and refit the retaining ring (photo). Ensure that the retaining ring is correctly located, as noted during removal, and as shown in the accompanying illustrations.

9   Hold the clutch friction disc against the flywheel (photo), with the greater projecting boss incorporating the torsion springs facing away from the engine. Refit the flywheel and the six retaining bolts. Tighten the bolts finger tight so that the friction disc is gripped, but can still be moved.

10  The clutch friction disc must now be centralised to allow the gearbox input shaft to pass through the friction disc hub splines. This can be done by obtaining the manufacturer's special service tool, or by making up a tool as shown in Fig. 5.7 to fit the flywheel aperture of either 5.118 in (130 mm) or 5.197 in (132 mm) diameter. Alternatively centre the disc using vernier calipers or a pair of dividers (photo). Once the clutch disc is centred correctly, tighten the retaining bolts in a diagonal sequence to the specified torque and recheck the centralisation.

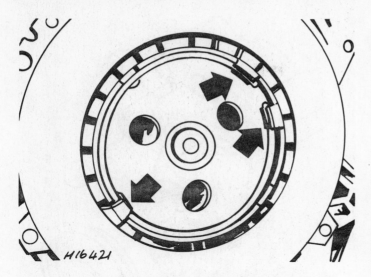

Fig. 5.5 Correct location of release plate retaining ring – 1.3 litre models (Sec 5)

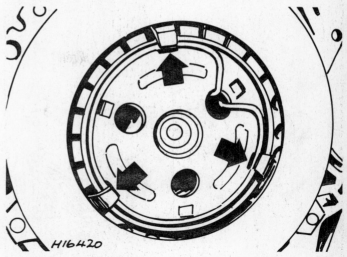

Fig. 5.6 Correct location of release plate retaining ring – 1.6 litre models (Sec 5)

5.9 Fit the clutch friction disc and flywheel with the greater projecting boss of the disc facing away fom the engine

5.10 Vernier calipers or dividers can be used to ensure that the distance between clutch disc hub and flywheel is equal all round, thus centralising the disc

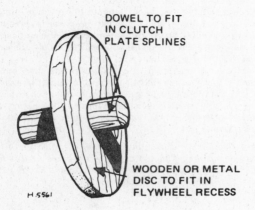

DOWEL TO FIT IN CLUTCH PLATE SPLINES

WOODEN OR METAL DISC TO FIT IN FLYWHEEL RECESS

Fig. 5.7 Home made tool for centralising the clutch friction disc (Sec 5)

## 6 Clutch assembly – inspection

1 With the clutch assembly removed, clean off all traces of asbestos dust using a dry cloth. This is best done outside or in a well ventilated area; *asbestos dust is harmful, and must not be inhaled.*

2 Examine the linings of the friction disc for wear and loose rivets, and the disc for rim distortion, cracks, broken torsion springs and worn splines. The surface of the friction linings may be highly glazed, but, as long as the friction material pattern can be clearly seen, this is satisfactory. If there is any sign of oil contamination, indicated by a continuous, or patchy, shiny black discolouration, the disc must be renewed and the source of the contamination traced and rectified. This will be either a leaking crankshaft oil seal or gearbox input shaft oil seal – or both. Renewal procedures are given in Chapter 1 and Chapter 6 respectively. The disc must also be renewed if the lining thickness has worn down to, or just above, the level of the rivet heads.

3 Check the machined faces of the flywheel and pressure plate. If either is grooved, or heavily scored, renewal is necessary. The pressure plate must also be renewed if any cracks are apparent, or if the diaphragm spring is damaged or its pressure suspect.

4 With the gearbox removed it is advisable to check the condition of the release bearing, as described in the following Sections.

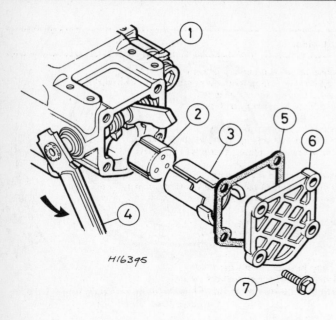

**Fig. 5.8 Release bearing assembly components – four-speed gearbox (Sec 7)**

| | | | |
|---|---|---|---|
| 1 | Gearbox | 5 | Gasket |
| 2 | Release bearing | 6 | End cover |
| 3 | Sleeve | 7 | End cover bolt |
| 4 | Operating lever | | |

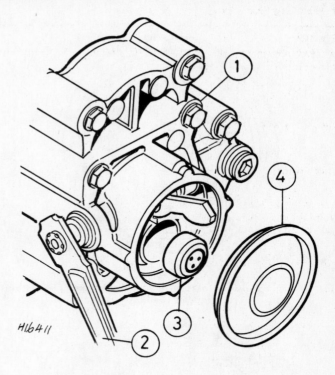

**Fig. 5.9 Release bearing assembly components – five-speed gearbox (Sec 8)**

| | | | |
|---|---|---|---|
| 1 | Gearbox | 3 | Release bearing |
| 2 | Operating lever | 4 | End cap |

### 7 Clutch release bearing (four-speed gearbox) – removal, inspection and refitting

1   If the gearbox has not been removed, apply the handbrake, prise off the wheel trim and slacken the left-hand front roadwheel nuts. Jack up the front left-hand side of the car and support it securely on axle stands. Remove the roadwheel.

2   From under the wheel arch, undo and remove the retaining screws and lift away the access panel from the inner wing.

3   Refer to Section 3 and disconnect the clutch cable from the gearbox operating lever and bracket.

4   Place a suitable receptacle beneath the gearbox end cover as there is likely to be some oil spillage when the cover is removed.

5   Undo and remove the four retaining bolts and lift off the end cover. Recover the gasket.

6   Move the operating lever sufficiently to allow the release bearing and sleeve to be withdrawn, and then remove the bearing from the sleeve.

7   Check the release bearing for smoothness of operation and renew it if there is any roughness or harshness as the bearing is spun.

8   Refitting is the reverse sequence to removal, bearing in mind the following points.

(a) Use a new end cover gasket, lightly smeared with jointing compound

(b) Tighten the end cover retaining bolts to the specified torque in a progressive diagonal sequence

(c) Adjust the clutch cable, as described in Section 2, and top up the gearbox oil, if necessary

### 8 Clutch release bearing (five-speed gearbox) – removal, inspection and refitting

1   If the gearbox has not been removed, apply the handbrake, prise off the wheel trim and slacken the left-hand front roadwheel nuts. Jack up the front left-hand side of the car and support it securely on axle stands. Remove the roadwheel.

2   From under the wheel arch, undo and remove the retaining screws and lift away the access panel from the inner wing.

3   Refer to Section 3, and disconnect the clutch cable from the gearbox operating lever and bracket.

4   Place a suitable receptacle beneath the gearbox end cap as there is likely to be some oil spillage when the cover is removed.

5   Using a suitable sharp instrument, pierce the end cap and lever it out of its location in the gearbox housing. Discard the end cap, as a new one will be needed when refitting.

6   Remove the operating lever stop clip and then move the lever sufficiently to allow the release bearing to be withdrawn.

7   Check the release bearing for smoothness of operation and renew it if there is any roughness or harshness as the bearing is spun.

8   Refitting is the reverse sequence to removal, bearing in mind the following points.

(a) Use a block of wood or suitable drift to drive in a new end cap and ensure that the cap is kept square as it is fitted

(b) Adjust the clutch cable, as described in Section 2, and top up the gearbox oil, if necessary

**9 Fault diagnosis – clutch**

| Symptom | Reason(s) |
| --- | --- |
| Judder when taking up drive | Loose or worn engine/gearbox mountings<br>Friction disc linings contaminated with oil or worn<br>Faulty pressure plate assembly<br>Clutch cable sticking or frayed |
| Clutch fails to disengage | Incorrect cable adjustment<br>Friction disc sticking on input shaft splines<br>Faulty pressure plate assembly |
| Clutch slips | Incorrect cable adjustment<br>Friction disc linings worn or contaminated with oil<br>Faulty pressure plate assembly |
| Noise when depressing clutch pedal | Worn release bearing<br>Defective release mechanism<br>Faulty pressure plate assembly |
| Noise when releasing clutch pedal | Faulty pressure plate assembly<br>Broken friction disc torsion springs<br>Gearbox internal wear (see Chapter 6) |

# Chapter 6 Gearbox

*For modifications, and information applicable to later models, see Supplement at end of manual*

## Contents

## Specifications

Type .................................................................................................. Four or five forward speeds (all synchromesh) and reverse. Final drive integral with main gearbox

### Gearbox ratios

Four-speed gearbox:

| | |
|---|---|
| 1st | 3.45 : 1 |
| 2nd | 1.94 : 1 |
| 3rd | 1.29 : 1 |
| 4th | 0.91 : 1 |
| Reverse | 3.17 : 1 |

3+E gearbox:

| | |
|---|---|
| 1st | 3.45 : 1 |
| 2nd | 1.75 : 1 |
| 3rd | 1.06 : 1 |
| E | 0.70 : 1 |
| Reverse | 3.17 : 1 |

Five-speed gearbox (except MG 1600):

| | |
|---|---|
| 1st | 3.45 : 1 |
| 2nd | 1.94 : 1 |
| 3rd | 1.29 : 1 |
| 4th | 0.91 : 1 |
| 5th | 0.71 : 1 |
| Reverse | 3.17 : 1 |

Five-speed gearbox (MG 1600):

| | |
|---|---|
| 1st | 3.45 : 1 |
| 2nd | 2.12 : 1 |
| 3rd | 1.44 : 1 |
| 4th | 1.13 : 1 |
| 5th | 0.91 : 1 |
| Reverse | 3.17 : 1 |

### Final drive ratios

| | |
|---|---|
| 1.3 and 1.3L models | 4.17 : 1 |
| 1.3 HLE; 1.6L, 1.6HLS and Vanden Plas models | 3.89 : 1 |
| MG models | 3.65 : 1 |

### Gearbox overhaul data

| | |
|---|---|
| 3rd gear axial movement | 0 to 0.008 in (0 to 0.20 mm) |
| Axial movement adjustment | Selected circlips |
| Minimum baulk ring to gear clearance: | |
| 1st and 2nd gear | 0.023 in (0.60 mm) |
| 3rd gear | 0.026 in (0.65 mm) |
| 4th and 5th gear | 0.031 in (0.80 mm) |

### Lubricant type/specification

Lubricant type/specification .......................................................... Hypoid gear oil, viscosity SAE 80EP (Duckhams Hypoid 80)

## Lubricant capacity

| | |
|---|---|
| Four-speed gearbox | 2.75 pt (1.5 litres) |
| Five-speed gearbox | 3.5 pt (2.0 litres) |

## Torque wrench settings

| | lbf ft | Nm |
|---|---|---|
| Gearbox to adaptor plate: | | |
|     M7 bolts | 4 | 5 |
|     M12 bolts | 67 | 90 |
| Main casing to gear carrier housing | 18 | 25 |
| End cover bolts: | | |
|     Four-speed gearbox | 11 | 15 |
|     Five-speed gearbox | 18 | 25 |
| Selector shaft locking screw | 15 | 20 |
| Engine mounting bracket to end cover or casing | 30 | 40 |
| Mainshaft bearing retaining nuts or screws | 11 | 15 |
| Pinion shaft bearing retaining plate bolts | 30 | 40 |
| Shift fork set retaining bolts | 18 | 25 |
| Reverse idler shaft retaining bolt: | | |
|     Four-speed gearbox | 15 | 20 |
|     Five-speed gearbox | 22 | 30 |
| 5th gear synchro-hub retaining screw | 110 | 150 |
| Oil filler/level plug and drain plug | 18 | 25 |
| Reverse lamp switch | 22 | 30 |

## 1 General description

The gearbox is of Volkswagen manufacture and is equipped with either four forward and one reverse gear or five forward and one reverse gear, according to model. Synchromesh gear engagement is used on all forward gears.

The final drive (differential) unit is integral with the main gearbox and is located between the main casing and the bearing housing. The gearbox and differential both share the same lubricating oil.

Gearshift is by means of a floor mounted lever connected by a remote control housing and shift rod to the gearbox selector shaft and relay lever.

If gearbox overhaul is necessary, due consideration should be given to the costs involved, since it is often more economical to obtain a service exchange or good secondhand gearbox rather than fit new parts to the existing unit.

## 2 Maintenance and inspection

1 At regular intervals (see Routine Maintenance) inspect the gearbox joint faces and oil seals for any sign of damage, deterioration or oil leakage.

2 At the same service interval check and, if necessary, top up the gearbox oil. The filler plug is located on the end of the gearbox casing and the oil level should be maintained up to the level of the filler plug orifice. Removal of the filler plug entails the use of a large Allen key. A suitable alternative, however, is to lock two nuts together on the thread of a suitable bolt, insert the hexagonal head of the bolt into the filler plug and then unscrew the plug using a spanner on the innermost nut.

3 Although not considered necessary by the manufacturers, the diligent home mechanic may wish to renew the gearbox oil, in the interests of extended gearbox life, every 24 000 miles (40 000 km) or two years.

4 It is also advisable to check for excess free play or wear in the gear linkage joints and levers, and check the gear lever adjustment, as described in Section 24.

## 3 Gearbox — removal and refitting

1 Disconnect the battery negative terminal.

2 Slide back the rubber cap and disconnect the two reversing lamp switch wires from the switch terminals (photo).

3 Undo and remove the bolt securing the speedometer cable or speed transducer cable retaining plate to the gearbox casing. Withdraw the cable and pinion assembly squarely, and without twisting, from the housing (photo). If the cable is not withdrawn squarely, the pinion may become dislodged from the cable and fall into the gearbox.

3.2 Disconnect the reversing lamp switch wires

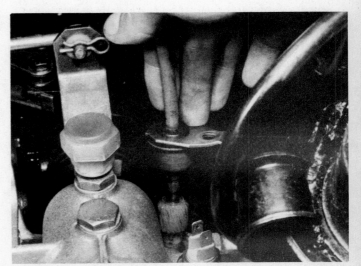

3.3 Remove the retaining bolt and lift out the speedometer or speed transducer cable

3.4 Remove the clutch cable retaining clip and seating plate (A), disengage the rubber retainer (B) and withdraw the cable

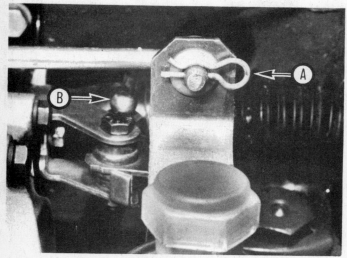

3.5 Remove the gearchange rod clip (A) and selector rod balljoint (B) – shown removed – to allow removal of the linkage

3.8 Remove the wiring harness retaining clip nut and bolt

**Fig. 6.1 Exploded view of the four-speed gearbox (Sec 1)**

| | |
|---|---|
| 1 | Plastic cap |
| 2 | Circlip |
| 3 | Spring washer |
| 4 | Drive coupling |
| 5 | Differential oil seal |
| 6 | Blanking plug |
| 7 | Gear carrier housing |
| 8 | Shim |
| 9 | Bearing outer race |
| 10 | Pinion shaft bearing |
| 11 | Pinion shaft |
| 12 | Pinion shaft bearing |
| 13 | Bearing outer race and retaining plate assembly |
| 14 | Retaining plate bolt |
| 15 | Thrust washer |
| 16 | Needle roller bearing |
| 17 | 1st gear |
| 18 | 1st gear baulk ring |
| 19 | Synchro key |
| 20 | Spring |
| 21 | 1st/2nd gear synchroniser hub |
| 22 | 1st/2nd gear synchroniser sleeve and reverse gear |
| 23 | Baulk ring |
| 24 | Needle roller bearing inner race |
| 25 | Needle roller bearing |
| 26 | 2nd gear |
| 27 | 3rd gear |
| 28 | Selected circlip |
| 29 | 4th gear |
| 30 | Circlip |
| 31 | Bearing retaining screw |
| 32 | Needle roller bearing |
| 33 | Shim |
| 34 | Bearing outer race |
| 35 | Taper roller bearing |
| 36 | Thrust washer |
| 37 | Differential shaft |
| 38 | Circlip |
| 39 | Final drive gear |
| 40 | Bolt, lock plate and nut |
| 41 | Differential cage |
| 42 | Reverse lamp switch and washer |
| 43 | Selector shaft detent plunger and washer |
| 44 | Selector shaft oil seal |
| 45 | Selector shaft boot |
| 46 | Main casing |
| 47 | Casing retaining bolt |
| 48 | Clutch pushrod |
| 49 | Release bearing |
| 50 | Release bearing sleeve |
| 51 | Dowel |
| 52 | Magnet |
| 53 | Drain plug |
| 54 | Differential gear |
| 55 | Pinion pin |
| 56 | Circlip |
| 57 | Differential pinion |
| 58 | Mainshaft bearing retaining clamps |
| 59 | Clutch release shaft |
| 60 | Release shaft oil seal |
| 61 | Filler/level plug |
| 62 | Clutch return spring |
| 63 | Circlip |
| 64 | Clutch lever |
| 65 | Main casing end cover |
| 66 | End cover bolt |
| 67 | Reverse idler gear |
| 68 | Bush |
| 69 | Reverse idler shaft |
| 70 | Selector shaft |
| 71 | Yoke |
| 72 | Circlip |
| 73 | Selector finger |
| 74 | Spring |
| 75 | Oil deflector |
| 76 | End cover |
| 77 | Selector rod |
| 78 | Circlip |
| 79 | Relay lever pivot post |
| 80 | Pivot post retaining bolt |
| 81 | Reverse gear relay lever |
| 82 | 1st/2nd selector fork |
| 83 | Reverse selector fork |
| 84 | 3rd/4th selector fork |
| 85 | Needle roller bearing |
| 86 | Clutch pushrod oil seal |
| 87 | Clutch pushrod bush |
| 88 | Mainshaft |
| 89 | Needle roller bearing |
| 90 | 3rd gear |
| 91 | Baulk ring |
| 92 | Synchro key |
| 93 | Spring |
| 94 | 3rd/4th synchroniser hub |
| 95 | 3rd/4th synchroniser sleeve |
| 96 | Circlip |
| 97 | Baulk ring |
| 98 | Needle roller bearing |
| 99 | 4th gear |
| 100 | Mainshaft bearing |
| 101 | Circlip |
| 102 | Shim (if fitted) |
| 103 | Reverse idler shaft bolt |
| 104 | Selector finger* |
| 105 | Yoke* |
| 106 | Spring* |
| 107 | Detent plate* |
| 108 | Shaft* |
| 109 | Roll pin* |
| 110 | Peg bolt* |

*Alternatives to items 43, 70, 71 and 73

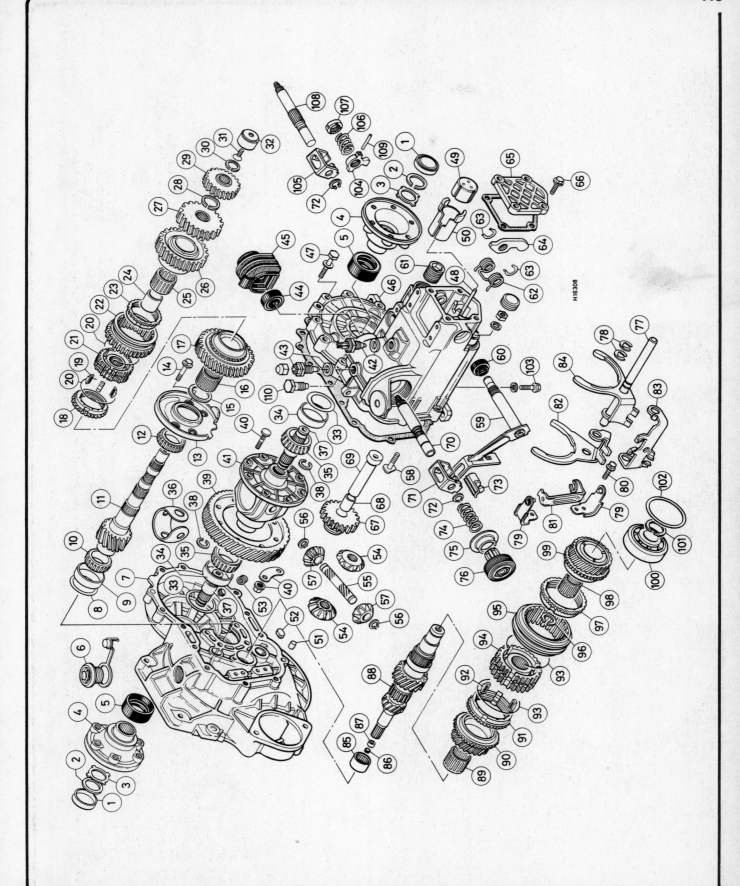

H16308

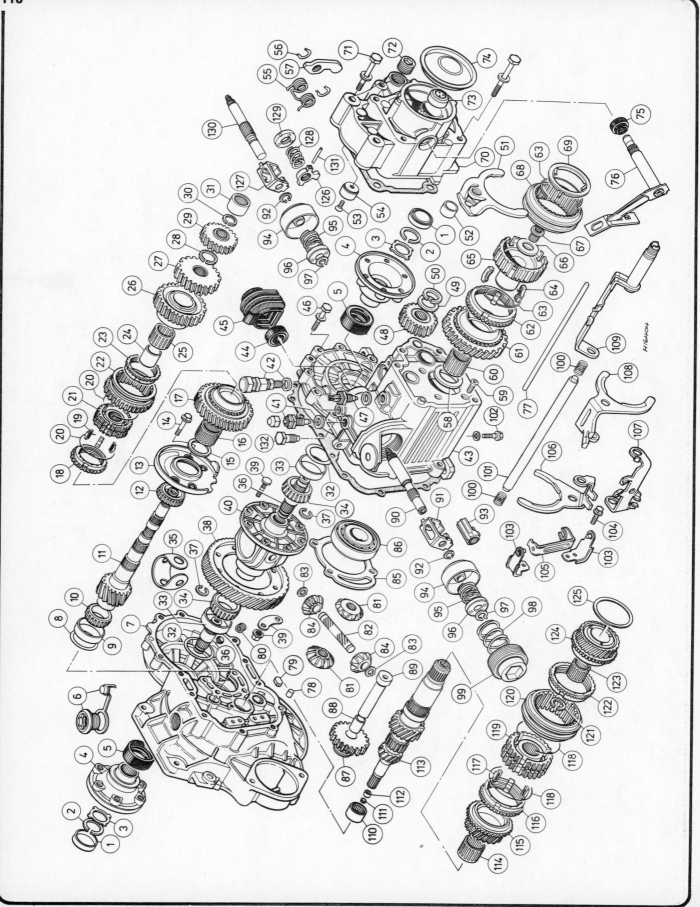

**Fig. 6.2 Exploded view of the five-speed gearbox (Sec 1)**

1 Plastic cap
2 Circlip
3 Spring washer
4 Drive coupling
5 Differential oil seal
6 Blanking plug
7 Gear carrier housing
8 Shim
9 Bearing outer race
10 Pinion shaft bearing
11 Pinion shaft
12 Pinion shaft bearing
13 Bearing outer race and retaining plate assembly
14 Retaining plate bolt
15 Thrust washer
16 Needle roller bearing
17 1st gear
18 1st gear baulk ring
19 Synchro key
20 Spring
21 1st/2nd gear synchroniser hub
22 1st/2nd gear synchroniser sleeve and reverse gear
23 Baulk ring
24 Needle roller bearing inner race
25 Needle roller bearing
26 2nd gear
27 3rd gear
28 Selected circlip
29 4th gear
30 Circlip
31 Needle roller bearing
32 Shim
33 Bearing outer race
34 Taper roller bearing
35 Thrust washer

36 Differential shaft
37 Circlip
38 Final drive gear
39 Bolt, lock plate and nut
40 Differential cage
41 Selector shaft detent plunger and washer
42 5th gear detent plunger and washer
43 Main casing
44 Selector shaft oil seal
45 Selector shaft boot
46 Casing retaining bolt
47 Reverse lamp switch and washer
48 5th gear
49 Thrust washer
50 Circlip
51 5th gear selector fork
52 Spacer bush
53 Bearing retainer screw
54 Needle roller bearing
55 Clutch return spring
56 Circlip
57 Clutch lever
58 Thrust washer
59 Bearing retaining plate screw
60 Needle roller bearing
61 5th gear
62 Baulk ring
63 Spring
64 Synchro key
65 5th gear synchroniser hub
66 Washer
67 Synchroniser hub screw
68 5th gear synchroniser sleeve

69 Stop plate
70 End cover
71 End cover bolt
72 Filler/level plug
73 Clutch release bearing
74 End cap
75 Operating shaft oil seal
76 Clutch release shaft
77 Clutch pushrod
78 Dowel
79 Magnet
80 Drain plug
81 Differential gear
82 Pinion pin
83 Circlip
84 Differential pinion
85 Mainshaft bearing retaining plate
86 Mainshaft bearing
87 Reverse idler gear
88 Bush
89 Reverse idler shaft
90 Selector shaft
91 Yoke
92 Circlip
93 Selector finger
94 Sleeve
95 Spring
96 Spring plate
97 Circlip
98 Spring
99 End cover
100 Spring
101 Selector rod
102 Reverse idler shaft bolt
103 Relay lever pillar
104 Pillar bolt

105 Reverse gear relay lever
106 1st/2nd selector fork
107 Reverse selector fork
108 3rd/4th selector fork
109 5th gear selector link and tube
110 Needle roller bearing
111 Clutch pushrod oil seal
112 Clutch pushrod bush
113 Mainshaft
114 Needle roller bearing
115 3rd gear
116 Baulk ring
117 Synchro key
118 Spring
119 3rd/4th synchroniser hub
120 3rd/4th synchroniser sleeve
121 Circlip
122 Baulk ring
123 Needle roller bearing
124 4th gear
125 Shim (if fitted)
126 Selector finger*
127 Yoke*
128 Spring*
129 Detent plate*
130 Shaft*
131 Roll pin*
132 Peg bolt*
*Alternatives to items 41, 90, 91 and 93

4    Remove the clutch cable retaining clip and seating plate from the end of the cable, disengage the rubber retainer from the guide sleeve and pull the cable and guide sleeve out of the operating lever and gearbox bracket (photo).

5    Extract the clip securing the gearchange rod to the selector shaft lever and slide the rod out of the lever bush (photo). Prise off the rear selector rod nylon balljoint from the relay lever using a screwdriver and move the rod to one side.

6    Make a note of the wiring harness connections at the starter motor solenoid and disconnect them.

7    Using an Allen key and suitable spanner, undo and remove the starter motor retaining bolts and lift off the starter motor.

8    Undo and remove the nut and bolt securing the wiring harness clip to the top of the gearbox and lift away the clip (photo).

9    Undo and remove the bolt securing the engine earth strap to the bracket below the left-hand side engine mounting (photo).

10   Prise off the left-hand front wheel trim and slacken the wheel nuts. Jack up the car, support it securely on axle stands and remove the roadwheel.

11   Undo and remove the retaining screws and lift off the access panel from under the wheel arch.

12   From underneath the front of the car, mark the drive flange to inner constant velocity joint flange relationship using paint or a file.

13   Lift off the protective covers and then undo and remove the bolts securing the constant velocity joints to the drive flanges, using an Allen key. Tie the driveshafts out of the way using string or wire.

14   Using a suitable jack and interposed block of wood, support the engine and gearbox assembly under the engine sump.

15   From above, undo and remove the left-hand engine mounting through-bolt and large flat washers (photo).

16   Position a second jack beneath the gearbox and remove all the bolts securing the gearbox to the engine adaptor plate. Make a note of the different lengths of the bolts and their locations, and also note that a bolt is concealed behind the engine to adaptor plate stiffener bracket, necessitating its removal for access (photos).

17   With all the bolts removed, make a final check that everything attached to the gearbox has been disconnecteed.

18   With the help of an assistant, lower the jacks until sufficient clearance exists to enable the gearbox to be drawn off the side of the engine. Keep the gearbox supported on the jack, as it is quite heavy, and after releasing the gearbox from the adaptor plate dowels, lower the unit slowly and carefully to the ground.

19   Refitting the gearbox is the reverse sequence to removal, bearing in mind the following points:

(a)   Tighten all retaining and mounting bolts to the specified torque

(b)   Refill the gearbox with the specified lubricant to the level of the filler plug orifice

(c)   Align the marks on the drive flanges and inner constant velocity joints before refitting the retaining bolts. Tighten the bolts to the specified torque and fit new protective caps

(d)   Lubricate the selector linkage rod and gearchange rod with a lithium based grease before refitting

3.9 Remove the engine earth strap (arrowed)

3.15 Remove the left-hand engine mounting through-bolt and flat washers

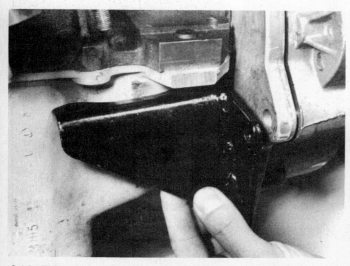

3.16a The engine to gearbox stiffener plate must be removed ...

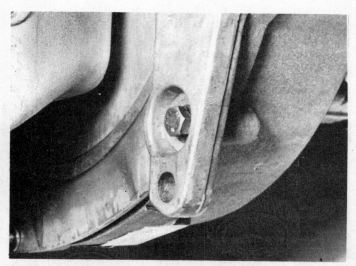

3.16b ... to gain access to a gearbox retaining bolt

## 4 Gearbox overhaul – general

The overhaul of the gearbox requires the use of a number of special tools, and also certain critical adjustments, if the job is to be done successfully. For this reason it is not recommended that a complete overhaul be attempted by the home mechanic unless he has access to the tools required and feels reasonably confident after studying the procedure. However, the gearbox can at least be dismantled into its major assemblies without too much difficulty, and the following Sections describe this, and the overhaul procedures.

Repair or overhaul of the differential unit is not considered to be within the scope of the home mechanic, since special jigs and fixtures are required for this work.

Before starting any repair work on the gearbox, drain the oil and thoroughly clean the exterior of the casings, using paraffin or a suitable solvent. Dry the unit with a lint-free rag. Make sure that an uncluttered working area is available with some small containers and trays handy to store the various parts. Label everything as it is removed.

Before starting reassembly all the components must be spotlessly clean and should be lubricated with the recommended grade of gear oil during assembly.

## 5 Gearbox (four-speed) – separating the housings

1   Remove the clutch pushrod. Undo the four bolts securing the gearbox end cover plate and remove the cover plate. This will give access to the clutch release mechanism. Lift out the clutch release bearing and sleeve.

2   There are two circlips, one on each side of the clutch release lever. Remove these and slide the operating shaft out of the main casing, collecting the return spring and release lever as the shaft is withdrawn. Note that there is a master spline on the shaft and that the release lever will fit on the shaft in one way only.

3   Prise out the plastic cap from the centre of the left-hand side drive flange and remove the circlip and spring washer. Withdraw the flange using a suitable puller (photos). There is no need to remove the opposite driveshaft flange at this stage.

4   Remove the selector shaft detent plunger or peg bolt and the lockbolt for the reverse gear shaft (photos). Remove the reversing lamp switch (photo).

5   On the side of the main casing below the clutch withdrawal shaft is the cover for the selector shaft. Using a plug spanner, remove this cover and lift off the oil deflector, then remove the detent spring (photo). Note that the gearbox must be in neutral for this operation.

6   Withdraw the selector shaft from the main casing (photo).

7   On the end of the main casing (where the clutch withdrawal mechanism is located) are two plastic caps. Prise these out and undo the nuts underneath them (photo). There is a third nut inside the casing from which the clutch withdrawal mechanism was removed; this must also be removed (photo). If these nuts are not removed, the mainshaft bearing cannot be pulled out of the casing and the casing will fracture if pressure is applied to draw it off.

8   Undo and remove the 14 bolts securing the two casings together. Twelve of these bolts are M8 x 50 and two are M8 x 36, note where the shorter bolts are fitted.

9   The casings are now ready for separation. Photos 15.16a and 15.16b show a suitable tool being used to draw the casing off the mainshaft on a five-speed gearbox. The arrangement is the same on the four-speed unit. Secure the tool in the holes for the cover plate with two 7 mm bolts and then screw the centre screw down on the top of the mainshaft until it just touches. Fasten a bar or piece of angle iron across the clutch housing, in such a manner as to support the end of the mainshaft, and then continue to screw in the centre screw of the tool until the casing is pulled away, leaving the mainshaft bearing complete on the mainshaft. Lift away the main casing (photo). On top of the bearing there may be one or more shims, collect them and label them to ensure that they can be identified at reassembly. The needle bearing for the pinion shaft will remain in the main casing: it can be removed, if necessary, using a suitable extractor.

10   Recover the three clamping screws which retain the mainshaft bearing – they will drop into the gearbox as the casing is being removed. Remove the magnet from the gear carrier housing.

5.3a Remove the drive flange plastic cap ...

5.3b ... extract the circlip and spring washer ...

5.3c ... and remove the flange with a puller

5.4a Remove the selector shaft detent plunger

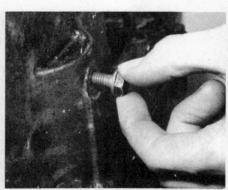
5.4b Remove the reverse gear shaft lockbolt ...

5.4c ... and the reversing lamp switch

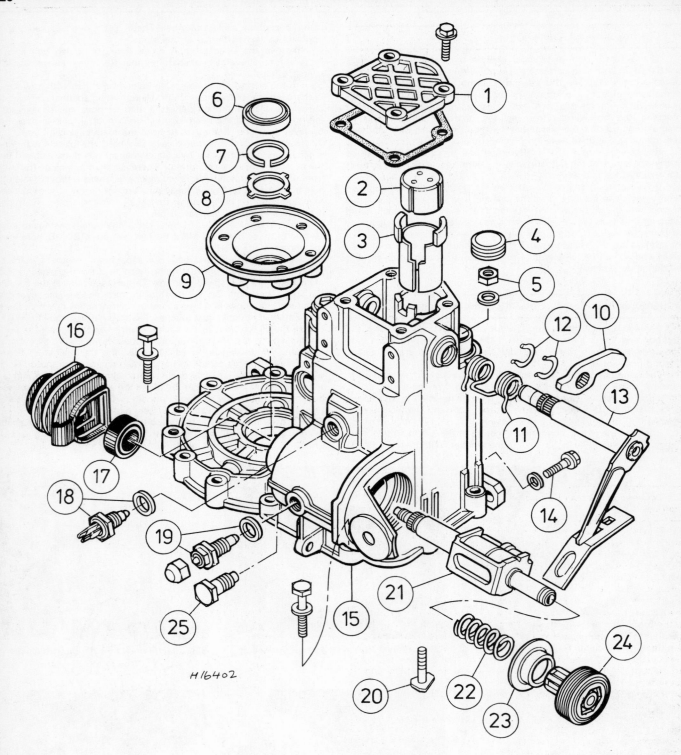

**Fig. 6.3 Main casing components – four-speed gearbox (Sec 5)**

| | | | | |
|---|---|---|---|---|
| 1 Main casing end cover | 6 Plastic cap | 12 Circlip | 17 Selector shaft seal | 21 Selector shaft assembly |
| 2 Clutch release bearing | 7 Circlip | 13 Clutch operating shaft | 18 Reverse lamp switch | 22 Spring |
| 3 Release bearing sleeve | 8 Spring washer | 14 Reverse idler shaft | 19 Selector shaft detent | 23 Oil deflector |
| 4 Rubber plug | 9 Drive coupling | bolt | plunger | 24 End cap |
| 5 Bearing retaining nut and washer | 10 Clutch lever | 15 Main casing | 20 Mainshaft bearing retaining clamp | 25 Peg bolt - alternative to item 19 |
| | 11 Return spring | 16 Selector shaft rubber boot | | |

H16402

5.5 Unscrew the selector shaft cover, oil deflector and spring

5.6 Withdraw the selector shaft

5.7a Remove the plastic caps to expose the mainshaft bearing clamp retaining nuts

5.7b A third nut is located inside the casing

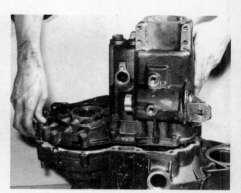

5.9 Lift off the main casing after releasing the bearing

## 6 Gearbox (four-speed) mainshaft, pinion shaft and differential – removal

1   The mainshaft assembly can be removed quite easily, but the pinion shaft assembly must be partially dismantled before the pinion shaft and the differential unit can be removed.

2   Remove the two shift fork shaft circlips (photo) and withdraw the shaft from the gear carrier housing, then lift away the shift fork set (photo).

3   Remove the circlip retaining 4th gear on the pinion shaft (photo), then lift the mainshaft out of its bearing in the gear carrier housing and at the same time remove 4th gear from the pinion shaft. The mainshaft needle bearing and oil seal will remain in the gear carrier housing.

4   Remove the circlip retaining 3rd gear on the pinion shaft (photo). This circlip is used to adjust the axial movement of 3rd gear and must be refitted in the same position, so label it for identification at reassembly. Remove 3rd gear (photo).

5   Remove 2nd gear and then the needle bearing from over its inner sleeve (photos).

6   To remove the rest of the gears a long-legged puller will be required. Before pulling off the synchroniser unit and 1st gear, remove the reverse gear by tapping the reverse gear shaft out of its seating, then lift the shaft and gear away.

7   Remove the plastic stop button from the end of the pinon shaft and fit the puller under 1st gear. Note that the pinion shaft bearing retainer has two notches to accommodate the puller legs. Pull the gear and synchro-hub off the shaft. Tape the synchro unit together to prevent it coming apart.

8   Remove the needle bearing and thrust washer (photos). Note that the flat side of the washer is towards 1st gear.

9   Remove the four nuts or bolts securing the pinion bearing retainer and lift off the retainer (photos). Note that the retainer incorporates the reverse gear stop. The pinion shaft is seated in a taper roller bearing, and can now be removed from the gear carrier housing.

10   Remove the second drive flange, as described in Section 5,

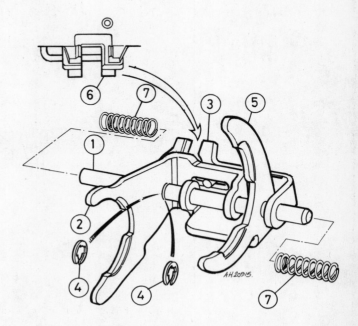

**Fig. 6.4 Selector shift fork set – four-speed gearbox (Sec 6)**

| | | | |
|---|---|---|---|
| 1 | Selector shaft | 5 | 3rd/4th selector fork |
| 2 | 1st/2nd selector fork | 6 | Alignment of selector |
| 3 | Reverse selector fork | | recesses |
| 4 | Circlip | 7 | Coil spring |

6.2a Extract the shift fork shaft circlips (upper circlip arrowed) ...

6.2b ... and withdraw the shift fork set

6.3 Remove the circlip securing 4th gear to the pinion shaft

6.4a Remove the 3rd gear retaining circlip ...

6.4b ... and remove 3rd gear from the pinion shaft

6.5a Lift off 2nd gear ...

6.5b ... followed by its needle roller bearing

6.8a Lift off 1st gear needle roller bearing ...

6.8b ... and the thrust washer

6.9a Unscrew the retaining bolts ...

6.9b ... and withdraw the pinion bearing retaining plate

6.10 Lift out the differential from the gear carrier housing

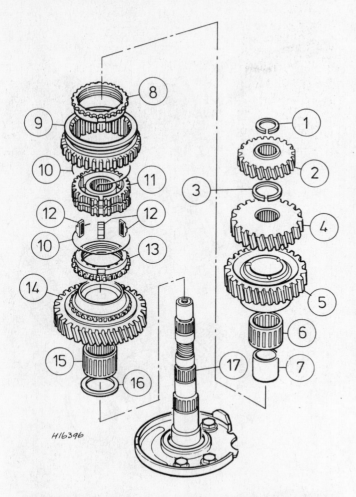

**Fig. 6.5 Pinion shaft components – four-speed gearbox (Sec 6)**

| | | | |
|---|---|---|---|
| 1 | Circlip | 9 | 1st/2nd synchro sleeve |
| 2 | 4th gear | 10 | Retaining spring |
| 3 | Selected circlip | 11 | 1st/2nd synchro-hub |
| 4 | 3rd gear | 12 | Synchro key |
| 5 | 2nd gear | 13 | 1st gear baulk ring |
| 6 | Needle roller bearing | 14 | 1st gear |
| 7 | Needle roller bearing | 15 | Needle roller bearing |
| | inner race | 16 | Thrust washer |
| 8 | Baulk ring | 17 | Pinion shaft |

paragraph 3, and then lift the differential unit out of the gear carrier housing (photo). We do not recommend trying to overhaul the differential unit; if it is in any way suspect seek advice from your BL dealer.

## 7 Gearbox (four-speed) gear carrier housing – overhaul

1   Clean the housing using paraffin, or a suitable solvent.
2   Prise or drift out the oil seals and fit new seals using a socket or tube and hammer to drive them in (photos). Fill the space between the seal lips with a multi-purpose grease before fitting.
3   The mainshaft needle roller bearing may be removed, if necessary, using a suitable extractor. Do not remove the bearing unless it is defective as it is likely to be damaged during removal (photo).
4   If the outer races of the differential bearings are in need of renewal, then this, and the renewal of the corresponding inner races and bearings on the differential, should be left to a BL dealer, as a complicated setting up procedure is involved.
5   The fit of the starter motor armature should be tried in the starter bush. If undue wear is apparent, renew the bush.

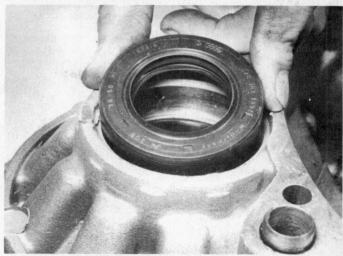

7.2a Fit a new differential drive flange oil seal to the gear carrier housing ...

7.2b ... and drive it fully into place

7.3 Mainshaft needle roller bearing in the gear carrier housing

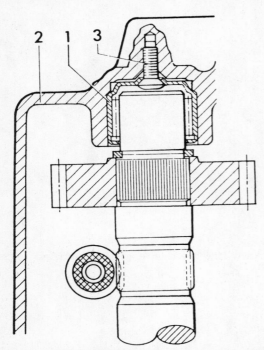

**Fig. 6.6 Sectional view of the pinion shaft needle roller bearing –
four-speed gearbox (Sec 8)**

1   *Needle roller bearing*
2   *Main casing*
3   *Self-tapping screw*

## 8   Gearbox (four-speed) main casing – overhaul

1   The three oil seals in the main casing should be renewed by prising
them out, noting their fitted direction, and fitting new seals using a
block of wood, large socket or tube to drive them in. Fill the lips of the
seals with multi-purpose grease before fitting.
2   The needle roller bearing for the pinion shaft is retained by a screw
and can be withdrawn for renewal after removal of the screw.
3   If the differential bearing outer race requires renewal, this should
be left to a BL dealer, as the bearings also require accurate setting up
using jigs and fixtures.

## 9   Gearbox (four-speed) pinion shaft bearings – renewal

1   The large and small bearings accurately locate the pinion shaft
gear with the crownwheel of the differential. If either bearing is
defective then both must be renewed. In the removal process the
bearings are destroyed. New ones have to be shrunk on and the shim
under the smaller bearing changed for one of the correct size.
2   This operation is quite complicated and requires special
equipment for preloading of the shaft and measurement of the torque
required to rotate the new bearings. In addition the shim at the top of
the mainshaft and the axial play at the circlip of the 3rd gear on the
pinion shaft will be affected. This will mean selection of a new shim
and circlip. There are six different thicknesses of circlip. Therefore it is
recommended that if these bearings require renewal, the work should
be left to your BL agent.

## 10   Gearbox (four-speed) mainshaft – dismantling and reassembly

1   Remove the ball-bearing retaining circlip and then, with the legs of
a two-legged puller positioned under 4th gear, pull the bearing and
gear off the mainshaft.
2   Withdraw the 4th gear needle bearing and baulk ring (photo).
3   Remove the circlip, then support 3rd gear and press the mainshaft

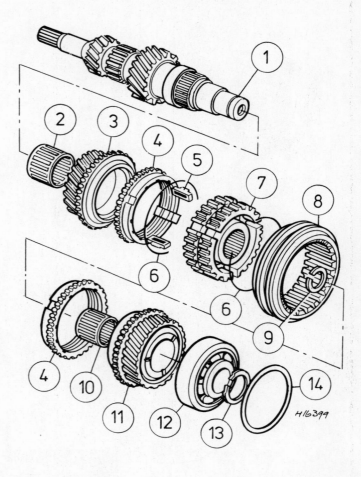

**Fig. 6.7 Mainshaft components – four-speed gearbox (Sec 10)**

| | |
|---|---|
| 1   *Mainshaft* | 8   *Synchro sleeve* |
| 2   *Needle roller bearing* | 9   *Circlip* |
| 3   *3rd gear* | 10  *Needle roller bearing* |
| 4   *Baulk ring* | 11  *4th gear* |
| 5   *Synchro key* | 12  *Mainshaft bearing* |
| 6   *Retaining spring* | 13  *Circlip* |
| 7   *Synchro-hub* | 14  *Shim (where fitted)* |

through the 3rd/4th synchro-hub. Tape the synchro unit together to
prevent its coming apart.
4   Remove the needle bearing to complete the dismantling of the
shaft (photos).
5   If the gears on either shaft are to be renewed, then the mating
gear on the other shaft must be renewed as well. They are supplied in
pairs only.
6   The inspection of the synchro units is dealt with in Section 11.
7   When reassembling the mainshaft, lightly oil all the parts.
8   Fit the 3rd gear needle bearing, 3rd gear and the 3rd gear baulk
ring. Press on the 3rd/4th gear synchro-hub and fit the retaining circlip
(photos). When pressing on the synchro-hub and sleeve, turn the rings
so that the keys and grooves line up. The chamfer on the inner splines
of the hub must face 3rd gear.
9   The mainshaft ball-bearing should now be pressed into the main
casing (photo). Ensure that the same shim(s) removed at dismantling
are refitted between the bearing and the casing. The bearing is fitted
with the closed side of the ball-bearing cage towards 4th gear. Insert
the clamping screws and tighten the clamping screw nuts to the
specified torque (photo).
**Note**: *The endplay will have to be adjusted if either of the bearings,
the thrust washer or mainshaft has been renewed, so the help of a BL
agent with the necessary special tools and gauges will be required.*

10.2 Withdraw the 4th gear needle roller bearing from the mainshaft

10.4a Open the cage to allow removal of the 3rd gear needle roller bearing

10.4b The mainshaft completely dismantled

10.8a Fit the 3rd gear ...

10.8b ... the 3rd gear baulk ring ...

10.8c ... the 3rd/4th synchro unit ...

10.8d ... and the synchro unit retaining circlip to the mainshaft

10.9a Fit the mainshaft ball-bearing into the main casing ...

10.9b ... and secure with the clamps and retaining nuts

## 11 Gearbox (four-speed) synchroniser units – inspection

1 The synchroniser unit hubs and sleeves are supplied as a matched set and must not be interchanged. Before dismantling the units, mark the sleeve and hub in relation to each other.

2 When renewing the synchro baulk rings it is advisable to fit new sliding keys and retaining springs.

3 When examining the units for wear bear in mind the following:

   (a) *With the keys removed, the hub and sleeve should slide easily with minimum backlash or axial rock*

   (b) *With the baulk rings in position the clearance from the face of the baulk ring to the face of the gear, measured with feeler gauges (photo), must not be less than the dimension given in the Specifications*

   (c) *Check for excess movement between the selector forks and their grooves in the sleeve. If in doubt compare the clearance with that of new components*

4 To reassemble the synchroniser units lay them out on the bench with the identifying marks made during removal uppermost (photo).

5 Slide the synchro sleeve over the hub, with the slots in the sleeve splines (photo) aligned with the cutaways in the hub. Note also that the selector fork groove on the 1st/2nd synchro unit must be fitted away from the side of the hub having the identifying grooves (photo).

6 Fit the keys into the hub and sleeve grooves (photo) and then place one of the retaining springs in position with its hooked end engaged with a key (photo).

7 Turn the synchro unit over and fit the other retaining spring, in the opposite direction to the first, and with its end engaged in a different key.

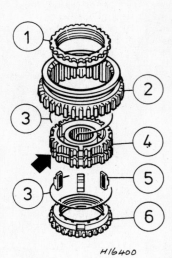

Fig. 6.8 Exploded view of the 1st/2nd synchroniser unit – four and five-speed gearboxes (Sec 11)

1  2nd gear baulk ring
2  Synchro sleeve
3  Retaining spring
4  Synchro-hub
5  Synchro key
6  1st gear baulk ring

Arrow indicates identification grooves in synchro-hub

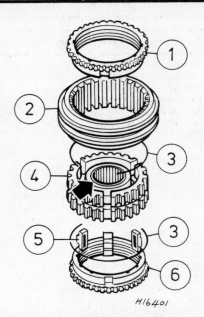

Fig. 6.9 Exploded view of the 3rd/4th synchroniser unit – four and five-speed gearboxes (Sec 11)

1  4th gear baulk ring
2  Synchro sleeve
3  Retaining spring
4  Synchro-hub
5  Synchro key
6  Baulk ring

Arrow indicates identification groove on hub boss

11.3 Checking baulk ring wear using feeler gauges

11.4 Lay out the synchroniser unit components, the correct way up, prior to assembly

11.5a The slots in the synchro sleeve must align with the cutaways in the hub

11.5b The selector fork groove in the sleeve must be fitted away from the side of the hub with identifying grooves (arrowed) on 1st/2nd synchro units

11.6a Fit the keys to the grooves in the hub and sleeve ...

11.6b ... and secure them with the retaining springs with their hooked ends (arrowed) engaged with the keys

## 12 Gearbox (four-speed) differential unit – inspection

1   As described earlier in this Chapter, dismantling and overhaul of the differential are considered beyond the scope of the home mechanic. If the differential assembly is obviously in need of renewal it will be necessary to obtain a complete unit and entrust the work to a dealer, as critical adjustments are required.

2   If the problem with the differential is purely one of noise, and if the noise is more of a whine than a rumble, the unit may continue working for some considerable time without getting any worse. Again, the help or advice of a dealer is recommended for deciding the course of action to be taken.

## 13 Gearbox (four-speed) differential, pinion shaft and mainshaft – reassembly

1   Refit the differential unit into the gear carrier housing. Refit the drive flange to the differential shaft and tap it into place using a tubular drift. Refit the spring washer, retaining circlip and a new plastic cap.

2   Check that the mainshaft ball-bearing is correctly fitted in the main casing, plastic cage towards the casing, and that the bearing clamp bolt nuts are tight.

3   Fit the pinion shaft complete with its taper bearings into the gear carrier housing, so that the pinion gear meshes with the crownwheel (photo).

4   Fit the bearing retaining plate and the four securing bolts (photo). Fit the 1st gear thrust washer with its flat side up (towards 1st gear). Fit the needle roller cage.

5   Slide 1st gear over the needle bearing and fit the 1st gear baulk ring (photos). The synchro-hub will slide on if heated to 248°F (120°C) – it can then be tapped into position. Make sure that the cut-outs are in line with the synchro keys in the 1st/2nd synchro unit to avoid damage to the baulk ring on reassembly. The shift fork groove in the operating sleeve should be nearer 2nd gear and the groove on the hub nearer 1st gear (photos). Fit the 2nd gear synchro baulk ring.

6   The inner race for the 2nd gear needle bearing must be fitted next and pressed down as far as it will go.

7   Fit the reverse idler gear and shaft with the shaft aligned as shown in Fig. 6.10. Use a plastic hammer to drive the shaft into the casing.

8   Fit the 2nd gear needle bearing on the pinion shaft and the 2nd gear with the shoulder downwards.

9   Warm the 3rd gear and press it down over the splines with the collar thrust face towards the 2nd gear.

10   Fit the 3rd gear retaining circlip and using feeler gauges measure the play between the gear and circlip (3rd gear axial movement). If the play is in excess of the specified amount, an oversize circlip must be fitted. Circlips are available in a range of thicknesses from 0.098 in (2.5 mm) to 0.118 in (3.0 mm), in 0.004 in (0.1 mm) increments.

11   At this stage the mainshaft must be fitted in position on the gear carrier housing. Slide it into the needle bearing in the casing and fit the shift forks in the operating sleeves. Insert the retaining circlips. Fit the reverse gear shift fork (photos).

12   Fit the 4th gear and its retaining circlip on the pinion shaft. Finally insert the stop button, where fitted, for the pinion shaft needle bearing in the end of the pinion shaft. Fit the magnet in its location in the gear carrier housing.

13   The gear carrier housing and shafts are now ready for the assembly of the main casing.

## 14 Gearbox (four-speed) – reassembling the housings

1   Check that the reverse gear shaft is in the correct position (see Fig. 6.10) and set the geartrain in neutral. Fit a new gasket on the gear carrier housing flange.

2   Lower the main casing over the gears, checking that the pinion shaft is aligned with the pinion shaft needle bearing in the casing. Drive the mainshaft into its bearing, using a suitable mandrel on the inner race. A piece of suitable diameter steel tube can be used. Ensure that the mainshaft is supported on a block of wood when driving the mainshaft into the bearing.

3   Insert the 14 bolts which secure the two housings together and

13.3 Fit the pinion shaft to the gear carrier housing

13.4 Tighten the pinion bearing retaining plate bolts to the specified torque

13.5a Fit the 1st gear ...

13.5b ... the 1st gear baulk ring ...

13.5c ... and the 1st/2nd synchro unit ...

13.5d ... then drive the synchro unit onto the pinion shaft using a suitable tube and hammer

13.11a Fit the assembled mainshaft to the gear carrier housing ...

13.11b ... refit the shift fork set ...

13.11c ... and shift fork shaft

13.11d Fit the reverse shift fork pivot posts ...

13.11e ... and the reverse shift fork assembly ...

13.11f ... ensuring that the fork engages on the reverse idler gear

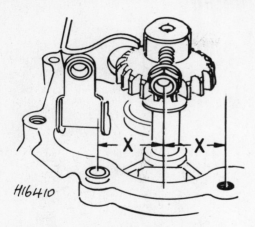

Fig. 6.10 Correct positioning of reverse idler shaft — four and five-speed gearboxes (Sec 14)

*Dimensions 'X' must be equal*

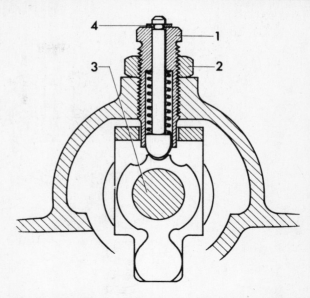

Fig. 6.11 Sectional view of the selector shaft detent plunger — four and five-speed gearboxes (Sec 14)

| | |
|---|---|
| *1  Adjusting sleeve* | *3  Selector shaft* |
| *2  Locknut* | *4  Lockring* |

14.4a Fit the mainshaft circlip working through the release bearing hole ...

14.4b ... and then insert the clutch pushrod into the mainshaft

tighten them to the specified torque.

4  Fit the circlip over the end of the mainshaft, working through the release bearing hole (photo). Insert the clutch pushrod into the mainshaft (photo). Ensure that the circlip is properly seated, then fit the clutch release bearing and sleeve assembly.

5  Fit the clutch release shaft and lever. Ensure that the spring is hooked over the lever in the centre and that the angled ends rest against the casing. The shaft can be inserted in the lever in one position only. Fit the two circlips, one each side of the lever.

6  Fit the clutch release sleeve and bearing.

7  Position a new gasket on the end of the casing and fit the end cover plate and four securing screws. Tighten the screws to the specified torque.

8  Lubricate the selector shaft and insert it into the casing. When it is in position, fit the spring(s) and screw in the shaft cover with a plug box spanner, tightening it to the specified torque.

9  Fit the selector shaft detent plunger (or peg bolt). This has a plastic cap. Only if the housing, selector shaft or plunger are faulty and new ones are required will the plunger need adjusting. If necessary, adjust as follows with neutral engaged:

(a)  Refer to Fig. 6.11. Slacken the locknut and screw in the adjusting sleeve until the lockring lifts off the adjusting sleeve

(b)  Screw the adjusting sleeve out until the lockring just contacts the sleeve

(c)  Check that the lockring lifts as soon as the shaft is turned. Tighten the locknut and fit the plastic cap

10  Fit the reverse gear shaft lockbolt and the reversing lamp switch.

## 15  Gearbox (five-speed) — separating the housings

1  Remove the clutch pushrod from the centre of the mainshaft.

2  Undo and remove the retaining bolts and withdraw the main casing end cover and engine mounting bracket. Remove the clutch release bearing and the gasket.

3  Move the selector shaft lever to the neutral position.

4  Unscrew the selector shaft detent plunger or peg bolt, the 5th gear detent plunger and the reversing lamp switch.

5  Undo and remove the nut securing the selector shaft lever to the shaft. Withdraw the lever and the rubber boot.

6  Using a suitable box spanner, such as a spark plug spanner, undo and remove the selector shaft end cap and lift out the spring. Carefully slide out the selector shaft assembly.

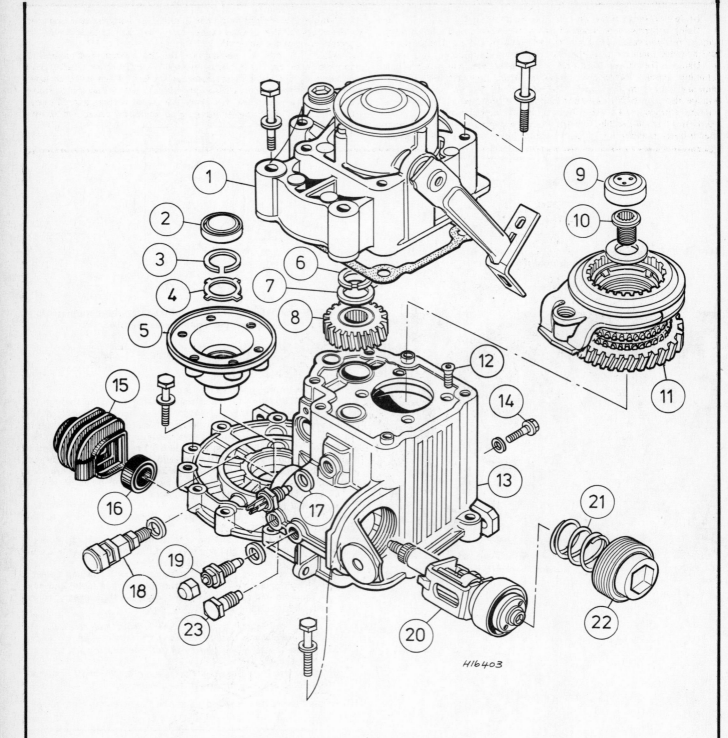

**Fig. 6.12 Main casing components – five-speed gearbox (Sec 15)**

1　Main casing end cover
2　Plastic cap
3　Circlip
4　Spring washer
5　Drive coupling
6　Circlip
7　Thrust washer
8　5th gear
9　Clutch release bearing
10　5th gear synchro-hub

　　retaining screw
11　5th speed gear, selector
　　fork and synchroniser
　　assembly
12　Main shaft bearing
　　retainer screws
13　Main casing
14　Reverse idler shaft bolt
15　Selector shaft rubber
　　boot

16　Selector shaft seal
17　Reverse lamp switch
18　5th gear detent plunger
19　Selector shaft detent
　　plunger
20　Selector shaft assembly
21　Spring
22　End cap
23　Selector shaft peg bolt
　　– alternative to item 19

7   Undo and remove the reverse idler shaft lockbolt.
8   Using a screwdriver inserted through the selector shaft opening,
engage 5th and reverse gears simultaneously by moving the front and
rear selector forks towards the clutch housing (photo).
9   Using a Torx driver socket bit, unscrew the 5th gear synchro-hub
retaining screw. **Note:** *this screw is extremely tight and is also
retained with a thread locking compound.* It will be necessary to
engage the help of an assistant to hold the gearbox as the screw is
undone. Remove the washer from under the screw head.
10  Using a small fine file, remove the two indentations in the 5th gear
spacer bush to allow the 5th gear selector tube to turn inside the bush.

11  Using a pair of right-angle circlip pliers, or a similar tool engaged
in the slots of the selector tube, turn the tube anti-clockwise to
unscrew it from the selector fork.
12  When the fork is released, lift off the synchro-hub assembly
complete with 5th gear, thrust washer, needle roller bearing and
selector fork. *Do not pull the selector rod out of the selector tube,
otherwise the selector fork assembly will fall apart inside the gearbox.*
13  Extract the circlip and withdraw the thrust washer and 5th gear
from the pinion shaft. Lever the gear up carefully, using two screwdrivers if it is tight.

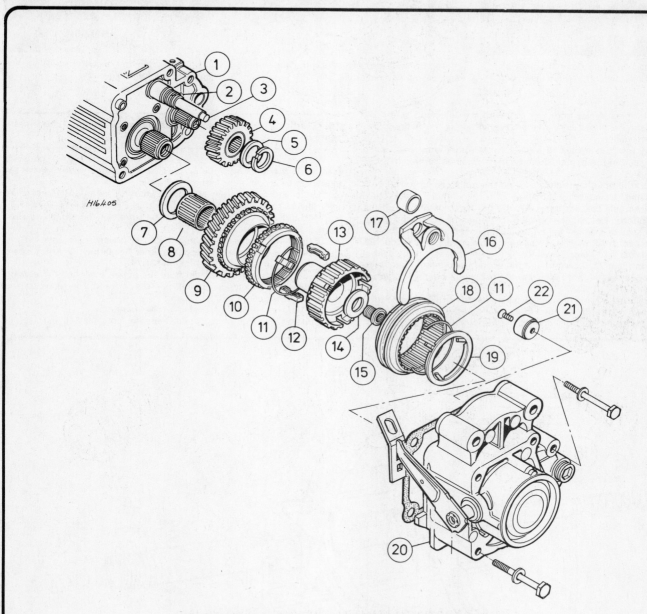

H16405

**Fig. 6.13 5th gear components – five-speed gearbox (Sec 15)**

| | | |
|---|---|---|
| 1  Main casing | 10  Baulk ring | 17  Spacer bush |
| 2  Selector tube | 11  Retaining spring | 18  Synchro sleeve |
| 3  Selector rod | 12  Synchro key | 19  Stop plate |
| 4  Pinion shaft 5th gear | 13  Synchro-hub | 20  End cover |
| 5  Thrust washer | 14  Washer | 21  Pinion shaft needle |
| 6  Circlip | 15  Synchro-hub retaining | roller bearing |
| 7  Thrust washer | screw | 22  Needle roller bearing |
| 8  Needle roller bearing | 16  Selector fork | retaining screw |
| 9  Mainshaft 5th gear | | |

15.8 Engage two gears simultaneously by moving the selector forks with a screwdriver

15.16a Suitable apparatus for removing the main casing – in position

15.16b By tightening the centre screw the casing is drawn off the bearing

14 Prise the plastic cap from the centre of the left-hand side drive flange, extract the circlip and washer, and withdraw the flange using a two-legged puller.

15 Using a Torx driver bit and ratchet or bar, undo and remove the four bolts securing the mainshaft bearing retainer to the gearbox housing.

16 Undo and remove the bolts securing the main casing to the gear carrier housing. Using strips of angle iron, or suitable alternatives, make up a removal bracket to enable the casing to be drawn off the mainshaft (photo). Fasten a bar or piece of angle iron across the clutch housing in such a manner as to support the end of the mainshaft. Tighten the centre screw of the casing separator tool until it touches a suitable thrust pad placed over the end of the mainshaft (or a steel ball placed in the hollow centre) and then continue tightening until the casing is pulled away (photo), leaving the mainshaft bearing complete on the mainshaft.

17 Lift the casing off and recover the shim located against the bearing outer race (where fitted). Remove the gasket and the magnet from the gear carrier housing, and disconnect the removal brackets.

## 16 Gearbox (five-speed) mainshaft, pinion shaft and differential – removal

1 Withdraw the selector fork rod from the gear carrier housing, disengage the forks from the synchro sleeves and remove the fork set sideways as a complete assembly.

2 Undo and remove the two bolts securing the reverse gear relay lever pillars to the housing and lift off the pillars and relay lever.

3 Withdraw the reverse idler shaft and remove the shaft and gear from the gear carrier housing.

4 Extract the circlip from the end of the pinion shaft, then lift the mainshaft assembly out of the gear carrier housing while at the same time sliding 4th gear off the pinion shaft.

5 Extract the remaining circlip from the pinion shaft and then, using a suitable long two-legged puller, pull the 3rd and 2nd gears off the pinion shaft together.

6 Withdraw the 2nd gear needle roller bearing.

7 Position the legs of the puller beneath 1st gear and pull off the

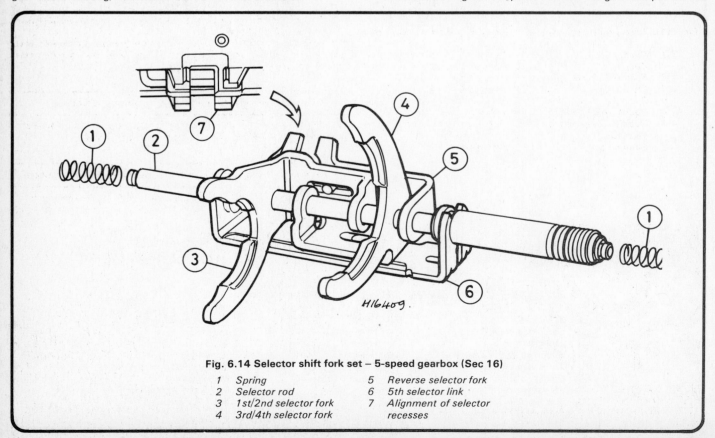

**Fig. 6.14 Selector shift fork set – 5-speed gearbox (Sec 16)**

1  Spring
2  Selector rod
3  1st/2nd selector fork
4  3rd/4th selector fork
5  Reverse selector fork
6  5th selector link
7  Alignment of selector recesses

needle roller bearing inner race, 1st/2nd synchro unit and 1st gear together as an assembly.

8    Withdraw the 1st gear needle roller bearing and thrust washer.

9    Undo and remove the four bolts securing the bearing retaining plate, then remove the plate and the pinion shaft from the gear carrier housing. Note that the retaining plate incorporates the reverse gear stop which locates beneath the reverse gear.

10  Remove the remaining differential drive flange, as described in Section 15, paragraph 14.

## 17  Gearbox (five-speed) gear carrier housing – overhaul

1    The procedure for overhaul of the gear carrier housing is identical to that for the four-speed gearbox, and reference should be made to Section 7.

2    The three oil seals in the main casing should be removed by prising them out, noting their fitted direction, and fitting new seals using a block of wood, large socket or tube to drive them in. Fill the lips of the seals with multi-purpose grease before fitting.

3    If required the needle roller bearing for the pinion shaft can be removed using a suitable extractor. Do not remove the bearing unless renewal is necessary as it will probably be damaged during removal.

4    If the differential outer race requires renewal, this should be left to a BL dealer, as the bearings must also be renewed – requiring accurate setting up using jigs and fixtures.

5    If the mainshaft has been dismantled, or if the mainshaft bearing has been removed, it should now be fitted to the main casing.

6    Position the bearing on the casing with the plastic side facing outward. If there were any shims recovered during dismantling, these should be fitted between the bearing and casing.

7    Drive the bearing into position and then refit the bearing retaining plate (photos). Secure the plate with the four Torx screws (photo).

8    To remove the clutch release mechanism from the end cover, pierce the end cap using a sharp tool and prise it out. A new cap must be obtained when refitting.

9    Extract the two circlips retaining the release lever in position on the shaft.

10  Withdraw the release arm and shaft and remove the lever and spring.

11  Inspect the components for signs of wear and renew as necessary. Renew the shaft oil seal.

12  Refit the components of the release mechanism to the end cover using the reverse sequence to removal. Tap a new end cap into place using a hammer and block of wood.

## 18  Gearbox (five-speed) pinion shaft bearings – renewal

1    The procedure is identical to that described for the four-speed gearbox, and reference should be made to Section 9.

## 19  Gearbox (five-speed) mainshaft – dismantling and reassembly

1    Extract the circlip securing the ball-bearing to the mainshaft.

2    Using a press, or a hydraulic puller with its legs positioned beneath

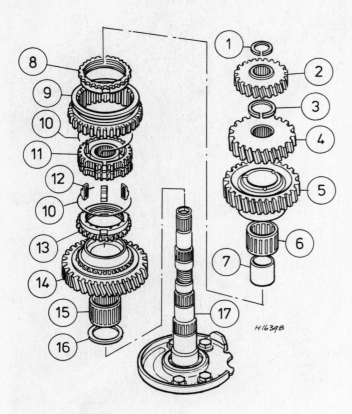

**Fig. 6.15 Pinion shaft components – five-speed gearbox (Sec 16)**

| | | | |
|---|---|---|---|
| 1 | Circlip | 9 | 1st/2nd synchro sleeve |
| 2 | 4th gear | 10 | Retaining spring |
| 3 | Selected circlip | 11 | 1st/2nd synchro-hub |
| 4 | 3rd gear | 12 | Synchro key |
| 5 | 2nd gear | 13 | 1st gear baulk ring |
| 6 | Needle roller bearing | 14 | 1st gear |
| 7 | Needle roller bearing | 15 | Needle roller bearing |
| | inner race | 16 | Thrust washer |
| 8 | Baulk ring | 17 | Pinion shaft |

H1639B

17.7a Refit the mainshaft bearing to the main casing ...

17.7b ... fit the bearing retaining plate ...

17.7c ... and secure the plate with the Torx screws

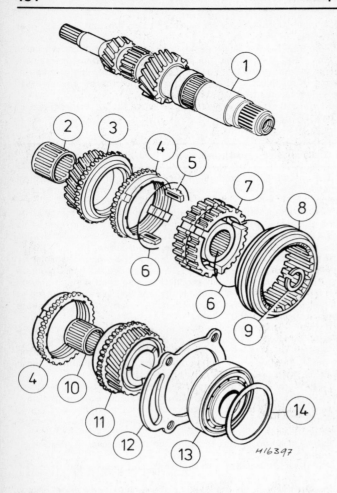

Fig. 6.16 Mainshaft components – five-speed gearbox (Sec 19)

| | | | |
|---|---|---|---|
| 1 | Mainshaft | 8 | Synchro sleeve |
| 2 | Needle roller bearing | 9 | Circlip |
| 3 | 3rd gear | 10 | Needle roller bearing |
| 4 | Baulk ring | 11 | 4th gear |
| 5 | Synchro hub | 12 | Bearing retaining plate |
| 6 | Retaining spring | 13 | Mainshaft bearing |
| 7 | Synchro-hub | 14 | Shim (where fitted) |

19.6a Slide the 3rd gear needle roller bearing ...

19.6b ... and 3rd gear onto the mainshaft

19.6c Place the baulk ring on the gear

4th gear, draw the gear and bearing off the mainshaft.
3   Remove the 4th gear needle roller bearing and extract the circlip securing the 3rd/4th gear synchro-hub to the shaft.
4   Again using a press or hydraulic puller remove 3rd gear and the 3rd/4th synchro-hub from the mainshaft as an assembly.
5   Withdraw the 3rd gear needle roller bearing.
6   Begin reassembly by sliding the 3rd gear needle roller bearing and 3rd gear onto the mainshaft (photos). Place the baulk ring onto 3rd gear (photo).
7   Heat the 3rd/4th synchro-hub in an oven to approximately 248°F (120°C). Place the hub on the mainshaft with the identifying groove in the hub boss towards 4th gear, and drive the synchro-hub assembly into position using a hammer and suitable tube. Make sure that the slots in the baulk ring engage with the keys in the synchro-hub assembly as it is fitted.
8   Secure the synchro-hub in position using the circlip (photo).
9   Place the baulk ring against the synchro-hub assembly with the slots aligned with the keys (photo).
10  Slide the needle roller bearing onto the mainshaft and refit 4th gear (photos).

19.8 Refit the 3rd/4th synchro unit and secure with the circlip

19.9 Fit the baulk ring to the synchro unit with the slots engaged with the synchro keys

19.10a Slide the needle roller bearing onto the mainshaft ...

19.10b ... and fit 4th gear

22.1 Lay the differential in place in the gear carrier housing

22.4a With the pinion bearings in position ...

22.4b ... place the pinion shaft in the gear carrier housing

22.5a Refit the bearing retaining plate ...

22.5b ... and tighten the bolts to the specified torque

22.6 Fit the thrust washer to the pinion shaft

22.7a Slide on 1st gear needle roller bearing ...

22.7b ... followed by 1st gear ...

## 20 Gearbox (five-speed) synchroniser units – inspection

1    The procedure is the same as for the four-speed gearbox, and reference should be made to Section 11.
2    Note that when reassembling the 5th gear synchroniser, the chamfer on the sleeve splines must face toward the hub boss.

## 21 Gearbox (five-speed) differential unit – inspection

The procedure is the same as for the four-speed gearbox, and reference should be made to Section 12.

## 22 Gearbox (five-speed) differential, pinion shaft and mainshaft – reassembly

1    Refit the differential unit in the gear carrier housing (photo).
2    Fit the right-hand drive flange and drive it fully into position using a hammer and a suitable tube.
3    Refit the spring washer, retaining circlip and a new plastic cap. In order to overcome the resistance of the spring washer, locate the circlip on the washer and then compress both the washer and circlip with a piece of tubing. The circlip will then snap into its groove.
4    With the bearings in position on the pinion shaft (photo), place the shaft in the gear carrier housing and mesh it with the differential gear (photo).
5    Fit the bearing retaining plate and tighten the bolts to the specified torque (photos).
6    Place the thrust washer over the pinion shaft with the shoulder on its internal diameter towards the pinion (photo).
7    Slide on the 1st gear needle roller bearing followed by 1st gear and the baulk ring (photos).
8    Heat the assembled 1st/2nd synchro unit in an oven to approximately 248°F (120°C) and then, with the identifying groove in the hub circumference towards 1st gear, drive the unit onto the pinion shaft using a hammer and a suitable tube or a press. As the unit is fitted align the slots in the 1st gear baulk ring so that they engage with the keys of the synchro unit.

9    Heat the 2nd gear needle roller bearing inner race and slide it over the pinion shaft and position it in contact with the shoulder on the shaft (photo).
10    Position the needle roller bearing over the inner race (photo) and then refit the baulk ring and 2nd gear (photos).
11    Place the 3rd gear on the pinion shaft with its boss facing 2nd gear (photo), and drive or press it onto the shaft (photo).
12    Fit the circlip to the pinion shaft groove above 3rd gear and then, using feeler gauges, measure the clearance between the gear and circlip (3rd gear axial movement) (photo). If the clearance is in excess of the specified amount, an oversize circlip must be fitted. Circlips are available in a range of thicknesses from 0.098 in (2.5 mm) to 0.118 in (3.0 mm), in 0.004 in (0.1 mm) increments.
13    At this stage the mainshaft must be fitted in position on the gear carrier housing (photo). Engage its end into the needle roller bearing and bring the gears into mesh.
14    Place 4th gear, boss upwards, on the pinion shaft (photo) and secure with the retaining circlip (photo).
15    Ensure that the reverse gear stop is in place on the pinion shaft bearing retaining plate and then refit the reverse idler gear and shaft (photo).
16    Locate the magnet in its location in the gear carrier housing (photo).
17    Engage the selector forks with their respective gears and position the forks and selector rod in the housing (photo).
18    Engage the forked end of the reverse gear relay lever with the reverse idler gear, and secure the relay lever pillars with the two retaining bolts (photo).

## 23 Gearbox (five-speed) – reassembling the housings

1    Check that the reverse idler shaft is positioned correctly, as shown in Fig. 6.10, and set the geartrain by moving the selector forks to neutral.
2    Fit a new gasket on the gear carrier flange and then carefully lower the main casing over the gears, shafts and selector rod (photo).
3    Support the clutch housing end of the mainshaft with an angle iron bracket and thrust screw, as described during removal, or on a

22.7c ... and the baulk ring

22.9 Fit the 2nd gear needle roller bearing inner race

22.10a Place the needle roller bearing over the inner race

22.10b Fit the baulk ring ...

22.10c ... and slide on 2nd gear

22.11a Place 3rd gear on the pinion shaft ...

22.11b ... and drive it into place using a tube and hammer

22.12 Fit the 3rd gear retaining circlip and measure the 3rd gear axial movement

22.13 Position the assembled mainshaft on the gear carrier housing

22.14a Fit 4th gear to the pinion shaft ...

22.14b ... and secure with the retaining circlip

22.15 Fit the reverse idler gear and shaft

22.16 Place the magnet in its location in the housing

22.17 Refit the selector forks and rod to the housing

22.18 Engage the relay lever with the reverse idler gear and refit the relay lever pillar retaining bolts

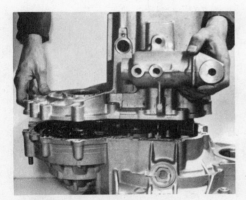

23.2 Refit the main casing to the gear carrier housing

23.3 Use a suitable tube and hammer to drive the bearing onto the mainshaft

23.4 Refit the reverse idler shaft lockbolt

block of wood. Using a tube against the mainshaft bearing inner race in the main casing, drive the bearing and the casing fully into position (photo).

4    Refit and tighten the reverse idler shaft lockbolt (photo), and then secure the gear carrier housing and main casing together — with the retaining bolts tightened to the specified torque.

5    Heat the 5th gear to 248°F (120°C) and fit it to the pinion shaft with the groove near its centre facing away from the main casing (photo).

6    Secure 5th gear with the thrust washer and circlip (photo).

7    Place the needle roller bearing and thrust washer in the mainshaft 5th gear, and place a new spacer bush in the selector fork. With the fork engaged with the synchroniser fit this assembly over the mainshaft and engage the selector fork and spacer over the selector rod (photo).

8    Hold the selector rod and, using right-angled circlip pliers or another suitable tool, turn the selector tube clockwise to engage the fork (photo). Screw the tube into the fork until the upper edge of the tube protrudes above the fork face by 0.197 in (5.0 mm) (photo).

9    Engage 5th and reverse gears simultaneously, as described in the removal procedure.

10   Apply a thin smear of thread locking compound to the threads of a new 5th gear synchroniser retaining screw and refit the screw and washer (photo). Tighten the screw to the specified torque.

11   Move the selector forks back to the neutral position and refit the selector shaft assembly, spring and end cover (photos). Apply a thin smear of thread locking compound to the threads of the end cover and tighten it using a spark plug box spanner or a suitable bolt with two nuts locked together on the bolt thread (photo).

12   Refit the selector shaft detent plunger or peg bolt (photo). If a detent plunger is fitted it should only be adjusted if the housing, selector shaft or detent plunger have been renewed.

   *(a)   Refer to Fig. 6.11. Slacken the locknut and screw in the adjusting sleeve until the lockring lifts off the adjusting sleeve*
   *(b)   Screw the adjusting sleeve out until the lockring just contacts the sleeve*
   *(c)   Check that the lockring lifts as soon as the shaft is turned, tighten the locknut and refit the plastic cap*

23.5 Fit 5th gear to the pinion shaft with its groove facing away from the casing

23.6 Secure 5th gear with the thrust washer and circlip

23.7 Fit the 5th gear synchronizer and selector fork assembly to the mainshaft

23.8a Turn the selector tube clockwise ...

23.8b ... until the tube protrudes above the fork face by the specified amount

23.10 Apply thread locking compound to the 5th gear synchroniser retaining screw and fit the screw and washer

23.11a Refit the selector shaft assembly ...

23.11b ... and the spring and end cover, with thread locking compound on the end cover

23.11c Tighten the end cover using a bolt head

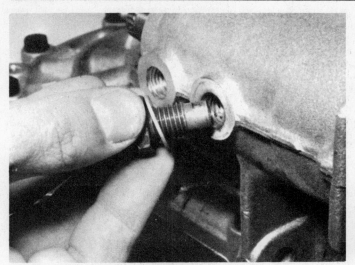

23.12 Refit the selector shaft peg bolt

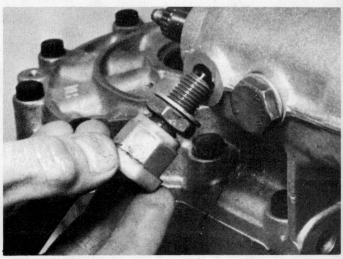

23.13 Refit the 5th gear detent plunger

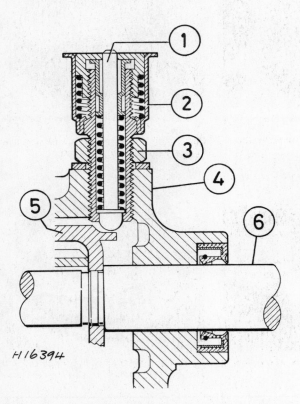

H16394

**Fig. 6.17 Sectional view of the 5th gear detent plunger – five-speed gearbox (Sec 23)**

| | | | |
|---|---|---|---|
| 1 | Centre pin | 4 | Main casing |
| 2 | Plunger | 5 | Selector shaft yoke |
| 3 | Locknut | 6 | Selector shaft |

13  Refit the 5th gear detent plunger (photo) and adjust it as follows if the casing, selector shaft or detent plunger have been renewed, or if too little or too much force is needed to overcome the 5th gear detent.

(a)  Select neutral and remove the plunger plastic cap
(b)  Slacken the locknut and screw in the plunger until the centre pin starts to lift
(c)  Slacken the plunger $\frac{1}{3}$ of a turn and tighten the locknut

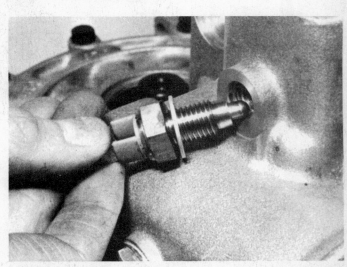

23.14 Refit the reversing lamp switch

14  Refit the reversing lamp switch (photo).
15  Make sure that the selector tube protrusion is still as described in paragraph 8, and then engage 5th gear. Check that, with 5th gear engaged and the selector fork held away from the gearbox to take up any free play, the synchro sleeve overlaps the hub teeth by at least 0.040 in (1.0 mm).
16  Mark the spacer bush 0.748 in (19 mm) below the upper edge of the selector tube (photo).
17  Peen the spacer bush in two places around its circumference at the places just marked (photo). Make sure that, after peening, the selector rod is still free to move up and down in the tube under its spring pressure (photo).
18  Place the clutch release bearing in its housing (photo) and, with a new gasket in place, refit the end cover to the main casing (photo).
19  Refit and tighten the end cover retaining bolts, noting that the two short bolts are fitted either side of the oil level/filler plug.
20  Refit the engine mounting bracket to the end cover (photo).
21  Refit the remaining differential drive flange, spring washer, circlip and plastic cap (photos).
22  Refit the selector shaft rubber boot (photo), position the selector shaft lever on the shaft and secure with the retaining nut (photo).
23  Attach the linkage support bracket to the main casing retaining bolt (photo).
24  Finally slide the clutch operating pushrod into the mainshaft (photo).

23.16 Mark the spacer bush at the specified position ...

23.17 ... and peen the bush in two places at that position

23.18a Fit the clutch release bearing to the end cover ...

23.18b ... and fit the end cover to the main casing

23.20 Refit the engine mounting bracket to the end cover

23.21a Fit the remaining differential drive flange ...

23.21b ... spring washer ...

23.21c ... retaining circlip ...

23.21d ... and plastic cap

## 24 Gear lever – adjustment

**Note:** *If the gearchange linkage is adjusted at any time, the selector rod lever must be renewed. This is necessary since serrations on the rod will have cut identical serrations in the bore of the lever, interfering with accurate adjustment. Refer also to Section 10 of Chapter 12 for details of a special tool which is now available for the adjustment.*

1   Jack up the front of the car and support it securely on axle stands.
2   From under the car, remove the plastic cap from the gear lever linkage rubber boot. Ensure that the gearbox is in neutral.
3   Slacken the clamp bolt securing the selector rod to the linkage and make sure that both the linkage and the rod move freely.
4   Refer to Fig. 6.19 and position the gear lever reverse stop as shown. Tighten the clamp bolt and check that all the gears can be engaged smoothly and positively and that the reverse stop is effective.
5   Refit the plastic cap to the rubber boot and lower the car to the ground.

## 25 Gear lever and linkage – removal and refitting

1   Jack up the front of the car and support it securely on stands.
2   From under the car, remove the plastic cap from the gear linkage rubber boot. Undo and remove the nut, washer and through-bolt securing the gear lever to the selector rod.
3   From inside the car, remove the centre console, as described in Chapter 11, undo and remove the two nuts and washers securing the gear lever to the floor and lift out the lever assembly.
4   To remove the selector rod and remote control linkage, extract the retaining clip and slide the gearchange rod out of the bush on the gearbox selector lever.
5   Disconnect the rear selector rod from the relay lever on the gearbox housing by prising off the balljoint using a screwdriver.
6   Undo and remove the two bolts securing the selector rod support bracket to the vehicle floor, and the nuts and bolts securing the linkage support bracket to the steering gear (photo).

23.22a Refit the selector shaft rubber boot ...

23.22b ... and the selector shaft lever

23.23 Attach the linkage support bracket to the main casing

23.24 Slide the clutch operating pushrod into the mainshaft

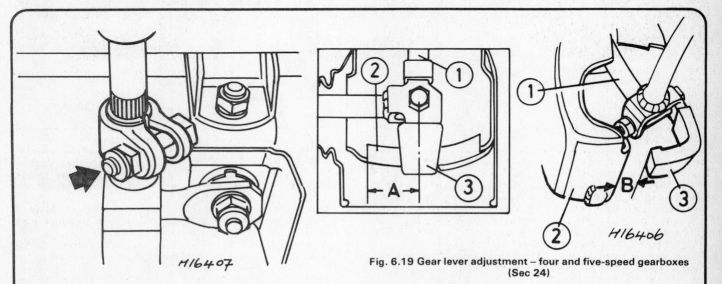

Fig. 6.18 Selector rod to linkage clamp bolt location – four and five-speed gearboxes (Sec 24)

Fig. 6.19 Gear lever adjustment – four and five-speed gearboxes (Sec 24)

1 Gear lever  A = 1.3 in (33 mm)
2 Stop plate  B = 0.61 in (15 mm)
3 Reverse stop

25.6 Gearshift linkage clamp bolt (A), selector rod support bracket retaining bolts (B) and (C)

7   Withdraw the linkage from under the car.
8   Refit in the reverse sequence to removal. When fitting the gear lever, ensure that the balljoint is well packed with grease. Adjust the gear lever as described in Section 24.

## 26 Differential oil seals – renewal

1   The differential oil seals may be renewed without removing the transmission from the vehicle. Mark the driveshaft-to-inboard flange alignment.
2   Disconnect the inboard ends of the driveshafts as described in Chapter 7 for manual gearbox models, and Chapter 12 for automatic transmission models.
3   Prise the end plug from the coupling flange, and then extract the circlip and spring washer.
4   Using a two- or three-legged puller as described in Chapter 6, Section 5, withdraw the coupling flange.
5   Lever out the oil seal and discard it.
6   Fit the new oil seal squarely, and fill its lips with grease.
7   Fit the coupling flange, spring washer and circlip after referring to Section 22.
8   Top up the oil or fluid level in the gearbox (manual gearbox) or final drive (automatic transmission).

## 27 Fault diagnosis – gearbox

| Symptom | Reason(s) |
| --- | --- |
| Gearbox noisy in neutral | Mainshaft (input shaft) bearings worn |
| Gearbox noisy only when moving (in all gears) | Pinion shaft (output shaft) bearings worn<br>Differential bearings worn |
| Gearbox noisy in only one gear | Worn, damaged, or chipped gear teeth |
| Jumps out of gear | Worn synchro-hubs or baulk rings<br>Worn selector shaft detent plunger or spring<br>Worn selector forks |
| Ineffective synchromesh | Worn baulk rings or synchro-hubs |
| Difficulty in engaging gears | Clutch fault<br>Gearshift mechanism out of adjustment |

# Chapter 7 Driveshafts

*For modifications, and information applicable to later models, see Supplement at end of manual*

## Contents

## Specifications

**Type** ................................................................................ Unequal length, solid (left-hand), tubular (right-hand), splined to inner and outer constant velocity joints

*Lubrication*
Assembly only – see text
Type:
    Outer constant velocity joint ............................................ Molycote grease VN2461/C, or equivalent
    Inner constant velocity joint ............................................. Mobil 525 grease, or equivalent
    Hub bearing water shield .................................................. Duckhams LBM 10 grease, or equivalent
Quantity:
    Outer constant velocity joint:
        1.3 litre models ........................................................ 78 cc
        1.6 litre models ........................................................ 90 cc
    Inner constant velocity joint:
        All models ................................................................. 180 cc

### Torque wrench settings

| | lbf ft | Nm |
|---|---|---|
| Driveshaft nut* | 140 to 160 | 190 to 220 |
| Inner joint to drive flange | 33 | 45 |
| Roadwheel nuts | 53 | 72 |

*Refer to Chapter 12, Section 12 for tightening procedure

## 1 General description

Drive is transmitted from the differential to the front wheels by means of two unequal length driveshafts. The right-hand driveshaft is a hollow construction and is of a larger diameter than the solid left-hand shaft. This is necessary to balance the torsional stiffness of both driveshafts so that an equal torque is applied to the front wheels under acceleration.

Both driveshafts are fitted with constant velocity joints at each end. The outer joints are of the Rzeppa ball and cage type and are splined to accept the driveshaft and wheel hub drive flange. The inner joints are of the sliding tripode type allowing lateral movement of the driveshaft during suspension travel. The inner joints are splined to the driveshafts and bolted to the differential drive flanges.

## 2 Maintenance and inspection

1 At regular intervals (see Routine Maintenance) carry out a thorough inspection of the driveshafts and joints as follows.
2 Jack up the front of the car and support it securely on axle stands.
3 Slowly rotate the roadwheel and inspect the condition of the outer joint rubber boots. Check for signs of cracking, splits or deterioration of the rubber which may allow the grease to escape and lead to water and grit entry into the joint. Also check the security and condition of the retaining clips. Repeat these checks on the inner constant velocity joints. If any damage or deterioration is found, the joints should be attended to, as described in Sections 4 or 5.
4 Continue rotating the roadwheel and check for any distortion or damage to the driveshafts. Check for any free play in the joints by holding the driveshaft firmly and attempting to rotate the wheel. Repeat this check whilst holding the differential drive flange. Any noticeable movement indicates wear in the joints, wear in the driveshaft splines, or loose joint retaining bolts or hub nut.
5 Lower the car to the ground, prise off the wheel trim, extract the split pin and check the tightness of the hub retaining nut. Fit a new split pin after aligning the holes and slots in the joint and hub nut. Refit the wheel trim.
6 Road test the car and listen for a metallic clicking from the front, as the car is driven slowly in a circle on full lock. If a clicking noise is heard this indicates wear in the outer constant velocity joint caused by excessive clearance between the balls in the joint and the recesses in which they operate. Remove and inspect the joint, as described in Section 5.
7 If vibration, consistent with roadspeed, is felt through the car when accelerating, there is a possibility of wear in the inner constant velocity joint. Remove and inspect the joint, as described in Section 4.

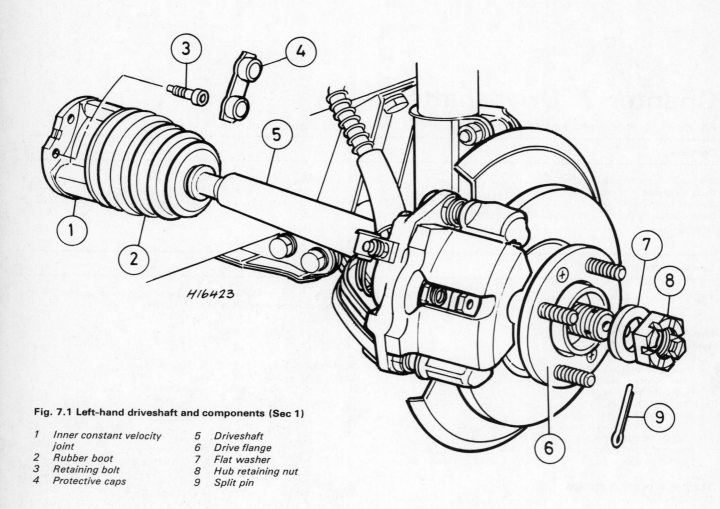

H16423

**Fig. 7.1 Left-hand driveshaft and components (Sec 1)**

| | |
|---|---|
| *1   Inner constant velocity* | *5   Driveshaft* |
| *     joint* | *6   Drive flange* |
| *2   Rubber boot* | *7   Flat washer* |
| *3   Retaining bolt* | *8   Hub retaining nut* |
| *4   Protective caps* | *9   Split pin* |

## 3   Driveshaft – removal and refitting

1   While the vehicle is standing on its wheels, firmly engage the handbrake and put the transmission in gear.

2   Prise off the wheel trim and extract the driveshaft nut retaining split pin. Using a suitable socket and bar, slacken the nut, but do not remove it at this stage.

3   Slacken the wheel nuts, jack up the front of the car and support it on axle stands. Remove the roadwheel and return the transmission to neutral. Remove the driveshaft nut and washer.

4   From underneath the car, make an alignment mark between the inner constant velocity joint flange and the differential drive flange, as an aid to reassembly.

5   Remove the protective caps over the inner joint retaining bolts and using an Allen key or suitable socket bit adaptor of the appropriate size, unscrew and remove the bolts (photos).

6   The procedure now varies slightly depending on whether the left-hand or right-hand driveshaft is being removed.

### Left-hand driveshaft

7   Ease the inner constant velocity joint away from the differential drive flange and lower the inner end of the shaft.

8   Withdraw the outer constant velocity joint from the wheel hub, lower the driveshaft to the ground and remove it from under the car. Withdraw the bearing water shield from the outer joint.

### Right-hand driveshaft

9   Extract the retaining clip and flat washer from the gearchange linkage pivot point directly above the inner constant velocity joint. Release the linkage from its pivot location and place it to one side.

10   Undo and remove the retaining screws and lift off the access cover from the inner wheel arch.

11   Ease the inner constant velocity joint away from the differential drive flange, raise the inner end of the shaft and allow the joint to rest on the flange.

12   Withdraw the outer constant velocity joint from the wheel hub (photo) and remove the driveshaft from under the wheel arch (photo). Withdraw the bearing water shield from the outer joint.

### Refitting

13   Refitting both driveshafts is the reverse sequence to removal, bearing in mind the following points:

(a)   *Fill the bearing water shield with the specified grease and position the shield on the outer joint flange before fitting the joint to the hub*

(b)   *If the original inner constant velocity joint is being refitted, ensure that the marks on the joint and differential drive flange made during removal are aligned*

(c)   *Tighten the inner joint retaining bolts to the specified torque and fit new protective caps. Tighten the driveshaft nut (refer to Chapter 12, Section 12 for tightening procedure). Do not attempt to fully tighten the driveshaft nut until the weight of the car is on its wheels*

3.5a Remove the protective caps ...

3.5b ... to expose the inner constant velocity joint retaining bolts (arrowed)

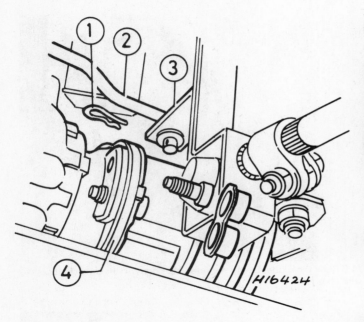

**Fig. 7.2 Gearchange linkage disconnection point (Sec 3)**

| 1 | Retaining clip | 4 | Inner constant velocity |
|---|----------------|---|-------------------------|
| 2 | Linkage arm   |   | joint |
| 3 | Pivot          |   | |

3.12a Withdraw the outer constant velocity joint from the wheel hub

3.12b Remove the driveshaft from the car

## 4 Inner constant velocity joint – removal, inspection and refitting

1   Remove the driveshaft from the car, as described in Section 3.
2   With the driveshaft on the bench, carefully prise up the tags securing the grease retaining plate (where fitted) to the joint outer member. Lift off the plate.
3   Cut off the outer metal retaining clip and inner rubber ring securing the rubber boot to the driveshaft and joint outer member.
4   Using circlip pliers, extract the circlip securing the joint inner member to the driveshaft.
5   Make an alignment mark between the end of the driveshaft and joint inner member to ensure correct reassembly. Withdraw the inner member, outer member, and the rubber boot.
6   Thoroughly clean the constant velocity joint inner and outer members using paraffin, or a suitable solvent. Dry with a lint-free rag,

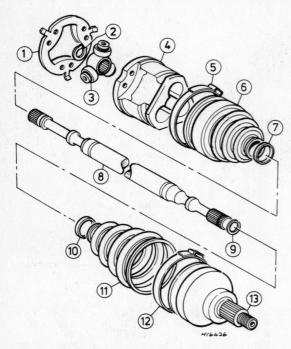

**Fig. 7.3 Exploded view of the constant velocity joints (Secs 4 and 5)**

| | |
|---|---|
| 1   *Grease retaining plate** | 7   *Retaining ring* |
| 2   *Circlip* | 8   *Driveshaft* |
| 3   *Inner joint inner member* | 9   *Circlip* |
| 4   *Inner joint outer member* | 10   *Retaining clip* |
| 5   *Retaining clip* | 11   *Rubber boot* |
| 6   *Rubber boot* | 12   *Retaining clip* |
| | 13   *Outer joint* |

**\*Note:** *Not fitted to all models*

or compressed air, and then inspect the joint as follows.

7   Examine the bearing tracks in the outer member for signs of scoring, wear ridges or evidence of lack of lubrication. Similarly examine the three bearing caps on the inner member. Check that each bearing cap turns evenly and smoothly on its roller bearings with no trace of tight spots. Insert the inner member into the outer member and check for excessive side movement of the bearing caps in their tracks, and of the inner member in the bearing caps.

8   If any of the above checks indicate wear in the joint, it will be necessary to renew the driveshaft and inner joint as an assembly; they are not available separately. If the joint is in satisfactory condition, obtain a repair kit consisting of a new rubber boot, retaining clips, and the correct quantity of grease (photo).

9   Apply a little rubber grease to the boot inner rubber retaining ring and slide it onto the shaft up to the shoulder (photo).

10   Slide on the new rubber boot (photo) and ease the retaining ring over its end to secure it in position (photo).

11   Place the joint outer member in position and carefully ease the rubber boot over its inner end using a screwdriver, or other suitable flat tool (photo).

12   Position the metal retaining ring over the rubber boot and engage one of the slots in the clip end over the small tag. Make sure the clip is as tight as possible and, if necessary, use a screwdriver to ease the slot over the tag (photo).

13   Fully tighten the clip by squeezing the raised portion with pliers (photo).

14   Pack the joint inner and outer members with the specified quantity of the grease supplied in the kit (photo) and then slide the inner member onto the shaft (photo). Ensure that the reference marks made during removal are aligned.

15   Secure the joint inner member with the retaining circlip (photo).

16   Place the grease retaining plate (where fitted) over the end of the outer member, and bend over the tags to secure it in place (photo).

17   The driveshaft can now be refitted to the car as described in Section 3.

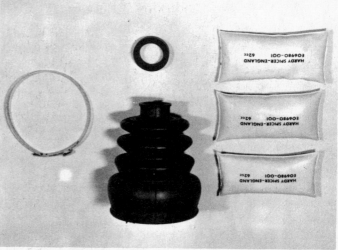

4.8 Components of the inner constant velocity joint repair kit

4.9 Slide the rubber boot inner retaining ring onto the driveshaft up to the shoulder

4.10a Fit the rubber boot ...

4.10b ... and secure the inner end of the boot with the retaining ring

4.11 Ease the other end of the boot over the joint outer member

4.12 Hook the retaining clip slot over the clip tag, making sure it is tight

4.13 Tighten the clip fully by squeezing the raised portion

4.14a Pack the outer member with the special grease ...

4.14b ... and then slide on the inner member

4.15 Secure the inner member with the retaining circlip

4.16 Secure the grease retaining plate in position by bending over the tags

## 5 Outer constant velocity joint – removal, inspection and refitting

1  Remove the driveshaft, as described in Section 3.
2  With the driveshaft on the bench, cut off the two rubber boot retaining clips and fold back the boot to expose the outer joint.
3  Firmly grasp the driveshaft, or support it in a vice. Using a hide, or plastic mallet, sharply strike the outer edge of the joint and drive it off the shaft. The outer joint is retained on the driveshaft by an internal circular section circlip and striking the joint in the manner described forces the circlip to contract into a groove, so allowing the joint to slide off.
4  With the constant velocity joint removed from the driveshaft, thoroughly clean the joint using paraffin, or a suitable solvent, and dry it, preferably using compressed air. Carry out a careful visual inspection of the joint, paying particular attention to the following areas.

5  Move the inner splined driving member from side to side to expose each ball in turn at the top of its track. Examine the balls for cracks, flat spots or signs of surface pitting.
6  Inspect the ball tracks on the inner and outer members. If the tracks have widened, the balls will no longer be a tight fit. At the same time check the ball cage windows for wear or for cracking between the balls. Wear in the balls, ball tracks and ball cage windows will lead to the characteristic clicking noise on full lock described previously.
7  If any of the above checks indicate wear in the joint it will be necessary to renew it complete, as the internal parts are not available separately. If the joint is in a satisfactory condition, obtain a repair kit consisting of a new rubber boot, retaining clips, and the correct quantity of grease.
8  The help of an assistant will be necessary whilst refitting the joint to the driveshaft. Ensure that the circlip is undamaged and correctly located in its groove in the driveshaft. Position the new rubber boot over the shaft and locate its end in the shaft groove.
9  Place the retaining clip over the rubber boot and wrap it round

until the slot in the clip end can be engaged with the tag. Make sure the clip is as tight as possible using pliers, or a screwdriver, if necessary. Fully tighten the clip by squeezing the raised portion with pliers.

10 Fold back the rubber boot and position the constant velocity joint over the splines on the driveshaft until it abuts the circlip.

11 Using two small screwdrivers placed either side of the circlip, compress the clip and at the same time have your assistant firmly strike the end of the joint with a hide, or plastic, mallet.

12 The joint should slide over the compressed circlip and into position on the shaft. It will probably take several attempts until you achieve success. If the joint does not spring into place the moment it is struck, remove it, reposition the circlip and try again. Do not force the joint, otherwise the circlip will be damaged.

13 With the joint in position against the retaining collar, pack it thoroughly with the specified quantity of the grease supplied in the repair kit. Work the grease well into the ball tracks while twisting the joint, and fill the rubber boot with any excess.

14 Ease the rubber boot over the joint and secure it with the retaining clip, as described in paragraph 9.

15 The driveshaft can now be refitted to the car, as described in Section 3.

## 6 Fault diagnosis – driveshafts

| Symptom | Reason(s) |
| --- | --- |
| Vibration and/or noise on turns | Worn constant velocity outer joint(s) |
| Vibration when accelerating | Worn constant velocity inner joint(s)<br>Bent or distorted driveshaft |
| Noise on taking up drive | Worn driveshaft or constant velocity joint splines<br>Loose driveshaft-to-hub nut<br>Worn constant velocity joints |

*See also Fault diagnosis – suspension and steering*

# Chapter 8 Braking system

*For modifications, and information applicable to later models, see Supplement at end of manual*

## Contents

## Specifications

**System type** .............................................. Diagonally split, dual circuit hydraulic with discs at the front and drums at the rear. Gravity pressure (GP) regulating valve in rear hydraulic circuit. Cable operated handbrake on rear wheels. Servo-assistance on all models

**Brake fluid type/specification** ..................... Hydraulic fluid to FMVSS 116 DOT 4 or SAE J1703 C (Duckhams Universal Brake and Clutch Fluid)

### Front brakes
Type ........................................................... Disc with single piston sliding calipers
Disc diameter ............................................... 9.5 in (241.3 mm)
Disc thickness .............................................. 0.497 to 0.507 in (12.623 to 12.878 mm)
Minimum pad thickness ................................... 0.125 in (3.175 mm)

### Rear brakes
Type ........................................................... Single leading shoe drum, self-adjusting
Drum diameter .............................................. 8 in (203 mm)
Lining width ................................................. 1.5 in (38.1 mm)
Minimum lining thickness ................................ 0.0625 in (1.588 mm)
Wheel cylinder diameter .................................. 0.687 in (17.449 mm)
Handbrake lever stop endfloat ......................... 0 to 0.080 in (0 to 2.032 mm)

### General
Master cylinder bore diameter ........ .................. 0.81 in (20.57 mm)
Servo unit boost ratio ..................................... 3:1

### Torque wrench settings

|  | lbf ft | Nm |
|---|---|---|
| Bleed screws | 7 | 10 |
| Brake caliper-to-swivel hub bolts | 53 | 72 |
| Twin GP valve mounting bolts | 9 | 12 |
| Guide pin bolts | 24 | 33 |
| Master cylinder mounting nuts | 9 | 12 |
| Servo mounting nuts | 9 | 12 |
| Wheel cylinder-to-backplate bolts | 5 | 7 |
| Rear hub retaining nut | 50 | 68 |
| Wheel nuts | 53 | 72 |
| Brake disc to drive flange | 8 | 11 |

## 1 General description

The braking system is of the servo-assisted, dual circuit hydraulic type with disc brakes at the front and drum brakes at the rear. A diagonally split dual circuit hydraulic system is employed in which each circuit operates one front and one diagonally opposite rear brake from a tandem master cylinder. Under normal conditions both circuits operate in unison; however, in the event of hydraulic failure in one circuit, full braking force will still be available at two wheels. A pressure regulating device or 'twin GP' (Gravity Pressure) valve is incorporated in the rear brake hydraulic circuit. This valve regulates the pressure applied to each rear brake and reduces the possibility of the rear wheels locking under heavy braking.

The front disc brakes are operated by single piston sliding type calipers. At the rear, leading and trailing brake shoes are operated by twin piston wheel cylinders and are self-adjusting by footbrake application.

The handbrake provides an independent mechanical means of rear brake application.

Driver warning lights are provided for brake pad wear, low brake hydraulic fluid level and handbrake applied.

## 2    Maintenance and inspection

1    The brake hydraulic level should be checked weekly and, if necessary, topped up with the specified fluid to the MAX mark on the reservoir.

2    At regular intervals (see Routine Maintenance) the hydraulic pipes, hoses and unions should be carefully inspected for chafing, cracks, leaks and corrosion. Details will be found in Section 14. At the same time, check the disc pads and rear brake linings for wear, as described in Sections 3 and 6 respectively, and renew them and lubricate the exposed cables and linkages. If necessary adjust the handbrake cable, as described in Section 16. Check the condition and security of the brake servo vacuum hose.

3    The three braking system warning lights should also be checked at this service interval. Check the operation of the handbrake warning light by applying the handbrake with the ignition switched on. The light should illuminate when the handbrake is applied. To test the low brake hydraulic fluid level warning light, place the car in gear, release the handbrake and switch on the ignition. The light should illuminate when the flexible contact cover in the centre of the brake fluid reservoir filler cap is depressed. To check the disc pad wear warning indicator, locate the twin terminal black plastic socket which is in the wiring harness adjacent to the right-hand brake caliper. Switch on the ignition and connect a bridging wire between the terminals of one socket and earth; the pad wear warning light should be illuminated on the instrument panel. If any of the lights fail to illuminate in the test condition, then either the bulb is blown, a fuse is at fault, or there is

a fault in the circuit.

4    At less frequent intervals (see Routine Maintenance) renew the brake hydraulic fluid by draining the system and refilling with fresh fluid, as described in Section 15.

5    The flexible brake hoses and rubber seals in the brake calipers, wheel cylinders and master cylinder should also be renewed regularly (see Routine Maintenance). At the same time the air filter and non-return valve in the servo unit should be renewed. Details of these operations will be found in the relevant Sections of this Chapter.

## 3    Front disc pads – inspection and renewal

1    Apply the handbrake, prise off the front wheel trim and slacken the wheel nuts. Jack up the front of the car and support it securely on axle stands. Remove the roadwheels.

2    The thickness of the disc pads can now be checked by viewing through the slot in the front of the caliper body. If the lining on any of the pads is at, or below, the minimum specified thickness all four pads must be renewed as a complete set.

3    To renew the pads, first remove the protective cap over the caliper bleed screw (photo). Obtain a plastic or rubber tube of suitable diameter to fit snugly over the bleed screw and submerge the free end in a jar containing a small quantity of brake fluid.

4    Open the bleed screw half a turn and pull the caliper body toward you. This will push the piston back into its bore to facilitate removal and refitting of the pads. When the piston has moved in as far as it will go, close the bleed screw, remove the tube and refit the protective cap.

5    Disconnect the pad wear indicator wiring connector (right-hand caliper only) and, using a suitable spanner, unscrew the lower guide pin bolt while holding the guide pin with a second spanner.

6    The caliper body can now be pivoted upwards, allowing removal of the pads, as shown in Fig. 8.1. For greater access the upper guide pin bolt can also be removed (photo), enabling the caliper to be lifted clear (photo).

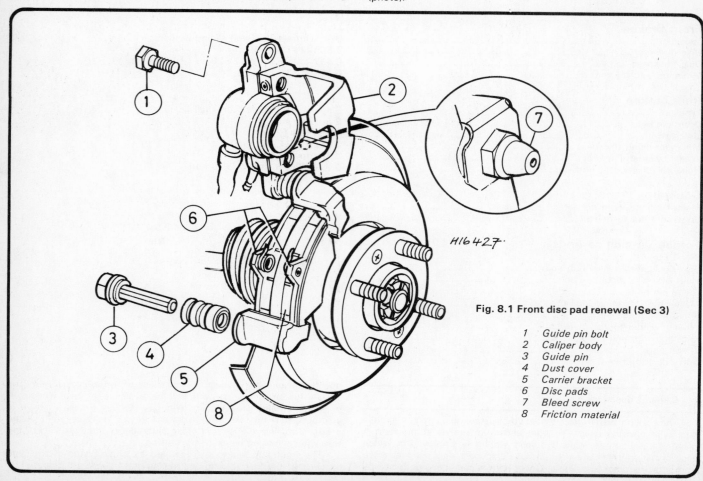

H16427.

**Fig. 8.1 Front disc pad renewal (Sec 3)**

1    Guide pin bolt
2    Caliper body
3    Guide pin
4    Dust cover
5    Carrier bracket
6    Disc pads
7    Bleed screw
8    Friction material

3.3 Front caliper bleed screw (A) and pad wear indicator wiring connector (B)

3.6a Removal of the caliper upper guide pin bolt (arrowed)

3.6b Removing the brake caliper body

3.7 With the caliper removed, lift out the disc pads

7   Withdraw the two disc pads (photo) and, where fitted, the anti-squeal shim.
8   Brush the dust and dirt from the caliper, piston, disc and pads, but **do not inhale**, as it is injurious to health.
9   Rotate the brake disc by hand and scrape away any rust and scale. Carefully inspect the entire surface of the disc and if there are any signs of cracks, deep scoring or severe abrasions, the disc must be renewed. Also inspect the caliper for signs of fluid leaks around the piston, corrosion, or other damage. Renew the piston seals or the caliper body as necessary.
10  To refit the pads first attach the anti-squeal shim (if fitted) to the outer pad. Very slightly smear the pad and caliper contact areas with a silicone grease, ensuring that no grease is allowed to come into contact with the friction material.
11  Place the pads in position against the disc, noting that the pad with the wear indicator lead is fitted to the inner position on the right-hand caliper.
12  Place the caliper body over the pads and refit the guide pin bolts. Tighten the bolts to the specified torque.
13  Reconnect the wear indicator wiring connector (where applicable), and refit the roadwheels – do not tighten the wheel nuts fully until the weight of the car is on the wheels.
14  Depress the brake pedal several times to bring the piston into contact with the pads and then lower the car to the ground. Check and, if necessary, top up the fluid in the master cylinder reservoir.

## 4  Front brake caliper – removal, overhaul and refitting

1   Apply the handbrake, prise off the front wheel trim and slacken the wheel nuts. Jack up the front of the car and support it securely on axle stands. Remove the roadwheel.
2   Using a suitable spanner, unscrew the guide pin bolts while holding the guide pins with a second spanner.
3   Disconnect the pad wear indicator wiring connector (right-hand side caliper only) and lift away the caliper body, leaving the disc pads and carrier bracket still in position. It is not necessary to remove the carrier bracket unless it requires renewal because of accident damage or severe corrosion.
4   With the flexible brake hose still attached to the caliper body, very slowly depress the brake pedal until the piston has been ejected just over halfway out of its bore.
5   Using a brake hose clamp or self-locking wrench with protected jaws, clamp the flexible brake hose. This will minimise brake fluid loss during subsequent operations.
6   Slacken the brake hose-to-caliper body union, and then, while holding the hose, rotate the caliper to unscrew it from the hose. Lift away the caliper and plug or tape over the end of the hose to prevent dirt entry.
7   With the caliper on the bench wipe away all traces of dust and dirt, but *avoid inhaling the dust as it is injurious to health.*

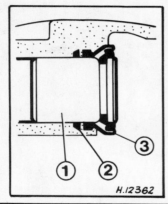

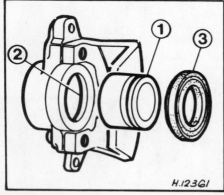

**Fig. 8.2 Front brake caliper components (Sec 4)**

| | | |
|---|---|---|
| 1 | Piston | 3 | Dust cover |
| 2 | Piston seal | | |

8   Withdraw the partially ejected piston from the caliper body and remove the dust cover.

9   Using a suitable blunt instrument, such as a knitting needle, carefully extract the piston seal from the caliper bore.

10   Clean all the parts in methylated spirit, or clean brake fluid, and wipe dry using a lint-free cloth. Inspect the piston and caliper bore for signs of damage, scuffing or corrosion and if these conditions are evident renew the caliper body assembly. Also renew the guide pins if bent or damaged.

11   If the components are in a satisfactory condition, a repair kit consisting of new seals and dust cover should be obtained.

12   Thoroughly lubricate the components and new seals with clean brake fluid and carefully fit the seal to the caliper bore.

13   Position the dust cover over the innermost end of the piston so that the caliper bore sealing lip protrudes beyond the base of the piston. Using a blunt instrument, if necessary, engage the sealing lip of the dust cover with the groove in the caliper. Now push the piston into the bore until the other sealing lip of the dust cover can be engaged with the groove in the piston. Having done this, push the piston fully into its bore. Ease the piston out again slightly, and make sure that the cover lip is correctly seating in the piston groove.

14   Remove the guide pins from the carrier bracket and smear them with a high melting-point brake grease. Fit new dust covers to the guide pins and refit them to the carrier bracket.

15   Hold the flexible brake hose and screw the caliper body back onto the hose.

16   With the piston pushed fully into its bore, refit the caliper and secure it with the guide pin bolts. Tighten the bolts to the specified torque.

17   Fully tighten the brake hose union and remove the clamp. If working on the right-hand caliper, reconnect the pad warning light wiring connector.

18   Refer to Section 15 and bleed the brake hydraulic system, noting that if precautions were taken to minimise fluid loss, it should only be necessary to bleed the relevant front wheel.

19   Refit the roadwheel and lower the car to the ground before fully tightening the wheel nuts and refitting the wheel trim.

## 5   Front brake disc – removal and refitting

1   Apply the handbrake, remove the front wheel trim and slacken the wheel nuts. Jack the front of the car up and support it securely on axle stands. Remove the roadwheel.

2   Rotate the disc by hand and examine it for deep scoring, grooving or cracks. Light scoring is normal, but, if excessive, the disc must be renewed. Any loose rust and scale around the outer edge of the disc can be removed by lightly tapping it with a small hammer while rotating the disc.

3   To remove the disc undo and remove the two bolts securing the carrier bracket to the swivel hub. Withdraw the caliper assembly, complete with pads, off the disc and support it to one side. Avoid straining the flexible brake hose.

4   Undo and remove the two screws securing the disc to the drive flange and withdraw the disc.

5   Refitting is the reverse sequence to removal. Ensure that the mating face of the disc and drive flange are thoroughly clean and tighten all retaining bolts to the specified torque.

## 6   Rear brake shoes – inspection and renewal

**Note:** *Although lining wear can be checked on later models by prising out the plug from the backplate, removal of the brake drum is recommended for a thorough inspection.*

1   Chock the front wheels, remove the rear wheel trim and slacken the rear wheel nuts. Jack up the rear of the car and support it securely on axle stands. Remove the roadwheel and release the handbrake.

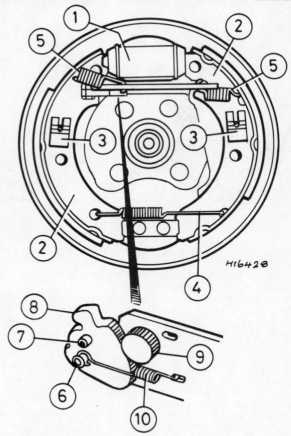

**Fig. 8.3 Rear brake assembly – left-hand side (Sec 6)**

| | | | |
|---|---|---|---|
| 1 | Wheel cylinder | 6 | Self-adjust quadrant |
| 2 | Brake shoes | | pivot pin |
| 3 | Hold-down springs | 7 | Hollow pin |
| 4 | Lower return spring | 8 | Quadrant |
| 5 | Upper return springs | 9 | Ratchet wheel |
| | | 10 | Operating spring |

6.3 Rear hub retaining nut and flat washer

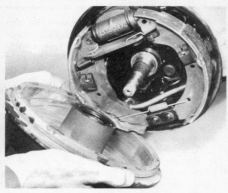

6.4 Removing the hub and brake drum assembly from the stub axle

6.8 Layout and position of the rear brake components

6.9 Brake shoe hold-down springs and pins

6.10 Brake shoe lower return spring

6.11 Removing the brake shoe upper return spring

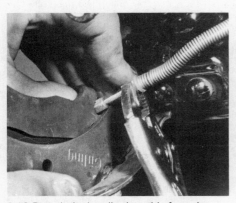

6.12 Detach the handbrake cable from the operating lever on the trailing shoe

6.13a Apply a trace of silicone grease to the brake shoe contact areas (arrowed)

6.13b Brake shoe self-adjust mechanism

6.15 Self-adjust mechanism is fully retracted when the hollow pin (arrowed) locates in the cutaway of the operating lever

6.17 Ensure the brake shoe locates correctly around the hollow pin (arrowed)

2   By judicious tapping and levering remove the hub cap and extract the split pin from the hub retaining nut.

3   Using a large socket and bar, undo and remove the hub retaining nut and flat washer (photo). *Note that the left-hand nut has a left-hand thread and the right-hand nut has a conventional right-hand thread.* **Take care not to tip the car from the axle stands.** If the hub nuts are particularly tight, temporarily refit the roadwheel and lower the car to the ground. Slacken the nut in this more stable position and then raise and support the car before removing the nut.

4   Withdraw the hub and brake drum assembly from the stub axle (photo). If it is not possible to withdraw the hub due to the brake drum binding on the brake shoes, the following procedure should be adopted. Refer to Section 16, if necessary, and slacken off the handbrake cable at the adjuster. From the rear of the brake backplate, prise out the handbrake lever stop, which will allow the brake shoes to retract sufficiently from the hub assembly to be removed. It will, however, be necessary to remove the brake shoes and fit a new handbrake lever stop to the backplate.

5   With the brake drum assembly removed, brush or wipe the dust from the brake drum, brake shoes and backplate. *Take great care not to inhale the dust, as it is injurious to health.*

6   Measure the brake shoe lining thickness. If it is worn down to the specified minimum amount, or if it is nearly worn down to the rivets, renew all four rear brake shoes. The shoes must also be renewed if any are contaminated with brake fluid or grease, or show signs of cracking or glazing. If contamination is evident, the cause must be traced and cured before fitting new brake shoes.

7   If the brake shoes are in a satisfactory condition proceed to paragraph 19; if removal is necessary, proceed as follows.

8   First make a careful note of the location and position of the various springs and linkages as an aid to refitting (photo).

9   Depress the brake shoe hold-down springs (photo) while supporting the hold down pin from the rear of the backplate with your finger. Turn the springs through 90° and lift off. Withdraw the hold down pins.

10  Using a screwdriver, if necessary, release the shoes from their lower pivots and disengage the lower return spring (photo).

11  Using long-nosed pliers, release the upper return spring from the leading shoe and the arm of the self-adjust mechanism (photo). Detach the leading shoe from the wheel cylinder and self-adjust mechanism, and remove it from the backplate.

12  Withdraw the trailing shoe from the backplate, move the handbrake operating lever away from the shoe and unhook the handbrake cable (photo). Release the upper return spring and detach the self-adjust mechanism from the trailing brake shoe.

13  Before fitting the new brake shoes clean off the brake backplate with a rag and apply a trace of silicone grease to the brake shoe contact areas (photo). Clean the self-adjust mechanism and make sure that it is free to move in its elongated slot (photo).

14  Refit the self-adjust mechanism to the trailing brake shoe and secure with the return spring.

15  Position the self-adjust mechanism in the fully retracted position by moving the quadrant away from the ratchet wheel and turning it until the hollow pin locates the inner cutaway (photo).

16  Connect the handbrake cable to the operating lever and position the trailing shoe on the backplate.

17  Refit the leading shoe to the backplate, ensuring that the shoe is properly located around the pin on the self-adjust mechanism (photo).

18  Refit the upper and lower return springs and the hold-down springs and pins.

19  Refit the brake drum and hub assembly, flat washer and hub retaining nut. Tighten the hub retaining nut to the specified torque and then tighten further until a split pin hole is aligned. Fit a new split pin and tap on the hub cap.

20  Refit the roadwheel, but do not fully tighten the wheel nuts.

21  If it was necessary to slacken the handbrake cable to enable the brake drum to be removed, adjust the cable as described in Section 16.

22  Lower the car to the ground, tighten the wheel nuts to the specified torque and refit the wheel trim. Depress the footbrake two or three times to operate the brake adjusters.

---

**7   Rear wheel cylinder – removal and refitting**

---

1   Begin by removing the rear hub and brake drum assembly, as described in Section 6, paragraphs 1 to 5 inclusive.

2   Using a screwdriver, or other suitable tool, carefully ease the upper end of the leading brake shoe (the one nearest the front of the car) away from the wheel cylinder piston. Take care not to damage the wheel cylinder rubber boot as you do this. As the leading shoe is moved away from the wheel cylinder, the self-adjust mechanism will expand and hold both brake shoes in the expanded position. This will provide sufficient clearance to allow removal of the wheel cylinder.

3   Using a brake hose clamp, or self-locking wrench with protected jaws, clamp the flexible brake hose just in front of the rear axle pivot mounting. This will minimise brake fluid loss during subsequent operations.

4   At the rear of the brake backplate unscrew the union nut securing the brake pipe to the wheel cylinder. Carefully ease the pipe out of the cylinder and plug or tape over its end to prevent dirt entry.

5   Undo and remove the two bolts securing the wheel cylinder to the backplate and withdraw the cylinder from between the brake shoes.

6   To refit the wheel cylinder, place it in position on the backplate and engage the brake pipe and union. Screw in the union nut two or three turns to ensure the thread has started.

7   Refit the wheel cylinder retaining bolts and tighten them to the specified torque. Now fully tighten the brake pipe union nut.

8   Using a screwdriver or other suitable tool, as before, ease the leading brake shoe away from the wheel cylinder and retract the self-adjust mechanism. To do this move the quadrant, in its elongated slot, away from the ratchet wheel and turn it until the hollow pin contacts the cutaway in the operating lever. As you do this, ease the brake shoes back into their upper locations in the wheel cylinder pistons.

9   Refit the brake drum and hub assembly, flat washer and hub retaining nut. Tighten the hub retaining nut to the specified torque and then tighten further until a split pin hole is aligned. Fit a new split pin and tap on the hub cap.

10  Remove the clamp from the brake hose and bleed the brake hydraulic system, as described in Section 15. Providing suitable precautions were taken to minimise loss of fluid, it should only be necessary to bleed the relevant rear wheel.

11  If it was necessary to slacken the handbrake cable to remove the brake drum, adjust the cable, as described in Section 16.

12  Refit the roadwheel, but do not tighten the wheel nuts fully.

13  Lower the car to the ground and tighten the wheel nuts. Depress the footbrake two or three times to operate the brake adjusters.

---

**8   Rear wheel cylinder – overhaul**

---

**Note:** *Before commencing a rear wheel cylinder overhaul, be certain that any suspected leak actually exists; it is possible to misinterpret the very small amounts of hydraulic fluid and assembly grease normally found under the dust seals as being indicative of a leak.*

1   Remove the wheel cylinder from the car, as described in the previous Section.

2   With the wheel cylinder on the bench, remove the dust cover retainers, where fitted, and withdraw the dust covers from the ends of the pistons and cylinder body.

3   Withdraw the pistons and piston spring. Remove the seals from the pistons and unscrew the bleed screw from the cylinder body.

4   Thoroughly clean all the components in methylated spirits or clean brake fluid, and dry with a lint-free rag.

5   Carefully examine the surfaces of the pistons and cylinder bore for wear, score marks or corrosion and, if evident, renew the complete wheel cylinder. If the components are in a satisfactory condition, obtain a repair kit consisting of new seals and dust covers.

6   Dip the new seals and pistons in clean brake fluid and assemble the components wet, as follows.

7   Using your fingers, fit the new seals to the pistons with their sealing lips facing inwards.

8   Lubricate the cylinder bore with clean brake fluid and insert the spring followed by the two pistons. **Note:** *The piston with the slot in its end must face toward the front of the car when fitted.*

9   Place the dust covers over the pistons and cylinder and, where applicable, refit the dust cover retainers.

10  Screw the bleed screw into the cylinder body and then refit the wheel cylinder to the car, as described in the previous Section.

## 9 Rear brake backplate – removal and refitting

The rear brake backplate is removed in conjunction with the stub axle and details of this procedure will be found in Chapter 10, Section 12.

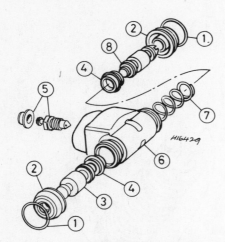

**Fig. 8.4 Exploded view of the right-hand rear wheel cylinder (Sec 8)**

| | |
|---|---|
| 1   Dust cover retainers (where fitted) | 5   Bleed screw and dust cap |
| 2   Dust cover | 6   Wheel cylinder body |
| 3   Trailing shoe piston | 7   Piston spring |
| 4   Piston seal | 8   Leading shoe piston |

## 10 Master cylinder – removal and refitting

1   Working under the front of the car, remove the dust cover from the bleed screw on each front brake caliper. Obtain two plastic or rubber tubes of suitable diameter to fit snugly over the bleed screws, and place the other ends in a suitable receptacle.

2   Open the bleed screws half a turn and operate the brake pedal until the master cylinder reservoir is empty. Tighten the bleed screws and remove the tubes. Discard the expelled brake fluid.

3   Disconnect the wiring connectors from the reservoir filler cap terminals.

4   Unscrew the two brake pipe union nuts and carefully withdraw the pipes from the master cylinder. Plug or tape over the ends of the pipes to prevent dirt entry, and place rags beneath the master cylinder to protect the surrounding paintwork.

5   Undo and remove the two retaining nuts and washers and withdraw the master cylinder from the servo unit.

6   Refitting the master cylinder is the reverse sequence to removal. Tighten the retaining nuts to the specified torque and, on completion, bleed the brake hydraulic system, as described in Section 15.

## 11 Master cylinder – overhaul

1   Remove the master cylinder from the car, as described in the previous Section. Drain any fluid remaining in the reservoir and prepare a clean uncluttered working surface, ready for dismantling.

2   Remove the primary piston assembly and then mount the cylinder horizontally in a soft-jawed vice. Using a parallel pin punch, drive out the two roll pins securing the reservoir to the cylinder body.

3   Lift off the reservoir and withdraw the two reservoir sealing washers from the master cylinder inlet ports.

4   Using a blunt instrument, push the secondary piston in as far as it will go and withdraw the secondary piston stop pin from its location in the secondary inlet port.

5   Slowly release the secondary piston, remove the cylinder from the vice, and tap it on a block of wood to release the secondary piston from the cylinder bore.

6   Note the location and position of the components on the secondary piston and then remove the piston spring. Withdraw the seal retainer followed by the seal and washer. Now remove the remaining seal from the other end of the secondary piston.

7   The primary piston should not be dismantled, as parts are not available separately. If the master cylinder is in a serviceable condition, and is to be reused, a complete new primary piston assembly is included in the repair kit.

8   With the master cylinder completely dismantled, clean all the components in methylated spirits, or clean brake fluid, and dry with a lint-free rag.

9   Carefully examine the cylinder bore and secondary piston for signs of wear, scoring or corrosion, and if evident renew the complete cylinder assembly.

10   If the components are in a satisfactory condition, obtain a repair kit consisting of new seals, springs and primary piston assembly.

11   Lubricate the master cylinder bore, pistons and seals thoroughly in clean brake fluid, and assemble them wet.

12   Fit the washer and seal onto the inner end of the secondary piston using your fingers only. Use the notes made during dismantling and the accompanying illustrations as a guide to the direction of fitment of the seal. Place the seal retainer over the seal and refit the spring. Fit the remaining seal to the other end of the secondary piston.

13   Insert the secondary piston into the cylinder bore, taking care not to turn over the lips of the seals as the piston is inserted.

14   Push the secondary piston down the cylinder bore as far as it will go and refit the stop pin into its hole in the inlet port.

15   Insert the new primary piston assembly into the cylinder bore, again taking care not to turn over the seal lips as they enter the bore.

16   Place the two reservoir seals into the inlet ports and refit the reservoir. Secure the reservoir with the two roll pins.

17   The master cylinder can now be refitted to the car, as described in the previous Section.

## 12 Twin GP valve – description and testing

1   The twin GP valve is mounted in the engine compartment and contains two gravity/pressure valves, one for each hydraulic circuit (photo).

2   The purpose of the valve is to distribute brake fluid to the front and rear brakes, and to limit the fluid pressure supplied to the rear brakes under heavy braking.

3   The operation of the valve may be suspect if one rear wheel continually locks during normal braking. It is essential, however, before condemning the valve, to ensure the fault does not lie with the brake shoe assemblies or wheel cylinders, and that adverse road conditions are also not responsible.

4   In the event of failure of the valve it must be renewed as an assembly, as parts are not available separately.

## 13 Twin GP valve – removal and refitting

1   Remove the master cylinder reservoir filler cap and place a piece of polythene over the filler neck. Secure the polythene in place with an elastic band ensuring that an airtight seal is obtained. This will minimise brake fluid loss during subsequent operations.

2   Place some rags around the valve to protect the paintwork from brake fluid spillage. Wash off any brake fluid that comes into contact with the body immediately, using copious amounts of cold water. Brake fluid is a very effective paint stripper.

3   Clean the area around the brake pipe unions thoroughly and unscrew the union nuts. Note that the nuts securing the primary brake pipes are of a smaller diameter than the secondary nuts. Very carefully withdraw the brake pipes from the valve.

4   Undo and remove the two bolts securing the valve to the inner member and withdraw the unit from the engine compartment.

5   Refitting is the reverse sequence to removal. Refer to Fig. 8.6 if in any doubt about the pipe locations, and bleed the brake hydraulic system, as described in Section 15, after refitting.

## 14 Hydraulic pipes and hoses – inspection, removal and refitting

1   At intervals given in Routine Maintenance carefully examine all

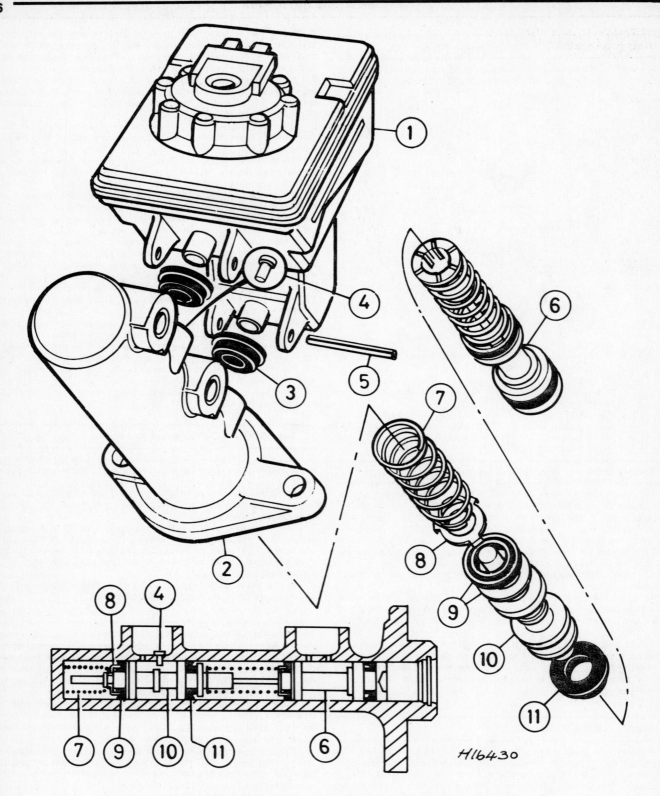

**Fig. 8.5 Master cylinder components and assembly details (Sec 11)**

1  Reservoir
2  Cylinder body
3  Reservoir sealing
   washers
4  Secondary piston stop pin

5  Roll pin
6  Primary piston assembly
7  Secondary piston spring
8  Seal retainer

9  Secondary piston seal
   and washer
10  Secondary piston
11  Secondary piston seal

H16430

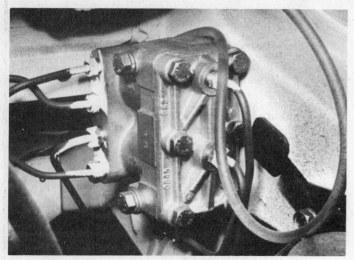

12.1 Location of the twin GP valve in the engine compartment

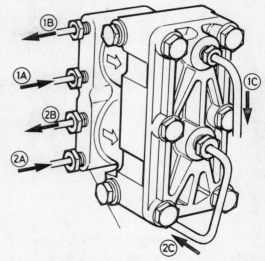

Fig. 8.6 Hydraulic pipe arrangement at twin GP valve (Sec 13)

1    Primary circuit hydraulic pipes (11 mm unions)
1A   *From master cylinder*
1B   *To right-hand front brake*
1C   *To left-hand rear brake*
2    Secondary circuit hydraulic pipes (13 mm unions)
2A   *From master cylinder*
2B   *To left-hand front brake*
2C   *To right-hand rear brake*

brake pipes, hoses, hose connections and pipe unions.
2   First check for signs of leakage at the pipe unions. Then examine the flexible hoses for signs of cracking, chafing and fraying.
3   The brake pipes must be examined carefully and methodically. They must be cleaned off and checked for signs of dents, corrosion or other damage. Corrosion should be scraped off, and, if the depth of pitting is significant, the pipes renewed. This is particularly likely in those areas underneath the vehicle body where the pipes are exposed and unprotected.
4   If any section of pipe or hose is to be removed, first unscrew the master cylinder reservoir filler cap and place a piece of polythene over the filler neck. Secure the polythene with an elastic band ensuring that an airtight seal is obtained. This will minimise brake fluid loss when the pipe or hose is removed.
5   Brake pipe removal is usually quite straightforward. The union nuts at each end are undone, the pipe and union pulled out and the centre section of the pipe removed from the body clips. Where the union nuts are exposed to the full force of the weather they can sometimes be quite tight. As only an open-ended spanner can be used, burring of the flats on the nuts is not uncommon when attempting to undo them. For this reason a self-locking wrench is often the only way to separate a stubborn union.
6   To remove a flexible hose, wipe the unions and bracket free of dirt and undo the union nut from the brake pipe end(s).
7   Next extract the hose retaining clip, or unscrew the nut, and lift the end of the hose out of its bracket (photos). If a front hose is being removed, it can now be unscrewed from the brake caliper.
8   Brake pipes can be obtained individually, or in sets, from most accessory shops or garages with the end flares and union nuts in place. The pipe is then bent to shape, using the old pipe as a guide, and is ready for fitting to the car.
9   Refitting the pipes and hoses is a reverse of the removal sequence. Make sure that the hoses are not kinked when in position and also make sure that the brake pipes are securely supported in their clips. After refitting, remove the polythene from the reservoir and bleed the brake hydraulic system, as described in Section 15.

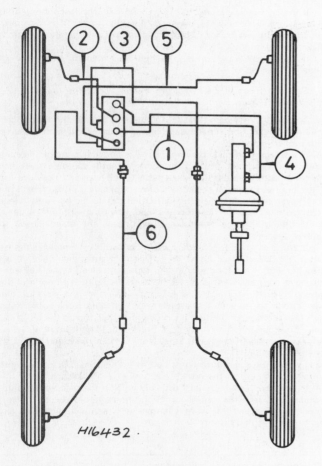

H16432.

Fig. 8.7 Layout of brake hydraulic pipes and hoses (Sec 14)

**Secondary circuit**
1   *Master cylinder to GP valve*
2   *GP valve to left-hand front hose*
3   *GP valve to right-hand rear hose*
**Primary circuit**
4   *Master cylinder to GP valve*
5   *GP valve to right-hand front hose*
6   *GP valve to left-hand rear hose*

## 15  Hydraulic system – bleeding

1   The correct functioning of the brake hydraulic system is only possible after removal of all air from the components and circuit; this

14.7a Rear brake hose and retaining clip (arrowed)

14.7b Front brake hose and retaining nut (arrowed)

15.11 One-man brake bleeding kit attached to front caliper bleed screw

is achieved by bleeding the system. Note that only clean unused brake fluid, which has remained unshaken for at least 24 hours, must be used.

2   If there is any possibility of incorrect fluid being used in the system, the brake lines and components must be completely flushed with uncontaminated fluid and new seals fitted to the components.

3   *Never* reuse brake fluid which has been bled from the system.

4   During the procedure, do not allow the level of brake fluid to drop more than halfway down the reservoir.

5   Before starting work check that all pipes and hoses are secure, unions tight, and bleed screws closed. Take great care not to allow brake fluid to come into contact with the car paintwork, otherwise the finish will be seriously damaged. Wash off any spilled fluid immediately with cold water.

6   There are a number of one-man, do-it-yourself, brake bleeding kits currently available from motor accessory shops. Always follow the instructions supplied with the kit. It is recommended that one of these kits is used wherever possible, as they greatly simplify the bleeding operation, and also reduce the risk of expelled air and fluid being drawn back into the system. If one of these kits is not available, it will be necessary to gather together a clean jar and a suitable length of clear plastic tubing which is a tight fit over the bleed screw, and also to engage the help of an assistant.

7   If brake fluid has been lost from the master cylinder due to a leak in the system, ensure that the cause is traced and rectified before proceeding further.

8   If the hydraulic system has only been partially disconnected and suitable precautions were taken to prevent further loss of fluid it should only be necessary to bleed that part of the system (ie primary or secondary circuit).

9   If the complete system is to be bled then it should be done in the following sequence:

*Secondary circuit: Left-hand front then right-hand rear*
*Primary circuit: Right-hand front then left-hand rear*

10   To bleed the system, first clean the area around the bleed screw and fit the bleed tube. If necessary, top up the master cylinder reservoir with brake fluid.

11   *If a one-man brake bleeding kit is being used,* open the bleed screw half a turn and position the unit so that it can be viewed from the car (photo). Depress the brake pedal to the floor and slowly release it; the one-way valve in the kit will prevent expelled air from returning to the system. Repeat the procedure then top up the brake fluid level. Continue bleeding until clean brake fluid, free from air bubbles, can be seen coming through the tube. Now tighten the bleed screw and remove the tube.

12   *If a one-man brake bleeding kit is not available,* immerse the free end of the bleed tube in the jar and pour in sufficient brake fluid to keep the end of the tube submerged. Open the bleed screw half a turn and have your assistant depress the brake pedal to the floor and then slowly release it. Tighten the bleed screw at the end of each downstroke to prevent the expelled air and fluid from being drawn back into the system. Repeat the procedure, then top up the brake fluid level. Continue bleeding until clean brake fluid, free from bubbles, can be seen coming through the tube. Now tighten the bleed screw and remove the tube.

13   Repeat the procedure described in paragraphs 10 to 12 on the remaining wheels, in the correct sequence, as necessary.

14   When completed, recheck the fluid level in the reservoir, top up if required and refit the cap. Depress the brake pedal several times; it should feel firm and free from 'sponginess' which would indicate air is still present in the system.

## 16  Handbrake cable – adjustment

1   Chock the front wheels, jack up the rear of the car and support it securely on axle stands. Release the handbrake.

2   Apply the footbrake firmly two or three times to ensure full movement of the self-adjust mechanism on the rear brake shoes. This is particularly important if the brake drums have recently been removed.

3   From beneath the car, pull the handbrake inner cable downwards and release sharply in order to centralise the cable and linkage.

4   From under the rear of the car measure the endfloat of the

handbrake lever stops located on the rear of each brake backplate (photo). If the movement of the stops is not as given in the Specifications, adjustment is necessary and is carried out as follows.

5　Turn the cable adjuster, located just in front of the rear axle (photo), clockwise to increase the cable tension and anti-clockwise to decrease it. The direction of rotation assumes the adjuster is being viewed from the rear of the car, ie facing forwards.

6　Turn the cable adjuster until the endfloat of the handbrake lever stops is as specified. Check that it is possible to rotate both stops by hand. Do not overtighten the cable.

7　After adjustment ensure that the wheels are free to turn without binding when the handbrake is released, and then lower the car to the ground.

## 17　Handbrake cable (front) – removal and refitting

1　Chock the front wheels, jack up the rear of the car and support it securely on axle stands.

2　From under the rear of the car slacken the handbrake cable adjuster to remove all tension from the cable. Refer to Section 16, if necessary.

3　From inside the car remove the centre console, as described in Chapter 11.

4　Slide both the front seats fully forward then undo and remove the rear bolts securing the inner seat rails to the floor. Now remove the centre console rear mounting bracket.

5　Undo and remove the seat belt centre stalk mounting bolts and

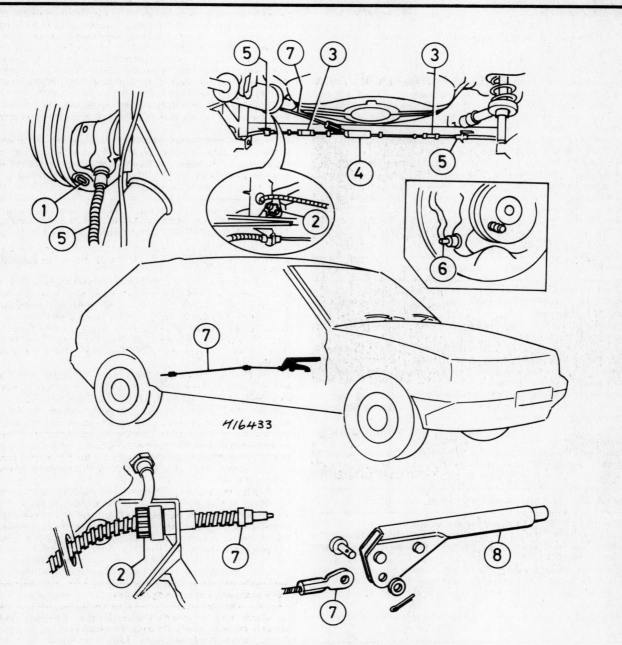

**Fig. 8.8 Layout of the handbrake mechanism (Secs 16 to 19)**

| | | | | | |
|---|---|---|---|---|---|
| 1 | Brake shoe inspection aperture | 3 | Cable connector | 6 | Handbrake lever stop |
| 2 | Handbrake cable adjuster | 4 | Compensator assembly | 7 | Handbrake cable – front |
| | | 5 | Handbrake cable – rear | 8 | Control lever |

16.4 Location of the right-hand handbrake lever stop (arrowed) on the rear brake backplate

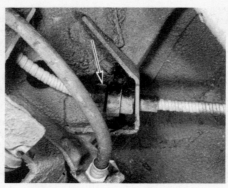

16.5 Location of the handbrake cable adjuster (arrowed) in front of the rear axle

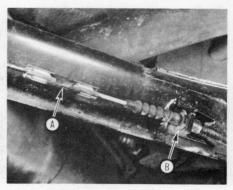

18.2 Handbrake cable connector (A) and rear cable retaining circlip location (B)

remove the two stalks.

6    Undo and remove the bolt securing the left-hand seat belt to the inner sill. Remove the carpet retaining screws and lift up the rear carpet sufficiently to gain access to the handbrake cable cover plate. Remove the cover plate and seal.

7    Extract the split pin and withdraw the clevis pin securing the handbrake cable to the handbrake lever. Remove the cable from the lever and feed it through the cover plate aperture.

8    Disconnect both rear cables from the connectors located to the rear of the rear axle transverse member. Release the cable from its mounting bushes and withdraw it from under the car.

9    Refitting the cable is the reverse sequence to removal. Ensure that the seat belt mounting bolts are tightened to the specified torque (Chapter 11) and adjust the cable, as described in Section 16, after fitting.

## 18    Handbrake cable (rear) – removal and refitting

1    Chock the front wheels, prise off the rear wheel trim and slacken the wheel nuts. Jack the car up and support it securely on axle stands. Remove the roadwheel.

2    Disconnect the rear cable at the connector just behind the rear axle transverse member (photo).

3    Using circlip pliers extract the retaining circlip and withdraw the rear cable from its mounting bracket on the rear cable.

4    Refer to Section 6, paragraphs 2 to 4 inclusive, and remove the rear hub and brake drum assembly.

5    With the drum removed, ease the handbrake operating lever on the trailing brake shoe forward, and disengage the inner cable nipple from the elongated slot on the lever.

6    Withdraw the cable from the brake backplate and remove the spring collar and felt seal.

7    Refitting is the reverse sequence to removal. Adjust the cable, as described in Section 16, after refitting.

## 19    Handbrake lever and switch – removal and refitting

1    Refer to Chapter 11, and remove the centre console.

2    If only the warning light switch is to be removed, disconnect the wires from the switch terminals, remove the securing screws and withdraw the switch.

3    To remove the lever assembly, extract the split pin, withdraw the clevis pin and detach the handbrake cable from the lever.

4    Undo and remove the two mounting bolts and lift away the handbrake lever assembly.

5    Refitting is a straightforward reversal of the removal sequence.

## 20    Footbrake pedal – removal and refitting

1    From inside the car extract the split pin and withdraw the clevis pin and washer securing the servo unit pushrod to the brake pedal.

2    Undo and remove the nut and washer at the clutch pedal end of the pedal pivot bolt.

3    Draw the pivot bolt toward the side of the car to release the clutch pedal. Recover the washer from the pivot shaft (where fitted), unhook the top of the clutch pedal from the cable and withdraw the pedal.

4    Fully remove the pivot bolt and withdraw the brake pedal after detaching the return spring. Where fitted, recover the pivot bolt washers.

5    With the pedals removed, examine the pivot bushes and, if worn, renew them.

6    Refitting the pedals is the reverse sequence to removal. Smear the pivot bolt and bushes with a little lithium-based grease prior to fitting.

## 21    Stoplight switch – removal, refitting and adjustment

1    To remove the switch first disconnect the battery negative terminal.

2    Undo and remove the bolts on the right-hand side of the pedal securing the switch bracket in position.

3    Disconnect the wiring connector and remove the switch. Unscrew the switch from the plastic insert.

4    To refit the switch, screw it fully into the plastic insert and position the switch with the terminal in the vertical position.

5    Refit the wiring connector and secure the switch bracket to the pedal bracket with the bolts, finger tight only at this stage.

6    To adjust the switch, reconnect the battery negative terminal and switch on the ignition.

7    Depress the brake pedal by 0.25 in (6 mm) and adjust the switch position so that the stoplights just come on.

8    Tighten the switch bracket retaining bolts and recheck the stoplight operation.

## 22    Vacuum servo unit – description

A vacuum servo unit is fitted into the brake hydraulic circuit in series with the master cylinder, to provide assistance to the driver when the brake pedal is depressed. This reduces the effort required by the driver to operate the brakes under all braking conditions.

The unit operates by vacuum obtained from the inlet manifold and comprises basically a booster diaphragm, control valve, and a non-return valve.

The servo unit and hydraulic master cylinder are connected together so that the servo unit piston rod acts as the master cylinder pushrod. The driver's braking effort is transmitted through another pushrod to the servo unit piston and its built-in control system. The servo unit piston does not fit tightly into the cylinder, but has a strong diaphragm to keep its edges in constant contact with the cylinder wall, so assuring an airtight seal between the two parts. The forward chamber is held under vacuum conditions created in the inlet manifold of the engine and, during periods when the brake pedal is not in use, the controls open a passage to the rear chamber so placing it under vacuum conditions as well. When the brake pedal is depressed, the vacuum passage to the rear chamber is cut off and the chamber opened to atmospheric pressure. The consequent rush of air pushes the servo piston forward in the vacuum chamber and operates the main pushrod to the master cylinder.

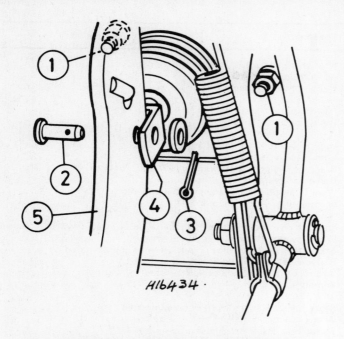

**Fig. 8.9 Vacuum servo unit attachments (Sec 23)**

1   Servo unit securing nuts   4   Servo pushrod
2   Clevis pin                 5   Brake pedal
3   Split pin

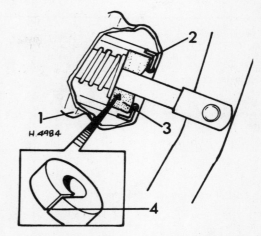

**Fig. 8.10 Servo unit air filter renewal (Sec 24)**

1   Dust cover   3   Filter
2   End cap      4   Position of cut in filter

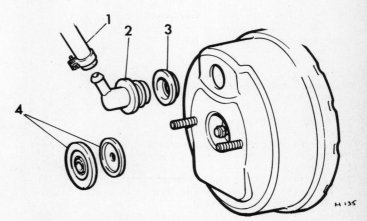

**Fig. 8.11 Servo unit non-return valve, seal and plate assembly (Sec 24)**

1   Vacuum hose        3   Grommet
2   Non-return valve   4   Seal and plate

The controls are designed so that assistance is given under all conditions and, when the brakes are not required, vacuum in the rear chamber is established when the brake pedal is released. All air from the atmosphere entering the rear chamber is passed through a small air filter.

## 23 Vacuum servo unit – removal and refitting

1   Undo and remove the two nuts and washers securing the brake master cylinder to the servo unit. Carefully withdraw the master cylinder, taking great care not to strain the brake pipes, and tie it to one side, just clear of the servo.
2   Unscrew the vacuum hose retaining clip and pull the hose off the non-return valve on the front of the servo.
3   From inside the car, extract the split pin and withdraw the clevis pin securing the servo pushrod to the brake pedal.
4   Undo and remove the two nuts and washers securing the servo to the bulkhead and withdraw the unit from the engine compartment.
5   Refitting the servo unit is the reverse sequence to removal. Tighten the servo and master cylinder retaining nuts to the specified torque and use a new split pin in the servo pushrod clevis pin.

## 24 Vacuum servo unit – servicing

1   At the intervals given in Routine Maintenance the servo unit air filter, seal and plate assembly and non-return valve should be renewed as follows. Note that this is the only work that can be carried out on the servo and no attempt should be made to dismantle the unit or alter the setting of the domed nut in the output rod (where fitted).
2   Begin by removing the servo unit from the car, as described in the previous Section.
3   To renew the air filter, pull back the rubber dust cover at the pushrod end, release the end cap and extract the old filter. Cut the new filter, as shown in Fig. 8.10, place it over the pushrod and push the filter into the neck of the servo. Refit the end cap and dust cover.
4   To fit a new non-return valve, note the angular position of the valve neck, then insert a wide-bladed screwdriver between the valve and grommet, prise out the valve and extract the grommet.
5   Fit a new grommet to the servo. Lubricate the ribs of the new valve with rubber grease, position it so that the valve neck is in the same angular position as the one removed and then press the valve fully into the grommet.
6   Remove the seal and plate assembly from the output rod end of the servo, noting the direction of fitting and relationship of the seal to the plate. Refit the new components in the same position.
7   The servo can now be refitted to the car, as described in the previous Section. To test the operation of the servo after fitting, depress the footbrake and then start the engine. As the engine starts there should be a noticeable 'give' in the brake pedal. Allow the engine to run for at least two minutes and then switch it off. If the brake pedal is now depressed again, it should be possible to hear a loud hiss from the unit when the pedal is depressed. After about four or five applications no further hissing will be heard and the pedal will feel considerably firmer.

**25 Fault diagnosis – braking system**

| Symptom | Reason(s) |
| --- | --- |
| Excessive pedal travel | Rear brake self-adjust mechanism inoperative<br>Air in hydraulic system<br>Faulty master cylinder |
| Brake pedal feels spongy | Air in hydraulic system<br>Faulty master cylinder |
| Judder felt through brake pedal or steering wheel when braking | Excessive run-out or distortion of front discs or rear drums<br>Brake pedals or linings worn<br>Brake backplate or disc caliper loose<br>Wear in suspension or steering components or mountings – see Chapter 10 |
| Excessive pedal pressure required to stop car | Faulty servo unit, disconnected, damaged or insecure vacuum hose<br>Wheel cylinder(s) or caliper piston seized<br>Brake pads or brake shoe linings worn or contaminated<br>Brake shoes incorrectly fitted<br>Incorrect grade of pads or linings fitted<br>Primary or secondary hydraulic circuit failure |
| Brakes pull to one side | Brake pads or linings worn or contaminated<br>Wheel cylinder or caliper piston seized<br>Seized rear brake self-adjust mechanism<br>Brake pads or linings renewed on one side only<br>Faulty twin GP valve<br>Tyre, steering or suspension defect – see Chapter 10 |
| Brakes binding | Wheel cylinder or caliper piston seized<br>Handbrake incorrectly adjusted<br>Faulty master cylinder |
| Rear wheels locking under normal braking | Rear brake shoe linings contaminated<br>Faulty twin GP valve |

# Chapter 9 Electrical system

*For modifications, and information applicable to later models, see Supplement at end of manual*

## Contents

## Specifications

### System type ........................................................ 12 volt, negative earth

### Battery
Type ...................................................................... Lucas or Chloride – 'sealed for life'
Capacity ................................................................. 36 amp hr, 44 amp hr or 55 amp hr

### Alternator
Type ...................................................................... Lucas A133
Maximum output ..................................................... 55 amps
Brush length:
   New ................................................................ 0.8 in (20 mm)
   Minimum .......................................................... 0.4 in (10 mm)
Brush spring tension (brush face flush with brushbox) ......... 4.7 to 9.8 ozf (1.3 to 2.7 N)

### Starter motor
Type:
   1.3 litre models ................................................. Lucas 8M90 pre-engaged
   1.6 litre models ................................................. Lucas 9M90 pre-engaged
Minimum brush length ............................................... 0.4 in (10 mm)
Brush spring tension ................................................. 32 to 36 ozf (9 to 10 N)
Commutator minimum skimming thickness ..................... 0.08 in (2 mm)

### Wipers
Wiper blades (front and rear) ...................................... Champion X-5103
Wiper arms (front and rear) ........................................ Champion CCA6

### Relays and control units

| Component: | Location |
| --- | --- |
| Heated rear window relay .......................................... | Relay panel on glovebox top cover |
| Windscreen wiper control unit (if fitted) ..................... | Relay panel on glovebox top cover |
| Direction indicator/hazard warning flasher unit ............ | Relay panel on glovebox top cover |
| Electric window switch relay (if fitted) ........................ | Relay panel on glovebox top cover |
| Carburettor electronic control unit – ECU (if fitted) ........ | Behind the facia shelf on the driver's side |
| Electric window switch isolation relays (if fitted) ........... | Behind the passenger's door inner trim panel |
| Voice synthesiser cut-out relay (if fitted) .................... | Behind the trip computer |

## Fuses

**Fuse colour coding:**

| | Current rating |
|---|---|
| Violet | 3 amp |
| Tan | 5 amp |
| Red | 10 amp |
| Blue | 15 amp |
| Green | 30 amp |

## Bulbs

| | Wattage |
|---|---|
| Headlamps | 60/50 |
| Sidelamps | 4 |
| Direction indicators | 21 |
| Reverse lamps | 21 |
| Stop/tail lamps | 21/5 |
| Tail lamps | 5 |
| Foglamps | 21 |
| Number plate lamps | 4 |
| Interior lamps | 10 |
| Glovebox lamp | 5 |
| Switch panel illumination | 2 |
| Instrument panel illumination and warning lamps | 1.2 |
| Ignition warning lamp | 2 |
| Heater control illumination | 1.2 |
| Ashtray illumination | 0.36 |

## Torque wrench settings

| | lbf ft | Nm |
|---|---|---|
| Alternator adjustment arm to alternator | 18 | 25 |
| Alternator adjustment arm to engine: | | |
| 1.3 litre models | 28 | 38 |
| 1.6 litre models | 16 | 22 |
| Alternator mounting bolts: | | |
| 1.3 litre models | 16 | 22 |
| 1.6 litre models | 20 | 27 |
| Alternator pulley nut | 28 | 38 |
| Starter motor retaining bolts | 38 | 51 |
| Wiper arm retaining nuts | 7 | 10 |
| Wiper linkage arm to spindle | 3 | 4 |

## 1  General description

The electrical system is of the 12 volt negative earth type, and consists of a 12 volt battery, alternator, starter motor and related electrical accessories, components and wiring. The battery is of the maintenance free, 'sealed for life' type and is charged by an alternator which is belt-driven from the crankshaft pulley. The starter motor is of the pre-engaged type incorporating an integral solenoid. On starting, the solenoid moves the drive pinion into engagement with the flywheel ring gear before the starter motor is energised. Once the engine has started, a one-way clutch prevents the motor armature being driven by the engine until the pinion disengages from the flywheel.

Further details of the major electrical systems are given in the relevant Sections of this Chapter.

**Caution:** *Before carrying out any work on the vehicle electrical system, read through the precautions given in Safety First! at the beginning of this manual and in Section 2 of this Chapter.*

## 2  Electrical system – precautions

It is necessary to take extra care when working on the electrical system to avoid damage to semi-conductor devices (diodes and transistors), and to avoid the risk of personal injury. In addition to the precautions given in Safety First! at the beginning of this manual, observe the following items when working on the system.

1  *Always remove rings, watches, etc before working on the electrical system.* Even with the battery disconnected, capacitive discharge could occur if a component live terminal is earthed through a metal object. This could cause a shock or nasty burn.

2  *Do not reverse the battery connections.* Components such as the alternator or any other having semi-conductor circuitry could be irreparably damaged.

3  If the engine is being started using jump leads and a slave battery, connect the batteries *positive to positive* and *negative to negative.* This also applies when connecting a battery charger.

4  Never disconnect the battery terminals, or alternator multi-plug connector, when the engine is running.

5  The battery leads and alternator multi-plug must be disconnected before carrying out any electric welding on the car.

6  Never use an ohmmeter of the type incorporating a hand cranked generator for circuit or continuity testing.

## 3  Maintenance and inspection

1  At regular intervals (see Routine Maintenance) carry out the following maintenance and inspection operations on the electrical system components.

2  Check the operation of all the electrical equipment, ie wipers, washers, lights, direction indicators, horn etc. Refer to the appropriate Sections of this Chapter if any components are found to be inoperative.

3  Visually check all accessible wiring connectors, harnesses and retaining clips for security, or any signs of chafing or damage. Rectify any problems encountered.

4  Check the alternator drivebelt for cracks, fraying or damage. Renew the belt if worn or, if satisfactory, check and adjust the belt tension. These procedures are covered in Chapter 2.

5  Check the condition of the wiper blades and if they are cracked or show signs of deterioration, renew them, as described in Section 34. Check the operation of the windscreen and tailgate washers (if fitted). Adjust the nozzles using a pin, if necessary.

6  Check the battery terminals, and if there is any sign of corrosion disconnect and clean them thoroughly. Smear the terminals and battery posts with petroleum jelly before refitting the plastic covers. If there is any corrosion on the battery tray, remove the battery, clean the deposits away and treat the affected metal with an anti-rust preparation. Repaint the tray in the original colour after treatment.

7  Top up the windscreen and rear window washer reservoirs and check the security of the pump wires and water pipes.

8  It is advisable to have the headlight aim adjusted using optical beam setting equipment.

9  While carrying out a road test check the operation of all the instruments and warning lights, and the operation of the direction

indicator self-cancelling mechanism.

10  At less frequent intervals (see Routine Maintenance) renew the alternator drivebelt, as described in Chapter 2.

## 4  Battery – removal and refitting

1  The battery is located on the right-hand side of the engine compartment.

2  Lift the plastic cover from the negative (-) terminal, loosen the clamp bolt and lift the terminal off the battery post (photo).

3  Lift the plastic cover from the positive (+) terminal, loosen the clamp bolt and lift the terminal off the battery post.

4  Undo and remove the retaining bolt and lift off the battery clamp plate (photo).

5  Withdraw the battery from the carrier tray.

6  Refitting is the reverse sequence to removal, but make sure that the polarity is correct before connecting the leads, and do not overtighten the clamp bolts.

## 5  Battery – charging

1  In winter when a heavy demand is placed on the battery, such as when starting from cold and using more electrical equipment, it may be necessary to have the battery fully charged from an external source. *Note that both battery leads must be disconnected before charging in order to prevent possible damage to any semi-conductor electrical components.*

2  The terminals of the battery and the leads of the charger must be connected *positive to positive* and *negative to negative*.

3  Due to the design of certain maintenance-free batteries, rapid charging is not recommended. If in any doubt about the suitability of certain types of charging equipment for use with maintenance-free batteries, consult a BL dealer or automotive electrical specialist.

## 6  Alternator – removal and refitting

1  Disconnect the battery negative terminal.

2  Release the retaining clip and remove the multi-plug from the rear of the alternator (photo).

3  Slacken the adjustment arm bolt and the mounting pivot bolt(s) and move the unit in towards the engine. Slip the drivebelt off the three pulleys.

4  Remove the adjustment arm bolt and washers. Remove the pivot bolt(s), nuts and washers, taking note of the position of any additional spacers. Withdraw the alternator from the engine.

5  Refitting is a reverse of the removal procedure, but before tightening the mounting bolts and the adjustment arm bolt, tension the drivebelt, as described in Chapter 2.

## 7  Alternator – fault tracing and rectification

Due to the specialist knowledge and equipment required to test or repair an alternator, it is recommended that, if the performance is suspect, the car be taken to an automobile electrician who will have the facilities for such work. Because of this recommendation, information is limited to the inspection and renewal of the brushes. Should the alternator not charge, or the system be suspect, the following points should be checked before seeking further assistance:

*(a)  Check the drivebelt condition and tension*
*(b)  Ensure that the battery is fully charged*
*(c)  Check the ignition warning light bulb, and renew it if blown*

## 8  Alternator brushes – removal, inspection and refitting

1  Remove the alternator, as described in Section 6.

4.2 Removal of the battery negative terminal

4.4 Battery clamp plate and retaining bolt

6.2 Alternator multi-plug retaining clip (A) and multi-plug (B)

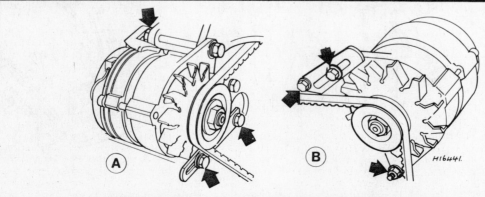

**Fig. 9.1 Alternator adjustment arm and mounting bolt locations (Sec 6)**

*A    1.3 litre models      B    1.6 litre models*

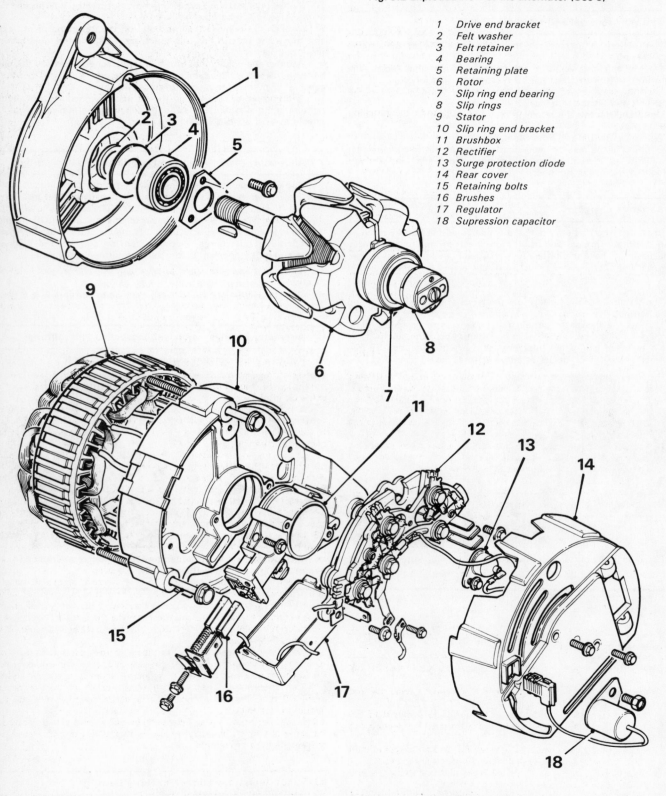

Fig. 9.2 Exploded view of the alternator (Sec 8)

1 Drive end bracket
2 Felt washer
3 Felt retainer
4 Bearing
5 Retaining plate
6 Rotor
7 Slip ring end bearing
8 Slip rings
9 Stator
10 Slip ring end bracket
11 Brushbox
12 Rectifier
13 Surge protection diode
14 Rear cover
15 Retaining bolts
16 Brushes
17 Regulator
18 Supression capacitor

2    Disconnect the electrical lead and remove the suppression capacitor from the rear of the alternator.

3    Undo and remove the two retaining screws, or nuts, and lift off the plastic rear cover.

4    Disconnect the surge protection diode electrical lead from the rectifier, undo the retaining screw and lift off the diode.

5    Make a careful note of the location and colour of the regulator electrical leads at the rectifier and brushbox, then disconnect the leads.

6    Undo and remove the screw securing the regulator to the brushbox and then lift off the regulator. Note that the screw also retains the inner brush mounting plate.

7    Undo and remove the two brushbox retaining screws and lift off the brushbox.

8    Remove the inner brush from the brushbox, undo the retaining screw and remove the outer brush and sealing pad.

9    Measure the brush length and, if less than the specified minimum dimension given in the Specifications, renew the brushes.

10   Refit the brushes and springs to the brushbox and check the brush spring pressure. Renew the brushes and springs if the pressure is outside the specified value.

11   Refitting is the reverse sequence to removal, but make sure that the brushes move freely in their holders. If necessary, clean them with petrol and, if this is not sufficient, use a fine file. Wipe the slip rings with a petrol-moistened cloth before refitting the brushbox.

### 9    Starter motor – testing in the car

1    If the starter motor fails to operate, first check the condition of the battery by switching on the headlamps. If they glow brightly then gradually dim after a few seconds, the battery is in an uncharged condition.

2    If the battery is satisfactory, check the starter motor main terminal and the engine earth cable for security. Check the terminal connections on the starter solenoid – located on top of the starter motor.

3    If the starter still fails to turn, use a voltmeter, or 12 volt test lamp and leads, to ensure that there is battery voltage at the solenoid main terminal (containing the cable from the battery positive terminal).

4    With the ignition switched on and the ignition key in position III, check that voltage is reaching the solenoid terminal with the Lucar connector, and also the starter main terminal.

5    If there is no voltage reaching the Lucar connector there is a wiring or ignition switch fault. If voltage is available, but the starter does not operate, then the starter or solenoid is likely to be at fault.

### 10    Starter motor – removal and refitting

1    Disconnect the battery negative terminal.

2    Detach the electrical leads at the solenoid terminals noting their respective locations (photo).

3    Using a suitable Allen key, undo and remove the two bolts, nuts and washers securing the starter to the gearbox flange and lift the unit off.

4    Refitting the starter motor is the reverse sequence to removal, but tighten the retaining bolts to the specified torque.

### 11    Starter motor – overhaul

1    Remove the starter motor from the car, as described in the previous Section.

2    At the rear of the solenoid, unscrew the nut and lift away the lead from the solenoid 'STA' terminal.

3    Undo and remove the two screws securing the solenoid to the drive end housing. Disengage the solenoid plunger from the engaging lever and withdraw the solenoid.

4    Withdraw the end cap from the commutator end housing and then prise off the 'spire' retaining washer from the armature shaft.

5    Undo and remove the two through-bolts and withdraw the end housing sufficiently to gain access to the brushes.

6    Release the field brushes from their brushbox locations and then remove the end housing.

7    Mark the relationship of the field coil assembly to the drive end housing, unscrew the two housing retaining screws and withdraw the

10.2 Electrical lead locations at the starter solenoid

drive end housing.

8    Slide the armature and drive assembly out of the field coil assembly.

9    Mount the armature in a vice and, using a suitable tubular drift, tap the thrust collar on the end of the shaft toward the pinion, to expose the jump ring. Prise the jump ring out of its groove and slide it off the shaft. Withdraw the thrust collar and the drive assembly.

10   With the starter motor now completely dismantled, clean all the components in paraffin or a suitable solvent, and wipe dry.

11   Check the length of the brushes and the tension of the brush springs. If the length and tension are not as given in the Specifications renew the brushes and springs. Note that the field brushes must be soldered in place.

12   Check that the brushes move freely in their holders, and clean the holders and brushes with a petrol-moistened rag if they show any tendency to stick. If necessary use a fine file on the brushes if they still stick after cleaning.

13   Check the armature shaft for distortion, and examine the commutator for excessive scoring, wear or burns. If necessary, the commutator may be skimmed in a lathe and then polished with fine glass paper. Make sure that it is not reduced below the specified minimum thickness and do not undercut the mica insulation.

14   Check the taping of the field coils, check all joints for security and check the coils and commutator for signs of burning.

15   Check the drive pinion assembly, drive end housing, engaging lever and solenoid for wear or damage. Make sure that the drive pinion one-way clutch permits movement of the pinion in one direction only and renew the complete assembly, if necessary.

16   Check the condition of the bush in the commutator end housing and, if necessary, renew it. Note that the armature is supported at the drive end by a bush in the gearbox housing, and that access to this bush entails removal of the gearbox from the car unless the BL special removing tool can be obtained. Soak the new bushes in engine oil for 24 hours before fitting.

17   Accurate checking of the armature, commutator and field coil windings and insulation requires the use of special test equipment. If the starter motor was inoperative when removed from the car and the previous checks have not highlighted the problem, then it can be assumed that there is a continuity or insulation fault and the unit should be renewed.

18   If the starter is in a satisfactory condition, or if a fault has been traced and rectified, the unit can be reassembled using the reverse of the dismantling procedure.

### 12    Fuses, relays and control units – general

*Fuses*

1    The fusebox is situated under a mat on top of the facia on the passenger's side. To gain access to the fuses, remove the mat and lift

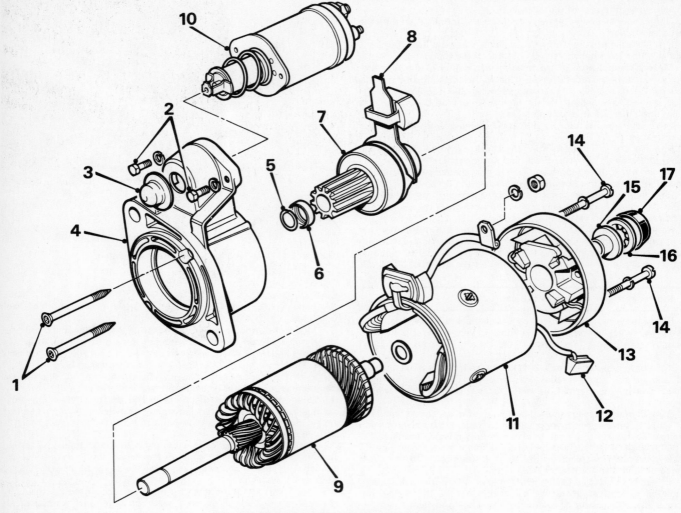

**Fig. 9.3 Exploded view of the starter motor (Sec 11)**

| | | |
|---|---|---|
| 1 Drive end housing bolts | 7 Drive assembly | 13 Commutator end housing |
| 2 Solenoid retaining screws | 8 Engaging lever | 14 Through-bolt |
| 3 End cap | 9 Armature | 15 Bush |
| 4 Drive end housing | 10 Solenoid | 16 'Spire' washer |
| 5 Jump ring | 11 Field coil assembly | 17 End cap |
| 6 Thrust collar | 12 Field brush | |

off the fusebox lid (photo). The fuse locations, current rating and circuits protected are shown on the lid. Each fuse is colour coded and has its rating stamped on it. To remove a fuse from its location, use a coin to prise it free and then lift it out (photo).

2    Always renew a fuse with one of an identical rating. *Never renew a fuse more than once without finding the source of the trouble.*

3    Circuits protected by fuses C1 and C3 operate when the ignition switch is in position I or II. Circuits A1, A2, C2, C5 and C6 only operate when the ignition switch is at position II. All other circuits operate irrespective of ignition switch position.

4    Spare fuses are located in positions A7, B7 and C7 and are of 30 amp, 5 amp and 15 amp rating respectively. Note, however, that no spare locations are provided for 3 amp and 10 amp fuses and it is a good idea to obtain these and carry them in the glovebox.

*Relays and control units*

5    The locations of the relays and control units are given in the Specifications.

6    The relays can be removed by simply pulling them from their respective locations. If a system controlled by a relay becomes inoperative, and the relay is suspect, operate the system and if the

relay is functioning it should be possible to hear it click as it is energized. If this is the case, the fault lies with the components of the system. If the relay is not being energized then the relay is not receiving a main supply voltage, a switching voltage, or the relay itself is faulty.

## 13  Direction indicator and hazard flasher system – general

1    The flasher unit is located on the relay panel which is on the glovebox top cover (photo).

2    Should the flashers become faulty in operation, check the bulbs for security and make sure that the contact surfaces are not corroded. If one bulb blows or is making a poor connection due to corrosion, the system will not flash on that side of the car.

3    If the flasher unit operates in one direction and not the other, the fault is likely to be in the bulbs, or wiring to the bulbs. If the system will not flash in either direction, operate the hazard flashers. If these function, check for a blown fuse in position C5. If the fuse is satisfactory renew the flasher unit.

12.1a The fusebox is located under a mat on top of the facia on the passenger's side

12.1b To remove a fuse, prise it free with a coin and then lift it out

13.1 The relay panel is located on the glovebox top cover

15.3 Steering column right-hand cowl retaining screws (arrowed)

15.4 Steering column multi-function switch clamp screw (arrowed)

## 14 Ignition switch/steering column lock — removal and refitting

The ignition switch is an integral part of the steering column lock, and removal and refitting procedures are given in Chapter 10.

## 15 Steering column multi-function switch — removal and refitting

1    Disconnect the battery negative terminal.
2    Remove the steering wheel, as described in Chapter 10.
3    Undo and remove the screws securing the two halves of the steering column cowl (photo). Lift off the right-hand cowl followed by the left-hand cowl and disconnect the lighting switch wiring multi-plug.
4    Slacken the switch clamp screw (photo), disconnect the wiring multi-plugs from under the facia and withdraw the switch from the steering column.
5    The switches can be separated after removing the insulation tape joining the wiring harnesses and removing the three screws securing the wiper/washer switch to the mounting plate.
6    Before installing the existing or a new switch assembly, check the pins in the wiring connector for corrosion or discoloration. If noted, either clean the contact surfaces with switch cleaner, or in bad cases, fit new connector terminal pins or a new connector as necessary. The connectors and parts are available through Austin Rover dealers.
7    Refitting is the reverse sequence to removal. Position the switch striker bush with the arrow pointing towards the direction indicator switch before refitting the steering wheel.

## 16 Instrumentation — description

Two completely different instrumentation packs are used to present information to the driver. The first pack, used on all models except the MG and Vanden Plas versions, has conventional electro-mechanical instruments and consists of a speedometer, fuel gauge, coolant temperature gauge and, on some versions, a tachometer. The instruments are arranged in a panel in front of the driver, and all electrical interconnections are by a printed circuit at the rear of the unit.

MG and Vanden Plas versions of the Maestro range are equipped with sophisticated solid-state instrumentation in two modules. Module 1 is mounted in the centre of the facia and consists of a mother board, display board and odometer. This module displays roadspeed, engine speed, coolant temperature, fuel level and total mileage. Module 2 is located to the left of Module 1 and consists of a voice synthesis unit and trip computer. The trip computer displays time and date, trip distance and fuel consumption information on request. The voice synthesis unit issues messages to identify the trip computer display, and also provides additional information to emphasize warning light operation. All the information received from the various transducers is processed by the mother board in Module 1. The information is then passed to the display board, trip computer and voice synthesis unit. Information received at the display board causes fluorescent segments to illuminate within three separate display tubes. The first display shows roadspeed in digital form, the second shows engine speed as a bar graph and the third shows fuel level and coolant temperature, also as bar graphs. In addition to the information received from the mother board, the trip computer receives signals from the fuel flow transducer, enabling fuel consumption to be computed and displayed.

The voice for the voice synthesis unit is held on a single memory chip in English language form, and is activated by the mother board. The correct sounds are selected from the memory and arranged to produce the desired phrase. When a phrase is transmitted, a relay cuts out the radio/cassette player, if switched on, and connects the synthesizer to the driver's front speaker. The voice is then transmitted at an audible tone and volume.

**Note:** *The instrumentation fitted to Maestro models is extremely delicate and must be handled with great care.* The solid-state instrumentation consists of fragile electronic circuit boards which can be easily damaged. Removal and refitting procedures are given for the solid-state instrumentation, but it is recommended that the two modules are not dismantled in any way. Fault diagnosis on these instruments entails the use of a sophisticated electronic tester, and, if a fault develops, repair should be left to a suitably equipped BL dealer.

## 17 Instrument panel and instruments (electro-mechanical type) – removal and refitting

1   Disconnect the battery negative terminal.
2   Carefully withdraw the instrument panel surround from its location (photo), and recover the retaining clips.
3   Undo and remove the four screws securing the instrument panel to the facia (photo).
4   Withdraw the panel from its location until sufficient clearance exists to enable the speedometer cable to be detached from the rear of the panel (photo). It may be necessary to push the cable through the bulkhead grommet from the engine compartment side to facilitate removal.
5   Tip the instrument panel forwards, and disconnect the wiring harness multi-plugs. Withdraw the panel from the facia.
6   With the instrument panel on the bench, release the retaining wires and carefully remove the shroud and window assembly.
7   On models equipped with a tachometer, carefully prise the needle

shroud from the tachometer and disconnect the fibre optic element. Undo and remove the two nuts and washers securing the tachometer in place and lift the printed circuit tags off the studs. Undo and remove the four nuts securing the fuel and temperature gauges and carefully manoeuvre all three gauges from their locations.
8   On models without a tachometer, carefully prise the needle shroud from the fuel and temperature gauge and disconnect the fibre optic elements. Undo and remove the four nuts and washers securing the fuel and temperature gauges and carefully withdraw the gauges from their locations.
9   On all models, carefully prise the needle shroud from the speedometer and disconnect the fibre optic elements. Undo and remove the two screws securing the speedometer and ease the speedometer from its location in the panel.
10  Refitting the instruments to the panel and the panel to the facia is the reverse sequence to removal. Ensure that the fibre optic element is located through the aperture in the gauges before securing the gauges in position.

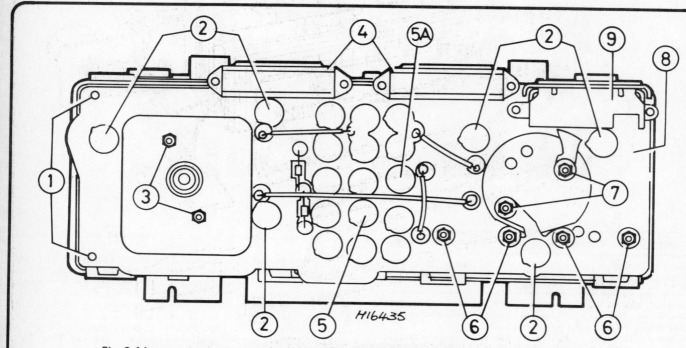

Fig. 9.4 Instrument panel connections and component location – electro-mechanical type (Sec 17)

1  Printed circuit locating peg
2  Panel illumination bulbs
3  Speedometer retaining screws
4  Wiring harness connectors
5  Warning light bulb
5A Ignition warning lamp
6  Fuel and temperature gauge retaining nuts
7  Tachometer retaining nuts (where fitted)
8  Printed circuit
9  Voltage stabilizer

17.2 Removal of the instrument panel surround from the facia

17.3 Location of the instrument panel retaining screws (arrowed)

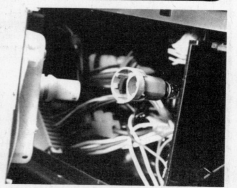

17.4 Withdraw the instrument panel just sufficiently to detach the speedometer cable from behind the panel

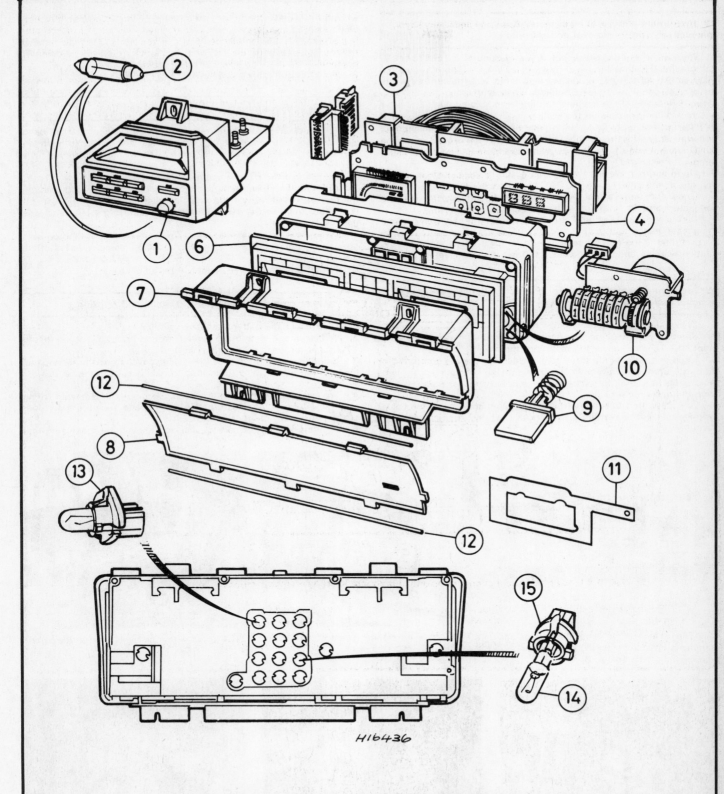

**Fig. 9.5 Exploded view of the solid-state instrument panel components (Sec 19)**

1  Trip computer and
   voice synthesis unit
2  Illumination bulb
3  Mother board
4  Display board

5  Instrument centre
   panel
6  Face plate
7  Shroud
8  Lens

9  Convert button and
   return spring
10  Odometer
11  Light filter
12  Retaining wire

13  Warning lamp and
    holder
14  Ignition warning lamp
15  Ignition warning lamp
    bulb holder

## 18 Instrument panel printed circuit and voltage stabilizer (electro-mechanical type) – removal and refitting

1   Remove the instrument panel, as described in Section 17, paragraphs 1 to 5 inclusive.
2   Remove all the panel and warning lamp bulb holders from the instrument panel by turning anti-clockwise and lifting out (photo). Note the location of the ignition warning lamp holder which is shorter and of a different colour to the rest.
3   If a tachometer is fitted, undo and remove the two retaining nuts and washers and lift the printed circuit tags off the studs.
4   Undo and remove the four nuts and washers securing the fuel and temperature gauges.
5   Undo and remove the two screws securing the voltage stabilizer and lift off the unit.
6   Undo and remove the four screws securing the wiring harness connectors and lift away the connectors.
7   Carefully ease the printed circuit off its locating pegs and remove it from the instrument panel.
8   Refitting is the reverse sequence to removal. Make sure that the ignition warning lamp bulb holder is refitted in its original location.

## 19 Instrument panel and trip computer (solid-state type) – removal and refitting

1   Disconnect the battery negative terminal.
2   Carefully withdraw the instrument panel surround from its location (photo 17.2), and recover the retaining clips.
3   Undo and remove the three screws securing the trip computer to the facia. Carefully withdraw the unit slightly and disconnect the two multi-plugs from the trip computer circuit board and also the two main wiring harness multi-plugs.
4   Withdraw the trip computer and, if required, disconnect the voice synthesis cut-out relay multi-plug, remove the relay securing nuts and the relay.

5   Undo and remove the four screws securing the instrument panel to the facia.
6   Move the instrument panel to the left to clear the switch panel and ease it from its location. Disconnect the two wiring harness multi-plugs and remove the instrument panel from the facia.
7   Refitting is the reverse sequence to removal.

## 20 Clock and econometer – removal and refitting

The clock and econometer are located in a panel on the left-hand side of the instrument panel. On models not equipped with an econometer, the space is used for an ashtray, or is covered by a blanking plate.
1   Disconnect the battery negative terminal.
2   Carefully withdraw the instrument panel surround from its location (photo 17.2), and recover the retaining clips.
3   Undo and remove the three screws securing the left-hand side panel (photo).
4   Withdraw the clock assembly from its location (photo), and disconnect the clock wiring multi-plug. If an econometer is fitted, detach the vacuum pipe. Withdraw the assembly from the facia.
5   Refitting is the reverse sequence to removal.

## 21 Switch panel and switches – removal and refitting

1   Disconnect the battery negative terminal.
2   Withdraw the instrument panel surround from its location (photo 17.2), and recover the retaining clips.
3   Carefully prise off the switch panel cover from the vent panel (photo), and withdraw it sufficiently to gain access to the rear of the switches.
4   To remove a switch from the panel, disconnect the relevant wiring multi-plug (photo), depress the side catches and push the switch out of the panel from the rear (photo).
5   Refitting is the reverse sequence to removal, but make sure that

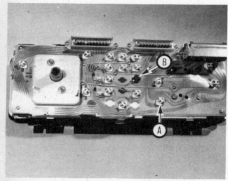

18.2 Typical instrument panel illumination and warning lamp bulb holder (A) and ignition warning lamp bulb holder (B)

20.3 Remove the retaining screws (arrowed) ...

20.4 ... and withdraw the left-hand side panel

21.3 Removal of the switch panel cover from the vent panel

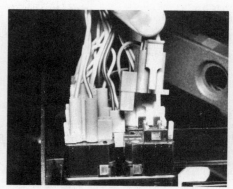

21.4a Disconnect the multi-plug ...

21.4b ... to allow the switch to be removed after depressing the side catches

the switches and panel seat fully in their respective locations.

## 22 Lighting switch – removal and refitting

1 Disconnect the battery negative terminal.
2 Undo and remove the screws securing the steering column cowl halves and lift off the left-hand cowl.
3 Disconnect the wiring multi-plug from the switch, depress the retaining tags and withdraw the switch from its location.
4 Refitting is the reverse sequence to removal.

## 23 Courtesy light switches – removal and refitting

### Front
1 Disconnect the battery negative terminal.
2 Open the door and locate the front courtesy light switch on the door pillar.
3 Remove the retaining screw and withdraw the switch.
4 Disconnect the supply wire and tie a loose knot in it to prevent it dropping into the pillar. Remove the switch.
5 Refitting is the reverse sequence to removal.

### Rear
6 Disconnect the battery negative terminal.
7 Open the tailgate and locate the switch on the left-hand side interior trim panel.
8 Disconnect the wires from the switch terminals, depress the retaining lugs and withdraw the switch from the panel (photo).
9 Refitting is the reverse sequence to removal.

## 24 Headlamp and sidelamp bulbs – renewal

1 From within the engine compartment, turn the headlamp cover anti-clockwise and tip it back to gain access to the bulbs (photos).
2 To renew the headlamp bulb, pull off the wiring connector, release the bulb retaining clip (photo) and withdraw the bulb from its location in the headlamp (photo). *Take care not to touch the bulb glass with your fingers;* if touched, clean the bulb with methylated spirits.
3 Fit the bulb, ensuring that the lug on the bulb engages with the slot on the headlamp. Refit the retaining clip, wiring connector and headlamp cover.
4 To renew the sidelamp bulb, withdraw the bulb holder from the headlamp and remove the bulb from the holder by turning anti-clockwise (photo).
5 Fit the bulb in the holder and push the holder into the headlamp. Refit the headlamp cover.

## 25 Headlamp lens assembly – removal and refitting

1 Open the bonnet then undo and remove the upper screws securing the grille to the front body panel.

2 Lift the grille to disengage the lower locating lugs and remove it from the car.
3 Remove the headlamp and sidelamp bulbs, as described in the previous Section.
4 Undo and remove the two screws securing the lens assembly to the body panel (photo).
5 Tip the lens assembly forward to release the two lower retaining lugs and remove it from the car.
6 If required, the glass can be removed from the lens body after prising off the side retaining clips (photos).

## 26 Front direction indicator bulb – renewal

1 Working in the engine compartment, release the spring retainer (photo) and ease the lamp body and seal from the body panel (photo). Release the bulb holder by turning anti-clockwise.
2 Remove the bulb from the holder by turning anti-clockwise.
3 Fit the bulb and holder to the lamp body, locate the lamp flange behind the panel and push the unit into position. Make sure the seal seats correctly.
4 Secure the lamp body with the spring retainer.

## 27 Rear lamp cluster bulbs – renewal

1 Release the rear edge of the luggage compartment side cover.
2 Undo and remove the three plastic retaining nuts (photo) and ease the lamp cluster away from its location.
3 Disconnect the wiring multi-plug (photo) and remove the lamp cluster.
4 Push the bulb holder panel towards the two retaining studs (photo), and lift the end nearest the single retaining stud. Withdraw the bulb holder panel (photo).
5 The bulbs can now be removed from the panel (photo). All the bulbs except the tail lamp bulb are removed by turning anti-clockwise. The tail lamp bulb is a push fit.
6 Fit the bulbs, holder panel and lamp cluster, using the reverse of the removal procedure.

## 28 Number plate lamp bulb – renewal

1 Using a small screwdriver, depress the catch in the side of the lens assembly and ease the unit out of its location in the bumper (photo).
2 Depress the retainers and lift the lens off the lamp body (photo). Remove the bulb by turning anti-clockwise.
3 Fit the bulb, refit the lens to the lamp body and press the assembly into the bumper.

## 29 Interior courtesy lamp bulbs – renewal

1 Ease the front, or rear, lamp lens assemblies from their locations (photos) and then withdraw the bulbs by turning anti-clockwise.
2 Fit the bulb and push the unit into place.

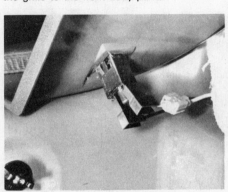

23.8 Rear courtesy light switch location on left-hand interior trim panel

24.1a Turn the cover anti-clockwise ...

24.1b ... to gain access to the bulbs

24.2a Remove the wiring multi-plug, release the bulb retaining clip ...

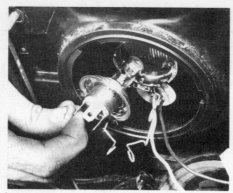

24.2b ... and withdraw the headlamp bulb. Avoid touching the bulb glass

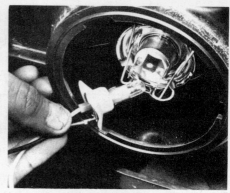

24.4 Withdraw the sidelamp bulb holder and turn the bulb anti-clockwise to remove

25.4 Headlamp lens assembly retaining screw locations (arrowed)

25.6a To remove the lens glass, prise off the retaining clips ...

25.6b ... and lift the lens off the body

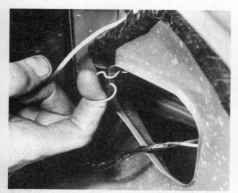

26.1a Release the direction indicator lamp body spring retainer ...

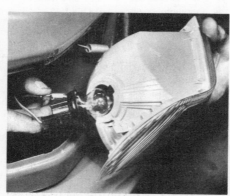

26.1b ... to gain access to the bulb holder and bulb

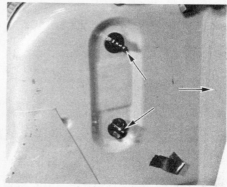

27.2 Rear lamp cluster plastic retaining nut locations (arrowed)

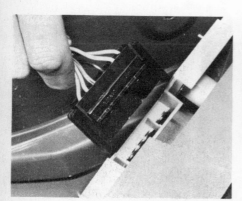

27.3 Remove the wiring multi-plug and lift away the cluster

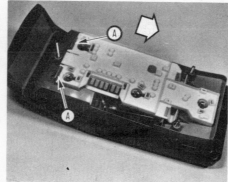

27.4a Move the bulb holder panel in the direction shown until the two catches (A) are released ...

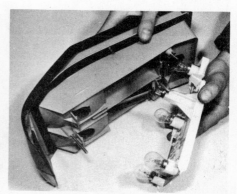

27.4b ... then tip the panel up and remove it from lens assembly

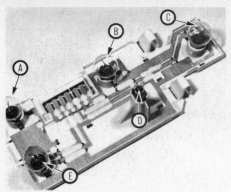

27.5 Bulb identification in the rear bulb holder panel
A  *Direction indicator*   D  *Tail*
B  *Reversing*             E  *Stop/tail*
C  *Foglamp*

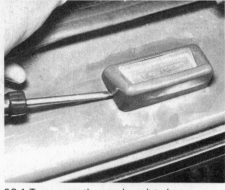

28.1 To remove the number plate lamp, depress the catch in the side of the lens

28.2 To gain access to the bulb depress the retainers and lift off the lens

29.1a Removal of the front ...

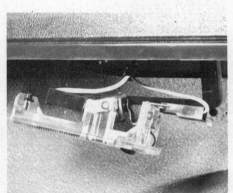

29.1b ... and rear, interior courtesy lamp assemblies

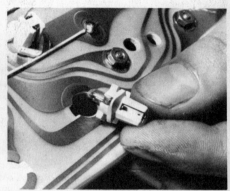

30.2 Remove the instrument panel bulb holders by turning them anti-clockwise

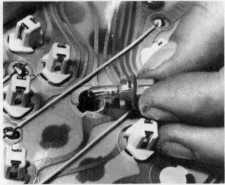

30.3 The ignition warning lamp bulb holder is shorter and of a different colour than the rest

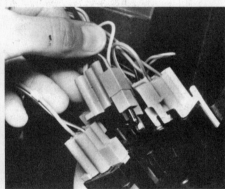

31.2 The switch panel illumination bulbs are located in the multi-plugs at the rear of the switches

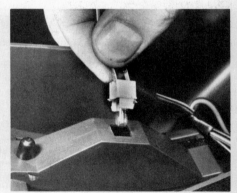

32.2 Removal of a heater control illumination bulb from the rear of the heater cover panel

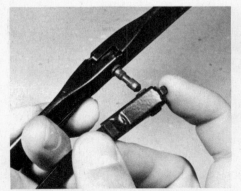

34.3 Remove the wiper blade from the arm by releasing the spring retainer catch and sliding it off

34.5 Lift the hinged cover to gain access to the wiper arm retaining nut

35.2 Bonnet seal panel retaining screw (arrowed)

## 30 Instrument panel illumination and warning lamp bulbs – renewal

1    Remove the instrument panel from the facia, as described in Section 17 for models with electro-mechanical instruments, or Section 19 for models with solid-state instruments.
2    With the instrument panel removed, release the bulb holders by turning anti-clockwise (photo).
3    The ignition warning lamp bulb holder is shorter and of a different colour than the rest of the bulb holders (photo). Only this bulb can be renewed independently of its holder.
4    Fit the bulb and then refit the instrument panel, as described in Section 17 or 19.

## 31 Switch panel illumination bulbs – renewal

1    Remove the switch panel, as described in Section 21, paragraphs 1 to 3 inclusive.
2    Withdraw the wiring multi-plug from the switch containing the bulb (photo), and remove the bulb by turning anti-clockwise.
3    Fit the bulb and multi-plug, then refit the switch panel, as described in Section 21.

## 32 Heater control and ashtray illumination bulbs – renewal

1    Remove the heater cover panel, as described in Chapter 11, Section 35, paragraphs 3 and 4.
2    With the panel removed, withdraw the heater control illumination bulb holders (photo), and withdraw the push-fit bulbs.
3    On models equipped with an ashtray at the front of the centre console an additional illumination bulb is located at the base of the heater cover panel, and renewal is as described above.
4    Fit the bulbs and bulb holders, and then refit the heater cover panel, as described in Chapter 11.

## 33 Headlamp aim – adjustment

1    At regular intervals (see Routine Maintenance) headlamp aim should be checked and, if necessary, adjusted.
2    Due to the light pattern of the homofocal headlamp lenses fitted to Maestro models, optical beam setting equipment must be used to achieve satisfactory aim of the headlamps. It is recommended therefore that this work is entrusted to a BL dealer.
3    Holts Amber Lamp is useful for temporarily changing the headlight colour to conform with the normal usage on Continental Europe.

## 34 Wiper blades and arms – removal and refitting

### Wiper blades
1    The wiper blades should be renewed when they no longer clean the windscreen or tailgate window effectively.
2    Lift the wiper arm away from the window.
3    Release the spring retaining catch and separate the blade from the wiper arm (photo).
4    Insert the new blade into the arm, making sure that the spring retainer catch is engaged correctly.

### Wiper arms
5    To remove a wiper arm, lift the hinged cover and unscrew the retaining nut (photo).
6    Using a screwdriver, carefully prise the arm off the spindle.
7    Before refitting the arm switch the wipers on and off, allowing them to return to the 'park' position.
8    Refit the arm to the spindle, with the arm and blade positioned at the bottom edge of the screen in the normal 'parked' position.
9    Refit and tighten the retaining nut and close the hinged cover.

## 35 Windscreen wiper motor – removal and refitting

1    Disconnect the battery negative terminal.
2    Undo and remove the retaining screws at each end of the bonnet

seal panel on the engine compartment bulkhead (photo). Withdraw the rubber seal from the lip of the panel and lift the panel off.
3    Undo and remove the nut and washer securing the wiper linkage arm to the motor spindle and pull off the arm (photo).
4    Undo and remove the three bolts securing the wiper motor mounting bracket to the body (photo 35.3). Recover the washers.
5    Trace the wiper motor wiring harness back to its grommet in the bulkhead and prise the grommet out.
6    From inside the car undo and remove the screws securing the glovebox lid to the facia, release the retaining straps and remove the glovebox lid.
7    Undo and remove the screws securing the top cover to the roof of the glovebox and lower the cover.
8    Reach into the opening and locate the wiper motor wiring harness connector and multi-plug. Disconnect the wiring and pull the harness through the bulkhead into the engine compartment.
9    Withdraw the motor and mounting bracket from the engine compartment. Undo and remove the three bolts and separate the motor from the bracket.
10   Refitting is the reverse sequence to removal. Before refitting the linkage arm to the motor spindle, reconnect the battery and switch the wipers on and off. This will set the motor in the 'park' position. Move the linkage so that the wiper blades are also in the 'park' position at the bottom of the screen, then refit the linkage arm, washer and nut.

## 36 Windscreen wiper linkage – removal and refitting

1    Disconnect the battery negative terminal.
2    Remove the wiper arms from the spindles, as described in Section 34.
3    Undo and remove the retaining screws at each end of the bonnet seal panel on the engine compartment bulkhead (photo 35.2). Withdraw the rubber seal from the lip of the panel and lift the panel off.
4    Undo and remove the nut and washer securing the wiper linkage arm to the motor spindle and pull off the arm.
5    Undo and remove the nut and washer securing each wiper spindle to the bodywork. Lift off the spacers and push the spindles through the body. Withdraw the linkage assembly from the car.
6    Refitting is the reverse sequence to removal.

## 37 Tailgate wiper motor and gearbox – removal and refitting

1    Disconnect the battery negative terminal.
2    Remove the wiper arm from the spindle, referring to Section 34 if necessary, then lift off the spindle boot.
3    Undo and remove the spindle retaining nut and lift off the flat washer and ferrule.
4    Open the tailgate and carefully prise off the inner trim panel.
5    Make a note of the colour coding and location of the motor wires and then disconnect them at the wiring connectors (photo). Unscrew the earthing point screw and detach the wiper motor earth lead.
6    Undo and remove the two screws securing the motor support bracket to the tailgate (photo 37.5) and withdraw the motor and gearbox assembly from its location. Recover the spacer on the motor spindle.
7    Refitting is the reverse sequence to removal.

## 38 Washer reservoir and pump – removal and refitting

1    Undo and remove the retaining screws, and withdraw the reservoir from its location.
2    Empty the washer fluid and then disconnect the pump wiring connectors, noting their locations (photo).
3    Pull the washer hose off the pump nozzles and remove the reservoir.
4    To remove the pump(s), insert a screwdriver into the reservoir and locate the blade in the slot in the pump retaining sleeve.
5    Unscrew the pump and remove the retaining sleeve from within the reservoir. Withdraw the sealing washer from the pump.
6    To refit the pump, place a new sealing washer in position on the pump and locate the retaining sleeve in a 15 mm ring spanner.
7    Position the ring spanner and sleeve inside the reservoir so that the pump can be located and screwed into the sleeve.

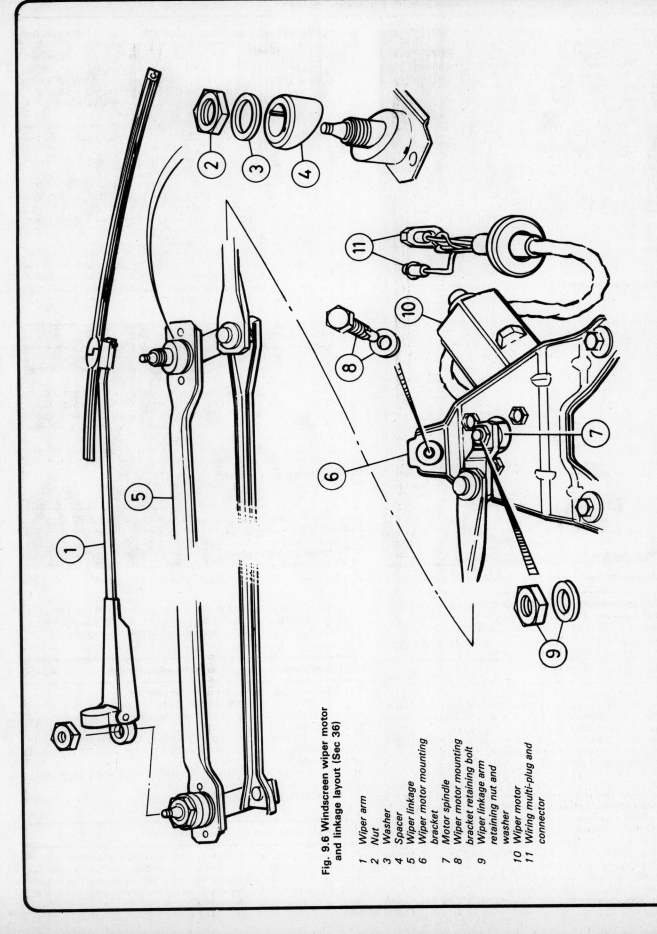

**Fig. 9.6 Windscreen wiper motor and linkage layout (Sec 36)**

1 Wiper arm
2 Nut
3 Washer
4 Spacer
5 Wiper linkage
6 Wiper motor mounting bracket
7 Motor spindle
8 Wiper motor mounting bracket retaining bolt
9 Wiper linkage arm retaining nut and washer
10 Wiper motor
11 Wiring multi-plug and connector

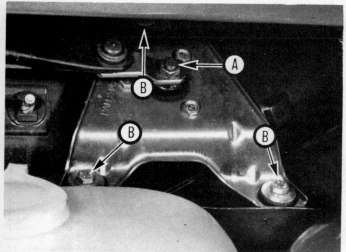

35.3 Wiper linkage arm retaining nut (A) and mounting bracket retaining bolts (B)

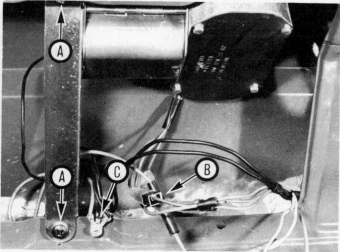

37.5 Tailgate wiper motor support bracket retaining screws (A), wiring connectors (B) and earthing screw (C)

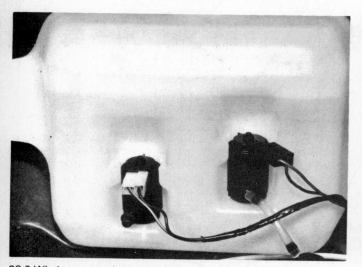

38.2 Windscreen washer pump wiring and hose connections

39.3 Horn wiring connector (A) and retaining screw (B)

8  Using light hand pressure, tighten the pump. Remove the spanner, refit the washer hose and wiring connector.
9  Refit the reservoir to the car and fill the reservoir with water.

### 39  Horn – removal and refitting

1  Disconnect the battery negative terminal.
2  Undo and remove the upper screws securing the grille to the front body panel. Tip the grille forwards and lift it up to release the lower mounting lugs from their locations.
3  Pull off the wiring connector, undo and remove the retaining screw and withdraw the horn from its location (photo).
4  Refitting is the reverse sequence to removal.

### 40  Speedometer cable – removal and refitting

1  Refer to Section 17, paragraphs 1 to 4 inclusive, and detach the speedometer cable from the instrument panel.
2  Release the grommet from the bulkhead and pull the cable through into the engine compartment.
3  Undo and remove the bolt securing the cable retaining plate to the gearbox and withdraw the cable and pinion assembly. *Take care to withdraw the cable squarely without twisting*, otherwise the pinion

may foul the housing and become detached. If this happens the gearbox must be removed and dismantled to retrieve the pinion.
4  Refitting the cable is the reverse sequence to removal.

### 41  Radio/cassette player – removal and refitting

1  Disconnect the battery negative terminal.
2  Pull off the knobs and bezels from the radio/cassette player controls, unscrew the retaining nuts and lift off the finisher and masking plate.
3  Push the radio/cassette player back into its aperture and remove the two packing plates. On some models, clips are used, the centres of which should be pressed inwards.
4  Withdraw the unit, disconnect the wiring, speaker and aerial leads, then remove it from the heater cover panel.
5  Refitting is a reversal of removal.

### 42  Central door locking – description

1  A central door locking system is fitted as standard equipment, or offered as an option, on certain Maestro models. The system enables the passenger's front door lock, both rear door locks, and the tailgate lock, to be operated simultaneously by the action of the driver's interior lock button or exterior private lock.

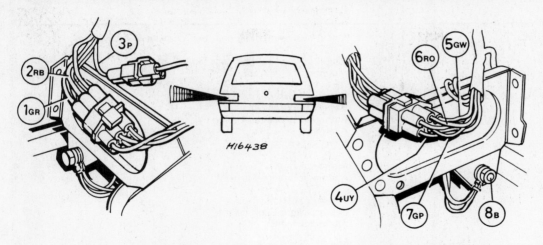

1   Left-hand indicator
2   Left-hand tail lamp
3   Interior light (live feed)
4   Rear foglamp
5   Right-hand indicator
6   Right-hand tail lamp
7   Stop lamp
8   Earthing point

**Cable colour code**
B   Black
G   Green
N   Brown
O   Orange
P   Purple
R   Red
U   Blue
W   White
Y   Yellow
*The second code letter indicates the tracer clour*

**Fig. 9.7 Wiring harness connections for towing bracket installation (Sec 44)**

2   The passenger's front door, both rear doors and the tailgate each have an electric motor fitted inside the door which is connected to the lock in place of the private lock and interior lock button.

3   The driver's door is equipped with the normal private lock and interior lock button arrangement, and is also fitted with a control unit. Operation of the driver's door lock causes the control unit to supply an electric current to each of the door lock motors, thus locking, or unlocking, the doors in unison with the driver's door.

4   To remove the lock motors or control unit, refer to Chapter 11 and remove the relevant inner trim panel. Disconnect the battery negative terminal and then disconnect the wiring multi-plug on the motor, or control unit harness. Detach the operating links, remove the retaining screws and withdraw the unit from its location.

5   Refitting is the reverse sequence to removal.

## 43  Electric windows – description

1   Certain Maestro models are available with electricaly operated front windows as standard or optional equipment. The system enables both front windows to be raised or lowered independently by two switches on the driver's door armrest. A single switch on the passenger's door armrest allows independent operation of the passenger's window. Each window is operated by an electric motor acting on the window regulator. A relay mounted in the relay panel on the glovebox top cover controls the electrical supply to the circuit, and two additional relays inside the passenger's door isolate the control switches from each other. Each motor contains a cut-out which will

cut off the motor supply should any objects jam the window during operation.

2   The motor and regulator assemblies are removed from the door in the same manner as the manually operated units, after disconnecting the wiring multi-plugs. Removal and refitting procedures are given in Chapter 11.

## 44  Accessory wiring – general

1   If an electrical accessory is to be fitted, electrical connections should be made at the fusebox, on the feed side of the following fuses.

   *(a)  If the accessory is to operate with the ignition switch at position I or II, connect to fuse C1, C2 or C3 (light green/white wire)*
   *(b)  If the accessory is to operate with the ignition switch at position II only, connect to fuse C5 or C6 (white wire)*
   *(c)  If the accessory is to operate irrespective of ignition switch position, connect to fuse A6 (brown wire)*

2   Always use a separate line fuse of the appropriate rating to protect the accessory being fitted.

3   For towing bracket installations, connections for the towing socket can be made at the wiring harness behind the rear light clusters. To gain access, fold back the floor covering and release the rear of the side panel covers. The cable colours, locations and their respective circuits are shown in Fig. 9.7. Note that a special relay is required.

## 45  Fault diagnosis – electrical system

**Note:** *Due to the sophistication of the circuitry and components, faults occurring in the solid-state instrumentation, trip computer or voice synthesis unit, on models so equipped, should be referred to a BL dealer*

| Symptom | Reason(s) |
| --- | --- |
| Starter fails to turn engine | Battery discharged or defective |
|  | Battery terminal and/or earth leads loose |
|  | Starter motor connections loose |
|  | Starter solenoid faulty |
|  | Starter brushes worn or sticking |
|  | Starter commutator dirty or worn |
|  | Starter field coils earthed |
| Starter turns engine very slowly | Battery discharged |
|  | Starter motor connections loose |
|  | Starter brushes worn or sticking |

| Symptom | Reason(s) |
|---|---|
| Starter spins but does not turn engine | Pinion or flywheel ring gear teeth broken or badly worn |
| Starter noisy | Pinion or flywheel ring gear teeth badly worn<br>Mounting bolts loose |
| Battery will not hold charge for more than a few days | Battery defective internally<br>Battery terminals loose<br>Alternator drivebelt slipping<br>Alternator or regulator faulty<br>Short circuit |
| Ignition light stays on | Alternator faulty<br>Alternator drivebelt broken |
| Ignition light fails to come on | Warning bulb blown<br>Indicator light open circuit<br>Alternator faulty |
| Instrument readings increase with engine speed | Voltage stabilizer faulty |
| Fuel or temperature gauge gives no reading | Wiring open circuit<br>Sender unit faulty |
| Fuel or temperature gauge give maximum reading all the time | Wiring short circuit<br>Gauge faulty |
| Lights inoperative | Bulb blown<br>Fuse blown<br>Battery discharged<br>Switch faulty<br>Wiring open circuit<br>Bad connection due to corrosion |
| Failure of component motor | Commutator dirty or burnt<br>Armature faulty<br>Brushes sticking or worn<br>Armature bearings dry or misaligned<br>Field coils faulty<br>Fuse blown<br>Wiring loose or broken |
| Failure of an individual component | Wiring loose or broken<br>Fuse blown<br>Bad circuit connection<br>Switch faulty<br>Component faulty |

**Fig. 9.8 Symbols used in the Wiring Diagrams**

1   Component earthed by a lead
2   Component earthed by its fixing
3   If fitted
4   Instrument pack link harness
5   Line connector
6   Sealed joint
7   Printed circuit

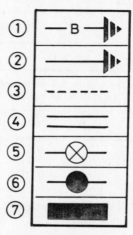

**Colour code**

| | |
|---|---|
| B | Black |
| G | Green |
| K | Pink |
| LG | Light green |
| N | Brown |
| O | Orange |
| P | Purple |
| R | Red |
| S | Slate |
| U | Blue |
| W | White |
| Y | Yellow |

H16439.

**Key to the wiring diagram for all models up to June 1984 except the MG and Vanden Plas**

1   Battery 12V
2   Starter motor solenoid
3   Starter motor
4   Fusebox
5   Ignition switch
6   Ignition warning lamp
7   Ignition coil
8   Ignition amplifier
9   Distributor
10  Tachometer (if fitted)
11  Alternator
12  Horn
13  Horn push
14  Lighting switch
15  Main headlamp
16  Main beam warning lamp
17  Dip headlamp
18  Dip headlamp switch
19  Headlamp flasher/dip switch
20  Sidelamp RH
21  Sidelamp LH
22  Sidelamp warning lamp
23  Tail lamp RH
24  Tail lamp LH
25  Number plate illumination lamp
26  Stop-lamps
27  Stop-lamp switch
28  Direction indicator hazard flasher unit
29  Direction indicator switch
30  RH front direction indicator lamp
31  Direction indicator warning lamps
32  LH front direction indicator lamp
33  Direction indicator repeater flasher (if fitted)
34  RH rear direction indicator lamp
35  LH rear direction indicator lamp
36  Hazard warning switch
37  Hazard warning lamp
38  Reversing lamp
39  Reversing lamp switch
40  Rear foglamp
41  Rear foglamp switch
42  Rear foglamp warning lamp
43  Panel illumination lamps
44  Switch illumination lamps
45  Fuel gauge tank unit
46  Fuel level warning lamp
47  Fuel level indicator
48  Fuel cut-off solenoid

49  Throttle switch
50  Oil pressure switch
51  Oil pressure warning lamp
52  Radiator cooling fan thermostat
53  Radiator cooling fan motor
54  Coolant temperature indicator
55  Coolant temperature transducer
56  Coolant temperature warning lamp
57  Ambient temperature sensor
58  Windscreen wiper motor
59  Windscreen wiper delay unit
60  Windscreen wash/wipe switch
61  Windscreen washer motor
62  Rear screen wiper motor
63  Rear screen wiper switch
64  Rear screen washer switch
65  Rear screen washer motor
66  Heated rear screen switch
67  Heated rear screen
68  Heated rear screen warning lamp
69  Heated rear screen relay
70  Blocking diode
71  Brake failure warning lamp
72  Brake fluid level switch
73  Brake pad wear sensor
74  Brake pad wear warning lamp
75  Handbrake warning lamp switch
76  Handbrake warning lamp
77  Heater control illumination
78  Heater switch
79  Heater motor
80  Interior lamp
81  Interior lamp switches
82  Load space lamp
83  Load space lamp switch
84  Econometer (if fitted)
85  Stepping motor
86  Spare warning lamp
87  Glovebox illumination lamp
88  Glovebox illumination lamp switch
89  Ashtray illumination lamp
90  Cigar lighter
91  Cigar lighter illumination lamp (if fitted)
92  Radio/cassette unit
93  Speaker
94  Clock (if fitted)
95  ECU mixture control (if fitted)
96  Towing warning lamp

**For a key to the colour code and symbols used refer to Fig. 9.8**

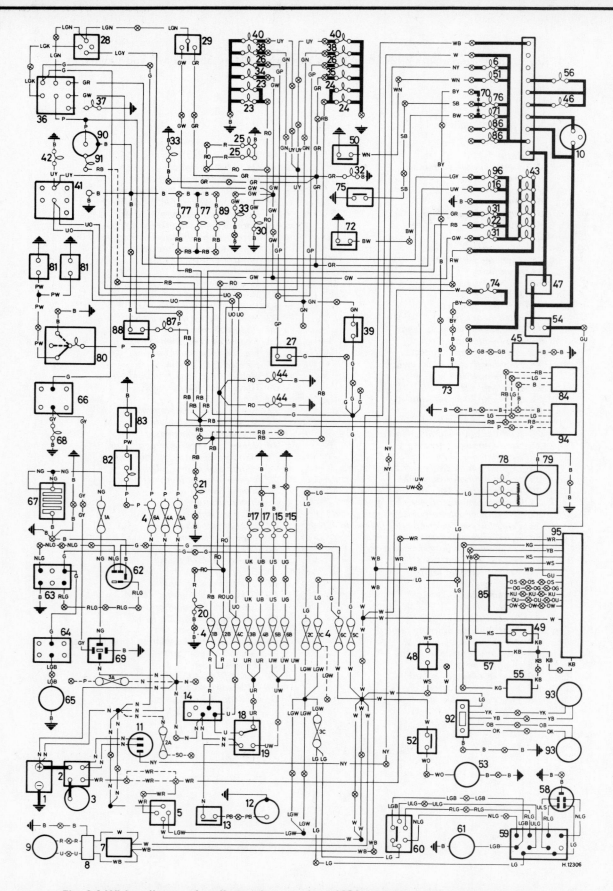

**Fig. 9.9 Wiring diagram for all models up to June 1984 except the MG and Vanden Plas**

## Key to the wiring diagram for MG models up to June 1984

| | |
|---|---|
| 1 Battery 12V | 54 Oil pressure switch |
| 2 Starter motor solenoid | 55 Oil pressure warning lamp |
| 3 Starter motor | 56 Radiator cooling fan thermostat |
| 4 Fusebox | 57 Radiator cooling fan motor |
| 5 Ignition switch | 58 Coolant temperature transducer |
| 6 Ignition warning lamp | 59 Temperature transducer signal |
| 7 Ignition coil | 60 Windscreen wiper motor |
| 8 Ignition amplifier | 61 Windscreen wiper delay unit |
| 9 Ignition 12 volt positive | 62 Windscreen wash/wipe switch |
| 10 Distributor | 63 Windscreen washer motor |
| 11 Tachometer signal | 64 Rear screen wiper motor |
| 12 Alternator | 65 Rear screen wiper switch |
| 13 Horn | 66 Rear screen washer switch |
| 14 Horn push | 67 Rear screen washer motor |
| 15 Lighting switch | 68 Heated rear screen switch |
| 16 Main headlamp | 69 Heated rear screen |
| 17 Main beam warning lamp | 70 Heated rear screen warning lamp |
| 18 Dip headlamp | 71 Heated rear screen relay |
| 19 Dip headlamp switch | 72 Brake fluid warning lamp |
| 20 Headlamp flasher/dip switch | 73 Brake fluid level switch |
| 21 Sidelamp RH | 74 Brake pad wear sensor |
| 22 Sidelamp LH | 75 Brake pad wear signal |
| 23 Sidelamp, warning lamp | 76 Brake pad wear warning lamp |
| 24 Tail lamp RH | 77 Speed transducer |
| 25 Tail lamp LH | 78 Speed transducer signal |
| 26 Number plate illumination lamp | 79 Handbrake warning lamp switch |
| 27 Stop-lamps | 80 Handbrake warning lamp |
| 28 Stop-lamp switch | 81 Heater control illumination |
| 29 Direction indicator hazard flasher unit | 82 Heater switch |
| 30 Direction indicator switch | 83 Heater motor |
| 31 RH front direction indicator lamp | 84 Driver's window switch |
| 32 RH direction indicator warning lamp | 85 Passenger's window switch |
| 33 LH front direction indicator lamp | 86 Window lift motor |
| 34 LH direction indicator warning lamp | 87 Window lift relay |
| 35 Direction indicator repeater flasher (if fitted) | 88 Door lock motor |
| 36 RH rear direction indicator lamp | 89 Door lock motor control unit |
| 37 LH rear direction indicator lamp | 90 Interior lamp |
| 38 Hazard warning switch | 91 Interior lamp switches |
| 39 Hazard warning lamp | 92 Load space lamp |
| 40 Reversing lamp | 93 Load space lamp switch |
| 41 Reversing lamp switch | 94 Potentiometer |
| 42 Rear foglamp | 95 Blocking diode |
| 43 Rear foglamp switch | 96 Spare warning lamp |
| 44 Rear foglamp warning lamp | 97 Earth |
| 45 Solid-state instrument pads | 98 Glovebox illumination lamp |
| 46 Panel illumination (dimmer) | 99 Glovebox illumination lamp switch |
| 47 Dimmer control | 100 Ashtray illumination lamp |
| 48 Switch illumination lamps | 101 Cigar lighter |
| 49 Trip computer/voice synthesis unit | 102 Cigar lighter illumination lamp |
| 50 Voice synthesis cut-out relay | 103 Radio/cassette unit |
| 51 Fuel gauge tank unit | 104 Balance control |
| 52 Fuel gauge tank unit signal | 105 Speaker |
| 53 Fuel flow sensor | 106 Combined mixture control (choke) and warning lamp (if fitted) |

For a key to the colour code and symbols used refer to Fig. 9.8

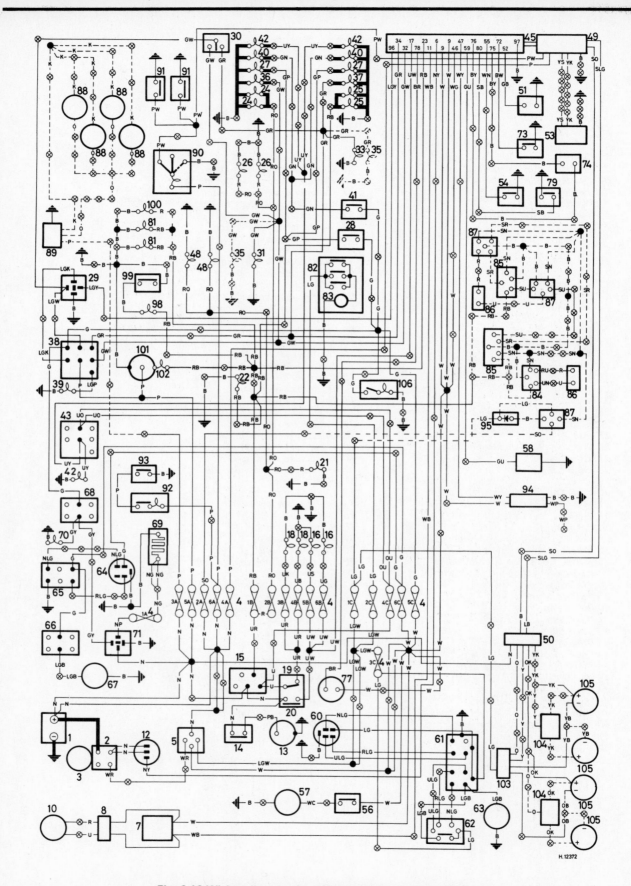

**Fig. 9.10 Wiring diagram for MG models up to June 1984**

H.12372

**Key to the wiring diagram for Vanden Plas models up to June 1984**

1 Battery 12V
2 Starter motor solenoid
3 Starter motor
4 Fusebox
5 Ignition switch
6 Ignition warning lamp
7 Ignition coil
8 Ignition amplifier
9 Ignition 12 volt positive
10 Distributor
11 Tachometer signal
12 Alternator
13 Horn
14 Horn push
15 Lighting switch
16 Main headlamp
17 Main beam warning lamp
18 Dip headlamp
19 Dip headlamp switch
20 Headlamp flasher/dip switch
21 Sidelamp RH
22 Sidelamp LH
23 Sidelamp warning lamp
24 Tail lamp RH
25 Tail lamp LH
26 Number plate illumination lamp
27 Stop-lamps
28 Stop-lamp switch
29 Direction indicator hazard flasher unit
30 Direction indicator switch
31 RH front direction indicator lamp
32 RH direction indicator warning lamp
33 LH front direction indicator lamp
34 LH direction indicator warning lamp
35 Direction indicator repeater flasher (if fitted)
36 RH rear direction indicator lamp
37 LH rear direction indicator lamp
38 Hazard warning switch
39 Hazard warning lamp
40 Reversing lamp
41 Reversing lamp switch
42 Rear foglamp
43 Rear foglamp switch
44 Rear foglamp warning lamp
45 Solid-state instrument pack
46 Panel illumination (dimmer)
47 Dimmer control
48 Switch illumination lamps
49 Trip computer/voice synthesis unit
50 Voice synthesis cut-out relay
51 Fuel gauge tank unit
52 Fuel gauge tank unit signal
53 Fuel cut-off solenoid
54 Fuel flow sensor
55 Throttle switch

56 Oil pressure switch
57 Oil pressure warning lamp
58 Radiator cooling fan thermostat
59 Radiator cooling fan motor
60 Coolant temperature transducer
61 Ambient temperature sensor
62 Temperature transducer signal
63 Windscreen wiper motor
64 Windscreen wiper delay unit
65 Windscreen wash/wipe switch
66 Windscreen washer motor
67 Rear screen wiper motor
68 Rear screen wiper switch
69 Rear screen washer switch
70 Rear screen washer motor
71 Heated rear screen switch
72 Heated rear screen
73 Heated rear screen warning lamp
74 Heated rear screen relay
75 Brake fluid warning lamp
76 Brake fluid level switch
77 Brake pad wear sensor
78 Brake pad wear signal
79 Brake pad wear warning lamp
80 Speed transducer
81 Speed transducer signal
82 Handbrake warning lamp switch
83 Handbrake warning lamp
84 Heater control illumination
85 Heater switch
86 Heater motor
87 Driver's window switch
88 Passenger's window switch
89 Window lift motor
90 Window lift relay
91 Door lock motor
92 Door lock motor control unit
93 Interior lamp
94 Interior lamp switches
95 Load space lamp
96 Load space lamp switch
97 Electric control unit choke
98 Potentiometer
99 Stepping motor
100 Blocking diode
101 Spare warning lamp
102 Earth
103 Glovebox illumination lamp
104 Glovebox illumination lamp switch
105 Ashtray illumination lamp
106 Cigar lighter
107 Cigar lighter illumination lamp
108 Radio/cassette unit
109 Balance control
110 Speaker

**For a key to the colour code and symbols used refer to Fig. 9.8**

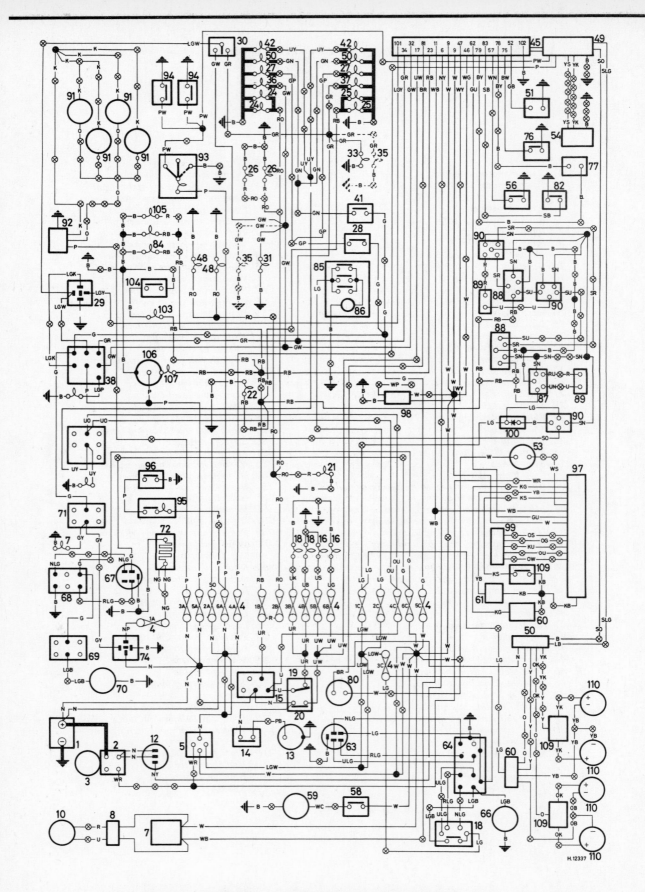

**Fig. 9.11 Wiring diagram for Vanden Plas models up to June 1984**

**Key to supplementary wiring diagram for solid-state instruments**

1   Fusebox
2   Radio/cassette unit
3   Balance control
4   Speakers
5   Speed transducer
6   Potentiometer
7   Voice cut-out relay
8   Solid state instrument pack
9   Trip computer/voice synthesis unit
10  Fuel flow sensor

a   Temperature transducer signal
b   Fuel gauge tank unit signal
c   Speed transducer signal
d   Brake pad wear signal
e   Panel illumination (dimmer)
f   Ignition 12 volt positive
g   Dimmer control
h   Brake fluid warning lamp
i   Handbrake warning lamp
j   Brake pad wear warning lamp
k   Oil pressure warning lamp
l   Direction indicator warning lamp RH
m   Sidelamp warning light
n   Direction indicator warning lamp LH
o   Earth
p   Main beam warning lamp
q   Spare warning lamp
r   Ignition warning lamp
s   Ignition 12 volt positive
t   Tachometer signal

**For a key to the colour code and symbols used refer to Fig. 9.8**

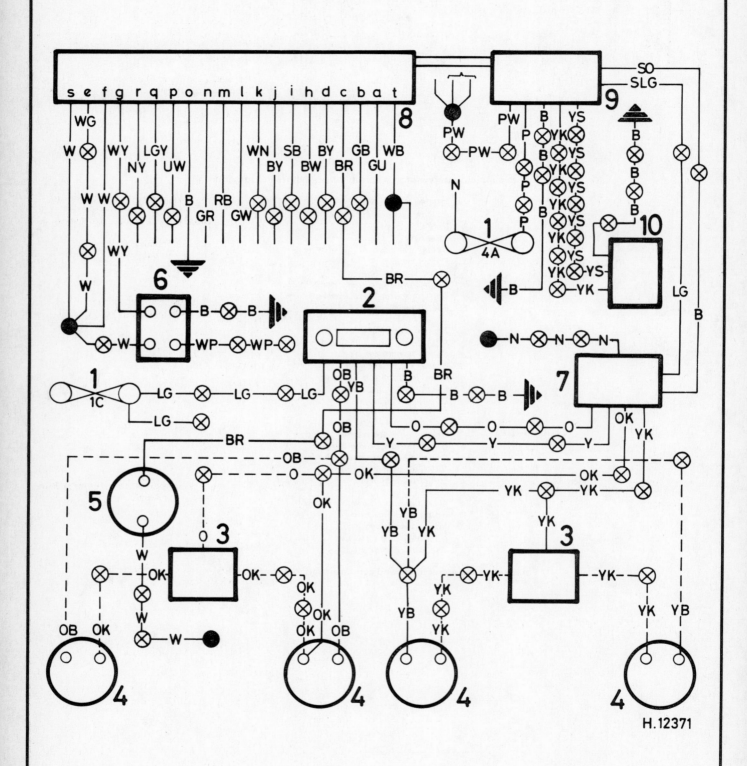

**Fig. 9.12 Supplementary wiring diagram for solid-state instruments**

H.12371

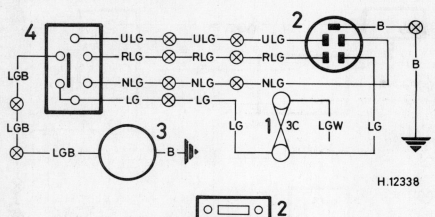

**Fig. 9.13 Supplementary wiring diagram for the wiper circuit on 1.3 litre models**

**Key**
1 Fusebox
2 Windscreen wiper motor
3 Windscreen washer motor
4 Windscreen wash/wipe switch

**For a key to the colour code and symbols used refer to Fig. 9.8**

H.12338

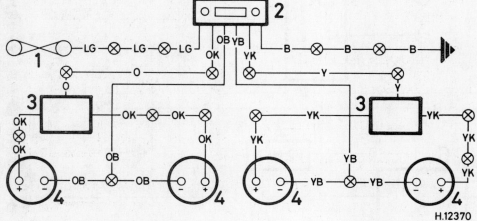

**Fig. 9.14 Supplementary wiring diagram for a four speaker radio/cassette player installation**

1 Fusebox
2 Radio/cassette
3 Balance control
4 Speakers

**For a key to the colour code and symbols used refer to Fig. 9.8**

H.12370

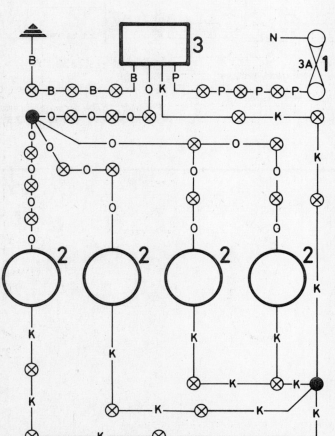

**Fig. 9.15 Supplementary wiring diagram for central door locking systems**

1 Fusebox
2 Door lock motor
3 Driver's door lock control unit

**For a key to the colour code and symbols used refer to Fig. 9.8**

H.12369

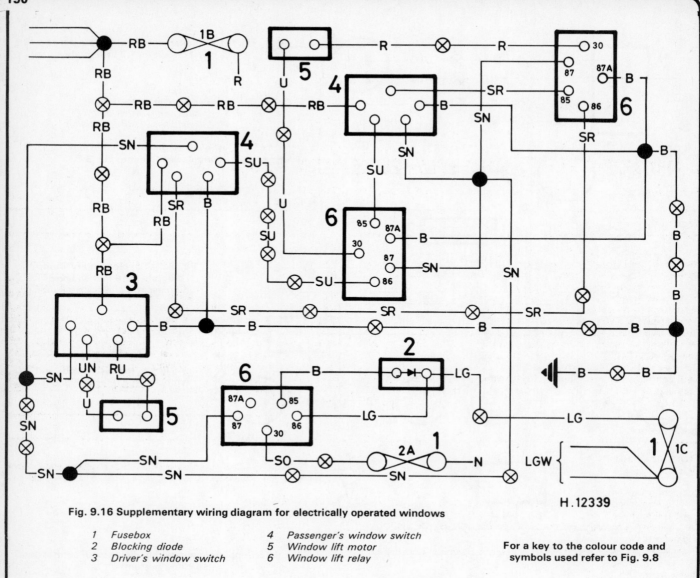

**Fig. 9.16 Supplementary wiring diagram for electrically operated windows**

1  Fusebox
2  Blocking diode
3  Driver's window switch
4  Passenger's window switch
5  Window lift motor
6  Window lift relay

For a key to the colour code and symbols used refer to Fig. 9.8

H.12339

# Chapter 10 Suspension and steering

*For modifications, and information applicable to later models, see Supplement at end of manual*

## Contents

## Specifications

### Front suspension

| | |
|---|---|
| Type .......................................................................................... | Independent by MacPherson type struts with coil springs and integral telescopic shock absorbers. Anti-roll bar on 1.6 litre models only |
| Coil spring free length: | |
| 1.3 litre models ...................................................................... | 14.48 in (368.6 mm) |
| 1.6 litre models ...................................................................... | 15.18 in (385.7 mm) |
| Trim height (measured from the centre of the front hub to the edge of the wheel arch) ............................................................. | 14.3 to 15.3 in (363 to 389 mm) |
| Trim height permissible side difference ..................................... | 0.39 in (10 mm) |

### Rear suspension

| | |
|---|---|
| Type .......................................................................................... | Trailing twist axle with coil springs and telescopic shock absorbers |
| Coil spring free length ............................................................... | 13.5 in (343 mm) |
| Trim height (measured from the centre of the rear hub to the edge of the wheel arch) ............................................................. | 14.6 to 15.6 in (371 to 396 mm) |
| Trim height permissible side difference ..................................... | 0.39 in (10 mm) |
| Rear wheel toe setting .............................................................. | 0° 30' to 1° 0' toe-in |
| Rear wheel camber angle .......................................................... | 0° to 1° negative |

### Steering

| | |
|---|---|
| Type .......................................................................................... | Rack and pinion |
| Turns lock to lock ..................................................................... | 3.6 |
| Steering wheel diameter ........................................................... | 15 in (381 mm) |
| Steering angles ......................................................................... | See Chapter 12 Specifications |
| Steering gear lubricant ............................................................. | BP Energrease, FGL Fluid Grease |

### Roadwheels

| | |
|---|---|
| Wheel size: | |
| 1.3 litre models ...................................................................... | 4½J x 13 |
| 1.6 litre models ...................................................................... | 5J x 13 |
| 1.3 and 1.6 litre models with alloy wheels ............................. | 5J x 13 |
| MG models ............................................................................. | 5½J x 14 |

### Tyres

| | |
|---|---|
| Tyre size: | |
| 1.3 litre models ...................................................................... | 145 SR 13, 155 SR 13, steel braced radial ply |
| 1.6 litre models ...................................................................... | 165 SR 13 steel braced radial ply |
| MG models ............................................................................. | 175/65 HR 14 radial ply |

| Tyre pressures (cold): | lbf/in² | bar |
|---|---|---|
| 145 SR 13: | | |
|     Front | 30 | 2.1 |
|     Rear | 32 | 2.2 |
| 155 SR 13: | | |
|     Front | 26 | 1.8 |
|     Rear | 28 | 1.9 |
| 165 SR 13: | | |
|     Front | 26 | 1.8 |
|     Rear | 28 | 1.9 |
| 175/65 HR 14: | | |
|     Front | 28 | 1.9 |
|     Rear | 26 | 1.8 |

## Torque wrench settings

| | lbf ft | Nm |
|---|---|---|
| *Front suspension* | | |
| Anti-roll bar bush-to-lower arm nut | 13 | 18 |
| Anti-roll bar clamp bolts | 33 | 45 |
| Balljoint-to-lower arm (service replacement bolts) | 22 | 30 |
| Balljoint-to-swivel hub clamp nut | 33 | 45 |
| Driveshaft nut | 150 | 203 |
| Suspension strut-to-swivel hub nuts | 66 | 90 |
| Suspension strut upper retaining nut | 41 | 55 |
| Suspension strut bearing retaining nut | 22 | 30 |
| Lower arm rear mounting bolts | 33 | 45 |
| Lower arm front mounting bolt | 53 | 72 |
| Subframe (crossmember) to body | 67 | 90 |
| Subframe supports to body | 55 | 75 |
| Subframe supports to subframe | 67 | 90 |
| | | |
| *Rear suspension* | | |
| Rear axle pivot bolts (standard) | 33 | 45 |
| Rear axle pivot bolts (marked '8.8') | 63 | 85 |
| Rear hub retaining nut | 50 | 68 |
| Stub axle-to-trailing arm nuts | 33 | 45 |
| Suspension strut lower mounting | 53 | 72 |
| Suspension strut upper mounting nut | 33 | 45 |
| Suspension strut spring retainer nut | 30 | 40 |
| | | |
| *Steering* | | |
| Steering column mounting bolts | 18 | 25 |
| Intermediate shaft clamp nuts | 18 | 25 |
| Rack and pinion assembly mounting bolts | 33 | 45 |
| Steering wheel nut | 35 | 48 |
| Tie-rod inner balljoint to rack | 60 | 80 |
| Tie-rod outer balljoint to steering arm | 22 | 30 |
| | | |
| *Roadwheels* | | |
| Wheel nuts (all models) | 53 | 72 |

## 1  General description

The independent front suspension is of the MacPherson strut type, incorporating coil springs and integral telescopic shock absorbers. Lateral and longitudinal location of each strut assembly is by pressed-steel lower suspension arms utilizing rubber inner mounting bushes and incorporating a balljoint at their outer ends. On 1.6 litre models both lower suspension arms are interconnected by an anti-roll bar. The front swivel hubs, which carry the wheel bearings, brake calipers and the hub/disc assemblies, are bolted to the MacPherson struts and connected to the lower arms via the balljoints.

The rear suspension is of the trailing twist axle type, whereby the two trailing arms are welded to an 'L' section transverse member. This arrangement allows considerable independent up-and-down movement of each trailing arm whilst providing lateral rigidity and anti-roll capability in a structure of minimum unsprung weight. Suspension and damping is by strut assemblies containing coil springs and integral telescopic shock absorbers.

The steering gear is of the conventional rack and pinion type, located behind the front wheels. Movement of the steering wheel is transmitted to the steering gear by an intermediate shaft containing two universal joints. The front wheels are connected to the steering gear by tie-rods, each having an inner and outer balljoint.

## 2  Maintenance and inspection

1  At regular intervals (see Routine Maintenance) a thorough inspection of all suspension and steering components should be carried out using the following procedure as a guide.

### Front suspension and steering

2  Apply the handbrake, jack up the front of the car and support it securely on axle stands.

3  Visually inspect the lower balljoint dust covers and the steering rack and pinion rubber gaiters for splits, chafing, or deterioration. Renew the rubber gaiters or the balljoint assembly, as described in Sections 21 and 8 respectively, if any damage is apparent.

4  Grasp the roadwheel at the 12 o'clock and 6 o'clock positions and try to rock it. Very slight free play may be felt, but if the movement is appreciable further investigation is necessary to determine the source. Continue rocking the wheel while an assistant depresses the footbrake. If the movement is now eliminated or significantly reduced, it is likely that the hub bearings are at fault. If the free play is still evident with the footbrake depressed, then there is wear in the suspension joints or mountings. Pay close attention to the lower balljoint and lower arm mounting bushes. Renew any worn components, as described in the appropriate Sections of this Chapter.

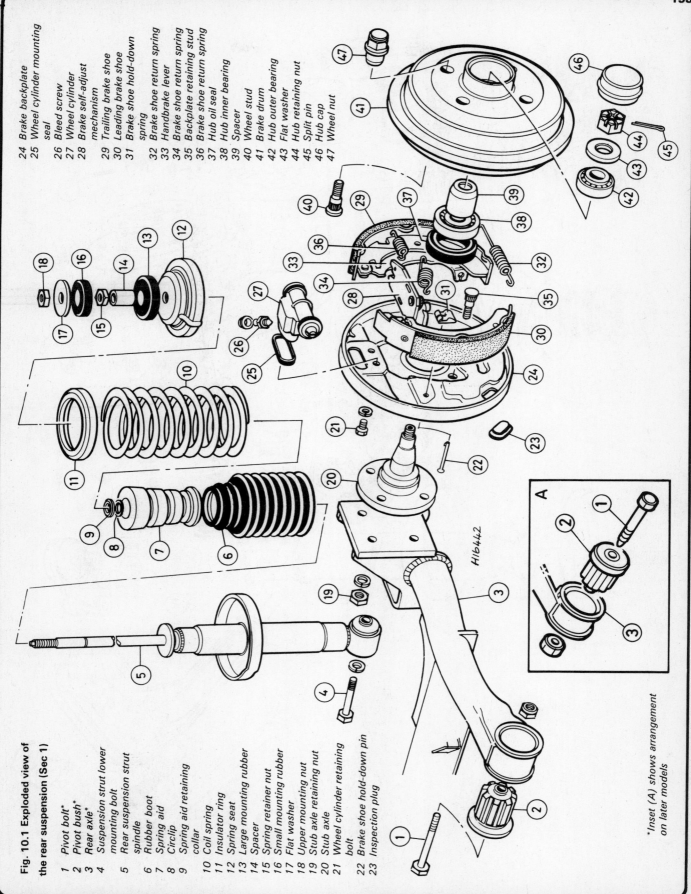

**Fig. 10.1 Exploded view of the rear suspension (Sec 1)**

1 Pivot bolt*
2 Pivot bush*
3 Rear axle*
4 Suspension strut lower mounting bolt
5 Rear suspension strut
6 Rubber boot
7 Spring aid
8 Circlip
9 Spring aid retaining collar
10 Coil spring
11 Insulator ring
12 Spring seat
13 Large mounting rubber
14 Spacer
15 Spring retainer nut
16 Small mounting rubber
17 Flat washer
18 Upper mounting nut
19 Stub axle retaining nut
20 Stub axle
21 Wheel cylinder retaining bolt
22 Brake shoe hold-down pin
23 Inspection plug

24 Brake backplate
25 Wheel cylinder mounting seal
26 Bleed screw
27 Wheel cylinder
28 Brake self-adjust mechanism
29 Trailing brake shoe
30 Leading brake shoe
31 Brake shoe hold-down spring
32 Brake shoe return spring
33 Handbrake lever
34 Brake shoe return spring
35 Backplate retaining stud
36 Brake shoe return spring
37 Hub oil seal
38 Hub inner bearing
39 Spacer
40 Wheel stud
41 Brake drum
42 Hub outer bearing
43 Flat washer
44 Hub retaining nut
45 Split pin
46 Hub cap
47 Wheel nut

*Inset (A) shows arrangement on later models

H16440

**Fig. 10.2 Exploded view of the front suspension (Sec 1)**

| | | | |
|---|---|---|---|
| 1 | Anti-roll bar | 11 | Front suspension strut |
| 2 | Mounting block | 12 | Lower insulator ring |
| 3 | Clamp | 13 | Rubber bush |
| 4 | Clamp retaining bolts | 14 | Rear mounting bracket |
| 5 | Lower arm front mounting bolt | 15 | Mounting bolt |
| 6 | Rubber bush | 16 | Coil spring |
| 7 | Lower suspension arm | 17 | Upper mounting nut |
| 8 | Anti-roll bar mounting bush | 18 | Washer |
| 9 | Lower suspension arm balljoint | 19 | Cup and washer assembly |
| 10 | Rivet (replaced by nut and bolt after balljoint renewal) | 20 | Upper mounting rubber |
| | | 21 | Bearing retainer nut |
| | | 22 | Bearing housing |
| | | 23 | Upper bearing |
| | | 24 | Spring seat |

| | | | |
|---|---|---|---|
| 25 | Spring aid | 36 | Swivel hub |
| 26 | Upper insulator ring | 37 | Hub outer bearing |
| 27 | Rubber boot | 38 | Outer oil seal |
| 28 | Strut-to-swivel hub retaining bolt | 39 | Disc shield halves |
| 29 | Bearing water shield | 40 | Disc shield retaining bolt |
| 30 | Inner oil seal | 41 | Wheel stud |
| 31 | Oil seal spacer | 42 | Drive flange |
| 32 | Hub inner bearing | 43 | Brake disc |
| 33 | Brake caliper mounting bolt | 44 | Disc retaining screw |
| 34 | Disc shield retaining screw and clip | 45 | Flat washer |
| 35 | Lower balljoint clamp bolt | 46 | Driveshaft nut |
| | | 47 | Split pin |
| | | 48 | Wheel nut |

| | |
|---|---|
| 49 | Bleed screw |
| 50 | Guide pin bolt |
| 51 | Caliper body |
| 52 | Inner brake pad |
| 53 | Outer brake pad |
| 54 | Piston |
| 55 | Guide pin |
| 56 | Dust cover |
| 57 | Piston dust cover |
| 58 | Carrier bracket |

5    Now grasp the wheel at the 9 o'clock and 3 o'clock positions and try to rock it as before. Any movement felt now may again be caused by wear in the hub bearings or the steering tie-rod inner or outer balljoints. If the outer balljoint is worn the visual movement will be obvious. If the inner joint is suspect it can be felt by placing a hand over the rack and pinion rubber gaiter and gripping the tie-rod. If the wheel is now rocked, movement will be felt at the inner joint if wear has taken place. Repair procedures are described in Section 20 and 23 respectively.

6    Using a large screwdriver or flat bar check for wear in the anti-roll bar mountings (where fitted) and lower arm mountings by carefully levering against these components. Some movement is to be expected, as the mountings are made of rubber, but excessive wear should be obvious. Renew any bushes that are worn.

7    With the car standing on its wheels, have an assistant turn the steering wheel back and forth about one eighth of a turn each way. There should be no lost movement whatever between the steering wheel and roadwheels. If this is not the case, closely observe the joints and mountings previously described, but in addition check the intermediate shaft universal joints for wear and also the rack and pinion steering gear itself. Any wear should be visually apparent and must be rectified, as described in the appropriate Sections of this Chapter.

*Rear suspension*

8    Chock the front wheels, jack up the rear of the car and support it securely on axle stands.

9    Visually inspect the rear suspension components, attachments and linkages for any visible signs of wear or damage.

10   Grasp the roadwheel at the 12 o'clock and 6 o'clock positions and try to rock it. Any excess movement here indicates wear in the hub bearings which may also be accompanied by a rumbling sound when the wheel is spun. Repair procedures are described in Section 11.

*Wheels and tyres*

11   Carefully inspect each tyre, including the spare, for signs of uneven wear, lumps, bulges or damage to the sidewalls or tread face. Refer to Section 25 for further details.

12   Check the condition of the wheel rims for distortion, damage and excessive run-out. Also make sure that the balance weights are secure with no obvious signs that any are missing. Check the torque of the wheel nuts and check the tyre pressures.

*Shock absorbers*

13   Check for any signs of fluid leakage around the shock absorber body or from the rubber boot around the piston rod. Should any fluid be noticed the shock absorber is defective internally and renewal is necessary.

14   The efficiency of the shock absorber may be checked by bouncing the car at each corner. Generally speaking the body will return to its normal position and stop after being depressed. If it rises and returns on a rebound, the shock absorber is probably suspect. Examine also the shock absorber upper and lower mountings for any sign of wear. Renewal procedures are contained in Sections 6 and 14.

**3    Front swivel hub assembly – removal and refitting**

1    Securely apply the handbrake, chock the rear wheels and remove the wheel trim from the centre of the front roadwheel.

2    Extract the split pin, then using a socket and long bar, slacken, but do not remove, the driveshaft nut.

3    Slacken the roadwheel retaining nuts then jack up the front of the car and support it securely on axle stands. Remove the roadwheel. Remove the driveshaft retaining nut and washer (photo).

4    Undo and remove the two bolts securing the disc brake caliper to the carrier bracket. Slide the caliper, complete with brake pads, off the carrier bracket and suspend it from a convenient place under the wheel arch using string or wire. Take care not to strain the flexible hydraulic hose.

5    Undo and remove the nut securing the tie-rod outer balljoint to the steering arm on the swivel hub. Release the balljoint from the steering arm using a suitable extractor (see Section 20).

6    At the base of the swivel hub unscrew and remove the nut and washer, then withdraw the lower balljoint clamp bolt (photo).

7    Undo and remove the nuts and washers, then withdraw the two bolts securing the suspension strut to the upper part of the swivel hub (photo).

3.3 Remove the driveshaft nut and flat washer

3.6 Unscrew the nut and withdraw the lower balljoint clamp bolt (arrowed)

3.7 Remove the two nuts and bolts (arrowed) securing the swivel hub to the suspension strut

3.8 Withdraw the hub assembly from the driveshaft

3.9a If the drive flange is tight in the bearings, use a hammer and socket, or tube, to drive out the flange ...

3.9b ... and then withdraw the drive flange and disc assembly from the hub

3.11a Position the water shield on the driveshaft flange before fitting the hub

3.11b Make sure the driveshaft retaining nut is tightened to the specified torque

8    Release the swivel hub from the strut and then lift the hub, while pushing down on the suspension arm, to disengage the lower balljoint. Withdraw the swivel hub assembly from the driveshaft and remove it from the car (photo).

9    Secure the swivel hub in a vice, undo the two bolts and remove the brake caliper carrier bracket. Separate the drive flange and disc from the hub using a hammer and suitable tube or socket, if necessary (photos).

10   If required, the two halves of the disc shield can now be removed after unscrewing the retaining bolt and screw.

11   Refitting the swivel hub is the reverse of the removal sequence, bearing in mind the following points:

(a)   *Ensure that the bearing water shield is in position on the driveshaft (photo) before fitting the swivel hub. Fill the groove in the water shield with a general purpose grease*

(b)   *Where applicable, tighten all retaining nuts and bolts to the specified torque.* **Do not attempt to fully tighten the driveshaft nut until the weight of the car is on the roadwheels**

(c)   *Tighten the driveshaft retaining nut as described in Chapter 12, Section 12. Always use a new split pin*

## 4   Front hub bearings – removal and refitting

1    Remove the swivel hub assembly from the car, as described in the previous Section.

2    With the hub assembly on the bench, prise out the inner and outer oil seals using a screwdriver or suitable flat bar. Note that there is a spacer fitted between the inner oil seal and the bearing.

3    With the hub supported on blocks use a hammer and drift to drive out one of the bearing inner races from the centre of the hub. Take care not to lose the balls which will be dislodged as the inner race is released. Turn the hub over and repeat the procedure for the other inner race. The outer races can now be driven out in the same way.

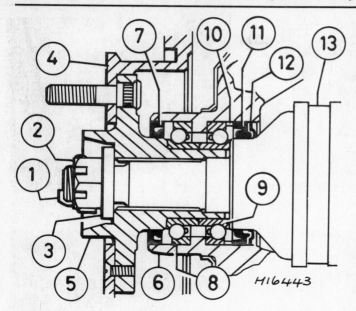

**Fig. 10.3 Cross-sectional view of the front hub (Sec 4)**

| | |
|---|---|
| 1   Split pin | 8   Outer bearing |
| 2   Hub nut | 9   Inner bearing |
| 3   Flat washer | 10  Spacer |
| 4   Brake disc | 11  Inner oil seal |
| 5   Drive flange | 12  Bearing water shield |
| 6   Hub | 13  Drive shaft |
| 7   Outer oil seal | |

4    Wipe away any surplus grease from the bearings and swivel hub and then clean these components thoroughly using paraffin, or a suitable solvent. Dry with a lint-free rag. Remove any burrs or score marks from the hub bore with a fine file or scraper.

5    Carefully examine the bearing inner and outer races, the balls and ball cage for pitting, scoring or cracks, and if at all suspect renew the bearings as a pair. It will also be necessary to renew the oil seals as they will have been damaged during removal.

6    If the old bearings are in satisfactory condition and are to be reused, reassemble the ball cage, holding the balls in position with grease, and then place this assembly in the outer race. Lay the inner race over the balls and push it firmly into place.

7    Before refitting the bearings to the hub, pack them thoroughly with a high melting-point grease.

8    Place one of the bearings in position on the hub with the word THRUST, or the markings stamped on the edge of the inner race, facing away from the centre of the hub (photo).

9    Using a tube of suitable diameter, a large socket or a soft metal drift, drive the bearing into the hub bore until it contacts the shoulder in the centre of the hub. Ensure that the bearing does not tip slightly and bind as it is being fitted. *If this happens the outer race may crack, so take great care to keep it square.*

10   Turn the hub over and repeat this procedure for the other bearing.

11   Dip the new oil seals in oil and carefully fit them to the hub using a tube of suitable diameter or one of the old seals to drive them in. Note that both oil seals are fitted with their sealing lips inward (photo) and that the inner seal has a second lip on its outer face. Don't forget to fit the spacer between the bearing and inner oil seal (photos).

12   The swivel hub can now be refitted to the car, as described in the previous Section.

## 5   Front suspension strut – removal and refitting

1    Securely apply the handbrake, chock the rear wheels and remove the trim from the centre of the front roadwheel.

2    Slacken the roadwheel retaining nuts, then jack up the front of the car and support it securely on axle stands. Remove the roadwheel.

3    From within the engine compartment prise off the small plastic cap in the centre of the strut upper mounting (photo).

4    Insert an Allen key of the appropriate size into the centre of the strut spindle and, while holding the key to prevent the spindle turning, unscrew the mounting nut (photo). Lift off the spring washer and the cup and washer assembly.

5    Undo and remove the two nuts, bolts and spring washers securing the suspension strut to the swivel hub (photo). Release the strut from the hub and withdraw it from under the wheel arch (photo).

6    Refitting is the reverse sequence to removal. Ensure that all retaining nuts and bolts are tightened to the specified torque, where applicable.

## 6   Front suspension strut – dismantling and reassembly

**Note:** *Before attempting to dismantle the front suspension strut, a suitable tool to hold the coil spring in compression must be obtained. Adjustable coil spring compressors are readily available and are recommended for this operation. Any attempt to dismantle the strut without such a tool is likely to result in damage or personal injury.*

1    Proceed by removing the front suspension strut, as described in the previous Section.

2    Position the spring compressors on either side of the spring (photo) and compress the spring evenly until there is no tension on the upper spring seat or upper mounting.

3    Lift off the upper mounting rubber (photo) and bearing housing (photo).

4    To remove the bearing retainer nut it will be necessary to make up a suitable tool which will engage in the slots of the nut enabling it to be unscrewed. A tool can be made out of a large nut, slightly larger than the front suspension strut upper mounting nut, with one end suitably shaped by cutting or filing so that two projections are left which will engage with the slots in the retainer nut (Fig. 10.4).

5    While holding the strut spindle with an Allen key, unscrew the bearing retainer nut. Lift off the upper bearing, spring seat and insulator ring.

6    The coil spring can now be removed, with compressors still in position if desired, followed by the spring aid, rubber boot and lower insulator ring.

7    With the strut completely dismantled, the components can be examined as follows.

8    Examine the strut for signs of fluid leakage. Check the strut spindle for signs of wear or pitting along its entire length and check the strut body for signs of damage or elongation of the mounting bolt holes. Test the operation of the strut, while holding it in an upright position, by moving the spindle through a full stroke and then through short strokes of 2 to 4 in (50 to 100 mm). In both cases the resistance felt should be smooth and continuous. If the resistance is jerky, or uneven, or if there is any visible sign of wear or damage to the strut, renewal is necessary.

9    If any doubt exists about the condition of the coil spring, remove the spring compressors and check the spring for distortion. Also measure the free length of the spring and compare the measurement with the figure given in the Specifications. Renew the spring if it is distorted or outside the specified length.

10   Begin assembly by fitting the rubber boot and spring aid to the strut.

11   Place the lower insulator ring in position, followed by the spring, ensuring that the end of the bottom coil locates in the step of the spring seat.

12   With the spring suitably compressed, withdraw the strut spindle as far as it will go and refit the upper insulator ring and spring seat. Make sure that the end of the spring upper coil locates in the step of the spring seat.

13   Place the bearing, with the small internal diameter downwards, over the spindle and refit the bearing retainer nut. Tighten to the specified torque and remove the spring compressors.

14   Finally refit the bearing housing and the upper mounting rubber, large open ng uppermost.

15   The strut can now be refitted to the car, as described in the previous Section.

## 7   Front lower suspension arm – removal and refitting

1    Apply the handbrake, chock the rear wheels and remove the front wheel trim. Slacken the wheel nuts. Jack up the front of the car, support it securely on axle stands and remove the roadwheel.

4.8 The hub bearings must be fitted with the word THRUST (arrowed), or the markings stamped on the outer race, facing away from the centre of the hub

4.11a Fit the outer oil seal with its sealing lip inwards

4.11b Place the spacer in position over the bearing ...

4.11c ... and then fit the inner oil seal, with its sealing lip also facing inwards

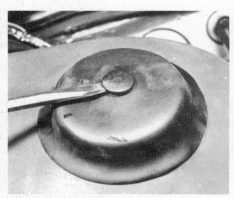

5.3 Prise off the plastic cap, and lift off the front strut upper mounting cover

5.4 Hold the strut spindle with an Allen key and unscrew the upper mounting nut

5.5a Undo and remove the strut to swivel hub securing nuts and bolts (arrowed) ...

5.5b ... and withdraw the strut assembly from under the wheel arch

6.2 The tension in the coil spring must be relieved using spring compressors before dismantling the strut

6.3a Lift off the upper mounting rubber ...

6.3b ... and bearing housing (arrowed) to gain access to the bearing retainer nut

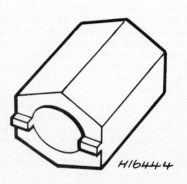

Fig. 10.4 Suspension strut bearing retainer nut removal tool (Sec 6)

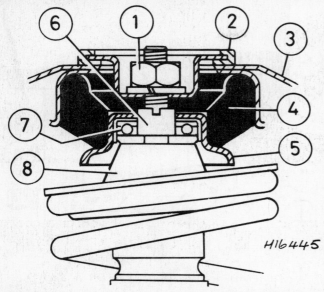

Fig. 10.5 Front suspension strut upper mounting details (Sec 6)

| | | | |
|---|---|---|---|
| 1 | Mounting nut | 5 | Bearing housing |
| 2 | Cup and washer assembly | 6 | Bearing retainer nut |
| 3 | Inner front wing valance | 7 | Upper bearing |
| 4 | Upper mounting rubber | 8 | Spring seat |

7.4 Front suspension arm rear mounting retaining bolts (arrowed)

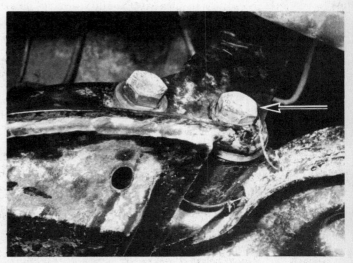

7.5 Front suspension arm front mounting retaining bolt (arrowed)

2   Undo and remove the nut and washer and then withdraw the clamp bolt securing the lower balljoint to the swivel hub.

3   Lever the lower suspension arm downwards to release the balljoint from the hub.

4   Undo and remove the three bolts securing the suspension arm rear mounting to the underbody (photo).

5   Undo and remove the nut and bolt securing the front mounting to the crossmember (photo).

6   On models equipped with an anti-roll bar, undo and remove the nut and washer securing the anti-roll bar mounting bush to the suspension arm.

7   Ease the front mounting out of the subframe lift the suspension arm to disengage the anti-roll bar (where fitted) and manoeuvre the arm out from beneath the vehicle.

8   With the arm removed from the car, carefully examine the rubber mounting bushes for swelling or deterioration, the balljoint for slackness and check for damage to the rubber boot. Renewal of the balljoint is described in Section 8. Renewal of the suspension arm mounting bushes may be carried out as follows.

9   Using a two-legged puller, or similar tool, draw the rear bush assembly off its spigot. The rear bush can be removed from its mounting bracket by pressing it out in a vice with the aid of tubes of suitable length and diameter. Removal of the front bush in the arm follows the same procedure.

10   To refit the new bushes first liberally lubricate them with rubber grease and then press them fully into place using a vice. Slide the rear bush assembly onto its spigot on the suspension arm. Note that the rear bush housings are handed and must not be interchanged from side to side. When fitted the small hole in the bush housing must be toward the centre of the car.

11   Refitting the lower suspension arm is the reverse sequence to removal. Ensure that all retaining nuts and bolts are tightened to the specified torque.

## 8   Front lower suspension arm balljoint – removal and refitting

1   Remove the lower suspension arm, as described in the previous Section.

2   Drill out the heads of the three rivets securing the balljoint to the arm and drive out the rivets with a punch.

3   Withdraw the balljoint from the suspension arm.

4   Replacement balljoint kits are supplied with nuts and bolts to secure the joint in place of the factory fitted rivets. Slide the new

balljoint into position and fit the bolts so that the bolt heads are located above the arm. Screw on the nuts and tighten them to the specified torque.

5   The lower suspension arm can now be refitted to the car, as described in the previous Section.

## 9   Anti-roll bar – removal and refitting

**Note:** *For this operation the front suspension must be kept in a laden condition. If a vehicle lift or inspection pit are not available, it will be necessary to drive the front of the car up on ramps.*

1   Undo and remove the nuts and washers securing the anti-roll bar mounting bush, one each side, to the lower suspension arms.

2   Undo and remove the four bolts securing the anti-roll bar clamps to the subframe. Lift away the clamps, disengage the mounting bushes from the lower suspension arms and lower the anti-roll bar to the ground.

3   If the mounting blocks require renewal, slip them off the bar and place new blocks in position after lubricating liberally with rubber grease.

4   To renew the mounting bushes first measure and record the distance from the outer face of the bush to the end of the anti-roll bar. Now draw off the bushes using a two-legged puller.

5    Lubricate the new bushes with rubber grease and drive them onto the anti-roll bar using a hammer and tube of suitable diameter. Use the measurement recorded during removal as a setting dimension.
6    To refit the anti-roll bar to the car, first locate the bush assemblies in the lower suspension arms and fit the washers and retaining nuts finger tight.
7    Place the clamps over the mounting blocks and refit the retaining bolts, noting that the long bolts locate in the rear holes.
8    First tighten the clamp bolts to the specified torque, followed by the bush retaining nuts.
9    Lower the car to the ground (if applicable).

## 10  Rear hub assembly – removal and refitting

1    Chock the front wheels, remove the rear wheel trim and slacken the wheel nuts. Jack up the rear of the car and support it securely on axle stands. Remove the roadwheel and release the handbrake.
2    By judicious tapping and levering extract the hub cap and withdraw the retaining split pin from the hub retaining nut.
3    Using a large socket and bar, undo and remove the hub retaining nut and flat washer. *Note that the left-hand nut has a left-hand thread and the right-hand nut has a conventional right-hand thread.* **Take care not to tip the car from the axle stands.** If the hub nuts are particularly tight, temporarily refit the roadwheel and lower the car to the ground. Slacken the nut in this more stable position and then raise and support the car before removing the nut.
4    Withdraw the hub and brake drum assembly from the stub axle. If it is not possible to withdraw the hub due to the brake drum binding on the brake shoes, the following procedure should be adopted. Refer to Chapter 8, if necessary, and slacken off the handbrake cable at the cable adjuster. From the rear of the brake backplate, prise out the handbrake lever stop, which will allow the brake shoes to retract sufficiently for the hub assembly to be removed. It will, however, be necessary to remove the brake shoes and fit a new handbrake lever stop to the backplate.
5    Refitting the hub assembly is the reverse sequence to removal. Tighten the hub retaining nut to the specified torque and then align the next split pin hole. Always use a new split pin.

## 11  Rear hub bearings – removal and refitting

1    Remove the rear hub assembly from the car, as described in the previous Section.
2    With the hub on the bench, prise out the rear oil seal using a stout screwdriver or suitable flat bar.
3    Support the hub on blocks and, using a soft metal drift, tap out the two bearing inner races. Take care not to lose any of the balls which will be released from the ball cage as the inner races are removed.
4    Withdraw the spacer located between the two bearings and then drive the two outer races from the centre of the hub.
5    Wipe away any surplus grease and then thoroughly clean all the parts in paraffin or a suitable solvent. Dry with a lint-free rag.
6    Carefully examine the bearing inner and outer races, the ball cage and the balls for scoring, pitting or wear ridges. Renew both bearings as a set if any of these conditions are apparent. The hub oil seal must

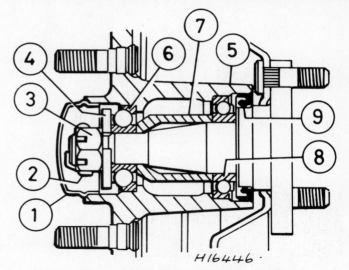

**Fig. 10.6 Cross-sectional view of the rear hub (Sec 11)**

| | | | |
|---|---|---|---|
| 1 | Hub cap | 6 | Outer bearing |
| 2 | Split pin | 7 | Spacer |
| 3 | Hub retaining nut | 8 | Inner bearing |
| 4 | Flat washer | 9 | Oil seal |
| 5 | Hub and brake drum assembly | | |

be renewed as it will have been damaged during removal. If the bearings are in a satisfactory condition, reassemble the balls and ball cage on the outer race, holding them in place with grease, and then press the inner race back into position (photo).
7    Before refitting the bearings, remove any burrs that may be present in the bore of the hub using a fine file or scraper.
8    Pack the bearings with a high melting-point grease and place the outer bearing in position with the word THRUST, or the markings stamped on the edge of the inner race, facing outwards. Drive the bearing into position using a tube of suitable diameter, or a drift, in contact with the bearing outer race. Take great care to keep the bearing square as it is installed, otherwise it will jam in the hub bore which could crack the outer race.
9    Dip a new oil seal in clean engine oil and position it over the outer bearing with its sealing lip facing inwards. Using a hammer and block of wood, tap the seal into the hub until it is flush with the end face of the hub.
10   Turn the hub over and lay the spacer over the installed outer bearing, with the smaller diameter of the spacer facing outwards (photo).
11   Fit the inner bearing and oil seal to the hub, using the same procedure as for the outer bearing, with the word THRUST, or the bearing markings, also facing out from the hub centre (photos).
12   The rear hub assembly can now be refitted to the car, as described in the previous Section.

11.6 Reassemble the balls in the cage of the hub bearings and then gently press the inner race into position

11.10 The spacer is fitted between the bearings with its smaller diameter facing outwards

11.11a Fit the bearings with the word THRUST, or the markings on the inner race, facing outwards from the hub centre

11.11b Drive the bearings into the hub using a tube, or drift, ensuring that the bearings are kept square

11.11c Fit the oil seal with its sealing lip facing in towards the hub centre

## 12 Rear stub axle – removal and refitting

1   Remove the rear hub assembly as described in Section 10.
2   Working under the car, disconnect the handbrake inner cable at the cable connector located beneath the rear axle transverse member.
3   Using circlip pliers, extract the circlip securing the handbrake outer cable to the bracket on the rear axle.
4   Using a brake hose clamp, or self-locking wrench with protected jaws, clamp the flexible brake hose located just in front of the rear axle. This will minimise brake fluid loss during subsequent operations.
5   Unscrew the brake pipe union nut at the rear of the wheel brake cylinder and carefully ease the pipe out of the cylinder. Plug the end of the pipe to prevent dirt entry.
6   Undo and remove the four nuts and spring washers securing the stub axle to the trailing arm and lift away the stub axle and brake backplate as an assembly.
7   Support the stub axle in a vice and drive out the four mounting studs using a soft metal drift. Take care not to damage the ends of the threads during this operation.
8   With the studs removed, separate the backplate from the stub axle.
9   Refitting the stub axle is the reverse sequence to removal. Tighten all retaining nuts and bolts to the specified torque and, on completion, bleed the brake hydraulic system, as described in Chapter 8. If suitable

precautions were taken to minimise fluid loss, as described, it should only be necessary to bleed the relevant wheel and not the entire system.

## 13 Rear suspension strut – removal and refitting

1   Chock the front wheels, prise off the rear wheel trim and slacken the wheel nuts. Jack up the rear of the car and support it securely on axle stands. Remove the roadwheel.
2   As a safety precaution place jack or suitable blocks beneath, and in contact with, the suspension trailing arm.
3   From inside the luggage compartment release the plastic cap from the strut upper mounting by rotating it whilst at the same time lifting upwards.
4   Engage a suitable small spanner on the flats of the strut spindle to prevent it turning and unscrew the upper mounting nut (photo). Lift off the flat washer and small mounting rubber.
5   From underneath the car, undo and remove the bolt securing the strut lower mounting to the rear suspension trailing arm (photo). Withdraw the strut from under the wheel arch and remove the large mounting rubber.
6   Refitting the suspension strut is the reverse sequence to removal. Ensure that the upper and lower mountings are tightened to the specified torque.

13.4 Rear suspension upper mounting, accessible from inside the car

13.5 Rear suspension strut lower mounting bolt (arrowed)

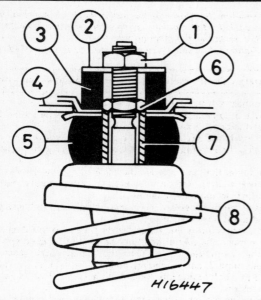

Fig. 10.7 Rear suspension strut upper mounting details (Sec 13)

| | |
|---|---|
| 1  Upper mounting nut | 5  Large mounting rubber |
| 2  Flat washer | 6  Spring retainer nut |
| 3  Small mounting rubber | 7  Spacer |
| 4  Rear wheel arch | 8  Spring seat |

15.8 Rear axle pivot bolt retaining nut (arrowed)

## 14  Rear suspension strut – dismantling and reassembly

**Note:** *Before attempting to dismantle the rear suspension strut, a suitable tool to hold the coil spring in compression must be obtained. Adjustable coil spring compressors are readily available and are recommended for this operation. Any attempt to dismantle the strut without such a tool is likely to result in damage or personal injury.*

1  Proceed by removing the rear suspension strut, as described in the previous Section.
2  Position the spring compressors on either side of the spring and compress the spring evenly until all the tension on the spring retainer nut is released.
3  With a spanner engaged with the flats of the strut spindle to stop it turning, unscrew the spring retainer nut. Lift off the spacer, spring seat and insulator ring.
4  The coil spring can now be removed, with the compressors still in position, if desired.
5  Carefully tap the spring aid retaining collar off the strut spindle then lift off the spring aid and the protective rubber boot.
6  With the strut completely dismantled, the components can be examined as follows.
7  Examine the strut body for signs of damage or corrosion, and for any trace of fluid leakage. Check the strut spindle for distortion, wear, pitting, or corrosion along its entire length. Test the operation of the strut, while holding it in an upright position, by moving the spindle through a full stroke and then through short strokes of 2 to 4 in (50 to 100 mm). In both cases the resistance felt should be smooth and continuous. If the resistance is jerky or uneven, or if there is any sign of wear or damage to the strut, renewal is necessary.
8  If the strut is in a satisfactory condition check the condition of the circlip on the strut spindle and, if it is in any way damaged or distorted, fit a new circlip.
9  If any doubt exists about the condition of the coil spring, remove the spring compressors and check the spring for distortion. Also measure the free length of the spring and compare the measurement with the figure given in the Specifications. Renew the spring if it is distorted or not of the specified length.
10  Begin reassembly by fitting the rubber boot to the strut, followed by the spring aid and retaining collar.
11  Place the spring in position, ensuring that the end of the bottom coil locates in the step of the retainer.
12  With the spring suitably compressed, withdraw the strut spindle as far as it will go and refit the insulator ring and spring seat, ensuring

that the end of the coil locates in the step of the spring seat.
13  Refit the spacer, followed by the spring retainer nut. Tighten the nut to the specified torque.
14  The spring compressors can now be removed and the strut assembly refitted to the car, as described in the previous Section.

## 15  Rear axle – removal and refitting

1  Chock the front wheels, prise off the rear wheel trim and slacken the wheel nuts. Jack up the rear of the car and support it securely on axle stands. Remove the roadwheel and release the handbrake.
2  Disconnect the two rear handbrake inner cables at the connectors located behind the rear axle transverse member.
3  Using two brake hose clamps, or self-locking wrenches with protected jaws, clamp the brake hydraulic flexible hoses, one located on each side of the car, adjacent to the rear axle front pivot bolts. This will minimise brake fluid loss during subsequent operations.
4  Undo and remove the two rear brake pipe unions at their connections with the flexible hoses. Plug or tape over the pipe and hose ends after disconnection to prevent dirt entry.
5  Using pliers extract the retaining clips and release the flexible hoses from the brackets on the rear axle.
6  Place a jack beneath one of the rear axle trailing arms and just take the weight of the axle.
7  Undo and remove the single bolt each side securing the rear suspension strut lower mountings to the rear axle trailing arms.
8  Undo and remove the nuts from the rear axle pivot bolts (one each side) (photo). Suitably support the axle beneath the transverse member and drift the pivot bolts from their locations.
9  Lever the axle out of its pivot mountings, lower it to the ground and withdraw it from under the car.
10  If necessary the axle can be completely dismantled by removing the rear hub assemblies and stub axles, as described in Sections 10 and 12 respectively.
11  If the axle pivot bushes require renewal, the old ones may be prised out and new ones inserted after lubricating them thoroughly in rubber grease.
12  Refitting the axle to the car is a straightforward reverse of the removal sequence. Ensure that all nuts and bolts are tightened to the specified torque and, on completion, bleed the brake hydraulic system, as described in Chapter 8.

## 16  Steering wheel – removal and refitting

1  Set the front wheels in the straight-ahead position.
2  Ease off the steering wheel pad to provide access to the retaining nut (photo).

16.2 Ease off the steering wheel pad to provide access to the retaining nut

3    Using a socket and bar, undo and remove the retaining nut and lockwasher.
4    Mark the steering wheel and inner column in relation to each other and withdraw the wheel from the inner column splines. If it is tight, tap it upwards near the centre, using the palm of your hand. *Refit the steering wheel retaining nut two turns before doing this, for obvious reasons.*
5    Refitting is the reverse of removal, but align the previously made marks and tighten the retaining nut to the specified torque. Note that there is a small arrow stamped on the striker bush of the multi-function switch and this must point towards the direction indicator switch when fitting the steering wheel.

## 17 Steering column assembly – removal, overhaul and refitting

1    Disconnect the battery negative terminal.
2    Remove the steering wheel, as described in the previous Section.
3    Undo and remove the four screws securing the two steering column cowls to the column. Remove the right-hand cowl, lift the left-hand cowl, disconnect the lighting switch multi-plug and remove the cowl.
4    Disconnect the ignition switch, windscreen wiper/washer switch and direction indicator switch multi-plugs, located under the facia.
5    From under the facia, remove the steering column cover and seal and then, to assist refitting, mark the inner column in relation to the intermediate shaft.
6    Undo and remove the intermediate shaft clamp bolt and nut securing the intermediate shaft to the inner column.
7    Undo and remove the upper and lower steering column mounting bolts, lift the column off the intermediate shaft and remove the assembly from the car.
8    Slacken the clamp screw and lift the multi-function switch off the steering column. Release the wiring from the clip.
9    Carefully support the outer column in a vice and withdraw the inner column from the top of the outer column.
10   Lift out the top bush, bend back the retaining tag and extract the bottom bush.
11   Clean the parts in paraffin, or a suitable solvent, and wipe dry. Examine the bushes for wear and renew, if necessary.
12   Reassembly and refitting is a reverse of removal and dismantling, bearing in mind the following points:

(a)   *Smear the outer surfaces and inner grooves of the bushes with graphite grease before fitting*
(b)   *Ensure that the marks made on the inner column and intermediate shaft are aligned when fitting the column*
(c)   *Adjust the position of the outer column so that it is 3.25 in (82.6 mm) below the top of the inner column before tightening the retaining bolts*

(d)   *Position the arrow on the striker bush of the multi-function switch so that it points towards the direction indicator switch before fitting the steering wheel*
(e)   *Tighten all retaining nuts and bolts to the specified torque*

## 18 Steering column intermediate shaft – removal and refitting

1    Disconnect the battery negative terminal.
2    Apply the handbrake, chock the rear wheels, jack up the front of the car and support it securely on axle stands.
3    From inside the car, pull back the carpet and unscrew the nut and bolt securing the intermediate shaft lower universal joint to the pinion shaft.
4    From under the facia remove the steering column cover and seal.
5    Unscrew the nut and bolt securing the intermediate shaft upper universal joint to the inner column.
6    Release the intermediate shaft from the pinion and inner column, and withdraw it from the car.
7    Before refitting it is first necessary to centralize the steering gear. To do this move the rubber band on the rack housing to one side to expose the centralizing hole. Turn the pinion shaft or move the roadwheels until a corresponding hole in the rack is in alignment. Insert a 6 mm bolt or drill into the hole to hold the steering gear in the central position.
8    From inside the car, engage the intermediate shaft upper universal joint with the inner column. Refit the clamp bolt and nut and tighten to the specified torque.
9    Position the steering wheel in the straight-ahead position and engage the intermediate shaft lower universal joint with the pinion shaft. Refit and tighten the clamp nut and bolt.
10   Refit the steering column cover and seal and place the carpet in position.
11   Remove the centralizing bolt or drill from the rack housing, refit the rubber band over the hole and lower the car to the ground. Reconnect the battery.

## 19 Steering column lock/ignition switch – removal and refitting

**Note:** *Where a new steering column lock/ignition switch is to be fitted as a result of damage sustained during an attempted theft, always check for damage to other steering components which may have been affected. Specifically, check the steering wheel hub and splines and steering joints. Also check for damage to the steering column (bending of the column, or damage to the steering column lock keyway).*

1    Remove the steering column, as described in Section 17.
2    With the column assembly on the bench, drill out the shear bolt heads and remove the clamp plate and lock/ignition switch from the outer column.
3    Locate the new lock body centrally over the slot in the outer column. Lightly bolt the clamp plate into position, but take care not to shear the bolt heads.
4    Refit the steering column, as described in Section 17, but before fitting the cowls check that the lock and ignition switch operate correctly.
5    Tighten the shear bolts until the heads break off, and then refit the cowls.

## 20 Tie-rods outer balljoint – removal and refitting

1    Apply the handbrake, chock the rear wheels, prise off the front wheel trim and slacken the wheel nuts. Jack up the front of the car and support it securely on axle stands. Remove the roadwheel.
2    Using a suitable spanner, slacken the balljoint locknut on the tie-rod by a quarter of a turn.
3    Undo and remove the locknut securing the balljoint to the steering arm and then release the tapered ball-pin using a balljoint separator tool (photos).
4    Unscrew the balljoint from the tie-rod.
5    Refitting is the reverse sequence to removal. Tighten the nuts to the specified torque and check the front wheel alignment, as described in Section 24.

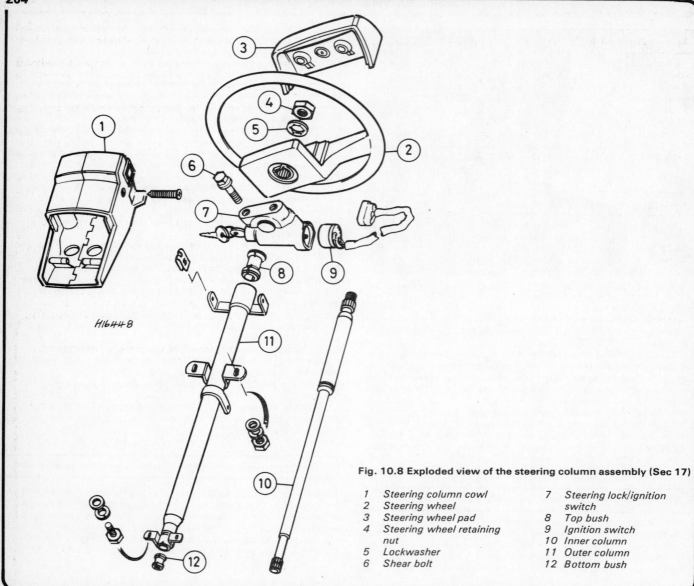

H16448

**Fig. 10.8 Exploded view of the steering column assembly (Sec 17)**

| | | | |
|---|---|---|---|
| 1 | Steering column cowl | 7 | Steering lock/ignition switch |
| 2 | Steering wheel | | |
| 3 | Steering wheel pad | 8 | Top bush |
| 4 | Steering wheel retaining nut | 9 | Ignition switch |
| 5 | Lockwasher | 10 | Inner column |
| 6 | Shear bolt | 11 | Outer column |
| | | 12 | Bottom bush |

20.3a Using a balljoint separator tool to release the tie-rod outer balljoint from the steering arm

20.3b With the taper released, the balljoint can be removed

## 21 Steering rack rubber gaiter – removal and refitting

1  Remove the tie-rod outer balljoint, as described in the previous Section.
2  Release the retaining wire or unscrew the securing clip screws and slide the gaiter off the rack and pinion housing and tie-rod.
3  Lubricate a new rubber gaiter with rubber grease and position it over the housing and tie-rod.
4  Using new clips, or two or three turns of soft iron wire, secure the gaiter in position.
5  Refit the outer balljoint, as described in the previous Section.

## 22 Rack and pinion steering gear – removal and refitting

1  Disconnect the battery negative terminal.
2  Apply the handbrake, chock the rear wheels and remove the trim from both front roadwheels. Slacken the wheel nuts before jacking up the front of the car and then support it securely on axle stands. Remove the roadwheels.
3  Unscrew the nuts securing the tie-rod outer balljoints to the steering arms and release the tapered ballpins using a balljoint separator tool.

4  From inside the car pull back the carpet and unscrew the nut and bolt securing the intermediate shaft lower universal joint to the pinion shaft.
5  Using a sharp knife make diagonal cuts in the sound-deadening material around the pinion shaft to provide access to the pinion cover plate. The pinion cover plate can now be removed.
6  Undo and remove the two nuts and washers securing the gearchange linkage relay lever bracket to the rack housing. Move the linkage clear of the steering gear.
7  Undo and remove the two bolts and washers securing the pinion end of the steering gear to the bulkhead. Now remove the two bolts and washers, clamp plate and plastic seating securing the other end of the rack housing to the bulkhead.
8  Ease the pinion shaft out of the intermediate shaft splines, manoeuvre the pinion clear of the body and withdraw the steering gear from the passenger's side of the engine compartment.
9  To refit the steering gear, manoeuvre it into position through the passenger's side of the engine compartment and position the pinion in the bulkhead aperture.
10  Fit the retaining bolts, finger tight, to the pinion end of the steering gear. At the other end, place the plastic seating and clamp in position, refit the retaining bolts and tighten them to the specified torque. Now tighten the pinion end retaining bolts to the specified torque.
11  Move the rubber band on the rack housing to one side to expose the centralizing hole. Move the rack as necessary, by turning the

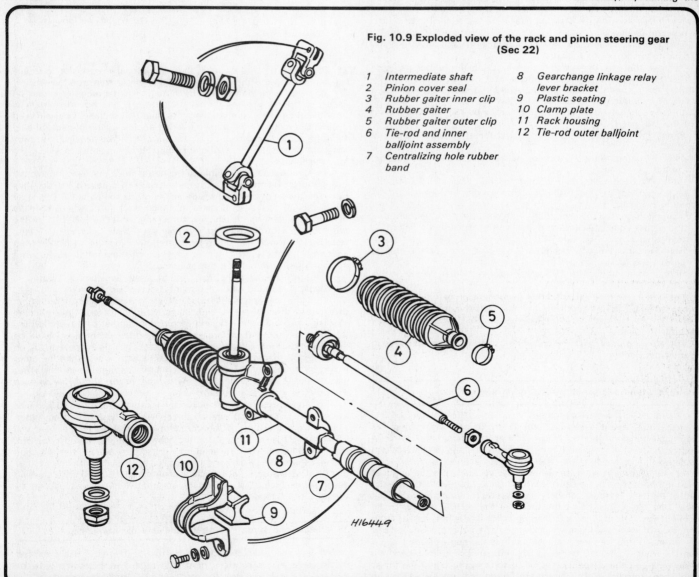

**Fig. 10.9 Exploded view of the rack and pinion steering gear (Sec 22)**

1  Intermediate shaft
2  Pinion cover seal
3  Rubber gaiter inner clip
4  Rubber gaiter
5  Rubber gaiter outer clip
6  Tie-rod and inner balljoint assembly
7  Centralizing hole rubber band
8  Gearchange linkage relay lever bracket
9  Plastic seating
10  Clamp plate
11  Rack housing
12  Tie-rod outer balljoint

H16449

pinion, until a 6 mm drill or bolt can be inserted through the hole in the housing and into the corresponding hole in the rack.

12  From inside the car, refit the pinion cover plate, position the steering wheel in the straight-ahead position and refit the intermediate shaft universal joint to the pinion shaft. Refit and tighten the clamp bolt and nut.

13  Reposition the sound-deadening material around the pinion shaft and tape over the diagonal cuts. Refit the carpets.

14  Remove the centralizing bolt or drill and cover the hole with the rubber band.

15  Refit the two nuts and washers securing the gearchange linkage bracket to the rack housing.

16  Refit the tie-rod outer balljoints to the steering arms and secure with the retaining nuts tightened to the specified torque.

17  Refit the roadwheels and wheel nuts, lower the car to the ground before fully tightening the wheel nuts. Refit the wheel trim.

## 23  Rack and pinion steering gear – dismantling and reassembly

**Note**: *The rack and pinion steering gear fitted to Maestro models cannot be fully dismantled for repair or overhaul and, with one exception, individual parts are not available separately. Should repair of the steering gear be necessary, due to wear or damage, a complete assembly must be obtained. It is, however, possible to renew the tie-rods individually and this Section describes the procedure.*

1  Begin by removing the steering gear from the car, as described in the previous Section.

2  Slacken the tie-rod outer balljoint locknut and unscrew the balljoint, followed by the locknut.

3  Remove the wire or retaining clips securing the rubber gaiter to the rack housing. Slide the gaiter off the rack housing and tie-rod.

4  Turn the pinion to extend the rack fully and support the exposed portion of rack between protected vice jaws.

5  Unscrew the ballhousing and withdraw the tie-rod and ballhousing from the rack.

6  Repeat paragraphs 2 to 5 inclusive for the other tie-rod, if required.

7  Liberally lubricate the tie-rod and ballhousing, using the specified lubricant.

8  Refit the ballhousing and tie-rod to the rack and tighten the housing fully. Secure the ballhousing by staking its edge into the groove in the rack.

9  Liberally lubricate the rack teeth with the specified lubricant and refit the rubber gaiter. Secure the gaiter with the retaining clips or two to three turns of soft iron wire.

10  Refit the outer balljoint locknut and balljoint to the tie-rod, but do not tighten the locknut at this stage.

11  Repeat paragraphs 7 to 10 inclusive for the other tie-rod, if this was also removed.

12  Position the two balljoints so that the dimension between the ball-pin centres is 53.78 in (136.6 mm) with an equal number of exposed threads visible on each tie-rod. Now secure the balljoints with the locknuts.

13  The steering gear can now be refitted to the car, as described in the previous Section.

## 24  Front wheel alignment and steering angles

1  Accurate front wheel alignment is essential to provide positive steering and prevent excessive tyre wear. Before considering the steering/suspension geometry, check that the tyres are correctly inflated, the front wheels are not buckled and the steering linkage and suspension joints are in good order, without slackness or wear.

2  Wheel alignment consists of four factors: Camber is the angle at which the front wheels are set from the vertical when viewed from the front of the car. 'Positive camber' is the amount (in degrees) that the wheels are tilted outward at the top from the vertical. Castor is the angle between the steering axis and a vertical line when viewed from each side of the car. 'Positive castor' is when the steering axis is inclined rearward. Steering axis inclination is the angle (when viewed from the front of the car) between the vertical and an imaginary line drawn between the suspension strut upper mounting and the lower suspension arm balljoint. Toe setting is the amount by which the distance between the front inside edges of the roadwheels (measured

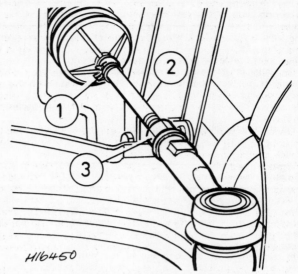

H16450

**Fig. 10.10 Toe setting adjustment (Sec 24)**

| 1 | Rubber gaiter clip | 3 | Outer balljoint locknut |
| 2 | Tie-rod | | |

at hub height) differs from the diametrically opposite distance measured between the rear inside edges of the front roadwheels.

3  With the exception of the toe setting all other steering angles on Maestro models are set during manufacture and no adjustment is possible. It can be assumed, therefore, that unless the car has suffered accident damage all the preset steering angles will be correct. Should there be some doubt about their accuracy it will be necessary to seek the help of a BL dealer, as special gauges are needed to check the steering angles.

4  Two methods are available to the home mechanic for checking the toe setting. One method is to use a gauge to measure the distance between the front and rear inside edges of the roadwheels. The other method is to use a scuff plate in which each front wheel is rolled across a movable plate which records any deviation, or scuff, of the tyre from the straight-ahead position as it moves across the plate. Relatively inexpensive equipment of both types is available from accessory outlets to enable these checks, and subsequent adjustments, to be carried out at home.

5  If, after checking the toe setting using whichever method is preferable, it is found that adjustment is necessary, proceed as follows.

6  Turn the steering wheel onto full left lock and record the number of exposed threads on the right-hand steering tie-rod. Now turn the steering onto full right lock and record the number of threads on the left-hand tie-rod. If there are the same number of threads visible on both tie-rods then subsequent adjustments can be made equally on both sides. If there are more threads visible on one side than the other it will be necessary to compensate for this during adjustment. *After adjustment there must be the same number of threads visible on each tie-rod. This is most important.*

7  To alter the toe setting slacken the locknut on the tie-rod and turn the rod using a self-grip wrench to achieve the desired setting. When viewed from the side of the car, turning the tie-rod clockwise will increase the toe-in, turning it anti-clockwise will increase the toe-out. Only turn the tie-rods by a quarter of a turn each time and then recheck the setting using the gauges, or scuff plate.

8  After adjustment tighten the locknuts and reposition the steering gear rubber gaiters, if necessary, to remove any twist caused by turning the tie-rods.

## 25  Wheels and tyres – general care and maintenance

Wheels and tyres should give no real problems in use provided that a close eye is kept on them with regard to excessive wear or damage. To this end, the following points should be noted.

Ensure that tyre pressures are checked regularly and maintained correctly. Checking should be carried out with the tyres cold and not immediately after the vehicle has been in use. If the pressures are checked with the tyres hot, an apparently high reading will be obtained owing to heat expansion. Under no circumstances should an attempt be made to reduce the pressures to the quoted cold reading in this instance, or effective underinflation will result.

Underinflation will cause overheating of the tyre owing to excessive flexing of the casing, and the tread will not sit correctly on the road surface. This will cause a consequent loss of adhesion and excessive wear, not to mention the danger of sudden tyre failure due to heat build-up.

Overinflation will cause rapid wear of the centre part of the tyre tread coupled with reduced adhesion, harsher ride, and the danger of shock damage occurring in the tyre casing.

Regularly check the tyres for damage in the form of cuts or bulges, especially in the sidewalls. Remove any nails or stones embedded in the tread before they penetrate the tyre to cause deflation. If removal of a nail *does* reveal that the tyre has been punctured, refit the nail so that its point of penetration is marked. Then immediately change the wheel and have the tyre repaired by a tyre dealer. Do *not* drive on a tyre in such a condition. If in any doubt as to the possible consequences of any damage found, consult your local tyre dealer for advice.

Periodically remove the wheels and clean any dirt or mud from the inside and outside surfaces. Examine the wheel rims for signs of rusting, corrosion or other damage. Light alloy wheels are easily damaged by 'kerbing' whilst parking, and similarly steel wheels may become dented or buckled. Renewal of the wheel is very often the only course of remedial action possible.

The balance of each wheel and tyre assembly should be maintained to avoid excessive wear, not only to the tyres but also to the steering and suspension components. Wheel imbalance is normally signified by vibration through the vehicle's bodyshell, although in many cases it is particularly noticeable through the steering wheel. Conversely,

it should be noted that wear or damage in suspension or steering components may cause excessive tyre wear. Out-of-round or out-of-true tyres, damaged wheels and wheel bearing wear/maladjustment also fall into this category. Balancing will not usually cure vibration caused by such wear.

Wheel balancing may be carried out with the wheel either on or off the vehicle. If balanced on the vehicle, ensure that the wheel-to-hub relationship is marked in some way prior to subsequent wheel removal so that it may be refitted in its original position.

General tyre wear is influenced to a large degree by driving style – harsh braking and acceleration or fast cornering will all produce more rapid tyre wear. Interchanging of tyres may result in more even wear, but this should only be carried out where there is no mix of tyre types on the vehicle. However, it is worth bearing in mind that if this is completely effective, the added expense of replacing a complete set of tyres simultaneously is incurred, which may prove financially restrictive for many owners.

Front tyres may wear unevenly as a result of wheel misalignment. The front wheels should always be correctly aligned according to the settings specified by the vehicle manufacturer.

Legal restrictions apply to the mixing of tyre types on a vehicle. Basically this means that a vehicle must not have tyres of differing construction on the same axle. Although it is not recommended to mix tyre types between front axle and rear axle, the only legally permissible combination is crossply at the front and radial at the rear. When mixing radial ply tyres, textile braced radials must always go on the front axle, with steel braced radials at the rear. An obvious disadvantage of such mixing is the necessity to carry two spare tyres to avoid contravening the law in the event of a puncture.

In the UK, the Motor Vehicles Construction and Use Regulations apply to many aspects of tyre fitting and usage. It is suggested that a copy of these regulations is obtained from your local police if in doubt as to the current legal requirements with regard to tyre condition, minimum tread depth, etc.

## 26 Fault diagnosis – suspension and steering

**Note:** *Before diagnosing steering or suspension faults, be sure that the trouble is not due to incorrect tyre pressures, mixture of tyre types or binding brakes*

| Symptom | Reason(s) |
| --- | --- |
| Vehicle pulls to one side | Incorrect wheel alignment<br>Wear in front suspension or steering components<br>Accident damage to steering on suspension components |
| Steering stiff or heavy | Lack of steering gear lubricant<br>Seized balljoint<br>Wheel alignment incorrect<br>Steering rack or column bent or damaged |
| Excessive play in steering | Worn steering or suspension joints<br>Wear in intermediate shaft universal joints<br>Worn rack and pinion assembly |
| Wheel wobble and vibration | Roadwheels out of balance<br>Roadwheels buckled or distorted<br>Faulty or damaged tyre<br>Worn steering or suspension joints<br>Wheels nuts loose<br>Worn rack and pinion assembly |
| Tyre wear uneven | Wheel alignment incorrect<br>Worn steering or suspension components<br>Wheels out of balance<br>Accident damage |

# Chapter 11 Bodywork

*For modifications, and information applicable to later models, see Supplement at end of manual*

## Contents

## Specifications

### Torque wrench settings

| | lbf ft | Nm |
|---|---|---|
| Seat belt mountings | 24 | 32 |
| Bumpers: | | |
|     Front | 6 | 8 |
|     Rear | 18 | 25 |
| Bumper end caps | 6 | 8 |
| Front body panel | 6 | 8 |
| Door locks | 6 | 8 |
| Door striker pins | 33 | 45 |
| Tailgate support strut ball pegs | 9 | 12 |
| Bonnet lock | 6 | 8 |

## 1 General description

The bodyshell and underframe is of all-steel welded construction and is of computer based design. The assembly and welding of the main body unit is completed entirely by computer controlled robots, and the finished unit is checked for dimensional accuracy using modern computer and laser technology.

The front wings are bolted in position and are detachable should renewal be necessary after a front end collision.

## 2 Maintenance – bodywork and underframe

1 The general condition of a vehicle's bodywork is the one thing that significantly affects its value. Maintenance is easy but needs to be regular. Neglect, particularly after minor damage, can lead quickly to further deterioration and costly repair bills. It is important also to keep watch on those parts of the vehicle not immediately visible, for instance the underside, inside all the wheel arches and the lower part of the engine compartment.

2 The basic maintenance routine for the bodywork is washing – preferably with a lot of water, from a hose. This will remove all the loose solids which may have stuck to the vehicle. It is important to flush these off in such a way as to prevent grit from scratching the finish. The wheel arches and underframe need washing in the same way to remove any accumulated mud which will retain moisture and tend to encourage rust. Paradoxically enough, the best time to clean the underframe and wheel arches is in wet weather when the mud is thoroughly wet and soft. In very wet weather the underframe is usually cleaned of large accumulations automatically and this is a good time for inspection.

3 Periodically, except on vehicles with a wax-based underbody protective coating, it is a good idea to have the whole of the underframe of the vehicle steam cleaned, engine compartment included, so that a thorough inspection can be carried out to see what minor repairs and renovations are necessary. Steam cleaning is available at many garages and is necessary for removal of the accumulation of oily grime which sometimes is allowed to become thick in certain areas. If steam cleaning facilities are not available, there are some excellent grease solvents available such as Holts Engine Degreasant, which can be brush applied. The dirt can then be simply hosed off. Note that these methods should not be used on vehicles with wax-based underbody protective coating or the coating will be removed. Such vehicles should be inspected annually, preferably just prior to winter, when the underbody should be washed down and any damage to the wax coating repaired using Holts Undershield. Ideally, a completely fresh coat should be applied. It would also be worth considering the use of such wax-based protection for injection into door panels, sills, box sections, etc, as an additional safeguard against rust damage where such protection is not provided by the vehicle manufacturer.

4 After washing paintwork, wipe off with a chamois leather to give an unspotted clear finish. A coat of clear protective wax polish, like the many excellent Turtle Wax polishes, will give added protection against chemical pollutants in the air. If the paintwork sheen has dulled or oxidised, use a cleaner/polisher combination such as Turtle Wax Hard Shell to restore the brilliance of the shine. This requires a little effort, but such dulling is usually caused because regular washing has been neglected. Care needs to be taken with metallic paintwork, as special non-abrasive cleaner/polisher is required to avoid damage to the finish. Always check that the door and ventilator opening drain holes and pipes are completely clear so that water can be drained out. Bright work should be treated in the same way as paint work. Windscreens and windows can be kept clear of the smeary film which often appears, by the use of a proprietary glass cleaner like Holts Mixra. Never use any form of wax or other body or chromium polish on glass.

## 3 Maintenance – upholstery and carpets

Mats and carpets should be brushed or vacuum cleaned regularly to keep them free of grit. If they are badly stained remove them from the vehicle for scrubbing or sponging and make quite sure they are dry before refitting. Seats and interior trim panels can be kept clean by wiping with a damp cloth and Turtle Wax Carisma. If they do become stained (which can be more apparent on light coloured upholstery) use a little liquid detergent and a soft nail brush to scour the grime out of the grain of the material. Do not forget to keep the headlining clean in the same way as the upholstery. When using liquid cleaners inside the vehicle do not over-wet the surfaces being cleaned. Excessive damp could get into the seams and padded interior causing stains, offensive odours or even rot. If the inside of the vehicle gets wet accidentally it is worthwhile taking some trouble to dry it out properly, particularly where carpets are involved. *Do not leave oil or electric heaters inside the vehicle for this purpose.*

## 4 Minor body damage – repair

*The colour bodywork repair photographic sequences between pages 32 and 33 illustrate the operations detailed in the following sub-sections.*

**Note:** *For more detailed information about bodywork repair, Haynes Publishing publish a book by Lindsay Porter called The Car Bodywork Repair Manual. This incorporates information on such aspects as rust treatment, painting and glass fibre repairs, as well as details on more ambitious repairs involving welding and panel beating.*

### Repair of minor scratches in bodywork

If the scratch is very superficial, and does not penetrate to the metal of the bodywork, repair is very simple. Lightly rub the area of the scratch with a paintwork renovator like Turtle Wax Color Back, or a very fine cutting paste like Holts Body + Plus Rubbing Compound, to remove loose paint from the scratch and to clear the surrounding bodywork of wax polish. Rinse the area with clean water.

Apply touch-up paint to the scratch using a fine paint brush; continue to apply fine layers of paint until the surface of the paint in the scratch is level with the surrounding paintwork. Allow the new paint at least two weeks to harden; then blend it into the surrounding paintwork by rubbing the scratch area with a paintwork renovator or a very fine cutting paste, such as Holts Body + Plus Rubbing Compound or Turtle Wax Color Back. Finally, apply wax polish from one of the Turtle Wax range of wax polishes.

Where the scratch has penetrated right through to the metal of the bodywork, causing the metal to rust, a different repair technique is required. Remove any loose rust from the bottom of the scratch with a penknife, then apply rust inhibiting paint, such as Turtle Wax Rust Master, to prevent the formation of rust in the future. Using a rubber or nylon applicator fill the scratch with bodystopper paste like Holts Body + Plus Knifing Putty. If required, this paste can be mixed with cellulose thinners, such as Holts Body + Plus Cellulose Thinners, to provide a very thin paste which is ideal for filling narrow scratches. Before the stopper-paste in the scratch hardens, wrap a piece of smooth cotton rag around the top of a finger. Dip the finger in cellulose thinners, such as Holts Body + Plus Cellulose Thinners, and then quickly sweep it across the surface of the stopper-paste in the scratch; this will ensure that the surface of the stopper-paste is slightly hollowed. The scratch can now be painted over as described earlier in this Section.

### Repair of dents in bodywork

When deep denting of the vehicle's bodywork has taken place, the first task is to pull the dent out, until the affected bodywork almost attains its original shape. There is little point in trying to restore the original shape completely, as the metal in the damaged area will have stretched on impact and cannot be reshaped fully to its original contour. It is better to bring the level of the dent up to a point which is about ⅛ in (3 mm) below the level of the surrounding bodywork. In cases where the dent is very shallow anyway, it is not worth trying to pull it out at all. If the underside of the dent is accessible, it can be hammered out gently from behind, using a mallet with a wooden or plastic head. Whilst doing this, hold a suitable block of wood firmly against the outside of the panel to absorb the impact from the hammer blows and thus prevent a large area of the bodywork from being 'belled-out'.

Should the dent be in a section of the bodywork which has a double skin or some other factor making it inaccessible from behind, a different technique is called for. Drill several small holes through the metal inside the area – particularly in the deeper section. Then screw long self-tapping screws into the holes just sufficiently for them to gain a good purchase in the metal. Now the dent can be pulled out by pulling on the protruding heads of the screws with a pair of pliers.

The next stage of the repair is the removal of the paint from the damaged area, and from an inch or so of the surrounding 'sound' bodywork. This is accomplished most easily by using a wire brush or abrasive pad on a power drill, although it can be done just as effectively by hand using sheets of abrasive paper. To complete the preparation for filling, score the surface of the bare metal with a screwdriver or the tang of a file, or alternatively, drill small holes in the affected area. This will provide a really good 'key' for the filler paste.

To complete the repair see the Section on filling and re-spraying.

### Repair of rust holes or gashes in bodywork

Remove all paint from the affected area and from an inch or so of the surrounding 'sound' bodywork, using an abrasive pad or a wire brush on a power drill. If these are not available a few sheets of abrasive paper will do the job just as effectively. With the paint removed you will be able to gauge the severity of the corrosion and therefore decide whether to renew the whole panel (if this is possible) or to repair the affected area. New body panels are not as expensive as most people think and it is often quicker and more satisfactory to fit a new panel than to attempt to repair large areas of corrosion.

Remove all fittings from the affected area except those which will act as a guide to the original shape of the damaged bodywork (eg headlamp shells etc). Then, using tin snips or a hacksaw blade, remove all loose metal and any other metal badly affected by corrosion. Hammer the edges of the hole inwards in order to create a slight depression for the filler paste.

Wire brush the affected area to remove the powdery rust from the surface of the remaining metal. Paint the affected area with rust inhibiting paint like Turtle Wax Rust Master; if the back of the rusted area is accessible treat this also.

Before filling can take place it will be necessary to block the hole in some way. This can be achieved by the use of aluminium or plastic mesh, or aluminium tape.

Aluminium or plastic mesh, or glass fibre matting, is probably the best material to use for a large hole. Cut a piece of the approximate size and shape of the hole to be filled, then position it in the hole so that its edges are below the level of the surrounding bodywork. It can be retained in position by several blobs of filler paste around its periphery.

Aluminium tape should be used for small or very narrow holes. Pull a piece off the roll and trim it to the approximate size and shape required, then pull off the backing paper (if used) and stick the tape over the hole; it can be overlapped if the thickness of one piece is insufficient. Burnish down the edges of the tape with the handle of a screwdriver or similar, to ensure that the tape is securely attached to the metal underneath.

### Bodywork repairs – filling and re-spraying

Before using this Section, see the Sections on dent, deep scratch, rust holes and gash repairs.

Many types of bodyfiller are available, but generally speaking those proprietary kits which contain a tin of filler paste and a tube of resin hardener are best for this type of repair, like Holts Body + Plus or Holts No Mix which can be used directly from the tube. A wide, flexible plastic or nylon applicator will be found invaluable for imparting a smooth and well contoured finish to the surface of the filler.

Mix up a little filler on a clean piece of card or board – measure the hardener carefully (follow the maker's instructions on the pack) otherwise the filler will set too rapidly or too slowly. Alternatively, Holts No Mix can be used straight from the tube without mixing, but daylight is required to cure it. Using the applicator apply the filler paste to the prepared area; draw the applicator across the surface of the filler to achieve the correct contour and to level the filler surface. As soon as a contour that approximates to the correct one is achieved, stop working the paste – if you carry on too long the paste will become sticky and begin to 'pick up' on the applicator. Continue to add thin layers of filler paste at twenty-minute intervals until the level of the filler is just proud of the surrounding bodywork.

Once the filler has hardened, excess can be removed using a metal plane or file. From then on, progressively finer grades of abrasive paper should be used, starting with a 40 grade production paper and finishing with 400 grade wet-and-dry paper. Always wrap the abrasive paper around a flat rubber, cork, or wooden block – otherwise the surface of the filler will not be completely flat. During the smoothing of the filler surface the wet-and-dry paper should be periodically rinsed in water. This will ensure that a very smooth finish is imparted to the filler at the final stage.

At this stage the 'dent' should be surrounded by a ring of bare metal, which in turn should be encircled by the finely 'feathered' edge of the good paintwork. Rinse the repair area with clean water, until all of the dust produced by the rubbing-down operation has gone.

Spray the whole repair area with a light coat of primer, either Holts Body+Plus Grey or Red Oxide Primer – this will show up any imperfections in the surface of the filler. Repair these imperfections with fresh filler paste or bodystopper, and once more smooth the surface with abrasive paper. If bodystopper is used, it can be mixed with cellulose thinners to form a really thin paste which is ideal for filling small holes. Repeat this spray and repair procedure until you are satisfied that the surface of the filler, and the feathered edge of the paintwork are perfect. Clean the repair area with clean water and allow to dry fully.

The repair area is now ready for final spraying. Paint spraying must be carried out in a warm, dry, windless and dust free atmosphere. This condition can be created artificially if you have access to a large indoor working area, but if you are forced to work in the open, you will have to pick your day very carefully. If you are working indoors, dousing the floor in the work area with water will help to settle the dust which would otherwise be in the atmosphere. If the repair area is confined to one body panel, mask off the surrounding panels; this will help to minimise the effects of a slight mis-match in paint colours. Bodywork fittings (eg chrome strips, door handles etc) will also need to be masked off. Use genuine masking tape and several thicknesses of newspaper for the masking operations.

Before commencing to spray, agitate the aerosol can thoroughly, then spray a test area (an old tin, or similar) until the technique is mastered. Cover the repair area with a thick coat of primer; the thickness should be built up using several thin layers of paint rather than one thick one. Using 400 grade wet-and-dry paper, rub down the surface of the primer until it is really smooth. While doing this, the work area should be thoroughly doused with water, and the wet-and-dry paper periodically rinsed in water. Allow to dry before spraying on more paint.

Spray on the top coat using Holts Dupli-Color Autospray, again building up the thickness by using several thin layers of paint. Start spraying in the centre of the repair area and then work outwards, with a side-to-side motion, until the whole repair area and about 2 inches of the surrounding original paintwork is covered. Remove all masking material 10 to 15 minutes after spraying on the final coat of paint.

Allow the new paint at least two weeks to harden, then, using a paintwork renovator or a very fine cutting paste such as Turtle Wax Color Back or Holts Body+Plus Rubbing Compound, blend the edges of the paint into the existing paintwork. Finally, apply wax polish.

## 5  Major body damage – repair

Where serious damage has occurred, or large areas need renewal due to neglect, it means that completely new sections or panels will need welding in, and this is best left to professionals. If the damage is due to impact, it will also be necessary to completely check the alignment of the bodyshell structure. Due to the principle of construction, the strength and shape of the whole car can be affected by damage to one part. In such instances the services of a BL agent with specialist checking jigs are essential. If a body is left misaligned, it is first of all dangerous, as the car will not handle properly, and secondly uneven stresses will be imposed on the steering, engine and transmission, causing abnormal wear or complete failure. Tyre wear may also be excessive.

## 6  Maintenance – hinges and locks

1   Oil the hinges of the bonnet, tailgate and door with a drop or two of light oil at regular intervals (see Routine Maintenance).
2   At the same time, lightly oil the bonnet release mechanism and all door locks.
3   Do not attempt to lubricate the steering lock.

## 7  Door rattles – tracing and rectification

1   Check first that the door is not loose at the hinges, and that the latch is holding the door firmly in position. Check also that the door lines up with the aperture in the body. If the door is out of alignment, adjust it, as described in Sections 22 and 28.
2   If the latch is holding the door in the correct position, but the latch still rattles, the lock mechanism is worn and should be renewed.
3   Other rattles from the door could be caused by wear in the window operating mechanism, interior lock mechanism, or loose glass channels.

## 8  Bonnet – removal, refitting and adjustment

1   Support the bonnet in its open position and place some cardboard, or rags, beneath the corners, by the hinges.
2   Detach the windscreen washer hose from the pump outlet on the washer reservoir. Plug the pump outlet after detaching the hose.
3   Mark the location of the hinges with a soft pencil, then loosen the four retaining nuts and bolts (photo).
4   With the help of an assistant, release the stay, unscrew and remove the retaining bolts, and withdraw the bonnet from the car.
5   Refitting is a reversal of removal, but adjust the hinges to their original positions. The bonnet rear edge should be flush with the scuttle, and the gaps at either side equal.

## 9  Bonnet lock – adjustment

1   Adjustment is only possible at the lockpin mounted on the bonnet (photo).
2   Slacken the locknut and use a screwdriver to adjust the length of the lockpin so that the bonnet closes easily and is held firmly in place.
3   Tighten the locknut.

## 10  Bonnet lock and release cable – removal and refitting

1   Working inside the car, remove the bonnet release lever and disconnect the cable.
2   Working in the engine compartment, release the outer cable from the support bracket on the lock, and detach the inner cable from the lock lever.
3   Release the cable from its retaining clips, pull the cable through the bulkhead grommet, and remove it from the car.
4   To remove the lock, undo and remove the retaining bolts and remove the lock assembly through the aperture in the front body panel.
5   Refitting is the reverse sequence to removal. Adjust the bonnet

8.3 Right-hand side hinge-to-bonnet retaining bolts

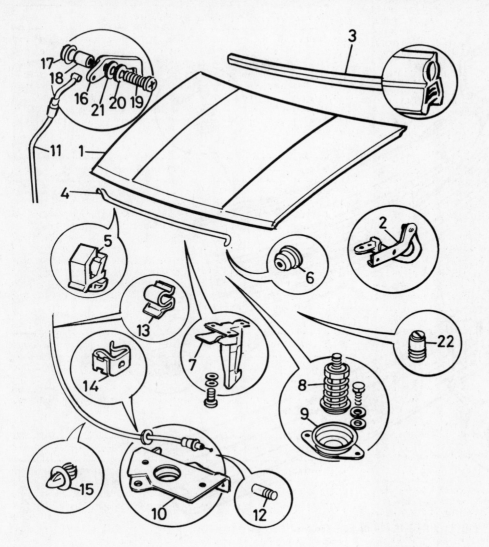

**Fig. 11.1 Details of the bonnet and bonnet lock components (Secs 8, 9 and 10)**

1   *Bonnet*
2   *Bonnet hinge*
3   *Bonnet seal*
4   *Bonnet prop*
5   *Bonnet prop clip*
6   *Bonnet prop bush*
7   *Bonnet safety catch*
8   *Lockpin assembly*
9   *Locking cup*
10  *Bonnet lock*
11  *Release cable*
12  *Inner release cable connector*
13  *Cable-to-body retaining clip*
14  *Cable-to-lock retaining clip*
15  *Cable-to-body retaining clip*
16  *Release lever*
17  *Washer*
18  *Bush*
19  *Release lever retaining screw*
20  *Washer*
21  *Washer*
22  *Bonnet buffer*

9.1 Bonnet lock adjustment points – locknut (A) and lockpin (B)

lock, as described in the previous Section, if necessary.

## 11 Radiator grille – removal and refitting

1   Undo and remove the screws securing the upper part of the grille to the front body panel.
2   Tip the grille outward at the top and lift it up to disengage the lower retaining lugs. Remove the grille from the car.
3   To remove the lower grille fitted to certain 1.3 litre models, remove the retaining screws and lift off the grille.
4   Refitting is the reverse sequence to removal.

## 12 Front body panel – removal and refitting

1   Remove the bonnet lock and cable from the panel, as described in Section 10, and the radiator grille, as described in the previous Section.
2   Detach the air cleaner cold air intake hose from the panel.
3   Undo and remove the three screws each side securing the panel to the body side-members.
4   Release the bonnet stay, lift up the panel and remove it from the car.
5   Refitting is the reverse sequence to removal. Ensure that the lugs on the radiator and cooling fan cowl are correctly located in the body panel as it is fitted.

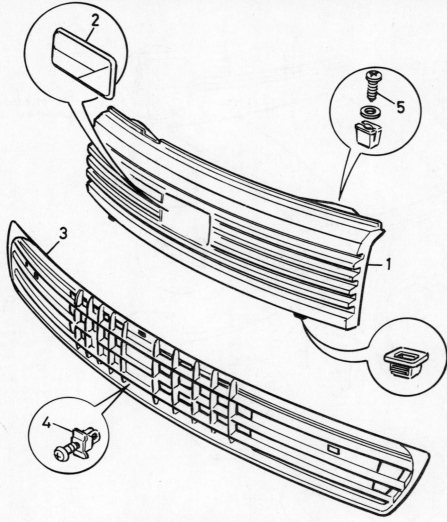

**Fig. 11.2 Radiator grille components (Sec 11)**

1  Radiator grille
2  Grille motif (Vanden Plas models)

3  Lower grille (1.3 base models)

4  Lower grille retaining screw

5  Grille upper retaining screw

## 13  Front wing – removal and refitting

1   Open the bonnet and support it in the raised position.
2   Remove the headlamp and front direction indicator lamp assembly, as described in Chapter 9.
3   Remove the front bumper, as described in Section 33 of this Chapter.
4   Refer to the accompanying illustrations and remove the wing retaining bolts from their locations – this varies according to model.
5   Carefully ease the front wing off its mating flanges and remove it from the car.
6   Refitting is the reverse sequence to removal, but use a sealing compound to seal the wing to the body.

## 14  Tailgate – removal and refitting

1   Disconnect the battery negative terminal.
2   Unhook the parcel shelf support cords and remove the shelf.
3   Carefully prise out the tailgate inner trim panel.
4   Disconnect the tailgate wiper wiring connectors and detach the earth lead at the earthing screw.
5   Disconnect the heated rear window element leads from the left-hand side of the glass. Detach the window washer hose from the

washer jet. If fitted, disconnect the tailgate central locking electrical leads.
6   Attach separate strings to the wiper leads, heating element leads, washer hose and central locking electrical leads, if fitted, as an aid to rethread the leads when the tailgate is refitted.
7   Release the heating element lead grommet from the tailgate, the harness sleeve clip from the hinge, and the harness sleeve from the tailgate.
8   Pull the leads and hose through the tailgate, untie the strings from the leads and leave them in position in the tailgate.
9   Release the seal from the top edge of the tailgate aperture, release the rear part of the headlining and withdraw the foam pad covering the hinge retaining nuts. On certain models the headlining is secured by Velcro strips, and can be released at the sides and rear after removing the grab handles.
10  Support the tailgate securely. Prise out the locking clips in the ends of the tailgate support strut end joints, and release the support struts from the tailgate.
11  Engage the help of an assistant to further support the tailgate, and then remove the hinge retaining nuts. Carefully lift the tailgate off the car.
12  Refitting the tailgate is the reverse sequence to removal. Adjust the position of the hinges and the tailgate striker (photo), as necessary, until the gap all round is equal, and the tailgate shuts and catches without force.

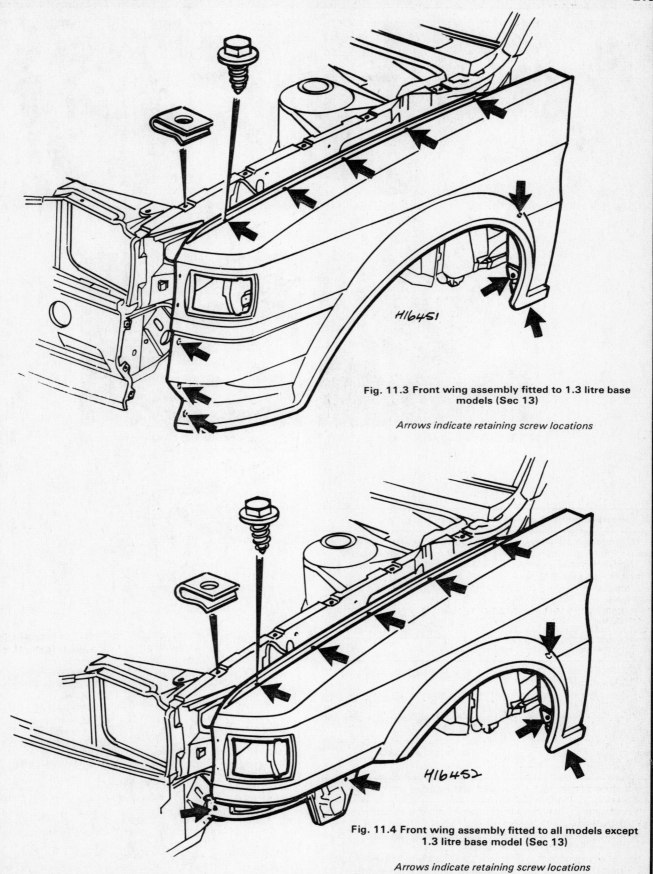

H16451

**Fig. 11.3 Front wing assembly fitted to 1.3 litre base models (Sec 13)**

*Arrows indicate retaining screw locations*

H16452

**Fig. 11.4 Front wing assembly fitted to all models except 1.3 litre base model (Sec 13)**

*Arrows indicate retaining screw locations*

14.12 Tailgate striker and retaining bolts

15.2 Prise out the tailgate support strut locking clips ...

15.3 ... to allow removal of the strut end joint from the ball pegs

16.3 Tailgate lock and mounting bolts

17.2 Tailgate private lock operating rod clip retainer (A) and large nut (B)

### 15  Tailgate support strut – removal and refitting

1    With the tailgate open, unhook the parcel shelf support cords and support the tailgate using a stout length of wood or an assistant.
2    Using a small screwdriver, prise out the locking clips in the ends of the strut end joints (photo).
3    Withdraw the end joints from the ball pegs on the tailgate and body (photo), and lift away the strut.
4    Refitting is the reverse sequence to removal.

### 16  Tailgate lock – removal and refitting

1    Carefully prise out the tailgate inner trim panel to gain access to the lock assembly.
2    Release the clip retainer and slide the operating rod out of its bush on the lock lever.
3    Undo and remove the three lock mounting bolts (photo) and withdraw the lock assembly from the tailgate.
4    Refitting is the reverse sequence to removal, but adjust the striker plate so that the tailgate shuts and catches without force.

### 17  Tailgate private lock – removal and refitting

1    Carefully prise out the tailgate inner trim panel to gain access to the lock assembly.
2    Release the clip retainer and slide the operating rod out of its bush on the private lock retainer lever (photo).
3    Undo and remove the large nut securing the private lock to the lock retainer. Withdraw the lock, washer and lock retainer from the tailgate.
4    Refitting is the reverse sequence to removal.

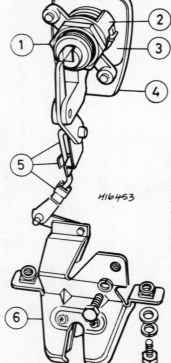

H16453

Fig. 11.5 Tailgate lock assembly (Secs 16 and 17)

1    Private lock large nut
2    Private lock retainer
3    Washer
4    Private lock
5    Operating rod and clip retainers
6    Tailgate lock

20.1 Remove the five door bin retaining screws (arrowed)

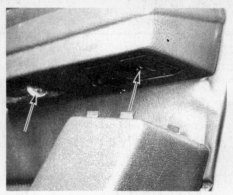

20.2 Disconnect the bin and remove the armrest retaining screws (arrowed)

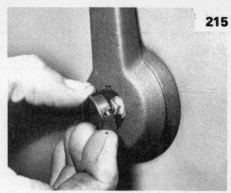

20.3 Remove the trim cap covering the regulator handle retaining screw

20.4a Remove the trim cap and internal release lever surround retaining screw ...

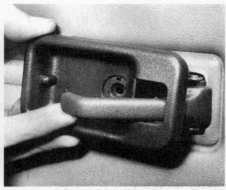

20.4b ... then slide the surround off the release lever

20.6a Remove the upper trim capping retaining screws (arrowed) ...

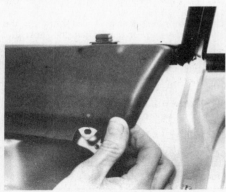

20.6b ... and lift the capping up and off

20.7 Carefully pull back the polythene sheet to gain access to the door internal components

22.3 Exterior door handle operating rod bush (A) and handle retaining nuts (B)

22.4 Private lock operating rod retaining clip (A) and lock horseshoe-shaped retaining clip (B)

22.5 Remove the internal release lever retaining screw (A) and slide the lever rearwards to release it

22.10 Door striker pin and nut

## 18 Windscreen – removal and refitting

All Maestro models are equipped with a flush glazed, laminated windscreen, secured to the bodyshell by direct bonding. Due to this method of retention, special tools and equipment are required to remove and refit the screen, and this task is definitely beyond the scope of the home mechanic. If it is necessary to have the windscreen removed, this job should be left to a suitably equipped specialist or BL dealer.

## 19 Tailgate window – removal and refitting

The tailgate window, like the windscreen, also features direct bonding retention, and its removal and refitting should be entrusted to a specialist or a BL dealer.

## 20 Front door inner trim panel – removal and refitting

1 Where fitted, undo and remove the five screws securing the door bin to the door (photo). Disengage the upper retaining tags from the armrest and lift away the bin.
2 Undo and remove the two screws securing the door pull handle armrest to the door (photo) and lift it off. On models equipped with electrically operated windows, disconnect the armrest switch wires at the wiring connectors.
3 Carefully prise out the trim cap (photo) and unscrew the window regulator handle retaining screw. Pull off the handle.
4 Prise out the trim cap and unscrew the door release lever surround retaining screw (photo). Remove the surround by sliding it over the release lever (photo).
5 Starting at the lower rear corner, release the trim panel retaining clips by carefully levering between the panel and door with a screwdriver or suitable flat bar.
6 Undo and remove the screws securing the upper trim capping to the door (photo), lift the rear of the capping over the lock button and lift off (photo).
7 To gain access to the door components, carefully pull back the polythene condensation barrier, as necessary (photo).
8 Refitting is the reverse sequence to removal.

## 21 Front door – removal and refitting

1 On models equipped with central door locking, electrically operated windows, or door speakers, remove the door inner trim panel, as described in Section 20. Disconnect the relevant wiring connectors and withdraw the harness from the door.
2 Lift up the rubber door seal and remove the lower sill trim panel to provide access to the lower door hinge.
3 Carefully mark the outline of the door hinges on the pillar using a soft pencil.
4 With the help of an assistant to support the door, undo and remove the upper bolts and lower nuts securing the door hinges to the pillar and lift away the door.
5 Refitting is the reverse sequence to removal. Align the hinges with the pencil marks made during removal.
6 Check that the door closes correctly, and that the door seal touches at all points around the door. If necessary, make minor corrections to the door adjustment and seal positioning to obtain a sound, weatherproof seal, or wind noise may result.

## 22 Front door lock – removal, refitting and adjustment

1 Remove the door inner trim panel, as described in Section 20.
2 Unscrew the interior lock button, temporarily refit the window regulator handle and wind the window fully up.
3 Prise the operating rod out of its retaining bush on the door exterior handle operating lever (photo).
4 Release the retaining clip and withdraw the operating rod from the private lock lever (photo).
5 Undo and remove the screw securing the internal release lever to the door. Release the operating rod from its steady clip and slide the lever rearwards to release it from its location (photo).

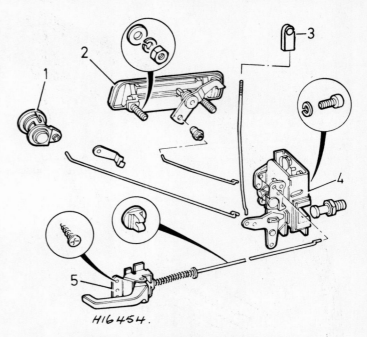

H16454.

**Fig. 11.6 Front door lock components (Secs 22 and 23)**

1  *Private lock*                      4  *Lock assembly*
2  *Door exterior handle*        5  *Internal release lever*
3  *Interior lock button*

6 Undo and remove the screw securing the rear window channel to the door. Release the channel from the felt guide and remove the channel from the door.
7 Undo and remove the three retaining screws and withdraw the lock assembly, complete with operating rods, from the door aperture.
8 The external handle can also be removed after unscrewing the two nuts and washers.
9 Refitting is the reverse sequence to removal, but adjust the lock striker pin as follows.
10 Check that the latch disc is in the open position then loosen the striker pin nut (photo) and position the pin so that the door can be closed easily and is held firmly. Close the door gently, but firmly, when making this adjustment.
11 Tighten the striker pin nut.

## 23 Front door private lock – removal and refitting

1 Remove the door interior trim panel, as described in Section 20, and wind the window fully up.
2 Release the retaining clip and withdraw the operating rod from the private lock lever (photo 22.4).
3 Prise out the horseshoe-shaped retaining clip and withdraw the lock and seating washer from the door.
4 To remove the lock barrel, extract the circlip and remove the spring washer and lock lever. Withdraw the lock barrel from the lock body.
5 Refitting is the reverse sequence to removal.

## 24 Front door glass and regulator – removal and refitting

1 Wind the window fully up and then remove the inner trim panel, as described in Section 20.
2 Using wooden wedges, support the window in the raised position.
3 Undo and remove the two bolts securing the regulator assembly to the door. Undo and remove the nuts securing the auxiliary slide, which are accessible from the bottom of the door, and withdraw the slide.
4 Disengage the regulator arm from the glass lifting channel and remove the regulator through the door aperture.
5 Undo and remove the screws securing the glass front and rear support channels and move the channels to one side.

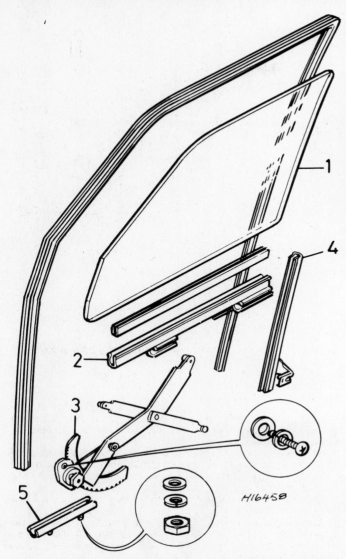

25.2a Carefully prise off the front door cheater panel ...

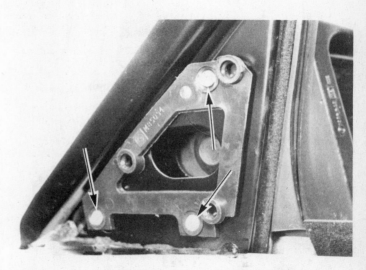

25.2b ... to provide access to the exterior mirror retaining screws (arrowed)

**Fig. 11.7 Front door glass and regulator components (Sec 24)**

| | | | |
|---|---|---|---|
| 1 | *Door glass* | 4 | *Glass rear support* |
| 2 | *Lifting channel* | | *channel* |
| 3 | *Window regulator* | 5 | *Auxiliary slide* |

6   Lower the glass carefully to the bottom of the door and release it from the support channels.
7   Remove the inner and outer waist seals from the door, as necessary, tilt the glass so that the rear top corner is uppermost and carefully lift the glass out through the top of the door. If required the lifting channel can now be removed from the door glass.
8   Refitting is the reverse sequence to removal.

## 25 Front door exterior mirror – removal and refitting

1   Open the front door, and, if the mirror is of the remotely controlled type, remove the adjusting lever by pulling it to the rear.
2   Carefully prise off the cheater panel internal finisher to provide access to the mirror retaining screws (photos).
3   Undo and remove the three screws, lift off the retaining plate and withdraw the mirror from the door.
4   Refitting is the reverse sequence to removal.
5   The design of the mirror is such that it will give slightly under impact, against spring tension, thus minimising the risk of damage or injury. On remotely controlled mirrors this will cause the adjusting lever to disengage from the internal mechanism and become

inoperative. The lever can be refitted, without removing the mirror, as follows.
6   Open the door and lower the window.
7   Gently move the mirror head toward the front of the car to give a working clearance between the mirror head and the base.
8   With the mirror held in this position, grasp the ball plate with one hand and the ball-head of the adjusting lever with the other. Firmly push the ball head into the socket on the ball plate until it fully engages. Release the mirror head and check the operation.

## 26 Rear door inner trim panel – removal and refitting

1   If a pull handle is fitted, prise back the edge cappings and remove the two retaining screws. Lift the pull handle off the door panel. If an armrest is fitted, remove the two screws under the armrest and lift the rear away (photo).
2   Carefully prise out the trim cap and unscrew the window regulator handle retaining screw. Lift off the handle (photo).
3   Prise out the trim cap and unscrew the door release lever surround retaining screw. Remove the surround by sliding it over the release lever.
4   Starting at the lower rear corner, release the trim panel retaining clips by carefully levering between the panel and door with a

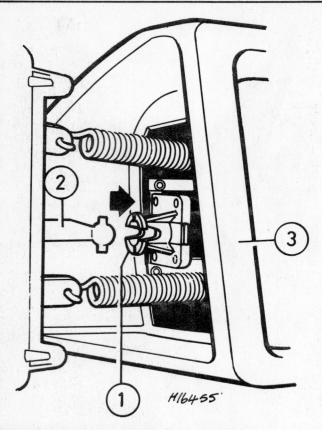

**Fig. 11.8 Remote control exterior mirror (Sec 25)**

1  Ball plate
2  Adjusting lever
3  Mirror head

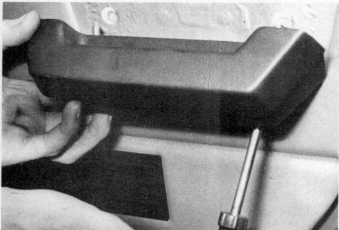

26.1 Remove the armrest retaining screws and lift off the armrest

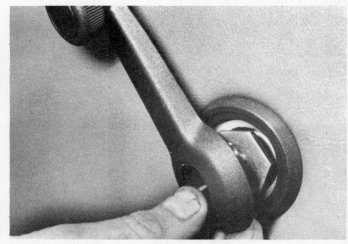

26.2 Remove the trim cap, screw and regulator handle

screwdriver or flat bar.
5   To gain access to the door components, carefully pull back the polythene condensation barrier, as necessary.
6   To remove the upper trim capping, undo and remove the retaining screws (photo) and lift the capping off.
7   Refitting is the reverse sequence to removal.

## 27  Rear door – removal and refitting

1   Carefully mark the outline of the door hinges on the pillar, using a soft pencil.
2   With the help of an assistant to support the door, undo and remove the bolts securing the upper and lower hinges to the pillar (photos) and lift away the door.
3   Refitting is the reverse sequence to removal. Align the hinges with

the pencil marks made during removal.
4   Check that the door closes correctly, and that the door seal touches at all points around the door. If necessary, make minor corrections to the door adjustment and seal positioning to obtain a sound, weatherproof seal, or wind noise may result.

## 28  Rear door lock – removal, refitting and adjustment

1   Remove the door inner trim panel and capping, as described in Section 26.
2   Temporarily refit the window regulator handle and wind the window fully up. Unscrew the interior lock button.
3   Prise the operating rod out of its retaining bush on the door exterior handle operating lever.
4   Undo and remove the screw securing the internal release lever to

26.6 Rear door upper trim capping retaining screws (arrowed)

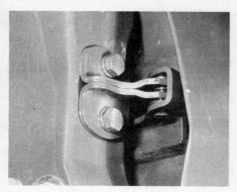

27.2a Rear door upper ...

27.2b ... and lower hinges and retaining bolts

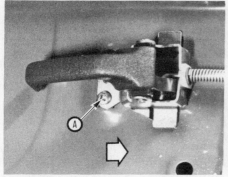

28.4 Remove the rear internal release lever retaining screw (A) and slide the lever rearwards to release it

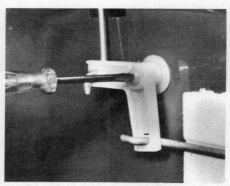

28.5a Press out the locking pin from the centre of the bellcrank lever ...

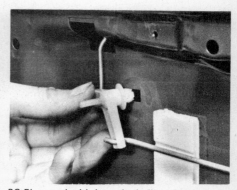

28.5b ... and withdraw the bellcrank and pivot

28.6a Remove the three retaining screws ...

28.6b ... and remove the lock assembly from the door aperture

the door (photo). Release the operating rod from its steady clip and slide the lever rearwards to release it from its location.

5    Using a small screwdriver or punch, press out the locking pin from the centre of the bellcrank lever (photo), and withdraw the bellcrank and pivot (photo). Detach the lock operating rod from the bellcrank and from its steady clip.

6    Undo and remove the three screws securing the lock to the door (photo) and withdraw the unit, complete with operating rods, from the door aperture (photo).

7    Refitting is the reverse sequence to removal, but adjust the lock striker pin as follows.

8    Check that the latch disc is in the open position, then loosen the striker pin nut (photo 22.10) and position the pin so that the door can be closed easily, and is held firmly. Close the door gently, but firmly, when making this adjustment.

9    Tighten the striker pin nut.

## 29 Rear door private lock – removal and refitting

Removal and refitting of the private lock is the same as described in Section 23 for the front door unit. Remove the inner trim panel, as described in Section 26, and then refer to Section 23 for the remainder of the procedure.

## 30 Rear door glass and regulator – removal and refitting

1    Wind the window fully up, and then remove the inner trim panel and capping, as described in Section 26.

2    Undo and remove the two bolts securing the window regulator to the door panel (photo). Support the glass, disengage the regulator arm from the door glass lifting channel, and withdraw the regulator through

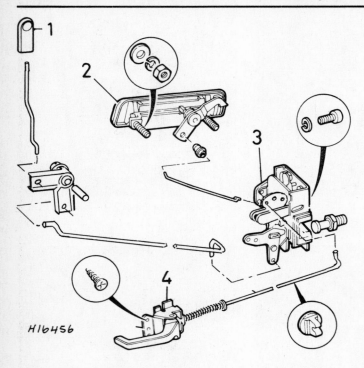

H16456

**Fig. 11.9 Rear door lock components (Secs 28 and 29)**

1   Interior lock button      3   Lock assembly
2   Door exterior handle      4   Internal release lever

the door aperture (photo).
3   Lower the glass to the bottom of the door and then remove the
rear guide channel retaining bolt. Release the channel from the glass
and remove the felt from the channel.
4   Remove the inner and outer waist seals from the door.
5   Drill out the rivets securing the cheater panel to the door frame
and lift off the panel. Drill an access hole in the bottom of the cheater
panel and shake out the rivet debris.
6   Drill out the rivets securing the rear guide channel to the door,
withdraw the channel, and remove the rivet studs.
7   Carefully lift the glass upwards and out of the door. The lifting
channel can now be removed from the glass, if necessary.
8   Refitting is the reverse sequence to removal.

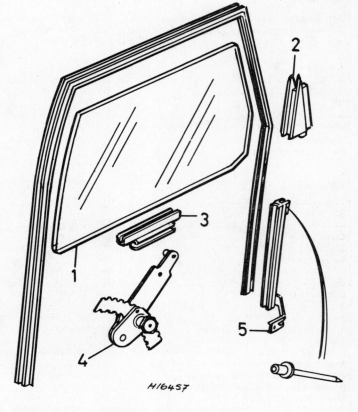

H16457

**Fig. 11.10 Rear door glass and regulator components (Sec 30)**

1   Door glass          4   Window regulator
2   Cheater panel       5   Rear guide channel
3   Lifting channel

30.2a Remove the window regulator retaining bolts (arrowed) ...

30.2b ... and withdraw the regulator through the door aperture

## 31 Seats – removal and refitting

1 A special splined Torx driver, or bit, should be used to remove the seat mounting bolts.

### Front seat
2 Adjust the seat for access to the seat runner retaining bolts, remove the bolts and withdraw the seat through the door aperture.

### Rear seat
3 Undo and remove the bolts securing the rear seat front mountings.
4 Remove the rear parcel shelf, unlock the rear seat squabs, and fold the seat forward.
5 Where applicable, fold back the carpet and rear floor covering, undo and remove the rear retaining bolts and lift out the rear seat.

### Front and rear seats
6 Refitting is the reverse sequence to removal, but before tightening the rear seat rear mountings, tighten the front mountings with the seats unfolded to ensure correct alignment.

## 32 Seat belts – removal and refitting

**Caution**: *If the vehicle has been involved in an accident in which structural damage was sustained, all the seat belt components must be renewed.*
1 Move the front seats fully forward, ease the door seal from around the central door pillar, and remove the interior trim covering the seat belt mechanism.
2 Prise off the trim capping from the top mounting. Undo and remove the top, bottom and inertia reel mounting bolts, noting the position of the spacers and washers, and remove the assembly from the car.
3 Press out the belt guide from the interior trim and remove the belt from the trim.
4 Pull off the trim cover then undo and remove the bolt securing the flexible stalk to the floor. Note the position of the washers and spacer, and remove the stalk.
5 Refitting is the reverse sequence to removal, *but ensure that the mounting bolts are tightened to the specified torque.*

## 33 Front and rear bumpers – removal and refitting

### One-piece type
1 If working on the front bumper, undo and remove the two bolts and shouldered tubular spacers securing each bumper front mounting tube to the body. If working on the rear bumper, disconnect the number plate lamp wiring connectors, then undo and remove the two bolts securing the bumper to the body.
2 Extract the retaining pegs which secure the bumper side mounting studs to the body side clips on each side, pulling the clips away from the bumper. Note that in the case of the rear bumper, these are hidden under a closing plate inside the wheelarch; this should be detached for access, after removing the screw which retains it.
3 With the help of an assistant, pull the bumper away from the car to free the side mounting studs from the clips on the body, and then lift off the bumper assembly.
4 If required, remove the side mounting studs and, on the rear bumper, the number plate lamp, with reference to Chapter 9.
5 Refitting is the reverse sequence to removal.

### Three-piece type
6 Undo and remove the bolt securing each bumper end cap to the side of the body and withdraw the end caps from the bumper.
7 If working on the rear bumper, disconnect the rear number plate lamps at the wiring connectors.
8 If working on the front bumper, undo and remove the two bolts and shouldered tubular spacers securing each bumper mounting tube to the body. If working on the rear bumper, undo and remove the two bolts securing the bumper to the body.
9 With the help of an assistant, withdraw the bumper from the car. If required, remove the number plate lamps from the rear bumper.
10 Refitting is the reverse sequence to removal.

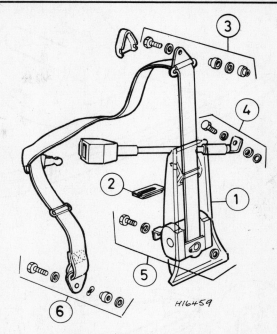

H16459

**Fig. 11.11 Front seat belts and mountings (Sec 32)**

| | |
|---|---|
| 1 *Interior trim* | 4 *Flexible stalk mounting* |
| 2 *Belt guide* | 5 *Inertia reel mounting* |
| 3 *Top belt mounting* | 6 *Bottom belt mounting* |

## 34 Sunroof – removal and refitting

### Sunroof panel
1 Open the trailing edge of the sunroof panel, ease each end of the panel liner down, and release the trim panel clips from the legs on the liner frame.
2 Close the sunroof and disengage the liner front clips from the deflector slides. Move the liner back between the panels and detach the panel liner tensioning springs.
3 Undo and remove the four screws on each side securing the sunroof panel to the slide and tilt mechanism. *Do not remove the tilt adjustment screws.*
4 Lift out the sunroof panel and, if required, remove the weatherstrip and trim panel clips.
5 If removed, refit the weatherstrip and trim panel clips, locate the sunroof panel in position and loosely secure.
6 Close the sunroof and check its alignment. Tighten the four securing screws in sequence and adjust the tilt arm as necessary.
7 Refit the tensioning springs, open the trailing edge of the sunroof and pull the liner forward, ensuring that the clips on the liner frame engage with the deflector slides.
8 Engage the trim panel clips on the legs of the liner frame and close the sunroof.

### Sunroof liner
9 Remove the sunroof panel, as previously described, and then remove the two deflector slides.
10 Slide the liner forward, disengage it from the frame and lift it upwards and out.
11 To refit the liner, locate it on the frame with the slides under the spigots. Slide the liner rearwards, refit the deflector slides and then refit the sunroof panel. Note that, if you need to fit a new liner to earlier models, the currently-supplied part cannot be fitted until the locating pegs used from VIN 649764 onwards have been removed with a hacksaw, the ends filed smooth, and the exposed metal painted to prevent corrosion problems.

### Sunroof frame
12 Remove the sunroof panel, sunroof liner and the wind deflector, as previously described.
13 Remove the operating handle.

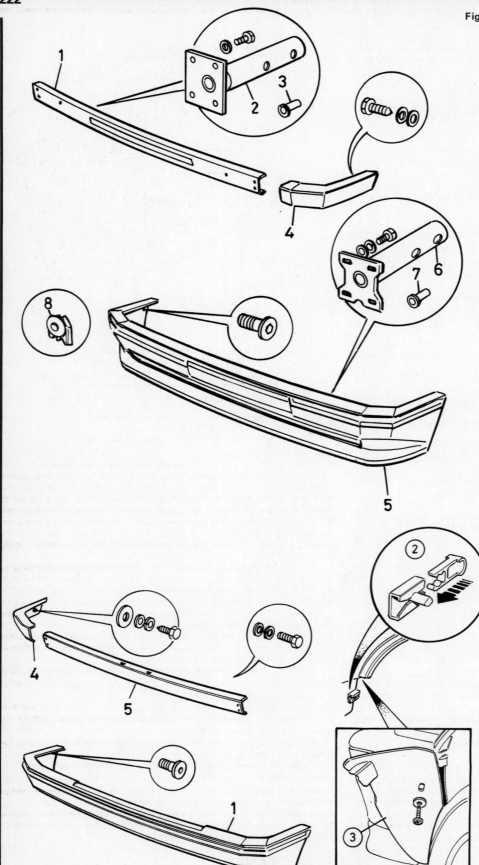

**Fig. 11.12 Front bumper component**
(Sec 33)

**Three-piece type**
1  Centre section
2  Mounting tube
3  Tubular spacer
4  End cap

**One-piece type**
5  Bumper and lower panel
6  Mounting tube
7  Tubular spacer
8  Side mounting clip

**Fig. 11.13 Rear bumper components**
(Sec 33)
1  Bumper and lower panel
   (one-piece type)
2  Bumper fixing peg and clip
   (one-piece type)
3  Wheelarch liner/closing panel
   (one-piece type)
4  End cap (three-piece type)
5  Centre section (three-piece type)

H.23952

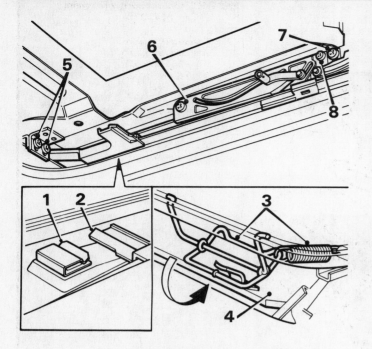

**Fig. 11.14 Sunroof panel attachments (Sec 34)**

1   *Trim panel front clip*
2   *Deflector slide*
3   *Trim panel clip and tensioning spring*
4   *Trim panel*
5   *Wind deflector slide retaining screws*
6   *Tilt arm front retaining screw*
7   *Tilt arm rear retaining screw*
8   *Tilt arm adjustment screw*

14   Release the aperture trim along the front edge and ease away the headliner. Undo and remove the two screws securing the winder mechanism to the frame and front bracket. Take care to protect the roof panel in front of the aperture.
15   Undo and remove the remaining screws securing the frame to the mounting assembly, move the frame forwards and lift it out, taking care to avoid scratching the surrounding paintwork.
16   To refit the frame, position it in the aperture and engage the guide pins in the rear support brackets. Refit the retaining screws loosely, locate the wind deflector and tighten all the retaining screws.
17   Refit the sunroof liner and sunroof panel.

### 35 Facia panel – removal and refitting

**Note**: *Removal of the facia is considerably involved, entailing extensive dismantling and the disconnection of many wiring harness plugs and connectors. Read through the entire Section before starting, and familiarize yourself with the procedure by referring to the photographs and illustrations. Identify all electrical connections with a label before removal and, if necessary, make notes during dismantling.*
1   Disconnect the battery negative terminal.
2   Open the glovebox and unscrew the strap retaining screws, unscrew the hinge retaining screws each side (photo) and remove the glovebox lid.
3   Pull the knobs and bezels off the radio controls, unscrew the retaining nuts and remove the radio finisher and masking plate. Push the radio back, remove the two packing plates, withdraw the radio and detach the aerial and electrical leads.
4   With the radio removed, undo and remove the two screws located above the radio aperture (photo). Pull the knobs off the heater controls (photo), remove the remaining screws securing the heater cover panel and lift away the panel (photos).
5   Refer to the relevant Sections of Chapter 9, and remove the

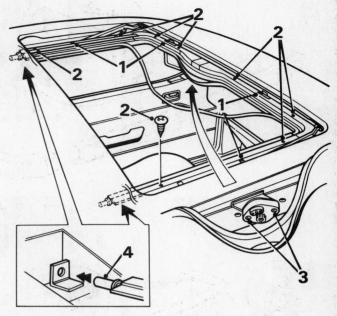

**Fig. 11.15 Sunroof frame attachments (Sec 34)**

1   *Wind deflector retaining screws*
2   *Frame retaining screws*
3   *Winder-to-front bracket retaining screws*
4   *Guide pin and rear support bracket*

instrument pack and surround, the switch panel and the side panel.
6   Refer to Chapter 10, and remove the steering column.
7   From within the glovebox, undo and remove the retaining screws and lower the glovebox top cover (photo). Make a very careful note of all the wiring locations and then disconnect the glovebox lamp leads, wiper control multi-plugs and earth lead, release the relays from the cover, detach any other optional electrical units that may be fitted and withdraw the top cover.
8   Disconnect the main feed multi-plugs from the fusebox, noting their locations.
9   Carefully ease away the door seals around the windscreen pillar to gain access to the pillar trim (photo). Remove the door pillar trim (photo) and lower finisher assembly.
10   Remove the retaining screws and lift off the facia end panels or, where fitted, the radio speaker grilles (photo). Detach the speaker leads and remove the grilles.
11   Release the side window and face level vent hoses from the left-hand side of the facia. Depress the catches and lift off the demister vents from the top of the facia (photo).
12   According to model and extras fitted, it may also be necessary to disconnect the dimmer switch, window lift, rear speaker and speaker balance control multi-plugs.
13   Remove the screws securing the facia to the mounting brackets (photo) and, with the help of an assistant, ease the facia carefully out of its location. Make sure all wiring is disconnected, and that all detached components are clear. Now carefully withdraw the facia out through the driver's door aperture.
14   Refitting is essentially the reverse of the removal sequence.

### 36 Centre console – removal and refitting

1   Withdraw the coin tray, ashtray or blanking plate at the front of the console, and then unscrew the two front retaining screws (photo).
2   Unscrew the two screws securing the rear of the console and unscrew the gearlever knob.
3   Lift the console and ease it off the handbrake gaiter and over the gearlever, then remove it from the car.
4   Refitting is the reverse sequence to removal.

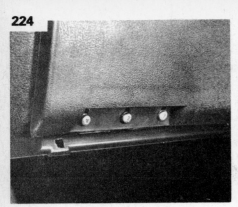

35.2 Glovebox hinge retaining bolts

35.4a With the radio removed, unscrew the heater cover panel centre securing screws (arrowed)

35.4b Pull off the heater control knobs ...

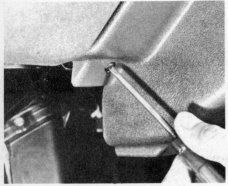

35.4c ... remove the lower retaining screws ...

35.4d ... and withdraw the heater cover panel

35.7 Lower the glovebox top cover to gain access to the relays and wiring connectors

35.9a Ease away the door seals around the windscreen pillar ...

35.9b ... and remove the pillar trim

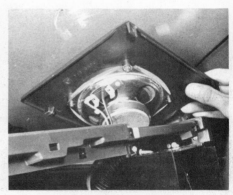

35.10 Remove the screws and lift off the speaker grilles

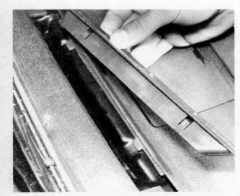

35.11 Lift off the demister vents from the top of the facia

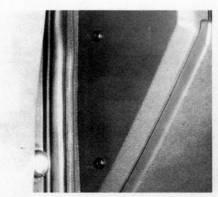

35.13 Facia side mounting screw locations

36.2 On certain models the centre console front mounting is located under the coin tray

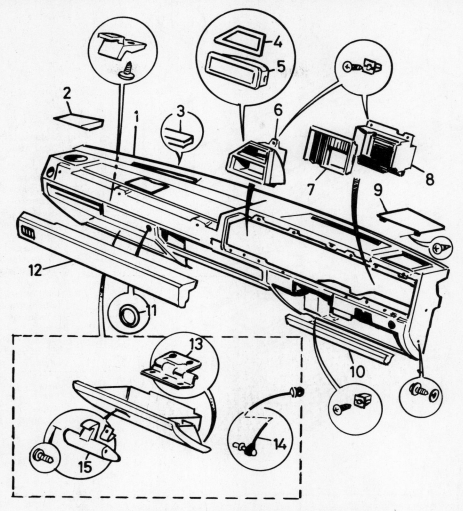

**Fig. 11.16 Facia panel attachments and components (Sec 35)**

1  Facia panel
2  Facia end panel
3  Finisher strip
4  Clock aperture blanking
   plate (where fitted)

5  Ashtray (where fitted)
6  Instrument side panel
7  Switch panel
8  Face level vent housing

9  Facia end panel
10  Lower facia rail
11  Cigar lighter blanking
   plate (where fitted)

12  Crash pad
13  Glovebox hinge
14  Glovebox retaining strap
15  Glovebox latch

## 37 Heater – adjustments

1  Remove the heater cover panel, as described in Section 35, paragraphs 3 and 4.

### Air distribution

2  Move the air distribution control lever to the SCREEN position.
3  Slacken the locking screw securing the air distribution control rod to the air distribution flap lever. Move the lever in a clockwise direction as far as it will go and then tighten the locking screw.

### Temperature control and face level distribution

4  Move the face level air control lever to the OFF position.
5  Slacken the locking screw securing the face level air control rod to the face level air flap lever. Move the lever in a clockwise direction as far as it will go and then tighten the locking screw.
6  Move the air temperature control lever to the COLD position.
7  Slacken the two locking screws securing the air temperature control rods to the air temperature flap levers.
8  Rotate the upper lever anti-clockwise until it is just clear of the face level outlet hose on the heater, and then tighten the locking screw.

9  Rotate the lower lever clockwise as far as it will go and then tighten the locking screw.
10  After adjustment refit the heater cover panel, as described in Section 35.

## 38 Heater – removal and refitting

1  Drain the cooling system, as described in Chapter 2, and then remove the facia, as described in Section 35 of this Chapter.
2  Working in the engine compartment, note the positioning of the heater hoses and then disconnect them at the heater outlets adjacent to the engine compartment bulkhead. Plug the heater outlets to prevent spillage inside the car as the heater is removed.
3  Disconnect the heater vacuum pipe from the connector in the main vacuum line near the carburettors. Pull the disconnected pipe through the retaining clips.
4  Undo and remove the bolt from the heater lower support strut and the screws securing the heater to the passenger's heater duct assembly.
5  Move the aerial lead to one side, then undo and remove the screws securing the demister duct outlets. Release the other end of the ducts and the face level vent tubes from the heater.

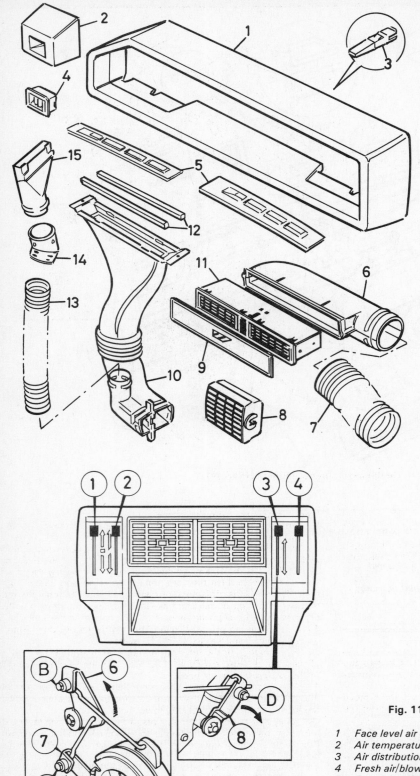

**Fig. 11.17 Facia panel vent and duct details (Sec 35)**

1  Instrument panel surround
2  Left-hand demister seal
3  Facia panel surround retaining clip
4  Left-hand side demister vent
5  Windscreen demister vents
6  Fresh air vent duct
7  Fresh air vent hose
8  Face level vent
9  Vent blanking plate (where fitted)
10  Windscreen demister duct
11  Fresh air vent
12  Windscreen demister seals
13  Side demister vent hose
14  Side demister vent elbow
15  Side demister vent duct

H16462

**Fig. 11.18 Heater adjustment points (Sec 37)**

1  Face level air control lever
2  Air temperature control lever
3  Air distribution control lever
4  Fresh air/blower control lever
5  Face level air flap lever
6  Air temperature flap upper lever
7  Air temperature flap lower lever
8  Air distribution flap lever
A  Face level air distribution control rod to flap lever locking screw
B  Air temperature control rod to upper flap lever locking screw
C  Air temperature control rod to lower flap lever locking screw
D  Air distribution control rod to flap lever locking screw
Arrows indicate directions of turn when setting the heater controls

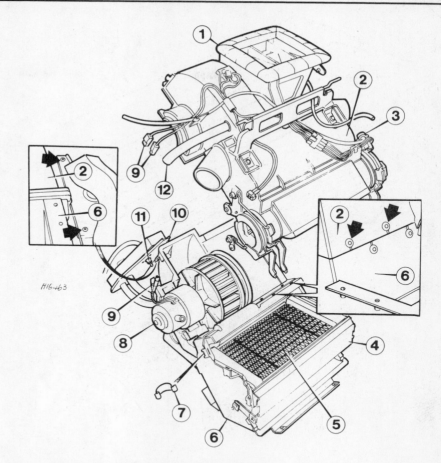

*1 Air inlet box*
*2 Upper casing*
*3 Vacuum switch*
*4 Matrix retaining panel*
*5 Heater matrix*
*6 Lower casing*
*7 Casing half retaining*
*clip*
*8 Blower motor*
*9 Motor wiring connectors*
*10 Heater pipe bracket*
*11 Vacuum non-return valve*
*12 Motor vent pipe*
*Arrows indicate rivet locations*

**Fig. 11.19 Heater assembly components (Sec 39)**

6   Disconnect the heater wiring harness multi-plug.
7   Undo and remove the heater upper retaining bolts and recover the clamp brackets.
8   Release the clips securing the main wiring harness to the heater.
9   Detach the heater drain tubes from the floor, and then carefully remove the heater from inside the car. As the heater is removed, pull the vacuum pipe through the bulkhead.
10  Refitting is the reverse sequence to removal. Refill the cooling system, as described in Chapter 2.

## 39   Heater – dismantling and reassembly

1   Undo and remove the screws securing the air inlet box to the heater body, and the single screw securing the resistor wiring harness clip to the air inlet box support bracket.
2   Withdraw the vacuum pipe from the vacuum switch and remove the tape securing the pipe to the heater. Lift the air inlet box off the heater body.
3   Disconnect the wiring connectors at the heater motor and pull off the motor vent pipe.
4   Slacken the screws securing the temperature control rod and air distribution control rod to their respective flap levers and withdraw the rods.
5   Drill out the single rivet securing the heater pipe support bracket to the upper casing and the two rivets securing the upper and lower casing halves together. Prise off the clips which also secure the two halves of the heater casing.
6   Detach the vacuum pipe from the non-return valve on the heater pipe support bracket and separate the upper and lower heater casings.
7   Lift out the heater motor assembly. If required, pull the rotor off the motor shaft and remove the rubber mounting strips from the motor housing and locating tag.
8   Drill out the retaining rivet and remove the heater pipes and

bracket assembly from the matrix.
9   Drill out the rivets, remove the heater matrix retaining panel and lift out the matrix.
10  With the heater dismantled, inspect the matrix for signs of leaks and, if any are apparent, renew the matrix. If the matrix appears serviceable, brush off any accumulation of dirt or debris from the fins and then reverse flush the core. Inpect the remaining heater components for any signs of damage or distortion. Note that only the motor, matrix and wiring harness are available as separate components, all other parts being supplied as part of a complete heater unit.
11  Begin reassembly by placing the matrix in position. Refit the retaining panel and secure with pop rivets.
12  If removed, refit the rotor to the motor shaft so that the outer face of the rotor is 4.04 to 4.06 in (102.5 to 103 mm) from the rear face of the tag on the motor body.
13  Apply adhesive to the rubber mounting strips and attach them to the motor housing. Refit the motor housing assembly ensuring that its tag locates in the heater casing lower half.
14  Apply a little grease to the pivots of the flaps and flap levers. Refit the upper and lower casing halves together, taking care to locate the flap pivots correctly. Ensure that the flaps move freely with no trace of binding.
15  Refit the retaining clips to the casing flanges, and secure the assembly with two pop rivets.
16  Lubricate the heater pipes and seals with a little soapy water and guide the pipes through the seals and onto the matrix. Secure the pipe bracket with pop rivets then attach the vacuum pipe to the non-return valve.
17  Refit the temperature and air distribution control rods to their flap levers. Adjust the rods, as described in Section 37.
18  Reconnect the heater motor vent pipe and wiring connectors.
19  Refit the air inlet box and resistor harness clip, and secure with the retaining screws. Connect the vacuum pipe to the vacuum switch and retain the pipe with adhesive tape.

# Chapter 12 Supplement:
# Revisions and information on later models

## Contents

## 1 Introduction

Since its introduction in 1983 the Austin Maestro has had a number of modifications and improvements made in order to keep pace with current technical and design innovations.

Those modifications made since the original publication of this manual which affect servicing and/or repairs are included in this supplementary Chapter. These are mainly concerned with the introduction of the 500 and 700 van, the 1.6 litre 'S' series engine and

automatic models.

In order to use this Supplement to the best advantage, it is suggested that it is referred to before the main Chapters of the manual; this will ensure that any relevant information can be noted and incorporated within the procedures given in Chapter 1 to 11. Time and cost will therefore be saved and the particular job will be completed correctly.

BL Cars Limited is now known as The Rover Group plc, with dealers operating under the flag of Austin Rover. All references to BL in the preceding eleven Chapters should be regarded with this in mind.

## 2 Specifications

*The specifications listed below are revised or supplementary to the main Specifications listed at the start of each Chapter*

### Engine – 1.3 litre (later models)

#### Crankshaft

Main journal diameter:
| | |
|---|---|
| No colour code | 2.0012 to 2.0017 in (50.83 to 50.84 mm) |
| Red colour code | 2.0005 to 2.0009 in (50.81 to 50.82 mm) |
| Green colour code | 2.0009 to 2.0013 in (50.82 to 50.83 mm) |
| Yellow colour code | 2.0013 to 2.0017 in (50.83 to 50.84 mm) |
| Main bearing running clearance | 0.0007 to 0.0023 in (0.017 to 0.058 mm) |
| Main journal minimum regrind diameter | 1.7297 in (43.93 mm) |
| Crankpin journal diameter | 1.7497 to 1.7504 in (44.44 to 44.46 mm) |
| Crankpin running clearance | 0.0015 to 0.0032 in (0.0381 to 0.0813 mm) |
| Crankpin minimum regrind diameter | 1.7297 in (43.93 mm) |
| Crankshaft endfloat | 0.002 to 0.003 in (0.051 to 0.076 mm) |
| Thrust washer thicknesses available | Standard, 0.003 in (0.076 mm) and 0.030 in (0.760 mm) oversize |

#### Pistons

Skirt clearance in cylinder:
| | |
|---|---|
| Top | 0.0029 to 0.0045 in (0.074 to 0.114 mm) |
| Bottom | 0.0009 to 0.0025 in (0.023 to 0.064 mm) |

#### Piston rings

| | |
|---|---|
| Clearance in groove (compression rings) | 0.0015 to 0.0035 in (0.038 to 0.089 mm) |

Fitted end gap:
| | |
|---|---|
| Top compression | 0.010 to 0.017 in (0.25 to 0.43 mm) |
| Second compression | 0.008 to 0.013 in (0.20 to 0.33 mm) |
| Oil control | 0.015 to 0.041 in (0.38 to 1.04 mm) |

#### Valves

| | |
|---|---|
| Head diameter – inlet (from engine Nos 12H 999 104 761 and 804 102 434) | 1.389 to 1.409 in (35.53 to 35.79 mm) |
| Seat angle | 45° 30' |

Head diameter – unleaded fuel engines:
| | |
|---|---|
| Inlet | 1.307 to 1.312 in (33.20 to 33.32 mm) |
| Exhaust | 1.151 to 1.156 in (29.24 to 29.36 mm) |

Head diameter – leaded fuel engines only:
Inlet..................................................................... 1.389 to 1.409 in (35.53 to 35.79 mm)
Exhaust................................................................ 1.150 to 1.160 in (29.24 to 29.36 mm)

## Engine – 1.6 litre from approximately July 1984

### General
Type........................................................................ Four-cylinder in-line, overhead camshaft
Designation............................................................ 'S' series
Bore........................................................................ 3.000 in (76.20 mm)
Stroke..................................................................... 3.448 in (87.58 mm)
Capacity................................................................. 1598 cc (97.5 cu in)
Firing order............................................................ 1-3-4-2 (No 1 cylinder at crankshaft pulley end)

### Crankshaft
Main journal diameter............................................ 2.2515 to 2.2520 in (57.19 to 57.20 mm)
Main bearing running clearance.............................. 0.002 to 0.0035 in (0.05 to 0.09 mm)
Main journal minimum regrind diameter.................. 2.2115 in (56.17 mm)
Crankpin journal diameter...................................... 1.8759 to 1.8765 in (47.65 to 47.66 mm)
Crankpin running clearance.................................... 0.0015 to 0.003 in (0.04 to 0.08 mm)
Crank minimum regrind diameter........................... 1.8359 in (46.63 mm)
Endfloat.................................................................. 0.004 to 0.007 in (0.10 to 0.18 mm)
Thrust washer thicknesses available....................... 0.089 in (2.26 mm), 0.090 in (2.28 mm), 0.091 in (2.31 mm) and 0.092 in (2.34 mm)

### Connecting rods
Length between centres.......................................... 5.830 in (148.08 mm)

### Pistons
Skirt clearance in cylinder:
Top......................................................................... 0.0028 to 0.0044 in (0.07 to 0.11 mm)
Bottom................................................................... 0.001 to 0.002 in (0.03 to 0.05 mm)
Oversizes available................................................ 0.020 in (0.51 mm)

### Piston rings
Clearance in grooves.............................................. 0.0015 to 0.0035 in (0.04 to 0.09 mm)
Fitted gap:
Compression.......................................................... 0.012 to 0.022 in (0.30 to 0.56 mm)
Oil control rails...................................................... 0.015 to 0.045 in (0.38 to 1.14 mm)

### Gudgeon pins
Diameter................................................................. 0.8123 to 0.8125 in (20.63 to 20.64 mm)
Clearance in piston................................................ Hand push fit at 20°C (68°F)
Interference fit in connecting rod........................... 0.0008 to 0.0015 in (0.02 to 0.04 mm)

### Camshaft
Journal diameter:
Front...................................................................... 1.9355 to 1.9365 in (49.16 to 49.19 mm)
Centre.................................................................... 1.9668 to 1.9678 in (49.96 to 49.98 mm)
Rear....................................................................... 1.998 to 1.999 in (50.75 to 50.77 mm)
Running clearance in bearings................................ 0.001 to 0.0023 in (0.025 to 0.058 mm)
Endfloat.................................................................. 0.002 to 0.007 in (0.05 to 0.18 mm)
Valve lift:
Inlet....................................................................... 0.342 to 0.344 in (8.69 to 8.74 mm)
Exhaust.................................................................. 0.338 to 0.340 in (8.58 to 8.64 mm)

### Tappets
Adjustment............................................................. Selected shims
Outside diameter.................................................... 1.1865 in (30.14 mm)
Shim size range available:
From shim no. 97................................................... 0.097 in (2.47 mm) in increments of 0.002 in (0.05 mm)
To shim no. 49....................................................... 0.149 in (3.78 mm)

### Valves
Seat angle.............................................................. 45.25°
Head diameter:
Inlet....................................................................... 1.500 in (38.1 mm)
Exhaust.................................................................. 1.218 in (30.9 mm)
Stem diameter (standard):
Inlet....................................................................... 0.3115 to 0.3120 in (7.91 to 7.92 mm)
Exhaust.................................................................. 0.3109 to 0.3114 in (7.90 to 7.91 mm)
Stem diameter (oversize)........................................ 0.3331 to 0.3336 in (8.46 to 8.47 mm)
Stem-to-guide (clearance)...................................... 0.0015 in (0.038 mm)
Valve spring free length......................................... 1.810 in (45.97 mm)
Valve timing (at tappet clearance of 0.021 in/0.53 mm)
Inlet opens............................................................. 17° BTDC
Inlet closes............................................................ 59° ABDC

| | |
|---|---|
| Exhaust opens | 57° BBDC |
| Exhaust closes | 19° ATDC |
| Tappet clearances (cold): | |
| Inlet | 0.014 to 0.015 in (0.36 to 0.38 mm) |
| Exhaust | 0.017 to 0.018 in (0.43 to 0.46 mm) |
| **Adjust only if less than** | 0.012 in (0.30 mm) |
| Valve sequence (from front of head): | |
| Inlet | 2, 3, 6, 7 |
| Exhaust | 1, 4, 5, 8 |

## Timing belt

| | |
|---|---|
| Tensioning method | Torque wrench engaged with hole in tensioner bracket |
| Tension: | |
| New belt | 15 lbf ft (20 Nm) |
| Used belt | 10 lbf ft (14 Nm) |

## Cylinder head

| | |
|---|---|
| Height: | |
| New | 3.312 to 3.322 in (84.12 to 84.38 mm) |
| Minimum | 3.302 in (83.87 mm) |
| Maximum clearance under straight-edge across surface | 0.002 in (0.05 mm) |

## Lubrication system

| | |
|---|---|
| Oil pump: | |
| Type | Bi-rotor |
| Outer rotor endfloat | 0.001 to 0.003 in (0.03 to 0.08 mm) |
| Outer rotor-to-body clearance | 0.007 to 0.009 in (0.18 to 0.23 mm) |
| Rotor lobe clearance | 0.010 to 0.011 in (0.25 to 0.28 mm) |
| System pressure: | |
| Idling | 10 lbf/in$^2$ (0.7 bar) |
| Over 2500 rpm | 55 lbf/in$^2$ (3.8 bar) |
| Pressure relief valve spring free length | 24.7 in (62.7 mm) |
| Warning light switch operating pressure | 6 to 10 lbf/in$^2$ (0.4 to 0.7 bar) |
| Oil filter | Champion C104 |

## Torque wrench settings

| | lbf ft | Nm |
|---|---|---|
| Timing belt tensioner bolts | 18 | 24 |
| Camshaft carrier bolts | 18 | 24 |
| Camshaft carrier cover bolts | 6 | 8 |
| Camshaft sprocket bolt | 41 | 56 |
| Connecting rod big-end cap nuts | 30 | 40 |
| Crankshaft pulley bolt | 34 | 46 |
| Cylinder head bolts (see text) | 60 | 80 |
| Gearbox adaptor plate: | | |
| M8 bolts | 18 | 24 |
| M10 bolts | 34 | 46 |
| M12 bolts | 67 | 91 |
| Knock sensor | 9 | 12 |
| Main bearing cap bolts | 67 | 91 |
| Oil pump-to-cylinder block bolts | 19 | 26 |
| Oil pressure switch | 18 | 24 |
| Sump drain plug | 18 | 24 |
| Sump bolts | 6 | 8 |
| Vacuum hose banjo union bolt | 37 | 50 |
| Tie-rods: | | |
| Tie-rod bracket to engine | 48 | 65 |
| Tie-rod bracket to sub-frame | 33 | 45 |
| Tie-rod to engine bracket | 66 | 90 |
| Tie-rod to sub-frame bracket | 33 | 45 |

## *Cooling system – 1.6 litre 'S' series engine*

| | |
|---|---|
| System capacity | 15.0 pints (8.5 litres) |

## Torque wrench setting

| | lbf ft | Nm |
|---|---|---|
| Coolant temperature thermistor | 11 | 15 |
| Thermostat housing bolts | 13 | 18 |
| Water inlet elbow to cylinder head | 18 | 24 |
| Water outlet elbow to thermostat housing | 18 | 24 |
| Water pump to cylinder block | 9 | 12 |

## *Fuel and exhaust systems*

## Fuel pump – MG 1600 with 'S' series engine

| | |
|---|---|
| Type | Pierburg 12 volt electric with 5 vane impeller |
| Delivery pressure | 4 lbf/in$^2$ (0.3 bar) |

Running current.................................................................... 1.5 amp maximum at 13.5 volts

## Carburettor cooling fan motor – MG 1600 with 'S' series engine
Light running current (without fan)...................................... 3.0 amp maximum at 13.5 volts
Light running speed (without fan)......................................... 3500 to 4000 rpm

## Air cleaner element
1.6 litre models with 'S' series engine (except MG 1600)...................... Champion W114

## SU carburettor – 1984 on
Type identification:
  1.3 HL.............................................................................. FZX 1422
  1.3 litre 500 and 700 van.................................................. FZX 1468
  1.6 litre models with 'R' series engine:
    Manual gearbox............................................................ FZX 1419
    Automatic gearbox........................................................ FZX 1420
  1.6 litre models with 'S' series engine:
    Manual gearbox............................................................ FZZ 1424 or 14563
    Automatic transmission................................................ FZX 1425
  1.6 litre models with manual choke.................................... FZX 1475
Needle identification:
  1.3 litre models............................................................... BCZ
  1.6 litre models with 'R' series engine.............................. BES
  1.6 litre models with 'S' series engine.............................. BFM
Idling speed:
  1.3, 1.3L, 1.3 HL.............................................................. 750 to 800 rpm
  1.3HLE........................................................................... 600 to 675 rpm
  500 and 700 van............................................................ 700 to 800 rpm
  1.6 litre models with 'R' series engine:
    Manual gearbox............................................................ 650 to 700 rpm
    Automatic transmission................................................ 800 to 850 rpm
  1.6 litre models with 'S' series engine:
    Manual gearbox............................................................ 700 to 800 rpm
    Automatic transmission................................................ 775 to 875 rpm
Fast idle speed:
  1.3 litre models except 500 and 700 vans:
    Up to VIN 154500.......................................................... 1000 to 1100 rpm
    From VIN 154500.......................................................... 1150 to 1225 rpm
  500 and 700 van............................................................ 1150 to 1225 rpm
  1.6 litre models with 'R' series engine and manual gearbox:
    Up to Vin 156290.......................................................... 900 to 1000 rpm
    From Vin 156290.......................................................... 1150 to 1225 rpm
  1.6 litre models with 'R' series engine and automatic
  transmission.................................................................. 1300 to 1375 rpm
  1.6 litre models with 'S' series engine:
    Manual gearbox............................................................ 1150 to 1250 rpm
    Automatic transmission................................................ 1300 to 1400 rpm
CO mixture:
  1.3 litre models............................................................... 1.5 to 3.5%
  1.6 litre models with 'R' series engine.............................. 1.5 to 3.5%
  1.6 litre models with 'S' series engine.............................. 2.0 to 3.5%
  1.6 litre models with manual choke.................................. 1.5 to 3.5%

## SU carburettor – 1.3 models, 1987 on
Type identification:
  1.3 lc engine.................................................................. FZX 1422
  1.3 hc engine................................................................. FZX 1468
Idle speed........................................................................... 700 to 800 rpm
Fast idle speed:
  With automatic choke...................................................... 1100 to 1200 rpm
  With manual choke.......................................................... 1150 to 1250 rpm
CO mixture.......................................................................... 1.5 to 3.5%
Fuel octane rating:
  1.3 lc engine.................................................................. 91 RON minimum, leaded
  1.3 hc engine................................................................. 97 RON minimum, leaded

## SU carburettor – unleaded fuel models, 1988 on
Type identification:
  1.3 lc and hc engines...................................................... FZX 1529
  1.6 engine, manual gearbox............................................. FZX 1488
  1.6 engine, automatic transmission.................................. FZX 1489
Idle speed:
  1.3 engines with catalytic converter ................................ 700 to 850 rpm
  All other 1.3 and 1.6 engines with manual gearbox .......... 700 to 800 rpm
  1.6 engines with automatic transmission ......................... 775 to 875 rpm

Fast idle speed ................................................................ 1150 to 1250 rpm
CO mixture:
   1.3 engines with catalytic converter – reading taken at
   front pipe take-off point ........................................... 1.0 to 2.0%
   All other 1.3 engines ................................................. 1.5 to 3.5%
   1.6 engines ............................................................... 1.5 to 3.0%
Minimum fuel octane rating:
   1.3 lc engines ........................................................... 95 RON unleaded to 91 RON leaded
   1.3 engines with catalytic converter ....................... 95 RON unleaded – leaded fuel **must not** be used
   All other 1.3 hc engines, and all 1.6 engines ........ 95 RON unleaded or 97 RON leaded

## Weber carburettor

Jet sizes:
   MG 1600 with 'R' series engine:
      Main ...................................................................... 145
      Air correction........................................................ 210
      Idle ....................................................................... 55
      Accelerator pump.................................................. 35
      Emulsion tube ...................................................... F22
   MG 1600 with 'S' series engine:
      Main ...................................................................... 145
      Air correction........................................................ 210
      Idle ....................................................................... 57
      Accelerator pump.................................................. 35
      Emulsion tube ...................................................... F36
CO mixture........................................................................ 2.0 to 3.5%

## Fuel octane rating

500 and 700 van and some later saloon models – low compression.    91 RON minimum
500 and 700 van – high compression........................... 97 RON minimum

## Fuel tank capacity

500 and 700 van ............................................................ 12 Imp gal (54 litres)

## Torque wrench settings – 1.6 litre models with 'S' engine

| | lbf ft | Nm |
|---|---|---|
| Carburettor retaining nuts | 18 | 24 |
| Fuel pump retaining nuts | 11 | 15 |
| Manifold retaining nuts and bolts | 21 | 28 |

## *Ignition system – 1.3 litre models from October 1984*

## Ignition coil – 1987 on
Type.................................................................................. GCL 143
Current consumption – engine idling................................ 0.5 amps
Primary resistance at 20°C (68°F)................................. 0.71 to 0.81 ohms

## HT leads ......................................................................... Champion LS-02 boxed set

## Distributor
500 and 700 van and later 1.3 models:
   Type............................................................................ Lucas 65 DM4

## Ignition amplifier
500 and 700 van and later 1.3 models:
   Type............................................................................ Lucas 9EM

## Ignition timing – up to 1988
Stroboscopic with vacuum pipe disconnected and plugged:
   1.3 HL ........................................................................ 12° BTDC at 1500 rpm
   1.3 litre hc engine ..................................................... 12° BTDC at 1500 rpm
   1.3 litre lc engine ...................................................... 9° BTDC at 1500 rpm

## Ignition timing – unleaded fuel models, 1989 on
Stroboscopic with vacuum pipe disconnected and plugged:
   1.3 lc engine.............................................................. 8 to 10° BTDC at 1500 rpm
   1.3 hc engine............................................................. 13 to 15° BTDC at 1500 rpm

## *Ignition system – 1.6 litre models with 'S' series engine*

## System type .................................................................. Microprocessor-controlled, programmed electronic ignition

## Ignition coil – up to 1987
Type.................................................................................. Unipart GCL 139
Current consumption – engine idling................................ 2.3 to 2.7 amps
Primary resistance at 20°C (68°F)................................. 0.82 ohms ± 5%

## Ignition coil – 1987 on
Type.................................................................................. GCL 143
Current consumption – engine idling..................................... 0.5 amps
Primary resistance at 20°C (68°F)........................................ 0.71 to 0.81 ohms

## HT leads...................................................................... Champion LS-05 boxed set

## Programmed ignition system
Electronic control unit type:
  All models except MG 1600........................................... Lucas AB17-84185
  MG 1600...................................................................... Lucas AB17-84383
Distributor cap type.............................................................. Lucas 544-03944
Rotor arm type..................................................................... Lucas 544-04286
Rotor arm rotation................................................................ Anti-clockwise
Knock sensor type................................................................ Lucas or Lamerholm VP50/1-M12
Crankshaft sensor type......................................................... Lucas 547-42886 or 84229

## Firing order.................................................................. 1-3-4-2
Location of No 1 cylinder...................................................... Crankshaft pulley end

## Spark plugs
Type:
  All models except MG 1600........................................... Champion RC9YCC or RC9YC
  MG 1600...................................................................... Champion RC7YCC or RC7YC
Spark plug gap.................................................................... 0.8 mm (0.031 in)

## Ignition timing – up to 1988*
1.6 litre automatic choke models except MG 1600:
  With vacuum pipe disconnected..................................... 16° to 18° BTDC at 1400 rpm
  With vacuum pipe connected........................................... 25° to 38° BTDC at 1400 rpm
MG 1600:
  With vacuum pipe disconnected..................................... 8° to 12° BTDC at 1000 rpm
  With vacuum pipe connected........................................... 18° to 22° BTDC at 1500 rpm
1.6 litre manual choke models:
  With vacuum pipe disconnected..................................... 10° BTDC at 750 rpm
  With vacuum pipe connected........................................... 20° BTDC at 750 rpm

## Ignition timing – unleaded fuel models 1988 on*
With vacuum pipe disconnected........................................... 11° BTDC at 1100 rpm
With vacuum pipe connected................................................. 26° to 30° BTDC at 1100 rpm

*Non-adjustable; for reference purposes only – see text*

## Torque wrench settings

| | lbf ft | Nm |
|---|---|---|
| Spark plugs | 13 | 18 |
| Knock sensor | 9 | 12 |

## *Clutch*

## Clutch disc diameter
1.3 litre models with 4- or 5-speed gearbox........................ 4.78 in (190 mm)
1.3 litre models with 3 + E or 4 + E gearbox........................ 7.87 in (200 mm)
1.6 litre models and van..................................................... 7.87 in (200 mm)

## Clutch pedal free play.................................................. 0.500 to 1.125 in (12 to 28 mm)

## Torque wrench settings – 1.6 litre models with 'S' series engine

| | lbf ft | Nm |
|---|---|---|
| Flywheel to pressure plate | 11 | 15 |
| Pressure plate to crankshaft (use new bolts) | 55 | 75 |

## *Gearbox*

## Gearbox ratios
4 + E gearbox:
  1st................................................................................. 3.45:1
  2nd................................................................................ 1.94:1
  3rd................................................................................. 1.29:1
  4th................................................................................. 0.91:1
  E................................................................................... 0.70:1
  Reverse.......................................................................... 3.17:1

## Final drive ratios – from approximately July 1984
1.3, 1.3L, 1.3HL................................................................. 4.25:1
1.3 HLE............................................................................. 3.94:1
500 van............................................................................. 4.25:1
1.3 litre 700 van................................................................ 4.60:1

1.6 litre 700 van:
   Gearbox type 6R.............................................................................   3.94:1
   Gearbox type 6S.............................................................................   4.25:1
1.6L, 1.6HL, 1.6HLS and Vanden Plas (with 'S' series engine).............   3.94:1
MG 1600 (with 'S' series engine)........................................................   3.67:1

### Gearbox overhaul data
Minimum baulk ring-to-gear clearance:
   1st and 2nd gear:
      New ring..................................................................................   0.043 to 0.067 in (1.1 to 1.7 mm)
      Wear limit...............................................................................   0.020 in (0.5 mm)
   3rd gear:
      New ring..................................................................................   0.045 to 0.069 in (1.15 to 1.75 mm)
      Wear limit...............................................................................   0.020 in (0.5 mm)
   4th and 5th Gear:
      New ring..................................................................................   0.051 to 0.075 in (1.3 to 1.91 mm)
      Wear limit...............................................................................   0.020 in (0.5 mm)

## Automatic transmission

### Type
Type.........................................................................................................   Hydraulically-controlled epicyclic geartrain with three element torque converter

### Gear ratios
1st...........................................................................................................   2.71:1
2nd..........................................................................................................   1.50:1
3rd...........................................................................................................   1.00:1
Reverse....................................................................................................   2.43:1
Final drive...............................................................................................   3.409:1

### Lubricant type/specification
Automatic transmission.........................................................................   Dexron II D type ATF (Duckhams Uni-Matic)
Final drive..............................................................................................   Hypoid gear oil, viscosity SAE 90EP (Duckhams Hypoid 90S)

### Lubricant capacities
Automatic transmission:
   Drain and refill...................................................................................   4.0 pints (2.3 litres)
   Total (dry unit including torque converter)........................................   10.5 pints (6.0 litres)
Final drive..............................................................................................   1.25 pints (0.71 litre)

### Torque wrench settings

| | lbf ft | Nm |
|---|---|---|
| Torque converter to driveplate | 22 | 30 |
| Oil strainer to valve block | 2 | 3 |
| Oil pan to transmission | 15 | 20 |
| Transmission to engine and adaptor plate: | | |
|    M10 bolts | 38 | 51 |
|    M12 bolts | 66 | 89 |
| Dipstick tube lower mounting bolt | 7 | 9 |
| Dipstick tube upper mounting bolt | 18 | 24 |

## Braking system

### Front brakes
Maximum disc thickness variation.........................................................   0.001 in (0.025 mm)
Maximum disc run-out............................................................................   0.006 in (0.15 mm)
Minimum disc thicknesses......................................................................   0.460 in (11.7 mm)

### Rear brakes
Drum diameter (500 and 700 van)..........................................................   9.0 in (228.6 mm)
Lining width (500 and 700 van)..............................................................   1.75 in (44.5 mm)
Wheel cylinder diameter (500 and 700 van)...........................................   0.81 in (20.57 mm)

### Torque wrench setting

| | lbf ft | Nm |
|---|---|---|
| Drive flange to disc bolts | 37 | 50 |

## Electrical system

### Alternator
Type – from July 1984............................................................................   Lucas 127/55 or A127/65
Drivebelt tension...................................................................................   0.16 to 0.32 in (4 to 8 mm) deflection between pulleys under load of 10 lbf (4.5 kgf)

### Starter motor – from 1987
Application:
   Models with manual transmission......................................................   Lucas M79
   Models with automatic transmission..................................................   Lucas M78R

Commutator minimum diameter.................................................................... 1.134 in (28.8 mm)
Minimum brush length (wear limit).............................................................. 0.14 in (3.5 mm)

## Relays and control units

| Component: | Location |
| --- | --- |
| Heated rear window relay............................................................ | Relay panel on glovebox top cover |
| Windscreen wiper control unit (if fitted)...................................... | Relay panel on glovebox top cover |
| Direction: indicator/hazard warning flasher unit............................ | Relay panel on glovebox top cover |
| Electric window switch relay (if fitted)........................................ | Relay panel on glovebox top cover |
| Ignition auxiliary circuits relay (if fitted).................................... | Relay panel on glovebox top cover |
| Inlet manifold heater relay (if fitted).......................................... | Relay panel on glovebox top cover |
| Starter solenoid relay................................................................ | Relay panel on glovebox top cover |
| Carburettor cooling fan relay (if fitted)....................................... | Relay panel on glovebox top cover |
| Fuel pump relay (if fitted).......................................................... | Relay panel on glovebox top cover |
| Fuel system electronic control unit (ECU)................................... | Behind the facia shelf on the driver's side |
| Programmed ignition system control unit (if fitted)...................... | Attached to engine compartment left-hand valance |
| Voice synthesizer cut-out relay (if fitted)................................... | Behind the trip computer |
| Electric window switch isolation relays and control unit (if fitted)... | Behind the door inner trim panel |
| Central locking control unit (if fitted)......................................... | Behind the door inner trim panel |

## Fuses

| Fuse colour coding: | Current rating |
| --- | --- |
| Violet....................................................................................... | 3 amp |
| Tan.......................................................................................... | 5 amp |
| Red.......................................................................................... | 10 amp |
| Blue......................................................................................... | 15 amp |
| Natural..................................................................................... | 25 amp |
| Green....................................................................................... | 30 amp |
| Fusible links: | |
| Link A...................................................................................... | 150 mm long, 28/0.3 wire |
| Link B...................................................................................... | 200 mm long, 28/0.3 wire |
| Link C...................................................................................... | 450 mm long, 14/0.3 wire |

## Bulbs

| | Wattage |
| --- | --- |
| Selector illumination lamp (automatic transmission models)................ | 3 |
| Side repeater lamps.................................................................... | 5 |
| Number plate lamp...................................................................... | 5 |

## *Suspension and steering*

### Front suspension – saloon from 1987

Bearing side play (maximum) at wheel rim.................................... 0.060 in (1.5 mm)

### Front suspension – 500 and 700 van

Coil spring free length............................................................... 11.22 in (285.0 mm) or 13.00 in (333 mm)
Trim height (measured from the centre of the front hub to the
edge of the wheelarch)................................................................ 14.7 to 15.7 in (373 to 399 mm)

### Rear suspension – 500 and 700 van

Type......................................................................................... Beam axle with single leaf semi-elliptic springs and telescopic shock absorbers
Spring free length (eye centre-to-eye centre)............................... 52.23 to 52.48 in (1327 to 1333 mm)
Trim height (measured from centre of hub to edge of wheelarch)..... 15.3 to 16.3 in (388 to 414 mm)

### Steering angles – up to 1986

Camber (at specified trim height):
    Saloon.................................................................................. 0° 15′ negative ± 0° 21′
    Van........................................................................................ 0° ± 0° 21′
Castor:
    Saloon.................................................................................. 0° 37′ ± 0° 30′
    Van........................................................................................ 0° 12′ ± 0° 30′
King pin inclination:
    Saloon.................................................................................. 12° 30′ ± 0° 30′
    Van........................................................................................ 12° 50′ ± 0° 30′
Front wheel alignment (toe)......................................................... Parallel ± 0° 8′

### Steering angles – from 1987 with modified strut (see text)

Camber (at specified trim height):
    Saloon.................................................................................. 0° 30′ positive ± 0° 21′
    Van........................................................................................ 0° 45′ positive ± 0° 21′

Castor angle:
　Saloon......................................................................................... 0° 37′ positive ± 0° 30′
　Van.............................................................................................. 0° 12′ positive ± 0° 30′
King pin inclination:
　Saloon......................................................................................... 12° 33′ ± 0° 30′
　Van.............................................................................................. 12° 16′ ± 0° 30′
Front wheel alignment (toe)........................................................... Parallel ± 0° 8′

## Power steering system

Application....................................................................................... Option on 1.6 models
Control type.................................................................................... Spool and torsion bar
Pump drivebelt deflection.............................................................. 0.28 to 0.47 in (7.0 to 12.0 mm)
Fluid type....................................................................................... Dexron II D type ATF (Duckhams Uni-Matic)
Rack lubricant................................................................................ Semi fluid grease (Duckhams Adgear 00)

## Roadwheels

Wheel size:
　1.3 and 1.6 models with alloy wheels......................................... 5J x 13 or 5½J x 15
　500 and 700 van........................................................................ 5J x 13

## Tyres

Tyre size:
　1.3 model with 5J x 13 wheels.................................................. 155 SR or 165 SR steel braced radial ply
　1.6 model with 5½J x 15 wheels............................................... 185/55 HR steel braced radial ply
　500 van..................................................................................... 155 SR 13, steel braced radial ply
　700 van..................................................................................... 165 SR 13, steel braced radial ply

| Tyre pressures (cold): | lbf/in$^2$ | bar |
|---|---|---|
| 500 van: | | |
| 　Front | 26 | 1.8 |
| 　Rear | 40* | 2.8* |
| 700 van: | | |
| 　Front | 26 | 1.8 |
| 　Rear | 46* | 3.2* |

* For continuous use in a lightly laden condition, reduce the rear tyre pressures by 10 lbf/in$^2$ (0.7 bar)

| Torque wrench setting | lbf ft | Nm |
|---|---|---|
| *500 and 700 van rear suspension* | | |
| Shock absorber lower mounting bolt | 53 | 72 |
| Shock absorber upper mounting locknut | 18 | 24 |
| Stub axle to axle beam | 37 | 50 |
| Rear hub retaining nut | 50 | 68 |
| Spring eye front mounting bolt | 68 | 92 |
| Spring eye rear mounting bolt to shackle | 68 | 92 |
| Spring rear shackle to body | 53 | 72 |
| Axle beam U-bolt nuts | 37 | 50 |
| *Power steering* | | |
| Hose-to-pump union | 20 | 27 |
| Pressure hose to rack | 11 | 15 |
| Pump-to-bracket bolts | 6 | 8 |
| Reservoir-to-bracket bolts | 18 | 25 |
| Rack housing mounting bolts | 33 | 45 |
| Pinion shaft coupling pinch-bolt | 18 | 25 |
| *Roadwheels* | | |
| Wheel nuts – van | 60 | 80 |

## General dimensions, weights and capacities

## Dimensions – vans

Turning circle (between kerbs)....................................................... 415.7 in (10.559 mm)
Wheelbase....................................................................................... 100.6 in (2555 mm)
Overall length................................................................................. 171.4 in (4354 mm)
Overall width.................................................................................. 76.4 in (1938 mm)
Overall height................................................................................. 64.0 in (1626 mm)
Ground clearance:
　Models up to 1987..................................................................... 4.7 in (119 mm)
　Models from 1987...................................................................... 6.3 in (160 mm)
Track:
　Front:
　　Original strut........................................................................... 57.5 in (1461 mm)
　　Modified strut.......................................................................... 57.3 in (1455 mm)
　Rear............................................................................................ 56.5 in (1434 mm)

## Dimensions – saloons from 1987

Overall width.................................................................................. 76.4 in (1938 mm)

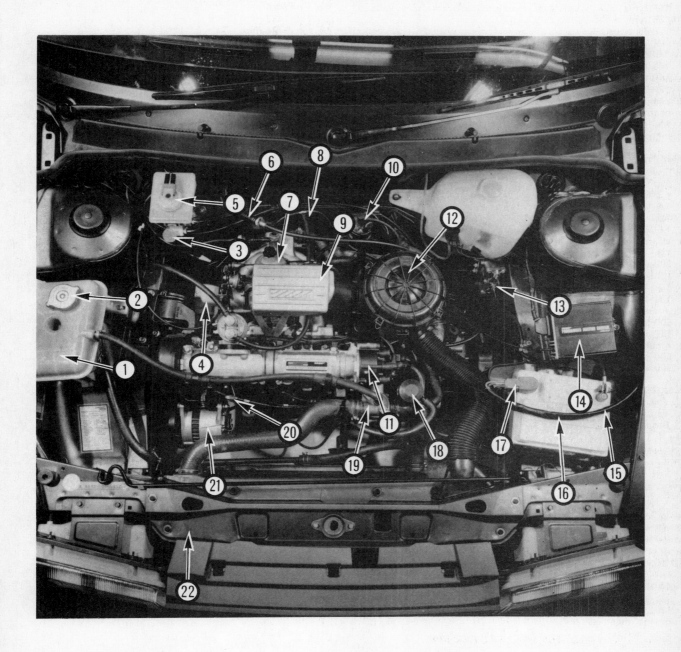

**1.6 litre 'S' series engine and underbonnet component
locations**

| | | | |
|---|---|---|---|
| 1 | Cooling system expansion tank | 6 | Clutch cable self-adjusting mechansim | 11 | Distributor | 16 | Fusible links |

1   Cooling system
    expansion tank
2   Cooling system filler
    cap
3   Brake master cylinder
4   Oil filter
5   Master cylinder reservoir
    filler cap

6   Clutch cable
    self-adjusting
    mechansim
7   Carburettor
8   Main vacuum line
9   Air cleaner plenum
    chamber
10  Ignition coil

11  Distributor
12  Air cleaner
13  Braking system twin GP
    valve
14  Ignition system
    electronic control unit
    (ECU)
15  Battery negative
    terminal

16  Fusible links
17  Battery positive terminal
18  Oil filler/breather cap
19  Water outlet elbow
    and thermostat
20  Oil dipstick
21  Alternator
22  Front body panel

Overall height:
    145 tyres.............................................................................    55.9 in (1419 mm)
    155 tyres.............................................................................    56.1 in (1424 mm)
    165 tyres.............................................................................    56.4 in (1432 mm)
    175/65 tyres.......................................................................    56.1 in (1424 mm)
Ground clearance:
    145 tyres.............................................................................    5.4 in (138 mm)
    155 tyres.............................................................................    5.6 in (143 mm)
    165 tyres.............................................................................    5.9 in (151 mm)
    175/65 tyres.......................................................................    5.6 in (143 mm)
Wheelbase..................................................................................    99.0 in (2514 mm)
Front track:
    Modified strut....................................................................    57.0 in (1455 mm)
Turning circle (between kerbs)..................................................    409.0 in (10.389 mm)

## Weights – 1985 to 1986
Kerb weight:
    500 and 700 van...............................................................    2116 lb (960 kg)
    1.3 HL..................................................................................    1995 lb (905 kg)
    1.6 HL..................................................................................    2094 lb (950 kg)
    1.6 Automatic.....................................................................    2172 lb (985 kg)
    1.6 Vanden Plas Automatic................................................    2227 lb (1010 kg)
Gross vehicle weight:
    1.3 litre models except 500 and 700 van.........................    3020 lb (1370 kg)
    500 van...............................................................................    3373 lb (1530 kg)
    1.3 litre 700 van................................................................    3814 lb (1730 kg)
    1.6 litre 700 van................................................................    3880 lb (1760 kg)
    1.6 litre models except 700 van.......................................    3175 lb (1440 kg)
Maximum front axle load:
    500 and 1.3 litre 700 van.................................................    1653 lb (750 kg)
    1.6 litre 700 van................................................................    1720 lb (770 kg)
Maximum rear axle load:
    500 van...............................................................................    1984 lb (900 kg)
    700 van...............................................................................    2337 lb (1060 kg)

## Weights – from 1987 where different to 1985/86 values
1.3 van........................................................................................    2116 lb (960 kg)
1.6 van........................................................................................    2183 lb (990 kg)
1.3 Base, City............................................................................    1973 lb (895 kg)
City X, LE...................................................................................    1984 lb (900 kg)
1.3L..............................................................................................    2028 lb (920 kg)
1.3HL............................................................................................    2040 lb (925 kg)
1.3HLE, Mayfair.........................................................................    2062 lb (935 kg)
1.6L..............................................................................................    2116 lb (960 kg)
1.6HL............................................................................................    2106 lb (955 kg)
1.6LX, Advantage......................................................................    2116 lb (960 kg)
1.6 Automatic.............................................................................    2172 lb (985 kg)
1.6HLS, Mayfair.........................................................................    2138 lb (970 kg)
Vanden Plas...............................................................................    2182 lb (990 kg)
Vanden Plas Automatic.............................................................    2238 lb (1015 kg)
MG 1600......................................................................................    2249 lb (1020 kg)

## Capacities
Engine oil (refill with filter change):
    1.6 litre with 'S' series engine.........................................    6.7 pints (3.8 litres)
Automatic transmission:
    Drain and refill..................................................................    4.0 pints (2.25 litres)
    Final drive (automatic transmission)................................    1.25 pints (0.75 litre)
Power steering reservoir...........................................................    0.87 pint (0.5 litre)
Cooling sytstem – 1.6 litre.......................................................    15 pints (8.5 litres)
Fuel tank:
    Saloon.................................................................................    11 gal (50 litres)
    Van......................................................................................    12 gal (54 litres)

## 3  Jacking and towing (500 and 700 van models)

To change a roadwheel, lower the spare wheel carrier by unscrewing the carrier retaining bolt located just inside the rear doors. The wheel brace provided in the tool kit can be used for this purpose. Remove the spare wheel from the carrier, and the jack from the tool kit. Apply the handbrake and chock the wheel diagonally opposite from the one to be changed. Make sure that the vehicle is located on firm level ground. Lever off the wheel trim and slacken the wheel nuts with the wheel brace. Position the jack directly under the jacking point nearest to the wheel to be changed and engage the jack head peg in the jacking bracket hole (1 or 2 in the illustration – Fig. 12.1). If a rear wheel is to be changed with the vehicle in a laden condition, position the jack under the rear spring just forward of the axle beam (5 in the illustration), but make sure that the spring leaf locates between the peg and lugs on the jack head. Do not raise the rear of the vehicle by positioning the jack directly under the axle beam. Raise the jack until the wheel is clear of the ground, unscrew the wheel nuts and remove the wheel. Fit the spare and secure with the wheel nuts, ensuring that their conical face is toward the wheel. Lower the jack and, with all four wheels on the ground, tighten the wheel nuts fully. Store the wheel in the carrier and wind it up. Refit the wheel trim to the spare wheel, replace the jack and wheel brace in the tool kit and remove the chock.

When jacking the van with a trolley jack, position the head of the jack under the jacking bracket/towing hook in the centre of the front crossmember (6 in the illustration) to raise both front wheels. To raise both rear wheels, use a suitable length of square steel tubing securely located beneath the rear axle beam U-bolt brackets (4 in the illustration) and running transversely across the rear of the car. Position the jack head under the centre of the tubing. **Do not** jack directly on the axle beam. To raise one side of the van at the front or rear, position the jack beneath the jacking points or alternatively, at the rear, under the rear spring U-bolt bracket. In all cases make sure that the handbrake is firmly applied and the wheels remaining on the ground are securely chocked. Always position axle stands or suitable supports under the side jacking brackets or under the rear chassis box sections (3 in the illustration) to support the van securely when it is raised. **Never** work on, around or under a raised vehicle unless the jack is supplemented with additional supports.

The van may be towed using the towing hook provided on the front crossmember. For towing another vehicle, or a trailer, an approved type of towing bracket should be used. It is not recommended that towing should be undertaken without such an installation.

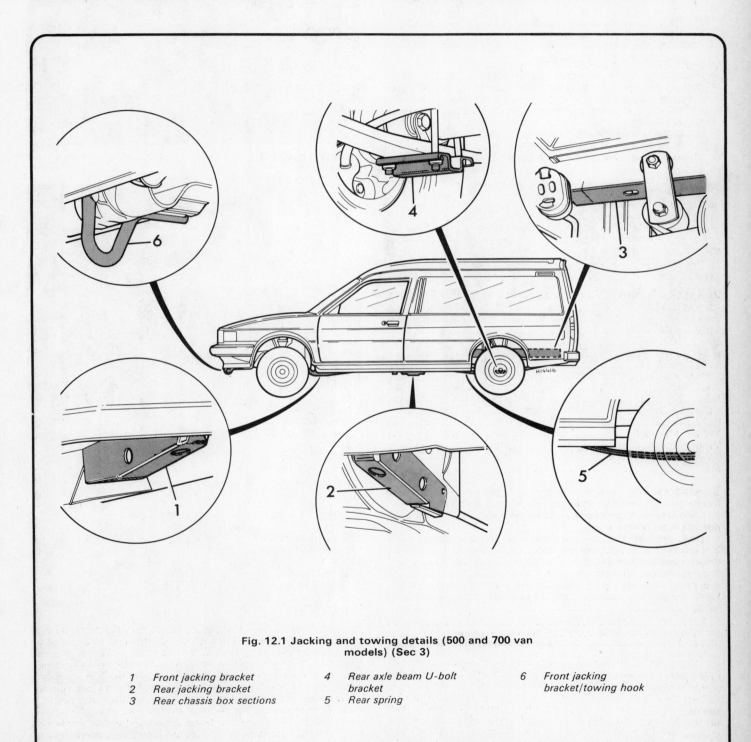

**Fig. 12.1 Jacking and towing details (500 and 700 van models) (Sec 3)**

| | | |
|---|---|---|
| 1   Front jacking bracket | 4   Rear axle beam U-bolt | 6   Front jacking |
| 2   Rear jacking bracket |     bracket |     bracket/towing hook |
| 3   Rear chassis box sections | 5   Rear spring | |

## 4  Engine (1.3 litre 'A+' series)

*Engine and gearbox assembly (1.3 litre models – removal and refitting)*

1  The procedure for removal and refitting of the engine and gearbox on 500 and 700 vans, and later hatchback saloon models is as follows.
2  Refer to Chapter 1, Section 6 and carry out the operations given in paragraphs 1 to 24, but note the following:

  (a) On models equipped with a manually operated choke control there are no multi-plugs to be disconnected at the carburettor, but the choke cable should be released, as described in Section 7 of this Supplement
  (b) Disconnect the clutch cable using the procedure described in Section 9 of this Supplement.

3  Remove the engine mountings, as follows.
4  From under the car, undo the two bolts and remove the thread plate securing the rear mounting to the crossmember. Undo the two nuts and bolts securing the rear mounting to the gearbox and remove the mounting (photo).
5  Undo and remove the screws securing the left-hand access panel under the wheel arch and lift out the panel.
6  Remove the axle stands and lower the car to the ground.

4.4 Engine rear mounting-to-gearbox retaining bolts and nuts (arrowed)

4.8 Engine front mounting body bracket bolts (A) and mounting through bolt (B)

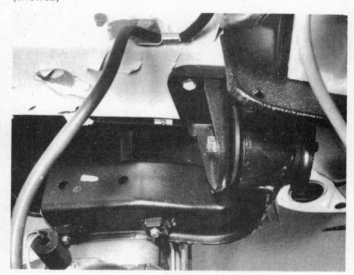
4.9 Engine left-hand mounting assembly

7  Attach a suitable hoist to the engine using chains or rope slings, or by attaching the chains or ropes to sturdy brackets bolted to the engine and gearbox. Raise the hoist or just take the weight of the engine and gearbox assembly.
8  Undo the two bolts securing the engine front mounting body bracket to the front body member. Undo the front mounting through-bolt and nut and remove the body bracket (photo).
9  Undo the two bolts securing the left-hand mounting to the gearbox and through-bolt securing the mounting to the body bracket (photo). Lower the engine and gearbox slightly and manipulate the mounting out of its location.
10  Undo the bolts securing the left-hand mounting body bracket to the chassis member and remove the bracket.
11  Undo the bolts securing the engine right-hand mounting support plate to the body and body bracket (photo).
12  From under the wheel arch, undo the two bolts securing the right-hand mounting body bracket to the body. Note the two spacers on the mounting bolts.
13  Undo the mounting through-bolt and remove the support plate and body bracket.
14  Make a final check that everything attaching the engine and gearbox to the car has been disconnected and that all detached components are well clear.
15  Lift the engine and gearbox slightly and, as soon as sufficient

4.11 Engine right-hand mounting support plate retaining bolts (arrowed)

clearance exists, release the driveshaft inner joints from the drive flanges. Support or tie up the driveshafts to avoid straining the outer joints.

16 Continue raising the engine assembly and, when it has been raised sufficiently, draw the hoist forward or push the car backwards and lower the engine and gearbox to the ground.

17 Refitting the engine and gearbox is the reverse of the removal sequence given in Chapter 1 and in the foregoing paragraphs. Note, however, the additional points listed in Chapter 1, Section 42 and also the following.

(a) On models equipped with a manually operated choke control, refit and adjust the cable as described in Section 7 of this Supplement.

(b) Refit and adjust the clutch cable, as described in Section 9 of this Supplement.

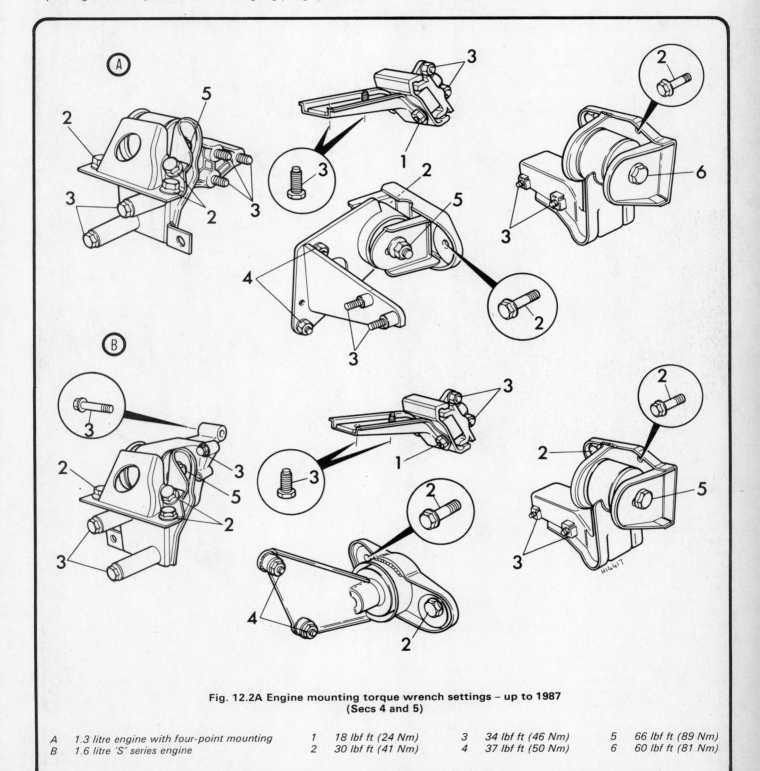

**Fig. 12.2A Engine mounting torque wrench settings – up to 1987
(Secs 4 and 5)**

| A | 1.3 litre engine with four-point mounting | 1 | 18 lbf ft (24 Nm) | 3 | 34 lbf ft (46 Nm) | 5 | 66 lbf ft (89 Nm) |
| B | 1.6 litre 'S' series engine | 2 | 30 lbf ft (41 Nm) | 4 | 37 lbf ft (50 Nm) | 6 | 60 lbf ft (81 Nm) |

244

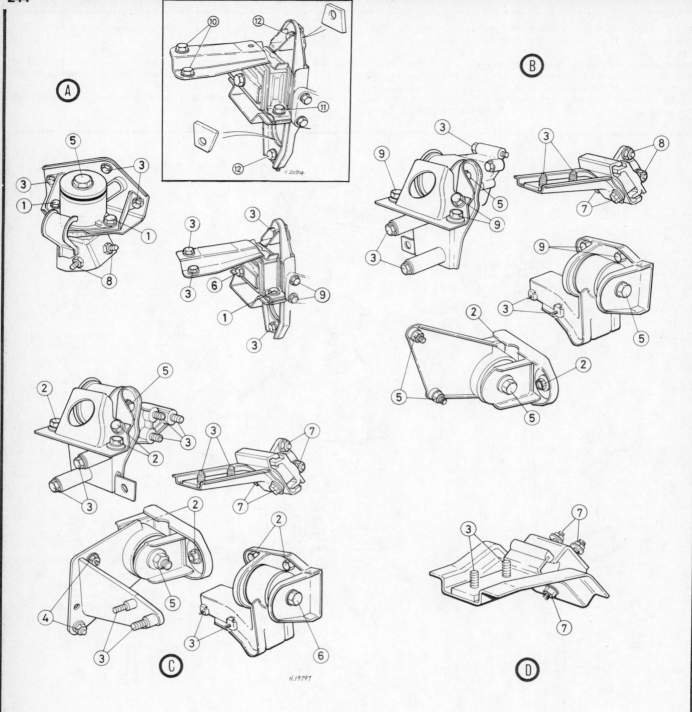

**Fig. 12.2B Engine mounting torque wrench settings – 1988 on (Secs 4 and 5)**

| A | 1.3 models (inset shows right-hand mounting with spacers – see text) | B | 1.6 models | 4 | 37 lbf ft (50 Nm) | 10 | 30 to 37 lbf ft (40 to 50 Nm) |
|---|---|---|---|---|---|---|---|
| | | C | Van models | 5 | 62 lbf ft (83 Nm) | | |
| | | D | Rear mounting | 6 | 108 lbf ft (135 Nm) | 11 | 37 to 48 lbf ft (50 to 65 Nm) |
| | | 1 | 18 lbf ft (25 Nm) | 7 | 24 lbf ft (33 Nm) | | |
| | | 2 | 30 lbf ft (40 Nm) | 8 | 18 lbf ft (25 Nm) | 12 | 33 to 40 lbf ft (45 to 55 Nm) |
| | | 3 | 33 lbf ft (45 Nm) | 9 | 34 lbf ft (45 Nm) | | |

## Engine mountings (1.3 litre models) – removal and refitting

18 On 500 and 700 van and later hatchback models the engine and gearbox are supported on a four-point mounting arrangement using mountings of a modified design. With this arrangement the engine tie-rod previously fitted to saloon models is no longer used. Removal and refitting procedures for the modified mountings are as follows.

**Left-hand mounting**

19 Place a jack beneath the gearbox with a block of wood between the jack head and gearbox. Raise the jack and just take the weight of the gearbox.

20 Turn the steering onto full right-hand lock, undo the retaining screws and remove the access panel from under the left-hand wheel arch.

21 Undo and remove the mounting through-bolt and the two bolts securing the mounting assembly to the gearbox.

22 Lower the jack and push down on the gearbox to free the mounting from the body bracket. Recover the two large washers.

23 Undo the bolts securing the body bracket to the body side-member, lift off the bracket and remove the left-hand mounting.

24 Refitting is the reverse sequence to removal, but refer to Fig. 12.2 for details of the torque wrench settings for the various retaining bolts.

**Right-hand mounting**

25 Refer to Chapter 9 and remove the alternator.

26 Disconnect the electrical lead at the coolant thermistor.

27 Turn the steering onto full left-hand lock, undo the retaining screws and remove the access panel from under the right-hand wheel arch.

28 Place a jack beneath the engine sump with a block of wood between the sump and jack head. Raise the jack and just take the weight of the engine.

29 Undo the bolts and securing screw and lift away the cooling system expansion tank support bracket.

30 Undo the bolts securing the mounting support plate to the body and body bracket.

31 From under the wheel arch, undo the two bolts securing the mounting body bracket to the body. Note the two spaces on the mounting bolts.

32 Undo the mounting through-bolt and remove the support plate and body bracket.

33 Undo the bolts securing the mounting to the cylinder block and remove the mounting assembly.

34 Refitting is the reverse sequence to removal. Note that the right-hand mounting on some models may incorporate spacers fitted to correct the alignment of the mounting bracket; modified torque settings are given for this arrangement. Refer to Fig. 12.2 for details of the torque wrench settings for the various retaining bolts. Refit the alternator, as described in Chapter 9.

**Front mounting**

35 Undo the bolts securing the front mounting body bracket to the chassis member and the through-bolt securing the mounting to the body bracket. Remove the body bracket.

36 Undo the bolts securing the mounting to the cylinder block and gearbox adaptor plate and remove the mounting.

37 Refitting is the reverse sequence to removal, but refer to Fig. 12.2 for details of the torque wrench settings for the various retaining bolts.

**Rear mounting**

38 Jack up the front of the vehicle and support it on axle stands.

39 Undo the two bolts and remove the thread plate securing the rear mounting support bracket to the crossmember.

40 Undo the two nuts and bolts securing the rear mounting to the gearbox and remove the mounting assembly.

41 Undo the two nuts and bolts then separate the mounting from the support bracket.

42 Refitting is the reverse sequence to removal, but refer to Fig. 12.2 for details of the torque wrench settings for the various retaining bolts.

## Crankshaft main bearings (1.3 litre models) – modifications

43 Later models (from VIN No. XC/312864) are fitted with lead indium main bearings. It should be noted that this bearing type can only be fitted to earlier models which have plain bottom bearing shells (without oil grooves) in the main bearing caps.

## Crankshaft main bearing colour codes – 1.3 litre models

44 The main bearings on later 1.3 litre engines may be colour-coded (red, green or yellow) in accordance with the crankshaft main bearing clearances. The colour code mark will either be 'R', 'G' or 'Y' (or be colour dyed) on the crankshaft centre web. All crankshafts fitted in service are colour-coded green.

45 When new colour-coded bearings are fitted to a non colour-coded cylinder block/crankshaft, it is important that the coding colour combinations comply. Check this with an Austin Rover dealer or engine reconditioner.

46 When new main bearings are fitted to a non colour-coded crankshaft, the main bearing-to-journal clearances must first be checked, compared against the specified requirement and the bearings selected to suit. Fit red bearings where the clearance is too great or yellow if too small, green if correct.

## Engine type identification – 1.3 litre models

47 Some 500 and 700 vans, and later 1.3 litre saloon models may be fitted with a low compression engine. A low compression engine can be identified from the engine number plate, attached to the cylinder block below the spark plugs. Reading from the *right*, the first letter which appears denotes the compression ratio. A letter H identifies the engine as a high compression type, while a letter L identifies a low compression engine.

## 5  Engine (1.6 litre 'S' series)

### General description

1 In July 1984 the 'R' series engine was discontinued and the all new 'S' series engine, originally used in the Montego range, was fitted to all 1.6 litre Maestro models. The new engine is of four-cylinder in-line overhead camshaft configuration and mounted transversely at the front of the car.

2 The major internal components of this engine are essentially as those described for the 'R' series engine (Chapter 1, Section 45), except that the camshaft is driven directly by a toothed belt.

3 The oil pump, pressure relief valve and full-flow oil filter are located in a housing attached to the front of the cylinder block. The rotor type oil pump is driven directly by the crankshaft.

4 The distributor rotor is driven directly by the camshaft whereas the fuel pump is operated by an eccentric camshaft lobe. The toothed timing belt also drives the water pump and a separate drivebelt is used for the alternator, driven by a pulley on the crankshaft.

### Maintenance and inspection

5 Refer to Chapter 1, Section 46, but note the following differences:

   (a) *The oil drain plug is located on the rear facing side of the sump*
   (b) *The oil filter is towards the right of the engine*
   (c) *The oil filler cap is located on a tube at the front of the engine*
   (d) *Adjust the tappet clearances, if necessary, with reference to this Section*
   (e) *The crankcase breather filter is located in the oil filler cap. At the recommended intervals (see Routine Maintenance) it should be cleaned using paraffin or a suitable solvent*
   (f) *Renew the timing belt at the specified intervals*

6 Refer to this Section for all procedures applicable to the 'S' series engine.

### Major operations possible with the engine in the car

7 The following operations can be carried out without having to remove the engine from the car:

   (a) *Removal, refitting and adjustment of the timing belt and tensioner*
   (b) *Removal and refitting of the camshaft and tappets*
   (c) *Removal and refitting of the cylinder head*
   (d) *Removal and refitting of the sump*
   (e) *Removal and refitting of the big-end bearings*
   (f) *Removal and refitting of the piston and connecting rod assemblies*
   (g) *Removal and refitting of the oil pump*
   (h) *Removal and refitting of the gearbox adaptor plate (after removal of the gearbox automatic transmission)*
   (i) *Removal and refitting of the engine mountings*

### Major operations requiring engine removal

8 Refer to Chapter 1, Section 48.

*Methods of engine removal*

9   The engine, complete with gearbox or automatic transmission, is removed by lifting it upwards and out of the engine compartment as a complete assembly. The gearbox or automatic transmission is then separated from the engine after removal. Due to the limited working clearances it is not possible to remove the engine on its own.

*Engine – removal with manual gearbox*

10  Remove the bonnet, as described in Chapter 11, and the battery, as described in Chapter 9.

11  Undo and remove the bolts securing the battery tray to the body and take out the tray. Note the arrangement of earth wires on the front retaining bolt (photos).

12  Drain the cooling system, as described in Chapter 2.

13  Remove the air cleaner assembly and the plenum chamber, as described in Chapter 3, or in Section 7 of this Supplement.

14  Slide back the protective cover, then disconnect the two reversing lamp wires at the gearbox switch (photo).

15  Undo the nut and bolt securing the earth strap and cable retaining clip to the gearbox casing (photo).

16  Make a note of the wiring connections at the starter motor solenoid and disconnect the wires.

17  Disconnect the crankshaft sensor wiring plug (photo) then, using a spanner and suitable Allen key, undo the two starter motor retaining bolts. Remove the starter, crankshaft sensor bracket and engine front snubber.

18  Disconnect the wiring plug at the knock sensor on the front face of the cylinder block (photo).

19  Spring back the clip and disconnect the wiring plug at the rear of the alternator.

20  Disconnect the wiring plug from the coolant temperature thermistor in the thermostat housing.

21  Disconnect the inlet manifold induction heater lead at the wiring

5.11A Earth wire arrangement on battery tray retaining bolt

5.11B Remove the battery tray

5.14 Disconnect the reversing lamp switch wires (arrowed)

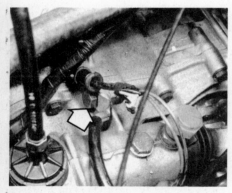

5.15 Remove the earth strap and cable clip retaining bolt (arrowed)

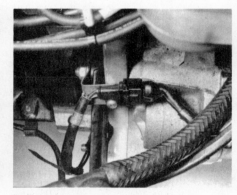

5.17 Disconnect the crankshaft sensor wiring plug ...

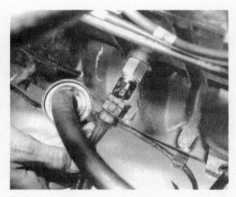

5.18 ... and knock sensor wiring plug

5.22 Disconnect the oil pressure switch wire

5.23A Disconnect the wiring at the carburettor stepping motor ...

5.23B ... and fuel shut-off valve solenoid

5.24 Remove the fuel inlet hose from the pump

5.25 Detach the float chamber vent hose (A) and crankcase breather hose (B)

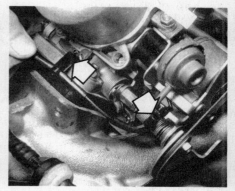

5.27 Detach the two ignition vacuum advance hose connectors (arrowed)

5.28 Remove the banjo union bolt and washers from the inlet manifold

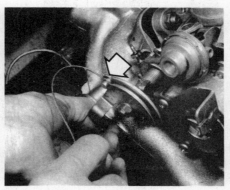

5.29A Slip the accelerator cable end (arrowed) out of the throttle lever ...

5.29B ... undo the lower accelerator cable locknut (arrowed) and remove the cable

5.31A Disconnect the hoses at the water inlet elbow ...

5.31B ... and water outlet elbow ...

5.31C ... and thermostat housing

connector and the two wires at the inlet manifold induction temperature sensor (where fitted).

22 Disconnect the wire at the oil pressure switch adjacent to the crankshaft pulley (photo).

23 On all models except MG 1600, disconnect the wiring plug at the carburettor stepping motor and the two leads at the fuel shut-off valve solenoid (photos).

24 Release the retaining clip and remove the fuel inlet hose from the fuel pump (photo). On MG 1600 models, disconnect the fuel hoses at the carburettor connectors. Plug all hoses after removal.

25 Pull the float chamber vent hose off the carburettor outlet and remove the hose and pipe from the engine (photo).

26 Detach the crankcase breather hoses at the carburettor, oil filler cap and oil separator, then remove the hose assembly.

27 Disconnect the two ignition vacuum advance hose connectors at the carburettor (photo).

28 Disconnect the vacuum hose from the inlet manifold banjo union,

undo the union bolt and recover the two washers (photo). Place the servo vacuum hose to one side.

29 Open the throttle linkage by hand and slip the accelerator cable end out of the slot on the throttle lever (photo). Slacken the outer cable locknuts, unscrew the lower locknut fully and release the cable from the support bracket (photo). On MG 1600 models, release the choke cable from the carburettor levers and flange. Place the disconnected cable clear of the engine.

30 Slacken the retaining clips and disconnect the heater hoses at the inlet manifold (where applicable).

31 Slacken the retaining clips and disconnect the heater hose and radiator bottom hose from the water inlet elbow (photo), followed by the expansion tank hose, radiator tap hose and heater hose from the water outlet elbow and thermostat housing (photos).

32 Refer to Section 9 of this Supplement and detach the clutch cable from the operating lever and gearbox bracket.

33 Undo and remove the bolt securing the speedometer cable or

speed transducer cable to the gearbox. Withdraw the cable and pinion assembly and place them aside (photo).

34 Remove the retaining clip and slide the gearchange rod out of the selector shaft lever. Disconnect the rear selector rod from the relay lever on the gearbox by prising off the balljoint socket with a screwdriver (photo).

35 Jack up the front of the car and support it securely on axle stands.

36 From underneath the car, undo the nuts securing the exhaust front pipes to the manifold. Separate the joint flange and recover the gasket.

37 Mark the relationship of the driveshaft inner constant velocity joints to the differential drive flanges. Lift off the protective caps and unscrew the joint-to-drive flange retaining bolts using a suitable Allen key or socket bit.

38 Undo the two nuts securing the rear engine mounting to the front crossmember (photo).

39 Undo the retaining screws and remove the left-hand and right-hand access panels from under the wheel arches.

40 Remove the axle stands and lower the car to the ground.

41 Attach a suitable hoist to the engine using chains or rope slings, or by attaching the chains or ropes to sturdy brackets bolted to the engine and gearbox. Raise the hoist to just take the weight of the engine.

42 Undo the screw securing the expansion tank to the support bracket and the two bolts securing the bracket to the body. Withdraw the bracket (photo).

43 From under the right-hand wheel arch, undo the two bolts securing the right-hand engine mounting to the body, noting the distance spacer on each bolt (photo).

44 Undo the bolts securing the right-hand engine mounting to the engine and remove the complete mounting assembly (photo).

45 Undo the two bolts securing the left-hand engine mounting to the gearbox, and the through-bolt and nut securing the mounting to the body bracket. Remove the mounting (photo).

46 Undo the three bolts securing the left-hand engine mounting bracket to the body and remove the bracket (photo).

5.33 Remove the speedometer cable and pinion assembly

5.34 Disconnect the gearchange rod after removing split pin (A) and prise off selector rod balljoint (B)

5.38 Undo the rear mounting-to-crossmember nuts (arrowed)

5.42 Remove the right-hand mounting support bracket

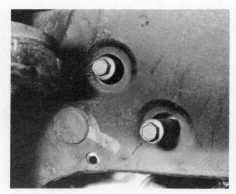

5.43 Undo the right-hand mounting to body bolts from under the wheel arch

5.44 Remove the right-hand mounting from the engine

5.45 Remove the left-hand mounting from the gearbox and body bracket ...

5.46 ... then undo the three bolts and remove the body bracket

47 Make a final check that everything attaching the engine and gearbox to the car has been disconnected and that all detached components are well clear.

48 Lift the engine and gearbox slightly and, as soon as sufficient clearance exists, release the driveshaft inner joints from the drive flanges. Support or tie up the driveshafts to avoid straining the outer joints.

49 Continue raising the engine and gearbox assembly and, when it has been raised sufficiently, draw the hoist forward or push the car backwards and lower the engine and gearbox to the ground.

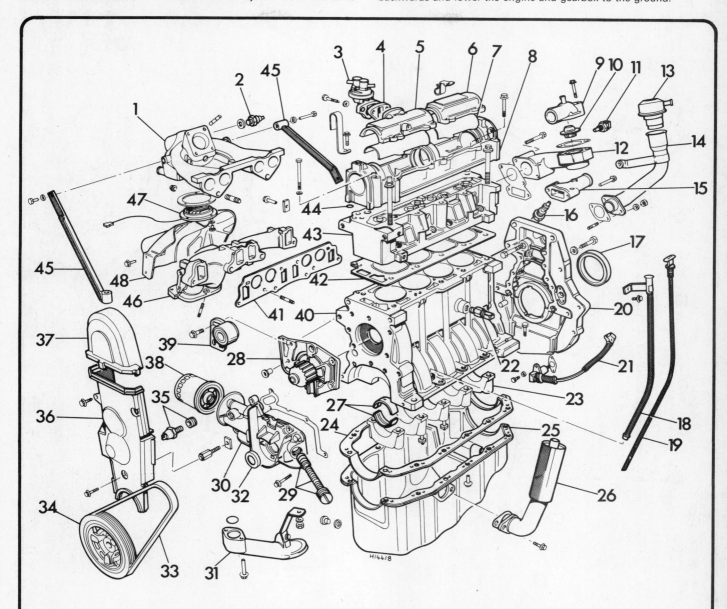

**Fig. 12.3 Exploded view of the 1.6 litre 'S' series engine external components (Sec 5)**

| | | | |
|---|---|---|---|
| 1 Inlet manifold | 13 Oil filler cap | 27 Main bearing shells | 39 Timing belt tensioner |
| 2 Inlet manifold induction temperature sensor | 14 Oil filler tube | 28 Water pump | 40 Cylinder block |
| | 15 Water inlet elbow | 29 Oil pressure relief valve | 41 Manifold gasket |
| 3 Fuel pump | 16 Spark plug | 30 Oil pump and housing | 42 Cylinder head gasket |
| 4 Insulating block | 17 Crankshaft rear oil seal | 31 Oil pick-up tube | 43 Cylinder head |
| 5 Camshaft carrier front cover | 18 Dipstick tube | 32 Crankshaft front oil seal | 44 Camshaft carrier O-ring seal |
| 6 Camshaft carrier rear cover | 19 Dipstick | 33 Alternator drivebelt | |
| 7 Cover gaskets | 20 Gearbox adaptor plate | 34 Crankshaft pulley | 45 Inlet manifold support struts |
| 8 Camshaft carrier | 21 Crankshaft sensor | 35 Oil pressure switch and adaptor | |
| 9 Water outlet elbow | 22 Knock sensor | | 46 Exhaust manifold |
| 10 Thermostat | 23 Main bearing cap | 36 Timing belt lower cover | 47 Inlet manifold induction heater |
| 11 Coolant temperature thermistor | 24 Sump gasket | 37 Timing belt upper cover | |
| | 25 Sump | 38 Oil filter | 48 Hot air box |
| 12 Thermostat housing | 26 Oil separator | | |

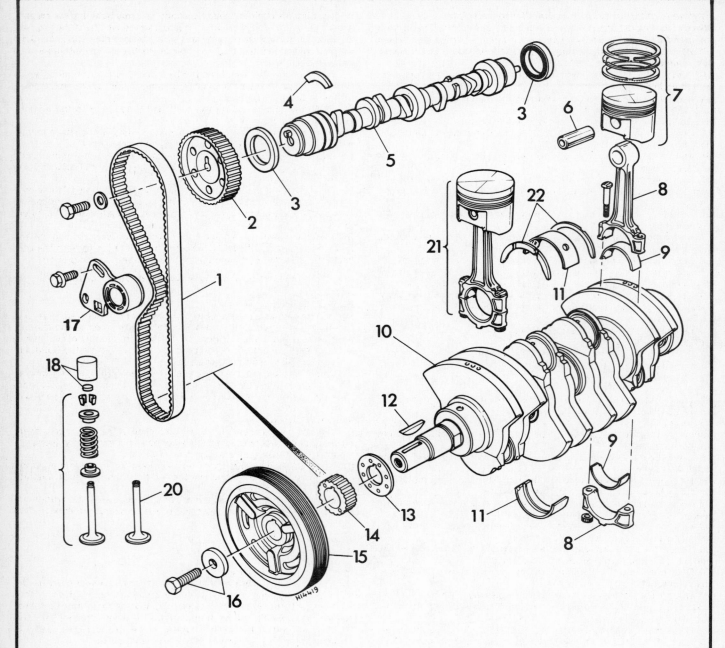

**Fig. 12.4 Exploded view of the 1.6 litre 'S' series engine internal components (Sec 5)**

| | | | | | |
|---|---|---|---|---|---|
| 1 | Timing belt | 10 | Crankshaft | 17 | Timing belt tensioner |
| 2 | Camshaft sprocket | 11 | Main bearing shells | 18 | Tappet bucket and shim |
| 3 | Camshaft oil seals | 12 | Woodruff key | 19 | Inlet valve components |
| 4 | Camshaft locating plate | 13 | Guide plate | 20 | Exhaust valve |
| 5 | Camshaft | 14 | Crankshaft sprocket | 21 | Piston and connecting |
| 6 | Gudgeon pin | 15 | Crankshaft pulley | | rod assembly |
| 7 | Piston and piston rings | 16 | Pulley retaining bolt | 22 | Crankshaft thrust washers |
| 8 | Connecting rod and cap | | and washer | | |
| 9 | Big-end bearing shells | | | | |

## Engine – removal with automatic transmission

**Note:** *The following procedure is also applicable to 1.6 litre models equipped with the 'R' series engine, but reference should be made to Chapter 1, Section 50 for details of engine fittings and attachments, where differences occur.*

50 Remove the bonnet, as described in Chapter 11, and the battery, as described in Chapter 9.

51 Undo and remove the bolts securing the battery tray to the body and take out the tray.

52 Drain the cooling system, as described in Chapter 2.

53 Remove the air cleaner assembly and the plenum chamber, as described in Chapter 3.

54 Make a note of the wiring connections at the starter motor solenoid and disconnect the wires.

55 Disconnect the crankshaft sensor wiring plug then, using a spanner and suitable Allen key, undo the two starter motor retaining bolts.

56 Remove the starter motor, crankshaft sensor bracket and the engine front snubber bracket.

57 Undo the nut and release the selector cable trunnion from the selector lever on the transmission.

58 Slip the kickdown cable end out of its operating lever on the transmission. Release the clevis pin and disconnect the other end of the kickdown cable from the carburettor linkage and support bracket.

59 Undo the retaining bolts securing the selector cable and kickdown cable support bracket to the transmission. Move the bracket and cables clear of the engine and transmission.

60 Disconnect the speedometer cable from its attachment on the transmission.

61 Disconnect the wiring plug at the knock sensor on the front face of the cylinder block.

62 Spring back the clip and disconnect the wiring plug at the rear of the alternator.

63 Disconnect the wiring plug from the coolant temperature thermistor in the thermostat housing.

64 Disconnect the inlet manifold induction heater lead at the wiring connector and the two wires at the inlet manifold induction temperature sensor.

65 Disconnect the wire at the oil pressure switch adjacent to the crankshaft pulley.

66 Disconnect the wiring plug at the carburettor stepping motor and the two leads at the fuel shut-off valve solenoid.

67 Release the retaining clip and remove the fuel inlet hose from the fuel pump. Plug the hose after removal.

68 Pull the float chamber vent hose off the carburettor outlet and remove the hose and pipe from the engine.

69 Detach the crankcase breather hoses at the carburettor, oil filler cap and oil separator, then remove the hose assembly.

70 Disconnect the two ignition vacuum advance hose connectors at the carburettor.

71 Disconnect the vacuum hose from the inlet manifold banjo union, undo the union bolt and recover the two washers. Place the servo vacuum hose to one side.

72 Open the throttle linkage by hand and slip the accelerator cable end out of the slot on the throttle lever. Slacken the outer cable locknuts, unscrew the lower locknut fully and release the cable from the support bracket. Place the cable to one side.

73 Slacken the retaining clips and disconnect the heater hoses at the inlet manifold.

74 Slacken the retaining clips and disconnect the heater hose and radiator bottom hose from the water inlet elbow, followed by the expansion tank hose, radiator top hose and heater hose from the water outlet elbow and thermostat housing.

75 Jack up the front of the car and support it securely on axle stands.

76 From underneath the car, undo the nuts securing the exhaust front pipes to the manifold. Separate the joint flange and recover the gasket.

77 Mark the relationship of the driveshaft inner constant velocity joints to the differential drive flanges. Lift off the protective caps and unscrew the joint-to-drive flange retaining bolts using a suitable Allen key or socket bit.

78 Undo the nuts securing the rear engine/transmission mounting to the crossmember.

79 Undo the retaining screws and remove the left-hand and right-hand access panels from under the wheel arches.

80 Remove the axle stands and lower the car to the ground.

81 Attach a suitable hoist to the engine using chains or rope slings, or by attaching the chains or ropes to sturdy brackets bolted to the engine and transmission. Raise the hoist to just take the weight of the engine.

82 Undo the screw securing the expansion tank to the support bracket and the two bolts securing the bracket to the body. Withdraw the bracket.

83 From under the right-hand wheel arch, undo the two bolts securing the right-hand engine mounting to the body, noting the distance spacer on each bolt.

84 Undo the bolts securing the right-hand mounting to the engine and remove the mounting.

85 Undo the bolt securing the left-hand mounting to the transmission and body then remove the complete mounting assembly.

86 Make a final check that everything attaching the engine and transmission to the car has been disconnected and that all attached components are well clear.

87 Lift the engine and transmission slightly and, as soon as sufficient clearance exists, release the driveshaft inner joints from the drive flanges. Support or tie up the driveshafts to avoid straining the outer joints.

88 Continue raising the engine and transmission assembly and, when it has been raised sufficiently, draw the hoist forward or push the car backwards and lower the engine and transmission to the ground.

## Engine – separation from manual gearbox or automatic transmission

**Manual gearbox**

89 With the engine and gearbox removed from the car, support the two units and undo all the bolts securing the gearbox to the engine adaptor plate. Note the locations of the different lengths of bolts and also the arrangement of retaining nut and captive nut on the bolt that secures the inlet manifold support strut.

90 When all the bolts have been removed, ease the gearbox off its locating dowels and withdraw it squarely from the engine. Do not allow the weight of the gearbox to hang unsupported on the gearbox shaft.

**Automatic transmission**

91 Turn the crankshaft as necessary until each of the torque converter retaining bolts becomes accessible through the starter motor aperture. Undo the bolts using a socket and extension bar.

92 Undo the bolts securing the transmission to the engine adaptor plate, noting the different bolt lengths and the arrangement of support brackets, where applicable.

93 Ease the transmission off the adaptor plate dowels and withdraw it from the engine, ensuring that the torque converter remains on the transmission shaft.

## Engine dismantling – general

94 Refer to Chapter 1, Section 8.

## Ancillary components – removal

95 If the engine has been removed from the car for major overhaul or repair the externally mounted ancillary components, as given in the following list, should first be removed. Removal is straightforward, but further information will be found in the relevant Sections of this Supplement and in the main Chapters of the Manual. The removal sequence need not necessarily follow the order given:

*Alternator*
*Timing belt covers (photos)*
*Fuel pump*
*Distributor cap and rotor arm (photos)*
*Oil filler tube*
*Thermostat housing and water inlet elbow*
*Alternator mounting bracket (photo)*
*Knock sensor (photo)*
*Crankshaft sensor (photo)*
*Spark plugs*
*Inlet and exhaust manifolds and carburettor(s)*
*Clutch and flywheel or driveplate*
*Water pump (after removal of the timing belt)*
*Oil filter*
*Dipstick*

## Timing belt – removal

96 Jack up the front of the car and support it on axle stands.

97 Remove the right-hand front roadwheel and the access panel under the wheel arch.

98 Disconnect the battery negative terminal.

5.95A Lift off the upper timing belt cover ...

5.95B ... then undo the screws (arrowed) and remove the lower cover

5.95C Remove the distributor cap and HT leads ...

5.95D ... followed by the rotor arm and shield

5.95E Undo the bolts (arrowed) and remove the alternator mounting bracket

5.95F Unscrew the knock sensor

5.95G Remove the crankshaft sensor

5.99 Remove the alternator drivebelt

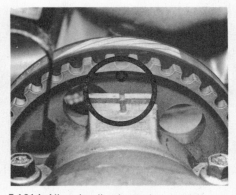

5.101A Align the dimple on the camshaft sprocket with the notch on the carrier ...

5.101B ... and the crankshaft pulley notch with the mark on the oil pump housing

5.102 Slacken the two tensioner retainer bolts (arrowed)

5.103 Remove the timing belt from the sprockets

99 Slacken the alternator pivot mounting bolt and the adjustment arm bolts. Move the alternator towards the engine and remove the drivebelt from the pulleys (photo).

100 Lift off the timing belt upper cover, then undo the screws and remove the lower cover (see photos 5.95A and 5.95B).

101 Using a socket or spanner on the crankshaft pulley bolt, turn the engine over until the dimple on the rear face of the camshaft sprocket is aligned with the notch on the camshaft carrier (photo). Check also that the notch on the crankshaft pulley is aligned with the timing mark on the oil pump housing (photo).

102 Slacken the two timing belt tensioner retaining bolts and move the tensioner away from the engine (photo).

103 Slip the timing belt off the three sprockets and remove it from the engine (photo).

104 If the original belt is to be reused, mark it with chalk to indicate its direction of rotation and also its outer facing edge. Store the belt on its edge while off the engine.

113 Release the retaining clip and remove the fuel inlet hose from the fuel pump. On MG 1600 models, disconnect the fuel hoses at the carburettor connectors. Plug all hoses after removal.

114 Pull the float chamber vent hose off the carburettor outlet and remove the hose and pipe from the engine.

115 Detach the crankcase breather hoses at the carburettor, oil filler cap and oil separator, then remove the hose assembly.

116 Disconnect the ignition vacuum advance hose connectors at the carburettor (photo).

117 Disconnect the vacuum hose from the inlet manifold banjo union, undo the union bolt and recover the two copper washers. Place the brake servo vacuum hose to one side.

118 Open the throttle linkage by hand and slip the accelerator cable end out of the slot on the throttle lever. Slacken the outer cable locknuts, unscrew the lower locknut fully and release the cable from the support bracket. On MG 1600 models, release the choke cable from the carburettor levers and flange. Place the disconnected cable

5.109 Undo the bolts (arrowed) and remove the alternator mounting bracket

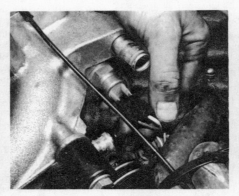

5.111 Disconnect the wires at the induction temperature sensor

5.116 Disconnect the vacuum hoses at the carburettor

### Cylinder head removal – engine in car

105 Remove the timing belt, as described in the previous paragraphs.

106 Drain the cooling system, as described in Section 6 of this Supplement.

107 Remove the air cleaner assembly and, on all models except MG 1600, the plenum chamber, as described in Section 7 of this Supplement.

108 Remove the alternator, as described in Section 14 of this Supplement.

109 Undo the three bolts securing the alternator mounting bracket to the cylinder head and block, then remove the bracket (photo).

110 Disconnect the wiring plug from the coolant temperature thermistor in the thermostat housing.

111 Disconnect the inlet manifold induction heater lead at the wiring connector and the two wires at the inlet manifold induction temperature sensor (where fitted) – photo.

112 On all models except MG 1600, disconnect the wiring plug at the carburettor stepping motor and the two wires at the fuel shut-off valve solenoid.

clear of the engine.

119 On vehicles equipped with automatic transmission, remove the clevis pin securing the kickdown cable to the throttle lever and remove the cable from the support bracket.

120 Slacken the retaining clips and disconnect the heater hose and radiator bottom hose from the water inlet elbow, followed by the expansion tank hose, radiator top hose and heater hose from the water outlet elbow and thermostat housing (photos).

121 Slacken the retaining clips and disconnect the heater hoses at the inlet manifold (where applicable).

122 Undo the small bolt and release the oil dipstick tube from the camshaft cover.

123 On all models except MG 1600, undo the two bolts securing the support struts to the inlet manifold (photo).

124 Undo the nuts securing the exhaust front pipes to the manifold. Separate the joint flange and recover the gasket.

125 Undo the two bolts securing the oil filler tube to the adaptor plate and remove the tube and gasket.

126 Disconnect the spark plug HT leads from the plugs then undo the

5.120A Disconnect the hoses at the water inlet elbow ...

5.120B ... and at the water outlet elbow and thermostat housing

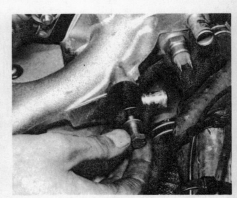

5.123 Undo the manifold support strut retaining bolts

two distributor cap retaining screws. Remove the cap and leads and place them to one side.

127 Place a suitable jack beneath the right-hand side of the engine with a block of wood between the jack head and the sump. Raise the jack and just take the weight of the engine.

128 Undo the bolts securing the right-hand engine mounting to the cylinder head. Slacken the mounting through-bolt and swivel the mounting as far away from the cylinder head as possible.

129 Gradually slacken the cylinder head retaining bolts, half a turn at a time, in the reverse order to that shown in Fig. 12.9. When all the bolts have been slackened, remove them from their locations noting where the bolts having upper thread extensions are fitted.

130 Lift the cylinder head and manifold assembly from the engine (photo). If it is stuck, tap it free with a soft-faced mallet, **do not** attempt to prise it free using a lever between the head and cylinder block, or the mating faces may be damaged.

131 Remove the cylinder head gasket from the cylinder block.

### Cylinder head removal – engine on bench

132 The procedure for removing the cylinder head with the engine on the bench is similar to that for removal when the engine is in the car with the exception of disconnecting the controls and services. Refer to the preceding paragraphs and follow the procedure given, as applicable.

### Camshaft and tappets – removal

**Note:** *If the engine is in the car, carry out the following operations with reference to the relevant Sections of this Supplement:*

(a) *Disconnect the battery negative terminal*
(b) *Remove the air cleaner*
(c) *Remove the timing belt*
(d) *Remove the fuel pump*
(e) *Remove the distributor cap, rotor arm and shield*

133 Undo the retaining bolts and lift off the two camshaft carrier covers (photo). Note the position of the cable and hose clips on the cover bolts.

134 Using a suitable socket, or spanner, undo the camshaft sprocket retaining bolt. Engage a stout screwdriver or bar through the sprocket holes and in contact with the carrier to prevent the camshaft turning. Remove the sprocket retaining bolt and washer then withdraw the sprocket from the camshaft. Carefully ease it off using two levers if it is tight.

135 Using pliers, withdraw the camshaft locating plate from the carrier (photo).

136 Progressively slacken the camshaft carrier retaining bolts and, when all tension on the bolts has been relieved, remove them.

137 Raise the camshaft carrier slightly and push down the tappet buckets until the cam lobes are clear.

138 Move the camshaft towards the rotor arm end until sufficient clearance exists to enable the oil seal at the sprocket end to be removed. Hook the seal out using a screwdriver.

139 Now move the camshaft towards the sprocket end and remove the remaining oil seal in the same way.

140 The camshaft can now be carefully removed from the rotor arm end of the carrier (photo).

141 Lift out each of the tappet buckets in turn and keep them in strict order (photo). Make sure that the small adjustment shim has remained in place inside the bucket.

142 Withdraw the camshaft carrier from the cylinder head (photo) noting the location of the O-ring oil seal.

### Cylinder head – dismantling

**Note:** *If the cylinder head was removed with the engine in the car, refer to the relevant Sections of this Supplement and remove the following components:*

(a) *Inlet and exhaust manifolds and carburettor*
(b) *Distributor cap, rotor arm and shield*
(c) *Thermostat housing and water inlet elbow*
(d) *Camshaft and tappets*

5.130 Removing the cylinder head, complete with manifolds and carburettor

5.133 Remove the camshaft carrier covers

5.135 Withdraw the camshaft locating plate

5.140 Carefully withdraw the camshaft from the carrier

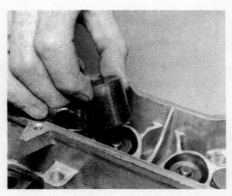

5.141 Lift out the tappet buckets, complete with shims

5.142 Remove the camshaft carrier from the cylinder head

143 Using a valve spring compressor, compress each valve spring in turn until the split collets can be removed (photo). Release the compressor and lift off the cap and spring.

144 If, when the valve spring compressor is screwed down, the valve spring cap refuses to free and expose the split collets, gently tap the top of the tool directly over the cap with a light hammer. This will free the cap.

145 Remove the valve through the combustion chamber then prise the valve stem oil seals off the valve guides using a screwdriver (photos).

146 It is essential that the valves are kept in their correct sequence unless they are so badly worn that they are to be renewed. If they are going to be kept and used again, place them in a sheet of card having eight holes numbered 1 to 8 – corresponding to the relative fitted positions of the valves. **Note that** No 1 valve is nearest to the crankshaft pulley end of the engine.

152 Withdraw the crankshaft pulley followed by the crankshaft sprocket and guide plate.

153 Undo the pump retaining bolts, noting their lengths and locations, and also the retaining plate fitted under the top centre bolt.

154 Withdraw the oil pump housing and recover the gasket.

### Gearbox adaptor plate – removal
**Note:** *If the engine is in the car, carry out the following operations with reference to the relevant Sections of this Supplement:*

   *(a) Remove the manual gearbox or automatic transmission*
   *(b) Remove the clutch assembly and flywheel*
   *(c) Remove the sump*
   *(d) Remove the oil filler tube*
   *(e) Remove the crankshaft sensor*

5.143 Compress the valve springs and lift out the split collets

5.145A Remove the valve ...

5.145B ... then prise off the valve stem oil seals

### Sump – removal
**Note:** *If the engine is still in the car, carry out the following operations:*

   *(a) Drain the engine oil*
   *(b) Disconnect the breather hose from the oil separator on the front face of the sump*

147 Undo the bolts securing the sump to the gearbox adaptor plate.

148 Progressively slacken the sump retaining bolts and then remove them. Make a note of the locations of the different lengths of bolts and of the ones which also secure cable clips and support brackets.

149 Tap the sump with a soft-faced mallet to free the joint face, then remove the sump from the crankcase. Recover the one-piece rubber gasket.

150 If necessary undo the two bolts and one nut securing the oil pick-up tube to the oil pump housing and main bearing cap and remove the tube. Recover the O-ring oil seal at the base of the pick-up tube.

### Oil pump and housing – removal
**Note:** *If the engine is in the car, carry out the following operations with reference to the relevant Sections of this Supplement:*

   *(a) Remove the timing belt*
   *(b) Remove the sump and oil pick-up tube*
   *(c) Disconnect the oil pressure switch wire*

151 Undo the bolt securing the crankshaft sprocket to the crankshaft. If the engine is in the car, engage 1st gear (manual transmission) and firmly apply the footbrake to prevent crankshaft rotation as the bolt is undone. On automatic transmission models it is necessary to remove the starter motor (Chapter 9) and prevent the crankshaft from turning by inserting a suitable bar into the driveplate ring gear. If the engine is on the bench refit two of the clutch pressure plate retaining bolts to the crankshaft and engage a stout bar between them.

155 Undo the bolts securing the adaptor plate to the cylinder block.

156 Tap the adaptor plate using a soft-faced mallet to free it from the locating dowels and remove it from the engine. Remove the two sump retaining bolts and gearbox retaining bolt from their captive recesses in the adaptor plate (photo).

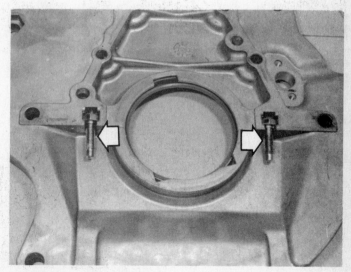

5.156 Sump retaining bolt locations (arrowed) in the gearbox adaptor plate

## Pistons and connecting rods – removal

157 Refer to Chapter 1, Section 65, but note the following differences:

(a) Refer to this Section for removal of cylinder head, sump and oil pick-up tube if the engine is still in the car
(b) If it is necessary to mark the caps and rods for identification, mark them 1 to 4 on the dipstick tube side to ensure correct refitting (photo). Note that No 1 is nearest to the crankshaft pulley end of the engine.

## Crankshaft and main bearings – removal

158 With the engine removed from the car and dismantled as described in the previous paragraphs of this Section, the crankshaft and main bearings can now be removed.
159 Check the crankcase and main bearing caps for identification marks and if no marks are present use a centre punch to mark them.
160 Undo the bolts securing the main bearing caps and remove the caps, complete with bearing shells.
161 Before removing the crankshaft, check that the endfloat is within the specified limits by inserting feeler blades between No 4 crankshaft web and the thrust washers (photo). If the clearance is not as specified, new thrust washers will be required for reassembly.
162 Lift the crankshaft out of the crankcase (photo) then remove the main bearing shell upper halves and the thrust washers (photo). Keep the main bearing shells in order with their respective caps.

5.157 Identify the connecting rod and cap with centre dots

5.161 Checking the crankshaft endfloat

5.162A Lift out the crankshaft ...

5.162B ... and remove the thrust washers and bearing shells

## Crankcase ventilation system – description

163 The crankcase ventilation system consists of an oil separator attached to the engine sump, a breather filter located in the oil filler cap and a hose connecting the oil separator and filler cap to the carburettor.
164 Air is drawn into the crankcase through the filter in the filler cap. Inlet manifold depression draws the crankcase fumes from the oil separator and oil filler tube through the hose into the carburettor airstream where they mix with the incoming fuel/air mixture passing to the cylinders for combustion.
165 The breather filter should be cleaned at the specified service intervals (see Routine Maintenance) and the hoses periodically checked for condition and security.

## Examination and renovation – general

166 With the engine completely dismantled, clean all the components and examine them for wear. Each part should be checked and where necessary renewed or renovated, as described in the following paragraphs. All oil seals, gaskets and O-rings should be renewed as a matter of course and also main and big-end shell bearings unless they have had little wear and are in perfect condition.

## Cylinder block and crankcase – examination and renovation

167 Refer to Chapter 1, Section 23, paragraphs 1 to 5

## Crankshaft and main bearings – examination and renovation

168 Refer to Chapter 1, Section 22.

## Pistons and connecting rods – examination and renovation

169 Refer to Chapter 1, Section 24, but note that when arranging the piston rings, the compression ring gaps should be positioned at 90° to each other towards the dipstick tube side of the cylinder block.

## Gearbox adaptor plate – examination and renovation

170 Refer to Chapter 1, Section 27.

## Oil pump and housing – examination and renovation

171 Remove the oil filter from the pump housing if not already done.
172 Undo the six screws and lift off the pump backplate (photo).
173 Lift out the two rotors from the pump body (photo)
174 Unscrew the pressure relief valve cap using a wide-bladed tool and remove the spring and plunger (photos).
175 Clean all the parts in paraffin or a suitable solvent and dry with a lint-free cloth. Examine the components for signs of scoring, wear ridges or other damage and renew the pump as a complete assembly if any of these conditions are apparent.

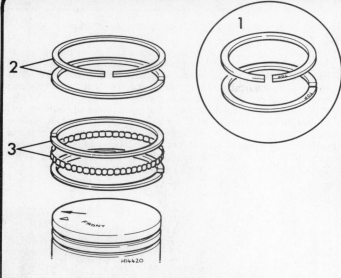

Fig. 12.5 Piston ring details (Sec 5)

1　Compression ring face marked 'TOP'
2　Compression ring gaps positioned at 90° to each other towards the dipstick tube side of the cylinder block
3　Oil control rings and spreader spring

5.172 Undo the screws and remove the oil pump backplate

5.173 Lift out the oil pump rotors

5.174A Unscrew the pressure relief valve cap ...

5.174B .. and withdraw the relief valve components

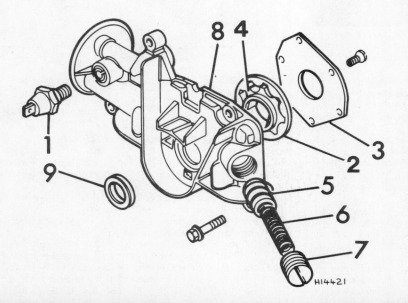

Fig. 12.6 Oil pump housing and pump components (Sec 5)

1　Oil pressure switch
2　Outer rotor
3　Pump backplate
4　Inner rotor
5　Pressure relief valve plunger
6　Pressure relief valve spring
7　Pressure relief valve cap
8　Oil pump housing
9　Crankshaft front oil seal

176 If the pump is satisfactory so far, refit the rotors to the pump body and check the rotor lobe clearance, outer rotor-to-body clearance and the outer rotor endfloat using feeler gauges and a straight-edge (photos). Renew the pump if any of the clearances are outside the figures given in the Specifications.

177 If the pump is serviceable, renew the crankshaft front oil seal in the pump housing. Tap the old seal out from the inside using a punch (photo) and fit a new seal using a tube, block of wood or socket by tapping it squarely into the housing (photo).

178 Lubricate the pressure relief valve plunger with clean engine oil and refit plunger followed by the spring and cap. Tighten the cap securely.

179 Liberally lubricate the two rotors with clean engine oil and place them in position in the pump housing.

180 Refit the pump backplate and secure with the six screws.

### Timing belt, sprockets and tensioner – examination and renovation

186 Carefully examine the belt for any sign of cracking, particularly at the root of the teeth, fraying, oil contamination or any other sign of deterioration. Renew the belt if any of these conditions are found, or as a matter of course if the belt is nearing the end of its recommended service life (see Routine Maintenance).

187 Check the sprockets for signs of cracked or chipped teeth and the tensioner for roughness of its bearings or excessive endfloat. Renew the sprockets or tensioner as necessary. Note that the water pump sprocket is an integral part of the pump and cannot be renewed separately. If this sprocket is damaged or if there is any play in the pump spindle, a complete water pump must be obtained.

5.176A Checking the oil pump rotor lobe clearance ...

5.176B ... outer rotor to body clearance ...

5.176C ... and the outer rotor endfloat

5.177A Remove the crankshaft front oil seal from the pump housing ...

5.177B ... and fit a new seal

### Camshaft and tappets – examination and renovation

181 The camshaft itself should show no signs of wear, but if very slight score marks on the cams are noticed, they can be removed by gently rubbing down with very fine emery cloth or an oilstone. *The greatest care must be taken to keep the cam profiles smooth.*

182 Carefully examine the camshaft bearing surfaces for wear and, if evident, the camshaft must be renewed.

183 Check the fit of the camshaft in the carrier and if excessive bearing journal clearance is apparent a new carrier must be obtained. The camshaft bearings run directly in the machined journals of the carrier; renewable bearings are not used.

184 The faces of the tappet buckets which bear on the camshaft lobes should exhibit no signs of pitting, scoring, cracks or other forms of wear and should be a smooth sliding fit in the carrier. Slight scuffing and blackening of the tappet bucket sides is normal, providing this is not accompanied by scoring or wear ridges.

185 The small shims found inside the tappet bucket should show no signs of indentation from contact with the valve stem. Renew the shim with one of an identical size if wear has taken place. Make sure that each shim is kept with its tappet bucket and not interchanged.

### Cylinder head – decarbonising, valve grinding and renovation

188 Refer to Chapter 1, Section 77.

### Engine mountings – removal and refitting
**Left-hand mounting**

189 Jack up the front of the car and support it on axle stands.

190 Remove the left-hand front roadwheel and the access panel under the wheel arch.

191 Remove the air cleaner cold air intake tube from the front body panel and air cleaner body.

192 Disconnect the two reversing lamp wires from the switch on top of the gearbox casing, where applicable.

193 Position a jack beneath the gearbox with an interposed block of wood, and just take the weight of the engine and gearbox assembly.

194 Undo the two bolts securing the mounting to the gearbox and the through-bolt securing the mounting to the body bracket.

195 Lower the gearbox slightly and manipulate the mounting out of its location.

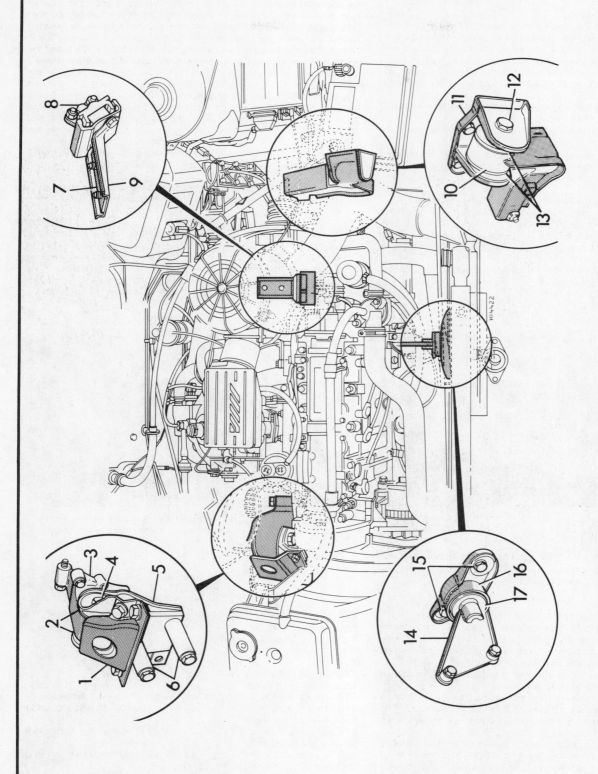

Fig. 12.7 Engine mounting components (Sec 5)

1 Right-hand mounting
  support plate
2 Washers
3 Right-hand mounting
4 Through-bolt

5 Right-hand mounting
  body bracket
6 Right-hand mounting
  distance spacers

7 Rear mounting thread
  plate
8 Rear mounting
9 Rear mounting support
  bracket

10 Left-hand mounting
11 Left-hand mounting
  body bracket
12 Through-bolt
13 Washers

14 Front snubber bracket
15 Snubber cup retaining bolts
16 Snubber cup
17 Snubber rubber

196 Refitting is the reverse sequence to removal. Tighten the retaining bolts to the specified torque (see Fig. 12.2) and centralize the front snubber, as described in paragraph 210.

**Right-hand mounting**

197 Position a jack beneath the engine sump with an interposed block of wood, and just take the weight of the engine.

198 Lift off the timing belt upper cover then undo the two upper bolts securing the lower cover.

199 Undo the bolts securing the right-hand mounting to the cylinder block and head.

200 Undo the through-bolt securing the mounting to the body bracket.

201 Undo the four bolts securing the support plate to the body and body bracket.

202 Ease the mounting out of the body bracket and manipulate it out of its location.

203 Refitting is the reverse sequence to removal. Tighten the retaining bolts to the specified torque (see Fig. 12.2) and centralize the front snubber, as described in paragraph 210.

**Rear mounting**

204 Jack up the front of the car and support it on axle stands.

205 Undo the two bolts securing the rear mounting support bracket to the crossmember. Recover the thread plate from the mounting bracket.

206 Undo the two nuts securing the mounting to the gearbox casing, slide the mounting off the casing studs and remove the assembly from under the car.

207 Refitting is the reverse sequence to removal. Tighten the retaining bolts to the specified torque (see Fig. 12.2) and centralize the front snubber, as described in paragraph 210.

**Front snubber**

208 Undo the nuts from the starter motor retaining bolts, remove the crankshaft sensor wiring plug bracket and lift off the front snubber bracket and snubber.

209 Refit the snubber using the reverse of this procedure, tightening the starter motor retaining bolts to the specified torque.

210 Slacken the snubber cup retaining bolts (photo), centralize the snubber cup around the snubber rubber then tighten the bolts. This should be done whenever **any** of the engine mountings are renewed or in any way disturbed.

*Engine reassembly – general*

211 To ensure maximum lift with minimum trouble from a rebuilt engine, not only must everything be correctly assembled, but it must also be spotlessly clean. All oilways must be clear, and locking washers and spring washers must be fitted where indicated. Oil all bearings and other working surfaces thoroughly with engine oil during assembly.

212 Before assembly begins, renew any bolts or studs with damaged threads.

213 Gather together a torque wrench, oil can, clean rags and a complete set of engine gaskets and oil seals, together with a new oil filter.

214 A tube of Loctite 574 sealant will be required for the camshaft carrier-to-cylinder head joint face, and an RTV silicone sealant for the remainder of the joint faces that do not have gaskets, with the exception of the camshaft carrier covers. For this joint face the manufacturers recommend the use of Gold Hermetite. These components, together with conventional gasket jointing compound, are available from Austin Rover dealers or leading motor factors.

5.210 Engine front snubber cup retaining bolts (arrowed)

5.216 Fit the main bearing shells to the cylinder block

5.217 Fit the thrust washers with their oilways facing away from the bearing

5.218A Lower the crankshaft into the crankcase ...

5.218B ... then fit the main bearing caps

5.221 Ensure that the word FRONT is towards the crankshaft pulley end of the engine

5.222 Apply RTV sealant to the adaptor plate mating face

5.224 Fit the adaptor plate to the cylinder block

## Crankshaft and main bearings – refitting

215 Clean the backs of the bearing shells and the bearing recesses in both the cylinder block and main bearing caps.

216 Press the main bearing shells into the cylinder block and caps and oil them liberally (photo).

217 Using a little grease, stick the thrust washers to each side of No 4 main bearing with their oilways facing away from the bearing (photo).

218 Lower the crankshaft into position, then fit the main bearing caps in their previously noted locations (photos).

219 Insert and tighten evenly the main bearing cap bolts to the specified torque.

220 Check that the crankshaft rotates freely, then check that the endfloat is within the specified limits by inserting a feeler blade between the crankshaft web and the thrust washers.

## Pistons and connecting rods – refitting

221 Refer to Chapter 1, Section 83, but note the following differences:

(a) The mark FRONT, A or an arrow on the piston crown should face the crankshaft pulley end of the engine (photo)

(b) If the engine is in the car, refit the sump and oil pick-up tube, and the cylinder head with reference to this Section

## Gearbox adaptor plate – refitting

222 Ensure that the mating faces of the cylinder block and adaptor plate are thoroughly clean then apply a bead of RTV sealant to the adaptor plate face (photo).

223 Make sure that the two sump retaining bolts and the gearbox

retaining bolt are fitted in their adaptor plate locations and apply additional sealant to their bolt heads.

224 Liberally lubricate the lips of the crankshaft rear oil seal in the adaptor plate then carefully fit the adaptor plate to the cylinder block (photo).

225 Refit the retaining bolts and tighten them evenly to the specified torque.

226 If the engine is in the car, refer to the gearbox adaptor plate removal procedures described earlier in this Section and refit the items listed, in the reverse sequence to removal.

## Oil pump and housing – refitting

227 Make sure that the mating faces of the pump and cylinder block are clean, then place a new gasket in position on the pump housing.

228 Wrap some insulating tape around the end of the crankshaft to protect the oil seal as the pump is fitted.

229 Liberally lubricate the lips of the oil seal and the insulating tape with engine oil.

230 Position the flats of the pump inner rotor to correspond with the flats on the crankshaft and carefully fit the pump to the cylinder block (photo). Remove the tape.

231 Refit the pump retaining bolts (photo) with the exception of the top centre bolt which also secures the water pump. This bolt is fitted later unless the water pump is already in place.

232 Tighten the bolts evenly to the specified torque.

233 If the engine is in the car, refer to the oil pump and housing removal procedures described earlier in this Section and refit the items listed, in the reverse sequence to removal.

5.230 Fit the oil pump housing to the cylinder block

5.231 Refit and tighten the oil pump housing retaining bolts (arrowed)

*Sump – refitting*

234 Insert a new O-ring seal into the groove in the oil pick-up tube then refit the tube to the oil pump housing and main bearing cap (photos). Refit the retaining bolts and nut and tighten them securely.

235 Ensure that all traces of old sealant are removed from the sump and cylinder block mating faces and from around the one-piece rubber gasket if this is intact and to be reused.

236 Apply a thick bead of RTV sealant to the semi-circular joint faces of the sump, oil pump housing and gearbox adaptor plate. Extend the bead of sealant about 0.5 in (12 mm) beyond the ends of the semi-circular joint faces (photo).

237 Place the rubber gasket on the sump, then position the sump on the engine (photo).

238 Refit the sump retaining bolts and nuts with the longer bolts, cable clips and brackets in the positions noted during removal. Progressively tighten the bolts in a diagonal sequence to the specified torque.

239 With a new gasket in place, fit the oil separator and secure with the two nuts (photo).

240 Refit the bolts securing the sump to the gearbox adaptor plate (photo).

241 If the engine is in the car, refer to the sump removal procedures described earlier in this Section and refit the items listed in the reverse sequence to removal.

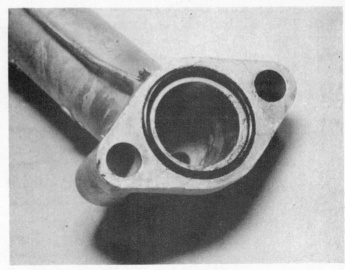

5.234A Insert a new O-ring into the oil pick-up groove ...

5.234B ... then secure the tube to the pump housing and bearing cap

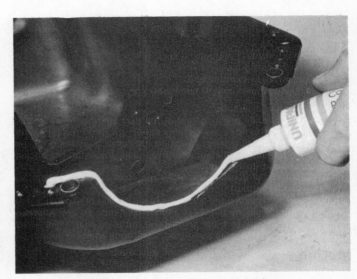

5.236 Apply RTV sealant to the semi-circular joint faces

5.237 Position the sump on the engine

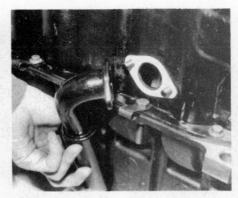

5.239 Fit the oil separator to the sump

5.240 Refit the sump-to-adaptor plate bolts

*Cylinder head – reassembly*

242 Place the new valve stem oil seals in place over the valve guides and push them fully into place using a small tube or socket (photos). Note that, if valves with oversize stems are being fitted, oil seals with two rings on their flange must be used (Fig. 12.8).

243 Oil the valve stems liberally and fit each valve to its original guide, or if new valves have been obtained, to the seat in which they have been ground (photo).

244 Working on one valve at a time, fit the spring and cap, then compress the spring with the compressor and insert the split collets (photos). Release the compressor and remove it.

5.242A Locate new valve stem oil seals over guides ...

5.242B ... then push them fully into place

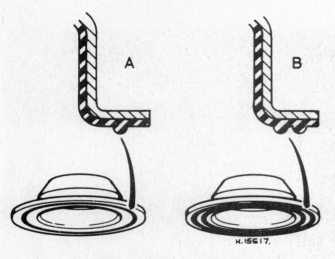

**Fig. 12.8 Valve stem oil seals (Sec 5)**

A   Standard size stem oil seal with one flange ring
B   Oversize stem oil seal with two flange rings

5.243 Fit the valves to their original guides

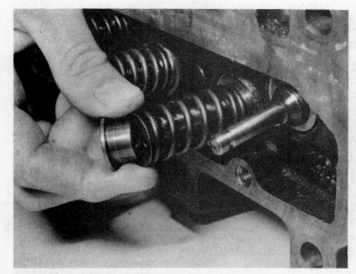

5.244A Fit the valve spring and cap ...

5.244B ... then compress the spring and insert the spring collets

245 Repeat the procedure given in paragraph 244 on the remaining valves. After fitting, tap the end of each valve stem with a mallet to settle the collets.

*Camshaft and tappets – refitting*

246 Smear the tappet shims with petroleum jelly and then locate the shims in the recesses of their respective tappet buckets.

247 Place the camshaft carrier in position on the cylinder head and fit the tappet buckets to their locations in the carrier.

248 Lift the carrier slightly, push the tappet buckets down and carefully insert the camshaft. Fit the camshaft locating plate to the carrier front bearing journal.

249 Fit the camshaft carrier retaining bolts and progressively tighten them to the specified torque.

250 Before proceeding further the tappet clearances should be checked and adjusted using the procedure described in paragraphs 279 to 284. For the purposes of tappet clearance checking the camshaft may be turned using an adjustable wrench on the square

protrusion between No 6 and 7 camshaft lobe (photo).

251 With the tappet clearance checked and the correct new shims obtained as necessary, remove the camshaft, camshaft carrier and the tappet buckets (if not already done).

252 Locate a new O-ring seal in the carrier recess, then fill the carrier groove with Loctite 574 sealant (photos).

253 Place the carrier in position on the cylinder head once more and insert the tappet buckets in their respective locations (photos).

254 Lift the carrier slightly, push down the tappet buckets and slide the camshaft into the carrier. Refit the camshaft locating plate.

255 Fit the camshaft carrier retaining bolts and progressively tighten them to the specified torque.

256 Thoroughly lubricate the lips of new camshaft front and rear oil seals and carefully locate them over the camshaft journals and into their positions in the carrier (photos). Tap the seals squarely into the carrier.

257 Place the camshaft sprocket on the camshaft and use the retaining bolt and washer to draw the sprocket fully home (photo). Tighten the

5.250 Camshaft square protrusion (arrowed) for spanner engagement

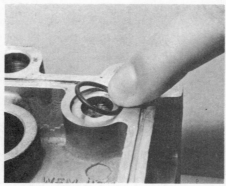

5.252A Locate a new O-ring in the camshaft carrier recess ...

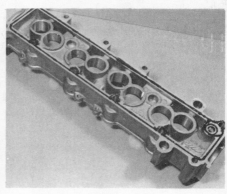

5.252B .. then fill the carrier groove with special sealant

5.253A Place the carrier in position on the cylinder head ...

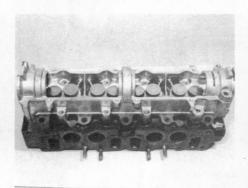

5.253B .. then fit the tappet buckets to their original bores

5.256A Fit a new camshaft front ...

5.256B ... and rear oil seal

5.257 Refit the camshaft sprocket and retaining bolt

5.258 Locate the rubber gaskets in the camshaft carrier covers

5.260 Fit the covers, noting the cable clip locations

5.263 Lay a new cylinder head gasket over the dowels ...

5.264 .. then lower the head onto the gasket

retaining bolt to the specified torque.

258 Locate the one-piece rubber gaskets in the camshaft carrier covers (photo) using new gaskets if necessary.

259 Apply a continuous bead of Gold Hermetite to the cover mating faces in the camshaft carrier.

260 Fit the two covers, retaining bolts and brackets, where applicable (photo). Tighten the cover bolts progressively to the specified torque.

261 If the engine is in the car, refer to the camshaft and tappets removal procedures described earlier in this Section and refit the items listed in the reverse sequence to removal.

### Cylinder head – refitting

262 Ensure that the cylinder block and head mating faces are perfectly clean and free from any traces of oil, grease or water.

263 Place a new head gasket in position over the cylinder block dowels (photo). The gasket is pre-coated and jointing compound **should not** be used.

264 Lower the cylinder head into position (photo) and, with their threads lightly oiled, refit the retaining bolts.

265 Tighten the cylinder head bolts in the sequence shown in Fig. 12.9 in two stages; first to half the specified torque, then to the full specified torque; and finally a further 1/4 turn (90°).

266 If the engine is in the car, refer to the cylinder head removal procedures described earlier in this Section and reverse the procedure given in paragraphs 106 to 128, then refit the timing belt, as described in the following paragraphs.

267 There is no need for any further tightening of the cylinder head bolts after warm-up.

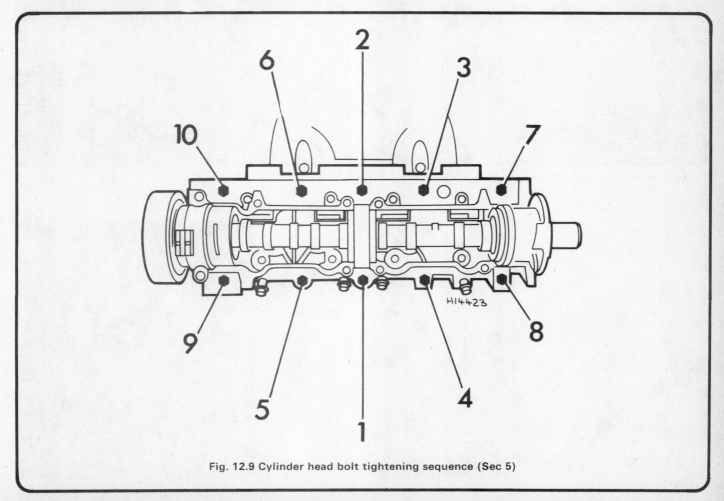

Fig. 12.9 Cylinder head bolt tightening sequence (Sec 5)

*Timing belt – refitting and adjustment*
268 If the engine is being reassembled after major overhaul, refer to Section 6 of this Supplement and refit the water pump.
269 Place the crankshaft sprocket guide plate on the crankshaft followed by the sprocket and crankshaft pulley (photos). Fit the pulley retaining bolt and washer and tighten the pulley to the specified torque (photo).
270 Turn the camshaft as necessary, using a spanner on the sprocket bolt, until the dimple on the rear face of the sprocket is aligned with the notch on the camshaft carrier (photo). Turn the crankshaft until the notch on the pulley is aligned with the timing mark on the oil pump housing.
271 Refit the timing belt tensioner, but do not tighten the two retaining bolts at this stage.
272 Slip the belt over the sprockets and around the tensioner so that it is taut on the straight (driving) side (photo).
273 To tension the belt, engage a torque wrench of the type having a dial gauge scale or sliding pointer scale and 3/8 in square drive into the hole in the tensioner bracket. Tension the belt to the torque figure given in the Specifications and tighten the two tensioner retaining bolts (photo).
274 Turn the crankshaft clockwise through three quarters of a turn so that the crankshaft pulley notch is a approximately 90° BTDC.

275 Slacken the tensioner retaining bolts again and re-tension the belt, as described in paragraph 273.
276 Turn the crankshaft clockwise through one and a quarter turns and realign the crankshaft pulley timing notch with the mark on the oil pump housing. Check that the camshaft sprocket and carrier timing marks are aligned. If not, repeat the belt refitting and adjustment procedure, starting at paragraph 270.
277 If the engine is in the car, refit the timing belt upper and lower covers, followed by the alternator drivebelt. Adjust the drivebelt as described in Section 14 of this Supplement.
278 Refit the access cover and roadwheel, lower the car to the ground and reconnect the battery.

*Tappet clearances – checking and adjustment*
279 To check the tappet clearances, disconnect the battery negative terminal then undo the retaining bolts and lift off the camshaft carrier covers. Note which bolts also secure cable and hose retaining clips.
280 Using a feeler gauge, check the clearance between the cam lobe and the tappet bucket of each valve (photo) in the order given in the following table and record each clearance. The engine may be turned using a spanner or socket on the crankshaft pulley bolt. If necessary remove the access panel from under the right-hand wheel arch to provide greater access to the pulley bolt.

5.269A Place crankshaft sprocket guide plate on the crankshaft ...

5.269B ... followed by the sprocket ...

5.269C ... and crankshaft pulley

5.269D Secure the pulley with the retaining bolt and washer

*Check No 1 tappet with No 8 valve fully open*
*Check No 3 tappet with No 6 valve fully open*
*Check No 5 tappet with No 4 valve fully open*
*Check No 2 tappet with No 7 valve fully open*
*Check No 8 tappet with No 1 valve fully open*
*Check No 6 tappet with No 3 valve fully open*
*Check No 4 tappet with No 5 valve fully open*
*Check No 7 tappet with No 2 valve fully open*

281 Once the readings have been tabulated for all valves it should be noted that, unless new parts have been fitted or the valve seats reground, adjustment of the valve tappet clearance to the standard setting is only necessary if the clearance of either inlet or exhaust is less than 0.012 in (0.30 mm).

282 If adjustment is necessary, remove the camshaft and tappets, as described earlier in this Section.

283 Remove the adjusting shim from each maladjusted tappet bucket in turn and note its thickness. The shim thickness is stamped on the face of the shim (photo) – see Specifications. By using the following calculation, determine the thickness of the new shim required to give the correct tappet clearance:

$A$ = *clearance measured in paragraph 280*
$B$ = *thickness of existing shim*
$C$ = *correct clearance*
*New shim thickness required* $= A + B - C$

5.270 Camshaft timing marks aligned

5.272 Slip the timing belt over the sprockets and tensioner

5.273 Using a torque wrench to adjust the timing belt tension

5.280 Checking tappet clearance with a feeler gauge blade

5.283 Tappet adjusting shim with size stamped on its face

284 With new shims obtained as necessary, refit the camshaft and tappets, as described earlier in paragraphs 252 to 261.

### Ancillary components – refitting
285 Refit the previously removed ancillary components detailed earlier, with reference to the applicable Sections of this Supplement where necessary.

### Engine – attachment to manual gearbox or automatic transmission
286 Refer to the removal procedure described earlier in this Section and attach the gearbox or automatic transmission using the reverse of the removal sequence. Tighten all nuts and bolts to the specified torque.

### Engine – refitting with manual gearbox or automatic transmission
287 Refer to the removal procedures described earlier in this Section and refit the engine and manual gearbox or automatic transmission using the reverse of the removal sequence. Note also the following additional points:

(a) *Do not tighten any of the engine mountings fully until all have been fitted, then tighten them in this order: right-hand mounting, left-hand mounting, rear mounting, front snubber. Centralize the front snubber as described in paragraph 210 of this Section, after tightening the other mountings*

(b) *Align the marks on the driveshaft joints and drive flanges made during removal. Secure the joints using **new** bolts and ensure that the correct torque setting is used*

(c) *On manual gearbox models, refit the clutch cable with reference to Section 9 of this Supplement*

(d) *On automatic transmission models, adjust the selector cable and kickdown cable, if necessary, as described in Section 11 of this Supplement*

(e) *Adjust the accelerator cable and, on MG1600 models, the choke cable with reference to Section 7 of this Supplement*

(f) *Refill the cooling system, as described in Section 6 of this Supplement, and refill the engine with oil, as described earlier in this Section*

### Engine – adjustments after major overhaul
288 With the engine refitted to the car, make a final check to ensure that everything has been reconnected and that no rags or tools have been left in the engine compartment.
289 Make sure that the oil and water levels are topped up and then start the engine; this may take a little longer than usual as the fuel pump and carburettor float chamber may be empty.
290 As soon as the engine starts, watch for the oil pressure light to go out and check for any oil, fuel or water leaks. Don't be alarmed if there are some odd smells and smoke from parts getting hot and burning off oil deposits.
291 Run the engine for at least 15 minutes or drive the car for approximately 5 miles then switch it off and allow it to cool. Recheck the oil and water levels.
292 If new pistons, rings or crankshaft bearings have been fitted the engine must be run-in for the first 500 miles (800 km). Do not exceed 45 mph (72 kph), operate the engine at full throttle or allow it to labour in any gear.

### Oil filter element and camshaft lubrication
293 An oil filter incorporating a pressure bypass valve is fitted to later 1.6 litre engine models, to prevent seizure of the camshaft due to lack of lubrication to the camshaft bearings.
294 A camshaft lubrication gallery restrictor is fitted at the timing belt end of the cylinder head, just below the cylinder head joint face. If this gallery becomes blocked the camshaft bearings will run dry and seize, and it is therefore important to check that the gallery is clear during an engine overhaul, or in the event of a camshaft seizure.
295 To unblock the gallery, withdraw the restrictor using a self-tapping screw to grip it and extract it. To clear the blockage, apply air pressure to the threaded oil filter adaptor at the oil pump. Leaving the restrictor out, fit a new oil filter and crank the engine over a few times to pump clean oil through the gallery, then refit the restrictor. **Do not**

apply air pressure through the restrictor from the other end (against the direction of oil flow).

### Engine type identification – 1.6 litre 'S' series models
296 Some 1.6 litre 700 vans, and later 1.6 saloon models may be fitted with a low compression engine. A low compression engine can be identified from the engine number plate, attached to the cylinder block below the spark plugs. Reading from the *right*, the first letter which appears denotes the compression ratio. A letter M identifies the engine as a high compression (9.6:1) type, while a letter L identifies a low compression (8.0:1) engine.

### Fault diagnosis – engine
297 Refer to Chapter 1, Section 96.

## 6 Cooling system (1.6 litre 'S' series models)

### General description
The cooling system is of the pressurised, pump-assisted thermo-syphon type comprising a radiator, water pump, thermostat, electric cooling fan, expansion tank and associated hoses. The system functions in the same manner as described in Chapter 2; the main differences being in the location of the various components (Fig. 12.10) and the water pump which is driven by the toothed timing belt and not by a conventional vee belt as on previous applications.

The contents of this Section covers changes in the system as applicable to the 1.6 litre, 'S' series engines only. All other cooling system operations are the same as for 1.6 litre 'R' series models described in Chapter 2.

### Cooling system – draining
1 The draining procedure is the same as described in Chapter 2, Section 3, but note that it is not possible to completely drain the 'S' series engine due to the absence of a cylinder block drain plug. To drain all the coolant from the engine, or to bring the level to below that of the water inlet elbow, it will be necessary to remove the water pump, as described later in this Section.

### Cooling system – flushing
2 To flush the system, first drain the coolant, as described in the previous paragraph.
3 Disconnect the top hose at the outlet elbow and leave the bottom hose disconnected at the radiator outlet.
4 Insert a hose into the top hose and allow water to circulate through the radiator until it runs clear from the outlet.
5 Disconnect the heater inlet hose from the thermostat housing. Insert the hose and allow water to circulate through the heater and out through the bottom hose until clear.
6 In severe cases of contamination the system should be reverse flushed. To do this remove the radiator, invert it and insert a hose in the bottom outlet. Continue flushing until clean water runs from the top hose outlet.
7 The engine should also be flushed. To do this remove the thermostat and insert the hose into the cylinder head or thermostat housing. Flush the system until clean water runs from the bottom hose.
8 The use of chemical cleaners should only be necessary as a last resort. The regular renewal of antifreeze should prevent the contamination of the system.

### Cooling system – filling
9 Where applicable, refit all hoses and components removed during the flushing operation.
10 Pour a couple of pints of water into the system through the expansion tank, and then add the correct quantity of antifreeze fluid – for system capacity, see 'Specifications' at the beginning of this Supplement. Top up with more water until the expansion tank is half full. The procedure takes into account the fact that the system cannot be completely drained. Do not refit the expansion tank cap at this stage.
11 Start the engine and run it at a fast idle for approximately one minute. During this time compress the top hose several times to release any air pockets in the system.
12 Stop the engine, top up the expansion tank to the indicated level then refit the filler cap.

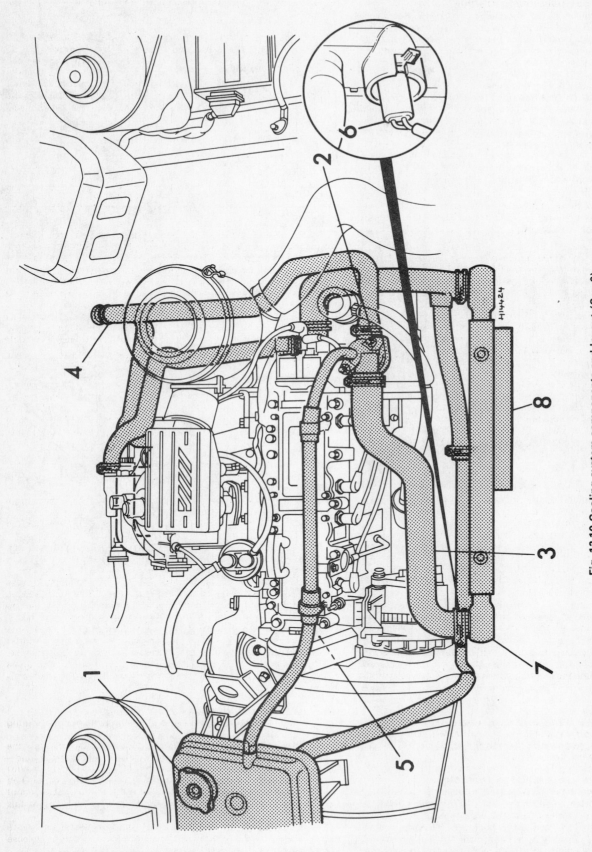

Fig. 12.10 Cooling system components and layout (Sec 6)

1 Expansion tank filler cap
2 Thermostat housing
3 Radiator top hose

4 Heater hoses
5 Water pump

6 Cooling fan thermostatic switch

7 Radiator
8 Cooling fan assembly

## Thermostat – removal, testing and refitting

13 The procedure is the same as described in Chapter 2, Section 8, except that the thermostat housing is located on the front left-hand side of the engine and the water outlet elbow is secured by two bolts instead of three.

## Water pump – removal and refitting

14 Disconnect the battery negative terminal.
15 Drain the cooling system, as described previously in this Section.
16 Refer to Section 5 of this Supplement and remove the timing belt.
17 Undo the two bolts and lift off the timing belt tensioner (photo).
18 Place a suitable container beneath the water pump to collect the coolant remaining in the cylinder block.
19 Using an Allen key, undo the water pump upper retaining bolt, then undo the remaining three bolts using a spanner or socket (photo). Recover the clamp plate on the lower bolt.

6.17 Timing belt tensioner retaining bolts (arrowed)

6.19 Water pump retaining bolts (arrowed)

20 Ease the water pump off the engine using a screwdriver to lever between the block and pump side flanges if necessary.
21 Refitting the pump is the reverse sequence to removal, bearing in mind the following points:

(a) Remove all traces of old sealant from the cylinder block and pump faces, and ensure that both mating surfaces are clean and dry

(b) Temporarily fit the water pump to the cylinder block and rotate the impeller by hand to ensure that it does not foul on the cylinder block. If it does, carefully file off the necessary amount from the impeller to allow a minimal clearance

(c) Apply a bead of RTV sealant around the pump mating faces (photo) and, with the pump in position, tighten the retaining bolts to the specified torque

(d) Refit and adjust the timing belt, as described in Section 5 of this Supplement

(e) Refill the cooling system, as described previously in this Section

## Cooling fan assembly – removal and refitting

22 Refer to the procedure given in Chapter 2, Section 11, but note that the fan is secured to the radiator by three nuts and spring washers. After undoing these the unit can be lifted away (photos).
23 If required the fan may be removed by pulling it off the motor shaft. Mark the outer face to ensure correct refitment. To remove the fan motor, drill off the rivet heads, tap out the rivets securing the motor to the cowl and lift off the motor.
24 Refitting is the reverse sequence to removal.

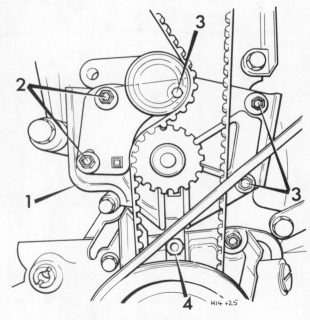

Fig. 12.11 Water pump removal –
1.6 litre 'S' series models (Sec 6)

1   Water pump
2   Timing belt tensioner
    retaining bolts
3   Water pump retaining
    bolts
4   Clamp plate

## Coolant temperature thermistor – removal and refitting

25 The coolant temperature thermistor incorporates a temperature-sensitive element, the resistance of which alters according to coolant temperature. The unit controls the operation of the temperature gauge and also influences the settings of the fuel and ignition system electronic control units.
26 Place a suitable container beneath the radiator bottom hose outlet. Slacken the retaining clip, disconnect the bottom hose and drain approximately 4 pints (2.3 litres) of coolant. Refit the hose and tighten the clip.
27 Disconnect the wiring plug from the thermistor which is located in the thermostat housing.
28 Unscrew the thermistor and remove it from the engine.
29 Refitting is the reverse sequence to removal, but top up the cooling system, as described earlier in this Section.

6.21 Apply RTV sealant to the pump mating face before fitting

6.22A Cooling fan upper ...

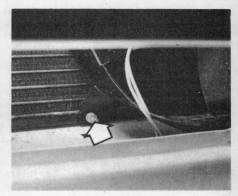

6.22B ... and lower retaining nuts (arrowed)

## 7  Fuel and exhaust systems

*Air cleaner and element (1.6 litre, 'S' series models) – description, removal and refitting*
1   The air cleaner fitted to 'S' series engine models, except the MG 1600, contains a disposable paper filter element and incorporates an automatic air temperature control system.
2   The system is controlled by a flap valve located at the junction of the air cleaner hot and cold air intakes. The flap is operated by inlet manifold vacuum acting on a thermac unit in conjunction with a temperature-sensitive thermac switch. The system allows hot or cold air to be delivered to the carburettor, depending on the position of the flap valve which varies according to engine temperature and load.

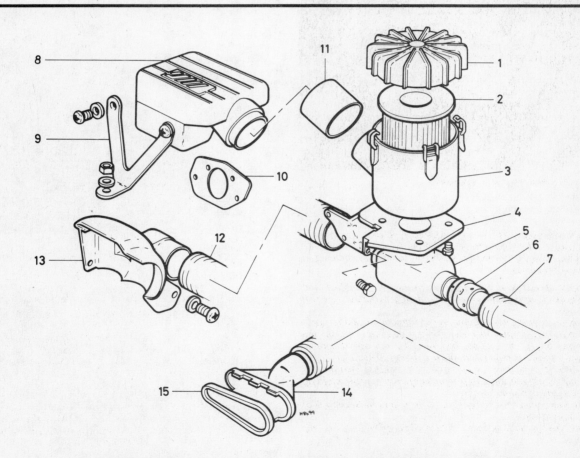

Fig. 12.12 Air cleaner and related components – 1.6 litre 'S' series models, except MG 1600 (Sec 7)

| | | | |
|---|---|---|---|
| 1   Top cover | 5   Thermac unit | 9   Support bracket | 13  Hot air box |
| 2   Paper element | 6   Adaptor sleeve | 10  Gasket | 14  Cold air intake hose |
| 3   Air cleaner body | 7   Cold air intake hose | 11  Connecting tube | adaptor |
| 4   Air cleaner mounting bracket | 8   Plenum chamber | 12  Hot air duct | 15  Gasket |

3  To remove the air cleaner element, spring back the retaining clips, lift off the top cover and withdraw the element (photo).

4  If the air cleaner body is to be removed, release the cold air intake hose from its attachments on the front body panel and thermac unit then remove the hose (photo).

5  Undo the three bolts securing the air cleaner mounting bracket to the engine.

6  Detach the air cleaner body from the plenum chamber and hot air ducts, disconnect the vacuum hose from the thermac unit (photo) and remove the air cleaner assembly from the engine.

7  To remove the plenum chamber, disconnect the vacuum hose from the thermac switch at the connector.

8  Undo the two screws and one nut securing the plenum chamber and support bracket. Withdraw the bracket then remove the plenum chamber from the carburettor.

9  Thoroughly clean the inside of the air cleaner body and check the vacuum pipes and thermac unit for condition and security.

10  To test the operation of the air temperature control system reconnect the vacuum hose from thermac unit to thermac switch, but leave the other vacuum hose from the thermac switch to T-piece disconnected.

11  Observe the position of the air temperature control flap in the thermac unit at the base of the air cleaner body. The flap should be set to receive air from the cold air intake. Apply suction to the disconnected vacuum hose and check that the flap moves to the hot air delivery position. The flap should return to the cold air delivery position when the ambient temperature reaches 30°C (85°F). This can be tested by heating the thermac switch in the plenum chamber with a hair dryer while applying suction to the hose. If the operation of the unit is in doubt, the thermac switch should be renewed.

12  Refitting the plenum chamber and air cleaner is the reverse sequence to removal. Renew the gasket between the plenum chamber and carburettor if the old one shows any signs of deterioration.

*Air cleaner and element (MG 1600 models) – description, removal and refitting*

13  The air cleaner fitted to MG 1600 models equipped with the 'S' series engine contains a disposable paper element and incorporates an automatic air temperature control system controlled by a flap valve at the junction of the hot and cold air intakes. The flap is operated by inlet manifold vacuum (taken from a five-way connector attached to each carburettor barrel and the ignition system ECU by small bore hoses) acting on a thermostatic air bleed valve inside the air cleaner.

14  An additional cold air intake at the front of the air cleaner allows cold air to be ducted around the carburettors. This air is supplied from a cooling fan mounted on the inner wing valance and controlled by a temperature switch in the air cleaner. The fan operates to maintain the ambient air temperature around the carburettors below 65°C (150°F).

15  To renew the paper element and service the air cleaner it must be removed from the engine, as follows.

16  Disconnect the vacuum hose at the flap valve and the two breather hoses from the top of the air cleaner body.

17  Disconnect the cold air intake hose from its attachment on the front body panel and remove the intake hose from the carburettor cooling fan and air cleaner front intake.

18  Undo and remove the bolts securing the front intake to the engine and slacken the clip securing the hot air intake to the air cleaner body.

19  Detach the cooling system expension tank hose from the two clips on the front of the engine.

20  Undo and remove the three retaining bolts, release the clips and lift the air cleaner and intake hose off the engine.

21  With the air cleaner cover removed, withdraw the filter element and clean the air cleaner body inside and out.

22  To remove the air cleaner baseplate, undo the nuts and washers then lift off the baseplate, together with the carburettor air intake throats.

23  Check the condition of the vacuum hoses and check the operation of the vacuum/temperature switch by applying suction. The switch should remain sealed at temperatures below 30°C (85°F). If suspect, heat the unit with a hair dryer and recheck the operation. Check the operation of the flap valve by applying suction to the hose. Renew any faulty components as necessary.

24  Fit a new element then refit the air cleaner using the reverse sequence to removal.

7.3 Air cleaner element renewal

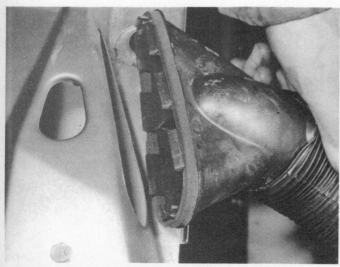

7.4 Cold air intake hose front body panel attachment

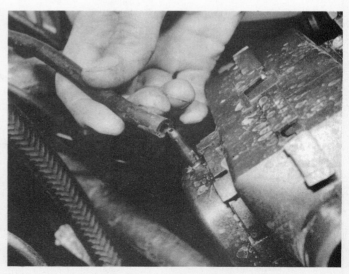

7.6 Vacuum hose attachment at air cleaner thermac unit

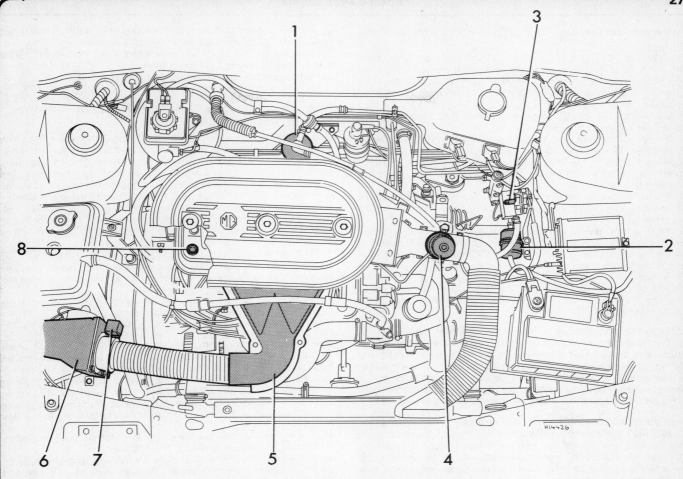

**Fig. 12.13 Fuel system layout – MG 1600 models (Sec 7)**

| | | |
|---|---|---|
| 1 | Vapour separator | 4 | Air cleaner air temperature | 6 | Carburettor cooling fan | 8 | Air temperature control |
| 2 | Fuel filter | | control flap valve | 7 | Carburettor cooling fan | | switch |
| 3 | Fuel flow transducer | 5 | Carburettor cold air intake | | control unit | | |

1    Vapour separator
2    Fuel filter
3    Fuel flow transducer

4    Air cleaner air temperature
     control flap valve
5    Carburettor cold air intake

6    Carburettor cooling fan
7    Carburettor cooling fan
     control unit

8    Air temperature control
     switch

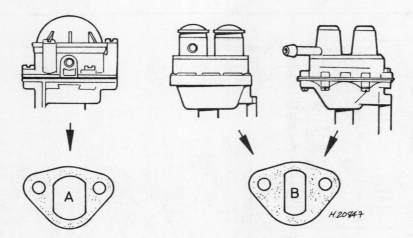

**Fig. 12.14 Fuel pump and spacer block fitted to 1.3 engine in Van models (Sec 7)**

*A   Early 700 Series*          *B   Later 800 Series*

### Carburettor cooling fan (MG 1600 models) – removal and refitting

25 A carburettor cooling fan is fitted to MG 1600 models equipped with the 'S' series engine to maintain the ambient temperature around the carburettors at a predetermined level. A brief description of its operation is given earlier in this Section; the removal and refitting procedures are as follows.

26 Disconnect the battery negative terminal then disconnect the cooling fan control unit wiring multi-plug.

27 Disconnect the cold air duct at the cooling fan and move it aside.

28 Undo and remove the nuts and bolts securing the cooling fan and mounting bracket to the inner wing valance. Support the unit then disconnect the leads from the fan motor and the multi-plug from the mounting bracket.

29 Disconnect the air intake hose and remove the assembly from the car. The mounting bracket can be removed if necessary by undoing the four retaining bolts.

30 Refitting is the reverse sequence to removal. **Note:** The cooling fan operates independently of the ignition switch and, if the temperature around the carburettors is above 30°C (85°F), the fan will operate as soon as the battery is reconnected. If this is the case the fan will run for approximately 10 minutes, then automatically switch off. If the ambient temperature is below the specified figure, test the unit by switching the ignition on, then off again. This will initiate the 10 minute running cycle.

### Fuel pump and spacer – Van with 1.3 engine

31 Two types of fuel pump have been used on this engine and the spacer block for each type differs. The correct spacer type must be used with the pump for which it was designed. An original spacer can be re-used with a pump of the correct type, but ensure that the mating faces are clean and locate a new gasket each side of the spacer. Refer to Fig. 12.14 for identification of the pump/spacer types.

### Fuel pump (MG 1600 models) – removal and refitting

32 MG 1600 models equipped with the 'S' series engine utilize a five vane impeller type electric fuel pump mounted under the car on the left-hand side of the body crossmember adjacent to the fuel tank. The pump only operates when the starter motor circuit is energized or when there is engine oil pressure.

33 Before removing the pump, position the car in a well ventilated area and observe the precautions listed in 'Safety First' at the beginning of this Manual.

34 Disconnect the battery negative terminal then jack up the rear of the car and support it on stands.

35 Disconnect the electrical lead at the pump terminal.

36 Clamp the fuel inlet hose from the tank to the pump using a brake hose clamp or other suitable tool. Disconnect the fuel inlet and outlet hoses at the pump and plug their ends after removal.

37 Remove the fuel pump and mounting bracket from under the car then remove the pump from the bracket.

38 Refitting is the reverse sequence to removal.

### Vapour separator (MG 1600 models) – general description, removal and refitting

39 MG 1600 models equipped with the 'S' series engine are fitted with a fuel vapour separator in the fuel inlet circuit between the fuel pump and the fuel filter. The unit is mounted on the engine compartment bulkhead and consists of a canister, gauze filter and a ball valve. The gauze filter allows free passage of fuel but restricts the passage of vapour which is returned to the fuel tank through the ball valve and down a separate return pipe. The ball valve opens and closes as necessary according to the amount of vapour present which will vary according to temperature. When no vapour is present a permanent bleed off allows a small quantity of fuel to be returned to the tank.

40 The unit is maintenance-free and no servicing is necessary.

41 To remove the vapour separator, disconnect the battery negative terminal then disconnect the fuel pipes at the vapour separator connectors. Plug the pipes after removal.

42 Undo the retaining bolts or nuts and remove the unit from the car.

43 Refitting is the reverse sequence to removal.

### Fuel filter – removal and refitting

44 All Maestro models equipped with solid-state instruments are fitted with an in-line fuel filter in the fuel inlet line just before the fuel flow transducer. The purpose of the filter is to prevent any minute foreign particles which may be present in the fuel from damaging the fuel flow transducer (which controls the operation of the trip computer – see Chapter 3) and to ensure accurate performance of the fuel flow transducer.

45 The in-line filter must be renewed at the intervals given in 'Routine Maintenance' at the beginning of this Manual.

46 Removal and refitting is straightforward and simply entails the disconnection of the two hoses and the slackening of the clamp bolt. Slide out the old filter and fit a new one with the arrow stamped on the unit facing the direction of fuel flow, ie towards the fuel flow transducer. Reconnect the hoses and tighten the clamp.

47 An in-line filter can be fitted to earlier 'R' series engine models using parts available from Austin Rover dealers and conforming to the installation diagram shown in Fig. 12.15. When fitting a filter to these engines ensure that the unit is inclined upwards at approximately 15° with the highest end towards the fuel flow transducer.

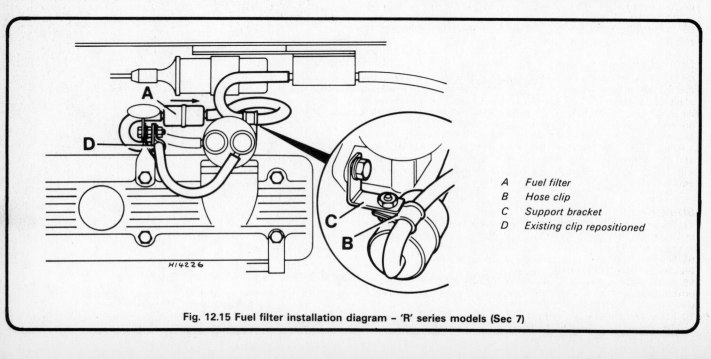

A    Fuel filter
B    Hose clip
C    Support bracket
D    Existing clip repositioned

**Fig. 12.15 Fuel filter installation diagram – 'R' series models (Sec 7)**

### Accelerator cable – removal and refitting

48 The procedure for removal and refitting of the accelerator cable on later models is basically the same as described in Chapter 3, but the end fitting at the carburettor has been altered on certain installations.
49 If the outer cable has two locknuts at the carburettor support bracket, proceed as follows.
50 Open the throttle linkage on the carburettor fully and slip the inner cable end out of the slot on the linkage lever.
51 Slacken the two locknuts securing the cable to the support bracket on the side of the carburettor. Unscrew the nut nearest the end of the cable fully, then slip the cable out of the slot on the bracket. The remainder of the procedure is now as described in Chapter 3.
52 Refitting is the reverse sequence to removal, but adjust the outer cable locknuts to provide a small amount of cable free play with the throttle closed.
53 On models equipped with automatic transmission, check the kickdown cable adjustment, as described in Section 11 of this Supplement.

### Choke control cable – removal and refitting

#### 500 and 700 van models
54 Disconnect the battery negative terminal and remove the air cleaner assembly, as described in Chapter 3.
55 Slacken the small screw securing the choke inner cable to the cable connector on the carburettor linkage.
56 Release the clip securing the outer cable to the support bracket and withdraw the cable from the carburettor. Recover the cable connector and store it safely as it is easily lost.
57 From inside the car, undo the retaining screws and lift off the two halves of the steering column cowls.
58 Undo the nut securing the choke cable to the cowl and pull the cable through the bulkhead grommet and into the car. Pull the cable through the cowl and remove it from the car.
59 Refitting is the reverse sequence to removal. Ensure that a small amount of free play exists at the carburettor end of the cable when the choke knob is pushed fully in.

#### MG 1600 models
60 The procedure for removal and refitting the choke cable on MG 1600 models equipped with the 'S' series engine is the same as described in Chapter 3, Section 9.

#### Cars (from 1986 on)
61 Slacken the trunnion screw and remove the outer cable clip, disconnect the cable from the carburettor.
62 Release the speedometer cable from the engine compartment rear bulkhead and feed the cable through the grommet.
63 Remove the cover from the fusebox and disconnect the lead from the mixture control warning lamp.
64 Remove the clip which holds the choke cable to the facia and withdraw the cable.
65 Refitting is a reversal of removal but ensure that the inner cable has a slight slackness when the choke is fully off.

### SU carburettor – general

66 Certain refinements have been carried out to the SU carburettor and associated components of the electronic mixture control system to improve the sensitivity and operational efficiency of the system under all operating conditions. These changes do not affect the procedures covered in Chapter 3, unless otherwise stated in the following sub-section. The layout of the components in the system fitted to all 1.6 litre models equipped with the 'S' series engine (except MG1600) and all 1.3 litre models (except those with manual choke) is shown in Fig. 12.16. Models fitted with a manually operated choke are not equipped with the electronic mixture control system.

### SU carburettor – adjustments

67 The procedure which follows is a slightly amended version of that in Chapter 3, Section 12. Use it in conjunction with the Specifications at the beginning of this Chapter.
68 For manual choke models proceed to paragraph 85.

#### Electronic mixture control models
69 Remove the air cleaner as described in paragraphs 3 to 6 inclusive of this Section, then refer to Chapter 3 and proceed as described in paragraphs 2 to 9 inclusive of Section 12.
70 Reconnect the vacuum hoses to the air cleaner or plenum chamber and lay the unit alongside the carburettor.

71 Start the engine and run it at a fast idle speed until it reaches its normal operating temperature. Continue to run the engine for a further five minutes before commencing adjustment.
72 Increase the engine speed to 2500 rpm for 30 seconds and repeat this at three minute intervals during the adjustment procedure. This will ensure that any excess fuel is cleared from the inlet manifold.
73 Disconnect the coolant thermistor (temperature gauge sensor) multi-plug – see Chapter 2 if necessary – and join the two plug terminals together using a suitable length of wire. This will ensure that the mixture control stepping motor is not actuated during adjustment.
74 If the cooling fan is running, wait until it stops then turn the idle speed adjustment screw as necessary until the engine is idling at the specified speed.
75 Switch off the engine.
76 Check the clearance between the fast idle pushrod and fast idle adjustment screw using feeler gauges (position B in Fig. 3.7 – Chapter 3). Turn the fast idle adjustment screw as necessary to obtain the specified clearance.
77 Check the throttle lever lost motion gap using feeler gauges (position A in Fig. 3.7 – Chapter 3) and, if necessary, turn the throttle lever adjustment screw to obtain the specified clearance.
78 Start the engine and slowly turn the mixture adjustment screw clockwise (to enrich) or anti-clockwise (to weaken) until the fastest idling speed which is consistent with smooth even running is obtained. If a CO meter is being used, adjust the mixture screw to obtain the specified idling exhaust gas content.
79 Reset the idling speed, if necessary, using the idle speed adjustment screw, then switch off the engine once more.
80 Adjustment of the fast idle speed is a task best entrusted to an Austin Rover dealer, due to the complexities of the system which requires the use of specialised test equipment to carry out accurate adjustment. However, if care is taken, a basic adjustment can be made as follows.
81 Remove the bridging wire from the thermistor multi-plug terminals (paragraph 73). Read the part number on the ECU under the facia shelf on the driver's side. If the number is 73245, 73247, 73248 or 73254, proceed as follows. (Other numbers, proceed to paragraph 82.)

*(a) Remove the ambient air temperature sensor from behind the right-hand headlamp (photo). Join the sensor wires together with a male-to-male connector or a suitable piece of wire*
*(b) Bridge the thermistor multi-plug terminals with a resistor, value 1000Ω (ECU Nos 73245A and 73247A) or 600Ω (ECU Nos 73245B, 73247B, 73248A/B and 73254A/B)*

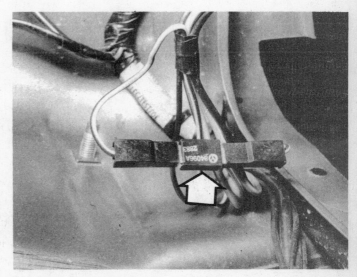

7.81 Ambient air temperature sensor location (arrowed) behind the right-hand headlamp

82 Start the engine again. The mixture control stepping motor should move the fast idle pushrod to the fast idle position. Compare the engine fast idle speed with the specified setting and if necessary adjust by turning the fast idle adjustment screw as required.

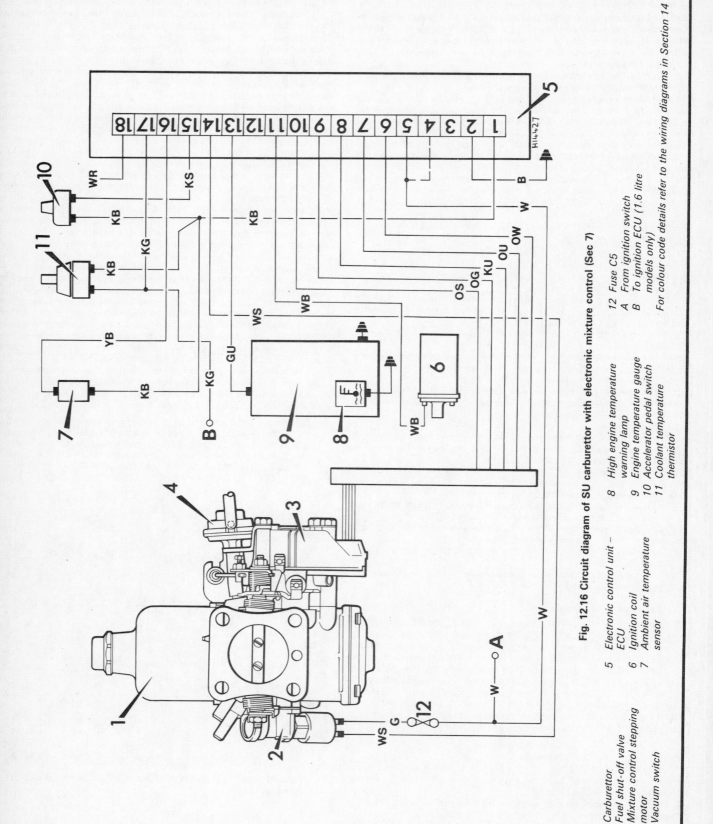

Fig. 12.16 Circuit diagram of SU carburettor with electronic mixture control (Sec 7)

1  Carburettor
2  Fuel shut-off valve
3  Mixture control stepping
   motor
4  Vacuum switch
5  Electronic control unit –
   ECU
6  Ignition coil
7  Ambient air temperature
   sensor
8  High engine temperature
   warning lamp
9  Engine temperature gauge
10 Accelerator pedal switch
11 Coolant temperature
   thermistor
12 Fuse C5
A  From ignition switch
B  To ignition ECU (1.6 litre
   models only)
For colour code details refer to the wiring diagrams in Section 14

83 Switch off the engine, reconnect the ambient air temperature sensor and coolant thermistor wiring plug. **Note:** after carrying out this adjustment, ensure that the specified minimum clearance still exists between pushrod and screw, as described in paragraph 76. Adjust the screw if the clearance is less than specified.

84 Make a final check that the idling speed and mixture are correct after refitting the air cleaner or plenum chamber then switch off the engine and disconnect the instruments.

**Manual choke models**

85 Refer to Chapter 3, Section 12 and carry out the operations described in paragraphs 1 to 9 inclusive.

86 Ensure that the choke control cable moves smoothly to the fully open and fully closed positions. Also make sure that there is a small amount of free play in the cable with the choke control pushed fully in and a small clearance between the fast idle adjusting screw and the cam.

87 Start the engine and run it at a fast idle until the cooling fan cuts in at least once. Continue to run the engine for a further five minutes before making any adjustments.

88 Open the throttle by hand to increase the engine speed to approximately 2500 rpm. Hold the throttle open for 30 seconds then allow the engine to idle once more. Repeat this operation at 3 minute intervals during the adjustment procedure to clear the inlet manifold of excess fuel.

89 If the idle speed and mixture adjustment screws have not been previously adjusted, they will still have the tamperproof seals in place over the screw heads. If so, hook these small metal sealing caps out of the adjustment screw recesses and discard them.

90 Turn the idle speed adjustment screw as necessary so that the engine is idling at the specified idling speed.

91 Slowly turn the mixture adjustment screw, a quarter of a turn at a time, clockwise to richen and anti-clockwise to weaken the mixture until the fastest possible engine speed is obtained. Now turn the screw anti-clockwise until the engine speed just commences to fall. If a CO meter is being used, adjust the mixture screw to obtain the specified idling exhaust content.

92 Readjust the idle speed screw to return the engine to the specified idling speed.

93 With the engine idling speed and mixture strength correctly set, pull out the choke control slightly until the arrow on the fast idle cam is aligned with the fast idle adjusting screw. Lock the choke control in this position.

94 Turn the fast idle adjusting screw until the specified fast idle speed is obtained. Release the choke control. Check that there is a clearance (A) (Fig. 12.17A).

95 It is now advisable to road test the car and carry out any minute adjustments to the mixture strength that may be necessary on the road. As a rough guide, if the engine tends to stall when coming down to idling speed the mixture is too weak, if the engine idles with a rhythmic unevenness or tends to roughen at high engine speed the mixture is too rich. Only make small corrections of the mixture screw, a quarter of a turn at a time, and test the car between each adjustment.

*SU carburettor – removal and refitting*

96 On later 1.3 litre and all 1.6 litre 'S' series engines the carburettor is secured to the inlet manifold with two nuts instead of four as used previously. This eliminates the accessibility problem at the lower right-hand nut and the need of a special spanner. Apart from this, and the revised accelerator cable attachment on certain models, as

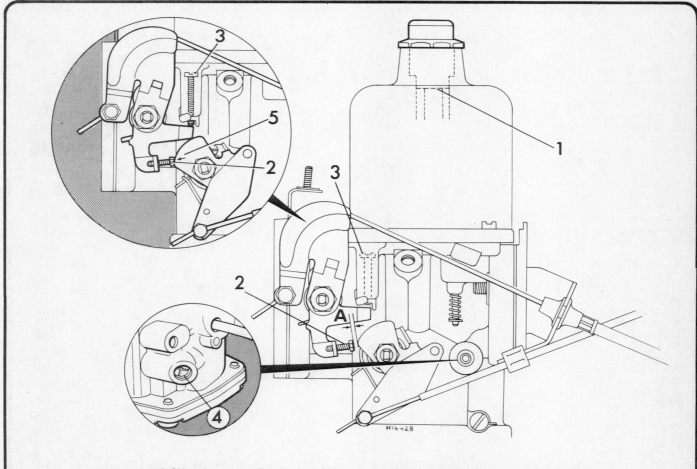

**Fig. 12.17A SU carburettor adjustment points – models with manually-operated choke (Sec 7)**

| | | |
|---|---|---|
| 1 Piston damper oil level | 3 Idle speed adjustment screw | 5 Cam position for fast idle |
| 2 Fast idle adjustment screw | 4 Mixture adjustment screw | adjustment |
| | | A Cam-to-screw clearance |

described earlier in this Supplement, the removal and refitting procedures are as given in Chapter 3. Note that where only two nuts are used to secure the carburettor, it is not necessary to remove the vacuum switch or the stepping motor and these units should not be disturbed.

97 On manual choke models the carburettors are not fitted with a vacuum switch, stepping motor or fuel shut-off valve and any reference to these components can be ignored. The choke cable and accelerator cable should be disconnected using the procedures described in Chapter 3 and earlier in this Supplement as applicable.

## SU carburettor – dismantling, overhaul and reassembly

98 Dismantling, overhaul and reassembly of the SU carburettor fitted to all models is the same as described in Chapter 3 with the exception of the stepping motor and vacuum switch. The stepping motor must **not** be removed as it is set during carburettor assembly and may not operate correctly if disturbed. If the stepping motor is faulty, renew the carburettor.

99 As mentioned earlier, the stepping motor, vacuum switch and fuel shut-off valve are not fitted to manual choke carburettors and any reference to these components may be ignored.

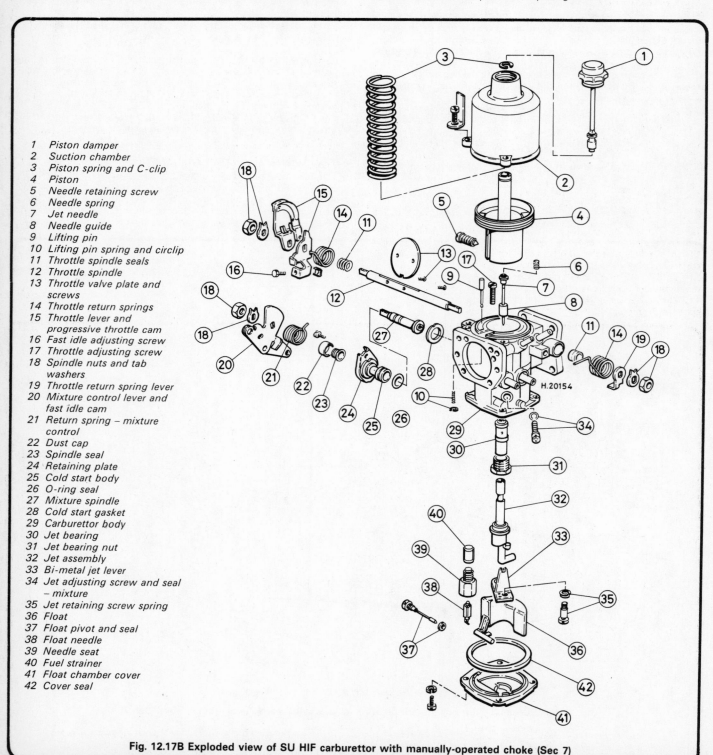

1  Piston damper
2  Suction chamber
3  Piston spring and C-clip
4  Piston
5  Needle retaining screw
6  Needle spring
7  Jet needle
8  Needle guide
9  Lifting pin
10  Lifting pin spring and circlip
11  Throttle spindle seals
12  Throttle spindle
13  Throttle valve plate and screws
14  Throttle return springs
15  Throttle lever and progressive throttle cam
16  Fast idle adjusting screw
17  Throttle adjusting screw
18  Spindle nuts and tab washers
19  Throttle return spring lever
20  Mixture control lever and fast idle cam
21  Return spring – mixture control
22  Dust cap
23  Spindle seal
24  Retaining plate
25  Cold start body
26  O-ring seal
27  Mixture spindle
28  Cold start gasket
29  Carburettor body
30  Jet bearing
31  Jet bearing nut
32  Jet assembly
33  Bi-metal jet lever
34  Jet adjusting screw and seal – mixture
35  Jet retaining screw spring
36  Float
37  Float pivot and seal
38  Float needle
39  Needle seat
40  Fuel strainer
41  Float chamber cover
42  Cover seal

Fig. 12.17B Exploded view of SU HIF carburettor with manually-operated choke (Sec 7)

## SU carburettor vacuum switch – removal and refitting

100 A faulty vacuum switch is indicated by a very rich mixture (black exhaust) high fuel consumption and inability to idle.

101 Disconnect the vacuum pipe and then prise the switch from its mounting bracket and connecting tubes. Remove the washer from the central nozzle.

102 If the switch is being renewed check the identification letter on the inner boss of the switch and pick a new switch as indicated in the following table:

| Mark on old switch | Mark on new switch |
| --- | --- |
| A | D |
| B | E |
| C | F |

103 Refitting is a reversal of removal; use a new washer at the central nozzle.

## Weber carburettor ('R' series models) – revised adjustment procedures

104 Make sure that the ignition timing, spark plugs and valve clearances are correctly set.

105 Operate the engine until it reaches normal working temperature.

106 Disconnect the cold and hot air intake ducts and release the air cleaner.

107 Disconnect the vacuum hose from the air intake temperature control and remove the air cleaner complete.

108 Remove the air intake throats, release the air cleaner baseplate and gasket and place them aside without disconnecting the vacuum hose from the thermostatic control unit.

109 Before starting to tune the carburettors, check the throttle lever interconnection and the air balance in the following way.

110 Make sure that the throttle valve plates open fully and that the operating cable has a slight slackness.

111 Check that the choke (cold start) levers are fully returned when the choke control is fully off.

112 With the engine idling, turn the idle speed screw until the engine speed is 900 rpm. A tachometer will be required.

113 Connect a vacuum gauge to the vacuum adaptor (20 – Fig. 3.14) on one carburettor barrel. Record the reading, reseal the vacuum adaptor and then repeat the check on the three remaining barrels.

114 If the vacuum readings are within ± 5.0 mm Hg then tuning may commence. If not, switch off the engine, unscrew the idle speed screw and the interconnection link screw until they are just clear of their levers.

115 Hold the right-hand carburettor throttles closed and turn the interconnection link screw until it just contacts its levers.

116 Turn the idle speed screw until it also just contacts its lever then give it one further complete turn.

117 If the carburettor has been fully dismantled and the mixture adjustment screws removed or tampered with, give them a basic setting, by screwing them in to lightly seat them and then unscrew them four complete turns each.

118 Start the engine and check the depression in each pair of carburettor barrels in the following way, using a vacuum gauge.

119 With the engine idling, connect the vacuum gauge to the vacuum adaptor of the inside barrel on one carburettor. Record the gauge reading, remove the gauge and seal the adaptor. Repeat the operations on the outside barrel.

120 If the vacuum readings are not identical, release the locknuts and lightly seat both air bypass screws (item 3, Fig. 3.13).

121 Unscrew the bypass screw on the barrel which indicated the higher vacuum reading by one half a turn. Now connect the vacuum gauge and turn the same bypass screw until the originally recorded lower vacuum reading (adjacent barrel, same carburettor) is obtained.

122 Tighten both locknuts. One bypass screw will of course still be lightly seated.

123 Repeat the vacuum balancing on the other carburettor.

124 Now check the vacuum readings between the adjacent barrels of the two carburettors. Obtain the same vacuum reading by adjusting the interconnection lever screw.

125 Turn the idle speed screw to set the idle speed to 900 rpm.

**Tuning**

126 Increase the engine speed to 2500 rpm for 30 seconds by holding the throttle open.

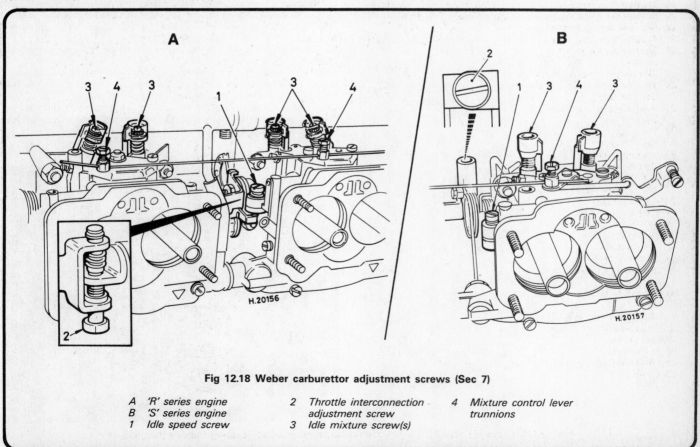

**Fig 12.18 Weber carburettor adjustment screws (Sec 7)**

| | | |
| --- | --- | --- |
| A 'R' series engine | 2 Throttle interconnection | 4 Mixture control lever |
| B 'S' series engine | adjustment screw | trunnions |
| 1 Idle speed screw | 3 Idle mixture screw(s) | |

127 If the following adjustment exceeds three minutes duration, repeat the clearing procedure before continuing.

128 The radiator cooling fan should not be running during this adjustment.

129 Turn one mixture adjustment screw clockwise until the engine speed just starts to fall, indicating a weakening of the mixture. Now turn the screw very slowly anti-clockwise until the highest idle speed is obtained.

130 Repeat these operations on each of the remaining idle screws. Reset the idle speed.

131 Ideally, the mixture should now be checked using an exhaust gas analyser (CO meter). To weaken the mixture, turn each mixture adjusting screw clockwise by an exactly similar amount. To enrich the mixture, turn the screws anti-clockwise.

132 On completion, refit the air cleaner and associated components and reconnect the air intake temperature control vacuum hose:

### Weber carburettor ('S' series models) – revised adjustment procedures

133 The mixture adjusting screws and the air bypass screws on these carburettors are normally fitted with tamperproof caps during production. The screws should not be disturbed unless essential following complete overhaul.

134 The balancing and tuning operations are very similar to those described for the 'R' series models in preceding paragraphs but do not disconnect the vacuum hose from the thermostatic switch in the air cleaner baseplate .

135 When attaching the vacuum gauge, first disconnect the hose which runs between the carburettor barrel adaptor and the five-way connector. Connect the gauge to the adaptor and then blank off the opening in the five-way connector.

### Weber carburettor ('S' series models) – removal and refitting

136 Disconnect the battery negative terminal then remove the air cleaner assembly, as described earlier in this Section.

137 Disconnect the electrical lead from the temperature switch and the vacuum pipe at the thermostatic switch.

138 Undo the retaining nuts and washers then lift off the air cleaner baseplate and carburettor intake throats.

139 Disconnect the accelerator cable, choke cable and choke cable link from their trunnions and support brackets.

140 Undo and remove the banjo union bolts securing the fuel pipes to each carburettor. Recover the copper washers from each side of the banjo union.

141 Detach the vacuum and breather hoses from the carburettor, noting their locations.

142 Undo and remove the nuts and washers securing each carburettor to the inlet manifold.

143 Lift the carburettors off the mounting studs and separate the throttle linkage. Withdraw the gaskets and the heat shield from the manifold.

144 Refitting is the reverse sequence to removal, bearing in mind the following points.

    (a) Use new gaskets between the carburettor and inlet manifold

    (b) With the carburettor fitted, unscrew the idle speed adjustment screw until it is clear of the lever. Hold the throttle of the left-hand carburettor closed and adjust the throttle interconnection screw to just contact the throttle lever. Now turn the idle speed adjustment screw clockwise half a turn.

    (c) Ensure that a small amount of free play, exists in the accelerator cable with the throttle closed

    (d) Connect the choke cable so that the choke levers on each carburettor move simultaneously and through the full range of their travel

    (e) After refitting the air cleaner, adjust the carburettors as described earlier in this Section.

### Inlet and exhaust manifolds (1.6 litre 'S' series models) – removal and refitting

145 Disconnect the battery negative terminal then remove the air cleaner and plenum chamber, and the carburettor, as described earlier in this Section.

146 Pull the vacuum hose off the banjo union connector in the centre of the inlet manifold. Undo and remove the banjo union bolt and recover the two washers. Place the servo vacuum hose to one side.

147 Disconnect the induction heater lead at the wiring connector (photo).

148 Disconnect the two wires at the induction temperature sensor (photo).

149 Remove the cooling system filler cap from the expansion tank. **Note:** If the engine is hot, unscrew the cap slowly to release the pressure and use a rag as a protection against scalding.

150 Place a suitable container beneath the inlet manifold and slacken the clips securing the three hoses to the manifold outlets. Ease off the hoses and allow the coolant to drain into the receptacle.

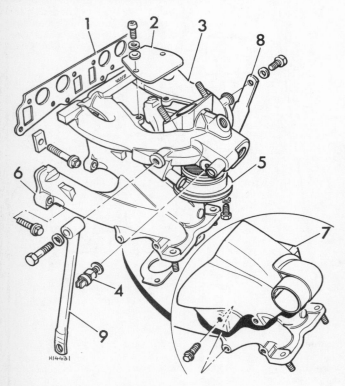

**Fig. 12.19 Inlet and exhaust manifolds – 1.6 litre 'S' series (Sec 7)**

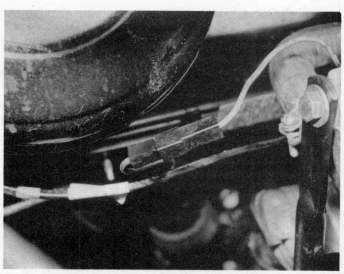

7.147 Manifold induction heater wiring connector

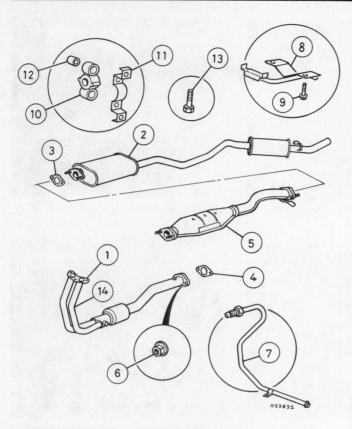

**Fig 12.20 Exhaust system – later 1.3 Saloon models equipped with a catalytic converter (Sec 7)**

1  Front section
2  Rear section
3  Gasket – catalytic converter to rear section
4  Gasket – catalytic converter to front section
5  Catalytic converter
6  Flange nut
7  Gas sampling pipe
8  Rear section mounting bracket
9  Bolt – mounting bracket to body
10  Mounting rubber
11  Mounting rubber retaining bracket
12  Spacer
13  Bolt – mounting bracket to body
14  CO measurement take-off point

151 Undo the bolts securing the left-hand and right-hand support struts to the manifold (photos).
152 Jack up the front of the car and securely support it on axle stands.
153 Undo the nuts securing the exhaust downpipes to the manifold and ease the flange off the manifold studs.
154 Undo the bolts securing the right-hand engine mounting to the cylinder head. Ease the engine away from the mounting sufficiently to allow removal of the manifold. Wedge the engine in this position.
155 Undo the two screws and remove the heat shield from the inlet manifold (photo).
156 Undo all the bolts, clamp plates and nuts securing the inlet manifold to the cylinder head and remove the manifold (photo). Recover the carburettor vent hose.
157 Undo the remaining nuts and bolts and remove the exhaust manifold (photo). Note that the two end bolts have plain washers.
158 Refitting the manifolds is the reverse sequence to removal. Use new gaskets and make sure all mating faces are clean. Tighten the manifold-to-cylinder head nuts and bolts evenly and to the specified torque before fully tightening the downpipe and steady bracket nuts and bolts. Refit the carburettor, air cleaner and plenum chamber, as described earlier in this Section, then top up the cooling system.

## Inlet and exhaust manifolds (MG 1600 models) – removal and refitting

159 Disconnect the battery negative terminal then remove the air cleaner and the carburettors, as described earlier in this Section.
160 Jack up the front of the car and securely support it on axle stands.
161 Undo the nuts securing the exhaust downpipes to the manifold and ease the flange off the manifold studs.
162 Lower the car to the ground.
163 Disconnect the brake servo vacuum hose at the manifold connection.
164 Slacken all the nuts and bolts securing the manifolds to the engine. Remove the nuts, bolts and clamp plates securing the inlet manifold and withdraw the manifold. Remove the remaining nuts and bolts and withdraw the exhaust manifold. Recover the gasket.
165 Refitting the manifolds is the reverse sequence to removal. Use a new gasket and make sure all mating faces are clean. Fit all the retaining nuts and bolts finger tight initially then progressively tighten, in a diagonal sequence, to the specified torque. Refit the carburettors and air cleaner, as described earlier in this Section.

## Unleaded petrol – general information and usage

166 Some engines in the Maestro range are suitable for use with 95 octane (RON) (minimum) unleaded fuel, whilst others can be adapted to suit by having the necessary 'Green Pack' modifications to the cylinder head. Note that later 1.3 models which are equipped with a catalytic converter must be run on unleaded fuel **only** to prevent irreparable damage being done to the catalytic converter (see below).
167 Serious damage will occur if unleaded fuel is used in an engine not adapted to suit. Engines which are suitable can be identified by the letter 'U' stamped between the engine number prefix and the number.
168 If in doubt on which type of fuel to use, consult an Austin Rover dealer for advice.

## Exhaust systems – general information

169 A number of different exhaust systems are fitted to models covered by this Supplement, but all are essentially the same apart from the number of silencers fitted and the shape of the intermediate pipe. The exception to this being the system fitted to later 1.3 models which are equipped with a catalytic converter (see below).
170 The procedures described in Chapter 3 for checking, removal and refitting are still applicable to later models, but note any differences during removal to use as a guide on refitting.

## Catalytic converter (later 1.3 models) – general information and precautions

171 On some later (from September 1990 onwards) 1.3 Saloon models, an un-regulated catalytic converter is incorporated in the exhaust system.
172 On these models the exhaust system consists of three sections: a front section, the catalytic converter and the rear section. The procedures described in Chapter 3 for checking, removal and refitting are largely still applicable, referring to Fig. 12.20 for further information. Note that on refitting all disturbed gaskets must be renewed and all flange joint nuts must be securely tightened.
173 When checking and adjusting the CO content on models equipped with a catalytic converter, as described earlier in the carburettor adjustment procedure, the CO meter must be connected to the take-off point on the exhaust front section left-hand downpipe and not placed in the end of the tailpipe. To do this, unscrew the threaded plug from the left-hand downpipe and screw in the gas sampling pipe adaptor into the threaded hole; the adaptor is available from any Austin Rover dealer. The CO meter should then be connected to the end of the sampling pipe. On completion of adjustment, unscrew the gas sampling pipe then refit the threaded plug ensuring that it is securely tightened.
174 The catalytic converter is a reliable and simple device which needs no maintenance in itself, but there are some facts of which an owner should be aware if the converter is to function properly for its full service life.

(a)  DO NOT use leaded petrol in a car equipped with a catalytic converter – the lead will coat the precious metals, reducing

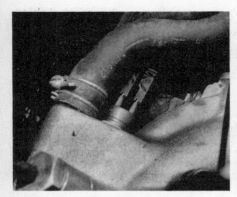

7.148 Wiring connectors at the induction temperature sensor

7.151A Inlet manifold left-hand support strut

7.151B Inlet manifold right-hand support strut

7.155 Manifold heat shield retaining screws (arrowed)

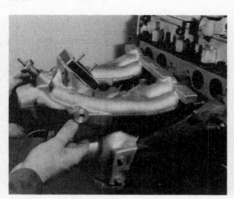

7.156 Removing the inlet manifold

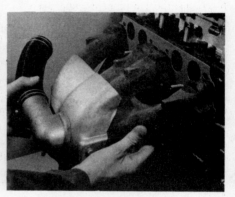

7.157 Removing the exhaust manifold

their converting efficiency and will eventually destroy the converter

(b)  Always keep the ignition and fuel systems well-maintained in accordance with the manufacturer's schedule – particularly, ensure that the air cleaner filter element, the fuel filter (where fitted) and the spark plugs are renewed at the correct interval – if the intake air/fuel mixture is allowed to become too rich due to neglect, the unburned surplus will enter and burn in the catalytic converter, overheating the element and eventually destroying the converter

(c)  If the engine develops a misfire, do not drive the car at all (or at least as little as possible) until the fault is cured – the misfire will allow unburned fuel to enter the converter, which will result in its overheating, as noted in (b) above

(d)  DO NOT push- or tow-start the car – this will soak the catalytic converter in unburned fuel, causing it to overheat when the engine does start – see (b) above

(e)  DO NOT switch off the ignition at high engine speeds – if the ignition is switched off at anything above idle speed, unburned fuel will enter the (very hot) catalytic converter, with the possible risk of its igniting on the element and damaging the converter

(f)  DO NOT use fuel or engine oil additives – these may contain substances harmful to the catalytic converter

(g)  DO NOT continue to use the car if the engine burns oil to the extent of leaving a visible trail of blue smoke – the unburned carbon deposits will clog the converter passages and reduce its efficiency; in severe cases the element will overheat

(h)  Remember that the catalytic converter operates at very high temperatures and the casing will become hot enough to ignite combustible materials which brush against it. DO NOT, therefore, park the car in dry undergrowth, over long grass or piles of dead leaves

(i)  Remember that the catalytic converter is FRAGILE – do not strike it with tools during servicing work, take great care when working on the exhaust system, ensure that the converter is well clear of any jacks or other lifting gear used to raise the

car and do not drive the car over rough ground, road humps, etc, in such a way as to 'ground' the exhaust system

(j)  In some cases, particularly when the car is new and/or is used for stop/start driving, a sulphurous smell (like that of rotten eggs) may be noticed from the exhaust. This is common to many catalytic converter-equipped cars and seems to be due to the small amount of sulphur found in some petrols reacting with hydrogen in the exhaust to produce hydrogen sulphide ($H_2S$) gas; while this gas is toxic, it is not produced in sufficient amounts to be a problem. Once the car has covered a few thousand miles the problem should disappear – in the meanwhile a change of driving style or of the brand of petrol used may effect a solution

(k)  The catalytic converter, used on a well-maintained and well-driven car, should last for between 50 000 and 100 000 miles – from this point on, careful checks should be made at all specified service intervals of the CO level to ensure that the converter is still operating efficiently – if the converter is no longer effective it must be renewed. With the catalytic converter removed from the car, you can check visually for internal damage by looking through the unit. If it appears to be blocked or broken, or has melted, the need for renewal is confirmed.

## 8  Ignition system

### General description

1    The ignition system fitted to later 1.3 litre Saloon and 1.3 litre 500 and 700 van models works on the same principle as earlier versions, but the ignition amplifier unit is integral with the distributor body rather than being mounted separately on the engine compartment bulkhead. A Lucas type 65 DM4 distributor is used and further details of this unit will be found in this Section. On later 1.3 models with a catalytic converter, a thermostatically-operated vacuum switch is incorporated into the vacuum line between the inlet manifold and the distributor vacuum unit; refer to paragraph 39 for further information.

2  1.6 litre models equipped with the 'S' series engine utilize a programmed electronic ignition system as part of their engine management system.

3  The programmed electronic ignition system operates on an advanced principle whereby the main functions of the distributor are replaced by an electronic control unit (ECU).

4  The mechanical operation of the contact breaker points in a conventional distributor is simulated electronically by the reluctor disc on the periphery of the clutch pressure plate and by the crankshaft sensor whose inductive head reads between the reluctor disc teeth. 34 teeth are used on the reluctor disc, spaced at 10° intervals with two spaces 180° apart which correspond to TDC for Nos 1 and 4 pistons and Nos 2 and 3 pistons respectively. As the crankshaft rotates, the reluctor disc teeth pass over the crankshaft sensor which transmits a pulse to the ECU every time a tooth passes over it. The ECU recognises the absence of a pulse every 180° and consequently establishes the TDC position. Each subsequent pulse then represents 10° of crankshaft rotation. This, and the time interval between pulses, allows the ECU to accurately determine engine position and speed.

5  A small bore pipe connecting the inlet manifold to a pressure transducer within the ECU, supplies the unit with information on engine load. From this constantly changing data the ECU selects a particular advance setting from a range of ignition characterisitics stored in its memory. This basic setting can be further advanced or retarded according to information sent to the ECU from the coolant temperature thermistor and knock sensor.

6  With the firing point established, the ECU triggers the ignition coil which delivers HT voltage to the spark plugs in the conventional manner. The cycle is then repeated many times a second for each cylinder in turn.

### Distributor (Lucas 65 DM4) – general

7  The Sections of Chapter 4 relating to the distributor and its associated functions are also applicable to the modular electronic ignition distributor fitted to later 1.3 litre models and the 1.3 litre 500 and 700 van models, except for the differences given in the following paragraphs and in the next sub-section.

8  When lubricating the distributor note that there is no anti-flash shield fitted, nor is there a felt pad in the centre of the cam spindle. Instead, with the distributor cap and rotor arm removed, apply two drops of engine oil to the spindle support bearing (photo).

9  When removing the distributor from the engine, as described in Chapter 4, Section 3, note that the distributor cap is retained by two screws, the ignition amplifier wiring harness plugs directly into the amplifier on the side of the distributor and a U-shaped clamp and single retaining bolt secure the unit to the engine (photos).

### Distributor (Lucas 65 DM4) – dismantling and reassembly

10  Remove the distributor from the engine, as described in Chapter 4, Section 3, and with reference to the previous paragraphs of this Section.

11  Lift off the rotor arm then undo the two screws and remove the ignition amplifier (photos). Do not dismantle the amplifier unit. If defective, it must be renewed.

12  Undo the two screws and separate the upper and lower halves of the distributor body (photos).

13  Lift off the grommet then release the plastic wiring connector from the side of the distributor body upper half (photo).

14  Invert the distributor body upper half and lift out the spacer ring, followed by the pick-up winding assembly (photos).

15  Undo the screw securing the vacuum unit to the body upper half (photo).

16  Using circlip pliers, extract the baseplate clip and withdraw the washer below the circlip (photos).

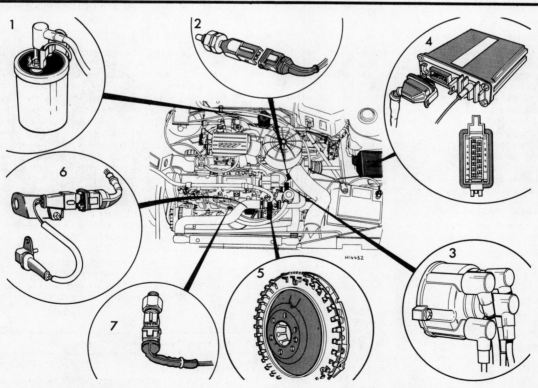

**Fig. 12.21 Programmed electronic ignition system component layout – 1.6 litre 'S' series (Sec 8)**

| | | |
|---|---|---|
| 1  Ignition coil | 4  Electronic control unit | 6  Crankshaft sensor |
| 2  Coolant thermistor | (ECU) | 7  Knock sensor |
| 3  Distributor cap | 5  Reluctor | |

17 Lift out the baseplate and remove the vacuum unit, noting how the peg on the vacuum unit arm engages with the slot on the baseplate. Recover the second washer located below the baseplate (photos).

18 The only component that can be renewed on the distributor body lower half is the driving dog at the base of the distributor spindle. If renewal is necessary, first mark or carefully note the relationship of the offset projections on the driving dog to the rotor arm slot on the other end of the distributor spindle. Ensure that the new driving dog is fitted in the same way. Tap out the retaining roll pin and draw the dog off the spindle (photo).

19 With the distributor dismantled, renew any parts that show signs of wear or damage and any that are known to be faulty. Pay close attention to the centrifugal advance mechanism (photo); checking for loose or broken springs, wear in the bob weight pivots and play in the spindle. If any of these components are worn a new distributor will be required as none of the parts on the distributor body lower half (except

the driving dog) are available separately.

20 Lightly lubricate the spindle and centrifugal advance mechanism with two or three drops of the engine oil then reassemble the distributor using the reverse of the dismantling sequence.

21 Before fitting the amplifier to the distributor body, smear the backplate with special heat conductive paste (obtainable from your dealer).

*Maintenance and inspection (1.6 litre 'S' series models)*

22 The only components of the system which require periodic maintenance are the distributor cap, HT leads and spark plugs. The HT leads and spark plugs should be treated in the same way as for earlier models, as described in Chapter 4, Section 8. Attend to the distributor cap and rotor arm, as described in the next sub-section.

23 On this system, dwell angle and ignition timing are a function of the electronic control unit and there is no provision for adjustment. It is

8.8 Oiling distributor shaft bearing

8.9A Disconnecting the ignition amplifier wiring plug

8.9B Distributor clamp plate and bolt

8.11A Removing rotor arm

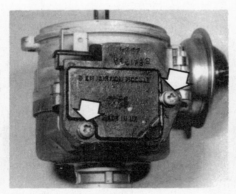

8.11B Ignition amplifier fixing screws (arrowed)

8.12A Removing a distributor body screw

8.12B Separating distributor body upper and lower sections

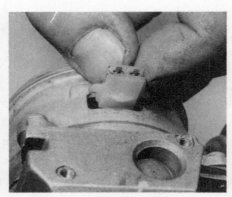

8.13 Extracting plastic wiring connector

8.14A Lifting out the spacer ring

possible to check the ignition advance using a stroboscopic timing light, but this should only be necessary as part of a fault finding procedure. Further details will be found later in this Section.

### Distributor cap and rotor arm (1.6 litre 'S' series models) – removal and refitting

24 Undo the two screws and lift the cap off the end of the camshaft carrier. Thoroughly clean the cap inside and out with a dry lint-free rag. Examine the four HT lead segments inside the cap. If the segments appear badly burned or pitted, renew the cap. Make sure that the carbon brush in the centre is free to move and stands proud of its holders. If renewal of the cap is necessary, mark the position of the HT leads then pull them off. Transfer the leads to a new cap, fitting them in the same position.

25 To remove the rotor arm, undo the retaining screw using a suitable Allen key and withdraw the rotor arm from the end of the camshaft. If necessary remove the rotor arm shield. In order to prevent seizure of the rotor arm fixing screw, always clean out the thread in the camshaft with an M6 tap before refitting the rotor.

26 Refitting the shield, rotor arm and distributor cap is the reverse sequence to removal.

### Crankshaft sensor (1.6 litre 'S' series models) – removal and refitting

27 Disconnect the battery negative terminal.

28 Disconnect the wiring multi-plug and undo the wiring plug screw. Undo the two bolts and withdraw the unit from the gearbox or automatic transmission adaptor plate.

29 To refit the sensor, ensure that the correct spacer is fitted to the sensor then position the unit on the adaptor plate and secure with two retaining bolts and one screw.

30 Reconnect the wiring multi-plug and the battery negative terminal.

8.14B Removing the pick-up winding assembly

8.15 Distributor vacuum unit retaining screw

8.16A Extracting baseplate retaining circlip

8.16B Withdrawing washer

8.17A Removing baseplate and vacuum unit

8.17B Removing baseplate lower washer

8.18 Distributor drive dog and roll pin (arrowed)

8.19 Centrifugal advance mechanism

## Knock sensor (1.6 litre 'S' series models) – removal and refitting

31 The knock sensor is located on the front facing side of the cylinder block in the centre. To remove the unit, disconnect the battery negative terminal and the wiring multi-plug then unscrew the sensor from its location.

32 Refitting is the reverse sequence to removal, but ensure that the sensor and cylinder block mating faces are clean.

## Electronic control unit (1.6 litre 'S' series models) – removal and refitting

33 Disconnect the battery negative terminal.

34 Release the catch and disconnect the wiring multi-plug from the front of the unit (photo).

35 Disconnect the ignition vacuum supply hose.

36 Undo the retaining screw, slip the unit out of the retaining tags and remove it from the engine compartment.

37 Refitting is the reverse sequence to removal.

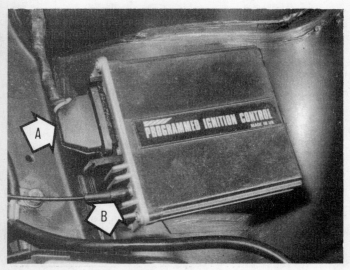

8.34 Ignition ECU multi plug (A) and vacuum connection (B)

## Spark plugs – modifications

38 All later models are fitted with copper core spark plugs. The later type plugs are fully interchangeable with the nickel core type plugs fitted to earlier models.

## Thermostatically-operated vacuum switch (later 1.3 models with catalytic converter) – general information, removal, testing and refitting

39 Later 1.3 models fitted with a catalytic converter have a thermostatically-operated vacuum switch screwed into the cylinder head water outlet elbow; the switch is connected into the vacuum hose linking the inlet manifold to the distributor vacuum unit. At coolant temperatures below approximately 70°C, the switch cuts off the vacuum supply to the diaphragm, and prevents the unit from advancing the ignition timing. This then causes the exhaust gas temperatures to rise, due to the retarded ignition timing, and brings the catalytic converter swiftly up to its operating temperature. Once coolant temperatures rise above approximately 70°C, the switch opens and allows the vacuum to reach the diaphragm unit, thus restoring normal advance and retard of the ignition timing. If when checking the ignition timing, it is noted that the advance mechanism is not functioning correctly, it could be that the vacuum switch is at fault.

40 To remove the switch, either drain the cooling system as described in Chapter 2, or be prepared for some loss of coolant as the switch is unscrewed. Disconnect and plug the switch vacuum pipes. Unscrew the switch, then remove it from the outlet elbow, and plug the opening to prevent the entry of dirt; if the cooling system has not been drained, work quickly to minimise coolant loss.

41 To test the switch, fit two suitable lengths of hose to the switch, and suspend the switch in a pan of water which is being heated. Measure the temperature of the water with a thermometer. Do not let either the switch or the thermometer touch the pan itself. Blow down one of the hoses which is attached to the switch; the switch should be closed (ie, passes no air) when the water temperature is below approximately 70°C. Above approximately 70°C, the switch should open and air should flow freely through the hoses. Allow the water to cool down, and check that the switch closes again around the 70°C mark. If the switch performance is significantly different from that specified, or if it does not work at all, it must be renewed.

42 On refitting, use a new sealing washer on the switch; screw it into position in the outlet elbow, working quickly if the cooling system has not been drained. Securely tighten the switch, and reconnect the vacuum hoses. Refill or top-up the cooling system as described in Chapter 2.

## Fault diagnosis – electronic ignition system with Lucas 65 DM4 modular distributor

**Engine fails to start or misfires when running**

| Test | Remedy |
| --- | --- |
| *Check battery voltage exceeds 11.7 volts | If not, charge battery |
| *With ignition switched on, check voltage at coil + terminal within 1 volt of battery voltage | If not, check wiring to coil +, battery earth and ignition switch |
| Check resistance between coil + and − terminals which should be between 0.4 and 0.9 ohms | If not, renew coil |
| Check resistance between coil + terminal and coil HT lead socket. The resistance should be between 5.0 and 15.0 kohms | If not, renew coil |
| Using a mains neon tester, connected to coil + and − terminals, crank the engine – the tester should flash | If not check amplifier harness plug |
| Check resistance of HT leads which should be less than 20 kohms | If not, renew leads |
| Check coil turret, distributor cap and rotor arm for tracking or other damage | Renew as necessary |
| Check condition of spark plugs | Renew if necessary |

*Applies only if engine will not start

| Test | Remedy |
|---|---|
| Check security of moulded harness plug to amplifier | Improve contact or renew plug |
| Remove amplifier from distributor and check that resistance of pick-up coil in distributor is between 950 and 1150 ohms | If not, renew pick-up coil |

## Fault diagnosis – programmed electronic ignition system (1.6 litre 'S' series models)

Problems associated with the programmed electronic ignition system can usually be grouped into one of the two areas; those caused by the more conventional HT side of the system such as spark plugs, HT leads, rotor arm and distributor cap, and those caused by the LT circuitry including the electronic control unit and its related components.

It is recommended that the checks described in Chapter 4, Section 9 under the headings 'Engine fails to start' or 'Engine misfires' should be carried out first, according to the symptoms. If the fault still exists the following step-by-step test procedure should be used. For these tests a good quality 0 to 12 voltmeter and an ohmmeter will be required.

**Engine fails to start**

| Test | Remedy |
|---|---|
| 1  Connect a voltmeter across pins 9 (+) and 12 (−) of the electronic control unit (ECU) wiring connector. Does the voltmeter indicate battery voltage 10 seconds after switching on the ignition? | Yes: Proceed to test 2<br>No: Check the wiring between the ignition switch and pin 9, and between pin 12 and earth. Rectify as required. |
| 2  Connect a voltmeter across pins 10 (+) and 12 (−) of the ECU wiring connector. Does the voltmeter indicate battery voltage 10 seconds after switching on the ignition? | Yes: Proceed to test 3<br>No: Check the wiring between the ignition switch and coil (+) terminal and between pin 10 and the coil (−) terminal. Rectify as required |
| 3  Connect an ohmmeter across the coil terminals. Is the coil primary winding resistance between 0.73 and 0.83 ohms? | Yes: Proceed to test 4<br>No: Renew the coil |
| 4  Connect a voltmeter between the battery (+) terminal and the coil (−) terminal. Does the reading on the voltmeter increase when the engine is cranking? | Yes: Engine should start. If not check ignition HT components, fuel system and engine internal components<br>No: Proceed to test 5 |
| 5  Switch ignition off and connect an ohmmeter across terminals 4 and 6 of the ECU. Does the ohmmeter register 1.5 kohms approximately? | Yes: Probable ECU fault<br>No: Check crankshaft sensor wiring and connections. If satisfactory, sensor is suspect |

**Engine misfires and performance is unsatisfactory**

| Test | Remedy |
|---|---|
| 1  Set engine at TDC with No 1 cylinder on compression. Highlight mark on crankshaft pulley with white chalk. Make a corresponding mark on timing belt cover. Connect a stroboscopic timing light, disconnect vacuum pipe at manifold and start engine. Does the pulley mark advance as engine speed is increased? | Yes: Proceed to test 2<br>No: Probable ECU fault |
| 2  With the engine operating as in test 1, apply suction to the end of the vacuum pipe. Does the pulley mark advance as vacuum is increased? | Yes: Ignition system is satisfactory, fault lies elsewhere<br>No: Check for leaks in vacuum pipe and connections. If satisfactory, ECU is faulty |

## 9  Clutch

### Clutch – modifications

1  From approximately July 1984 all Maestro models were equipped with a self-adjusting clutch; utilizing a ratchet and spring type self-adjusting mechanism incorporated in the clutch cable.
2  On 1.6 litre models equipped with the 'S' series engine the clutch pressure plate incorporates a reluctor disc on its periphery which is used in conjunction with the programmed electronic ignition system.
3  On models with 'A+' and 'S' series engines, the bolts used to secure the pressure plate to the crankshaft are of the encapsulated type and contain a thread locking and sealing compound. Once these bolts are disturbed they must be discarded and new encapsulated bolts obtained for reassembly.

4  It is important that the bolt threads in the crankshaft are cleaned before screwing in the new bolts. Use a tap to do this but, if one of the correct thread is not available, file three or four grooves at equidistant points down the length of an old bolt to serve as a thread clearing tap.
5  Removal and refitting procedures for the self-adjusting clutch cable and clutch assembly fitted to 'S' series engines are given in the following sub-sections. All other clutch operations are as described in Chapter 5 of this Manual.
6  Later 1.3 litre 'A+' series engine models are fitted with a modified clutch end cover which has the timing inspection hole blanked off. If replacing an earlier cover with the later type, it will be necessary to break out the aluminium blanking plug from the inspection hole prior to fitting. Transfer the blanking plate and screws from the old cover to the new.

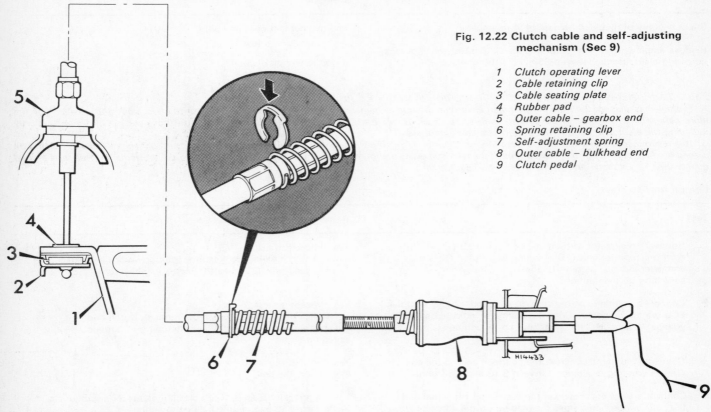

**Fig. 12.22 Clutch cable and self-adjusting mechanism (Sec 9)**

1  *Clutch operating lever*
2  *Cable retaining clip*
3  *Cable seating plate*
4  *Rubber pad*
5  *Outer cable – gearbox end*
6  *Spring retaining clip*
7  *Self-adjustment spring*
8  *Outer cable – bulkhead end*
9  *Clutch pedal*

### Clutch cable (self-adjusting) – removal and refitting

7  Working in the engine compartment, release the clutch cable from its retaining clips and cable ties.

8  Using pliers, withdraw the retaining clip from the cable at the end of the self-adjusting spring (photo).

9  Release the inner cable from the clutch operating lever by sliding out the retaining clip and cable seating plate located on the underside of the lever (photos).

10  Withdraw the inner cable end from the operating lever rubber pad, release the rubber retainer and withdraw the cable assembly from the gearbox bracket (photos).

11  From inside the car, unhook the cable end from the clutch pedal and withdraw the cable into the engine compartment. Remove the cable assembly from the car.

12  To refit the cable, feed the hooked end through the engine compartment bulkhead and connect it to the pedal. Ensure that the outer cable is located correctly in the bulkhead tube.

13  Route the cable through the engine compartment, locating it in its retaining clips and cable ties.

14  Feed the cable through the transmission bracket until the guide sleeve is seated squarely in the bracket.

15  Feed the inner cable through the rubber pad of the operating lever and slide on the cable seating plate and retaining clip.

16  Refit the retaining clip to the cable at the end of the self-adjusting spring. Press down on the clutch operating lever and at the same time pull up on the cable to operate the self-adjusting mechanism. Check that the clutch free play at the pedal is between 0.47 to 1.10 in (12 to 28 mm).

### Clutch assembly (1.6 litre 'S' series models) – removal and refitting

17  Refer to Chapter 6, or Section 10 of this Supplement, and remove the gearbox. Also remove the crankshaft sensor (Section 8).

18  In a diagonal sequence, half a turn at a time, slacken the six bolts securing the flywheel to the pressure plate. Use a screwdriver or stout bar engaged with the ring gear teeth and a suitable bolt to prevent the crankshaft turning (photos).

19  When all the bolts are slack, take them out and lift off the flywheel

9.8 Removing clutch cable clip

9.9A Clutch cable retaining clip

9.9B Clutch cable nipple seating plate

9.10A Clutch cable operating lever rubber pad

9.10B Disconnecting clutch cable from transmission

9.18A Flywheel-to-pressure plate retaining bolts (arrowed)

9.18B Starter ring gear locked against rotation

9.21 Clutch pressure plate locked against rotation

9.23A Locating clutch pressure plate

9.23B Fitting backplate

9.23C New clutch pressure plate fixing bolts

9.23D Tightening bolts to specified torque

and the clutch friction disc. It may be necessary to carefully ease the flywheel off using a screwdriver, due to the tight fit of the locating dowels.

20 Note the fitted position of the clutch release plate retaining ring as a guide to reassembly, and then prise the ring out using a screwdriver. Lift off the release plate.

21 It is not necessary to remove the pressure plate unless it is visibly worn or is to be renewed for other reasons. If the plate is to be removed, undo the retaining bolts in a diagonal sequence, lift off the locking plate and withdraw the pressure plate. To prevent the crankshaft turning as the bolts are undone, lock it using a screwdriver or stout bar located in one of the U-shaped cut-outs in the pressure plate and in contact with a bolt engaged in the starter top mounting bolt hole (photo). **Do not,** under any circumstances, lock the

crankshaft using the reluctor disc teeth on the pressure plate periphery. Note that after removal of the pressure plate retaining bolts, new bolts must be obtained before reassembly. The bolts are of the encapsulated type containing a thread locking and sealing compound the properties of which are impaired after removal. Clean out the bolt holes (paragraph 4).

22 With the clutch assembly removed from the engine, refer to Chapter 5, Section 6 and carry out a careful inspection of the components.

23 To refit the clutch, place the pressure plate and locking plate in position on the end of the crankshaft and secure with new encapsulated bolts, tightened to the specified torque (photos).

24 The remainder of the refitting procedure is as given in Chapter 5, Section 5, paragraphs 8 to 10.

## 10 Gearbox

### Gearbox modifications

1 Various modifications have been progressively introduced on both the 4- and 5-speed gearboxes fitted to later models. Apart from revised gear ratios the main changes which affect repair procedures are modifications to the driveshaft flange internal location, revised 5th gear selector fork retention and various alterations to the shift fork set and gear linkage. Additionally, due to the different engine mountings on the 'S' series engine, van and later 1.3 models, and the external attachment of various related components and services, the gearbox removal and refitting procedures are also revised.

2 Apart from the information in the following sub-sections, all other procedures remain unchanged and are as given in Chapter 6.

### Gearbox (later models) – removal and refitting

3 Disconnect the battery negative terminal.

4 Slide back the rubber cap and disconnect the two reversing lamp switch wires from the switch terminals.

5 Release the clutch cable adjustment by removing the retaining clip at the end of the cable self-adjusting spring.

6 Slide out the clip securing the clutch cable to the gearbox operating lever then withdraw the seating plate. Disengage the rubber retainer from the guide sleeve and pull the cable and guide sleeve out of the operating lever and gearbox bracket.

7 Undo and remove the bolt securing the speedometer cable or speed transducer cable to the gearbox casing. Carefully withdraw the cable and pinion assembly and place them aside.

8 Disconnect the battery earth cable and cable harness retaining clip from the top of the gearbox.

9 Extract the clip securing the gearchange rod to the selector shaft lever and slide the rod out of the lever bush. Prise off the rear selector rod nylon balljoint from the relay lever using a screwdriver and move the rod to one side.

10 Make a note of the wiring harness connections at the starter motor solenoids and disconnect them.

11 Undo the starter motor retaining bolts, withdraw the starter and, where fitted, the front snubber and its bracket.

12 On 1.3 and van models undo the bolts securing the engine front mounting to the chassis member.

13 Prise off the left-hand front wheel trim and slacken the wheel nuts. Jack up the car, support it securely on axle stands and remove the roadwheel.

14 Undo and remove the retaining screws and lift off the access panel from under the wheel arch.

15 From underneath the front of the car, mark the drive flange to inner constant velocity joint flange relationship using paint or a file.

16 Lift off the protective covers and then undo and remove the bolts securing the constant velocity joints to the drive flanges, using an Allen key. Tie the driveshafts out of the way using string or wire.

17 Using a suitable jack and interposed block of wood, support the engine and gearbox assembly under the engine sump.

18 Undo and remove the left-hand engine mounting through-bolt. On 1.6 models, undo the bolts securing the left-hand mounting to the gearbox and remove the mounting. Undo the nuts and bolts securing the rear engine mounting to the crossmember and gearbox and remove the mounting.

19 Position a second jack beneath the gearbox and remove all the bolts securing the gearbox to the engine adaptor plate. Make a note of the different lengths of bolts and their locations and also, on 1.6 litre models, the arrangement of nuts and washers at the inlet manifold support strut.

20 With all the bolts removed, make a final check that everything attached to the gearbox has been disconnected.

21 With the help of an assistant, lower the jacks until sufficient clearance exists to enable the gearbox to be drawn off the side of the engine. Keep the gearbox supported on the jack, as it is quite heavy, and, after releasing the gearbox from the adaptor plate dowels, lower the unit slowly and carefully to the ground.

22 Refitting the gearbox is the reverse sequence to removal, bearing in mind the following points.

  (a) Tighten all retaining and mounting bolts to the specified torque

  (b) Refill the gearbox with the specified lubricant to the level of the filler plug orifice

  (c) Align the marks on the drive flanges and inner constant velocity joints before refitting the retaining bolts. Tighten the bolts to the specified torque and fit new protective caps

  (d) Lubricate the selector linkage rod and gearchange rod with a lithium-based grease before refitting

  (e) On models equipped with a front snubber, slacken the snubber cup retaining bolts, position the cup centrally around the snubber then tighten the bolts

  (f) With the clutch cable connected, refit the spring retaining clip then press down on the operating lever and pull up on the outer cable to operate the self-adjusting mechanism

### Input shaft – modifications

23 If renewing the clutch pushrod bush in the input shaft, fit it to the depth shown in Fig. 12.23. This bush was originally manufactured in steel, but has been superseded by a bronze type.

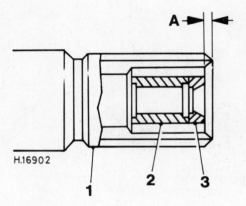

**Fig. 12.23 Clutch pushrod bush (2) and oil seal (3) positions in the input shaft (1) (Sec 10)**

*A = 0.039 in (1.0 mm)*

### Differential drive flange – modifications

24 When removing the differential drive flange, or coupling, as part of the procedure described in Chapter 6, Section 5, note that on later models there is a spring, spring collar and a thrust ring located behind the flange. These components can be withdrawn after removal of the flange. When refitting, ensure that the tapered face of the thrust ring and the plain side of the collar face toward the differential. This modification will be found on both four- and five-speed gearboxes.

### Selector shift fork set – modifications

25 On certain four-speed gearboxes a modified selector shift fork set is fitted which is virtually identical to the assembly used on the five-speed version and shown in Fig. 6.14 of Chapter 6.

26 When removing the modified assembly note that there are no circlips fitted to the selector shaft which is allowed to 'float' within the selector forks. If one of the springs at the end of the shaft remains in the gearbox when the shaft is removed, remember to retrieve it later after the gearbox is completely dismantled.

### 5th gear selector fork and synchroniser assembly – removal and refitting

27 To improve selection of 5th gear, the method of securing the selector fork to the selector tube has been improved. The spacer bush has been deleted on later gearboxes and in its place is fitted a lockplate.

28 When separating the gearbox housings using the procedure described in Chapter 6, Section 15, carry out the operations described in paragraphs 1 to 9 inclusive. Now carefully prise the 5th gear selector fork lockplate upwards to release it from the selector tube.

29 The remainder of the removal procedure is as described in Chapter 6.

30 When refitting the synchroniser assembly, as described in Chapter

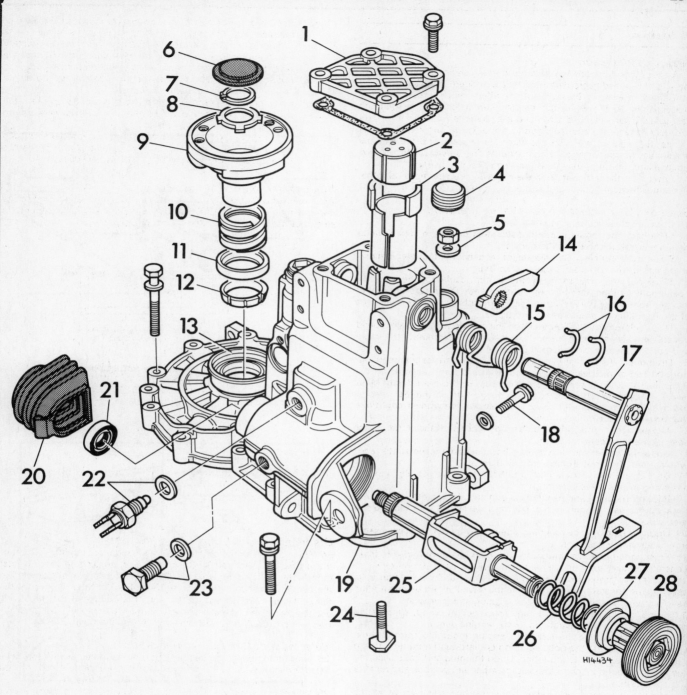

**Fig. 12.24 Exploded view of the transmission casing showing modified drive flange components – four-speed transmission (Sec 10)**

| | | | | | |
|---|---|---|---|---|---|
| 1 | Main casing end cover | 10 | Spring | 20 | Selector shaft seal |
| 2 | Clutch release bearing | 11 | Spring collar | 22 | Reverse lamp switch |
| 3 | Release bearing sleeve | 12 | Thrust cone | 23 | Selector shaft peg bolt |
| 4 | Rubber plug | 13 | Oil seal sleeve | 24 | Mainshaft bearing retaining |
| 5 | Bearing retaining nut and | 14 | Clutch lever | | clamp |
| | washer | 15 | Return spring | 25 | Selector shaft assembly |
| 6 | Plastic cap | 16 | Circlip | 26 | Spring |
| 7 | Circlip | 17 | Clutch operating shaft | 27 | Oil deflector |
| 8 | Spring washer | 18 | Reverse idler shaft bolt | 28 | End cap |
| 9 | Drive flange | 19 | Main casing | | |

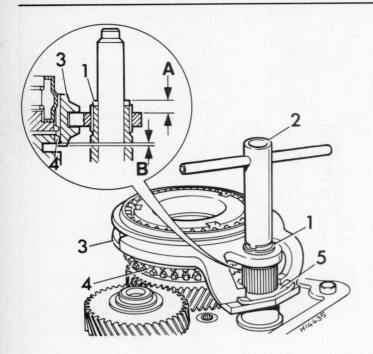

**Fig. 12.25 Modified 5th gear components and adjustment details (Sec 10)**

1  *Selector tube*
2  *Tool for turning selector tube*
3  *Synchro sleeve*
4  *Baulk ring*
5  *Lockplate*
A  *Selector tube protrusion = 0.197 in (5.0 mm)*
B  *Synchro sleeve overlap = 0.040 in (1.0 mm)*

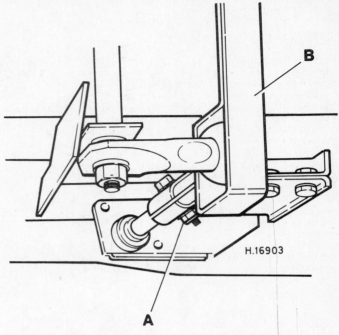

**Fig. 12.26 Gearchange linkage adjustment point (A) (Sec 10)**

B  *Selector rod lever*

6, Section 23, carry out the operations described in paragraphs 1 to 15 inclusive, but use a new selector fork lockplate during reassembly.
31 Using two pairs of pliers, one at each end of the lockplate and clamping the lockplate and selector fork bridge, secure the lockplate to the splines of the selector tube.
32 The remainder of the refitting procedure is as described in Chapter 6.

*Gear lever – adjustment*
33 If the gearchange linkage is reset at any time, the selector rod lever must be renewed. This is necessary since serrations on the rod will have cut identical serrations in the bore of the lever, interfering with accurate adjustment (Fig. 12.26).
34 To improve the accuracy of gear lever adjustment and to simplify the operation a special tool is now available for this purpose. If difficulties are experienced adjusting the gear lever using the procedure described in Chapter 6, Section 24, service tool 18G 1455 should be obtained and the following procedure adopted.
35 Jack up the front of the car and support it securely on axle stands.
36 From under the car remove the plastic cap from the gear lever rubber boot. Ensure that the gearbox is in neutral.
37 Slacken the clamp bolt securing the selector rod to the linkage and make sure that both the linkage and rod move freely.
38 Refer to Fig. 12.27 and fit tool 18G 1455 over the lip of the stop plate and with the gear linkage reverse stop engaged with the cutaway portion of the tool.
39 Pull the tool rearward so that the lug on the tool leading edge is in firm contact with the edge of the stop plate.
40 Insert an 0.028 in (0.7 mm) thick feeler gauge between the end of the reverse stop and the tool cutaway. Move the reverse stop until the feeler gauge is a tight sliding fit.
41 Have an assistant hold the selector shaft lever in the vertical position and tighten the selector rod clamp bolt.
42 Remove the feeler gauge and tool, refit the plastic cap to the rubber boot and lower the car to the ground.

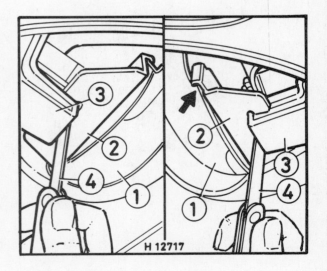

**Fig. 12.27 Gear lever adjustment (Sec 10)**

1  *Stop plate*
2  *Service tool 18G 1455*
3  *Reverse stop*
4  *Feeler gauges*

*Arrow shows lug on tool*

*Gear linkage – lubrication*
43 A special lubricant is now available for lubrication of the sliding surfaces of the gear linkage. The compound is Unipart Solid Lubricating Paste and should be applied to the sliding and contact surfaces of the linkage (with the exception of the nylon balljoints) whenever the linkage is dismantled, or if stiffness during gear selection is experienced.

## 11 Automatic transmission

### General description

A three-speed automatic transmission is fitted to Maestro Automatic models and offered as an option on certain other versions. The transmission consists of a torque converter, an epicyclic geartrain and hydraulically operated clutches and brakes (Fig. 12.28).

The torque converter provides a fluid coupling between engine and transmission which acts as an automatic clutch and also provides a degree of torque multiplication when accelerating.

The epicyclic geartrain provides each of the three forward or one reverse gear ratios according to which of its component parts are held stationary or allowed to turn. The components of the geartrain are held or released by brakes and clutches which are activated by hydraulic valves. An oil pump within the transmission provides the necessary hydraulic pressure to operate the brakes and clutches.

Drive control of the transmission is by a six position selector lever which allows fully automatic operation with a hold facility on the first and second gear ratios.

Due to the complexity of the automatic transmission any repair or overhaul work must be left to an Austin Rover dealer or automatic transmission specialist with necessary equipment for fault diagnosis and repair. The contents of the following sub-sections are therefore confined to supplying general information and any service information and instructions that can be used by the owner.

### Maintenance and inspection

1  Carry out the following maintenance operations with reference to the relevant paragraphs of this Section.
2  At the intervals specified in 'Routine Maintenance', carefully inspect the transmission joint faces and oil seals for any signs of damage, deterioration or oil leakage.
3  At the same service intervals check the transmission fluid level and the final drive gear oil level.
4  At less frequent intervals (see 'Routine Maintenance'), drain the transmission fluid, clean the oil strainer then refill with fresh fluid.
5  Carry out a thorough road test ensuring that all gear changes occur smoothly and, when under kickdown acceleration, at the speeds specified (paragraph 52). With the vehicle at rest, check the operation of the parking pawl when P is selected.

### Automatic transmission fluid – level checking

6  The automatic transmission fluid level should be checked when the engine is at normal operating temperature, preferably after a short journey.
7  With the car standing on level ground and with the engine running, apply the handbrake and slowly move the selector lever through all gear positions.
8  Return the selector lever to N and with the engine still idling, withdraw the dipstick from the filler tube and wipe it on paper or a lint-free cloth.
9  Reinsert the dipstick, withdraw it immediately and observe the fluid level. This should be between the upper and lower 'O' marks on the dipstick (Fig. 12.29).
10  If topping-up is necessary, switch off the engine and add the required quantity of the specified fluid through the dipstick tube. Use a funnel with a fine mesh screen to avoid spillage and to ensure that any foreign matter is trapped. Take care not to overfill the transmission; noting that the difference between the upper and lower 'O' marks on the dipstick is 0.75 pint (0.4 litre).
11  After topping-up, re-check the level again, as described above, refit the dipstick and switch off the engine.

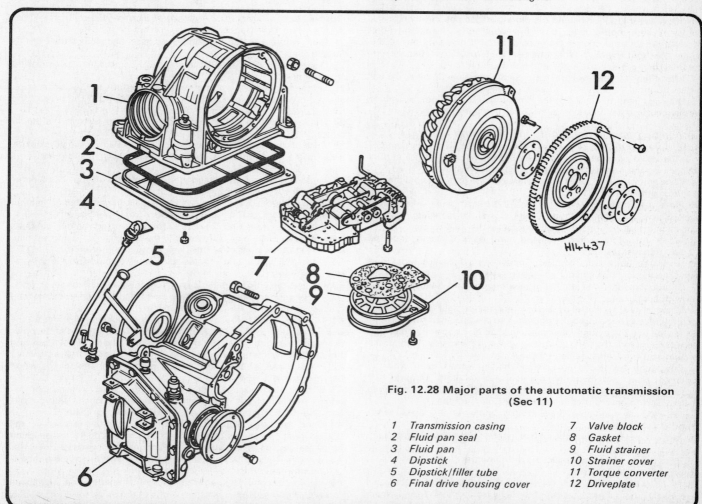

**Fig. 12.28 Major parts of the automatic transmission (Sec 11)**

| | | | |
|---|---|---|---|
| 1 | Transmission casing | 7 | Valve block |
| 2 | Fluid pan seal | 8 | Gasket |
| 3 | Fluid pan | 9 | Fluid strainer |
| 4 | Dipstick | 10 | Strainer cover |
| 5 | Dipstick/filler tube | 11 | Torque converter |
| 6 | Final drive housing cover | 12 | Driveplate |

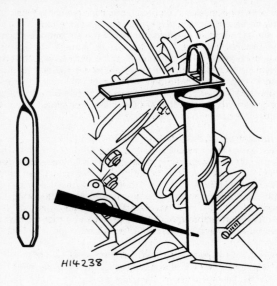

Fig. 12.29 Dipstick marking (Sec 11)

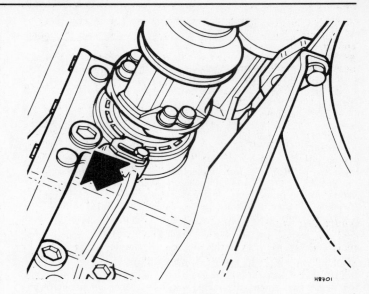

Fig. 12.30 Final drive oil level/filler plug (arrowed) (Sec 11)

*Final drive gear oil – level checking*

12 With the car raised to provide working clearance, but in a level position, wipe clean the area around the filler/level plug then unscrew the plug.

13 Allow any oil lodged behind the plug to trickle out and then check the level which should be up to the filler plug orifice. If topping-up is necessary, inject the correct grade of oil until it just runs out of the orifice then refit the plug. Note that gear oil is used for lubrication of the final drivegears – **not** automatic transmission fluid.

14 After checking the level and topping-up as required, lower the car to the ground.

15 Draining and refilling of the final drive oil is not a service requirement and no provision is made for this purpose.

*Automatic transmission fluid – draining and refilling*

**Note:** *To avoid the risk of scalding, only drain the fluid when cold or after the vehicle has been standing for some time.*

16 Jack up the front of the car and support it on stands.

17 Wipe around the oil pan-to-transmission case joint to avoid the risk of dirt or grit entry.

18 Place a suitable container beneath the transmission oil pan and slacken the oil pan retaining bolts. Carefully separate the oil pan-to-transmission joint if stuck, and allow the fluid to drain.

19 When most of the fluid has drained, remove the bolts and lift off the oil pan. Recover the seal.

20 Undo the bolts securing the oil strainer to the valve block and withdraw the strainer, strainer cover and gasket.

21 Thoroughly clean the strainer in paraffin, or a suitable solvent, and dry with compressed air.

22 Using a new gasket if necessary, refit the strainer assembly and secure with the retaining bolts tightened to the specified torque.

23 Ensure that the mating faces of the oil pan and transmission casing are clean and refit the pan, using a new seal if necessary. Tighten the retaining bolts to the specified torque.

24 Lower the car to the ground and fill the transmission with the specified type and quantity of transmission fluid through the dipstick/filler tube. Use a funnel with a fine mesh screen to avoid spillage and to ensure that any foreign matter is trapped.

25 With the car standing on level ground, apply the handbrake, select P and start the engine.

26 Move the selector lever through all gear positions, pausing at each position.

27 With the engine idling, select N, withdraw the dipstick and wipe it on paper or a lint-free cloth.

28 Reinsert the dipstick fully then withdraw it again and observe the fluid level. Top up if necessary until the level reaches the lower 'O' mark on the dipstick.

29 Run the engine until normal operating temperature is reached or, preferably, drive the car for a short journey. Carry out a final level check and top up, as described earlier in this Section.

*Automatic transmission – removal and refitting*

30 Disconnect the battery negative terminal.

31 Remove the air cleaner assembly, as described in Section 7 of this Supplement.

32 Disconnect the speedometer cable from its transmission attachment.

33 Undo the bolts securing the dipstick/filler tube to the transmission and remove the dipstick and tube. Note the O-ring at the base of the tube and also the cable clip on the upper retaining bolt.

34 Refer to Section 14 of this Supplement and remove the starter motor.

35 Prise off the left-hand front wheel trim and slacken the wheel nuts. Jack up the front of the car, support it on axle stands and remove the roadwheel.

36 Undo and remove the retaining screws and lift off the access panel from under the wheel arch.

37 From underneath the front of the car, mark the drive flange to inner constant velocity joint flange relationship using paint or a file.

38 Lift off the protective covers and then undo and remove the bolts securing the constant velocity joints to the drive flanges, using an Allen key. Tie the driveshaft out of the way using string or wire.

39 Undo the nut securing the selector cable trunnion to the selector lever. Slip the trunnion out of the lever.

40 Release the kickdown cable end from the transmission lever, undo the cable support bracket retaining bolts and place the cables and bracket to one side.

41 Turn the crankshaft as necessary using a socket or spanner on the pulley bolt until one of the torque converter retaining bolts becomes accessible through the starter motor aperture. Undo the bolt then turn the crankshaft and remove the remaining two bolts in the same way.

42 Place a jack beneath the engine sump with a block of wood between the jack head and sump.

43 Slacken, but do not remove, the upper front transmission-to-engine retaining bolt then remove all the other remaining bolts securing the transmission to the engine and adaptor plate.

44 Undo the bolts securing the left-hand mounting bracket to the body. Lower the engine slightly, undo the mounting-to-transmission bolts, remove the earth cable and the mounting assembly.

45 Remove the engine front snubber bracket and the rear mounting-to-crossmember assembly.

46 Place a second jack beneath the transmission with interposed block of wood and just take the weight of the unit.

47 Remove the remaining transmission-to-engine bolt then lower

both jacks until the transmission is clear of the body side-member.
48 Withdraw the transmission and torque converter from the engine and remove the assembly from the car.
49 Refitting the transmission is the reverse sequence to removal, bearing in mind the following points:

    (a) *Tighten all retaining and mounting bolts to the specified torque where applicable*

    (b) *Top up or refill the transmission and final drive with the specified lubricants, as described earlier in this Supplement*

    (c) *Align the marks on the drive flanges and inner constant velocity joints before refitting the retaining bolts. Tighten the bolts to the specified torque and fit new protective covers*

    (d) *Adjust the front snubber cup position so that it is central around the snubber rubber*

    (e) *Check and, if necessary, adjust the kick-down cable and selector cable, as described in the following sub-sections*

### Kickdown cable – adjustment

50 Fully depress the accelerator pedal and check that there is full movement at the carburettor linkage. If the kickdown cable is preventing full movement, slacken the locknut and back off the cable adjuster slightly (Fig. 12.31).

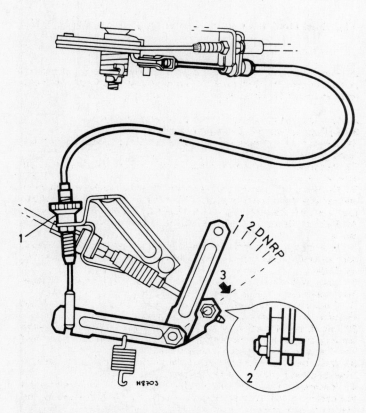

**Fig. 12.31 Kickdown cable and selector cable adjustment points (Sec 11)**

    *1 Kickdown cable adjuster and locknut*
    *2 Selector cable trunnion*
    *3 Selector lever position prior to tightening trunnion*

51 Drive the car until normal operating temperature is reached and then find a quiet, straight stretch of road.
52 Accelerate the car from rest with the selector lever in D and the accelerator pedal fully depressed in the kickdown position. Note the road speeds at which the 1st/2nd and 2nd/3rd gear changes occur; these should be:

| | |
|---|---|
| 1st to 2nd | 38 to 41 mph (61 to 66 km/h) |
| 2nd to 3rd | 67 to 69 mph (108 to 112 km/h) |

If the gearchange speeds are too low, decrease the cable tension. If the gearchange speeds are too high, increase the cable tension.
53 To adjust the cable tension, switch off the engine and slacken the kickdown cable locknut. Turn the cable adjuster to increase or decrease the cable tension as required, then screw the locknut back up to the bracket. Hold the locknut and tighten the adjuster by hand. Do not hold the adjuster and tighten the locknut.
54 Repeat the procedure described in paragraphs 52 and 53 making small adjustments each time until the gear changes occur at the specified speeds.

### Selector cable – adjustment

55 Move the selector lever to the P position.
56 Slacken the selector cable trunnion at the transmission selector lever then move the lever towards the left-hand roadwheel as far as it will go (Fig. 12.31).
57 Hold the lever in this position and tighten the trunnion.
58 Check that the trunnion pivots are without any free play, that the selector lever moves through all gear positions and that the starter only operates with the lever in the P or N positions.

### Selector cable – removal and refitting

59 Refer to Chapter 11 and remove the centre console.
60 Move the selector lever to the P position.
61 Extract the retaining spring clip and disconnect the cable end from the selector lever. Undo the outer cable locknut and release the cable from the selector lever housing.
62 Attach a drawstring to the disconnected cable end.
63 Working in the engine compartment, slacken the cable-to-transmission selector lever trunnion and the locknut securing the cable to the support bracket. Remove the cable from the trunnion and bracket.
64 Release the grommet from the engine compartment bulkhead, pull the cable through and into the engine compartment then untie the drawstring. Remove the cable from the car.
65 Attach the drawstring to the new cable and insert the cable into the bulkhead as far as possible.
66 Pull the carpet up from behind the left-hand side of the heater ducts. Pull the drawstring and guide the cable below the heater ducts and through the selector lever housing. Remove the drawstring.
67 Lubricate both ends of the inner cable with multi-purpose grease and connect the cable using the reverse of the removal sequence.
68 Refit the centre console then adjust the cable, as described in the previous sub-section.

### Starter inhibitor/reversing lamp switch – removal and refitting

69 Refer to Chapter 11 and remove the centre console.
70 Place the selector lever in N then undo the retaining Allen screw and remove the selector lever handle.
71 Remove the selector panel and light screen. Withdraw the bulb holders and remove the guide plate.
72 Disconnect the switch wiring connectors, undo the two screws and lift out the switch.
73 Before refitting the switch, check the condition and operation of the switch contact on the selector lever and renew the contact if worn. Also check that the selector cable trunnion on the transmission selector lever pivots freely but without free play. Free play in the trunnion or selector cable will affect the operation of the starter inhibitor/reversing lamp switch. If free play is evident, renew the nylon bush in the selector lever trunnion.
74 Fit the switch and secure with the two screws, finger tight only at this stage.
75 With the selector lever at N align the mark on the upper face of the switch with the mark on the contact bracket, then tighten the retaining screws.
76 Connect the wiring, refit the selector handle and check that the starter only operates in P or N and the reversing lamps operate in R. Realign the switch if necessary.
77 Remove the selector handle, refit the guide plate, bulb holders, light screen and selector panel.
78 Refit the selector handle, followed by the centre console.

### Selector lever assembly – removal and refitting

79 Refer to Chapter 11 and remove the centre console.
80 Place the selector lever in the P position.

81 Extract the spring clip securing the selector cable to the lever and disconnect the cable end. Undo the outer cable retaining locknut and withdraw the selector cable from the selector lever assembly.

82 Disconnect the electrical wiring at the starter inhibitor/reversing lamp switch.

83 Undo the retaining bolts and remove the selector lever assembly from the car.

84 Refitting is the reverse sequence to removal. Check the selector cable adjustment, as described earlier in this Section after refitting.

*Fault diagnosis – automatic transmission*

If a transmission fault is suspected, first check the fluid level, the kickdown cable adjustment and the selector cable adjustment as described earlier. If the fault persists, it will be necessary to determine

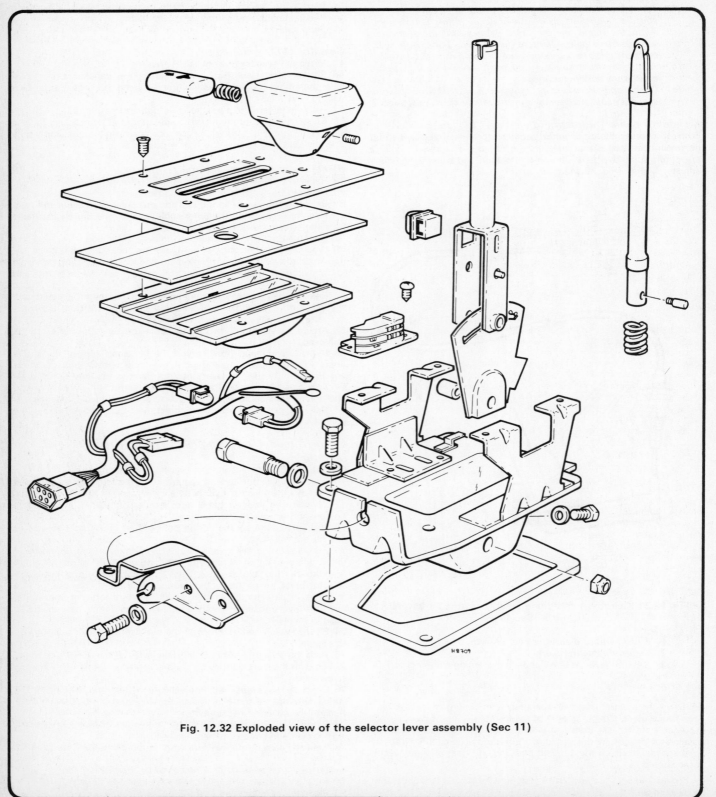

Fig. 12.32 Exploded view of the selector lever assembly (Sec 11)

whether it is of a mechanical or hydraulic nature and to do this the transmission must be in the car. Special test equipment is necessary for this purpose, together with a systematic test procedure, and the work should be entrusted to a suitably equipped Austin Rover dealer or automatic transmission specialist.

Do not remove the transmission from the car for repair or overhaul until professional fault diagnosis has been carried out.

## 12 Driveshafts

### *Driveshafts/front hubs – refitting*

1   The hub bearing repair kit may include three flat washers which have different thicknesses. When fitting the driveshaft/hub assembly, use the middle sized washer and tighten the nut to the specified torque setting. If the nut does not align with the split pin hole, use an alternative washer instead. Use the washer which allows the closest alignment of the split pin hole at the specified torque setting. Insert the split pin to secure. The alternative washers avoid the possibility of having to overtighten the driveshaft nut and consequently overloading the wheel bearings.

**Washer identification**
| | |
|---|---|
| Silver | 6.1 mm thick |
| Green | 6.2 mm thick |
| Dark grey | 6.3 mm thick |

2   On later models, a staking nut with integral washer is used in place of a castle nut, and the driveshaft has a longitudinal groove in the threaded end section (see Section 15 of this Chapter). In this instance, renew the old nut (a new nut is supplied in the repair kit). Tighten the nut to the specified torque, then stake the nut into the shaft groove to secure.

### *Driveshaft (automatic transmission models) – removal and refitting*

3   When removing the left-hand driveshaft on models equipped with automatic transmission, carry out the operations described in Chapter 7, Section 3, paragraphs 1 to 6, then proceed as follows.
4   Undo and remove the nuts and washers then withdraw the two bolts securing the suspension strut to the upper part of the swivel hub.
5   Separate the swivel hub from the strut, ease the inner constant velocity joint away from the differential drive flange and withdraw the outer constant velocity joint from the wheel hub. Remove the driveshaft from under the car and slide the bearing water shield off the outer joint.
6   The remainder of the procedure is as described in Chapter 7.

## 13 Braking system

### *Front brake pads and discs*

1   Later replacement front brake pad kits include new anti-squeal shims for the inboard and outboard brake pads in each caliper. The inboard and outboard shims are not interchangeable. Pad renewal is otherwise as described in Chapter 8.
2   The front brake disc on some models is secured to the hub drive flange by four bolts, rather than two screws (as described in Section 5 of Chapter 8). When inspecting the brake disc, irrespective of fixing method/type, check both the run-out and thickness of the disc. Check the disc thickness at eight points, 0.24 in (6 mm) in from the outer rim using a micrometer. The maximum variation in thickness must not exceed that specified. If necessary, renew the disc. **Do not** reface or grind the brake discs.
3   Check disc run-out using dial test indicator (clock gauge) and measure the run-out at a point 0.24 in (6 mm) in from the outer rim of the disc. If the run-out exceeds the specified maximum allowed, remove the disc and reposition it 180° from its previous position, then recheck its run-out. If the run-out is still excessive, the disc and/or the drive flange must be distorted and renewal is necessary.

### *Front brake disc (500 and 700 van models) – removal and refitting*

**Note**: This procedure applies to models with the two-piece hub bearing. When a one-piece bearing is fitted, remove the hub and disc as described in Section 15.

4   Securely apply the handbrake, chock the rear wheels and remove the wheel trim from the front roadwheel.

5   Extract the split pin then, using a socket and long bar, slacken, but do not remove, the driveshaft retaining nut.
6   Slacken the roadwheel nuts then jack up the front of the car and support it on axle stands. Remove the roadwheel followed by the driveshaft retaining nut and washer.
7   Undo and remove the two bolts securing the brake caliper carrier bracket to the swivel hub. Slide the caliper assembly off the disc and suspend it from a convenient place under the wheel arch using string or wire. Take care not to strain the brake hose.
8   Withdraw the hub and disc assembly from the swivel hub. If the two parts are to be separated, undo the four bolts and remove the hub from the disc.
9   Refitting is the reverse sequence to removal, bearing in mind the following points:

(a)   *Ensure that the mating faces of the hub and disc are perfectly clean before refitting*
(b)   *Tighten the driveshaft retaining nut to the specified torque, see paragraph 1, Section 12. The vehicle should be standing on its wheels for this operation. Always use a new split pin to retain the nut.*

### *Rear brake shoes (500 and 700 van models) – inspection and renewal*

**Note**: *Although lining wear can be checked by prising out the plug from the backplate, removal of the brake drum is recommended for a thorough inspection.*

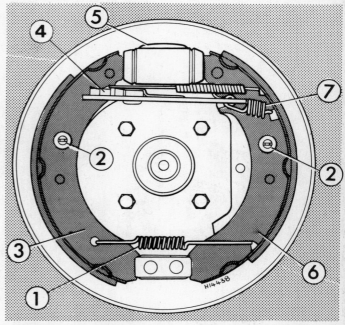

**Fig. 12.33 Left-hand rear brake assembly – 500 and 700 Van models (Sec 13)**

| | | | |
|---|---|---|---|
| 1 | *Lower return spring* | 4 | *Self-adjusting ratchet* |
| 2 | *Brake shoe hold-down* | 5 | *Wheel cylinder* |
| | *springs* | 6 | *Trailing brake shoe* |
| 3 | *Leading brake shoe* | 7 | *Small pull-off spring* |

10 Chock the front wheels, remove the rear wheel trim and slacken the rear wheel nuts. Jack up the rear of the car and support it securely on axle stands. Remove the roadwheel and release the handbrake.
11 By judicious tapping and levering remove the hub cap and extract the split pin from the hub retaining nut.
12 Using a large socket and bar, undo and remove the hub retaining nut and flat washer. *Note that the left-hand nut has a left-hand thread and the right-hand nut has a conventional right-hand thread.* **Take care not to tip the car from the axle stands.** If the hub nuts are particularly tight, temporarily refit the roadwheel and lower the car to

the ground. Slacken the nut in this more stable position and then raise and support the car before removing the nut.

13  Withdraw the hub and brake drum assembly from the stub axle.

14  With the brake drum assembly removed, brush and wipe the dust from the brake drum, brake shoes and backplate. Be careful not to inhale any brake dust.

15  Measure the brake shoe lining thickness. If it is worn down to the specified minimum amount renew all four rear brake shoes. The shoes must also be renewed if any are contaminated with brake fluid or grease, or show signs of cracking or glazing. If contamination is evident, the cause must be traced and cured before fitting new brake shoes.

16  If the brake shoes are in a satisfactory condition, proceed to paragraph 32; if removal is necessary, proceed as follows.

17  First make a careful note of the position of the various springs and linkages as an aid to refitting (photo).

18  Using pliers, depress the brake shoe hold-down spring caps while supporting the hold-down spring pin from the rear of the backplate with your fingers. Turn the caps through 90° and lift off then withdraw the spring, inner cap and pin (photos).

19  Pull the lower ends of the brake shoes outward against the pressure of the return springs and release them from their lower pivots (photo).

20  Ease the upper ends of the brake shoes out of their locations in the wheel cylinder pistons.

21  Holding the shoes together as an assembly, manipulate them as necessary so as to disengage the handbrake cable end from the handbrake operating link.

22  With the brake shoes removed, disengage the lower return spring from the leading and trailing shoe. Remove the upper return spring from both shoes followed by the small pull-off spring and the longer self-adjusting ratchet pull-off spring.

23  Remove the trailing shoes from the transfer link then disengage the

self-adjusting ratchet mechanism from the leading shoe.

24  Before fitting new brake shoes clean the brake backplate with a rag and apply a trace of silicone grease to the brake shoe contact areas (photo). Clean the self-adjusting mechanism and make sure that it is free to move.

25  Connect the small pull-down spring to the trailing shoe and transfer link and engage the link with the slots on the trailing shoe and handbrake operating link (photo).

26  Engage the self-adjusting mechanism on the transfer link with the leading brake shoe; then connect the self-adjusting ratchet pull-off spring (photos).

27  Connect the upper and lower return springs to the slots in the two brake shoes (photos).

28  Position the self-adjusting ratchet so that the mechanism is fully retracted (photo).

29  Holding the brake shoes together as an assembly, engage the handbrake cable end in the handbrake operating link. To do this push the spring on the cable back with pliers and hold it back while the cable end is engaged.

30  Engage the lower ends of the brake shoes in their pivots then locate the upper ends, one at a time in the wheel cylinder pistons.

31  Fit the hold-down spring pins, inner cap, spring and outer cap. Push the outer cap down against the spring and turn it through 90°.

32  Refit the brake drum and hub assembly, flat washer and hub retaining nut. Tighten the hub retaining nut to the specified torque and then tighten further until a split pin hole is aligned. Fit a new split pin and tap on the hub cap.

33  Depress the footbrake fully and listen for a clicking sound from the brake drum as the self-adjusting mechanism operates. Depress the footbrake two or three more times and check that the brake is locked when the pedal is held down, and free to turn when it is released.

34  Refit the roadwheel, lower the car to the ground and finally tighten the wheel nuts fully. Refit the wheel trim.

13.17  Right-hand rear brake assembly

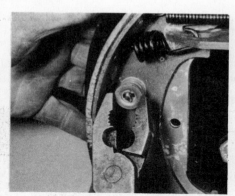
13.18A  Releasing a shoe hold-down spring cap

13.18B  Shoe hold-down spring

13.19  Releasing brake shoes from their lower pivot

13.24  Brake backplate grease application points (arrowed)

13.25  Shoe pull-off spring and transfer link

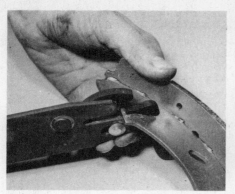

13.26A Fitting transfer self-adjusting link to shoe

13.26B Self-adjuster transfer link tension spring

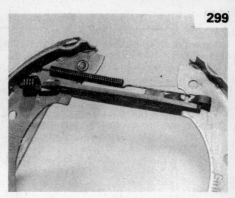

13.27A Shoe upper return spring

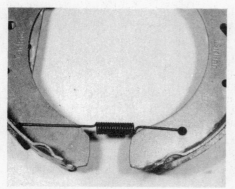

13.27B Shoe lower return spring

13.28 Self-adjuster ratchet set to fully retracted position

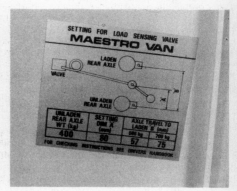

13.38 Load sensing valve decal

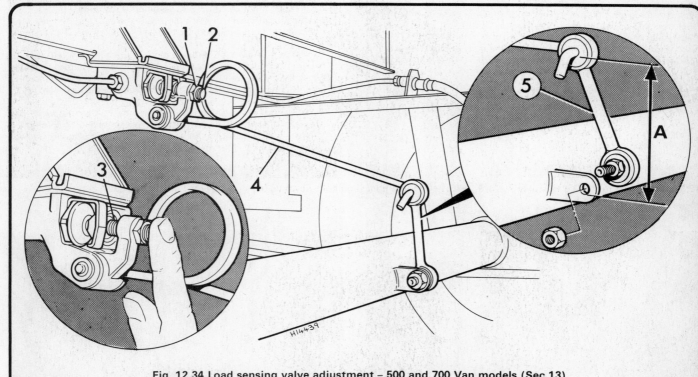

Fig. 12.34 Load sensing valve adjustment – 500 and 700 Van models (Sec 13)

1  Adjusting screw locknut
2  Adjusting screw
3  Valve bridge
4  Load sensing spring
5  Connecting arm and dimension 'A' measuring points

## Load sensing valve (500 and 700 van models) – description

35 Van models are equipped with a twin piston load sensing valve incorporated in the hydraulic circuit to the rear brakes. The purpose of the valve is to regulate the hydraulic fluid pressure to the rear brakes according to vehicle loading. The valve is located on the underbody at the rear and is connected to the rear axle by a load sensing spring. If the vehicle is fully laden the body will sit lower in relation to the rear axle which will cause the load sensing spring to act on the valve and regulate the pressure. In this case full hydraulic pressure will be available. When the van is empty and therefore light at the rear, the opposite will apply and very little pressure will be available thus reducing the risk of the rear brakes locking under heavy applications.
36 For the valve to work properly, adjustment is critical and should be checked if any new components are fitted to the rear suspension or if it is in any way dismantled. The adjustment should also be checked if rear brake performance is suspect or if the rear brakes continually lock under heavy applications.

**Warning:** *Under no circumstances must the vehicle ever be driven with the load sensing spring disconnected. In this condition the rear brakes are inoperative.*

## Load sensing valve (500 and 700 van models) – adjustment

37 Before checking or adjusting the valve the following conditions must apply:

(a) *The vehicle must be level and standing on its wheels. It will therefore be necessary to have it raised on a vehicle lift or driven over an inspection pit. Car ramps can be used but four will be needed to keep the valve level*

(b) *The vehicle must be in an unladen condition, but with a full tank and with the spare wheel stored in its carrier*

(c) *If the vehicle is fitted internally with special equipment which cannot be removed such as storage racks or bins etc, then it will be necessary to have the van weighed to establish the rear axle load before proceeding*

38 If the vehicle is unladen, open the bonnet and observe the loading label attached to the inside of the bonnet (photo). Note the Setting Dimension 'A' which is given on the label.
39 If it was necessary to first establish the rear axle load to satisfy the conditions given above, determine dimension 'A' from the following table.

| Rear axle load | | Dimension A |
|---|---|---|
| lb | kg | mm |
| 772 | 350 | 86 |
| 827 | 375 | 83 |
| 882 | 400 | 80 |
| 937 | 425 | 77 |

| Rear axle load | | Dimension A |
|---|---|---|
| lb | kg | mm |
| 992 | 450 | 75 |
| 1047 | 475 | 72 |
| 1102 | 500 | 69 |
| 1157 | 525 | 66 |
| 1212 | 550 | 64 |
| 1268 | 575 | 61 |
| 1323 | 600 | 58 |
| 1378 | 625 | 55 |
| 1433 | 650 | 53 |
| 1488 | 675 | 50 |
| 1543 | 700 | 47 |

40 Having now established dimension 'A', checking and, if necessary, adjustment can be carried out.
41 From under the rear of the vehicle, undo the nut and slip the connecting arm out of the bracket on the rear axle.
42 Without touching the load sensing spring, push the valve adjusting screw against the valve bridge with your finger and take a measurement from the underside of the end of the load sensing spring to the lower edge of the hole in the connecting arm bracket on the rear axle. This measurement is dimension 'A' and should be within 5 mm of the dimension given on the bonnet label or obtained from the axle loading table.
43 If this is not the case, slacken the valve adjusting screw locknut and turn the screw until the appropriate dimension is obtained. Tighten the locknut while holding the adjusting screw and then recheck that the setting is still within 2 mm of the specified dimension.
44 With adjustment complete, refit the connecting arm to the rear axle and return the vehicle to the ground.

## Load sensing valve (500 and 700 van models) – removal and refitting

45 Jack up the rear of the vehicle and support it on axle stands.
46 Open the bonnet, remove the brake master cylinder reservoir filler cap and place a piece of polythene over the filler neck. Secure the polythene in place ensuring that an air tight seal is obtained. This will minimise brake fluid loss during subsequent operations.
47 Working underneath at the rear, undo the nut and slip the load sensing valve connecting arm out of the bracket on the rear axle (photo).
48 Clean the area around the brake pipe unions and unscrew each of the four union nuts from the load sensing valve (photo). Carefully withdraw the pipes from the valve and seal their ends after removal.
49 Undo the two valve retaining bolts and remove the unit from under the vehicle.
50 Refitting is the reverse sequence to removal. After the valve has been refitted, bleed the hydraulic system, as described in Chapter 8. If a new load sensing valve is being fitted carry out the adjustment procedure described in the previous sub-section.

13.47 Load sensing valve link nut (arrowed)

13.48 Load sensing valve pipe unions (arrowed)

## *Handbrake cable (500 and 700 van models) – removal and refitting*

51 The handbrake cable assembly fitted to van models comprises a primary (front) cable, intermediate cable and two rear cables. Each cable is joined with a connector and all can be removed individually as follows.

### Primary front cable

52 Refer to Chapter 8, Section 17, and carry out the operations described in paragraphs 1 to 7 inclusive.

53 Separate the front cable from the intermediate cable by disconnecting it at the connector adjacent to the fuel tank under the car (photo).

54 Refitting is the reverse sequence to removal. Adjust the cable, as described in Chapter 8, Section 16, after fitting.

### Intermediate cable

55 Chock the front wheels, jack up the rear of the vehicle and support it securely on axle stands.

56 From under the rear of the vehicle, slacken the cable adjuster to remove all tension from the cable. Refer to Chapter 8, Section 16, if necessary.

57 Disconnect the intermediate cable from the front cable at the connector, release the cable adjuster from its bracket and pull the cable through the bracket (photo).

58 Disconnect the two rear cables from the intermediate cable assembly at the connector alongside the rear axle (photo).

59 Undo the bolt securing the cable support strap to the rear axle bracket, slide the compensator out of its guide and remove the cable from under the vehicle (photo).

60 Refitting is the reverse sequence to removal. Adjust the cable, as described in Chapter 8, Section 16, after fitting.

### Rear cables

61 Chock the front wheels, prise off the rear wheel trim and slacken the wheel nuts. Jack the van up and support it securely on axle stands. Remove the appropriate rear roadwheel.

62 Slacken the handbrake cable adjuster to remove all tension from the cable. Refer to Chapter 8, Section 16, if necessary.

63 Disconnect the rear cable at the connector alongside the rear axle.

64 Using a screwdriver, prise out the clip securing the rear cable to the support bracket on the axle (photo).

65 Remove the rear hub and brake drum assembly, as described earlier in this Section.

66 With the drum removed, ease the handbrake operating link on the trailing brake shoe forward and disengage the handbrake cable nipple from the elongated slot on the link.

67 Withdraw the cable from the brake backplate and remove the spring collar and felt seal.

68 Refitting is the reverse sequence to removal. Adjust the cable, as described in Chapter 8, Section 16, after fitting.

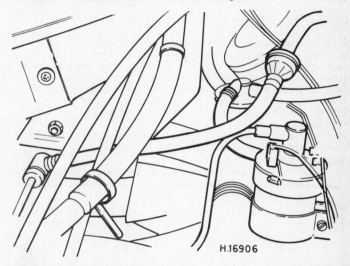

**Fig. 12.35 Brake vacuum hose correctly routed on MG 1600 models (Sec 13)**

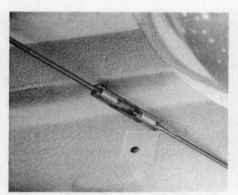

13.53 Handbrake primary-to-intermediate cable connector

13.57 Handbrake cable adjuster

13.58 Handbrake intermediate-to-rear cable connector

13.59 Handbrake cable compensator

13.64 Handbrake rear cable retaining clip (arrowed)

*Brake vacuum servo (MG 1600 'S' series models) – hose routing*

69 When refitting the brake servo unit or hose on this model, care must be taken to ensure that the hose is routed as shown (Fig. 12.35), running upwards and just clear of the hoses directly above it. This will avoid the possibility of damage or distortion to the hose due to heat from the exhaust manifold.

## 14 Electrical system

*Alternator drivebelt (1.6 litre 'S' series models) – adjustment*

1 The procedure is basically the same as described in Chapter 2, Section 13, except that the alternator is mounted the other way up, ie, the pivot mounting bolt is at the top and the adjusting arm bolt is below. The tension checking point is midway between the alternator and crankshaft pulleys. See Specifications for tension.

*Alternator brushes (later models) – removal, inspection and refitting*

2 Remove the alternator, as described in Chapter 9.
3 Disconnect the electrical lead and remove the suppression capacitor from the rear of the alternator.
4 Undo the retaining screws, lift off the regulator and brushbox assembly and disconnect the electrical lead.
5 Check the brush length and the brush spring tension against the figures given in the Specifications. New brushes are supplied as an assembly complete with brushbox and regulator.
6 Refitting is the reverse sequence to removal.

*Starter motor – Types 8M90 and 9M90 – removal and refitting*

7 Disconnect the battery negative terminal.
8 Disconnect the electrical leads at the solenoid terminals noting their respective locations.

**Manual gearbox models**

9 Using a suitable Allen key, undo and remove the two bolts, nuts and washers securing the starter to the gearbox flange and lift the unit off. Note that on 1.6 litre 'S' series models the starter motor bolts also retain the engine front snubber bracket and ignition system crankshaft sensor bracket.
10 Refitting the starter motor is the reverse sequence to removal, but tighten the retaining bolts to the specified torque.

**Automatic transmission models**

11 Jack up the front of the car and securely support it on axle stands.
12 From under the car undo and remove the three bolts securing the starter motor to the transmission and manipulate the motor out from under the car.
13 Refitting is the reverse sequence to removal, but tighten the retaining bolts to the specified torque.

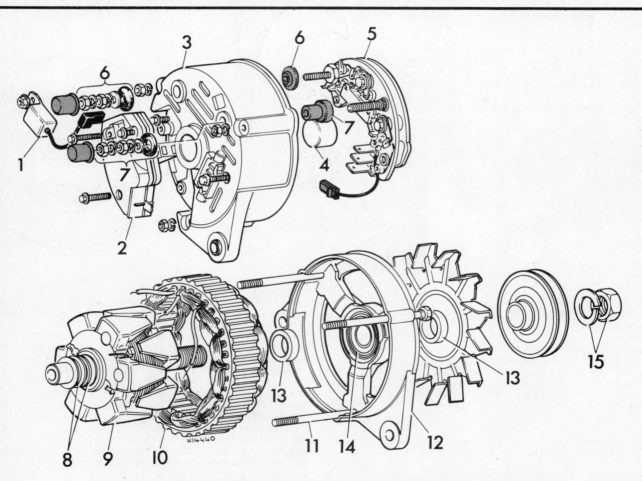

**Fig. 12.36 Exploded view of alternator fitted to later models (Sec 14)**

| | | |
|---|---|---|
| 1 Suppressor capacitor | 5 Rectifier | 8 Slip rings | 13 Spacers |
| 2 Regulator and brushbox assembly | 6 Phase terminal and washer assembly | 9 Rotor assembly | 14 Bearing |
| 3 Slip ring end bracket | 7 Main terminal and washer assembly | 10 Stator | 15 Pulley retaining nut and washer |
| 4 Bearing | | 11 Through-bolts | |
| | | 12 Drive end bracket | |

### Starter motor (automatic transmission models) – Type 9M90 – overhaul

14 Before removing the drive end housing, using the procedure described in Chapter 9, Section 11, slacken the locknut and unscrew the eccentric pivot pin from the side of the drive end housing.

15 When refitting the eccentric pivot pin screw it fully into the housing, unscrew it one full turn then align the mark with the arrow on the housing. Hold the pin in this position and tighten the locknut.

### Starter motor (from 1987) – description

16 Two different types of pre-engaged starter motors are fitted to later models depending upon whether manual or automatic transmission is fitted; see Specifications.

17 The starter motors, although of pre-engaged type, differ in detail from earlier versions, see Figs. 12.39 and 12.40.

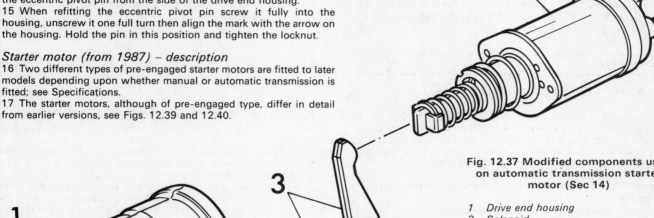

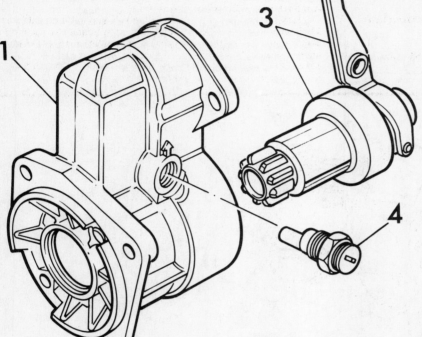

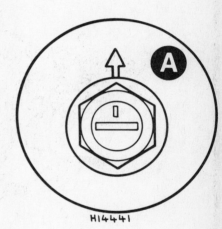

Fig. 12.37 Modified components used on automatic transmission starter motor (Sec 14)

1   Drive end housing
2   Solenoid
3   Drive end engaging lever assembly
4   Eccentric pivot pin
A   Eccentric pivot pin mark and housing arrow alignment

H14441

### Starter motor (from 1987) – removal and refitting

**1.6 models only**

18 Remove the air intake trunking and disconnect the intake air temperature sensor multi-plug.

19 Disconnect the breather hose from the diverter valve (if fitted).

20 Unbolt the air cleaner bracket from the transmission casing flange and move the air cleaner just enough to gain access to the outlet trunking. Unclip and release the trunking. Remove the air cleaner.

**All models**

21 Disconnect the battery and the leads from the starter solenoid terminals.

22 Unbolt and remove the starter motor from the engine.

23 Refitting is a reversal of removal.

### Starter motor (Lucas type M78R) – brush renewal

24 Disconnect the lead from the solenoid 'STA' terminal.

25 Remove the screws which secure the commutator end bracket and ease the bracket from the yoke.

26 Remove the grommet from the yoke and ease the brushbox from the commutator.

27 Detach the brush springs, unclip and remove the earth brushes, remove the insulation plate and withdraw the brushes complete with bus bar.

28 If the brushes have worn below the specified minimum length, renew them. Check that the brushes slide freely in their holders.

29 This should be regarded as the limit of overhaul. Worn bushes, a scored commutator or a damaged drive assembly should be rectified by replacing the starter motor complete with a new or factory reconditioned unit. This will be more economical than repairing the old one.

30 Clean the commutator with a fuel-moistened cloth. If the surface is badly stained or burned, polish it with very fine glasspaper.

31 Do not undercut the mica insulators between the copper segments.

32 Reassemble by placing the bus bar onto the brushbox, fit the brushes and the insulation plate.

33 Insert and fit the earth brushes and clips.

34 Place the assembly over the commutator and fit the brush springs.

35 Slide the armature and brushbox inside the field coils and fit the yoke grommet.

36 Fit the commutator end bracket to the yoke and reconnect the lead to the 'STA' terminal.

### Starter motor (Lucas type M79) – brush renewal

37 Disconnect the lead from the solenoid 'STA' terminal.

38 Remove the sealing cap and gasket from the commutator end bracket.

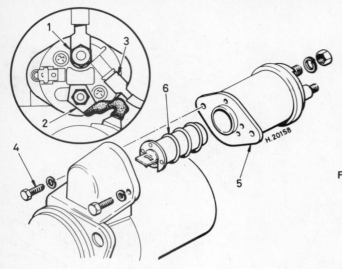

**Fig. 12.38 Starter solenoid (Sec 14)**

1  Battery terminal BAT
2  Starter terminal STA
3  Solenoid terminal 50
4  Retaining screws
5  Solenoid
6  Solenoid plunger

**Fig. 12.39 Exploded view of Lucas type M78R starter motor (Sec 14)**

1  Solenoid and plunger
2  Commutator end bracket
3  Brushes and insulator
4  Brush springs
5  Armature
6  Jump ring and thrust collar
7  Pivot and grommet
8  Shaft, bearing bracket and gears
9  Drive assembly
10  Bush
11  Bush
12  Bush
13  Drive end bracket
14  Tie-bolts
15  Intermediate bracket
16  Field coil yoke
17  Commutator end bracket
18  Drive end bracket
19  Oil seal
20  Bush
21  Drive assembly
A  Automatic transmission

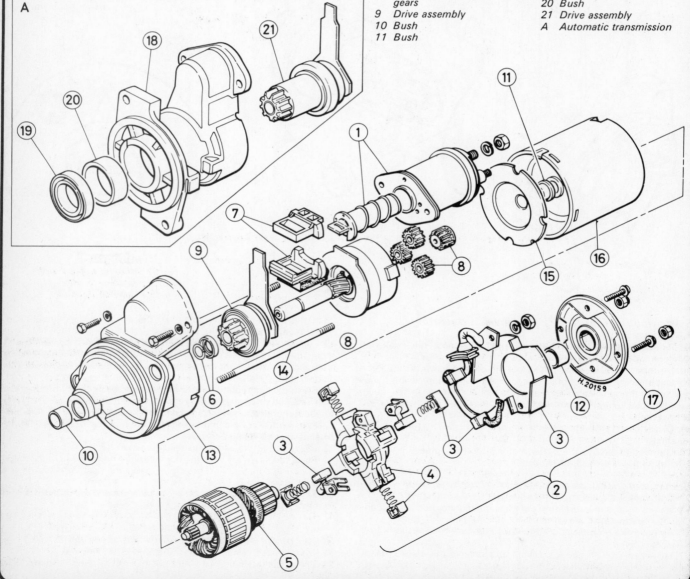

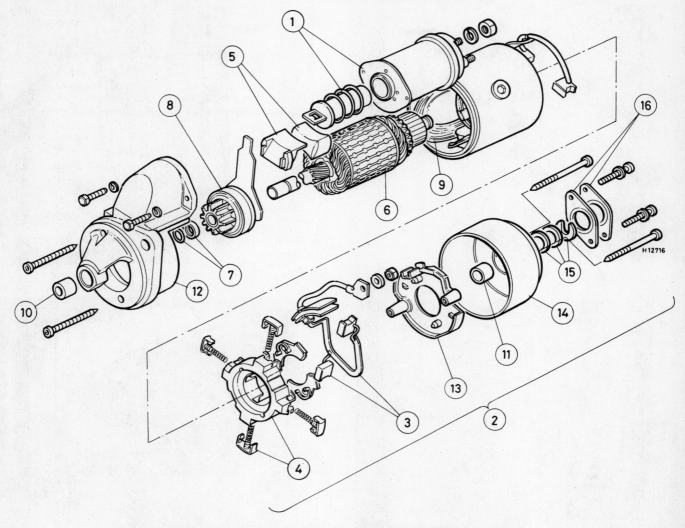

**Fig. 12.40 Exploded view of Lucas type M79 starter motor (Sec 14)**

| | | | |
|---|---|---|---|
| 1 | Solenoid and plunger | 5 | Pivot and grommet |
| 2 | Commutator end bracket | 6 | Armature |
| 3 | Brushes | 7 | Jump ring and thrust collar |
| 4 | Brush springs | 8 | Drive assembly |

| | | | |
|---|---|---|---|
| 9 | Field coils and yoke | 13 | Insulation plate |
| 10 | Bush | 14 | Commutator end bracket |
| 11 | Bush | 15 | Circlip and washers |
| 12 | Drive end bracket | 16 | End cap and gasket |

39 Extract the circlip and washers from the armature shaft.

40 Extract the fixing screws and withdraw the commutator end bracket from the yoke and brush grommet. Note the bracket to yoke alignment marks.

41 Remove the brush springs and withdraw the earth brushes.

42 Lift the brushbox from the commutator, remove the insulation plate and then withdraw the positive brushes complete with bus bar.

43 Check the brushes for wear, if they have worn below the specified minimum length, renew them. Check that the brushes slide freely in their holders.

44 This should be regarded as the limit of overhaul. Worn bushes, a scored commutator or a damaged drive assembly should be rectified by replacing the starter motor complete with a new or factory reconditioned unit. This will prove more economical than repairing the old one.

45 Clean and inspect the commutator (paragraphs 30 and 31).

46 Reassemble by reversing the dismantling operations.

### Fusible link – general

47 On later models certain electrical circuits are protected by fusible links which form the first part of the battery positive (+) cable. The links consist of fusible cable of different thicknesses and lengths according to the circuits they protect. The wire size and fusible link lengths are given in the Specifications.

48 If power to a number of related electrical circuits is lost, the relevant fusible link may be suspect. (As with an ordinary fuse, the link will have failed for a reason – probably a major short-circuit, which must be found and rectified before renewing the link.) The circuits protected by the fusible links are as follows.

*Link A Ignition circuit*
*Link B Window lift circuit*
*Link C Interior lights, lighter, clock circuit*

49 To renew a fusible link, disconnect the battery leads then remove the leads from the battery positive (+) terminal.

50 Carefully cut back the binding and pull the sleeve from the cables. Identify the link to be renewed by referring to the Specifications.

51 Remove the joint cover and unsolder the fusible link at both ends.

52 Solder a new fusible link into place and seal the joints with insulating tape. Retape the sleeve to the cables and reconnect the battery terminals.

14.53 Trim panel wing nuts (arrowed)

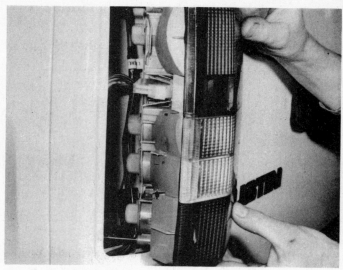

14.54 Withdrawing rear lamp cluster

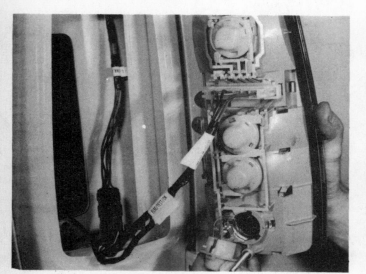

14.55 Rear lamp bulb holders

14.58 Rear number plate lamp bulb holder

*Rear lamp cluster bulbs (500 and 700 van models) – renewal*

53  Open the rear doors and release the trim panel by undoing the two plastic wing nuts (photo).

54  Lift off the trim panel from inside the van, then withdraw the lamp cluster assembly from outside (photo).

55  Release the bulb holders by pushing down and turning anticlock-wise; release the bulbs from the holders in the same way (photo).

56  Refitting is the reverse sequence to removal.

*Number plate lamp bulb (500 and 700 van models) – renewal*

57  Undo the two screws securing the number plate lamp assembly to the inner edge of the bumper.

58  Withdraw the lamp assembly and turn the bulb holder anticlock-wise to release it. Withdraw the bulb from the holder (photo).

59  Refitting is the reverse sequence to removal.

*Side repeater lamp bulb – renewal*

60  Press the lamp to the right and release the left-hand retainer. Withdraw the lamp from the body panel.

61  Turn the lamp holder anti-clockwise to release it from the lens.

62  Withdraw the bulb from the holder.

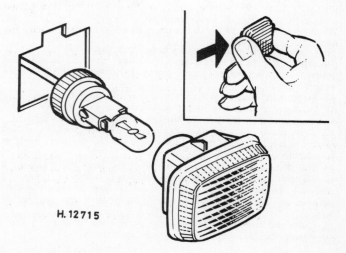

H. 12715

Fig. 12.41 Side repeater lamp removal (Sec 14)

**Fig. 12.42 Fusebox and relays – 1986 models (Sec 14)**

1   Ignition
2   Headlamps
3   Auxiliary ignition 2
4   Starter solenoid
5   Auxiliary ignition 1
6   Heated rear screen
7   Inlet manifold heater
8   Interior lamp
9   Windscreen wipers
10  Rear screen wiper
F   Flasher unit

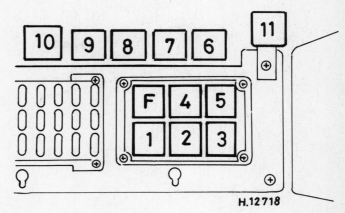

**Fig. 12.43 Fusebox and relays – models from 1987 (Sec 14)**

1   Ignition
2   Headlamps
3   Auxiliary ignition 2
4   Starter solenoid
5   Auxiliary ignition 1
6   Heated rear screen
7   Inlet manifold heater
8   Interior lamp
9   Windscreen wipers
10  Rear screen wiper
11  Dim-dip headlamps
F   Flasher unit

63  Fit the new bulb and refit the lamp by reversing the removal operations.

*Selector lever illumination bulbs (automatic transmission models) – renewal*
64  Remove the centre console sufficiently to gain access to the bulbs, using the procedure given in Chapter 11.
65  Pull the relevant bulb holder from the inside of the selector housing and remove the push-fit bulb.
66  Refitting is the reverse sequence to removal.

*Fusebox and relays (from 1986) – location*
67  The fusebox and main relay units are now located in the compartment beneath the steering column. The relays are numbered for identification as shown in Figs. 12.42 and 12.43.

*Horn*
68  From 1986, the horn is located under the left-hand front wing.

*Electrically-operated door mirror*
**Glass renewal**
69  Operate the mirror control switch until the top of the glass is tilted into the mirror casing as far as it will go.
70  Insert a forked tool at the bottom edge of the glass and ease the retainers out of engagement.
71  Now operate the control switch until the bottom of the glass moves into the casing.
72  Ease the top edge of the glass out of the retaining clips.
73  Disconnect the wiring and remove the glass.
74  When fitting the glass, centralise the motor housing by operating the control switch.
75  Connect the wiring and then align the pegs on the retaining ring and press the glass firmly to engage the retaining clips.
**Mirror – removal and refitting**
76  Remove the door interior trim panel as described in Chapter 11.
77  Peel away the waterproof sheet from the forward end of the door.
78  Release the mirror wiring harness and disconnect the multi-pin plug.
79  Prise off the triangular finisher panel to expose the mirror fixing screws and retaining plate. Remove the screws and withdraw the mirror.
80  Refitting is a reversal of removal.

*Dim-dip headlamp system*
81  This system is fitted to all models as from October 1986 in accordance with EEC regulations.

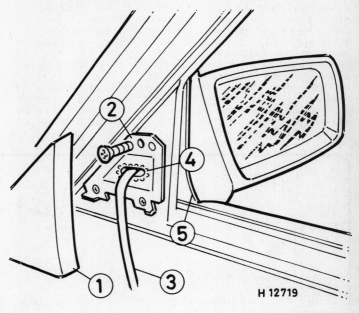

**Fig. 12.44 Electrically-operated door mirror (Sec 14)**

1   Finisher
2   Retaining plate
3   Wiring harness
4   Edge protector
5   Flange seal

82  The system is designed to prevent the car being driven with parking lamps only. Low power headlamp beams come on automatically once the ignition and parking lamps are switched on.
83  The main component of the system is a resistor which is accessible after removal of the radiator grille and left-hand headlamp.

*Ignition switch/steering column lock (from 1986) – modifications*
84  From 1986, all models are fitted with a modified ignition switch which prevents the starter motor from being energised again after initial actuation until after the switch has been returned to the 'AUX'

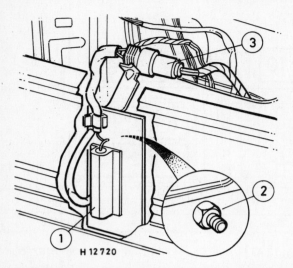

**Fig. 12.45 Headlamp dim-dip system resistor (1), mounting nut (2) and multi-plug (3) (Sec 14)**

position. This safeguards against the starter motor being energised whilst the engine is running.

### Instrument panel (from 1986) – removal and refitting

85 Disconnect the battery negative terminal and detach the speedometer cable retainer ties within the engine compartment.
86 Undo the retaining screws and carefully withdraw the instrument panel bezel from its location.
87 Disconnect the wiring connector from the clock and the vacuum pipe (if applicable). Detach the bezel unit.
88 Undo the five instrument unit retaining screws, then withdraw the unit from the facia by easing it down a little then pivoting it rearwards.
89 Disconnect the speedometer cable (press the moulded bar on the retainer ring) and detach the wiring multi-plugs. Withdraw the instrument panel unit.

90 Refit in the reverse order of removal.

### Clock and econometer (from 1986) – removal and refitting

91 Disconnect the battery negative terminal.
92 Undo the two instrument bezel retaining screws and withdraw the bezel. Disconnect the wiring multi-plug from the clock and, if applicable, the vacuum hose.
93 To remove the clock, lay the panel downwards onto its face, undo the retaining screws and carefully withdraw the clock.
94 To remove the econometer, press it at one end on its rear face and free a retainer, then using a small screwdriver, carefully ease out the opposing retainer and withdraw the econometer. The wiring connections to the econometer should be noted before they are disconnected from the plug. If the econometer unit is being renewed, cut free the wires from the connectors.
95 Refitting is a reversal of the removal procedures. If detached, solder the new econometer wires to the connectors before assembling the unit to the panel.
96 Note that if an original manufacturer's-type clock is being fitted to a model not previously fitted with a clock, a bezel will also be required to enable it to be correctly located.

### Speedometer cable (from 1986) – removal and refitting

97 Proceed as described in paragraphs 85 to 89 inclusive and disconnect the cable from the instrument panel.
98 Carefully detach the cable grommet at the bulkhead and pull the cable into the engine compartment. Undo the cable clamp plate at the gearbox end and withdraw the cable and pinion unit from the gearbox. Release the retainer clip and cable.
99 Refit in the reverse order of removal.

### Electric window switch unit (from 1986) – removal and refitting

100 Disconnect the battery negative lead.
101 Withdraw the control unit from the facia. Rotate the four retainers to bring the alignment marks nearest the switches and release them from the housing (see inset in Fig. 12.46).
102 Insert a small screwdriver as shown and release the face plate retainers from the housing at each end. Press the wiring harness connector pins into the housing, then carefully withdraw the face

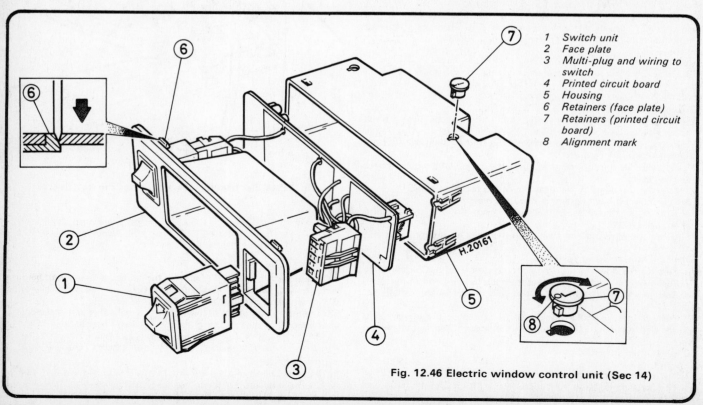

1 Switch unit
2 Face plate
3 Multi-plug and wiring to switch
4 Printed circuit board
5 Housing
6 Retainers (face plate)
7 Retainers (printed circuit board)
8 Alignment mark

**Fig. 12.46 Electric window control unit (Sec 14)**

plate, switches and printed circuit board (take care not to damage the latter).

103 Detach the wiring multi-plug, apply pressure to the retainers on each side of the switch and withdraw the switch from the face plate.

104 Refit in the reverse order of removal. As the unit is assembled, take care not to damage the printed circuit board, and ensure that the harness connecting pins are correctly and securely located.

### Electric window regulator motor (from 1986) – removal and refitting

105 Disconnect the battery earth lead.

106 Remove the door trim (see Chapter 11).

107 Wedge the door glass in the raised position, then detach the wiring harness multi-plug.

108 Undo the regulator and auxiliary slide securing nuts and remove the slide from the door.

109 Detach the regulator arm from the glass lift channel, then withdraw the regulator/lift motor unit.

110 Refit in the reverse order of removal.

### Earth point connectors (from 1986)

111 Refer to Fig. 12.47 for the earth point locations for models from 1986.

### Heated rear window timer switch

112 This is fitted to later models and will switch off the heating element automatically after ten minutes. The cycle can be terminated at any time by giving a second push to the switch button.

### Radio aerial – removal and refitting

113 Disconnect the battery negative lead.

114 Carefully prise up the cover trim at the base of the aerial and undo the baseplate retaining screws. Note the screening braid locations on one of the screws.

115 From inside the car, disconnect the aerial lead at the rear of the radio (for radio removal, see Chapter 9, Section 41) and withdraw the lead from the console and facia.

116 Tie a length of string to the end of the aerial lead as an aid to

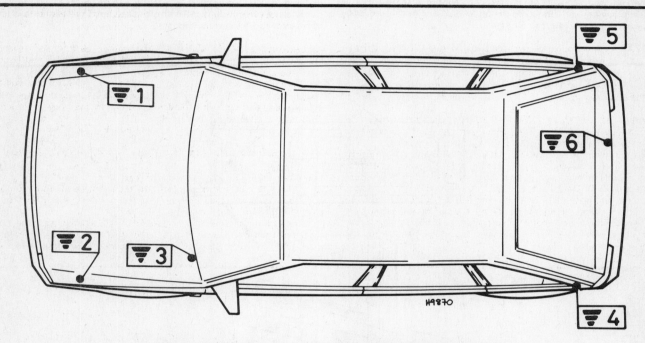

**Fig. 12.47 Earthing point location – models from 1986 (Sec 14)**

1  Right-hand inner wing (front)
2  Left-hand inner wing (front)
3  Top left-hand bulkhead (behind facia)

4  Left-hand wing (rear) behind trim panel
5  Right-hand wing (rear) behind trim panel
6  Tailgate, behind tailgate trim panel

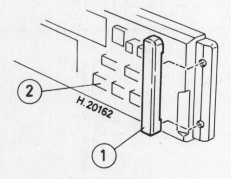

**Fig. 12.48 Radio/cassette player blanking plate (1), unit (2) (Sec 14)**

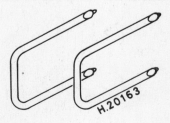

**Fig. 12.49 Radio removal tools (Sec 14)**

refitting and withdraw the aerial lead upwards and out from the windscreen pillar. Once the lead is clear, untie the string and leave it in position in the body.

117 Refitting is a reversal of the removal procedure. Use the string to pull the aerial lead down the pillar and through behind the facia. Ensure that the aerial has a good clean earth connection.

### Radio/cassette player (electronic tune type) – removal and refitting

118 Using a small screwdriver, prise off the blanking plate from each side of the radio. Not all units are fitted with these plates.

119 Two removal tools must now be inserted into the two pairs of holes in the front of the unit. Suitable tools can be purchased or made up from stiff wire.

120 Push the tools in until they are felt to engage with the radio/cassette player retaining clips. Press the tools outwards away from each other and then, using the tools as handles, withdraw the unit until the multi-plug and the radio aerial can be disconnected.

121 When refitting, the tools are not required, simply push the unit into its housing, having first connected the multi-plug and aerial lead, until the retaining clips are heard to engage.

### Tailgate washer tube – renewal

122 Carefully prise the washer nozzle from the tailgate.

123 Disconnect the nozzle from the washer tube.

124 Using adhesive tape, or a plastic tube connector, connect the new length of tubing to the original one.

125 Release the washer tube grommet from the tailgate, and pull the tube through the tailgate until the nozzle can be connected to the end of the new tube. Fit the nozzle to the tailgate.

126 Release the grommets from the rear of the body and the inner front wing, so that the washer tube can be drawn through the vehicle. Refit the grommets.

127 Disconnect the non-return valve which is adjacent to the fluid reservoir, and pull the tube until it protrudes through the bulkhead.

128 Disconnect the new tube from the original tube, cut the new tube to tne required length, and connect it to the non-return valve.

### Manifold heater (1.6 models)

129 An electrically-operated inlet manifold heater which operates when the coolant is below 30°C (86°F) and the ignition is switched on, is fitted to later 1.6 models.

130 As the current draw is 10 amps, disconnect the heater lead if the ignition is to be left on without the engine running.

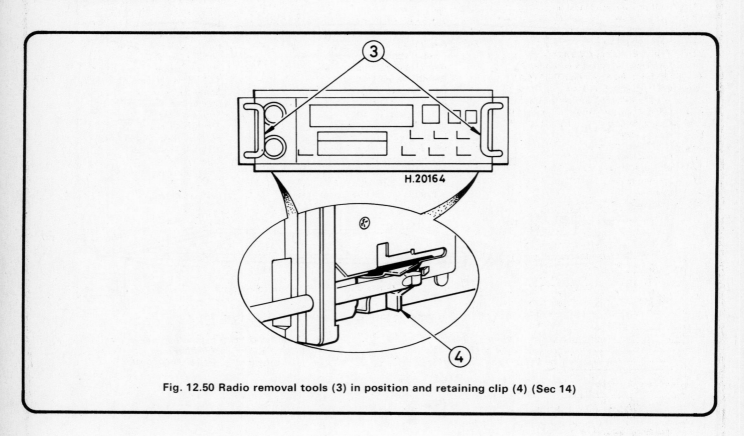

Fig. 12.50 Radio removal tools (3) in position and retaining clip (4) (Sec 14)

## Key to Fig. 12.51

| No | Description | No | Description | No | Description |
|---|---|---|---|---|---|
| 1 | Alternator | 36 | Oil pressure switch | 70 | Blocking diode/brake warning |
| 2 | Battery | 37 | Oil pressure warning lamp | 71 | Ambient temperature sensor |
| 3 | Starter motor solenoid | 38 | Ignition warning lamp | 72 | Rear screen wiper motor |
| 4 | Starter motor | 39 | Headlamp flasher/dip switch | 73 | Rear screen washer motor |
| 5 | Lighting switch | 40 | Coolant temperature indicator | 74 | Rear foglamp switch |
| 6 | Headlamp dip switch | 41 | Coolant temperature transducer | 75 | Rear foglamp warning light |
| 7 | Dip headlamp | 42 | Reverse lamp switch | 76 | Rear foglamp |
| 8 | Main headlamp | 43 | Reverse lamp | 77 | Fuel cut-off solenoid |
| 9 | Main beam warning light | 44 | Clock | 78 | Brake failure warning light |
| 10 | Sidelamp RH | 45 | Cigar lighter | 79 | Windscreen wiper delay unit |
| 11 | Sidelamp LH | 46 | Radio/cassette unit | 80 | Auxiliary circuits relay |
| 12 | Panel illumination lamps | 47 | Windscreen washer motor | 81 | Direction indicator hazard flasher unit |
| 13 | Number plate illumination lamps | 48 | Ashtray illumination lamp | 82 | Coolant temperature warning light |
| 14 | Stop-lamps | 49 | Switch illumination lamp | 83 | Brake pad wear warning light |
| 15 | Tail lamp RH | 50 | Tachometer | 84 | Brake pad wear sensor |
| 16 | Fusebox | 51 | Direction indicator repeater flashers | 85 | Speakers |
| 17 | Interior lamp | 52 | Heated rear screen switch | 86 | Rear screen wiper switch |
| 18 | Interior lamp switches | 53 | Heated rear screen | 87 | Rear screen washer switch |
| 19 | Tail lamp LH | 54 | Windscreen wash/wipe switch | 88 | ECU mixture control (choke) |
| 20 | Horn | 55 | Heated rear screen warning light | 89 | Load space lamp |
| 21 | Horn push | 56 | Hazard warning light | 90 | Load space lamp switch |
| 22 | Direction indicator switch | 57 | Hazard warning switch | 91 | Throttle switch |
| 23 | Direction indicator warning lamps | 58 | Handbrake warning light switch | 92 | Stepper motor |
| 24 | RH front direction indicator lamp | 59 | Handbrake warning light | 93 | Trailer towing warning light |
| 25 | LH front direction indicator lamp | 60 | Fuel level warning light | 94 | Spare warning light |
| 26 | RH rear direction indicator lamp | 61 | Radiator cooling fan thermostat | 95 | Econometer |
| 27 | LH rear direction indicator lamp | 62 | Radiator cooling fan motor | 96 | Knock sensor |
| 28 | Heater switch | 63 | Brake fluid level switch | 97 | Crank sensor |
| 29 | Heater motor | 64 | Cigar lighter illumination lamp | 98 | Programmed ignition ECU |
| 30 | Fuel level indicator | 65 | Heater control illumination | 99 | Manifold heater relay |
| 31 | Fuel level tank unit | 66 | Sidelamp warning light | 100 | Manifold heater |
| 32 | Windscreen wiper motor | 67 | Heated rear screen relay | 101 | Manifold heater switch |
| 33 | Ignition switch | 68 | Glovebox illumination lamp | 102 | Fusible link |
| 34 | Ignition coil | 69 | Glovebox illumination lamp switch | 103 | Stop lamp switch |
| 35 | Distributor | | | | |

H14442

### Symbols used in the wiring diagrams

1. Component earthed by a lead
2. Component earthed by its fixing
3. If fitted
4. Instrument pack link harness
5. Line connector
6. Sealed joint
7. Printed circuit
8. Printed circuit connector

### Colour code

| | | | | | | | |
|---|---|---|---|---|---|---|---|
| B | Black | LG | Light green | P | Purple | U | Blue |
| G | Green | N | Brown | R | Red | W | White |
| K | Pink | O | Orange | S | Slate | Y | Yellow |

*When two colour code letters are shown together, the first denotes the main wire colour and the second denotes the tracer colour*

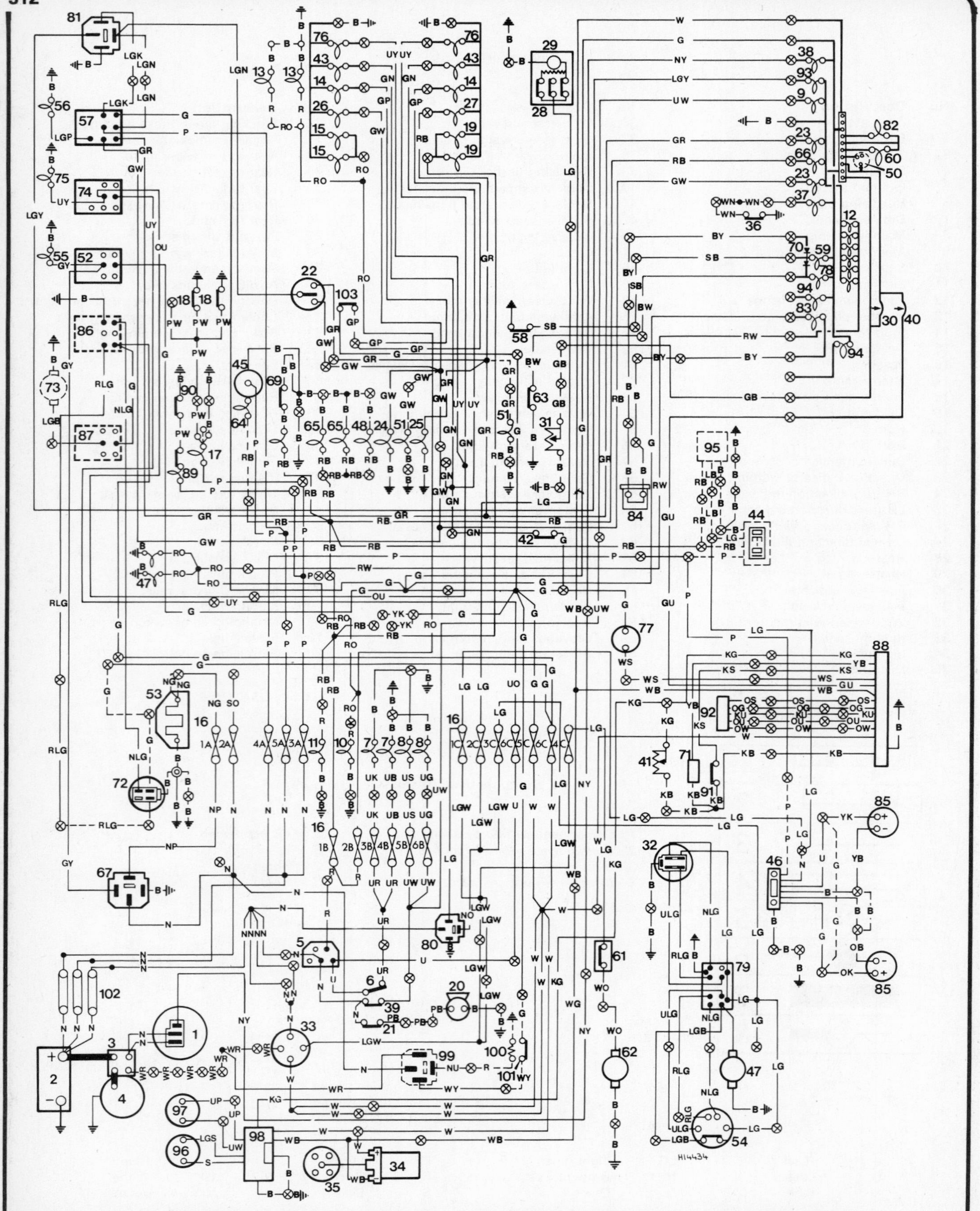

Fig. 12.51 Wiring diagram for all models except MG 1600 and Vanden Plas – July 1984 to 1985

## Key to Fig. 12.52

| No | Description | No | Description |
|----|-------------|----|-------------|
| 1 | Alternator | 57 | Heater control illumination |
| 2 | Battery | 58 | Window lift switch – drivers |
| 3 | Starter motor solenoid | 59 | Window lift switch – passengers |
| 4 | Starter motor | 60 | Window lift motor |
| 5 | Lighting switch | 61 | Heated rear screen relay |
| 6 | Headlamp dip switch | 62 | Glovebox illumination lamp |
| 7 | Dip headlamp | 63 | Glovebox illumination lamp switch |
| 8 | Main headlamp | 64 | Rear screen wiper motor |
| 9 | Sidelamp RH | 65 | Rear screen washer motor |
| 10 | Sidelamp LH | 66 | Rear foglamp switch |
| 11 | Number plate illumination lamps | 67 | Rear foglamp warning light |
| 12 | Stop-lamps | 68 | Rear foglamp |
| 13 | Tail lamp RH | 69 | Fuel pump relay |
| 14 | Stop-lamp switch | 70 | Windscreen wiper delay unit |
| 15 | Fusebox | 71 | Direction indicator hazard flasher unit |
| 16 | Interior lamp | 72 | Brake pad wear sensor |
| 17 | Interior lamp switches | 73 | Balance control |
| 18 | Tail lamp LH | 74 | Speakers |
| 19 | Horn | 75 | Rear screen wiper switch |
| 20 | Horn push | 76 | Rear screen washer switch |
| 21 | Direction indicator switch | 77 | Door lock motor |
| 22 | RH front direction indicator lamp | 78 | Door lock motor control unit |
| 23 | LH front direction indicator lamp | 79 | Load space lamp |
| 24 | RH rear direction indicator lamp | 80 | Load space lamp switch |
| 25 | LH rear direction indicator lamp | 81 | Speed transducer |
| 26 | Heater switch | 82 | Potentiometer |
| 27 | Heater motor | 83 | Voice synthesis cut-out relay |
| 28 | Fuel level tank unit | 84 | Solid-state instrument pack |
| 29 | Windscreen wiper motor | a | Temperature transducer signal |
| 30 | Ignition switch | b | Fuel level tank unit signal |
| 31 | Ignition coil | c | Speed transducer signal |
| 32 | Distributor | d | Brake pad wear signal |
| 33 | Fuel pump | e | Panel illumination (dimmer) |
| 34 | Oil pressure switch | f | Ignition 12 volt positive |
| 35 | Headlamp flasher/dip switch | g | Dimmer control |
| 36 | Coolant temperature transducer | h | Brake fluid warning light |
| 37 | Reverse lamp switch | i | Handbrake warning light |
| 38 | Reverse lamp | j | Brake pad wear warning light |
| 39 | Cigar lighter | k | Oil pressure warning light |
| 40 | Radio/cassette unit | l | Direction indicator warning light RH |
| 41 | Windscreen washer motor | m | Sidelamp warning light |
| 42 | Ashtray illumination lamp | n | Direction indicator warning light LH |
| 43 | Switch illumination lamp | o | Earth |
| 44 | Direction indicator repeater flashers | p | Main beam warning light |
| 45 | Heated rear screen switch | q | Spare warning light |
| 46 | Heated rear screen | r | Ignition warning light |
| 47 | Windscreen wash/wipe switch | s | Ignition 12 volt positive |
| 48 | Heated rear screen warning light | t | Tachometer signal |
| 49 | Hazard warning light | 85 | Trip computer/voice synthesis unit |
| 50 | Hazard warning switch | 86 | Fuel flow sensor |
| 51 | Handbrake warning light switch | 87 | Window lift relay |
| 52 | Radiator cooling fan thermostat | 88 | Combined choke switch and warning light |
| 53 | Radiator cooling fan motor | 89 | Knock sensor |
| 54 | Brake fluid level switch | 90 | Crankshaft sensor |
| 55 | Cigar lighter illumination lamp | 91 | Programmed ignition ECU |
| 56 | Blocking diode | 92 | Fusible link |

For colour code see key to Fig. 12.51

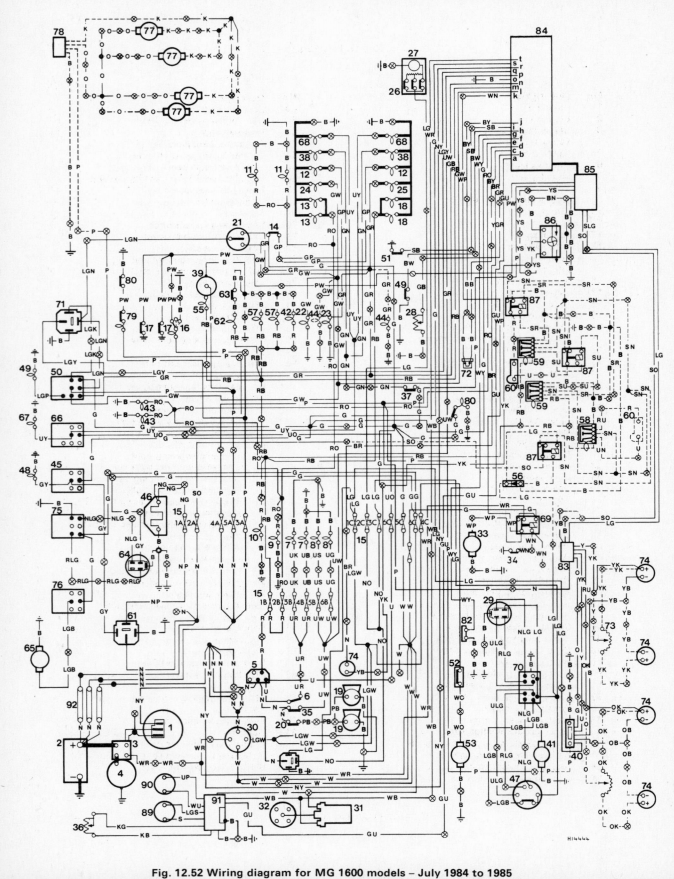

**Fig. 12.52 Wiring diagram for MG 1600 models – July 1984 to 1985**

H14444

## Key to Fig. 12.53

| No | Description | No | Description |
|----|-------------|----|-------------|
| 1 | Alternator | 60 | Rear foglamp switch |
| 2 | Battery | 61 | Rear foglamp warning light |
| 3 | Starter motor solenoid | 62 | Rear foglamp |
| 4 | Starter motor | 63 | Fuel cut-off solenoid |
| 5 | Lighting switch | 64 | Windscreen wiper delay unit |
| 6 | Dip headlamp | 65 | Auxiliary circuits relay |
| 7 | Main headlamp | 66 | Direction indicator hazard flasher unit |
| 8 | Side lamp, RH | 67 | Brake pad wear sensor |
| 9 | Side lamp, LH | 68 | Balance control |
| 10 | Numper plate lamps | 69 | Speakers |
| 11 | Stop lamps | 70 | Rear screen wiper switch |
| 12 | Tail lamp, RH | 71 | Rear screen washer switch |
| 13 | Stop lamp switch | 72 | Door lock motor |
| 14 | Fusebox | 73 | Door lock motor control unit |
| 15 | Interior lamp | 74 | ECU mixture control (choke) |
| 16 | Interior lamp switches | 75 | Load space lamp |
| 17 | Tail lamp, LH | 76 | Load space lamp switch |
| 18 | Horn | 77 | Throttle switch |
| 19 | Direction indicator switch | 78 | Speed transducer |
| 20 | RH front direction indicator lamp | 79 | Potentiometer |
| 21 | LH front direction indicator lamp | 80 | Voice synthesis cut-out relay |
| 22 | RH rear direction indicator lamp | 81 | Stepper motor |
| 23 | LH rear direction indicator lamp | 82 | Solid state instrument pack |
| 24 | Heater switch | a | Temperature transducer signal |
| 25 | Heater motor | b | Fuel level tank unit signal |
| 26 | Fuel level tank unit | c | Speed transducer signal |
| 27 | Ignition switch | d | Brake pad wear signal |
| 28 | Ignition coil | e | Panel illumination (dimmer) |
| 29 | Distributor | f | Ignition 12 volt positive |
| 30 | Oil pressure switch | g | Dimmer control |
| 31 | Coolant temperature transducer | h | Brake fluid warning light |
| 32 | Reverse lamp | i | Handbrake warning light |
| 33 | Cigar lighter | j | Brake pad wear warning light |
| 34 | Radio/cassette unit | k | Oil pressure warning light |
| 35 | Windscreen washer motor | l | Direction indicator warning light RH |
| 36 | Ashtray illumination lamp | m | Sidelamp warning light |
| 37 | Direction indicator repeater flashers | n | Direction indicator warning light LH |
| 38 | Heated rear screen switch | o | Earth |
| 39 | Heated rear screen | p | Main beam warning light |
| 40 | Windscreen wash/wipe switch | q | Spare warning light |
| 41 | Heated rear screen warning light | r | Ignition warning light |
| 42 | Hazard warning light | s | Ignition 12 volt positive |
| 43 | Hazard warning switch | t | Tachometer signal |
| 44 | Handbrake warning light switch | 83 | Trip computer/voice synthesis unit |
| 45 | Radiator cooling fan thermostat | 84 | Fuel flow sensor |
| 46 | Radiator cooling fan motor | 85 | Window lift relay |
| 47 | Brake fluid level switch | 86 | Knock sensor |
| 48 | Cigar lighter illumination lamp | 87 | Crank sensor |
| 49 | Blocking diode | 88 | Programmed ignition ECU |
| 50 | Heater control illumination | 89 | Manifold heater relay |
| 51 | Driver's window lift switch | 90 | Manifold heater |
| 52 | Passenger's window lift switch | 91 | Manifold heater switch |
| 53 | Window lift motor | 92 | Fusible link |
| 54 | Heated rear screen relay | 93 | Switch illumination lamp |
| 55 | Glovebox illumination lamp | 94 | Horn push |
| 56 | Glovebox illumination lamp switch | 95 | Windscreen wiper motor |
| 57 | Ambient temperature sensor | 96 | Headlamp flasher/dip switch |
| 58 | Rear screen wiper motor | 97 | Reverse lamp switch |
| 59 | Rear screen washer motor | | |

For colour code see key to Fig. 12.51

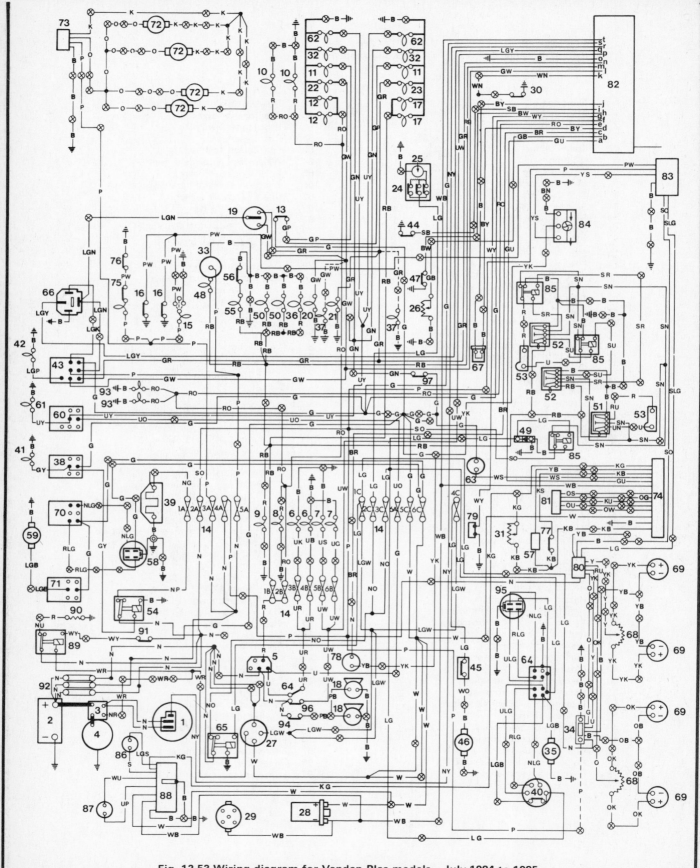

Fig. 12.53 Wiring diagram for Vanden Plas models – July 1984 to 1985

### Key to Fig. 12.54

| No | Description | No | Description |
|----|-------------|----|-------------|
| 1 | Alternator | 40 | Headlamp flash switch |
| 2 | Battery | 41 | Coolant temperature gauge |
| 3 | Starter motor solenoid | 42 | Water temperature transducer |
| 4 | Starter motor | 43 | Reverse lamp switch |
| 5 | Lighting switch – main | 44 | Reverse lamps |
| 6 | Headlamp dip switch | 45 | Cigar lighter |
| 7 | Headlamp dip beam | 46 | Radio |
| 8 | Headlamp main beam | 47 | Windscreen washer motor |
| 9 | Main beam warning lamp | 48 | Switch illumination lamps |
| 10 | RH sidelamp | 49 | Windscreen washer/wiper switch |
| 11 | LH sidelamp | 50 | Hazard warning lamp |
| 12 | Panel illumination lamps | 51 | Hazard warning switch |
| 13 | Number plate illumination lamps | 52 | Printed circuit – instrument panel |
| 14 | Stop-lamps | 53 | Handbrake warning light switch |
| 15 | RH tail lamp | 54 | Handbrake warning light |
| 16 | Stop-lamp switch | 55 | Radiator cooling fan thermostat |
| 17 | Fusebox | 56 | Radiator cooling fan motor |
| 18 | Interior lamps | 57 | Brake fluid level switch |
| 19 | Interior lamp door switches | 58 | Cigar lighter illumination lamp |
| 20 | LH tail lamp | 59 | Heater control illumination |
| 21 | Horn | 60 | Sidelamp warning light |
| 22 | Horn push | 61 | Foglamp switch |
| 23 | Direction indicator switch | 62 | Foglamp warning light |
| 24 | Direction indicator warning lamp(s) | 63 | Rear foglamps |
| 25 | RH front direction indicator lamp | 64 | Brake failure warning light |
| 26 | LH front direction indicator lamp | 65 | Auxiliary circuit relay |
| 27 | RH rear direction indicator lamp | 66 | Direction indicator/hazard flasher unit |
| 28 | LH rear direction indicator lamp | 67 | Brake pad wear warning light |
| 29 | Heater/fresh air motor switch | 68 | Brake pad wear sensor |
| 30 | Heater/fresh air motor | 69 | Speakers |
| 31 | Fuel level gauge | 70 | Load space light |
| 32 | Fuel level gauge tank unit | 71 | Load space lamp switch |
| 33 | Windscreen wiper motor | 72 | Breakerless ignition unit |
| 34 | Ignition/starter switch | 73 | Instrument pack multi-function unit |
| 35 | Ignition coil | 74 | Trailer indicator warning light |
| 36 | Distributor | 75 | Spare warning lamp |
| 37 | Oil pressure switch | 76 | Combined mixture control switch/warning light |
| 38 | Oil pressure warning lamp | | |
| 39 | Ignition/no charge warning lamp | 77 | Fusible link |

For colour code see key to Fig. 12.51

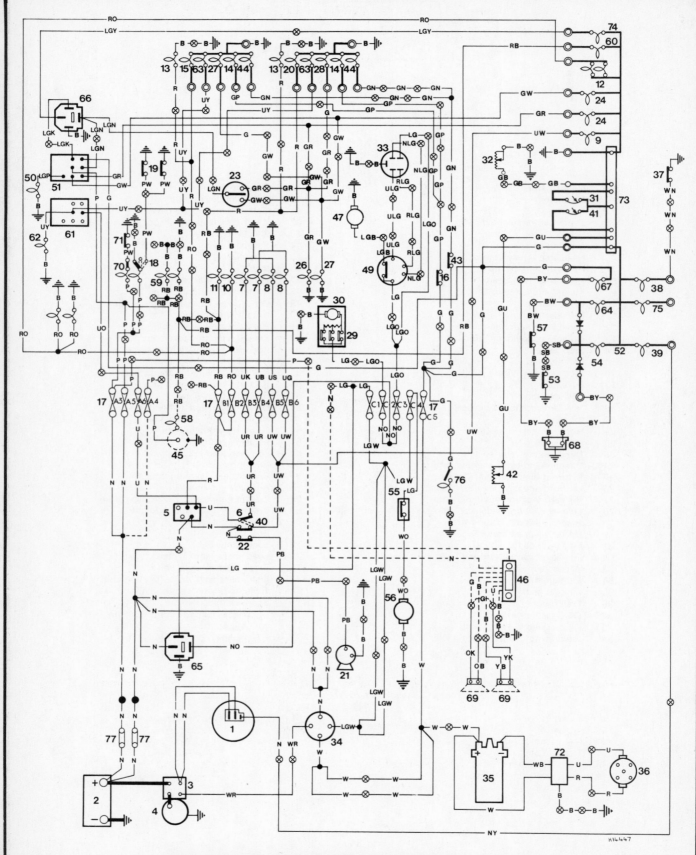

Fig. 12.54 Wiring diagram for 500 and 700 Van models – up to 1985

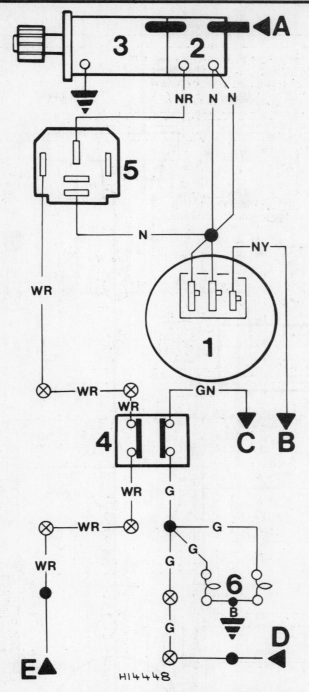

**Fig. 12.55 Supplementary wiring diagram – starter inhibitor switch and reversing lamp circuit (automatic transmission models)**

| No | Description | No | Description |
|----|-------------|----|-------------|
| 1 | Alternator | A | From battery |
| 2 | Starter motor solenoid | B | To ignition warning light |
| 3 | Starter motor | C | To reverse lamps |
| 4 | Combined reverse light and starter inhibitor switch | D | From fuse 5C |
| 5 | Starter motor solenoid relay | E | From ignition switch |
| 6 | Automatic gearbox quadrant illumination | | |

**Colour code**

| | | | | | |
|---|---|---|---|---|---|
| B | Black | N | Brown | S | Slate |
| G | Green | O | Orange | U | Blue |
| K | Pink | P | Purple | W | White |
| LG | Light green | R | Red | Y | Yellow |

*When two colour code letters are shown together, the first denotes the main wire colour and the second denotes the tracer colour*

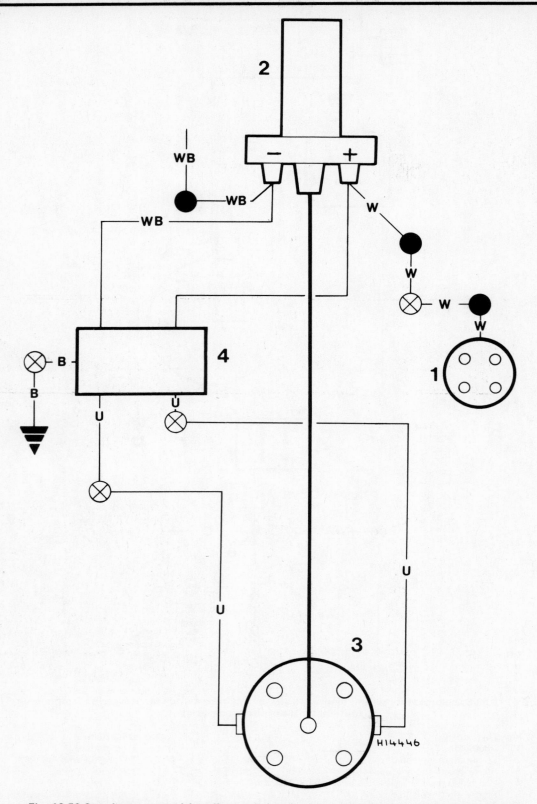

**Fig. 12.56 Supplementary wiring diagram – breakerless ignition circuit (1.3 litre models)**

| No | Description | No | Description |
|----|-------------|----|-------------|
| 1 | Ignition switch | 3 | Distributor |
| 2 | Ignition coil | 4 | Ignition amplifier |

### Key to Fig. 12.57

| No | Description | No | Description |
|----|-------------|----|-------------|
| 1 | Alternator | 50 | Direction indicator repeater flashers |
| 3 | Battery | 51 | Heated rear screen switch |
| 4 | Starter motor solenoid | 52 | Heated rear screen |
| 5 | Starter motor | 53 | Windscreen washer/wiper switch |
| 6 | Lighting switch | 54 | Heated rear screen warning lamp |
| 7 | Headlamp dip switch | 55 | Hazard warning lamp |
| 8 | Headlamp dip beam | 56 | Hazard warning switch |
| 9 | Headlamp main beam | 57 | Handbrake warning lamp switch |
| 10 | Main beam warning light | 58 | Handbrake warning lamp |
| 11 | RH sidelamp | 59 | Radiator cooling fan thermostat |
| 12 | LH sidelamp | 60 | Radiator cooling fan motor |
| 13 | Panel illumination lamps | 61 | Brake fluid level switch |
| 14 | Number plate illumination lamps | 62 | Cigar lighter lamp |
| 15 | Stop-lamps | 63 | Panel lamp rheostat |
| 16 | RH tail lamp | 64 | Heater control lamps |
| 17 | Stop-lamp switch | 65 | Mixture control (choke) warning light switch |
| 18 | Fusebox | 66 | Mixture control (choke) warning light |
| 19 | Interior lamps | 67 | Headlamp relay |
| 20 | Interior lamp door switches | 68 | Sidelamp warning lamp |
| 21 | LH tail lamp | 69 | Glovebox lamp |
| 22 | Horn | 70 | Glovebox lamp switch |
| 23 | Horn push | 71 | Blocking diode |
| 24 | Direction indicator switch | 72 | Rear screen wiper motor |
| 25 | Direction indicator warning lamps | 73 | Rear screen washer motor |
| 26 | RH front indicator lamp | 74 | Fog rearguard lamp switch |
| 27 | LH front indicator lamp | 75 | Fog rearguard warning light |
| 28 | RH rear indicator lamp | 76 | Fog rearguard lamps |
| 29 | LH rear indicator lamp | 77 | Brake failure warning lamp |
| 30 | Heater/fresh air motor switch | 78 | Windscreen wiper delay unit |
| 31 | Heater/fresh air motor | 79 | Ignition switch relay |
| 32 | Fuel level indicator | 80 | Direction indicator/hazard flasher unit |
| 33 | Fuel level gauge tank unit | 81 | Brake pad wear warning lamp |
| 34 | Windscreen wiper motor | 82 | Brake pad wear sensor |
| 35 | Ignition/starter switch | 83 | Rear screen wiper switch |
| 36 | Ignition coil | 84 | Rear screen washer switch |
| 37 | Distributor | 85 | Load space lamp |
| 38 | Oil pressure switch | 86 | Load space lamp switch |
| 39 | Oil pressure warning lamp | 87 | Trailer indicator warning lamp |
| 40 | Ignition/no charge warning lamp | 88 | Spare warning lamp |
| 41 | Headlamp flash switch | 89 | Column switch illumination |
| 42 | Coolant temperature indicator | 90 | Auxiliary ignition relay |
| 43 | Coolant temperature transducer | 91 | Centre console illumination |
| 44 | Reversing lamp switch | 92 | Fusible links |
| 45 | Reversing lamps | 93 | Low fuel LED |
| 46 | Clock | 94 | High temperature LED |
| 47 | Cigar lighter | 95 | Rear wash/wipe unit |
| 48 | Windscreen washer motor | 96 | Heated rear screen timer relay |
| 49 | Switch illumination lamps | A | Radio/cassette player circuit |

For colour code see key to Fig. 12.51

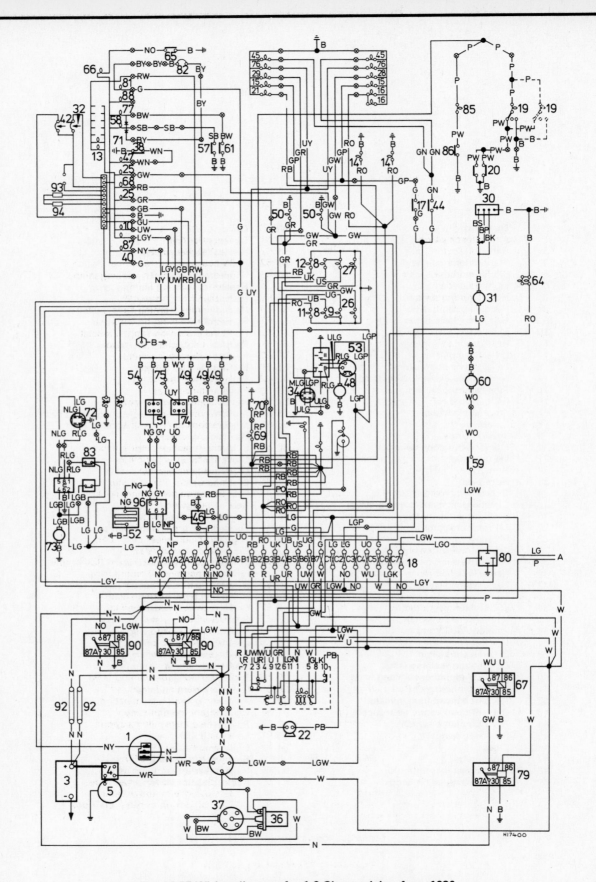

**Fig. 12.57 Wiring diagram for 1.3 City models – from 1986**

## Key to Fig. 12.58

| No | Description | No | Description |
|----|-------------|----|-------------|
| 1 | Alternator | 51 | Heated rear screen |
| 2 | Battery | 52 | Windscreen washer/wiper switch |
| 3 | Starter motor solenoid | 53 | Heated rear screen warning lamp |
| 4 | Starter motor | 54 | Hazard warning lamp |
| 5 | Lighting switch | 55 | Hazard warning switch |
| 6 | Headlamp dip switch | 56 | Handbrake warning lamp switch |
| 7 | Headlamp dip beam | 57 | Handbrake warning lamp |
| 8 | Headlamp main beam | 58 | Radiator cooling fan thermostat |
| 9 | Main beam warning light | 59 | Radiator cooling fan motor |
| 10 | RH sidelamp | 60 | Brake fluid level switch |
| 11 | LH sidelamp | 61 | Cigar lighter lamp |
| 12 | Panel illumination lamps | 62 | Heater control lamps |
| 13 | Number plate illumination lamps | 63 | Headlamp relay |
| 14 | Stop-lamps | 64 | Sidelamp warning lamp |
| 15 | RH tail lamp | 65 | Glovebox lamp |
| 16 | Stop-lamp switch | 66 | Glovebox lamp switch |
| 17 | Fusebox | 67 | Blocking diode |
| 18 | Interior lamps | 68 | Ambient temperature sensor |
| 19 | Interior lamp door switches | 69 | Rear screen wiper motor |
| 20 | LH tail lamp | 70 | Rear screen washer motor |
| 21 | Horn | 71 | Fog rearguard lamp switch |
| 22 | Horn push | 72 | Fog rearguard warning light |
| 23 | Direction indicator switch | 73 | Fog rearguard lamps |
| 24 | Direction indicator warning lamps | 74 | Fuel cut off solenoid |
| 25 | RH front indicator lamp | 75 | Brake failure warning lamp |
| 26 | LH front indicator lamp | 76 | Windscreen wiper delay unit |
| 27 | RH rear indicator lamp | 77 | Ignition switch relay |
| 28 | LH rear indicator lamp | 78 | Direction indicator/hazard flasher unit |
| 29 | Heater/fresh air motor switch | 79 | Brake pad wear warning lamp |
| 30 | Heater/fresh air motor | 80 | Brake pad wear sensor |
| 31 | Fuel level indicator | 81 | Rear screen wiper switch |
| 32 | Fuel level gauge tank unit | 82 | Rear screen washer switch |
| 33 | Windscreen wiper motor | 83 | Fuel ECU |
| 34 | Ignition/starter switch | 84 | Load space lamp |
| 35 | Ignition coil | 85 | Load space lamp switch |
| 36 | Distributor | 86 | Accelerator pedal switch |
| 37 | Oil pressure switch | 87 | Stepper motor |
| 38 | Oil pressure warning lamp | 88 | Trailer indicator warning lamp |
| 39 | Ignition/no charge warning lamp | 89 | Spare warning lamp |
| 40 | Headlamp flash switch | 90 | Column switch illumination |
| 41 | Coolant temperature indicator | 91 | Auxiliary ignition relay |
| 42 | Coolant temperature transducer | 92 | Centre console illumination |
| 43 | Reversing lamp switch | 93 | Fusible links |
| 44 | Reversing lamps | 94 | Low fuel LED |
| 45 | Clock | 95 | High temperature LED |
| 46 | Cigar lighter | 96 | Rear wash/wipe unit |
| 47 | Windscreen washer motor | 97 | Heated rear screen timer relay |
| 48 | Switch illumination lamps | A | Radio/cassette player circuit |
| 49 | Direction indicator repeater flashers | B | Central locking circuit – LHD only |
| 50 | Heated rear screen switch | | |

For colour code see key to Fig. 12.51

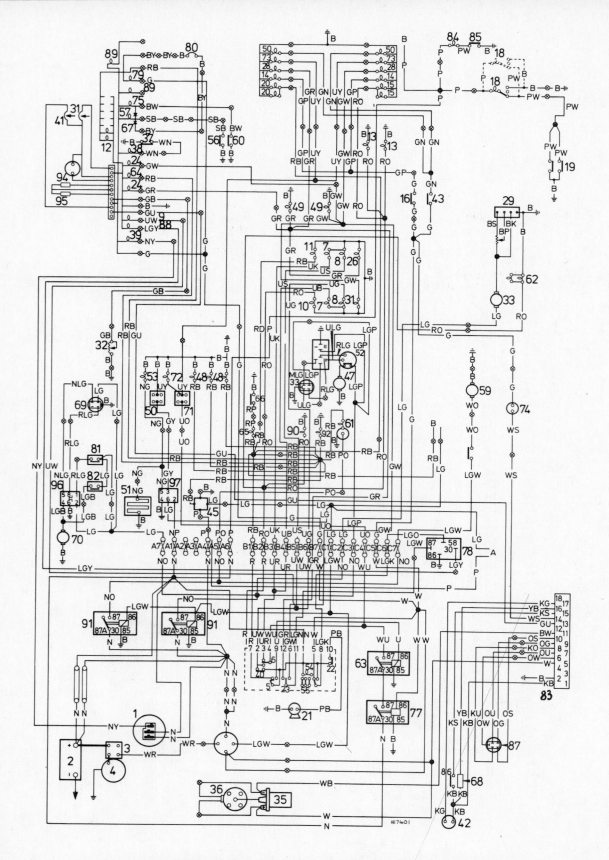

**Fig. 12.58 Wiring diagram for 1.3L and City X models – from 1986**

## Key to Fig. 12.59

| No | Description | No | Description |
|----|-------------|----|-------------|
| 1 | Alternator | 45 | Clock |
| 2 | Battery | 46 | Cigar lighter |
| 3 | Starter motor solenoid | 47 | Junction box – beacon |
| 4 | Starter motor | 48 | Windscreen washer motor |
| 5 | Lighting switch | 49 | Switch illumination lamps |
| 6 | Headlamp dip switch | 50 | Direction indicator repeater flashers |
| 7 | Headlamp dip beam | 51 | Windscreen washer/wiper switch |
| 8 | Headlamp main beam | 52 | Hazard warning lamp |
| 9 | Main beam warning light | 53 | Hazard warning switch |
| 10 | RH sidelamp | 54 | Handbrake warning lamp switch |
| 11 | LH sidelamp | 55 | Handbrake warning lamp |
| 12 | Panel illumination lamps | 56 | Radiator cooling fan thermostat |
| 13 | Number plate illumination lamps | 57 | Radiator cooling fan motor |
| 14 | Stop-lamps | 58 | Brake fluid level switch |
| 15 | RH tail lamp | 59 | Cigar lighter lamp |
| 16 | Stop-lamp switch | 60 | Heater control lamps |
| 17 | Fusebox | 61 | Mixture control (choke) warning light switch |
| 18 | Interior lamps | 62 | Mixture control (choke) warning light |
| 19 | Interior lamp door switches | 63 | Headlamp relay |
| 20 | LH tail lamp | 64 | Sidelamp warning lamp |
| 21 | Horn | 65 | Glovebox lamp |
| 22 | Horn push | 66 | Glovebox lamp switch |
| 23 | Direction indicator switch | 67 | Blocking diode |
| 24 | Direction indicator warning lamps | 68 | Fog rearguard lamp switch |
| 25 | RH front indicator lamp | 69 | Fog rearguard warning light |
| 26 | LH front indicator lamp | 70 | Fog rearguard lamps |
| 27 | RH rear indicator lamp | 71 | Brake failure warning lamp |
| 28 | LH rear indicator lamp | 72 | Windscreen wiper delay unit |
| 29 | Heater/fresh air motor switch | 73 | Ignition switch relay |
| 30 | Heater/fresh air motor | 74 | Direction indicator/hazard flasher unit |
| 31 | Fuel level indicator | 75 | Beacon master switch |
| 32 | Fuel level gauge tank unit | 76 | Master beacon switch warning lamp |
| 33 | Windscreen wiper motor | 77 | Brake pad wear warning lamp |
| 34 | Ignition/starter switch | 78 | Brake pad wear sensor |
| 35 | Ignition coil | 79 | Load space lamp |
| 36 | Distributor | 80 | Load space lamp switch |
| 37 | Oil pressure switch | 81 | Trailer indicator warning lamp |
| 38 | Oil pressure warning lamp | 82 | Spare warning lamp |
| 39 | Ignition/no charge warning lamp | 83 | Column switch illumination |
| 40 | Headlamp flash switch | 84 | Auxiliary ignition relay |
| 41 | Coolant temperature indicator | 85 | Centre console illumination |
| 42 | Coolant temperature transducer | 86 | Fusible links |
| 43 | Reversing lamp switch | 87 | Low/high beacon switch |
| 44 | Reversing lamps | A | Radio/cassette player circuit |

For colour code see key to Fig. 12.51

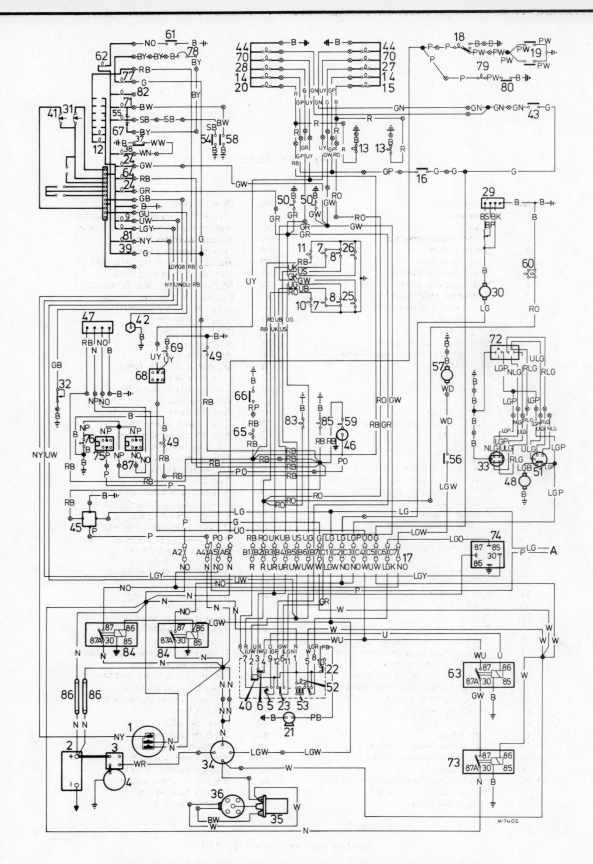

**Fig. 12.59 Wiring diagram for 1.3 City and L Van models – from 1986**

## Key to Fig. 12.60

| No | Description | No | Description |
|----|-------------|----|-------------|
| 1 | Alternator | 53 | Windscreen washer/wiper switch |
| 2 | Battery | 54 | Heated rear screen warning lamp |
| 3 | Starter motor solenoid | 55 | Hazard warning lamp |
| 4 | Starter motor | 56 | Hazard warning switch |
| 5 | Lighting switch | 57 | Handbrake warning lamp switch |
| 6 | Headlamp dip switch | 58 | Handbrake warning lamp |
| 7 | Headlamp dip beam | 59 | Radiator cooling fan thermostat |
| 8 | Headlamp main beam | 60 | Radiator cooling fan motor |
| 9 | Main beam warning light | 61 | Brake fluid level switch |
| 10 | RH sidelamp | 62 | Cigar lighter lamp |
| 11 | LH sidelamp | 63 | Panel lamp rheostat |
| 12 | Panel illumination lamps | 64 | Heater control lamps |
| 13 | Number plate illumination lamps | 65 | Headlamp relay |
| 14 | Stop-lamps | 66 | Sidelamp warning lamp |
| 15 | RH tail lamp | 67 | Glovebox lamp |
| 16 | Stop-lamp switch | 68 | Glovebox lamp switch |
| 17 | Fusebox | 69 | Blocking diode |
| 18 | Interior lamps | 70 | Ambient temperature sensor |
| 19 | Interior lamp door switches | 71 | Rear screen wiper motor |
| 20 | LH tail lamp | 72 | Rear screen washer motor |
| 21 | Horn | 73 | Fog rearguard lamp switch |
| 22 | Horn push | 74 | Fog rearguard warning light |
| 23 | Direction indicator switch | 75 | Fog rearguard lamps |
| 24 | Direction indicator warning lamps | 76 | Fuel cut-off solenoid |
| 25 | RH front indicator lamp | 77 | Brake failure warning lamp |
| 26 | LH front indicator lamp | 78 | Windscreen wiper delay unit |
| 27 | RH rear indicator lamp | 79 | Ignition switch relay |
| 28 | LH rear indicator lamp | 80 | Direction indicator/hazard flasher unit |
| 29 | Heater/fresh air motor switch | 81 | Brake pad wear warning lamp |
| 30 | Heater/fresh air motor | 82 | Brake pad wear sensor |
| 31 | Fuel level indicator | 83 | Rear screen wiper switch |
| 32 | Fuel level gauge tank unit | 84 | Rear screen washer switch |
| 33 | Windscreen wiper motor | 85 | Fuel ECU |
| 34 | Ignition/starter switch | 86 | Carburettor vent valve |
| 35 | Ignition coil | 87 | Load space lamp |
| 36 | Distributor | 88 | Load space lamp switch |
| 37 | Oil pressure switch | 89 | Accelerator pedal switch |
| 38 | Oil pressure warning lamp | 90 | Stepper motor |
| 39 | Ignition/no charge warning lamp | 91 | Trailer indicator warning lamp |
| 40 | Headlamp flash switch | 92 | Spare warning lamp |
| 41 | Coolant temperature indicator | 93 | Column switch illumination |
| 42 | Coolant temperature transducer | 94 | Auxiliary ignition relay |
| 43 | Reversing lamp switch | 95 | Centre console illumination |
| 44 | Reversing lamps | 96 | Fusible links |
| 45 | Clock | 97 | Low fuel LED |
| 46 | Cigar lighter | 98 | High temperature LED |
| 47 | Windscreen washer motor | 99 | Rear wash/wipe unit |
| 48 | Switch illumination lamps | 100 | Heated rear screen timer relay |
| 49 | Tachometer | A | Radio/cassette circuit |
| 50 | Direction indicator repeater flashers | B | Electric window circuit |
| 51 | Heated rear screen switch | C | Central locking circuit |
| 52 | Heated rear screen | D | Electric mirror circuit |

For colour code see key to Fig. 12.51

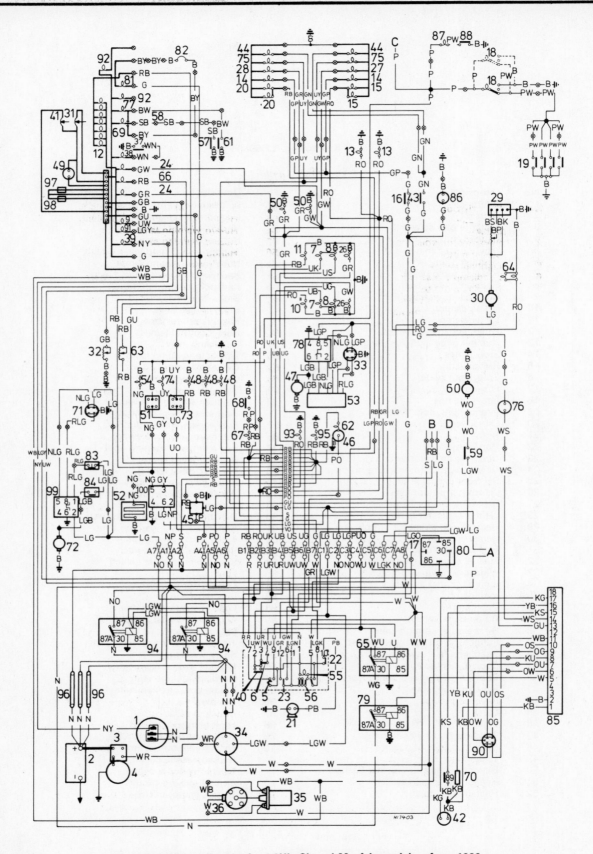

**Fig. 12.60 Wiring diagram for 1.3HL, SL and Mayfair models – from 1986**

## Key to Fig. 12.61

| No | Description | No | Description |
|---|---|---|---|
| 1 | Alternator | 53 | Heated rear screen warning lamp |
| 2 | Battery | 54 | Hazard warning lamp |
| 3 | Starter motor solenoid | 55 | Hazard warning switch |
| 4 | Starter motor | 56 | Handbrake warning lamp switch |
| 5 | Lighting switch | 57 | Handbrake warning lamp |
| 6 | Headlamp dip switch | 58 | Radiator cooling fan thermostat |
| 7 | Headlamp dip beam | 59 | Radiator cooling fan motor |
| 8 | Headlamp main beam | 60 | Brake fluid level switch |
| 9 | Main beam warning light | 61 | Cigar lighter lamp |
| 10 | RH sidelamp | 62 | Heater control lamps |
| 11 | LH sidelamp | 63 | Headlamp relay |
| 12 | Panel illumination lamps | 64 | Sidelamp warning lamp |
| 13 | Number plate illumination lamps | 65 | Glovebox lamp |
| 14 | Stop-lamps | 66 | Glovebox lamp switch |
| 15 | RH tail lamp | 67 | Blocking diode |
| 16 | Stop-lamp switch | 68 | Ambient temperature sensor |
| 17 | Fusebox | 69 | Rear screen wiper motor |
| 18 | Interior lamps | 70 | Rear screen washer motor |
| 19 | Interior lamp door switches | 71 | Fog rearguard lamp switch |
| 20 | LH tail lamp | 72 | Fog rearguard warning light |
| 21 | Horn | 73 | Fog rearguard lamps |
| 22 | Horn push | 74 | Fuel cut off solenoid |
| 23 | Direction indicator switch | 75 | Brake failure warning lamp |
| 24 | Direction indicator warning lamps | 76 | Windscreen wiper delay unit |
| 25 | RH front indicator lamp | 77 | Ignition switch relay |
| 26 | LH front indicator lamp | 78 | Direction indicator/hazard flasher unit |
| 27 | RH rear indicator lamp | 79 | Brake pad wear warning lamp |
| 28 | LH rear indicator lamp | 80 | Brake pad wear sensor |
| 29 | Heater/fresh air motor switch | 81 | Rear screen wiper switch |
| 30 | Heater/fresh air motor | 82 | Rear screen washer switch |
| 31 | Fuel level indicator | 83 | Fuel ECU |
| 32 | Fuel level gauge tank unit | 84 | Load space lamp |
| 33 | Windscreen wiper motor | 85 | Load space lamp switch |
| 34 | Ignition/starter switch | 86 | Accelerator pedal switch |
| 35 | Ignition coil | 87 | Stepper motor |
| 36 | Distributor | 88 | Trailer indicator warning lamp |
| 37 | Oil pressure switch | 89 | Spare warning lamp |
| 38 | Oil pressure warning lamp | 90 | Knock sensor |
| 39 | Ignition/no charge warning lamp | 91 | Crankshaft sensor |
| 40 | Headlamp flash switch | 92 | Column switch illumination |
| 41 | Coolant temperature indicator | 93 | Programmed ignition ECU |
| 42 | Coolant temperature transducer | 94 | Manifold heater relay |
| 43 | Reversing lamp switch | 95 | Manifold heater |
| 44 | Reversing lamps | 96 | Manifold heater switch |
| 45 | Clock | 97 | Auxiliary ignition relay |
| 46 | Cigar lighter | 98 | Centre console illumination |
| 47 | Windscreen washer motor | 99 | Fusible links |
| 48 | Switch illumination lamps | 100 | Low fuel LED |
| 49 | Direction indicator repeater flashers | 101 | High temperature LED |
| 50 | Heated rear screen switch | 102 | Rear wash/wipe unit |
| 51 | Heated rear screen | 103 | Heated rear screen timer relay |
| 52 | Windscreen washer/wiper switch | A | Radio/cassette player circuit |

For colour code see key to Fig. 12.51

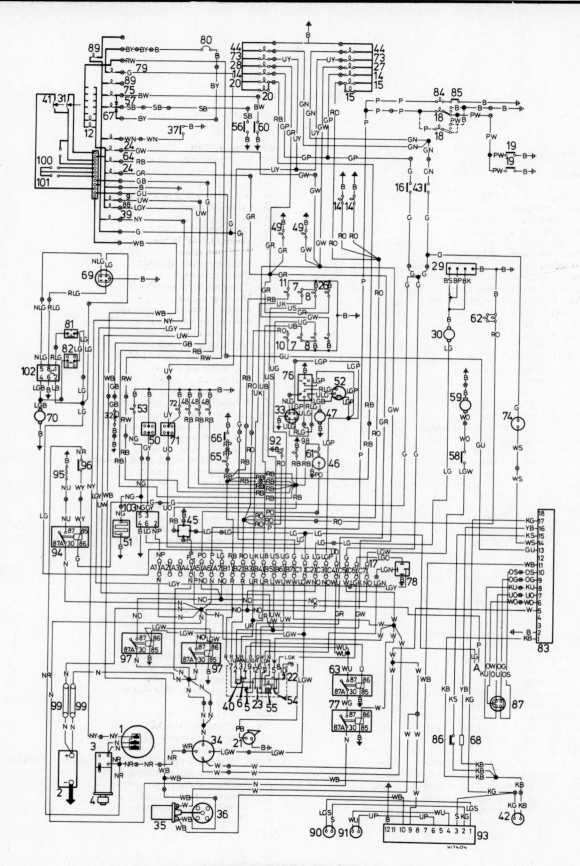

**Fig. 12.61 Wiring diagram for 1.6L models – from 1986**

## Key to Fig. 12.62

| No | Description | No | Description |
|----|-------------|----|-------------|
| 1 | Alternator | 59 | Handbrake warning lamp |
| 2 | Battery | 60 | Starter relay |
| 3 | Starter motor solenoid | 61 | Radiator cooling fan thermostat |
| 4 | Starter motor | 62 | Radiator cooling fan motor |
| 5 | Lighting switch | 63 | Brake fluid level switch |
| 6 | Headlamp dip switch | 64 | Cigar lighter lamp |
| 7 | Headlamp dip beam | 65 | Panel lamp rheostat |
| 8 | Headlamp main beam | 66 | Heater control lamps |
| 9 | Main beam warning light | 67 | Headlamp relay |
| 10 | RH sidelamp | 68 | Sidelamp warning lamp |
| 11 | LH sidelamp | 69 | Glovebox lamp |
| 12 | Panel illumination lamps | 70 | Glovebox lamp switch |
| 13 | Number plate illumination lamps | 71 | Blocking diode |
| 14 | Stop-lamps | 72 | Ambient temperature sensor |
| 15 | RH tail lamp | 73 | Rear screen wiper motor |
| 16 | Stop-lamp switch | 74 | Rear screen washer motor |
| 17 | Fusebox | 75 | Fog rearguard lamp switch |
| 18 | Interior lamps | 76 | Fog rearguard warning light |
| 19 | Interior lamp door switches | 77 | Fog rearguard lamps |
| 20 | LH tail lamp | 78 | Fuel cut off solenoid |
| 21 | Horns | 79 | Brake failure warning lamp |
| 22 | Horn push | 80 | Windscreen wiper delay unit |
| 23 | Direction indicator switch | 81 | Ignition switch relay |
| 24 | Direction indicator warning lamps | 82 | Direction indicator/hazard flasher unit |
| 25 | RH front indicator lamp | 83 | Brake pad wear warning lamp |
| 26 | LH front indicator lamp | 84 | Brake pad wear sensor |
| 27 | RH rear indicator lamp | 85 | Auto gearbox quadrant illumination |
| 28 | LH rear indicator lamp | 86 | Rear screen wiper switch |
| 29 | Heater/fresh air motor switch | 87 | Rear screen washer switch |
| 30 | Heater/fresh air motor | 88 | Fuel ECU |
| 31 | Fuel level indicator | 89 | Carburettor vent valve |
| 32 | Fuel level gauge tank unit | 90 | Load space lamp |
| 33 | Windscreen wiper motor | 91 | Load space lamp switch |
| 34 | Ignition/starter switch | 92 | Accelerator pedal switch |
| 35 | Ignition coil | 93 | Stepper motor |
| 36 | Distributor | 94 | Trailer indicator warning lamp |
| 37 | Oil pressure switch | 95 | Spare warning lamp |
| 38 | Oil pressure warning lamp | 96 | Knock sensor |
| 39 | Ignition/no charge warning lamp | 97 | Crankshaft sensor |
| 40 | Headlamp flash switch | 98 | Column switch illumination |
| 41 | Coolant temperature indicator | 99 | Programmed ignition ECU |
| 42 | Coolant temperature transducer | 100 | Manifold heater relay |
| 43 | Reversing lamp switch | 101 | Manifold heater |
| 44 | Reversing lamps | 102 | Manifold heater switch |
| 45 | Clock | 103 | Interior lamp delay unit |
| 46 | Cigar lighter | 104 | Auxiliary ignition relay |
| 47 | Windscreen washer motor | 105 | Centre console illumination |
| 48 | Switch illumination lamps | 106 | Fusible links |
| 49 | Tachometer | 107 | Low fuel LED |
| 50 | Direction indicator repeater flashers | 108 | High temperature LED |
| 51 | Heated rear screen switch | 109 | Rear wash/wipe unit |
| 52 | Heated rear screen | 110 | Heated rear screen timer relay |
| 53 | Windscreen washer/wiper switch | X | Combined reverse light and auto gearbox inhibitor switch connections to ignition switch |
| 54 | Combined reversing light and auto gearbox inhibitor switch | A | Radio/cassette player circuit |
| 55 | Heated rear screen warning lamp | B | Electric window circuit |
| 56 | Hazard warning lamp | C | Central locking circuit |
| 57 | Hazard warning switch | D | Electric mirror circuit |
| 58 | Handbrake warning lamp switch | | |

For colour code see key to Fig. 12.51

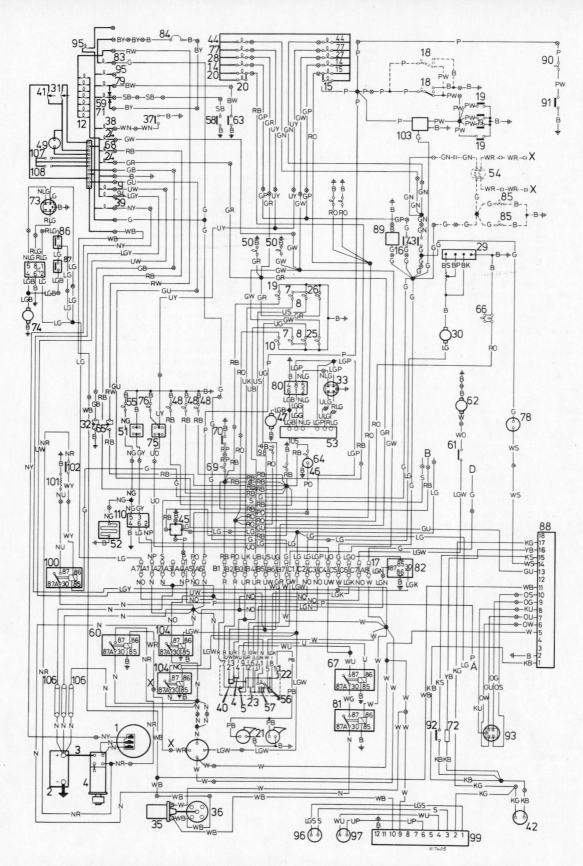

**Fig. 12.62 Wiring diagram for 1.6 HL, SL, Mayfair and Vanden Plas models – from 1986**

**Key to Fig. 12.63**

| No | Description | No | Description |
|----|-------------|----|-------------|
| 1 | Alternator | 45 | Junction box – beacon |
| 2 | Battery | 46 | Windscreen washer motor |
| 3 | Starter motor solenoid | 47 | Switch illumination lamps |
| 4 | Starter motor | 48 | Direction indicator repeater flashers |
| 5 | Lighting switch | 49 | Windscreen washer/wiper switch |
| 6 | Headlamp dip switch | 50 | Hazard warning lamp |
| 7 | Headlamp dip beam | 51 | Hazard warning switch |
| 8 | Headlamp main beam | 52 | Handbrake warning lamp switch |
| 9 | Main beam warning light | 53 | Handbrake warning lamp |
| 10 | RH sidelamp | 54 | Radiator cooling fan thermostat |
| 11 | LH sidelamp | 55 | Radiator cooling fan motor |
| 12 | Panel illumination lamps | 56 | Brake fluid level switch |
| 13 | Number plate illumination lamps | 57 | Heater control lamps |
| 14 | Stop-lamps | 58 | Mixture control (choke) warning light switch |
| 15 | RH tail lamp | 59 | Mixture control (choke) warning light |
| 16 | Stop-lamp switch | 60 | Headlamp relay |
| 17 | Fusebox | 61 | Sidelamp warning lamp |
| 18 | Interior lamps | 62 | Blocking diode |
| 19 | Interior lamp door switches | 63 | Fog rearguard lamp switch |
| 20 | LH tail lamp | 64 | Fog rearguard warning light |
| 21 | Horn | 65 | Fog rearguard lamps |
| 22 | Horn push | 66 | Brake failure warning lamp |
| 23 | Direction indicator switch | 67 | Ignition switch relay |
| 24 | Direction indicator warning lamps | 68 | Direction indicator/hazard flasher unit |
| 25 | RH front indicator lamp | 69 | Beacon master switch |
| 26 | LH front indicator lamp | 70 | Master beacon switch warning light |
| 27 | RH rear indicator lamp | 71 | Brake pad wear warning lamp |
| 28 | LH rear indicator lamp | 72 | Brake pad wear sensor |
| 29 | Heater/fresh air motor switch | 73 | Load space lamp |
| 30 | Heater/fresh air motor | 74 | Load space lamp switch |
| 31 | Fuel level indicator | 75 | Trailer indicator warning lamp |
| 32 | Fuel level gauge tank unit | 76 | Spare warning lamp |
| 33 | Windscreen wiper motor | 77 | Knock sensor |
| 34 | Ignition/starter switch | 78 | Crankshaft sensor |
| 35 | Ignition coil | 79 | Column switch illumination |
| 36 | Distributor | 80 | Programmed ignition ECU |
| 37 | Oil pressure switch | 81 | Manifold heater relay |
| 38 | Oil pressure warning lamp | 82 | Manifold heater |
| 39 | Ignition/no charge warning lamp | 83 | Manifold heater switch |
| 40 | Headlamp flash switch | 84 | Auxiliary ignition relay |
| 41 | Coolant temperature indicator | 85 | Centre console illumination |
| 42 | Coolant temperature transducer | 86 | Fusible links |
| 43 | Reversing lamp switch | 87 | Low/high beacon switch |
| 44 | Reversing lamps | A | Radio/cassette player circuit |

For colour code see key to Fig. 12.51

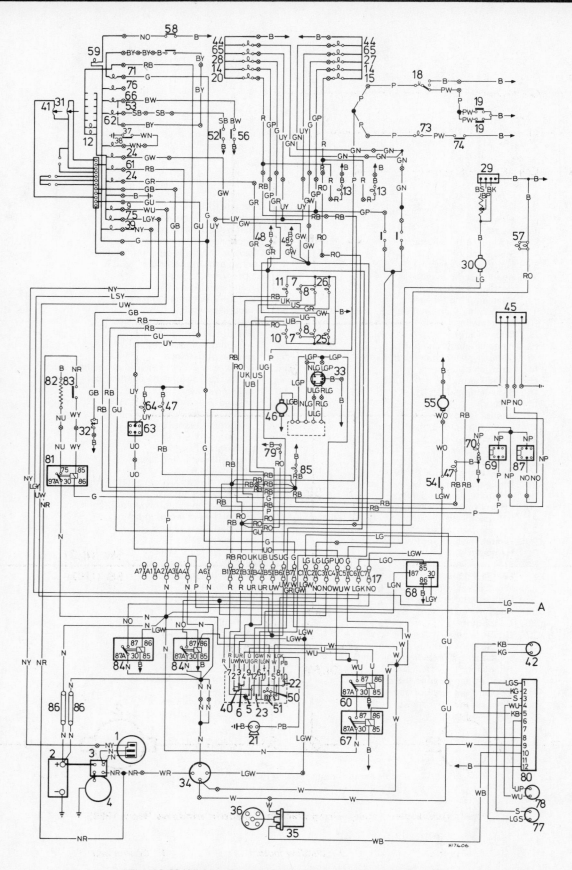

**Fig. 12.63 Wiring diagram for 1.6 Van models – from 1986**

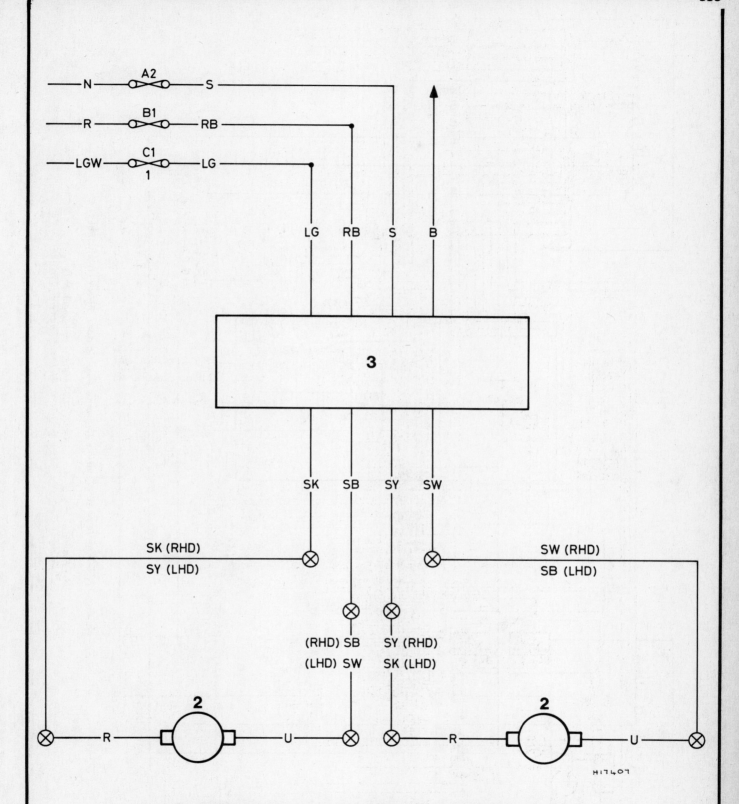

**Fig. 12.64 Supplementary wiring diagram – electric windows (from 1986)**

1 Fusebox 2 Window motors 3 Control unit

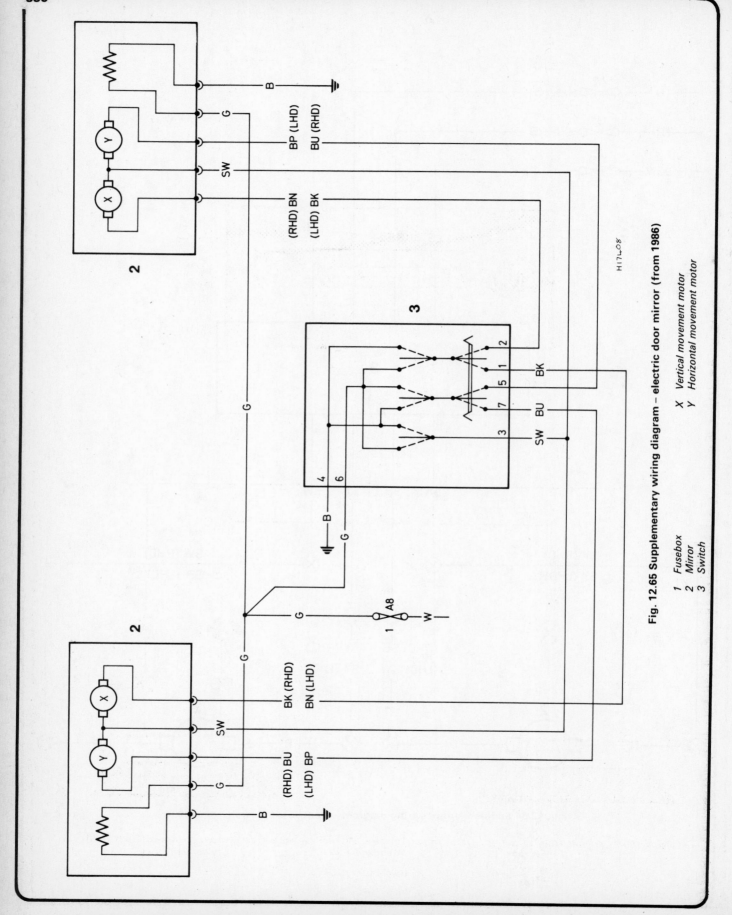

Fig. 12.65 Supplementary wiring diagram – electric door mirror (from 1986)

1 Fusebox
2 Mirror
3 Switch

X Vertical movement motor
Y Horizontal movement motor

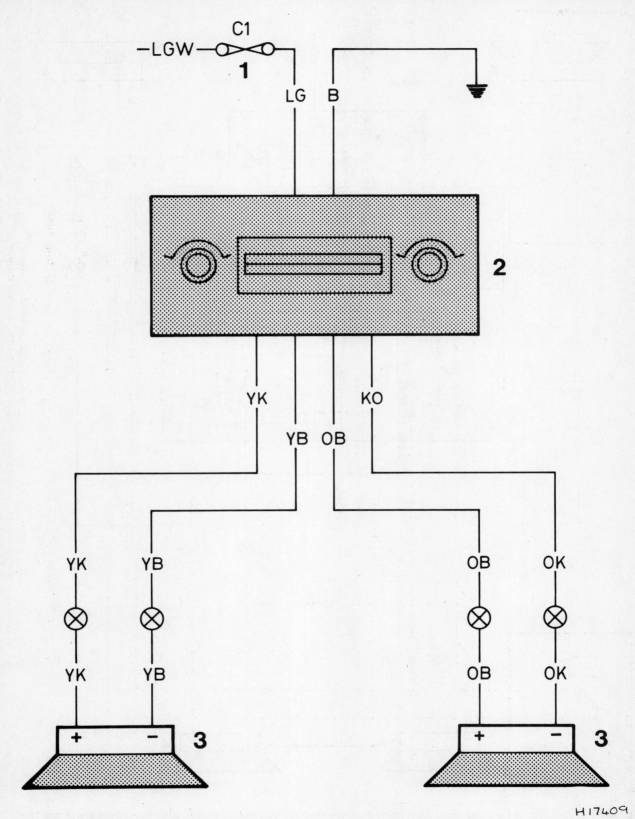

H17409

**Fig. 12.66 Supplementary wiring diagram – manually tuned radio/cassette player – two speakers (from 1986)**

1   *Fusebox*        2   *Radio/cassette player*        3   *Speakers*

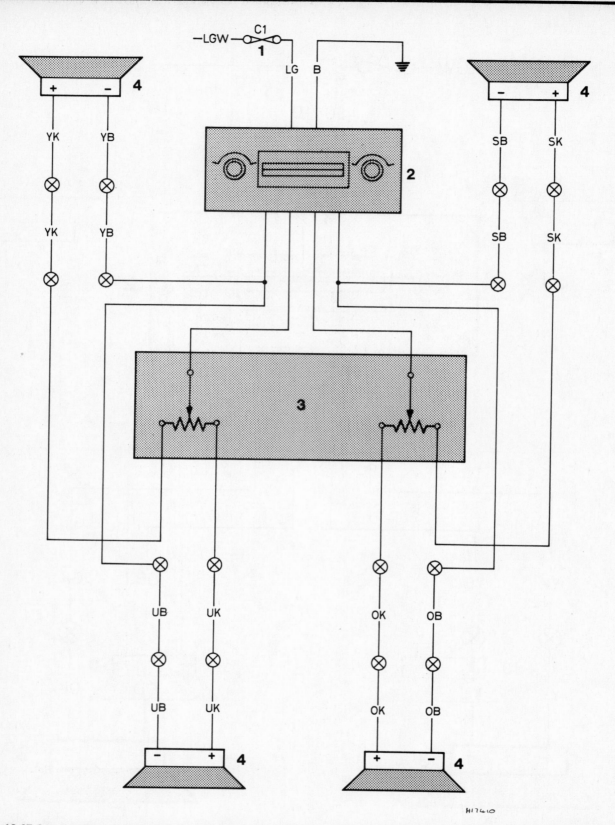

Fig. 12.67 Supplementary wiring diagram – manually-operated radio/cassette player with four speakers (from 1986)

1  Fusebox
2  Radio/cassette player

3  Balance control
4  Speakers

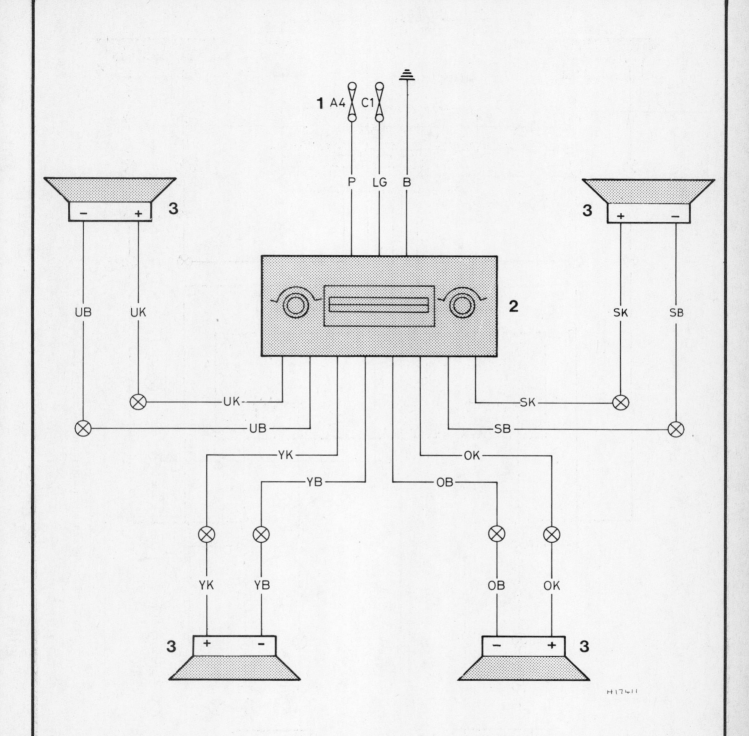

**Fig. 12.68 Supplementary wiring diagram – electronically tuned radio with four speakers (from 1986)**

1   *Fusebox*          2   *Radio/cassette player*          3   *Speakers*

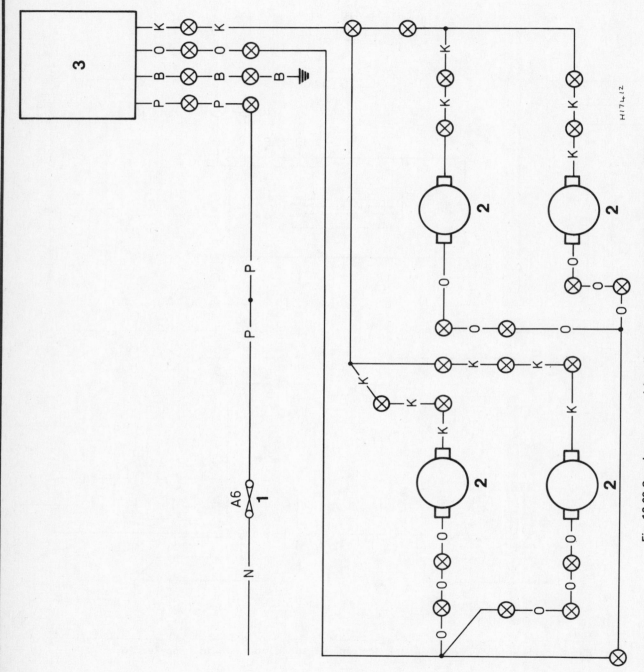

Fig. 12.69 Supplementary wiring diagram – central door locking (from 1986)

1  Fusebox        2  Door lock motor        3  Driver's control unit

H 174.12

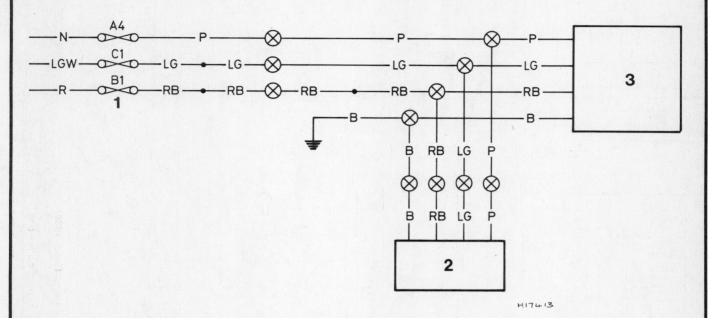

**Fig. 12.70 Supplementary wiring diagram – clock and econometer (from 1986)**

1  *Fusebox*  2  *Clock*  3  *Econometer*

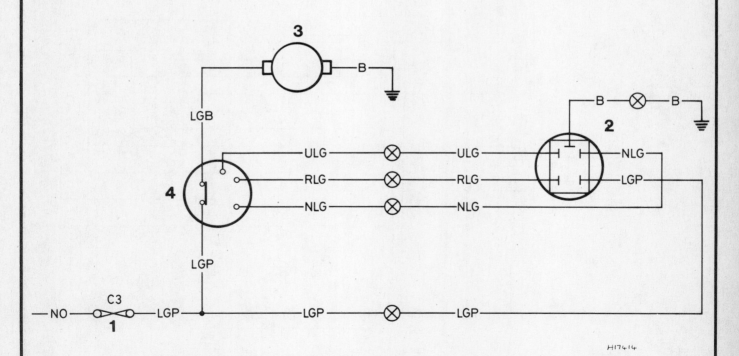

**Fig. 12.71 Supplementary wiring diagram – wiper circuit for 1.3 City Van (from 1986)**

1  *Fusebox*  3  *Windscreen washer motor*
2  *Windscreen wiper motor*  4  *Combination switch*

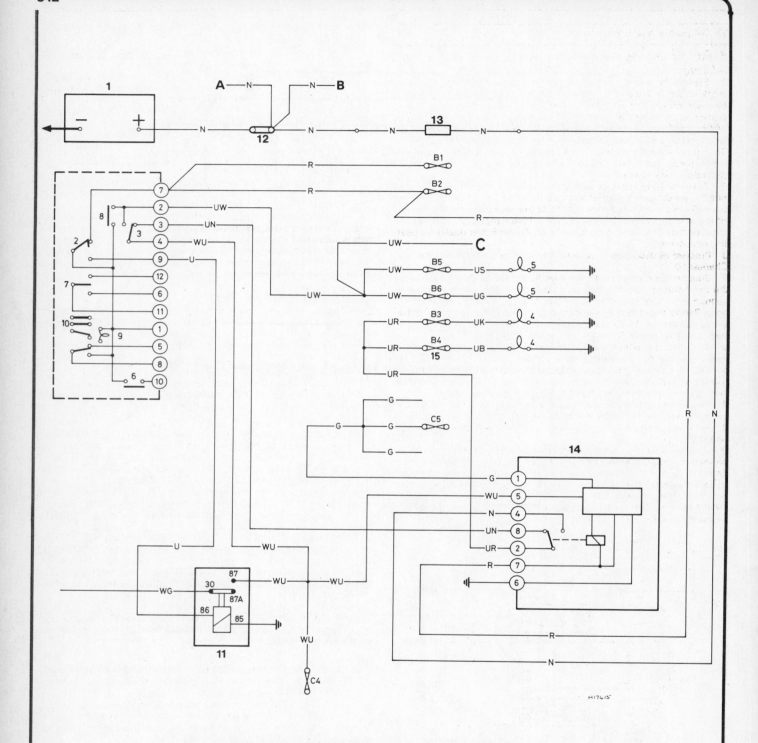

**Fig. 12.72 Supplementary wiring diagram – dim-dip headlamps**

| | | |
|---|---|---|
| 1 Battery | 7 Direction indicator switch | 13 Dim-dip resistor |
| 2 Main lighting switch | 8 Headlamp flasher switch | 14 Dim-dip relay |
| 3 Dip switch | 9 Hazard warning lamp | 15 Fusebox |
| 4 Dipped beam | 10 Hazard warning switch | A To headlamp washer relay |
| 5 Main beam | 11 Headlamp relay | B To sealed joint |
| 6 Horn push | 12 Fusible link | C To main beam warning lamp |

## 15 Suspension and steering

### Front hub bearing (single piece type) – removal and refitting

1 Some later models are fitted with a front hub unit which has a single-piece hub bearing rather than the separate inner and outer bearings shown and described in Chapter 10. This single-piece type of bearing is not interchangeable with the earlier type. As from February 1989, single-piece taper-roller bearings are used instead of the single-piece ball type bearings, in order to eliminate bearing 'drone'. The taper-roller bearings are directly interchangeable with the single-piece ball type, and removal, fitting and torque tightening procedures are identical.

2 When bearing renewal becomes necessary with these later type hubs, manufacturer's special tools are required to remove the bearing from the hub and drive flange, and to fit the new replacement. In view of this it is suggested that the hub and drive flange are removed and separated as described, then taken to an Austin Rover dealer for bearing replacement.

3 Proceed as described in paragraphs 1 to 8 inclusive in Section 3 of Chapter 10.

4 Support the hub unit with the drive flange facing down, then press the drive flange from the hub by applying pressure against the inner bearing track. Use special Austin Rover tool 18G 1284 if available. The drive flange **must not** be separated from the hub by driving it free using a hammer! As they are separated, the bearing outer half inner track and ball-race will remain on the drive flange.

5 As previously mentioned, the hub/drive flange bearing renewal is best entrusted to your Austin Rover dealer.

6 With the new hub bearing fitted and the hub and drive flange unit reassembled, locate the unit onto the driveshaft, fit the new driveshaft nut onto the driveshaft and hand tighten it only at this stage.

7 Refit the hub unit to the front strut, lower balljoint and tie-rod outer balljoint. Tighten the fastenings to the specified torque settings.

8 Refit the brake disc (if removed) and brake caliper (Chapter 8 refers).

9 With the hub and brake units fully assembled, the hub nut can be tightened. Get an assistant to apply the footbrake to prevent the front hub from turning whilst you tighten the hub nut to the specified torque wrench setting. Stake the nut into the groove in the driveshaft to secure it in the set position.

10 When the roadwheel is refitted, check that it rotates freely but without excessive play, before lowering the vehicle.

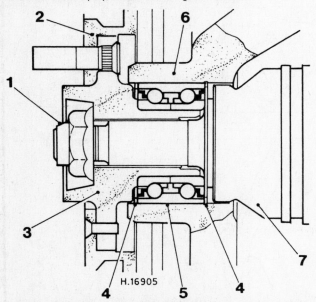

**Fig. 12.73 Sectional view of single-piece, ball type, front hub bearing (Sec 15)**

| | | | |
|---|---|---|---|
| 1 | Hub nut | 5 | Bearing |
| 2 | Brake disc | 6 | Hub |
| 3 | Drive flange | 7 | Driveshaft |
| 4 | Circlip | | |

### Rack and pinion steering gear (1.6 litre 'S' series models) – removal and refitting

11 Carry out the operations described in Chapter 10, Section 22, paragraphs 1 to 6 inclusive.

12 Slacken the front crossmember support strut bolts on the driver's side. Remove the two short bolts, but leave the long bolt in position. Pivot the support strut outward at the top.

13 The remainder of the procedure is now as described in Chapter 10, Section 22, except that the steering gear is removed through the driver's side wheel arch, the pinion cover being removed first.

### Suspension and steering (500 and 700 van models) – general description

14 The steering and front suspension on van models is as described in Chapter 10 except that the front hub is situated outboard of the disc and an anti-roll bar is fitted on 700 van versions.

15 The rear suspension on van models consist of a tubular rear axle housing the stub axles, rear brake assemblies and the wheel hubs. The axle is supported on single leaf semi-elliptic springs and damping is by telescopic shock absorbers. The rear hubs, bearings and stub axles are the same as hatchback saloon models and all repair procedures are as given in Chapter 10 except for the differences given later.

### Steering angles – from 1987

16 As from 1987, the front camber, castor and king pin inclination have been changed as the result of moving the position of the suspension strut-to-hub carrier lower fixing hole by 1.0 mm.

17 Refer to the Specifications at the beginning of this Supplement.

### Power steering system – description

18 This system was offered as an option on later 1.6 models.

19 Power assistance to the steering rack is provided hydraulically, pressure being generated by a belt-driven pump.

### Power steering system – fluid level checking and bleeding

20 At the intervals specified in 'Routine Maintenance', unscrew and withdraw the combined reservoir cap and dipstick. If the level is between the 'MIN' and 'MAX' marks, no further action need be taken. If it is below the 'MIN' mark, top up with the specified fluid.

21 The system will only require bleeding if the fluid has been drained and refilled as a result of dismantling a part or whole of the system.

22 Fill the system until the fluid reaches the 'MAX' mark on the dipstick.

23 Slacken the pump drivebelt (see next sub-section) and turn the pump pulley by hand in its normal direction of travel to prime the system. Retension the drivebelt and top up the reservoir if necessary.

24 Start the engine and allow it to idle then turn the steering wheel to full lock and then back again to the straight-ahead position. Top up the reservoir if necessary.

25 Repeat by turning to the opposite lock.

26 Turn the steering slowly from lock to lock several times and then return to the straight-ahead position. Check the fluid level, top up and switch off the engine.

### Power steering pump drivebelt – tensioning and renewal

27 Release the cooling system expansion tank hose and the fuel pump inlet hose from their retaining clips.

28 Unscrew the bolt and remove the timing belt upper cover.

29 The correct belt tension is achieved when the centre of the belt run between the power steering and camshaft pulleys can be deflected between (0.28 and 0.47 in) 7.0 and 12.0 mm.

30 If adjustment is required, slacken the pump adjustment and pivot bolts and nuts and move the pump by gripping its bracket **not** the reservoir. Tighten the bolts and nuts.

31 Refit the timing belt cover and clip the displaced hoses.

32 If a worn belt is to be renewed, slacken the belt tension as previously described and slip the belt from its pulleys. Refit the new belt and tension as previously described.

### Power steering pump – removal and refitting

33 Remove the pump drivebelt as previously described.

34 Place a container underneath the pump and disconnect the pressure hose banjo union hollow bolt (5) (Fig. 12.79). Cap or plug the open ends of hose and pump.

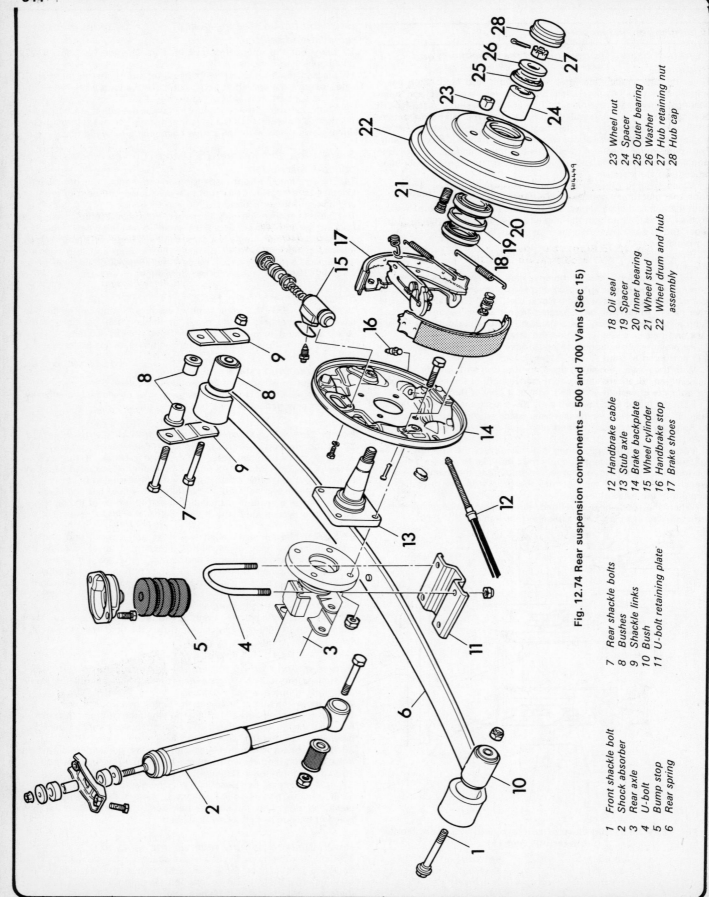

Fig. 12.74 Rear suspension components – 500 and 700 Vans (Sec 15)

| | | | |
|---|---|---|---|
| 1 | Front shackle bolt | 12 | Handbrake cable |
| 2 | Shock absorber | 13 | Stub axle |
| 3 | Rear axle | 14 | Brake backplate |
| 4 | U-bolt | 15 | Wheel cylinder |
| 5 | Bump stop | 16 | Handbrake stop |
| 6 | Rear spring | 17 | Brake shoes |
| 7 | Rear shackle bolts | 18 | Oil seal |
| 8 | Bushes | 19 | Spacer |
| 9 | Shackle links | 20 | Inner bearing |
| 10 | Bush | 21 | Wheel stud |
| 11 | U-bolt retaining plate | 22 | Wheel drum and hub |
| | | | assembly |
| | | 23 | Wheel nut |
| | | 24 | Spacer |
| | | 25 | Outer bearing |
| | | 26 | Washer |
| | | 27 | Hub retaining nut |
| | | 28 | Hub cap |

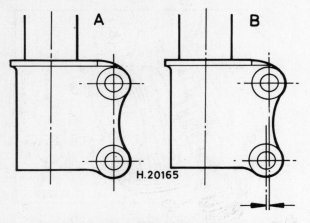

H.20165

**Fig. 12.75 Front strut lower fixing clamp hole modification (Sec 15)**

A   Old type          B   New type

**Fig. 12.76 Exploded view of the power-assisted steering gear (Sec 15)**

| | |
|---|---|
| 1   Seal | 12   Pipe (fluid feed from pump) |
| 2   Dust shield | |
| 3   Circlip | 13   Pipe (fluid return to pump) |
| 4   Fluid seal | |
| 5   Bearing | 14   Intermediate steering shaft |
| 6   Valve and pinion | |
| 7   Fluid seal | 15   Centralising plug (if fitted) |
| 8   Bush | |
| 9   Slipper | 16   Rack housing |
| 10   Spring | 17   Clip |
| 11   Plug | 18   Seal |
| | 19   Bush/fluid seal |
| | 20   Locking wire |
| | 21   Gaiter |
| | 22   Clip |
| | 23   Tie-rod end balljoint |
| | 24   Locknut |
| | 25   Tie rod |
| | 26   Cap |
| | 27   Self-locking nut |
| | 28   Bearing |
| | 29   Circlip |
| | 30   Pipe |
| | 31   Pipe |
| | 32   Support ring |
| | 33   Fluid seal |
| | 34   Rack |
| | 35   Piston |
| | 36   O-ring seal |
| | 37   Piston ring |

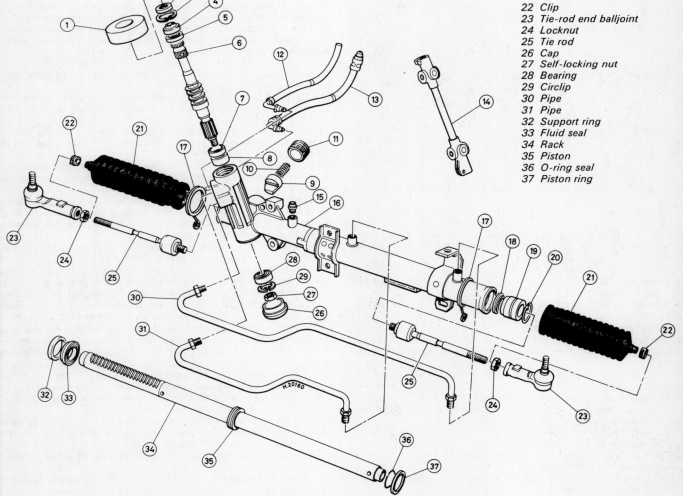

H.20160

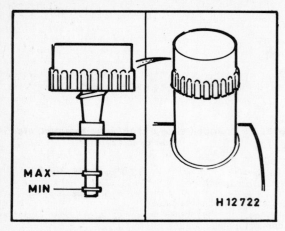

Fig. 12.77 Power steering fluid reservoir dipstick
markings (Sec 15)

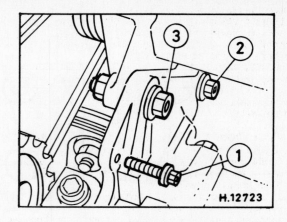

Fig. 12.78 Power steering pump drivebelt (Sec 15)

1   Timing belt upper cover        2   Pivot bolt
    bolt                           3   Adjustment bolt

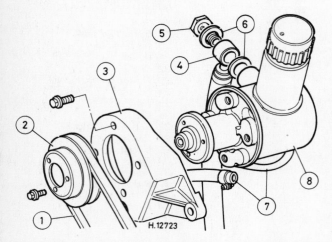

Fig. 12.79 Power steering pump components (Sec 15)

1   Drivebelt              5   Banjo union hollow bolt
2   Pulley                 6   Sealing washers
3   Mounting bracket       7   Fluid return pipe and hose
4   Pressure pipe          8   Pump

35 Disconnect the return hose from the fluid reservoir pipe. Seal the
open ends of hose and pipe.
36 Remove the adjustment and pivot bolts and nuts and withdraw the
pump.
37 Unbolt and remove the pulley.
38 Scribe alignment marks across the pump and its bracket as an aid
to reassembly then unscrew the bolts and separate the pump from the
bracket.
39 If the pump is faulty, it should be renewed as spare parts are not
available to overhaul it.
40 Fit the pulley and bracket to the new pump.
41 Reconnect the oil return hose to the pump reservoir pipe then
locate the pump on the engine with all bolts finger tight.
42 Connect the pressure hose to the pump, setting the hose at 30° to
the right-hand side. Tighten the hose union.
43 Top up the pump reservoir and turn the pulley by hand to prime the
system – see paragraphs 22 and 23.
44 Refit and tension the drivebelt as previously described. Refit the
other disturbed components.
45 Finish bleeding the system as described in paragraphs 24 to 26.

*Power steering gear – removal and refitting*
46 Disconnect the battery.
47 Unscrew and remove the pinch-bolt which connects the steering

column intermediate shaft coupling to the splined pinion shaft of the
steering gear.
48 Raise and securely support the front end of the car and remove the
front roadwheels.
49 Unscrew the steering tie-rod balljoint taper pin nuts and, using a
suitable 'splitter' tool, disconnect the balljoints from the steering arms.
50 Unbolt the suspension crossmember support bracket from the
driver's side. It may be necessary to support the crossmember with a
jack in order to remove the bolts.
51 Disconnect the exhaust downpipes from the manifold.
52 Disconnect the gearshift selector bracket and shaft bracket from
the steering rack housing.
53 Unscrew and remove the rack housing mounting bolts and
disengage the pinion shaft from the intermediate shaft by moving the
coupling upwards.
54 Working inside the car, peel back the carpet from the driver's
footwell, extract the screws which holds the rack pinion cover and lift
out the cover.
55 Disconnect the fluid pressure and return pipes from the pinion
housing, allow the fluid to drain into a suitable container and then cap
or plug the open ends of the pipes and housing.
56 Withdraw the steering gear from under the driver's side wheel arch.
57 It is not recommended that the steering gear is dismantled or
overhauled. If wear or faulty action is evident, replace the assembly
with a new or reconditioned unit.
58 Renewal of a rack gaiter and replenishment of rack lubricant is as
described for manual steering gear in Chapter 10.
59 Before fitting the steering gear, set the front roadwheels and the
steering wheel in the straight-ahead attitude, then centralise the rack.
On some models this can be done by removing the rack housing plug
and inserting a rod. Turn the pinion shaft until the rod is felt to drop
into an indentation in the rack. Where a centralising plug is not fitted,
scribe a mark at the exact centre of the rack housing for use as a
reference mark then measure to see that the ends of the tie-rods are
equidistant from the marked point. Turn the pinion shaft as necessary
to achieve this. Alternatively fit a cardboard disc to the pinion shaft and
turn the rack to full lock. Mark the disc and then turn the rack to full
opposite lock, counting the number of turns. Divide the number of
turns by two and turn the pinion shaft so that the disc rotates through
this smaller number of turns.
60 Offer the steering gear into position, screw in the mounting bolts
and then connect the pressure and return hoses and secure the unions
by bending up the lockwasher tabs.
61 Fit the gearshift brackets and connect the exhaust to the manifold
using a new gasket.
62 Fit the crossmember support bracket, but do not tighten the fixing
bolts to the specified torque until the car has been lowered.
63 Screw on the tie-rod end balljoints until the taper pins will just
drop into the eyes of the steering arms, with the roadwheels in the
straight-ahead position. Screw on and tighten the taper pin nuts.
Tighten the locknuts.
64 Connect the intermediate-to-pinion shaft coupling, fit the pinch-

bolt and tighten to the specified torque.

65 Tighten the rack housing mounting bolts to the specified torque.

66 Fit the rack pinion cover to the driver's footwell.

67 Lower the car to the floor and tighten the suspension crossmember bracket bolts to the specified torque.

68 Connect the battery.

69 Fill and bleed the steering system as described earlier in this Section.

70 Check and adjust the front wheel alignment as described in Chapter 10, Section 24.

### Rear shock absorber (500 and 700 van models) – removal and refitting

71 Chock the front wheels, remove the rear wheel trim and slacken the wheel nuts. Jack up the rear of the vehicle and support it on axle stands. Remove the roadwheel.

72 Undo and remove the nut and bolt securing the shock absorber lower mounting to the rear axle (photo).

73 Undo the nut and remove the flat washer and rubber bush securing the shock absorber upper mounting to the support bracket (photo).

74 Withdraw the upper and lower mountings from their locations and remove the shock absorber from under the wheel arch. Remove the remaining rubber bush and flat washer from the upper mounting.

75 Refitting is the reverse sequence to removal, but tighten the mounting nuts and bolts to the specified torque.

**Note:** *As of VIN 667466, a revised damper and top mounting arrangement has been used, to resolve a premature wear problem on some vehicles which resulted in knocking noises from the rear. The original type of damper remains available for direct replacement, but it is possible to fit the revised arrangement to earlier vehicles. To accomplish this, you will require the new type dampers (Part No. GSA 971101) and a rear damper top mounting kit (Part No. RPM 10001). Note that, if you elect to fit the modified dampers, they must be fitted as pairs only, using the new top mounting kit.*

### Rear road spring (500 and 700 van models) – removal and refitting

76 Chock the four wheels, remove the rear wheel trim and slacken the wheel nuts. Jack up the rear of the vehicle and support it on axle stands. Remove the appropriate rear roadwheel.

77 Place a jack or axle stands under the rear axle on the side being worked on.

78 Undo the nut and remove the load sensing valve connecting arm from the bracket on the rear axle.

79 Undo the four nuts, then withdraw the retaining plate and the two U-bolts securing the rear axle to the roadspring (photo).

80 Undo the nuts and remove the front and rear shackle bolts (photo). Withdraw the spring from its locations and remove it from under the vehicle.

81 Refitting is the reverse sequence to removal, bearing in mind the following points:

    (a) Fit the spring front and rear shackle bolts, but tighten the nuts finger tight only at this stage.

    (b) Refit the remainder of the spring attachments and components, then, with the vehicle standing on its wheels, tighten the shackle bolts. Ensure that all nuts and bolts are tightened to the specified torque.

    (c) If new springs have been fitted, bounce the vehicle at the rear to settle the components then adjust the braking system load sensing valve, as described in Section 13 of this Supplement. When the springs have settled fully (after approximately 1000 miles (1600 km) the valve must be checked and, if necessary, adjusted again.

### Rear axle (500 and 700 van models) – removal and refitting

82 Chock the front wheels, remove the rear wheel trim and slacken the wheel nuts. Jack up the rear of the vehicle and support it on axle stands. Remove the roadwheels.

83 Release the handbrake then slacken the handbrake adjuster to remove all tension from the cable.

84 Disconnect the handbrake front and intermediate cables at the cable connector alongside the fuel tank.

85 Using brake hose clamps or other suitable tools, clamp the two rear brake flexible hoses. Wipe clean the area around the pipe-to-hose unions on the rear axle then unscrew the brake pipe union nuts. Extract the retaining clips and remove the hoses from their support brackets on the rear axle.

86 Undo the retaining nut and remove the load sensing valve connecting arm from the bracket on the rear axle.

87 Undo the nuts and remove the bolts securing the shock absorber lower mountings to the rear axle.

88 Undo the four nuts each side securing the rear axle to the rear springs. Remove the retaining plates and withdraw the U-bolts.

89 Manipulate the rear axle over the rear springs and withdraw it from under the vehicle.

90 Refitting is the reverse sequence to removal, bearing in mind the following points:

    (a) Tighten all nuts and bolts to the specified torque

    (b) Bleed the braking system and adjust the handbrake cable, as described in Chapter 8

    (c) Check the load sensing valve adjustment, as described in Section 13 of this Supplement

### Rear hub bearings (500 and 700 van models) – removal and refitting

91 When working on the rear hub bearings on the above models, note that the hub and bearing arrangement is similar, but not identical, to that described for the saloons; the hub components are not interchangeable between the car and van models. The hub components can be dealt with as described in Chapter 10, Section 11, noting the following points.

92 The bearings do not have the THRUST markings described for the saloon models. Instead, when fitting the outer bearing, make sure that you position the plastic bearing cage adjacent to the road wheel. The hub should be packed with Shell Alvania RA (or equivalent) grease as specified by Austin Rover – in case of difficulty, consult an Austin Rover

15.72 Rear shock absorber lower mounting bolt (arrowed)

15.73 Rear shock absorber upper mounting

15.79 Rear roadspring U-bolts and nuts

15.80A Rear roadspring front shackle

15.80B Roadspring rear shackle

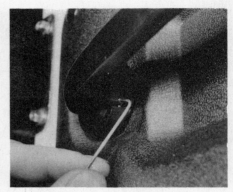

16.3 Door interior handle grub screw

dealer. Install the bearing spacer with the tapered end towards the outer bearing, then fit the inner bearing with the plastic cage nearest the brake backplate. Fit the hub oil seal with the projecting seal lip facing outwards towards the backplate.

93  Clean carefully the brake backplate where the hub oil seal contacts it. Pack the inside of the oil seal lip with the recommended Shell Alvania grease. This prevents contact between the hub and the backplate causing squealing in service. After installing the hub, wipe away any excess grease from around the hub, to prevent contamination of the brake surfaces.

## Anti-roll bar – 500 van

94  As from 1988, the 500 van is fitted with a front anti-roll bar. The removal and refitting operations are described in Chapter 10, Section 9.

## 16 Bodywork

### Central door locking system motor/switch

1  When fitting a central door locking motor/switch unit, locate it into position in the door panel so that it is in its normal position but with the unit forward as much as possible and with the front retaining screw in the centre to upper slot position.

2 Tighten the front retaining screw, then the rear screw keeping it in the central to upper position, see Fig. 12.81.

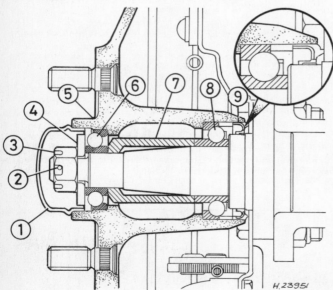

**Fig. 12.80 Rear hub bearing components (500 and 700 van models) (Sec 15)**

1  Hub cap
2  Split pin
3  Hub retaining nut
4  Washer
5  Hub
6  Outer bearing
7  Spacer
8  Inner bearing
9  Oil seal

*Inset shows projecting lip of oil seal packed with grease*

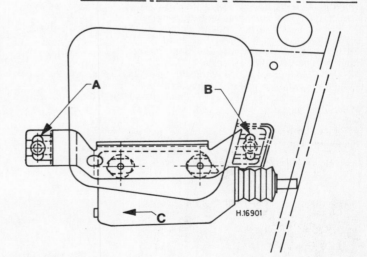

**Fig. 12.81 Central door locking switch unit (Sec 16)**

A  Front retaining screw
B  Rear retaining screw
C  Unit positioned fully forward

### Left-hand rear door latches (500 and 700 van models) – removal and refitting

3  Open the left-hand rear door and slacken the interior handle retaining grub screw using a suitable Allen key (photo).

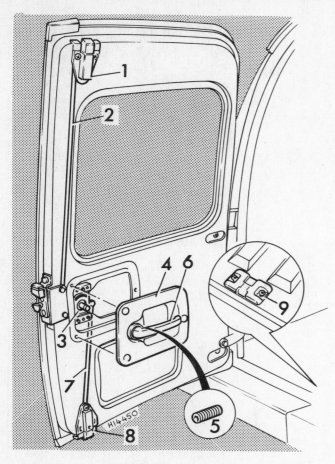

**Fig. 12.82 Left-hand rear door latch on 500 and 700 Van models (Sec 16)**

| | |
|---|---|
| 1  Upper latch | 6  Door interior handle |
| 2  Upper link rod | 7  Lower link rod |
| 3  Door handle mechanism | 8  Lower latch |
| 4  Trim cover panel | 9  Latch striker plate |
| 5  Grub screw | |

4  Withdraw the interior handle then remove the trim cover panel by prising out the plastic retaining buttons (Fig. 12.82).
5  Undo the bolts securing the door handle mechanism and disconnect the upper and lower link rods. Withdraw the handle mechanism from the door panel aperture.

6  Undo the three bolts and withdraw the upper and lower latches and link rods as required (photo).
7  Refitting is the reverse sequence to removal. Adjust the upper and lower latch strike plates as necessary so that the door shuts and locks securely (photo).

### Right-hand rear door latch (500 and 700 van models) – removal and refitting
8  With the door open, turn the latch claw anti-clockwise to its closed position.
9  Disconnect the operating rod at the door handle then release the retaining clip and remove the operating rod at the private lock (photo).
10  Undo the screws securing the latch mechanism to the door and remove it through the door panel aperture (photo). With the latch removed, rotate the claw clockwise to its open position.
11  Refitting is the reverse sequence to removal.

### Rear door private lock (500 and 700 van models) – removal and refitting
12  Open the rear doors and release the operating rod retaining clip at the private lock. Withdraw the rod from the lock (photo).
13  Prise out the retaining clip and withdraw the private lock from the door.
14  Refitting is the reverse sequence to removal.

### Rear door (500 and 700 van models) – removal and refitting
15  Open the rear doors then undo the bolts securing the check strap linkage to the bottom of the door (photo).
16  Mark the outline of the hinge arms on the door using a soft pencil.
17  With an assistant supporting the door, undo the upper and lower hinge retaining bolts (photo) and withdraw the door.
18  Refitting is the reverse sequence to removal, but align the marks made during removal before tightening the retaining bolts.

### Tailgate lock (from VIN 146812) – removal and refitting
19  The rear courtesy lamp switch is operated by the lock on these later models.
20  Remove the tailgate trim panel and disconnect the courtesy lamp leads.
21  Disconnect the operating rod from the lock lever.
22  Unscrew the lock mounting bolts and withdraw the lock from the tailgate.
23  Refitting is a reversal of removal. Adjust the position of the striker if necessary to give smooth, positive closure of the tailgate.

### Rear seat belts – general
24  Later models are equipped with rear seat belts as standard.
25  The outer belts are of inertia reel type connecting to a static belt which is located between the rear edge of the seat cushion and the bottom edge of the seat back. The central lap belt is of static type. The belt is adjustable for length by means of a buckle.
26  Removal and refitting operations are similar to those described for the front seat belts in Chapter 11.

16.6 Van rear door upper latch

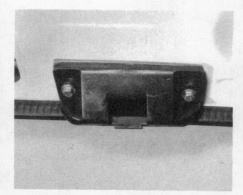

16.7 Van rear door latch striker plate

16.9 Van rear door handle (A) and lock (B) operating rods

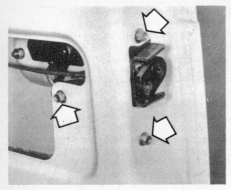

16.10 Van rear door latch retaining screws (arrowed)

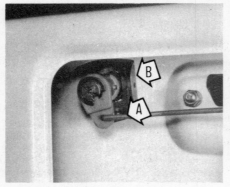

16.12 Van rear door lock operating rod clip (A) and lock retaining clip (B)

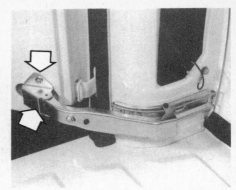

16.15 Van rear door check strap fixing bolts (arrowed)

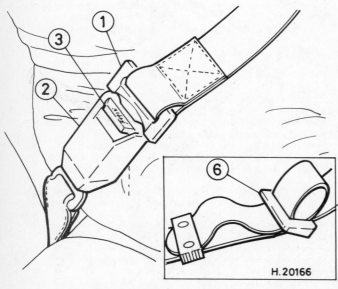

Fig. 12.83 Rear seat central belt (Sec 16)

| 1 | Torque | 3 | Release plunger |
|---|--------|---|-----------------|
| 2 | Lock   | 6 | Adjuster |

*Rear quarter bumper (500 and 700 van models) – removal and refitting*

27 Undo the two screws and withdraw the number plate lamp assembly from the end of bumper (Fig. 12.84).

28 Prise out the two plastic moulding caps then undo the bumper retaining bolts.

29 Withdraw the bumper and release the wiring harness from the cable clips on the bumper edge.

30 Refitting is the reverse sequence to removal.

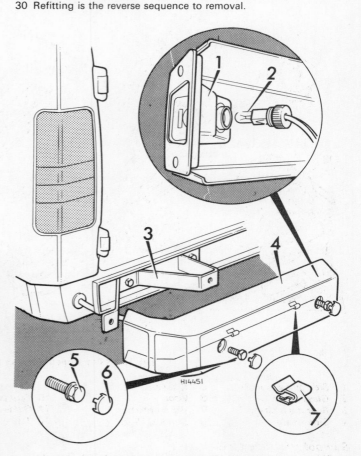

Fig. 12.84 Rear quarter bumper details – 500 and 700 van models (Sec 16)

| 1 | Number plate lamp assembly | 5 | Bumper retaining bolt |
|---|----------------------------|---|-----------------------|
| 2 | Bulb | 6 | Moulding cap |
| 3 | Bumper bracket | 7 | Wiring clip |
| 4 | Bumper | | |

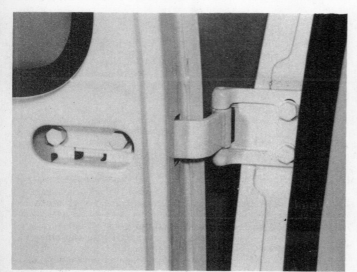

16.17 Van rear door hinge fixing bolts

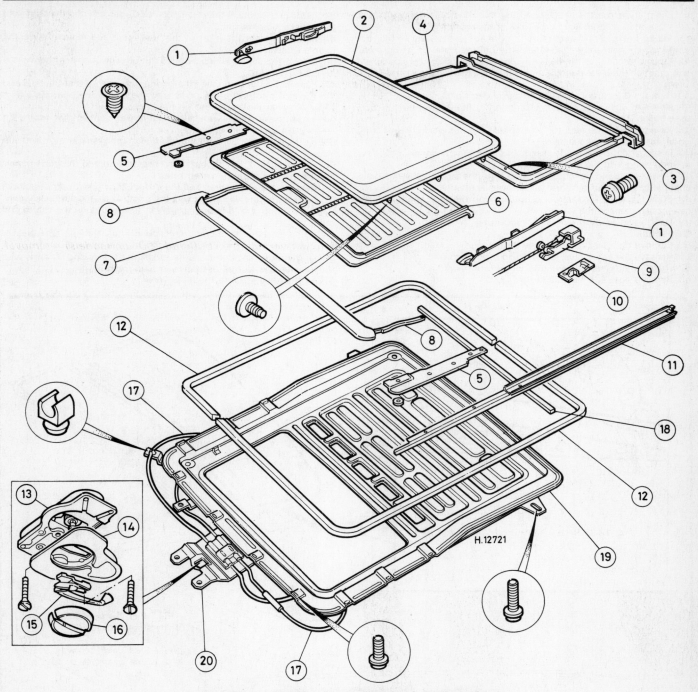

**Fig. 12.85 Components of the tilt/slide sunroof (Sec 16)**

| | | | | | | | |
|---|---|---|---|---|---|---|---|
| 1 | Side arm assembly | 5 | Slide rail | 9 | Rear guide/cable | 13 | Drive gear |
| 2 | Glass panel | 6 | Visor | 10 | Pilot plate | 14 | Escutcheon |
| 3 | Rear drain channel | 7 | Wind deflector | 11 | Guide rail | 15 | Crankhandle |
| 4 | Side shield | 8 | Deflector lighting arm | 12 | Tray seal | 16 | Bezel |

17 Cable guide and runout tubes
18 Tray rear seal
19 Tray
20 Front bracket

## Sunroof (tilt/slide type)

31  This type of sunroof is fitted to 1987 model vehicles. Operation is by means of a manual crank handle with reversible action.

32  Individual components of the sunroof may be removed and refitted in the following way.

**Glass panel and seal**

33  Check that the operating handle is in the closed (free play) position, then open the panel to the halfway position.

34  Release the screws which secure the side shield and rear drain channel assembly (3 and 4) (Fig. 12.85) to the glass panel.

35  Slide the cover, drain channel and visor towards the rear of the car into the recess above the headlining.

36  Close the glass panel and then tilt its rear edge.

37  Extract the screws which hold the glass panel to the side arms (1).

38  Lift off the glass panel and remove the seal.

39  Fit the seal firmly to the edge of the glass panel so that the rubber surface is inwards. Cut the seal where the ends meet to form a butt joint.

40  Set the operating mechanism in the closed position, then place the glass panel on the side arm assemblies and fit the screws.

41 Open and close the panel, checking that the front edge is flush or not more than 1.0 mm below the level of the roof panel. The rear edge should be flush or not more than 1.0 mm above the level of the roof panel. Where necessary adjust the setting of the panel on its brackets.
42 Open the panel to the half-way position and slide the side shield and drain channel assembly into position. Fit the securing screws.

**Visor**
43 Remove the glass panel as previously described.
44 Remove the pilot plates (10) (Fig. 12.85) and the side arm assemblies (1).
45 Remove the slide rails (5) and collect the flat washers, one from under the front of each slide rail.
46 Disengage the rear guide assemblies from their channels and allow them to hang into the roof opening.
47 Lower the wind deflector (7) and slide the side shield and drain channel forward and out through the roof opening.
48 Slide the visor forwards and out through the roof opening. Take care not to damage the guides.
49 Refit by reversing the removal procedure.

**Drivegear**
50 Remove the glass as previously described.
51 Remove the crank handle bezel and escutcheon.
52 Remove the finisher from around the roof opening.
53 Remove both sun visors and their clips.

54 Remove the grab handle from the passenger side and the stud from the driver's side headlining.
55 Carefully lower the front of the headlining and remove the crank handle screws.
56 Extract the screw which secures the drivegear, and withdraw the drivegear.
57 To refit, first position the lift arm and side arm so that the hole and the triangular cut-out are aligned with the slot in the pilot plate (Fig. 12.87). Repeat the alignment on the opposite arm.
58 Smear the drivegear with silicone grease and engage the cables. Fit and tighten the drivegear screw.
59 Fit the crank handle, refit the headlining grab handle, stud and sun visors.
60 Fit the finisher, handle bezel and escutcheon and the glass panel.

**Rear guide and cable assemblies**
61 Remove the glass panel and the drivegear as previously described.
62 Extract the screws and remove the pilot plates and front slide rails.
63 Detach both side/lift arm assemblies and withdraw the cables and guides.
64 When refitting, fill the guide tubes with non-staining type grease.
65 Push the cables through the grease into the guide tubes.
66 Fit the remaining components and align the side and lift arms with the cut-out and slot as described in paragraph 57.
67 Fit the drivegear and the glass panel.

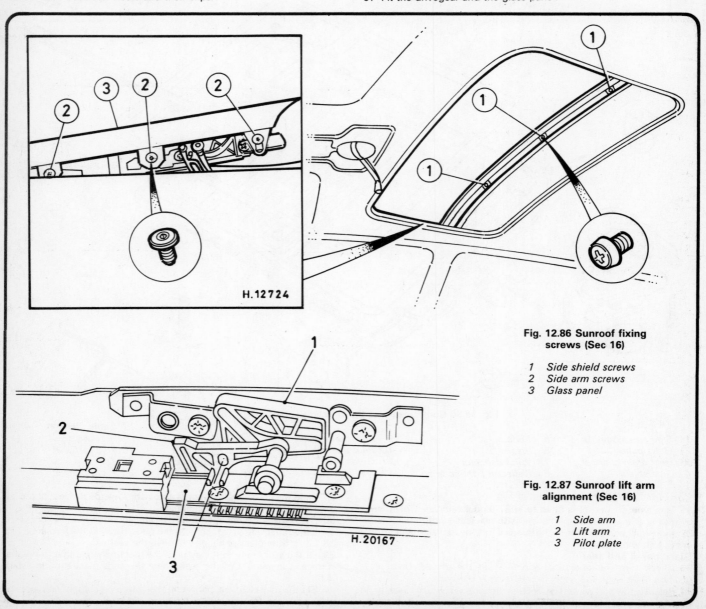

H.12724

**Fig. 12.86 Sunroof fixing screws (Sec 16)**

1 Side shield screws
2 Side arm screws
3 Glass panel

**Fig. 12.87 Sunroof lift arm alignment (Sec 16)**

1 Side arm
2 Lift arm
3 Pilot plate

H.20167

## Sunroof assembly – complete

68 Remove the glass panel as described previously.

69 Remove the bezel, escutcheon and crankarm.

70 Withdraw the headlining from around the roof opening.

71 Disconnect the drain tubes from the sunroof tray. Locate a block of wood above the front bracket and drill out the two rivets.

72 Fully recline the front seats and then extract the sunroof tray fixing screws. Lower the tray and withdraw it through the front passenger door. Remove the tray seal.

73 Refitting is a reversal of removal but, before installation, fit a new strip of 20 x 20 mm Compriband seal around the edge of the tray. This is available from your dealer.

74 Secure the front bracket with rivets.

### Plastic components – repair

75 With the use of more and more plastic body components by the vehicle manufacturers (eg bumpers, spoilers, and in some cases major body panels), rectification of more serious damage to such items has become a matter of either entrusting repair work to a specialist in this field, or renewing complete components. Repair of such damage by the DIY owner is not really feasible owing to the cost of the equipment and materials required for effecting such repairs. The basic technique involves making a groove along the line of the crack in the plastic using a rotary burr in a power drill. The damaged part is then welded back together by using a hot air gun to heat up and fuse a plastic filler rod into the groove. Any excess plastic is then removed and the area rubbed down to a smooth finish. It is important that a filler rod of the correct plastic is used, as body components can be made of a variety of different types (eg polycarbonate, ABS, polypropylene).

76 Damage of a less serious nature (abrasions, minor cracks etc) can be repaired by the DIY owner using a two-part epoxy filler repair material, like Holts Body + Plus or Holts No Mix which can be used directly from the tube. Once mixed in equal proportions (or applied direct from the tube in the case of Holts No Mix), this is used in similar fashion to the bodywork filler used on metal panels. The filler is usually cured in twenty to thirty minutes, ready for sanding and painting.

77 If the owner is renewing a complete component himself, or if he has repaired it with epoxy filler, he will be left with the problem of finding a suitable paint for finishing which is compatible with the type of plastic used. At one time the use of a universal paint was not possible owing to the complex range of plastics encountered in body component applications. Standard paints, generally speaking, will not bond to plastic or rubber satisfactorily, but Holts Professional Spraymatch paints to match any plastic or rubber finish can be obtained from dealers. However, it is now possible to obtain a plastic body parts finishing kit which consists of a pre-primer treatment, a primer and coloured top coat. Full instructions are normally supplied with a kit, but basically the method of use is to first apply the

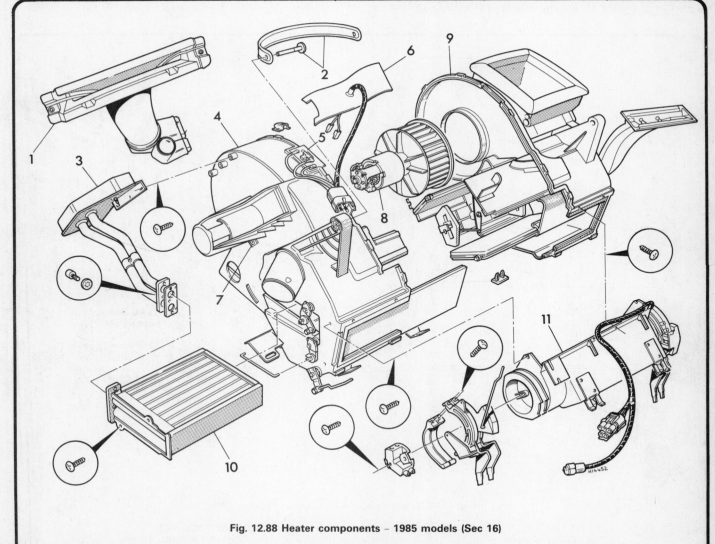

**Fig. 12.88 Heater components – 1985 models (Sec 16)**

| 1 | Face level vent | 4 | Left-hand heater body | 7 | Motor retaining plate | 10 | Matrix |
| 2 | Carrier strap and support pin | 5 | Resistor unit | 8 | Blower motor | 11 | Front panel and control |
| 3 | Matrix pipes | 6 | Blower motor cover | 9 | Right-hand heater body | | lever housing |

pre-primer to the component concerned and allow it to dry for up to 30 minutes. Then the primer is applied and left to dry for about an hour before finally applying the special coloured top coat. The result is a correctly coloured component where the paint will flex with the plastic or rubber, a property that standard paint does not normally possess.

### Heater (1985 and later models) – general

78 On 1985 models, a heater unit of modified design is fitted to all variants. The heater on these models functions in essentially the same way as earlier units except that the vacuum operation has been replaced by total mechanical operation giving greater control of air distribution and temperature.

79 On later models, the heater unit is similar to that fitted to the 1985 models, but the adjustment controls differ. There are just two control levers, the right-hand lever adjusts the air distribution and the left-hand lever adjusts the air temperature control. The blower motor has three speeds and is controlled by a rotary switch.

**Note:** *Should the heater fuse blow when the blower motor is switched on, on these later models, renew the 15 amp fuse with one of 20 amp rating.*

### Heater (1985 and later models) – removal and refitting

80 On later 1985 and 86/87 models the removal and refitting procedures are similar to those described for the earlier models in Section 38 of Chapter 11, but any reference to vacuum pipes can be ignored. The fixing points for the 86/87 models are shown in Fig. 12.90.

### Heater adjustments – 1985 models

81 Remove the heater cover panel, as described in Chapter 11, Section 35, paragraphs 3 and 4.

82 With reference to Fig. 12.91 carry out the adjustments as follows.

83 Move the face level air control to the fully raised position, slacken the securing screw (A) and hold the flap lever in the fully clockwise position. Tighten the securing screw.

84 Move the air temperature control to the fully raised position, slacken the securing screw (B) and hold the flap lever in the fully anti-clockwise position. Tighten the securing screw.

85 Move the air distribution control to the fully raised position, slacken the securing screw (C) and hold the flap lever in the fully clockwise position. Tighten the securing screw.

86 After adjustment, refit the heater cover panel, as described in Chapter 11, Section 35.

### Heater adjustments – 1986 and later models

87 Remove the cover from the fuse box and, if fitted, the closing panel above the pedals.

88 Fully raise the adjustment levers, then loosen the pinchbolt and move the air temperature flap fully down. Check that the air temperature control lever is still fully raised then tighten the pinchbolt (Fig. 12.92).

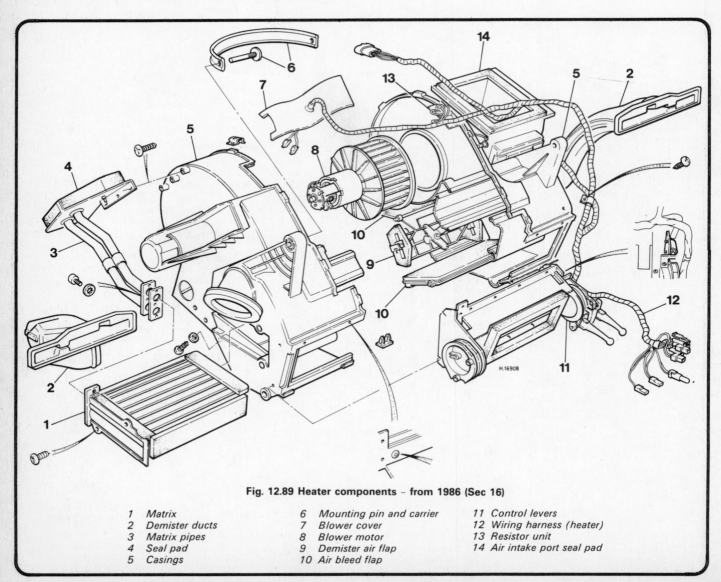

**Fig. 12.89 Heater components – from 1986 (Sec 16)**

| | | |
|---|---|---|
| 1  Matrix | 6  Mounting pin and carrier | 11  Control levers |
| 2  Demister ducts | 7  Blower cover | 12  Wiring harness (heater) |
| 3  Matrix pipes | 8  Blower motor | 13  Resistor unit |
| 4  Seal pad | 9  Demister air flap | 14  Air intake port seal pad |
| 5  Casings | 10  Air bleed flap | |

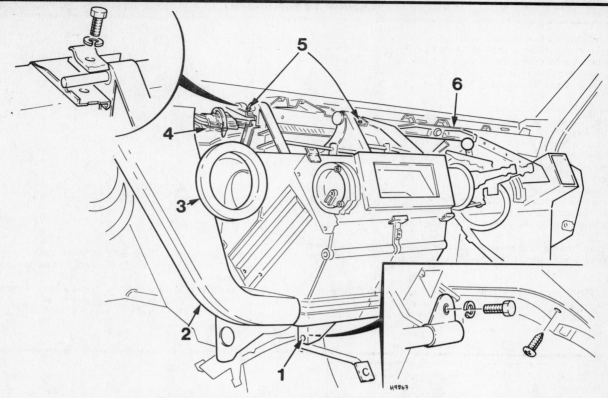

**Fig. 12.90 Heater fixing points – 1986/87 models (Sec 16)**

1 Lower fixing
2 Left-hand demister duct
3 Left-hand side vent duct
4 Heater blower wiring multi-plug connection
5 Top fixings
6 Right-hand side demister duct

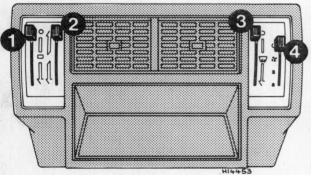

**Fig. 12.91 Heater control adjustments – 1985 models (Sec 16)**

1 Face level air control
2 Air temperature control
3 Air distribution control
4 Blower control
A Face level air control adjustment
B Air temperature control adjustment
C Air distribution control adjustment

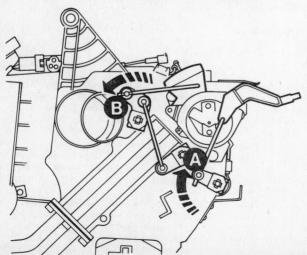
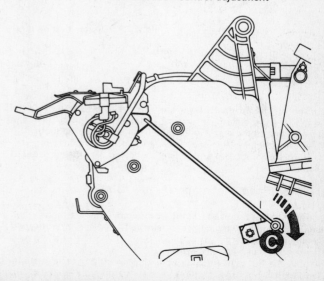

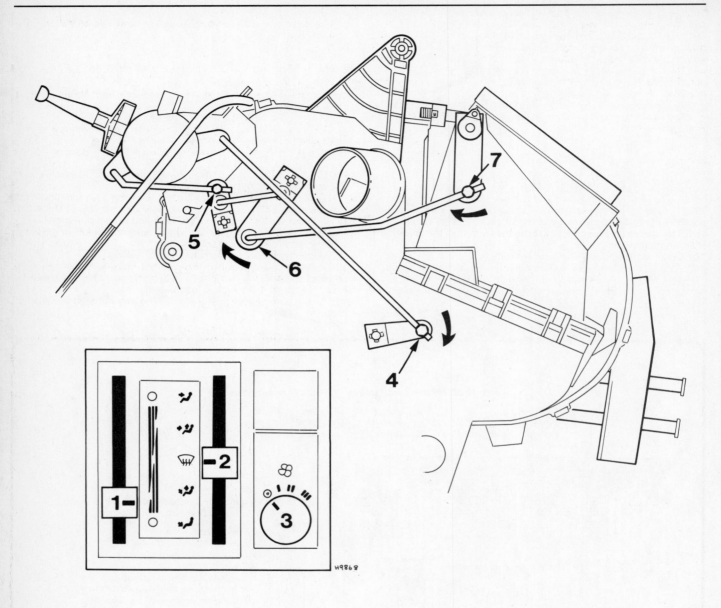

**Fig. 12.92 Heater flap linkage – 1986 and later models (Sec 16)**

1   Air temperature control          4   Air temperature flap lever          6   Demister flap lever
2   Air distributor control          5   Fresh air flap lever                7   Air intake flap lever
3   Blower switch

89  Loosen off the air intake lever and the fresh air lever pinchbolts, check that the air distributor control is fully raised, then push the demister air flap to the rear. Tighten the fresh air lever pinchbolt.
90  Push the air intake lever to the rear and tighten its pinchbolt.
91  Refit the fusebox cover and where applicable the closing panel to complete.

### Heater (1985 and later models) – dismantling and reassembly

92  With the heater removed from the car, remove the drain hose then release the retaining spring clips and remove the heater upper support pins and carrier strap.
93  Remove the side vent elbows.
94  Remove the Rokut rivets securing the heater control panel, remove the flap link rod from the trunnion, then move the control levers and panel to one side.

95  Undo the screws securing the matrix pipe bracket, pipe support clip and matrix flange. Lift out the matrix and pipes. Undo the retaining screws and remove the pipes and gasket from the matrix.
96  Undo the eight screws and two clips securing the heater motor terminal cover. Lift off the cover and disconnect the motor wiring harness plugs. Remove the harness clips.
97  On 1985 models, undo the two screws and washers securing the demist flaps. On later models, undo the screw and washer, then drill out the pop rivets retaining the left-hand side of the demister baffle to the heater case.
98  Drill out the pop rivet adjacent to the heater lower mounting. Remove the sealing tape from inside the heater control panel aperture.
99  Release the spring retaining clips and separate the two halves of the heater body. Withdraw the resistor unit and place the wiring harness to one side. Remove the two plastic hinge bushes from the flaps.

100 Using a flat screwdriver inserted between the heater body and the rear of the blower motor casing, carefully ease out the motor.

101 With the heater dismantled, inspect the matrix for signs of leaks and, if any are apparent, renew the matrix. If the matrix appears serviceable, brush off any accumulation of dirt or debris from the fins and then reverse flush the core. Inspect the remaining heater components for any signs of damage or distortion and renew as necessary.

102 Reassembly is the reverse sequence to dismantling, but adjust the heater flap linkage, as described previously on completion. New pop rivets will be required.

### Front seat belts with adjustable upper guide – removal and refitting

103 Slide the front seat fully forward.

104 Release the door seals from the central body pillar.

105 Prise off the plastic cap from the upper belt anchor bolt, and then unscrew the bolt and remove the anchor plate '2' (Fig. 12.93).

106 Remove the pillar upper cover, prise the knob from the adjustment slide, and remove the cover.

107 Unbolt and remove the adjustment slide.

108 Prise off the plastic cap and unscrew the sill anchor plate bolt.

109 Remove the lower cover from the pillar.

110 Unbolt the belt reel and withdraw it. Note the location of the spacer.

111 Slide the plastic cover upwards off the floor stalk, and then unbolt and remove it.

112 Refitting is a reversal of removal. The stalk release button must face inwards.

### Facia panel (1988 on) – removal and refitting

113 Disconnect the battery.

114 Remove the under covers (where fitted) from each side of the facia panel (Fig. 12.94).

115 Remove the steering column (Chapter 10).

116 Remove the instrument panel, radio and electric window switch assembly (Section 14 of this Supplement).

117 Release the heater blower switch panel and disconnect the illumination lamp.

118 Extract the screw and withdraw the heater control panel. Disconnect the electrical connections.

119 Open the glovebox, release the glovebox top cover and lower it.

120 Disconnect all facia wiring multi-plugs also the fuel ECU if fitted.

121 Take off the end caps from the facia and extract the screws.

122 Unscrew and remove the bolt which holds the middle of the lower stiffener rail to the support bracket.

123 Withdraw the facia assembly from the vehicle.

124 Refitting is a reversal of removal, but make sure that the radio aerial lead passes over the right-hand demister duct before pushing the facia fully forwards to engage the top panel clips.

125 Check the operation of all switches and lamps after the battery has been reconnected.

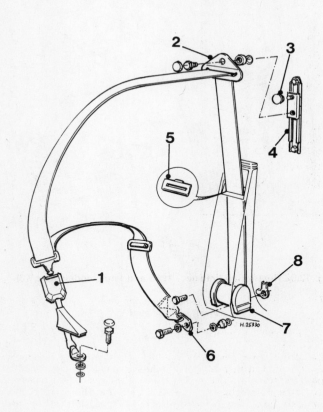

**Fig. 12.93 Components of adjustable upper guide type seat belt (Sec 16)**

| | | | | | |
|---|---|---|---|---|---|
| 1 | Stalk | 4 | Slide | 7 | Inertia reel |
| 2 | Anchor plate | 5 | Escutcheon | 8 | Reel locating |
| 3 | Knob | 6 | Lower anchor plate | | bracket |

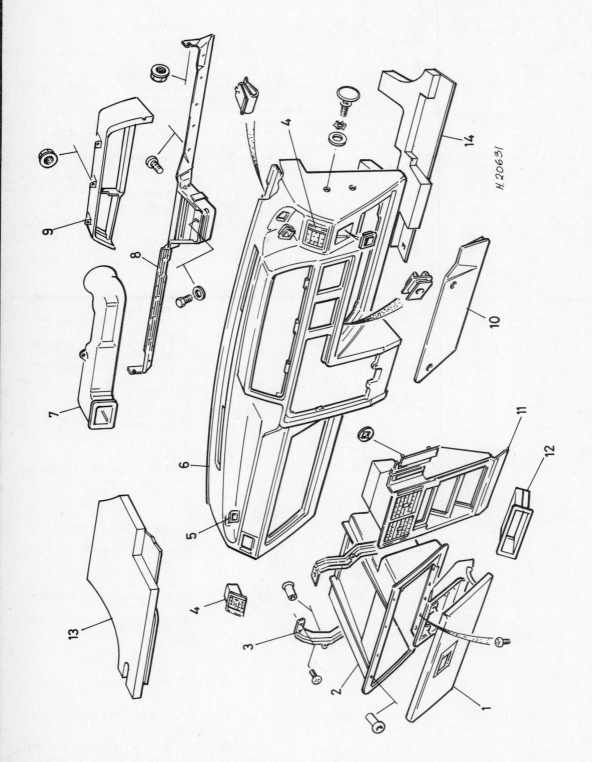

H. 20631

**Fig. 12.94 Facia components – 1988 on (Sec 16)**

| | | | | |
|---|---|---|---|---|
| 1 | Glovebox lid | 6 | Facia panel | 12 | Tidy tray |
| 2 | Glovebox | 7 | Fresh air cross duct | 13 | Facia under cover |
| 3 | Glovebox supports | 8 | Lower stiffening rail | 14 | Facia under cover |
| 4 | Fresh air vents | 9 | Instrument carrier | | |
| 5 | Side window demist escutcheon | 10 | Fusebox cover | | |
| | | 11 | Centre vent housing | | |

# Conversion factors

### Length (distance)

| | | | | | |
|---|---|---|---|---|---|
| Inches (in) | X 25.4 | = Millimetres (mm) | X 0.0394 | = Inches (in) |
| Feet (ft) | X 0.305 | = Metres (m) | X 3.281 | = Feet (ft) |
| Miles | X 1.609 | = Kilometres (km) | X 0.621 | = Miles |

### Volume (capacity)

| | | | | |
|---|---|---|---|---|
| Cubic inches (cu in; in³) | X 16.387 | = Cubic centimetres (cc; cm³) | X 0.061 | = Cubic inches (cu in; in³) |
| Imperial pints (Imp pt) | X 0.568 | = Litres (l) | X 1.76 | = Imperial pints (Imp pt) |
| Imperial quarts (Imp qt) | X 1.137 | = Litres (l) | X 0.88 | = Imperial quarts (Imp qt) |
| Imperial quarts (Imp qt) | X 1.201 | = US quarts (US qt) | X 0.833 | = Imperial quarts (Imp qt) |
| US quarts (US qt) | X 0.946 | = Litres (l) | X 1.057 | = US quarts (US qt) |
| Imperial gallons (Imp gal) | X 4.546 | = Litres (l) | X 0.22 | = Imperial gallons (Imp gal) |
| Imperial gallons (Imp gal) | X 1.201 | = US gallons (US gal) | X 0.833 | = Imperial gallons (Imp gal) |
| US gallons (US gal) | X 3.785 | = Litres (l) | X 0.264 | = US gallons (US gal) |

### Mass (weight)

| | | | | |
|---|---|---|---|---|
| Ounces (oz) | X 28.35 | = Grams (g) | X 0.035 | = Ounces (oz) |
| Pounds (lb) | X 0.454 | = Kilograms (kg) | X 2.205 | = Pounds (lb) |

### Force

| | | | | |
|---|---|---|---|---|
| Ounces-force (ozf; oz) | X 0.278 | = Newtons (N) | X 3.6 | = Ounces-force (ozf; oz) |
| Pounds-force (lbf; lb) | X 4.448 | = Newtons (N) | X 0.225 | = Pounds-force (lbf; lb) |
| Newtons (N) | X 0.1 | = Kilograms-force (kgf; kg) | X 9.81 | = Newtons (N) |

### Pressure

| | | | | |
|---|---|---|---|---|
| Pounds-force per square inch (psi; lbf/in²; lb/in²) | X 0.070 | = Kilograms-force per square centimetre (kgf/cm²; kg/cm²) | X 14.223 | = Pounds-force per square inch (psi; lbf/in²; lb/in²) |
| Pounds-force per square inch (psi; lbf/in²; lb/in²) | X 0.068 | = Atmospheres (atm) | X 14.696 | = Pounds-force per square inch (psi; lbf/in²; lb/in²) |
| Pounds-force per square inch (psi; lbf/in²; lb/in²) | X 0.069 | = Bars | X 14.5 | = Pounds-force per square inch (psi; lbf/in²; lb/in²) |
| Pounds-force per square inch (psi; lbf/in²; lb/in²) | X 6.895 | = Kilopascals (kPa) | X 0.145 | = Pounds-force per square inch (psi; lbf/in²; lb/in²) |
| Kilopascals (kPa) | X 0.01 | = Kilograms-force per square centimetre (kgf/cm²; kg/cm²) | X 98.1 | = Kilopascals (kPa) |
| Millibar (mbar) | X 100 | = Pascals (Pa) | X 0.01 | = Millibar (mbar) |
| Millibar (mbar) | X 0.0145 | = Pounds-force per square inch (psi; lbf/in²; lb/in²) | X 68.947 | = Millibar (mbar) |
| Millibar (mbar) | X 0.75 | = Millimetres of mercury (mmHg) | X 1.333 | = Millibar (mbar) |
| Millibar (mbar) | X 0.401 | = Inches of water (inH₂O) | X 2.491 | = Millibar (mbar) |
| Millimetres of mercury (mmHg) | X 0.535 | = Inches of water (inH₂O) | X 1.868 | = Millimetres of mercury (mmHg) |
| Inches of water (inH₂O) | X 0.036 | = Pounds-force per square inch (psi; lbf/in²; lb/in²) | X 27.68 | = Inches of water (inH₂O) |

### Torque (moment of force)

| | | | | |
|---|---|---|---|---|
| Pounds-force inches (lbf in; lb in) | X 1.152 | = Kilograms-force centimetre (kgf cm; kg cm) | X 0.868 | = Pounds-force inches (lbf in; lb in) |
| Pounds-force inches (lbf in; lb in) | X 0.113 | = Newton metres (Nm) | X 8.85 | = Pounds-force inches (lbf in; lb in) |
| Pounds-force inches (lbf in; lb in) | X 0.083 | = Pounds-force feet (lbf ft; lb ft) | X 12 | = Pounds-force inches (lbf in; lb in) |
| Pounds-force feet (lbf ft; lb ft) | X 0.138 | = Kilograms-force metres (kgf m; kg m) | X 7.233 | = Pounds-force feet (lbf ft; lb ft) |
| Pounds-force feet (lbf ft; lb ft) | X 1.356 | = Newton metres (Nm) | X 0.738 | = Pounds-force feet (lbf ft; lb ft) |
| Newton metres (Nm) | X 0.102 | = Kilograms-force metres (kgf m; kg m) | X 9.804 | = Newton metres (Nm) |

### Power

| | | | | |
|---|---|---|---|---|
| Horsepower (hp) | X 745.7 | = Watts (W) | X 0.0013 | = Horsepower (hp) |

### Velocity (speed)

| | | | | |
|---|---|---|---|---|
| Miles per hour (miles/hr; mph) | X 1.609 | = Kilometres per hour (km/hr; kph) | X 0.621 | = Miles per hour (miles/hr; mph) |

### Fuel consumption*

| | | | | |
|---|---|---|---|---|
| Miles per gallon, Imperial (mpg) | X 0.354 | = Kilometres per litre (km/l) | X 2.825 | = Miles per gallon, Imperial (mpg) |
| Miles per gallon, US (mpg) | X 0.425 | = Kilometres per litre (km/l) | X 2.352 | = Miles per gallon, US (mpg) |

### Temperature

Degrees Fahrenheit = (°C x 1.8) + 32

Degrees Celsius (Degrees Centigrade; °C) = (°F - 32) x 0.56

*It is common practice to convert from miles per gallon (mpg) to litres/100 kilometres (l/100km), where mpg (Imperial) x l/100 km = 282 and mpg (US) x l/100 km = 235

# Index